All you can eat

Tamasin Day-Lewis   1000 recipes

can eat

WEIDENFELD & NICOLSON

LIST of CONTENTS

The heart of good

IT IS TEN YEARS since I wrote my first cookbook, *West of Ireland Summers: A Cookbook*, and eight books later I think I'm beginning to know a little more about what the reader and, most importantly, the cook, really wants.

There are only so many recipes we ever need; beyond that, it is not the new dish we crave, it is being able to cook the old favourite better. I hope the days of cheffy, over-complicated recipes are over. We can go to restaurants when we want that kind of food. What I want from a cookbook is the mundane and the inspirational in one parcel—clear instructions, faith that the recipes will work, and ideas for something delicious but not off-puttingly esoteric for dinner. And I want a book that does it all in the right order, like recipe books used to do. That way you know exactly where to find things, and if you've forgotten the ingredients or the amounts for a sauce or a cake, you will be able to find the recipe again in a perfectly clear and cogent index.

This is a simple book. It will tell you what I have been cooking over the years and how my ways of cooking those dishes have refined; the fail-safe is in the detail. You cannot fail to succeed with these recipes. My daughters—and son—don't, so you won't either. The book is encyclopaedic in range

cooking

and reach, but that shouldn't deter you. You will be able to browse like you do at the market and decide on the most traditional and simple of things, or on how to slightly dress something up in the emperor's borrowed new robes. There are no pretensions in my food. It is hearty, earthy and delicious, and it relies on two serious virtues: the virtue of the obsessive ingredients shopper and of the perfectionist cook. No egg is too simple to take seriously, whether it be scrambled or boiled. Cook it right and you will delight everyone you cook for — and, most of all, yourself.

*B*uying right is not about spending more money always, but it is about spending more money sometimes. The great chicken debate is the tip of that enormous iceberg. What we buy says who we are and how much we care as much as what we can afford, and I believe we should always buy the best, even if the cut is a cheaper one. Buy less, eat less, waste less, spend more. I believe we should take bad food out of our lives at the root. If farmers didn't rear caged birds to 39 days old in densities that would make you blush and heave with disgust, no one would be able to buy and eat them. Chicken would be a treat and, like lamb or beef, we would accept that they cost more because that way they taste good. And you can use your prize bird in three incarnations — the roast, the risotto, the soup by augmenting it with extra vegetables.

In this country we spend less than 10 per cent of our income on food, whereas the proper food nations, like the French, the Italians, the Greeks, spend 15 per cent and the Spanish more than 17 per cent. A cultural tsunami is needed to make us all realise that good food equals healthy food. Instead of worrying about what is good for us and constantly studying meaningless labels such as low fat or salt or sugar, or being driven by the food industry's ludicrous scares and cynical incantations of new buzzwords like 'omega 3' or 'added vitamins', we should use our common sense and just buy the best ingredients, not processed, ready-made junk.

Nothing in this book should have you sobbing at the stove or wondering why the dish didn't turn out like you expected. When things work, my experience tells me you want to cook more often, not less, and you begin to enjoy the lovely unwinding and concentration that are at the heart of good cooking. You will get your hands dirty for pleasure, use all your senses, and look forward to turning the best raw materials into the best cooked ones.

Forget that exhortation to do something speedy in the kitchen. Put everything else down, forget work, switch on some good music, talk to your friends and family, get them to peel and chop, and enjoy that most convivial and satisfying of activities—cooking, second only to eating the result. Here is the bumper book of *All You Can Eat*. Get stuck in.

Tamasin Day-Lewis
March 2008

to EAT W
you

HILE

DRINK

Home-made Bloody Mary

MAKES 6–8 GLASSES

ripe organic tomatoes	1kg/2¼lb
celery, with leaves	2 small stalks
fresh coriander	small bunch
thyme, flat-leaf parsley & rosemary	a sprig of each
fresh horseradish, *grated*	1 tsp
onion, *grated*	1 tsp
lemons	juice of 2
molasses sugar	a pinch
sea salt	a pinch
Tabasco and Worcestershire sauce	few drops of each
vodka, *chilled*	about ⅓ bottle
ice cubes	½ a tray

This is my pre-Sunday lunch ritual. Once you have made the real McCoy you will never go back to your old habits. If you have a pretty glass jug, put it and the glasses in the freezer for 30 minutes before you make your Bloody Mary. That way everything has a rime of frosting when you serve it —quite beautiful.

→ Cut the TOMATOES into halves or quarters, depending on their size. Liquidise EVERYTHING BUT THE ALCOHOL in the food processor or blender, then push as much as you can through a sieve into a bowl, forcing it down hard with the back of a wooden spoon. Pour the COLD VODKA into the cold jug, add the contents of the bowl and mix well. Adjust the SEASONING and serve the Bloody Mary in cold glasses. If there are any would-be virgins among you, keep back some of the Virgin Mary before you add the vodka.

Cheddar and Grain Mustard Dip

farmhouse Cheddar	110g/4oz
cream cheese, *softened*	30g/1oz
unsalted butter, *softened*	85g/3oz
grain mustard	1 tsp
black peppercorns, *crushed coarsely*	¼ tsp
garlic, *very finely minced*	⅛ tsp
onion, *finely minced*	1½ tsp
celery, *finely diced and strung*	3 tbsp

Please, I beg of you, use a wonderful, unpasteurised farmhouse Cheddar for this dip, not a nasty processed cheese. You want the real thing—well-aged and tangy.

→ Crumble the CHEDDAR or chop it in a food processor. Mix ALL THE INGREDIENTS in a bowl and then refrigerate for at least an hour before you want to use the dip. You can also make a horseradish version of this by adding the hot stuff to taste. Buy fresh horseradish root if you can get it or the nearest to natural and unadulterated you can lay your hands on—not the creamy stuff! Grate it and add a teaspoon at a time so that you don't light the touch-paper too hot and have to retire hurt.

Garlic and Herb Dip

best cream cheese at room temperature	200g/7oz
crème fraîche	45g/1¾oz
spring onions, the white part only, *minced finely with a sharp knife*	2
parsley, *finely minced*	1 tbsp
chives, *finely snipped*	4 tbsp
black peppercorns, *scrunched in a mortar, or from a pepper mill*	¾ tsp
garlic, *minced fine with a little sea salt*	1 tsp
sea salt to taste	

This is as close to home-made Boursin as you can get, and all the better for being made with fresh ingredients. Do not use dried herbs for this.

→ Put ALL THE INGREDIENTS in a large bowl together and stir until well amalgamated.

Smoked Salmon and Cream Cheese Dip

wild smoked salmon trimmings, *chopped small*	110g/4oz
best cream cheese, *softened*	30g/1oz
unsalted butter, *softened*	110g/4oz
lemon	juice of ¼
black peppercorns, *crushed*	6

This is rich and glorious and I make it with wild smoked salmon as I have very strong feelings against the farming of these kings of fish, whether organically or otherwise. I know wild is more expensive, but this is such a small amount and I always buy for flavour and quality, even if it means having a treat less often.

→ Mix ALL THE INGREDIENTS together in a large bowl, adding more lemon juice to taste and a little knife-point of cayenne if you want to warm things up a little. Serve on fingers or triangles of toasted wholemeal bread.

Smoked Salmon Dip with Dill
→ You could also add finely chopped FRESH DILL to taste if you feel like something a little more Scandinavian, and serve the dip on toasted rye bread or rye crackers to complete the theme. Begin by adding just a tablespoon of dill and don't let the herb become too intrusive.

Cabrales or Blue Cheese Dip

good fresh walnuts	85g/3oz
Cabrales, *trimmed of its rind and crumbled by hand*	200g/7oz
best cream cheese, *softened*	140g/5oz
flat-leaf parsley, *finely chopped*	15g/½oz
tarragon, *finely chopped*	7g/¼ oz
black pepper	

Cabrales is an eye- and mouth-wateringly delicious raw milk blue cheese from Spain, but any feisty, good-quality blue from Stilton to Roquefort would be as good. Serve with slices of toasted walnut bread.

→ Toast the WALNUTS in the oven or in a pan until they have just taken on a little colour and begun to release their nutty scent. Don't let them get charred and blackened. Mix the WALNUTS with the CHEESE and HERBS together well in a bowl, adding a scrunch of BLACK PEPPER to taste.

Smoked Mozzarella Dip

smoked mozzarella	140g/5oz
best cream cheese, *softened*	340g/12oz
sundried tomatoes, *chopped very small*	45g/1½ oz
garlic, *finely minced with a little sea salt*	1 clove
onion, *finely minced*	20g/¾ oz
cayenne	a knife point, or to taste
lemon	juice of ¼

Smoky flavours make great appetisers—earthy and wondrous to the palate at the start of a good meal.

→ Blitz the MOZZARELLA in a food processor, but keep it in tiny bits, not crumbs. Fold ALL THE INGREDIENTS together in a large bowl, adding extra lemon juice or cayenne to taste. This is delicious served on hunks of toasted country or sourdough bread, which stands up well to the smoky taste.

Mediterranean Feta Dip

feta, a good sheep's milk one, *crumbled*	110g/4oz
ricotta, fresh if you can get it	55g/2oz
dry English mustard powder	½ tsp
smoked paprika	¼ tsp
spring onion, the white part only, *finely minced*	2 tsp
garlic, *minced fine with a little sea salt*	1 clove
black olives, *pitted and finely chopped*	a handful
sundried tomatoes, *finely chopped*	2 tbsp
black pepper	to taste

Strong flavours and colour make this a good start to any robust fishy or meaty lunch or supper. Use the glossy black Nyons olives if possible, but certainly not tinned or brined. Serve with some chilled rosé.

→ Place ALL THE INGREDIENTS in a big bowl and adjust the seasoning, garlic, paprika, spring onion and mustard powder to taste. Mix well.

Red Pepper, Roast Onion and Feta Purée

medium onions	2
red peppers or piquillo peppers in a jar	340g/12oz
sheep's milk feta, *crumbled*	285g/10z
good extra virgin olive oil	6 tbsp
sherry or red wine vinegar	2 tbsp
fresh thyme leaves	1 tsp
sea salt and black pepper	

You can make this with wood-smoked piquillo peppers from a jar, in which case be sure to buy a good brand, not one in brine. Otherwise, scorch the peppers yourself over the flame, holding them with tongs.

→ Preheat the oven to 200°C/400°F/Gas 6. Roast the ONIONS in their skins until soft right the way through when pierced with a skewer. This will take anything from 30–45 minutes. Meanwhile, char the PEPPERS all over until soft—you can just roast them in the oven too if you wish, but the effect won't be quite the same without the smokiness. Put them in a bowl immediately, cover with clingfilm and leave for 10 minutes. Then peel and seed the peppers.

→ Push the onions out of their skins and mash them with the peppers on a plate or in a shallow bowl with the crumbled FETA. Add the OIL, VINEGAR and THYME with some SEASONING. Be sparing with the salt because of the feta. The texture should be coarse, not smooth. Serve with slices of griddled pitta bread.

Parmesan Cheese Straws

best Parmesan cheese, *freshly grated*   up to 225g / 8oz

puff pastry, all butter, *straight from the fridge*   450g / 1lb

sesame, onion, celery seeds OR English mustard powder OR smoked paprika

These really are the best things to have with a drink before dinner or to nibble at whenever you have a got-to-have-cheese pang. You can sprinkle sesame, onion or celery seeds onto them or just a little smoked paprika down their length for added colour and bite. Or you can add a teaspoon of chopped fresh thyme and one of English mustard powder for a new twist. One thing you must not compromise is the quality of the puff pastry, which should be the best and made with butter. Make it yourself if you have the time and energy (see p. 517), otherwise buy a sheet of good puff pastry and the straws will occupy very little more of your time to make than it takes to search out, uncork and pour a good bottle of wine. The Parmesan, too, must be the best Parmigiano Reggiano, grated fresh on a medium grater.

→ Preheat oven to 220°C / 425°F / Gas 7. Scatter half the GRATED PARMESAN onto a marble slab or pastry board and set your sheet of PASTRY down on top of it. Roll the pastry out, scattering on the remaining cheese before it is completely rolled thin. Make sure the cheese is rolled into the pastry. If you are using THYME and MUSTARD, scatter it over the pastry sheet with the cheese and roll it in. Cut the pastry with a knife point down its length into strips 1cm / ½ inch or so. With one hand at each end, twist each strip as you would a rope, treating it gently so that it doesn't break. Place on a silicone or greaseproof sheet on a large baking tray. No butter needed as the pastry is quite buttery enough. Scatter over SEEDS or PAPRIKA if you are using them.

→ Bake the straws in the middle of the oven until they are gloriously golden along their whole length. If there are anaemic patches the pastry won't be cooked through in the middle. The straws take 10–15 minutes in my oven, but keep checking as they shouldn't darken and taste burnt. Remove to a rack to cool, but try and serve while still warm. They can be reheated on the day, or, at a pinch, the following day, but fresh is best with all pastry.

Parmesan Cheese Puffs
→ One day I thought it was time for a change. Instead of making straws I got a cutter and turned the pastry into lovely puffy, golden, freckled, circular suns, and everyone seemed just as keen. Same recipe as above, but a drastic change of shape.

Parmesan, Chilli and Anchovy Biscuits

MAKES 20–24

medium-hot chillies	3 or 4
extra virgin olive oil	1tsp
plain organic flour	110g/4oz
cold unsalted butter, *cut into small cubes*	110g/4oz
anchovies	55g/2oz
Parmesan cheese, *freshly grated*	110g/4oz

This dough is brilliantly laid-back about being made earlier, rolled into a cylinder and left in the fridge until you want it. The dough freezes well and the biscuits can be cut and baked as soon as it is defrosted enough for the knife to get through. If you hate anchovy just leave it out, but I love its fishy saltiness with the chilli and Parmesan.

→ Preheat oven to 220°C/425°F/Gas 7. Turn the CHILLIES in the OIL, then blister the skins by holding the chillies over a flame with a pair of tongs. If you don't have gas, you can roast the chillies in the hot oven until they are brown all over. Seal the chillies in a bowl under clingfilm until they're cool enough to peel easily. Then de-seed them and chop them really finely. Remove the ANCHOVIES from their oil and dry, or desalinate them under a cold tap and dry.

→ Work the BUTTER into the FLOUR with your fingertips or blitz briefly in a food processor to amalgamate. Chop the ANCHOVIES finely and mix them and the little flecks of chilli into the dough with the Parmesan. Knead to a paste by hand, roll into a fat cylinder about 5cm/2in in diameter and wrap in foil. Leave to chill in the fridge for at least 30 minutes. Cut into slices and place on silicone or Bakewell paper on a baking tray. Leave a little space between the biscuits as they will spread. Cook in the middle of the oven for about 10 minutes or until golden, but not brown. Using a palette knife, remove them to a wire rack to firm up and cool down. Eat while they are still warm.

Blue Cheese and Celery Seed Biscuits
→ You can also make these biscuits with crumbled blue cheese. Follow the method above, but forget the chilli and anchovies. Mix 100g/4oz of crumbled BLUE CHEESE into the dough and sprinkle some CELERY SEEDS over the biscuits on the baking tray.

Cheese Footballs

plain flour	110g/4oz
Parmesan, *freshly grated*	110g/4oz
black pepper	a good scrunch
English mustard powder and cayenne pepper	a pinch of each
sage or thyme (optional), *finely chopped*	1 tsp
unsalted butter, *melted*	110g/4oz

My grandmother, ever indulgent, used to let us eat plates of cheese footballs before Sunday lunch, and do you know what? They never seemed to diminish our appetites—wickedly salty, cheesy things just don't when you're hungry and growing. Utterly compulsive.

→ Preheat the oven to 180°C/350°F/Gas 4. Mix ALL THE DRY INGREDIENTS together in a bowl. Pour in the MELTED BUTTER so the mixture becomes like breadcrumbs, stirring as you go. You might need a little extra butter if the mixture seems too dry. Roll walnut-sized balls of mixture in your hands and put them on a silicone or buttered baking sheet. Cook for 15–20 minutes until lightly browned. Eat warm, or cool and keep in an airtight container.

Parmesan and Cheddar Crisps

Parmesan, *freshly grated*	85g/3oz
Cheddar, *freshly grated*	85g/3oz

These are at their best eaten warm and crisp with a drink. You can't believe how simple they are until you try them.

→ Preheat the oven to 180°C/350°F/Gas 4. Line a baking sheet with non-stick baking paper or use a silicone baking sheet. Mix the CHEESES together in a bowl. Place tablespoons of the mixture on the baking sheet, flattening them out a little, and leaving plenty of space between each one as you would with cookies. Bake in the centre of the oven for 8–10 minutes until the cheese has melted and is just beginning to bronze around the edges like an autumn leaf. Remove from the oven and leave for a couple of minutes to firm up before removing them to a rack.

→ If you prefer, you can shape these like tuiles by folding them over a rolling pin. Serve with a dish of tart, baked cherry tomatoes on the vine, dressed with a good few drops of aged balsamic vinegar and some grassy olive oil. Keep the crisps to the side so they don't wilt into a soggy morass.

Cheese Cigars

MAKES 16

feta cheese	200g/7oz
organic egg, *lightly beaten*	1
fresh mint, parsley OR dill, *very finely chopped*	a small bunch
filo pastry	16 sheets
unsalted butter, *melted* OR olive oil	3 tbsp

These little bundles of crisp deliciousness are perfect for pre-prandial, ambulatory scoffery as they won't collapse on you or stain your best dress with grease. The wonderful food writer Claudia Roden alerted me to this recipe.

→ Preheat the oven to 180°C/350°F/Gas 4. Mash the FETA CHEESE with a fork and mix it in a bowl with the EGG and HERBS. Take the FILO SHEETS out of the packet one at a time as you are about to use them, as they dry and crack otherwise.
→ Lightly brush half the sheet lengthways with MELTED BUTTER or OIL and fold it in half to make a long, narrow strip. Brush the top of the folded strip with butter or oil. Take a heaped tea-spoon of filling and place it at one side of the strip in a long thin sausage shape, about 2.5cm/1in from the top edge and the sides. Roll the strip up with the filling inside. About halfway through rolling, fold the edges in towards the middle so that the filling can't leak out and escape. Make all 16 cigars in this way—any child can do it and will love to join in.
→ Place the cigars close to each other on a greased baking sheet and brush the tops with the rest of the melted butter or oil. Bake in the oven for 30 minutes, or until crisp and golden. Leave for a few minutes before you tuck in.

Taramasalata

SERVES 6

piece of smoked cod's roe	200g/7oz
stale white bread, *crust removed*	1 slice
garlic, *chopped finely*	1 large clove
extra virgin olive oil	240ml/8fl oz
organic lemons	juice of 1–2
black pepper	

Tarama is traditionally made with the salted, pressed roe of the grey mullet or with smoked cod's roe. You can buy the cod's roe in its skin at good fishmongers, but leave it in water overnight to leach away some of its saltiness.

→ Soak the COD'S ROE, then remove it from its skin with a spoon. Wet the BREAD and squeeze it so it is damp rather than wringing wet and put it in a food processor with the pre-soaked cod's roe and the GARLIC. Blitz, adding a thin stream of OLIVE OIL. If the mixture over-thickens, slacken with a spoon or two of water. Add the LEMON JUICE, season with PEPPER, and taste to see if you need more lemon juice. Scoop into a bowl and pour a little more oil over the top. Serve with griddled pitta bread or toast.

Hummus bi Tahini

chickpeas, *soaked overnight in a bowl of water*	225g/8oz
onion, *spiked with a couple of cloves*	1
celery	2 sticks
leek tops	2
carrots, *chopped*	2
large lemons	juice of up to 3
organic tahini paste from dark or lightly roasted sesame seeds	2 tbsp
garlic cloves, *peeled and chopped*	3
olive oil	
sea salt and black pepper	
cumin seeds OR paprika (optional)	1 tsp
fresh coriander OR parsley, *finely chopped*	

An earthy Middle Eastern dish, which everyone tinkers with to find the proportions they like: lemony, less lemony, garlicky, with more or less tahini, made with either dark roast sesame seeds or the lighter ones and so on. There are those of you who will want to make it with tinned chickpeas, but just make it the proper way once and you will be converted.

→ Put the drained CHICKPEAS and the vegetables in a large heavy-bottomed casserole and cover with cold water to half a thumb above them. Bring to the boil, scum rigorously with a slotted spoon and some kitchen paper, then reduce to a simmer and cook with the lid on. In my experience, depending on the age of the chickpeas, they will take 1½–2 hours to cook. Drain them, keeping a little of the cooking water, which you may want to use some of to thin down the hummus.

→ Put the chickpeas in a food processor with the juice of 2 of the LEMONS, the TAHINI, the GARLIC, 3 tablespoons of OLIVE OIL and the SEASONING. Blitz to a thick paste, then taste. It may need thinning down with a tablespoon or two of cooking liquor, it might need more oil, more garlic, more lemon, more tahini. There is no right way, except the way you like it. The consistency should be that of a creamy paste or mayonnaise.

→ Put into a serving dish or terrine before cooling and serving. Top with a good splosh of OLIVE OIL and scatter over a teaspoon of CUMIN SEEDS roasted dry in a small frying pan for a minute then crushed in a mortar, or a teaspoon of PAPRIKA. Some finely chopped PARSLEY or CORIANDER is also good. Serve with griddled pitta bread or toast. Sourdough bread is also delicious with hummus.

Tzatziki

cucumber	1
thick Greek yoghurt	225g/8oz
extra virgin olive oil	2 tbsp
garlic cloves	4
sea salt	
fresh mint, *finely chopped*	1 tbsp
black pepper	

This lovely dish is simple to make and good to serve with griddled pitta bread, grilled meat or prawns, or sticks of raw vegetables. Don't leave it in the fridge longer than a couple of days or the garlic will develop a some-what rank and bitter flavour. Try to find good-quality thick Greek yoghurt.

→ Peel the CUCUMBER, halve lengthways and take out the seeds with a teaspoon. The seeds would make the finished dish watery. Peel the GARLIC and crush in a mortar with a little sea salt. Mix the CUCUMBER, YOGHURT, OLIVE OIL, SALTY GARLIC PASTE and MINT together in a bowl. Scrunch on some BLACK PEPPER and check the seasoning. Refrigerate for at least half a day to let the flavours marry and deepen.

Aubergine Purée with Tahini

SERVES 6–8

large aubergines	2
garlic, *chopped*	2–4 cloves
lemons	juice of up to 3
tahini, the dark roasted or light sesame paste	2 tbsp
sea salt and black pepper	
olive oil	
cumin seeds	1 tsp
parsley	1 tbsp
pomegranate seeds (optional)	

This is a creamy, smoky purée that you can make as part of a mezze or just eat on its own with griddled pitta bread. It is also delicious with lamb—roast leg or shoulder, chops or kebabs—the sweet meat and the smoky, lemony, garlicky purée a perfect taste and texture partnership.

→ Preheat the oven to 180°C/350°F/Gas 4. If you have a grill or a gas flame, sear the AUBERGINES until their skins begin to blacken and blister. Charcoal is the best for a smoky flavour, but unless you're having a barbie, hold each aubergine over the gas flame with a pair of tongs, turning it as it blackens, or put them under the grill, turning them likewise. Then put the aubergines on a baking tray and finish the cooking process, about another 30 minutes depending on their size, until they feel soft right the way through when pricked with a skewer. Dry roast the CUMIN SEEDS in a small frying pan for a minute then grind in a mortar

→ Allow the aubergines to cool to the point where you can skin them, then put them in chunks in the blender or food processor. Add 2 cloves of GARLIC to begin with, the juice of 2 LEMONS, 2 tablespoons of TAHINI and the SEASONING, and blitz. Add OLIVE OIL until you have a creamy textured paste, but don't overdo it; start with around 2–4 tablespoons. Taste and adjust anything: the lemon, the seasoning, the tahini, the garlic, the oil.

→ Pour into a serving bowl while still warm or spread on a plate, sprinkling with a little OIL, the CUMIN SEEDS and, if you like, some jewels of POMEGRANATE, which always give colour and glamour to this grey but divine-tasting dish. Serve with griddled pitta bread and some sticks of raw vegetables such as celery, carrots, cardoons or radishes.

Smoky Aubergine and White Bean Purée

aubergine	1
olive oil	
garlic cloves	2
cumin	1 tsp
coriander seeds	1 tsp
sea salt	1 tsp
fresh chilli paste	½ tsp
cannellini beans	400g/14oz tin, or cook your own
tahini	1 heaped tsp
lemon	juice of ½
fresh mint and coriander leaves	a handful of each
olive oil	
pepper	

→ Cut the AUBERGINE in half lengthwise, make slits diagonally in the flesh and brush with OLIVE OIL. If you have a griddle, brush oil over it lightly, then place the aubergine halves on it cut side down with the whole, unpeeled GARLIC. If not, cook them on a lightly oiled baking tray in a moderate to hot oven. Cook until soft and beginning to char. Meanwhile roast the CUMIN and CORIANDER seeds for 30 seconds in a pan until they exude their scent, then crush them in a mortar. You can also make your own chilli paste by crushing a seeded red chilli with a bit of sea salt in a mortar.

→ Scoop out the flesh of the aubergine and the garlic cloves into the food processor along with ALL THE OTHER INGREDIENTS, process until smooth, and check the seasoning. Serve with some hot, griddled pitta bread.

Piemontese Peppers

SERVES 4

organic red peppers	2
large organic tomatoes	2
good-quality anchovies	4–6
best olive oil	
unsalted butter	a generous knob
thyme	a sprig
garlic cloves	3
feta cheese, *crumbled or cubed, the best sheep's milk one you can find*	
sea salt, pepper	

I serve quarters of the peppers like warm boats transporting their cargo of salt anchovy, garlic, tomatoes, olive oil and herbed cheese. You can prepare the petits bateaux in advance, then put them in the oven just before your guests arrive. Hot, warm or cold, all are equally delicious.

→ Preheat the oven to 180°C/350°F/Gas 4. Halve the PEPPERS, remove the seeds and innards, then halve them again and place them on a flat roasting tray like small boats. On each deck, place two tiny chunks of TOMATO, three thin slices of GARLIC, half a chopped ANCHOVY in tiny bits, a sprinkling of THYME and a splosh of best OLIVE OIL. SEASON, add a dot of BUTTER, and bake in the oven for 40 minutes, or until the peppers are tender but slightly resistant.

→ Add some crumbled bits of good FETA CHEESE to the boats while still hot. Cool to whatever temperature you wish to serve them at and make sure you spoon back any escaped juices.

Anchoïade de Croze

SERVES 8

dried red chilli	1
whole blanched almonds	12
salted anchovies, *desalinated and de-spined*	6
OR anchovies in olive oil	12
dried figs, *roughly chopped*	3
small onion, *quartered*	1
garlic cloves, *chopped*	2
fennel fronds	2
parsley, chives and tarragon, *mixed*	55g/2oz
olive oil	
lemon juice	
orange-flower water	up to 1 tbsp

This is an elaborate version of a Provençal anchoïade with the strength of a tapenade—magical, particularly on a hot day. Serve it with fingers of country bread which you have brushed with some olive oil and baked in the oven.

→ Put the CHILLI, ALMONDS, ANCHOVIES, FIGS, ONION, GARLIC, FENNEL and HERBS in the food processor. Process to a thick paste, pouring in the OLIVE OIL in a steady stream, then adding the LEMON JUICE and any extra olive oil to taste. Finally add the ORANGE FLOWER WATER, a dessertspoon to start with — it must scent, not overwhelm.

Instead of serving the anchoïade on baked bread, you can oil the bottom of the bread, spread the mixture on the top and bake in a hot oven for 10 minutes.

Ann-Marie's Crostini

thick slices of bread, preferably Pugliese	1 per person
garlic clove	1 or more
good olive oil	
Carluccio's black olive and caper paste	
fresh goat's cheese	
prosciutto	1 slice per person
salad leaves	

→ Squeeze a GARLIC CLOVE into some good OLIVE OIL, and brush it over both sides of a thick slice of BREAD. Put the bread in a hot oven for 10–15 minutes, turning it once. Spread a layer of Carluccio's BLACK OLIVE AND CAPER PASTE over it, then some fresh GOAT'S CHEESE, which is softer than a crottin. Top with a slice of PROSCIUTTO, and serve with some dressed salad leaves.

Baked Goat's Cheese Crostini

→ Mix some goat's cheese with a spoonful or two of crème fraîche and season with a little salt and black pepper. Toast the bread as above but on one side only. Spread the goat's cheese mixture on the untoasted side and add a few slivers of char-grilled and skinned red peppers. Put in a hot oven for 5 minutes or until the cheese has started to melt and brown.

Spiced Chicken Livers

SERVES 6

cumin seeds	1½ heaped tsp
coriander seeds	1 tsp
sea salt crystals	1 tsp
black peppercorns	1 tsp
cayenne	tip of a tsp
plain flour	1–1½ tbsp
organic chicken livers	450g/1lb
olive oil or a good-sized knob of unsalted butter	

Wilted Endives

endives	3
best olive oil	4 tbsp
molasses sugar	1 tsp
sea salt and black pepper	
lemon juice	to taste

This is one of the simplest and most delicious titbits of a dish that I have ever cooked. It should be eaten straight from a communal plate, or even the frying pan, while you clutch a cold glass of something good with your free hand. I'm afraid I take a purist line here—only organic will do, since chemical residues collect in the liver and kidneys. Serve the livers by themselves or with wilted endives.

→ Temper the CUMIN and CORIANDER in a small frying pan over a gentle heat for 30 seconds to a minute, until the spices exude their scent. Tip into a mortar and crush with the SEA SALT and PEPPERCORNS. Add the CAYENNE, then the FLOUR, and stir well together. Set aside. Clean and de-vein the LIVERS, keeping them whole, and removing any green patches. Pat them dry and keep in the fridge until about 30 minutes before you want to cook them.

→ Just before cooking, roll each liver in the spice mixture in the mortar and put on a plate. Heat a good knob of UNSALTED BUTTER or OLIVE OIL, whichever you prefer, in a frying pan— I come down on the side of butter, with a tiny addition of oil to discourage burning. Throw in the livers when the fat is hot. Allow one side to spit and crisp for a couple of minutes, turn over and repeat, then test with a knife point. When gorgeously oozily pink, shunt the contents of the pan onto a white plate and consume.

Wilted Endives
→ Cut the base off the ENDIVES, core them and strip them into leaves. Heat the OLIVE OIL gently in a pan with the MOLASSES SUGAR, then throw in the endives and stir them in the warm oil. They will begin to wilt pretty quickly. Season with the SEA SALT and BLACK PEPPER, remove from the heat, and spritz on the LEMON JUICE.

Spiced Pork Meatballs with Guacamole

SERVES 8–10

minced organic pork	1.2kg/2½lb
sea salt	
red chilli, *finely chopped with its seeds*	1
root ginger, *grated*	1 tbsp
flat-leaf parsley, *chopped*	1 tbsp
fresh coriander, *chopped*	1 tbsp
fresh thyme, *chopped*	1 tsp
Dijon mustard	1 tbsp
zest of a lemon	
Guacamole	
ripe organic avocados	3
limes	juice of 3
chilli, *finely chopped with its seeds*	1
sea salt	
fresh coriander leaves, *chopped*	a handful

This is a brilliant stand-in-the-kitchen-and-eat dish, which you can prepare in advance, cook in front of your friends and serve straight from the pan with drinks. You raise the temperature with the spice, then cool it with the guacamole, all in one mouthful. Make sure the pork is fatty enough to stop the meatballs from drying out during the cooking.

→ Throw all the MEATBALL INGREDIENTS into a large bowl and mix together well with your fingers, making sure that you don't rub your eyes afterwards: chilli is lethal. Form into small balls, the size of walnuts. At this point, you can leave the meat for an hour or two until you need it. Remember, if you cover the meatballs and put them in the fridge, don't cook them until they have come back to room temperature.

→ I cook mine on a griddle with no fat—there is enough in the meatballs—until crusted and crisped all over and cooked through to the stage where there are no pink juices flowing out of the meat when you test it with a skewer. The GUACAMOLE can be chilled for up to an hour before you want it, so all you need to do is spoon it over the meatballs, cold with hot, when they are cooked.

Guacamole
→ Mash the AVOCADOS on a plate with a fork until they are smooth but with the odd lump for texture. Stir in the LIME JUICE, CHILLIES and SALT. Scrape into a bowl, cover and chill for an hour. Stir in the CORIANDER, taste and adjust the seasoning and citrus to taste. Lob spoons of it on to the pork meatballs hot from the griddle. If you want to eat this as a main course, make the pork balls into large, flat burgers. Grill them in the same way, top them with guacamole and put them inside a good floury bap or tortilla.

Spiced Meatballs with Tomato Sauce
→ For a change, make a fairly thick TOMATO SAUCE (p. 140), and serve spoonfuls with the meatballs as above.

SOUP

and

S

stock

Easy Roast Cherry Tomato Soup

SERVES 4–5

organic cherry tomatoes	1kg / 2½lb
garlic cloves, in their skins	3
chicken stock (see p. 54)	1.2 litre / 2 pints
muscovado sugar	1 heaped tsp
salt and pepper	

A perfect soup for a late summer lunch, deeply flavoured, yet made without butter, oil or cream.

→ Roast the TOMATOES in a roasting tin with the GARLIC for about an hour in a medium oven. The skins will have split, and the juices run. Allow to cool until you can handle them, then skin them and the garlic, and put in the blender with 2–3 ladles of the HOT STOCK. Whizz, then sieve, including the skins which you can press the flavour from.

→ Return to the pan with the rest of the STOCK, add the SUGAR and SEASONING to taste, and serve. I resist the urge for basil, butter, cream or parsley. This is an intensely enough flavoured soup as it is.

Sweet Potato and Cherry Tomato Soup

SERVES 6

medium-sized orange-fleshed sweet potatoes	6
onion	1
organic cherry tomatoes	450g/1lb
thyme	a sprig
olive oil	
chilli	a scrap
rosemary	a sprig
chicken stock (see p. 54)	1 litre / 1¾ pints
molasses sugar	1 heaped tsp

The mealy sweetness of sweet potato, with its beautiful orange flesh, and the sharp acidity of the cherry tomatoes with a smidgen of molasses sugar to add treacly back notes, is an unexpectedly good combination in a soup. And the colour is like an extravagantly unbelievable sunset.

→ Preheat the oven to 200°C/400°F/Gas 6. Cut the SWEET POTATOES, in their skins, into chunks, about 3 per potato. Cut the ONION into large chunks, and place both on a roasting tray. Splash over a little olive oil, scatter over some THYME LEAVES, some finely chopped ROSEMARY, a scrap of finely chopped, seeded RED CHILLI, SEA SALT and BLACK PEPPER and turn the vegetables in the mixture to coat. Bake for about 30 minutes; they will not be hard when you test them, but they will not have reached softness through and through either.

→ Slide in the TOMATOES, and a bit of extra OLIVE OIL if it looks as though there isn't enough to gloss them, and return the vegetables to the oven for 15–20 minutes, when everything should be done: the tomatoes weeping their luscious juices and beginning to split at the seams, the onion caramelised and the sweet potatoes totally tender.

→ Skin the SWEET POTATOES while still as hot as you can stand and throw them into a food processor with everything else, including the stock which you have brought to the boil, and the molasses sugar. Bring back just to the boil and taste for seasoning and sweetness. If the tomatoes have made the soup too sharp, add a little more sugar and serve.

Nelisha's Spiced Sweet Potato and Pumpkin Soup

SERVES 4

cumin seeds	1 tsp
coriander seeds	1 tsp
sesame seeds	1 tbsp
butter	30g/1oz
OR light olive oil	1 tbsp
medium red onion, *finely chopped*	1
garlic cloves, *finely chopped*	2
a thumb of fresh ginger, *peeled and chopped*	
green chillies, *seeded and chopped*	1–2
lime	zest and juice of 1
vegetable stock (see p. 55)	1.2 litres/2 pints
honey	1 tsp
sweet potato, *peeled and diced*	340g/12oz
pumpkin, *peeled and diced*	340g/12oz
coriander leaves, *roughly chopped*	a handful

Garnish

live yoghurt	120ml/4fl oz
OR coconut milk	1 tin
olive oil	

There was an ingredient I couldn't identify when I tried this magical soup, cooked by Sri Lankan chef Nelisha Wickremasinghe. It was the roasted sesame seeds.

→ Lightly roast the CUMIN, CORIANDER and SESAME SEEDS separately for about one minute, then grind them together. Heat the OIL or BUTTER in a heavy-bottomed pan and cook the ONION and GARLIC over a medium heat without browning, until they are softened.

→ Add the GROUND SPICES, GINGER, CHILLIES and LIME ZEST and stir them in. Cook for a minute to amalgamate the flavours. Add the STOCK, half the LIME JUICE, the HONEY, SWEET POTATO, PUMPKIN and the CORIANDER LEAVES and bring to the boil.

→ Then reduce to a simmer and cook until the vegetables are tender (about 20 minutes). Liquidise until very smooth, adding more stock to achieve the right consistency if you need to. Add the rest of the lime juice and seasoning to taste. Serve with a swirl of YOGHURT or COCONUT MILK and a few drops of OLIVE OIL.

Cream of Tomato Soup

SERVES 4–6

ripe organic tomatoes	450g / 1lb
unsalted butter	55g / 2oz
small onion, *peeled and diced*	1
small carrot, *peeled and diced*	1
stick celery, *diced*	1
garlic clove, *peeled and chopped*	1
vegetable, beef OR chicken stock (see pp. 54–55)	700ml / 1¼ pints
bay leaf	1
tomato purée	2 tsp
molasses OR dark muscovado sugar	1 tsp
nutmeg	a suspicion
sea salt and black pepper	
cream OR Jersey full-cream milk	150ml / 5fl oz
parsley OR chives, *chopped*	

You could add some torn leaves of basil at the end, but this is really the nursery not the Mediterranean version, so I like to keep it as close to childhood memories as possible, though without the farinaceous undertones of a certain proprietary brand!

→ First skin and seed your TOMATOES. Put the tomatoes in a bowl and pierce them with the blade of a sharp knife somewhere around their middle. Boil a kettle and pour the boiling water over the tomatoes. It MUST cover them for this to work. Count 30 seconds. Tip the scalding water out of the bowl and fill the bowl with cold water for just long enough to cool the tomatoes so you can handle them. The skins should now unpeel as easily as you would unwrap a parcel. Cut each tomato in quarters and push the seeds out with your fingers. Remove the nasty little core that really doesn't do any tomato dish any favours, hot or cold.

→ Heat the BUTTER in a pan and sauté the DICED ONION, CARROT, CELERY and GARLIC together gently for about 10 minutes, making sure they don't start to brown. Add the quartered TOMATOES, STOCK, BAY LEAF, TOMATO PURÉE and SUGAR and simmer briefly and slowly until the carrots are cooked through. Remove the bay leaf, liquidise and season to taste.

→ *If you are serving the soup hot*, scald the CREAM to boiling point in a pan, add it to the soup and reheat it without letting it boil. Sprinkle the PARSLEY or CHIVES over each bowl as you serve it.

→ *If you are serving the soup cold*, allow it to cool down and chill it in the fridge in a large bowl. Stir in the cold CREAM, SEASON more highly than you would for a hot soup and cool further. Sprinkle the PARSLEY or some chopped CHIVES over as you serve each bowl.

Carrot Soup

SERVES 4–6

organic carrots	450g / 1lb
unsalted butter OR half-and-half olive oil and butter	45g / 1½ oz
onion, *peeled and finely chopped*	1

You can add the juice of an orange at the end of the cooking time to give a citrussy sharpness to this sweet vegetable, or scatter over some chopped coriander leaves if you prefer, with or without a blob of crème fraîche.

→ Peel the CARROTS and cut them into small dice or slim coins. Heat the BUTTER gently in a heavy-bottomed pan and add the ONION, stirring and cooking it until it is softened and golden. Add the diced carrot and turn it in the butter, cooking it for a

vegetable OR chicken stock (see pp. 54–55)	1.2 litres/2 pints
parsley, *chopped*	1 tbsp
sea salt and black pepper	
orange (optional)	juice of 1
coriander leaves, *chopped*	
crème fraîche (optional)	

few minutes until it just begins to soften. Pour over the STOCK, add the chopped PARSLEY, SEASON, and bring it up to the boil. Simmer with a lid on until the carrots are completely soft, then liquidise and return to the pan, adjusting the SEASONING before you reheat it. As it gets to boiling point add the ORANGE JUICE if you are using it and remove from the heat. Ladle into bowls, sprinkle over CORIANDER and add a dollop of CRÈME FRAÎCHE if you want to.

Carrot and Ginger Soup
→ Simply add a finger of grated raw ROOT GINGER with the diced carrot to make this spicier version.

Cream of Asparagus Soup

SERVES 4

bundle of asparagus	about 450g/1lb
small onion OR shallot, *finely chopped*	1
unsalted butter	55g/2oz
potato flour OR flour	1 tbsp
water OR chicken stock (see p. 54)	1.2 litres/2 pints
sea salt, black pepper	
lemon juice	a little
double cream	150ml/5fl oz

Asparagus is a vegetable with a strong enough identity not to demand chicken stock when you turn it into soup. The cooking liquor takes on the scent of the asparagus and I would hardly want to diminish that, so choose between chicken stock and water, depending on how purist you are feeling.

→ Soak the ASPARAGUS in water to clean out any sand. Cut the bottoms of the asparagus stems off if they look dry and peel the bottom third of each stem with a potato peeler. This really does make a difference to the texture of the asparagus. Now cut the stems into 4 and throw them into the boiling salted water or stock, keeping back the tips. Simmer the stems for about 15 minutes.

→ Meanwhile, melt the BUTTER in a pan and gently soften the chopped ONION. Throw the TIPS into the pan with the stems and simmer for a further 10 minutes until tender. Remove the stems and tips to a plate, and sort them into two separate piles. Stir the FLOUR into the buttery onion for a couple of minutes and add the asparagus liquor and stems. Simmer them together for a few more minutes. Blitz in the liquidiser, then sieve to get rid of any woody bits. Season, adding a little LEMON JUICE. Stir in the CREAM and the ASPARAGUS TIPS and reheat to just under boiling point.

Fresh Thyme Soup

thyme	a whole handful
small onion, *finely chopped*	1
small new potatoes	2
butter	a knob
olive oil	
chicken stock (see p. 54)	750ml/1¼ pint
Jersey milk	450ml/1 pint
salt and pepper	

This is an intensely flavoured, beautiful soup to make in summer, when the thyme flowers have turned into new growth. It is simple, aromatic, and needs no embellishment. The chicken stock should be strong enough to jellify in the fridge.

→ Strip half the THYME STALKS, about 10 or 12 twigs, of their leaves and chop them to release the oils. Melt a knob of BUTTER and a couple of tablespoons of good OLIVE OIL in a heavy-bottomed casserole, then add the finely chopped ONION, the diced POTATOES and the THYME. Stir to coat for a few minutes, then ladle in the STOCK. Bring to the boil, add the MILK, bring to the boil again, turn down to a lazy simmer, adding the rest of the THYME STALKS tied in a bundle like a bouquet garni, salt and pepper.

→ Put the lid on, and continue to simmer for about 20 minutes. Remove the bouquet, check the seasoning, and put the soup through the thinnest of the three discs of a mouli-légumes. The result is utterly white, with tiny flecks of thyme. Do not add cream to this soup, or you will dilute the magical flavour, the essence of the herb.

Lovage and Potato Soup

butter	a knob
olive oil	2 tbsp
medium onion, *finely chopped*	1
medium potatoes, *diced*	3
lovage leaves, *stripped from their stalks*	55g/2oz
chicken stock (see p. 54)	1.2 litre / 2 pints

The Greeks and the Romans used lovage, as did the Tudors and the Stuarts, who also bathed in it. It has a sort of musky flavour and underscores a dish in just the same way as celery.

→ Heat the BUTTER and OIL together in a heavy-bottomed casserole, add the ONION and POTATO, and stir to coat. Add the finely chopped LOVAGE, stir for a couple of minutes, season, then add the STOCK. Bring to the boil, then turn down to a blip of a simmer, and put the lid on the pan for 15 minutes. Liquidise thoroughly, add SALT AND PEPPER to taste, and heat to scalding point again. I also ate this soup cold the next day, jellied and straight from the fridge, and it was delicious.

Cream of Fennel Soup

SERVES 4

fennel bulbs	3
small onion, *chopped*	1
olive oil	
butter	
dill seeds	1 tsp
chicken stock (see p. 54)	900ml/1½ pints
salt, pepper	
lemon juice	
single cream	a few tbsp

There are times when I feel like something mild and delicate. Florentine fennel, with its slightly medicinal astringency, has a flavour that can support this pale but interesting soup.

→ Remove the tough outer layers from the FENNEL and chop the bulbs and wispy fronds. Heat the OIL and BUTTER, a splosh of one, 30g/1oz or so of the other, in a heavy-bottomed pan. Add the fennel and ONION, with the DILL SEEDS and some SALT AND PEPPER, and soften gently with a lid on for 15–20 minutes, peeking occasionally and giving an encouraging stir. Then add the hot stock and simmer until the vegetables are soft, about 15 minutes, before you push everything through the coarse disc of a mouli-légumes (my preference) or liquidise and sieve if you haven't got a mouli.

→ Add a few tablespoons of CREAM, taste, adjust the SEASONING and cream and add a tiny spritz of LEMON if you feel like cutting the creaminess a little. Reheat to boiling point, but do not let it boil, and serve. You could, if you like, serve this soup with Parmesan crisps, or just with a good roll or a ficelle with fennel and poppy seeds.

Spinach and Rosemary Soup

SERVES 8

medium potatoes, *peeled and cubed*	2
medium onion, *peeled and chopped*	1
rosemary	4 or 5 sprigs
olive oil	
butter	
chicken stock (see p. 54)	1.5 litres/2¾ pints
spinach, washed, *tough stalks discarded*	675g/1½lb
salt, pepper, lemon juice	

→ Gently sauté the POTATO, ONION and 3 sprigs of finely chopped ROSEMARY in a little OLIVE OIL and butter in a heavy-bottomed casserole. Season. When the vegetables begin to soften and turn translucent, add the STOCK, bring to the boil, then simmer until the potatoes are just tender—about 10 minutes.

→ Meanwhile, strip the ROSEMARY from the other 2 sprigs, and put it in a mortar with a pinch of SEA SALT. Pound until the raw green herb is well crushed, introduce a spoonful of OLIVE OIL, and pound again until you have a beautiful verdant slick of oily green. Throw the washed SPINACH, with a bit of water still clinging to it, into another pan and stir briskly until the leaves begin to exude their own juice, a matter of a minute or two. Chop them down a bit before putting them into the pan with the stock and vegetables. Blitz in the food processor, return to the pan, heat until just at boiling point, squeeze on the juice of a scant half LEMON, stir in the ROSEMARY OIL off the heat, check the SEASONING and serve.

Parsnip and Baked Apple Soup

SERVES 6

large cooking apple	1
small onion, *peeled and finely chopped*	1
parsnips, *peeled and diced*	750g/1lb 10oz
unsalted butter	55g/2oz
chicken or vegetable stock (see pp. 54–55)	1.2 litres/2 pints
sage leaves, *tied in a bundle with string*	6
cream (optional)	150ml/5fl oz
salt, pepper, flat-leaf parsley	

What an amenable root the parsnip is. It is enhanced by spicing, so makes a stunning curried soup. It also allows its sweetness to be offset by a good, sharp cooking apple.

→ Score the COOKING APPLE around its circumference, core it and place it on a tray with 1cm/½in of water. Bake in a hot oven until tender right through when pierced with a skewer. Peel, ensuring that there are no nasty toenaily bits around the core.

→ Sweat the ONION and PARSNIP in the BUTTER gently for about 10 minutes, SEASONING early on, then pour in the STOCK and SAGE and simmer until tender. Remove the sage and liquidise the soup, adding the apple.

→ Check the seasoning, reheat with or without the CREAM and serve with a scattering of chopped PARSLEY.

Spicy Thai-style Celeriac Soup

SERVES 4

medium-sized celeriac	1
olive oil	2–3 tbsp
small onion, *peeled and finely chopped*	1
leek, *cleaned, white chopped*	1
red chilli, *quartered, seeded and finely chopped*	1
garlic clove, *finely chopped*	1
root ginger, *peeled and grated*	1 thumb
water	1.2 litres/2 pints
creamed coconut	about 1 tbsp
sea salt and black pepper	

All winter roots make velvety-thick winter soups, but celeriac wins as it is less sweet than so many roots and has an idiosyncratic medicinal whiff. Its flavour is strong enough to shine through hot spices and works well with water rather than stock on your stock-free days.

→ Peel the CELERIAC and cut into small cubes, removing any squashy bits. Heat the OLIVE OIL in a heavy-bottomed pot and add the ONION, sweating it over a medium heat until it has begun to soften and turn translucent. Throw in the LEEK and RED CHILLI followed by the GARLIC, and stir to soften. Add the cubes of celeriac and turn thoroughly to coat in the oil. Continue to cook for 5 minutes or so until they begin to brown, making sure they don't stick to the base of the pot.

→ Add the GINGER, some SEASONING and the hot water, followed by the shards of CREAMED COCONUT, which you can break up into the soup. Simmer gently for 10–15 minutes until the celeriac is cooked through. Check the seasoning and blend the soup to a thick, velvety texture. This is a soup with a clean, fresh flavour that benefits from the lack of butter or cream.

Cucumber Soup

SERVES 6

organic cucumbers	2
medium onion, *finely chopped*	1
butter	55g/2oz
flour	2 scant tsp
good jellied chicken stock (see p. 54)	1.5 litres/2¾ pints
organic egg yolks	2
cream	2 tbsp
flat-leaf parsley, *chopped*	

A perfect, mild-mannered, delicate soup to serve before or with a selection of Irish cheeses for lunch or supper.

→ Peel the CUCUMBERS and chop them into dice. Stew the ONION gently in the butter in a lidded saucepan for a few minutes, then throw in the CUCUMBER, stir, cover, and continue to stew for about 10 minutes until tender. Liquidise.
→ Beat the EGG YOLKS with a couple of tablespoons of THICK CREAM in a small bowl. Add a ladle of the soup and whisk it in, then return the mixture to the pan. Heat through gently but do not boil. Serve with a twist of PARSLEY in each bowl.

Roasted Beetroot and Dill Soup

SERVES 4

medium beetroots	6–8
good jellied chicken stock (see p. 54)	1.2 litres/2 pints
sea salt and black pepper	
fresh dill, *finely chopped*	

Keep their whiskery bits on when you clean the beetroot, then no blood will bleed away as they cook.

→ Preheat the oven to 200°C/400°F/Gas 6. Wash the BEETROOTS, leaving on the whiskery bits. Wrap them in foil and roast on a baking tray in the hot oven until they are soft when you pierce them right the way through with a skewer. Remove them from the foil, push off the skins with your fingers and chop the beetroot into cubes.
→ Throw the cubed beetroot into the liquidiser with the boiling hot STOCK, a little of each at a time, and whizz. Reheat and season, but don't prolong the cooking time or let the soup boil or it will change colour. Serve with a pinch of fresh green DILL in the middle of each bowl.

Garlic Bread

garlic cloves, *skinned and crushed to a paste*	6–8
flat-leaf parsley, *chopped*	a handful
unsalted butter, *softened*	110g/4oz
black pepper	
lemon juice (optional)	a spritz
baguette	1

This is the perfect accompaniment to most soups.

→ Preheat the oven to 180°C/350°F/Gas 4. Work the GARLIC and PARLEY into the BUTTER on a large flat plate with a fork, season with BLACK PEPPER and add a spritz of LEMON JUICE if you like.
→ Cut the BAGUETTE into slices, not quite down to the base of the loaf. Spread the garlic butter generously into the slices and wrap in foil in a baggy but sealed parcel. Place on a shallow roasting tray and bake for about 20 minutes. Serve in the opened-out foil. I cut my slices about 2.5cm/1in thick so that each one has enough butter soaked right into the bread.

Green Salad Soup

Serves 6

medium potato	1
butter	55g / 2oz
medium onion	1
organic rocket leaves	255g / 9oz
baby spinach	450g / 1lb
bunch watercress	255g / 9oz
milk	300ml / 10fl oz
chicken OR vegetable stock (see pp. 54–55)	900ml / 1½ pints
salt and black pepper	to taste
toasted almonds (optional)	a few
single cream (optional)	

→ Peel and chop the POTATO into small dice. Chop the ONION finely. Melt the BUTTER in a large saucepan and sweat the onion and potato until soft and transparent over a low heat for 5–10 minutes. Add all the GREEN LEAVES and sweat with the butter and onions until they have collapsed — about 5 minutes. Give them a stir from time to time. Add the STOCK and MILK and simmer on a low heat for 10 minutes. Blitz the soup until you have a smooth purée and add SALT AND PEPPER to taste.
→ Garnish with a few TOASTED ALMONDS and a swirl of SINGLE CREAM on each bowl before serving. The soup can be served hot or cold, and with or without the garnish.

Thai Lettuce and Pea Soup

Serves 6

coriander seeds	1 tsp
cumin seeds	1 tsp
medium onions, *roughly chopped*	2
olive oil	1 tbsp
garlic cloves, *peeled and chopped*	2
fresh ginger	
fresh chilli paste	½ tsp
medium potato, *peeled and cubed*	1
chicken OR vegetable stock (see pp. 54–55)	900ml / 1½ pints
tinned coconut milk	400ml / 13fl oz
fresh or frozen peas	300g / 10oz
lettuce	1

A recipe from Sally Edwards, who ran the River Café in Taunton. Sally makes her soup with a vegetable stock; I made my version with chicken stock. Experiment.

→ Roast the CORIANDER and CUMIN SEEDS briefly in a frying pan for only 30 seconds or so until they exude their scent; any longer and they burn. Peel and chop or grate the GINGER. Prepare the CHILLI PASTE. Sally uses Bart's Spices fresh hot chilli in sunflower oil, or you can use some seeded red chilli crushed in the mortar with a bit of salt
→ Sauté the ONION gently in a little OLIVE OIL. Add the GARLIC, ginger, spices and chilli and sauté for a few more minutes until softened and translucent. Add the POTATO and STOCK, then simmer together for 25–30 minutes. Add the COCONUT MILK, bring back to a simmer. Add the PEAS and LETTUCE and bring it back to a simmer before removing from the heat. Process in the blender, season and serve.

Cream of Portobello Mushroom Soup

SERVES 4

mushrooms	450g /1lb
lemon	1
unsalted butter	50–85g / 2–3oz
pinch of ginger	
onion, *finely chopped*	1 tbsp
garlic clove, *finely chopped*	1
flour	1 tbsp
chicken stock (see p. 54)	900ml/1½ pints
double cream	120ml / 4fl oz
salt and pepper	

Good supermarkets have Portobello mushrooms in autumn; if you can't find them or field mushrooms, use organic chestnut mushrooms.

→ Chop the MUSHROOMS finely and sprinkle them with LEMON JUICE. Melt a large knob of the BUTTER in a pan, and gently cook the ONION and GARLIC until softened and pale gold. Add the mushrooms, sprinkle with a pinch of GINGER, and cook until their juice has almost evaporated.

→ Melt another knob of BUTTER in a pan, then stir in the FLOUR until bubbling, and gradually add the HOT STOCK —you can use veal stock instead of chicken. Whisk until smooth, and simmer for about 10 minutes. Add the MUSHROOM MIXTURE and continue to simmer for another 10 minutes. Season and stir in the CREAM. Liquidise if you want a smooth, velvety soup.

Sweetcorn Soup with a Rouille

SERVES 6

corn cobs	6
unsalted butter	45g/1½ oz
medium onion, *peeled and finely chopped*	1
leek, white part only, *washed and chopped*	1
small carrot, *peeled and diced*	1
garlic cloves, *peeled and finely chopped*	2
chicken OR vegetable stock (see pp. 54–55)	1.2 litres / 2 pints
double cream	6 tbsp
salt, pepper, sugar and lemon juice	
fresh coriander, *chopped* (optional)	
Rouille	
pimentos / piquillo peppers	200g /7oz jar
garlic clove, *peeled*	1
red chilli peppers, *seeded*	2
olive oil	2 tbsp

→ Strip the kernels from the CORN COBS with a sharp knife. Melt the BUTTER, add the ONION and stew gently with the LEEK and CARROT in a heavy-bottomed pan until translucent. Add the GARLIC about 10 minutes into the cooking. Pour over the HOT STOCK, and carry on simmering for 10 minutes.

→ Add the kernels of corn, bring the soup back to the boil, then take the pan off the heat. Leave the pan for 5 minutes before puréeing in your blender. It will need a good 2 or 3 minutes before it is liquidised enough for you to push it through a sieve. Then stir in the CREAM and season to taste with SUGAR and LEMON as well as SALT AND PEPPER. If the corn is young and sweet enough, you will not need any sugar.

Rouille

→ Make the rouille by simply placing the PIMENTOS, GARLIC, CHILLI and OLIVE OIL in the blender with some SEASONING and whizzing them to a scarlet paste to be dropped into the centre of the corn yellow soup. Add a scattering of CORIANDER leaves over the summit if you feel like it.

Pea Soup

SERVES 4–6

unsalted butter	55g/2oz
medium onion, *peeled and finely chopped*	1
smoked streaky bacon, *snipped small* (optional)	2 rashers
shelled weight fresh or frozen peas	225g/8oz
OR dried split peas	110g/4oz
chicken stock (see p. 54)	1.2 litres/2 pints
OR ham stock with the ham bone left in it	
sea salt, black pepper	
fresh mint, *leaves chopped small at the last minute*	2–3 sprigs

Use fresh or frozen peas for this—add some of the pods if you like when using fresh. You can also make a thicker, muskier, but delicious soup with dried yellow or green split peas. If using split peas, soak them in cold water overnight.

→ Melt the BUTTER in a heavy-bottomed pan and sauté the ONION gently until it begins to soften and turn golden. Add the BACON if you are using it and continue to fry for a couple of minutes, stirring as you go. Tip in the PEAS, turn them briefly in the butter then pour in half the STOCK and simmer until the peas are cooked for 5–10 minutes depending on their size and freshness. Simmer the PEA PODS in the rest of stock if you are using them.

→ If you are making the soup with DRIED SPLIT PEAS, they will take up to an hour to cook, but check the peas are soft after 40 minutes, having skimmed the pan when they first come to the boil. Do not season the dried variety with salt until they are cooked or they will toughen. This applies to all dried lentils and beans as well.

→ Liquidise and dilute with more of the STOCK until you have the desired texture, SEASON and sprinkle over FRESH MINT just before serving. If you have used a ham bone, strip of any remaining meat to add to the soup.

You can also add the rind of a hunk of Parmesan to the soup when you are cooking it if you like a whiff of its flavour with the peas.

French Onion Soup

SERVES 6–8

onions	1kg/2¼ lb
unsalted butter	55g/2oz
light olive oil	2 tbsp
sea salt	
flour	55g/2oz
hot beef stock OR half beef, half chicken stock (see pp. 54–55)	1.5 litres/2¾ pints
sea salt and fresh black pepper	

The threads of gooey Gruyère, pulled like skeins from the softened toasts, make this the homeliest and sexiest of soups.

→ Slice the ONIONS thinly—use a mandolin if you have one. Melt the BUTTER and OLIVE OIL in a heavy-bottomed pan. Throw in the onions and sprinkle them with salt so that they start exuding their juices. Cook, stirring from time to time, over a low heat for about 20 minutes until they turn a gorgeous golden brown colour and are wilted. Scatter the FLOUR over them and stir for a couple of minutes. Pour the HOT STOCK over the onions and stir before partially covering the pan and letting it blip away at a low simmer for about 30–40 minutes. Season with SALT AND PEPPER to taste.

baguette	1
olive oil to brush the bread with	
garlic clove, *cut in half*	1
Beaufort or other good Gruyère, *grated*	110g/4oz
Parmesan, *freshly grated*	55g/2oz

→ While the soup is simmering, preheat the oven to 170°C/325°F/Gas 3. Slice the BAGUETTE into 12–16 slices, 2.5cm/1in thick. Place the slices on a baking tray and toast for 10–15 minutes on one side. Then brush both sides with OLIVE OIL and toast the other side. Rub the slices with the cut GARLIC.

→ When the soup is ready, either float a couple of slices of baguette in each filled bowl and pass the cheese round, or gratinée them the REAL onion soup way. To do this, place the slices of baguette in the pot of soup or individual bowls—you need ovenproof bowls for this—sprinkle cheese on top and sprinkle a few drops of olive oil onto each one. Turn up the oven temperature to 190°C/375°F/Gas 5. Put the pot or bowls in the oven for 10 minutes or until the cheese has melted, then slip under a hot grill to brown.

Cauliflower Cheese and Grain Mustard Soup

SERVES 4

unsalted butter	55g/2oz
onion, *peeled and finely chopped*	1
garlic clove, *peeled and finely minced*	1
large cauliflower in florets	1
bay leaf	1
large potato, *peeled and cubed*	1
chicken stock (see p. 54)	1.2 litres/2 pints
double cream	4 tbsp
grain mustard	1 tbsp
farmhouse Cheddar, *coarsely grated*	170g/6oz

This is also delicious made with half cauliflower, half broccoli, so just do what your store cupboard and taste dictate. A real winter warmer of a soup.

→ Melt the BUTTER in a heavy-bottomed pan and throw in the ONION and GARLIC to soften and turn translucent. Do not let them brown. Meanwhile, throw the CAULIFLOWER FLORETS into the boiling STOCK in another pan and cook until tender, about 7 or 8 minutes. Add the BAY LEAF to the onion, followed by the cauliflower in its stock and the CUBED POTATO, and continue to simmer for 15 minutes.

→ Remove the bay leaf and process the soup in batches in the liquidiser until smooth, before tipping it back into the pan. Stir in the CREAM and then the MUSTARD and a little scrunch of BLACK PEPPER. Scatter in the CHEDDAR and stir briefly before removing from the heat and serving. Do not add salt until you have tasted the soup with the cheese in it. Cheddar is salty.

Quick Cauliflower Soup

SERVES 4

small cauliflower	1
large potato, *peeled and cubed*	1
garlic cloves, *peeled and finely minced*	2
semi-skimmed milk	1.2 litres/2 pints
unsalted butter	
Parmesan cheese, *grated*	30g/1oz
sea salt and white pepper	

→ Break the CAULIFLOWER into small florets and put it in a large pan with the POTATO, GARLIC and MILK. Simmer gently until the potato is soft. Add the BUTTER and PARMESAN and blend in a liquidiser until velvety smooth. Strain through a sieve, season, reheat and serve.

Leek, Broccoli and Stilton Soup

SERVES 4

small onion	1
olive oil	2 tbsp
butter	30g/1oz
broccoli	a head
leeks, whites only, *finely chopped*	3
chicken stock (see p. 54)	1.2 litres/2 pints
cream	150ml/5fl oz
Stilton OR other blue cheese	up to 55g/2oz
black pepper	

The important thing with this soup is to add the Stilton crumb by crumbled crumb at the end and to keep tasting. The cheese is very salty and very strong and you don't want it to overwhelm. If you don't have Stilton, use Roquefort, Cashel Blue, Beenleigh Blue, Fourme d'Ambert or any other good blue.

→ Chop the ONION very finely and cook it gently in the OIL AND BUTTER for a few minutes. Divide the BROCCOLI into florets, peel the stalks and chop into slices. Add the LEEKS and broccoli to the onions and turn to coat them. Let them sweat, cook down and begin to soften for about 5 minutes before you add the HOT STOCK. Simmer very gently until the broccoli is cooked through but hasn't lost its colour and barely-tender feel. Add the cream and blitz in the liquidiser.

→ Return to the pan and heat gently without boiling, slowly adding little crumbly bits of STILTON and some BLACK PEPPER until you have the right balance of cheese and vegetable. You might not need any salt as the Stilton is very salty.

Walnut Soup

SERVES 6

shelled walnuts	170g / 6oz
large garlic clove	1
chicken stock (see p. 54)	1.2 litres / 2 pints
cream	150ml / 5fl oz
sea salt and freshly ground black pepper	

This is delicate and robust at the same time and highly unusual. You need to use very high-quality fresh walnuts.

→ Crush the WALNUTS and GARLIC to a paste with a little of the STOCK in a mortar or a liquidiser. Incorporate the rest of the stock slowly until the mixture has the consistency of single cream. If the walnuts have been liquidised they will probably take up most of the stock; if they've been pounded in a mortar they'll take about 850ml / 1½ pints.

→ Pour the soup through a sieve into a saucepan and bring to the boil. Add the CREAM and correct the seasoning with SALT AND PEPPER. Serve straight away.

Chestnut and Thyme Soup with Juniper

SERVES 4

olive oil	1 tbsp
unsalted butter	30g / 1oz
small onion, *finely chopped*	1
good sprig of thyme, *leaves stripped and chopped*	1
juniper berries, *crushed in a mortar*	4–6
chestnuts, *roughly chopped*	200g / 7oz
chicken stock (see p. 54)	900ml / 1½ pints
sea salt and black pepper	
crème fraîche (optional)	

I use a jar of Sierra Rica organic chestnuts for this, which good delis, supermarkets and organic stores sell. The French or Italian vacuum-packed ones are very good too, and so little trouble.

→ Heat the OLIVE OIL and butter together in a heavy-bottomed pan and add the ONION, stirring to coat. Cook over a medium heat until it softens and begins to turn golden. Add the THYME, which will release its astringent oily scent almost immediately, then add 4 of the crushed JUNIPER BERRIES and stir them in with the thyme. Add the CHESTNUTS, followed by the HOT STOCK. Bring to the boil, SEASON and turn to a mere burble of a simmer for 15–20 minutes. Liquidise until smooth.

→ Test the seasoning and juniper, which needs to be a background hint only, adding more if you need. Serve with a spoon of CRÈME FRAÎCHE if you like, but I prefer to keep this soup light. Delicate, restorative and fragrant.

Brazil Nut and Lemon Soup

SERVES 6

unsalted butter	30g / 1oz
medium onion, *sliced*	1
chicken stock (see p. 54)	1.2 litres / 2 pints
Brazil nuts, *shelled*	110g / 4oz
zest of a lemon, *cut into thick strips*	
sea salt and freshly ground black pepper	
single cream	60ml / 2fl oz

I first cooked this soup from Joyce Molyneaux's lovely The Carved Angel Cookery Book *years ago. As she says, if you have any leftover Brazil nuts after Christmas it's a good way to use them up. This is an unusual and delicately refreshing soup.*

→ Melt the BUTTER in a heavy-bottomed pan. Sweat the ONION, covered, for 15 minutes. Add the HOT STOCK, NUTS and LEMON ZEST, SEASON, cover and simmer gently for a further 20 minutes. Process in a liquidiser until smooth. Return the soup to the pan and stir in the CREAM. Check the seasoning and reheat before serving.

Potage Bonne Femme with Dumplings

unsalted butter	45g / 1½ oz
large leeks, *cleaned, finely sliced*	2
carrots, *diced*	3
potatoes, *peeled, diced*	450g / 1lb
water	1.2 litres / 2 pints
sea salt and black pepper	
sugar	1 tsp
cream (optional)	a little
flat-leaf parsley and chervil	

Cornmeal Dumplings

wholemeal bread, *finely torn into pieces*	200g / 7oz
organic egg	2
duck fat (OR melted butter)	2 tbsp
smoked streaky bacon, *minced*	55g / 2oz
fresh horseradish, *grated*	2 heaped tbsp
polenta	85g / 3oz
sea salt and black pepper	

A soup of substance that you can serve as a lunch or supper dish in its own right in the winter.

→ Melt the BUTTER and add the LEEKS and CARROTS. Make sure they are coated in butter before adding the POTATOES, 1.2 litres / 2 pints of WATER, SEASONING and SUGAR. Simmer for 20 minutes before adding the dumplings.

→ Mix the DUMPLING INGREDIENTS in a large bowl. Roll into about 12 balls and cook in the gently simmering soup for about 15 minutes. Remove and keep warm. Adjust the SEASONING to the soup, liquidise it, and add a little CREAM if you like. Put the dumplings back as you serve the soup and sprinkle with chopped CHERVIL and flat-leaf PARSLEY.

New England Clam Chowder

SERVES 4

clams	2kg / 4½lb
shallot, *chopped*	1
stick of celery, *roughly chopped*	1
smallish potatoes	3
organic smoked streaky bacon	2 rashers
medium onion, *finely chopped*	1
thyme	a sprig, enough for ½ tbsp
bay leaf	1
unsalted butter	30g/1oz
double cream	170ml/6fl oz
sea salt and black pepper	
flat-leaf parsley, *chopped*	1 tbsp

I make this classic chowder with beautiful carpetshell clams from the Devon coast. All creamy salt-sweetness with a little added starchiness from the potatoes and smoky crispness from the rashers, this is a perfect starter or can make a more substantial lunch or supper dish if you up the quantity.

→ Put the CLAMS into a large pan with a cup of COLD WATER, the SHALLOT and CELERY. Steam over a fierce heat until all the clams have opened. Pour the cooking liquor through a sieve and set it aside. Remove the clams from their shells once they have cooled down a little.

→ Peel the POTATOES, cut into 1cm/½ in cubes and set aside. Snip the BACON RASHERS into small pieces with a pair of scissors and cook them in the pan until the fat runs. Stir in the finely chopped ONION, THYME, BAY LEAF and BUTTER and cook until the onions have turned translucent. Add the reserved CLAM LIQUOR and the POTATOES, and simmer until the potatoes are cooked through. Stir in the CLAMS and CREAM and simmer for 4–5 minutes before seasoning and adding the PARSLEY. Serve with bread, or American-style with crackers.

Smoked Fish and Shrimp Chowder

SERVES 6 AS A STARTER
OR 4 AS A MAIN COURSE

naturally smoked haddock fillet	225g/8oz
unsalted butter	30g/1oz
onion, *peeled, finely chopped*	1
back bacon, *unsmoked, snipped into small strips*	4 rashers
carrots, *cut into small cubes*	2
celery sticks, *strung, finely sliced*	2
medium potatoes, *peeled, cubed*	2
plain flour	30g / 1oz
full-cream milk	1.2 litres/2 pints
small, shelled cooked shrimps	110g/4oz
flat-leaf parsley	2 tbsp
Parmesan, *grated*	110g / 4oz

The pairing of fish and cheese is a matter of debate, but on the subject of smoked haddock and cheese there seems little or no dissent. Cheddar and Parmesan are the ones, and there is nothing quite like a warming bowl of cheesy, smoky chowder with perhaps some bacon or chorizo thrown in.

→ Poach the HADDOCK for a few minutes in some hot milk, then skin it. Melt the BUTTER in a large, heavy bottomed pan and then throw in the ONION and BACON and cook gently until the onion has turned translucent. Add the CARROT, CELERY and POTATO and stir to coat, then sprinkle over the FLOUR and keep turning for a minute or so. Pour in a third of the HOT MILK and stir well, allowing the mixture to thicken before you add the rest of the milk and bring it just up to the boil. Add 140ml/¼ pint of HOT WATER, and when it has all come to the boil again, turn down to a simmer and cook until all the vegetables have softened, about 15 minutes.

→ Cut the HADDOCK into small, flaky bits, add it with the SHRIMP to the pot and cook for about 4 minutes. Season with PEPPER (the fish is salty), sprinkle with PARSLEY and serve in bowls with PARMESAN to pass around.

Smoked Haddock Soup

SERVES 4

smoked haddock	225g/8oz
cod, hake OR haddock	225g/8oz
butter	55g/2oz
large onion, *chopped*	1
flour	1 tbsp
milk	600ml/1 pint
large cooked prawns	225g/8oz
double cream	150ml/5fl oz
salt, pepper	
lemon	1
flat-leaf parsley, *chopped*	a handful

→ Put the smoked HADDOCK in a gratin dish, cover it with boiling water and leave for 10 minutes. Cut the WHITE FISH into cubes. Melt the BUTTER in a large pan and sauté the ONION gently, adding the FLOUR when the onion has softened. Cook for a minute or two, then add about 150ml/5fl oz of the haddock-soaking LIQUOR and the MILK.

→ Put the cubes of white fish in the pan with the haddock, skin, bone and all, and simmer for 10 minutes. Remove the bones, then liquidise the soup. Throw in the PRAWNS, add the CREAM and bring the soup to just below boiling point. Season cautiously—it may not need extra salt—and squeeze on a little LEMON JUICE before adding the PARSLEY and serving.

Oyster Soup

SERVES 6

large oysters	2 dozen
shallots, chopped	2
leek, the white part	1
celery	1 stick
butter	85g/3oz
flour	2 tbsp
light beef stock (see p. 54)	600ml/1 pint
sea salt, pepper, cayenne, nutmeg	
double cream	150ml/5fl oz
chives, *chopped*	1 handful
lemon	1

This is a lovely light, fishy soup, perfect for smarter or family gatherings.

→ First, shuck your OYSTERS. It is a murderous procedure for the beginner, but it gets easier, and the satisfaction of accomplishing the task is high. If you don't have an oyster knife with a protective shield, use a short, fat knife such as a penknife blade. If you are right-handed, wrap your left hand in a tea towel, pick up the oyster, flat side up, and curl your fingers over it. Push the knife blade between the two shells at the hinge end and twist to lever open. Free the oyster from the shell with the knife tip, and remove any shell particles. Do this over a bowl to catch the juice.

→ Clean the LEEK and chop. De-string the CELERY stick with a potato peeler and chop finely. Sauté the SHALLOTS, leek and celery gently in the BUTTER until they are soft and beginning to turn golden. Sprinkle in the FLOUR and cook for 30 seconds or so before adding the HOT STOCK and turning up the heat. Strain the OYSTER JUICE into the pan through a sieve and SEASON, going easy on the cayenne. Bring just short of boiling point and leave to simmer for about 20 minutes with the lid on.

→ Just before serving, pour in the CREAM and scatter in the CHIVES. Remove from the heat and add the oysters and a spritz of lemon juice.

Passatelli

SERVES 6

beef or veal stock (see p. 54)	1.4 litres / 2½ pints
Parmesan cheese, *freshly grated*	85g / 3oz
breadcrumbs, *made with stale bread*	6 tbsp
nutmeg	
organic lemon	*grated zest* of 1
organic eggs	2

The simplest and lightest of soups, this relies on a good basic broth made predominantly from beef and veal bones with the addition of a few chicken bones. The stock should be chilled and skimmed of fat. A mouli-légumes is the other imperative, through which the passatelli must be pressed.

→ Bring the STOCK slowly to the boil in a heavy-bottomed, uncovered pan. Meanwhile, combine the PARMESAN, BREAD-CRUMBS, a grating of NUTMEG and the LEMON ZEST together on a chopping board and make a well in the centre. Crack the EGGS into the well and knead everything together until it coheres.

→ Put the coarse grater on to a mouli-légumes. When the broth comes to boiling point, press the CHEESE MIXTURE through the mouli straight into it. Do this as high above the steam as you can. Cook at a gentle boil for a minute, then turn off the heat and leave the broth for 5 minutes. Serve with extra grated Parmesan in a bowl on the side.

Barley Broth

SERVES 8

neck of lamb OR mutton	1.5 kg / 3¼lb
organic barley	110g / 4oz
split peas	110g / 4oz
carrots, *peeled and diced*	2
turnip, *peeled and diced*	1
swede, *peeled and diced*	1
onions or fat leeks, *diced*	2
salt and pepper	
flat-leaf parsley, *chopped*	a handful

This is a soup of substance that is not really asking for anything to follow it. Quite the reverse, it is almost saying 'I bet you can't eat anything after this'.

→ Put the MEAT in the bottom of a large, heavy-bottomed pot, add 2.2–2.8 litres/4–5 pints of WATER, then the BARLEY and PEAS. Bring it to the boil slowly, skim until clear, then simmer slowly for an hour if it's mutton, 30 minutes if it's lamb. I mean so slowly that a bubble barely breaks the surface. Add the VEGETABLES and continue simmering until the meat is really tender. This could take as long as an hour.

→ When the meat is cooked, remove it and the vegetables, barley and pulses from the pot. Boil down the broth until you have a more intense flavour. SEASON, remove the meat from the bones if you feel like a modicum of refinement, and return everything to the pot to heat through. Throw a good handful of chopped PARSLEY into the pot and serve.

Chicken Soup

<small>Serves 8</small>

Stock

chicken carcasses from a cooked bird	1 large OR 2 small
onions, *halved, in their skins*	2 or 3
celery, *broken in two, with the leaves*	2 or 3 stalks
carrots, *chopped in chunks*	3 or 4
leeks, *cleaned and trimmed, use green and white parts*	2 or 3
parsley	a small bunch
peppercorns	6–8

Soup

chicken stock	2 litres / 3½ pints
celery stalks with their leaves	2
fennel bulb	1
small potato	1
parsnip, *peeled and chopped into tiny dice*	1
carrot, *peeled and chopped into tiny dice*	1
frozen petits pois	2 large handfuls
dark and light chicken meat	110–170g / 4–6oz
cornflour	2 tbsp
double cream	150ml / 5fl oz
sea salt and black pepper	
parsley	

This is the most comforting dish in the world and a dish you can play around with according to the season. Your base stock has to be good. Some like chicken soup thick, some like it thin; some like their vegetables puréed, some diced.

→ Strip any meat off the CARCASSES and cut into small pieces along the grain of the flesh. This can be added to the soup at the end of the cooking. Break the carcasses into two or three bits with your fingers and put them with the leftover bones and skin in a huge, heavy-bottomed pot. Heat gently, until the bones begin to brown and the skin starts to release its fat, then add the VEGETABLES, PARSLEY, PEPPERCORNS and enough WATER to cover. Bring to the boil slowly, then skim. Turn down to a simmer, put the lid on and bubble for a couple of hours.

→ Strain the liquid into a large bowl, pressing down on the vegetables. Throw all the contents of the strainer away. Allow the liquid to cool and refrigerate, if necessary, before using. Then remove the stock from the fridge and scoop off the solidified fat from the surface.

→ To make the soup, bring the STOCK to boiling point. Meanwhile, string the CELERY with a potato peeler and chop finely, and remove the outer leaves from the FENNEL and dice the rest. Add the POTATO to the stock. After five minutes of gentle simmering, throw in the PARSNIP and CARROT and, five minutes later, the celery and fennel. Cook until nearly softened before adding the PEAS for five minutes. Add the pieces of CHICKEN. Remove a couple of ladles of the hot stock from the pan to a bowl in which you've put the CORNFLOUR and stir with a small whisk until free of lumps. Return to the pan, add the CREAM, season, and bring to boiling point. Serve with a scattering of PARSLEY.

Turkey Soup

turkey carcass	
onions, *halved, in their skins*	2 or 3
celery stalks, *broken in two, with the leaves*	2 or 3

This soup is easier and quicker than the chicken soup above, but just as delicious. I wait until the carcass is nearly picked clean but there is just enough left to add to the soup at the end.

→ Strip off any remaining dark and light TURKEY MEAT to add at the end of cooking. Cut it into small pieces along the grain of the flesh. Break the CARCASS into two or three bits with your fingers and put them with any leftover bones and skin in a

carrots, *chopped in chunks*	3 or 4
leeks, *cleaned and trimmed, use green and white parts*	2 or 3
parsley	a small bunch
peppercorns	6–8
frozen petits pois	2 large handfuls
dark and light turkey meat	110–170g/4–6oz
cornflour (optional)	2 tbsp
double cream	150ml/5fl oz
sea salt and black pepper	
parsley	

huge, heavy-bottomed pot. Heat gently, until the bones begin to brown and the skin starts to release its fat, then add the VEGETABLES, PARSLEY, PEPPERCORNS and enough WATER to cover. Bring to the boil slowly, then skim. Turn down to a simmer, put the lid on and bubble for a couple of hours.

→ Add the pieces of TURKEY now. Put the CORNFLOUR into a bowl and pour in a couple of ladles of the hot stock from the pan. Stir with a small whisk until free of lumps. Not everyone likes their turkey or chicken soup thickened so ignore this if you wish.

→ Return to the pan, add the CREAM, SEASON, and bring to boiling point. Serve with a scattering of PARSLEY.

Chickpea Soup with Pasta

SERVES 6

dried chickpeas, *soaked overnight*	285g/10oz
vegetable stock (see p. 55) OR an organic stock cube, OR water	2 litres/3½ pints
rosemary	2 large sprigs
garlic cloves, *peeled and bruised with the back of a knife*	6
best olive oil	
organic tomatoes, *skinned and seeded*	300g/10oz
ditalini OR other tiny pasta	175g/6oz
Parmesan cheese, *freshly grated*	
salt and black pepper	

This soup does have guts, though they be vegetarian guts, and will quite happily stand alone as a main course. You can make the soup up to the point of cooking the pasta two or three days in advance and keep it in the fridge. You then reheat it, cook the ditalini and serve with a bowl of Parmesan. Start the day before by soaking the chickpeas overnight in plenty of water and a dessertspoon of bicarbonate of soda. You can use a stock cube if you like and a tin of tomatoes if there aren't any good ripe tomatoes around.

→ Drain and rinse the CHICKPEAS, put them in a large enamel pot and cover them with the VEGETABLE STOCK OR WATER. Add the sprigs of ROSEMARY (preferably inside muslin since they are not the easiest thing to fish out by their needles at the end), the GARLIC, and 2 tablespoons of OLIVE OIL. Put the lid on the pan and bring to the boil, then lower the heat to an unpersistent simmer and cook for 2 hours before you check to see if the chickpeas are soft. They will harden if you lift the lid early in the cooking or salt them before they are cooked.

→ When they are cooked, remove the garlic and rosemary and add the TOMATOES, which you have put through a mouli-légumes or processed. Season and simmer for 10 minutes more. Cook the PASTA separately and add to the pan when it is al dente.

→ You can omit the pasta if you feel like it, in which case you could purée half the soup for texture before returning it to the pan. It would be too thick to serve like this with pasta. Serve the soup in hot bowls, with a bowl of freshly grated PARMESAN cheese to hand round.

Lentil, Bacon and Pasta Soup

SERVES 6

olive oil	3 tbsp
small onions, *finely chopped*	2
garlic cloves, *finely chopped*	6
celery stalks, *peeled and finely chopped*	2
organic smoked streaky bacon, *snipped small* 110g/4oz	
Puy OR Umbrian lentils	225g/8oz
tinned organic tomatoes	2 × 400g/14oz
chicken OR vegetable stock, (see pp. 54–55) 1.5 litres/2¾ pints	
thyme	3 sprigs
fresh bay leaves	2
small, tubular pasta, but not as minute as ditalini 225g/8oz	
sea salt and black pepper	
flat-leaf parsley	a handful
Parmesan cheese, *freshly grated*	110g/4oz

Another meal in a bowl, or precursor to something light, say steamed or poached fish.

→ Heat the OIL in a large, heavy-bottomed casserole, add the ONIONS, CELERY and BACON and cook slowly until softened and translucent. Introduce the GARLIC after about 10 minutes, so it doesn't become bitter. Add the LENTILS and stir to coat them in the oil and bacon fat. Add the TOMATOES, chopping them down into the juice with a sharp knife, bring up to a bubble, then pour over the HOT STOCK. Add the THYME and BAY, and bring to the boil. Cover and simmer for about 40 minutes, until the lentils are cooked. If the lentils are absorbing too much liquid, and beginning to look too thick for a soup, add a ladleful more of water whenever necessary. Season when the lentils are cooked through.

→ Cook the PASTA separately until al dente, then add some to each soup bowl when ready. If you have enough soup left over to reheat, you need to cook fresh pasta for it, since pasta goes very soggy if it is left in soup and then reheated. This can be made a couple of days in advance, up to the point where you cook the pasta, and kept in the fridge until needed.

Split Pea Soup

SERVES 4–6

green split peas, *washed* 450g/1lb	
ham or chicken stock (see p. 54) OR water 1.5 litres/2¾ pints	
white wine	⅓ bottle
onions, *stuck with a couple of cloves each*	2
a bouquet of fresh bay, thyme, parsley and rosemary, *tied together*	
carrots, *roughly chopped*	3
celery stalks, *chopped*	2
leeks, green tops only	3
peppercorns	12
ham bone	1

Pea soup can be made with chicken stock, but the stock you've cooked a ham in is infinitely superior, with the little snippets of leftover meat pulled from it and thrown like pink jewels into a thick sea of green. With a hunk of burnt-crusted white bread and some good butter, I can't think of a nicer way to beat the winter chill.

→ Put the SPLIT PEAS in a large, heavy-bottomed casserole with the STOCK, WINE, ONIONS, BOUQUET OF HERBS, CARROTS, CELERY, LEEK TOPS, PEPPERCORNS and the HAM BONE and bring to the boil. Skim off the scum with a slotted spoon and some kitchen paper, then turn the heat down to a simmer and leave the pot on the stove for about an hour.

→ When the peas are cooked through, the other vegetables should be too. Remove the bone, leek tops, bouquet and the cloves from the onions and purée all the rest together in a blender. Return to the pan and SEASON to taste. You may not

chunks of meaty ham	225g / 8oz
fresh mint leaves	
butter (optional)	a little

need salt as the ham bone and stock may be salty enough. Add the chopped MINT, about 6 leaves, and a knob of BUTTER if you like, 30g/1oz or so, stirring it in as the soup heats through. Throw in the little chunks of HAM off the heat and serve.

Red Lentil Soup

SERVES 4

onion, *peeled and chopped*	1
olive oil	
cumin and coriander seeds, *toasted and crushed*	1 tsp
turmeric	1 tsp
red lentils, *washed*	450g / 1lb
stock (see p. 54)	1.5 litres / 2¾ pints
root ginger, *chopped*	1 finger
cinnamon stick	1 piece
cardamon pods	

→ Sauté the chopped ONION in a little OIL and add the toasted and crushed CUMIN and CORIANDER SEEDS and the TURMERIC. Throw in the LENTILS, then add STOCK or water, GINGER, a CINNAMON STICK and the CARDAMOM PODS and CLOVES. Simmer for 30–40 minutes until the lentils are soft. Take out the whole spices and liquidise half the soup, leaving the rest as it is for texture.

This dish can also be served as a dal if you use less stock or water.

Risi e Bisi, or Rice and Peas

SERVES 4

unsalted butter	30g / 1oz
mild extra virgin olive oil	2 tbsp
small onion, *very finely chopped*	1
flat-leaf parsley, *chopped*	3 tbsp
small, fresh peas (podded weight) OR frozen petits pois	450g / 1lb
risotto rice, preferably Vialone Nano	225g / 8oz
chicken stock (see p. 54)	up to 1.2 litres / 2 pints
sugar, sea salt and black pepper	
Parmesan, *freshly grated*	55g / 2oz

This is a classic Venetian dish which is turned into a soup, if you feel like it, by the addition of hot chicken stock at the end.

→ Put the BUTTER, OIL, ONION and a tablespoon of the chopped PARSLEY in a large, heavy-bottomed pot and sauté very gently for 5 minutes or so. Add the PEAS and cook, stirring all the time, for a couple of minutes. Stir in the RICE until all the grains are coated in the butter and oil, then pour in 700ml/1¼ pints of the HOT STOCK. Stir and bring to the boil before adding the FENNEL SEEDS and seasoning and boiling, covered, for 15–20 minutes or until the rice is cooked.

→ Remove from the heat and stir in the PARMESAN and the rest of the PARSLEY. Ladle into bowls into which you ladle extra CHICKEN STOCK to make them more soupy than risotto-like. If you are using fresh peas you can simmer the pea pods until tender then drain, reserving the cooking water to use instead of stock.

Iced Almond and Garlic Soup

This is a deliciously creamy-cold, absolutely white soup made with organic garlic and country market white bread. It dates back over 1,000 years to when the Moors ruled much of Spain.

SERVES 4

organic Spanish almonds	110g/4oz
white day-old bread, *crusts cut off*	225g/8oz
new season's garlic cloves, *peeled*	2
salt	
olive oil	2–3 tbsp
sherry vinegar OR white wine tarragon vinegar	2 tbsp
fridge-cold water	600ml/1 pint
seedless green grapes	a handful

→ Process the ALMONDS until ground. Wet the BREAD, then squeeze it out. Tear it into chunks and throw it in the blender with the chopped GARLIC, SALT and OLIVE OIL. Purée, then add the VINEGAR and ALMONDS, and slowly pour in the cold water with the blender running. Process until smooth and creamy.

→ Refrigerate for several hours, then ladle into bowls and toss in a few GRAPES.

Iced Plum Tomato Soup

Ripe, well-flavoured plum or heritage tomatoes are a must for this great summer soup. A lovely starter to prepare and cool in advance on a hot summer's day.

SERVES 4

ripe plum tomatoes, *halved and seeded*	450g/1lb
cherry tomatoes	450g/1lb
tomato juice	300ml/10fl oz
balsamic vinegar, a good one	3 tsp
sea salt and pepper	
fresh buffalo mozzarella	140g/5oz
basil and olive oil purée, *simply blitz the two together*	60ml/2fl oz
small basil leaves, purple if you can find them	a handful
mixed small tomatoes, yellow, red, *cut into small dice*	140g/5oz

→ Process the PLUM TOMATOES in the liquidiser with the CHERRY TOMATOES, JUICE, BALSAMIC VINEGAR and GARLIC. Pass the mixture through a sieve, pushing as much through as you can. Season and correct the flavour, adding a little more balsamic vinegar if you need to.

→ Chill the soup in the freezer for 30 minutes or in the fridge if you have more time. Serve in soup plates with small slices of MOZZARELLA, a little BASIL PURÉE, a few BASIL LEAVES and a spoon of DICED TOMATO.

Gazpacho

SERVES 6–8

tomatoes	450g/1lb
stale white bread, *crusts removed*	2 slices
small onion, *cut into chunks*	1
garlic cloves, *peeled and chopped*	2
best olive oil	2 tbsp
sea salt and cayenne	
cucumber, *half-peeled, quartered lengthwise and seeded*	1
red peppers	1½
best sherry vinegar	2 tbsp
very cold water straight from the fridge	600–850ml / 1–1½ pints

If you are making this at the last minute, it can be whacked into the freezer for a 30-minute freeze-down. If you have time, make it the day before you need it, keep it in the fridge overnight and allow the intense flavours to mingle. On the day, just add a jug of cold water and stir to the desired texture and strength. Use organic tinned tomatoes with their juice if you can't get good fresh tomatoes.

Chop the TOMATOES. I don't bother to skin them—you may prefer to—but I do halve and seed. Hold the BREAD under the cold tap, then squeeze out the water and put it in the food processor with the ONION, GARLIC, OLIVE OIL, a teaspoon of SEA SALT and the CAYENNE. The soup is meant to have warmth, not fire, so start with the tip of a teaspoon of cayenne, and correct at the end if it is not quite right. Blitz briefly to a pulp.
→ Add the CUCUMBER, PEPPERS, VINEGAR and TOMATO and blitz until liquid. The mixture will be coarse rather than puréed. Pour into a bowl, cover and chill as above. Just before serving, dilute with the FRIDGE-COLD WATER, stirring and tasting to the required texture and flavour. Adjust the SEASONING and serve in tall glasses or bowls. You can also serve little bowls of chopped egg, olives, peppers and ham and let people add what they like to their soup.

Avocado Soup

SERVES 4

ripe avocados, *stones removed*	2
whipping cream	250ml/8½fl oz
chicken stock, *chilled, gelled* (see p. 54)	1.2 litres/2 pints
lemon juice	
Tabasco sauce	
Worcestershire sauce	
sea salt and black pepper	
raw onion, *very finely minced*	1 tbsp
sugar	1 tsp
chives, *chopped*	2 tbsp
crème fraîche (optional)	

This soothing, cooling soup is thickly rich and creamy, with the oiliness of the avocado muted by lemon juice and a burst of chilli.

→ Put ALL THE INGREDIENTS except the chives and crème fraîche into the blender—start with the juice of half a lemon until you have tasted the mixture. Go easy on the Tabasco and Worcestershire as you don't want either of them to take over, just to warm and deepen the flavours. When you have the right balance, pour the soup into a glass bowl and chill for a few hours. Finish with a sprinkle of chopped CHIVES.
→ If you are serving the soup in individual bowls, add a dollop of CRÈME FRAÎCHE over which you scatter the chives.

Chilled Beetroot Soup

SERVES 6

small beetroots about 500g/1lb 2oz	
chicken OR vegetable stock (see pp. 54–55) 1.5 litres/2¾ pints	
2 tbsp good-sized organic tomatoes, *chopped*	3 or 4
salt and fresh black pepper	
lemon juice	
soured cream	150ml/5fl oz
chives, *chopped*	2 tbsp

The combination of garnet-hued beetroot, ivory sour cream and green snipped chives is as beautiful as it is delicious. The tomatoes add a sour note to the earthy sweetness of the beetroot.

→ Clean the BEETROOTS, leaving their whiskery bits intact. Bake the beetroots in individually wrapped foil parcels in a hottish oven until just tender when pierced with a skewer. Peel and cube them and add them to the HOT STOCK, keeping one or two back to perk up the colour later. Add the chopped TOMATOES, and keep the temperature at a blip for 20 minutes. Liquidise and sieve the soup, then let it cool and chill in the fridge.

→ Grate the remaining BEETROOT. SEASON the soup to taste, add a spritz of LEMON JUICE, and pour into bowls. Add a spoon of grated beetroot and one each of SOUR CREAM and CHIVES to each bowl. The stock should be really concentrated and jellied if possible.

Iced Broad Bean Soup

SERVES 4

onion, *chopped*	110g/4oz
unsalted butter	55g/2oz
chicken stock (see p. 54)	1 litre/1¾ pints
tiny broad beans (podded weight)	450g/1lb
sea salt, pepper, sugar	
cream	
lovage OR sage, *finely chopped*	a few leaves

→ Soften the ONION gently in the BUTTER in a heavy-bottomed casserole, sprinkling on some SEA SALT to draw out the moisture. Add three-quarters of the BEANS, stir for a minute and tip on the boiling CHICKEN STOCK. Cook the soup at a simmer until the beans are done, about 5 minutes. Season with more salt, pepper and a tiny scrap of SUGAR.

→ Cook THE REST OF THE BEANS even more briefly by throwing them into boiling salted water for a couple of minutes, draining and refreshing in cold water, then peeling them. Fiddly, but worth it—the baby emerald green beans lurking like jewels in the soup make all the difference. Liquidise the soup, sieve it, then throw in the SHELLED BEANS and allow it to cool in a bowl before leaving in the fridge for several hours before you drink it. You can stir in a bit of CREAM if you want a rich soup, I prefer not to. Sprinkle some LOVAGE over each bowl when you serve it.

→ You can also eat this soup hot, in which case try frying the lovage leaves in a bit of butter until crisp, and then scattering them over the hot soup.

Leek and Potato Soup or Crème Vichyssoise

SERVES 4–6

large leeks	4
unsalted butter	45g/1½ oz
small potatoes, *peeled and cubed*	3 or 4
parsley, *chopped*	a little
chicken stock (see p. 54)	1.2 litres / 2 pints
cream	300ml / 10fl oz
chives	a bunch
sea salt and black pepper	

This is one of those delectable dishes that has fallen from fashion, but when the young leeks and early spring chives are in season it is a perfect start to a cold lunch or supper. Use more leeks if they are spindly. If you prefer, you can use half-and-half water and full-cream milk instead of stock and cream, and finish with a little cream.

→ Remove the green tops from the LEEKS. Wash and chop the rest into rings. Melt the BUTTER in a heavy-bottomed pan over a low heat and add the leeks. Stir and cook them for a few minutes until they are beginning to soften and turn golden before adding the cubed POTATO. Turn it briefly in the butter, add the chopped PARSLEY, stock and seasoning and bring back to the boil stirring as you do. Simmer until the potatoes are cooked through, about 15–20 minutes.

→ Liquidise in the blender, adjust the SEASONING and add the CREAM if you are going to use it. Bring back to simmer point before removing from the heat. Ladle into bowls and sprinkle some snipped CHIVES over the top. You might prefer to use the rich milk in making the soup and not add cream, or add a little swirl of it or a blob of crème fraîche into the bowl, onto which you can scatter a teaspoon of CHIVES.

Crème Vichyssoise
→ If you are going to serve the soup cold, do not add the cream until the soup has cooled. Refrigerate until properly chilled, then serve with the chives on top.

Garlic Croutons

garlic clove	1
sourdough bread, *crusts cut off*	2 thick slices
olive oil	

→ Preheat the oven to 200°C/400°F/Gas 6. Cut the clove of GARLIC in half. Rub the BREAD with the garlic and brush with OLIVE OIL on both sides. Cut into croutons and bake briefly in a hot oven until they are crisp on both sides but not too brown.

Chicken stock

MAKES 1.5 LITRES / 2¾ PINTS

chicken carcass	
onions	2
cloves	2
celery stalks, *broken in half*	2–3
carrots	2
green tops of leeks and mushroom peelings if you have some, *washed*	
bouquet of fresh herbs—parsley, bay, thyme and rosemary, *tied together*	
a few black peppercorns	

→ Break up the CARCASS of your roast chicken into large pieces and make sure you save all the bones from people's plates to add. Brown the bones in the roasting tin if you can be bothered, then put them in a large, heavy-bottomed pan. Add a couple of ONIONS halved, skins still on for flavour and colour, each stuck with a CLOVE, and the CELERY and chopped CARROTS—chopping the vegetables imparts more flavour than leaving them whole. If you have them, throw in some cleaned GREEN TOPS OF LEEKS that are too tough to cook with, a few MUSHROOM PEELINGS, a small bouquet of FRESH HERBS—parsley, bay, thyme and rosemary or any combination of these—and a few BLACK PEPPERCORNS. You should also add the GIBLETS if you haven't already used them for your gravy.

→ Cover with COLD WATER, bring slowly to the boil, skim, then simmer three-quarters covered for a couple of hours. Any longer than this and the flavour doesn't improve. I suspect all the goodness has been released by the bones and the vegetables by then. Strain into a bowl and when cold, put in the fridge covered in clingfilm. Take the fat off when you want to use the stock. The fat can be clarified and used as dripping for your roast potatoes, so the cycle is complete and without waste.

Beef stock

beef bones	1kg/2¼lb
usual stock vegetables—onion, celery, carrot, leek tops, *roughly chopped*	
bouquet of bay leaves, parsley and thyme, *tied together*	

→ Brown the BEEF BONES in a roasting tin, then transfer to a large pot. Add the VEGETABLES and cover with water. Bring to the boil and skim, then simmer for 2 hours. Strain well.

Meat stock

MAKES 6 LITRES / 10½ PINTS

chicken bones AND/OR meat	1kg / 2¼lb
pork ribs AND/OR meat	1kg / 2¼lb
unsmoked bacon	1kg / 2¼lb
water	6 litres / 10½ pints

This is Matthew Fort's lovely slow-cooked meat stock, which you can use for the French onion soup (p. 38) or for any other soup that needs a deep full flavour. Boil it down further if you want a stronger stock.

→ Place ALL THE INGREDIENTS in a big pot. Put the pot into the oven overnight, or for not less than 8 hours, on an 'S' for slow setting—about 110°C / 225°F / Gas ¼. If you have an Aga, put the pot in the simmering oven overnight. That way, the contents come very slowly to the heat at which the flavours are leached from the meat and bones, so you're left with a naturally clear stock and don't have to do any skimming or clarifying.
→ Alternatively, bring the pan to the boil, boil vigorously while scum rises to the surface, and then skim it off. When the froth on top is white, turn down the heat to a gentle simmer and let it mutter away for 2 to 3 hours. Strain through a fine-mesh sieve or muslin and it's ready to use.

Vegetable stock

water	1.2 litres / 2 pints
dry white wine	240ml / 8fl oz
large carrots, *cut into chunks*	2
celery stalks, *cut in half*	2
medium onions, *unpeeled and stuck with 2 cloves*	2
shallots	4
leeks (green tops only)	3
whole tomatoes	2
fennel bulb, *chopped*	1
whole mushrooms OR mushroom peelings	a few
bouquet of fresh thyme, rosemary, parsley and bay	
white peppercorns	1 tbsp

→ Bring the WATER and WINE to the boil. Add the VEGETABLES and HERBS and return to the boil. Skim off any grey froth. When the surface is clear, add the PEPPERCORNS: if you add them earlier, you'll skim most of them off. Simmer gently for 40 minutes, then strain.

STARTE
and S

RS

ALADS

Tomato Cream

SERVES 8

good organic tomatoes	
gelatine	
whipping cream	240ml / 8fl oz
sea salt	to taste
Tabasco	to taste
Worcestershire sauce	to taste
sugar	a little

An old-fashioned ring mould is the thing I like best for making this tomato cream in. You can heap some tiger prawns grilled with chilli, garlic and olive oil in the middle, or add some tepid broad beans that you have stewed in olive oil, adding a spritz of lemon and some chopped chives at the end or simply some chopped tomatoes and cucumber.

→ Skin, process and sieve enough TOMATOES to give you 400g/14oz.

→ Mix in the GELATINE, following the instructions on the packet, and then add SALT, TABASCO, WORCESTERSHIRE SAUCE and a little SUGAR to taste. The flavour should be strong, since the cream will mute it. You could also add some chopped tarragon, parsley and spring onion, or some chopped basil.

→ Chill until the mixture has thickened to the consistency of egg whites, then fold in the CREAM, which you have whipped to stiffness but not rigidity. Check the seasoning again, scrape into an oiled mould, and set in the fridge overnight. Turn out and serve with chopped tomatoes dressed with herbs and oil.

Neapolitan Tomatoes

SERVES 4

ripe, firm, organic tomatoes	4
flat-leaf parsley, *chopped*	3 tbsp
garlic clove, *finely minced*	1
capers, *chopped, soaked and rinsed*	1 tbsp
white OR brown breadcrumbs	4 tbsp
marjoram, *chopped*	1 dsrtsp
olive oil	2 tbsp
sea salt and black pepper	

Sometimes a simple, pleasing starter that you can forage for in your fridge or store cupboard is the answer. Just make sure the tomatoes are of the heritage kind, big, fleshy, meaty and scented. This dish is also good with grilled meat or fish.

→ Preheat the oven to 180°C/350°F/Gas 4. Halve the TOMATOES, scoop out a little of the flesh and chop it into fine dice. Put the diced tomato into a bowl with ALL THE OTHER INGREDIENTS and mix everything together well.

→ Place the scooped-out tomato halves cut side up on an oiled baking tray and pile the mixture into them. Bake for 30 minutes. Turn the oven up to 190°C/375°F/Gas 5 if the tomato mixture needs crisping a little, but don't let the tomatoes soften too much. Cool to warm and serve with some good country or sourdough bread.

Tomatoes Baked with Olives, Mustard and Gruyère

SERVES 4

ripe, medium-sized organic tomatoes	8
sea salt and black pepper	
glossy, pitted black olives	16
fresh thyme	a sprig
black olive paste	1 tbsp
Dijon mustard	1 tbsp
breadcrumbs (use day-old bread)	a handful
Gruyère cheese, *grated*	110g/4oz
olive oil	

This is a marvellous dish, redolent of the Mediterranean, which you can eat as a starter or with some grilled or roasted meat or fish. Nyons black olives are best for this—don't use olives in brine.

→ Preheat the oven to 220°C/425°F/Gas 7. Cut the TOMATOES in half horizontally and scoop out the seeds and cores with a tea-spoon. Place them cut-side up on a baking tray, season, and plop a pitted OLIVE inside each half.

→ Rub a few THYME LEAVES from their sprig with your fingers into the OLIVE PASTE, then stir in the MUSTARD and brush it over the tomatoes.

→ Mix the BREADCRUMBS with half the grated GRUYÈRE and use to stuff the tomatoes. Put the rest of the grated cheese on top and pour a slug of OLIVE OIL over each tomato half. You are now ready to bake, but you can leave these prepared tomatoes for a few hours before cooking them if it suits you, adding the olive oil just before putting them in the oven. Bake for about 20 minutes and cool to warm to serve.

→ If the breadcrumbs look like they are drying out and darkening too much halfway through cooking, splosh on a little more oil, so that they emerge from the oven crisp and golden and gooey with cheese.

Tomatoes with Mozzarella and Breadcrumbs

SERVES 6

plum tomatoes	12
fresh breadcrumbs	170g/6oz
anchovy fillets, *rinsed, dried and chopped*	8
garlic cloves, *crushed*	2
black olive paste	1 tbsp
flat-leaf parsley, *chopped*	a handful
mozzarella, *finely diced*	1 ball
olive oil	6 tbsp
salt and black pepper	

Another excellent tomato recipe, this time from Nigel Slater.

→ Preheat the oven to 220°C/425°F/Gas 7. Slice the TOMATOES in half lengthways, scoop out the seeds and set them aside. Put the tomatoes, skin-side down, in a roasting tin, keeping them closely packed.

→ Mix the tomato scoopings with the BREADCRUMBS, ANCHOVY FILLETS, GARLIC, PARSLEY, MOZZARELLA and 2 tablespoons of the OLIVE OIL.

→ Season with BLACK PEPPER and SALT, then pile the filling into the tomato halves. Pour over the remaining olive oil. Bake in the hot oven for 25 minutes, until the filling is golden.

Caponata

SERVES 6

aubergines	1.4kg/3lb
sea salt and black pepper	
vegetable oil for frying	
olive oil	
celery sticks	3
large onion, *sliced*	1
molasses sugar	2 tsp
garlic clove, *chopped*	1
plum tomatoes	1 × 400g/14oz tin
red wine vinegar	4 tbsp
salted capers, *rinsed*	85g/3oz
good green olives, *pitted*	85g/3oz
flat-leaf parsley, *roughly chopped*	a handful

You can make the caponata a day in advance—indeed, it tastes better if you do—and leave it out of the fridge overnight to serve at room temperature. If you want to make it even further in advance, it will happily tolerate being kept in the fridge for a few days and then brought back to room temperature before serving.

→ Peel the AUBERGINES, cut them into 2.5cm/1in cubes. Sprinkle them with salt, weight them down with a plate and leave them to drain in a colander for an hour. Squeeze them out, and dry them on kitchen paper.

→ Pour the VEGETABLE OIL into a frying pan so you have a layer about 2.5cm/1in deep. When it is hot, drop in the cubes of AUBERGINE and fry until brown all over, watching that they don't burn. Drain them on kitchen paper. Cut the CELERY into matchstick strips and fry them in the oil until they are crisped and golden.

→ Heat a splosh of good OLIVE OIL in another pan and throw in the sliced ONION, GARLIC and a teaspoon of the SUGAR. Cook for about 5 minutes until the onions begin to colour, then add the tinned TOMATOES AND the rest of the sugar, and season to taste. Cook briskly for a couple of minutes before adding the VINEGAR and CAPERS. Halve the pitted OLIVES and add them and the aubergines and celery to the tomato mixture. Cook gently for about 30 minutes, adjust the seasonings, and leave to cool. When just warm and jammy, scatter over some roughly chopped PARSLEY and serve, or keep as suggested above.

Parmigiana di Melanzane

SERVES 4

aubergines	1kg/2¼lb
sea salt	
mozzarella di bufala	1 ball
garlic clove	1
good olive oil	a few tbsp
whole plum tomatoes, *drained and chopped*	1 × 400g/ 14oz tin
basil leaves	a handful
vegetable oil for frying	
black pepper	
Parmesan cheese, *freshly grated*	½ cup
organic eggs, *hard-boiled*	2

A delightful, old-style trat dish that is as substantial as you could wish for as an appetiser or can be served as a main course. Use a non-intrusive oil, such as peanut oil, for frying.

→ Preheat the oven to 200°C/400°F/Gas 6. Peel the AUBERGINES with a potato peeler and cut them lengthwise into 6mm/¼in slices like long tongues. Sprinkle them with SEA SALT and let them drain in a colander for a couple of hours before rinsing them and drying them on paper towels.

→ Chop the MOZZARELLA into small cubes. Peel the GARLIC and bruise it with the back of a knife. Heat a splosh of OLIVE OIL in a pan and add the TOMATOES, GARLIC and BASIL LEAVES which you have torn by hand. Season and cook down at a brisk heat for a few minutes, before puréeing through the coarse disc of a food mill or food processor, making sure that the basil gets through the holes.

→Heat an inch of VEGETABLE OIL in a roomy, heavy-bottomed frying pan and test by dropping in a tiny corner of bread: it should sizzle immediately. Put in a single layer of AUBERGINE slices and fry until golden brown on both sides, about 5 minutes. This method of salting, drying, and cooking in hot oil prevents the aubergines from absorbing copious quantities of fat and ending up hideously greasy.

→ Drain the aubergine slices on paper towels. Brush the bottom of a gratin dish with good OLIVE OIL, cover with a layer of aubergine, spread some of the tomato sauce on top, and dot with MOZZARELLA. Season with BLACK PEPPER and strew with some freshly grated PARMESAN. Then top with a few slices of EGG before repeating the process. Finish the dish with a layer of aubergine, onto which you dribble a little olive oil before baking for 25–30 minutes.

→ Allow to cool for 10 minutes before serving or you will taste nothing and scorch your tongue.

Roasted Red Peppers with Baked Ricotta and Olives

Here is a bright and elegant starter for a summer's day, which could also be served alongside barbecued meat if you prefer. If you have proper fresh ricotta, strain it through some cheesecloth placed in a sieve overnight. Ordinary commercial ricotta doesn't need straining.

SERVES 4

red peppers	4
fennel seeds	1 tsp
smoked paprika	1 tsp
olive oil	75ml/2½fl oz
garlic cloves, *sliced thin*	4
thyme leaves, *bruised with the base of a knife handle*	1 tbsp
Baked ricotta	
fresh ricotta, *drained*	450g/1lb
1 organic egg and an extra yolk	
Parmesan cheese, *grated*	3 tbsp
feta, *crumbled small*	110g/4 oz
green olives, *pitted and finely chopped*	4 tbsp
chilli flakes	¼ tsp
flat-leaf parsley, chives and basil	3 tbsp
olive oil	1 tbsp
sweet smoked paprika	½ tsp

→ Preheat the oven to 180°C/350°F/Gas 4. Halve the PEPPERS, scraping out the seeds and innards and leaving on the stems. Toast the FENNEL SEEDS in a small hot pan for a minute and crush them in a mortar. Mix the OLIVE OIL, GARLIC, FENNEL SEEDS, PAPRIKA and THYME together and spoon over the pepper halves on a baking tray. Season, and roast until just tender but not collapsed, 30 minutes or so, then leave to cool.
→ Put the RICOTTA, EGG, Parmesan, FETA, OLIVES, CHILLI and HERBS into a bowl and season. Oil a gratin dish and spoon the mixture into it, pressing down on the top with a fork. Sprinkle over the OIL and PAPRIKA and bake for about 40 minutes until firm and golden.
→ Cool completely. Arrange the pepper halves around the edge of a large serving plate. Cut the baked ricotta into triangular wedges and stack loosely and somewhat chaotically in the middle. You can serve the ricotta warm, but if you do, spoon it straight from the gratin dish so that it holds its shape better.

Sicilian Peppers

This Sicilian dish is great as a starter or a main course, or it can accompany game or cold roast meat with brio. Make it in advance, and eat it warm or cold. Use an aged, velvety black balsamic vinegar that is mellow rather than sharp.

SERVES 4

red peppers	4
onion, finely sliced	1
garlic cloves, chopped	2
organic vegetable bouillon cube	½
best extra virgin olive oil	3 tbsp
best balsamic vinegar	2 tbsp
fresh oregano	a small bunch
best glossy black olives, halved and stoned	18

→ Grill or char your PEPPERS until they are uniformly blackened and softened. Leave them to cool, and then the skins should peel away easily. Cut the prepared peppers into long strips.
→ Cook the ONION, GARLIC and OLIVE OIL gently in a covered pan, with a bit of salt and a couple of tablespoons of water. You want the onion to be softened to a purée. Remove the lid, and carry on cooking until the onion is golden, which will take about 40 minutes. Add the strips of pepper, the crumbled BOUILLON CUBE and the BALSAMIC VINEGAR. Cook uncovered for a further 30 minutes, stirring occasionally. You can always

salted anchovies, *rinsed and boned,*	2
OR anchovy fillets in olive oil	4
salted capers *rinsed under a cold tap*	1½ tbsp
sea salt and black pepper	

add an extra tablespoon or two of water if the mixture seems to be drying out.

→ Add ALL THE OTHER INGREDIENTS, and carry on slow cooking for 20 minutes at a very low temperature; anything more and the anchovies will turn bitter. Serve the peppers warm or at room temperature with good crusty bread, or with game or cold roast meat as above.

Stuffed Vine Leaves

MAKES 45–50

vine leaves in brine	1 jar
small onion, *peeled and very finely chopped, almost minced*	1
organic basmati rice, *cooked and drained*	100g/3½oz
raw minced organic lamb	225g/8oz
tomatoes, *skinned, seeded and chopped*	2
mint, flat-leaf parsley and celery leaves, *finely chopped*	3 tbsp each
pine nuts	55g/2oz
ground cinnamon	¼ tsp
ground allspice	¼ tsp
concentrated tomato purée	2 tbsp
garlic cloves, *cut into slivers*	6
good olive oil and the same quantity of water	150ml/5fl oz
lemons	juice of 1½
sea salt and freshly ground black pepper	

The therapeutic stuffing and rolling into parcels of this dish is as pleasurable as the eating. Make the dish hours before you want to eat it and serve it at room temperature. You can eschew the meat and do a vegetarian version if you would rather.

→ Drain the VINE LEAVES and put them in a bowl. Cover them with boiling water and soak for 20 minutes. Repeat the process twice more, but with cold water, before a final drain.

→ Peel the ONION and chop very finely so it is almost minced. In a large bowl mix together the onion, RICE, MINCED LAMB, TOMATOES, HERBS, PINE NUTS, SPICES and TOMATO PURÉE. Season. Place a VINE LEAF on your work surface, vein side up, the stem edge nearest to you. Put a heaped teaspoon of the mixture in the centre of the leaf near the stem. Fold up over the filling, then fold both sides of the leaf towards the middle, and roll into a little cigar. Do the same with the remaining 49. Children are very adept at this sort of repetitive action if you have any on hand to bribe, but I find some comfort and relaxation in the leisurely performing of this sort of task, which is not going to ruin if the telephone rings.

→ Line a heavy-bottomed casserole with a single layer of unstuffed VINE LEAVES, slightly overlapping, so that they come about a third of the way up the sides of the pan. Pack in the stuffed vine leaves, snuggled tightly together and one or two layers deep, placing occasional slivers of GARLIC between them. Add the OLIVE OIL, WATER and LEMON JUICE, and weight down with an upturned plate and a couple of weights.

→ Cook very gently on top of the stove for about 2 hours, until tender when pierced with a skewer. Check the liquid level after the first hour; you may need to add a bit more water. The sort of unhurried, uncomplicated but tremendously satisfying cooking that brings forth memories of the best kind of Greek taverna.

Leeks Vinaigrette

SERVES 4

leeks	12
Dijon mustard	2 tbsp
warm water	4 tbsp
red OR white wine vinegar	2 tbsp
olive oil	150ml/5fl oz or more to taste
salt and pepper	
organic eggs, *softly hard-boiled*	2
chives, *snipped*	a handful

A perfect summer starter, with the new season's taut white wands of leek, and that magical combination of chives, mustard and chopped egg. This is a real classic.

→ Wash the LEEKS very well and trim the green leaves to about 2.5cm/1in. Steam them until collapsed and tender. Drain, and allow them to cool, then halve them lengthwise.

→ Blitz the MUSTARD, WATER, VINEGAR, SALT and PEPPER in a blender, then, with the motor running, gradually pour in the OLIVE OIL until you have a thick, mustardy emulsion. Taste and adjust. You might need a little more water if it is too thick. Lay the leeks in a flat dish, pour on the dressing, then sprinkle over the finely chopped EGG and the snipped CHIVES.

Baby Artichokes Marinated in Olive Oil

SERVES 6

small artichokes	1.5 kg/3¼lb
lemons	4
extra virgin olive oil	150–170ml/ 5–6fl oz
thyme and parsley	2 sprigs each
bay leaves	
celery stalk	1
black peppercorns	12

→ Have a large bowl of cold water with the juice of half a lemon squeezed into it to hand while you trim the ARTICHOKES. Snap off and discard the dark outer leaves, trim the base and the stalk, and rub the other half of the LEMON over the cut surfaces as you go. Cut the top 1cm/½in off the remaining leaves, and throw the artichokes into the acidulated water to prevent discoloration.

→ Bring a large pan of water to the boil, add salt, and boil the artichokes until just tender. Drain well, and place in a bowl.

→ Make the marinade by putting ALL THE OTHER INGREDIENTS into a saucepan with the juice of the three remaining LEMONS and 850ml/1½pints of WATER. Simmer uncovered for 20 minutes, then pour the hot liquid over the artichokes and leave to cool. Cover and refrigerate for at least 3 days.

→ When you want to eat them, remove the artichokes with a slotted spoon and serve with an extra splash of olive oil.

Cannellini Beans with Garlic, Sage and Olive Oil

SERVES 4

dried cannellini beans, *soaked for at least 8 hours*	225g/8oz
rosemary and sage	a sprig of each
medium onion	1
celery stalks	2
garlic cloves	2 or 3
Tuscan olive oil	6 tbsp
fresh OR tinned tomatoes (optional)	3
salt and fresh black pepper	

In this most famous of Tuscan dishes, it is the libation of olive oil poured over the warm beans just before serving that makes it. It is as delicious made with the chalky-textured, speckledy borlotti beans. The tomatoes are optional—I prefer the dish without their distraction. Don't forget to soak the beans overnight or for at least 8 hours.

→ Drain and rinse the soaked BEANS. Cook the beans in plenty of water, with a sprig each of ROSEMARY and SAGE, the ONION and CELERY and a clove of GARLIC, until tender. Drain the beans, discarding the other vegetables, but keeping the cooking liquor.

→ Sauté another sprig of fresh sage in 3 tablespoons of olive oil with the two bruised cloves of garlic. When the garlic begins to frizzle, remove it. Skin, seed and chop the tomatoes if you are using them and add to the pot. Add the beans, and turn them in the oil, then pour over enough of the bean stock to cover the base of the saucepan. Season with salt and pepper—never season dried beans with salt during the initial cooking stage, it will merely toughen the skins to husks—and cook until most of the liquid has evaporated. Transfer to an earthenware dish to cool and pour over a good glug of olive oil, about 3 tablespoons, just before serving. Best served warm.

Asparagus, Fennel and Red Pepper Salad

SERVES 6

organic red peppers	2
asparagus bundles	2 × 450g/1lb
fennel bulbs	2
olive oil	
lemon juice	
salt and pepper	
chervil (optional)	a sprinkling

Loath as I am to eat asparagus in any form that isn't as near as dammit au natur, this salad, which my friend George Morley suggested we make one greedy weekend, quite converted me. It makes a brilliant starter, but allows the asparagus to play the starring role, so the peppers don't overwhelm.

→ Grill the PEPPERS on all sides and put them in a bowl under clingfilm so the skins begin to steam off. Skin, de-seed and cut them into thin strips. Cut the ASPARAGUS into 5cm/2in chunks, and steam the stalks on their own for a couple of minutes. Add the tips, and steam until cooked, about another 3 minutes.

→ Remove the outer layer of the FENNEL BULBS down to the firm heart, and slice them as thinly as you can, with a mandolin if you have one. Put all the vegetables into a bowl, then pour in your OIL AND LEMON DRESSING, and mix together gently by hand. Sprinkle with CHERVIL if you have some and serve with a good crusted bread.

Frittata Stuffed with Sprue

SERVES 4

large organic eggs	6
basil, *roughly torn*, set aside a few leaves	1 bunch
garlic clove, *peeled and finely chopped*	1
Parmesan cheese, *freshly grated*	2 tbsp
sprue, or fine-stemmed asparagus	225g/8oz
olive oil, salt and pepper	

Dipping verdant green spears of asparagus into runny boiled egg yolks is a real post-nursery delight, as is throwing the violet-tinged tips into a sea of creamy scrambled eggs. But try these little bundles of sprue wrapped in a basil-scented frittata.

→ Beat the EGGS in a bowl then add the BASIL, GARLIC, PARMESAN and SEASONING. Allow the mixture to rest a bit if you have time, for the basil to permeate the eggs. Cut the ASPARAGUS into 5cm/2in chunks, and steam the stalks on their own for a couple of minutes. Add the tips, and steam until cooked, about another 2 minutes. Drain, season, and dribble over a bit of OLIVE OIL.

→ Put a couple of tablespoons of OLIVE OIL into a frying pan on a medium heat, then pour in a quarter of the EGG MIXTURE and swirl it around as you would for a pancake. When it turns opaque, flip it over and cook the other side briefly. Cook the remaining frittatas. Put a little bundle of SPRUE at the edge of each frittata and roll up. Sprinkle on the remaining BASIL and a bit of extra PARMESAN and serve.

Broad Beans with Serrano Ham

SERVES 6

Serrano ham	170g/6oz
good olive oil	4 tbsp
onion, a mild one, *very finely chopped*	170g/6oz
garlic clove, *finely chopped*	1
broad beans	1kg/2¼lb
large organic eggs	4
sea salt and black pepper	
flat-leaf parsley, *chopped*	a handful

Use fingernail-size broad beans for this, not the giant toughies. If you can't get Serrano ham, use prosciutto or organic green back bacon.

→ Cut or tear the HAM into small strips and sauté it gently in the hot OLIVE OIL in a pan with the chopped ONION until the onion is softened. Add the GARLIC and soften briefly. Throw in the BROAD BEANS, cover, turn down the heat and cook until they are tender, about 6 or 7 minutes.

→ Hard-boil the EGGS for about 7 minutes, then peel them and chop them. Season the ham and beans, stir in the chopped egg and PARSLEY and serve warm.

Warm Broad Bean and Pea Purée with Vinaigrette

SERVES 4–6

broad beans (podded weight)	1lb/450g
fresh or frozen peas (podded weight)	1lb/450g
chicken stock (see p. 54) or water	
fresh mint	a handful
Vinaigrette	
garlic clove	1
sea salt	
Dijon mustard	1 tsp
white wine vinegar	½ tbsp
lemon	juice of ½
black pepper	
best olive oil	4–5 tbsp

→ First make the vinaigrette by crushing the GARLIC with the SEA SALT in a mortar, then adding the rest of the ingredients. Add the OLIVE OIL last and whisk into an emulsion as you go. Check the seasoning.

→ You need baby broad beans, unless you are prepared to take off the leathery jackets from older ones when they're cooked. Throw the BEANS and PEAS into boiling stock or water and cook for 5 minutes. Drain, purée in a food processor and stir in the chopped MINT. Dress the purée with vinaigrette when still warm.

Globe Artichokes in Balsamic Dressing

SERVES 4

globe artichokes	4
lemon	½
shallots, peeled and finely chopped	2–3
good olive oil	
balsamic vinegar, the best aged one you can find	
sea salt and black pepper	

→ Bring a large pan of water to the boil and acidulate it with half a squeezed LEMON. Throw in your ARTICHOKES and cook without a lid at a rolling boil until you can easily pull an outside leaf away from its parent stem, about 25–30 minutes. Remove and drain.

→ In a small pan, heat the finely chopped SHALLOT very gently in some good OLIVE OIL until it is softened. Remove from the heat and whisk in the BALSAMIC VINEGAR and seasoning to taste. Pour the warm dressing over the artichokes, and leave for as long as you can, preferably overnight. Before serving, spoon some of the escaped dressing over the artichokes.

Bagna Cauda

SERVES 4–6

butter	55g/2oz
garlic cloves, *peeled and very finely sliced*	4
salted anchovies, *rinsed and boned*	5
OR anchovy fillets in olive oil	10
olive oil	200ml/7fl oz
salt	

This 'hot bath' of a sauce is garlicky, salt with anchovy and the perfect thing to pass round warm with a selection of crisp raw vegetables and a glass of wine. Fennel, cardoons, carrots, radishes, celery and peppers work well, and cooked potatoes are also good.

→ Melt the BUTTER in a small, deep earthenware pot or in a very heavy-based saucepan over the lowest possible heat. As soon as the butter has melted, add the GARLIC and sauté for a few seconds. The garlic should not colour. Add the ANCHOVIES to the pot and pour in the OIL very gradually, stirring all the time. Cook for about 10 minutes on the lowest possible heat, stirring constantly. The dip is ready when the ingredients are well blended and smooth. Season if necessary and serve. The sauce must be kept hot, which the Piedmontese do in an earthenware pot over a spirit lamp. Special bagna cauda pots are available.

Fresh Fig and Mint Salad

SERVES 6

ripe figs	1kg/2¼lb
prosciutto, *fat removed*	3 thin slices
fresh mint leaves	12–15
lemon	juice of 1
salt	
Jersey cream	200ml/7fl oz

This recipe comes from the great food writer Richard Olney, an American who became an honorary Frenchman; he was so much more than a Francophile even before he moved to France. Olney refers to the fact that 'French friends find the recipe bizarre, but all who have tasted it have been delighted by the clean, clear, surprising combination of flavours and fragrance'. How right he is.

→ Olney peels the FIGS, I do not, before cutting halfway down from the stem end, making two incisions in the form of a cross. Press gently from the sides to open them slightly. Arrange the figs closely packed on a serving dish and chill for about an hour in the coldest part of the fridge.

→ Cut the HAM into fine julienne strips about 2.5cm/1in long and matchstick width. Crush about half of the MINT LEAVES in the lemon juice, leave to macerate for 20–30 minutes, then discard them. Dissolve the SALT into the LEMON JUICE and slowly stir in the CREAM — the acid of the lemon will thicken it somewhat, and adding the cream a little at a time while continuing to stir encourages the thickening. Taste for salt.

→ Sprinkle the figs with half the ham julienne and spoon over the cream sauce. Distribute the remaining ham on the surface and decorate with the remaining mint leaves.

Roast Figs Stuffed with Goat's Cheese

SERVES 4

Marsala	170ml / 6 fl oz
root ginger, *grated*	½ a finger
maple syrup	2 tbsp
ripe but not squishy figs	8
fresh goat's cheese	85g/3oz
a little watercress to strew around each plate	
leaves of a little gem lettuce	
basil leaves	1 small bunch
tarragon, *leaves stripped off*	2 sprigs
garlic clove, *crushed*	½
lemon juice	1 tsp
olive oil	
sea salt	

Sweet and savoury in a mouthful, this is a quick and delicious vegetarian starter. I've adapted the recipe from one at my favourite vegetarian café— Ottolenghi in London's Notting Hill.

→ Bring the MARSALA and GINGER to the boil in a small pan. Turn the heat down and let it bubble gently until reduced to about three tablespoons. Strain the juice and add the MAPLE SYRUP. Allow it to cool slightly.

→ Preheat the oven to 180°C / 350°F / Gas 4. Remove the stalk of the FIG and cut a cross halfway down each fruit. Crumble the CHEESE lightly and stuff each fig with it. Put the figs close together in a roasting tin so that they support each other, sprinkle with a little SALT and OLIVE OIL and bake for about 4 minutes or a little longer if the figs are not ripe.

→ Toss all the GREENS together with the GARLIC, LEMON JUICE, two tablespoons of extra virgin OLIVE OIL, salt and pepper and place a little on each serving plate. Top with a warm or room temperature fig and pour a little of the warm Marsala and maple syrup reduction over each one. Perfection!

Fennel à la Grecque

SERVES 4

large fennel bulbs	4
olive oil	6 tbsp
lemons	juice of 2
onion, *sliced into thin rings*	1
garlic cloves, *bruised*	2
coriander seeds	12
fennel seeds	1 tsp
a bouquet of thyme, bay, parsley and rosemary with a strip of orange peel, *tied with string*	
sea salt and black pepper	
flat-leaf parsley, *chopped*	

A classic, simple starter or a side dish for grilled pork or fish.

→ Remove the tough outer leaves from the FENNEL. Quarter the bulbs down through the core so that they don't break up. Lay them flat in one layer in a heavy-bottomed frying pan. Add ALL THE OTHER INGREDIENTS except the PARSLEY and just cover with boiling water. Bring to the boil, turn down to a simmer and cover. Cook for about 20 minutes until tender right through the core.

→ Remove the herbs and spoon the fennel and its cooking liquor onto a deep serving dish. Leave to cool and serve at room temperature or cold with plenty of parsley.

Leeks à la Grecque
→ Trim off the dark green leaves and slice the white part of the leeks in half. Lay in the pan and continue as above.

Baked Stuffed Field Mushrooms

SERVES 4–6

large, flat mushrooms	450g/1lb
olive oil	4–6 tbsp
fennel bulb, *finely chopped*	1
celery stick, *finely chopped*	1
small onion, *finely chopped*	1
garlic cloves, *finely chopped*	2
fresh thyme, *chopped*	1 tbsp
Parmesan cheese, *coarsely grated*	a handful
fresh parsley, *chopped*	a handful
fresh brown breadcrumbs	a handful
salt and pepper	
red wine	about 150ml/5fl oz
chicken stock (see p. 54) or water	about 150ml/5fl oz

Very good for the vegetarians in your party, this is perfect for a buffet as well as a starter, because the stuffing can be cooked in advance, the dish then assembled ready for the oven, and it is something you can happily serve warm rather than hot.

→ Preheat the oven to 180°C / 350°F / Gas 4. Wipe the MUSHROOMS clean with a damp cloth. Break off the stalks and chop the stalks finely. Make a duxelles by heating half the OIL in a frying pan and sautéing the FENNEL, CELERY, ONION and MUSHROOM STALKS with the GARLIC and THYME. Mix together the PARMESAN, PARSLEY and BREADCRUMBS for the topping.
→ Put a tablespoon of stuffing into each mushroom and season, then cover with a layer of the topping. Place in a roasting tin and dribble the remaining oil over the top. Put a couple of ladles of RED WINE and the same of WATER or STOCK into the roasting tin, and cook in the oven until the mushrooms can be pierced easily with a knife, and their tops are golden and crusty. Check after 20–30 minutes that the wine and water hasn't been absorbed—if it has, ladle in some more.

Mushrooms à la Grecque

SERVES 4–6

extra virgin olive oil	6 tbsp
lemons	juice of 2
onion, *sliced into thin rings*	1
garlic cloves, *bruised*	2
coriander seeds	12
a bouquet of thyme, bay, parsley and rosemary with a strip of orange peel, *tied with string*	
salt, pepper	
button mushrooms	450g/1lb
flat-leaf parsley, *chopped*	

→ Put ALL THE INGREDIENTS except the mushrooms and parsley in a pan and add 400ml boiling water. Bring to the boil, turn down the heat and simmer for 15–20 minutes. Add the MUSHROOMS and simmer for another 5 minutes.
→ Remove the mushrooms with a slotted spoon, then boil the cooking liquor until reduced. Pour over the mushrooms, add the chopped PARSLEY and serve at room temperature or cold.

Coriander Mushrooms

SERVES 2

button OR closed-cap mushrooms	170g / 6oz
lemon juice	
olive oil	
coriander seeds, *crushed*	1 tsp
bay leaves	2
salt, pepper	

The inimitable Mrs David in her Spices, Salt and Aromatics in the English Kitchen *observes that the flavourings in this dish are almost the same as those used for mushrooms à la Grecque, 'but the method is simpler, and the result even better'. Try it for yourself, it is one of those nigh-forgotten dishes that graces a cold table beautifully, makes a great starter, or, as Mrs David recommends, can be eaten hot with veal or chicken.*

→ Clean the MUSHROOMS, and halve them if they are on the large side. Brush a little LEMON JUICE over them. Heat a film of OLIVE OIL to cover the bottom of a heavy pan, and cook the CORIANDER SEEDS for a few seconds over a low heat. Add the mushrooms and bay leaves. Season. After a minute, cover the pan and cook for another 3–5 minutes, but no longer.
→ Pour the mushrooms with their cooking juices into a serving dish and sprinkle them with fresh OLIVE OIL and LEMON JUICE to taste. Serve chilled, or hot with veal or chicken.

Eliza Acton's Mushrooms au Beurre

mushrooms	1 pint
butter	1½oz
cayenne pepper, mace	
salt	

Eliza Acton's Modern Cookery for Private Families *(1845) includes this recipe which is simplicity itself, as elegantly so in her writing as in the dish, and to my mind it would be insulting to update her prose.*

→ Wipe the mushrooms clean with a damp cloth, then: 'For every pint of them thus prepared, put an ounce and a half of fresh butter into a thick iron saucepan, shake it over the fire until it JUST begins to brown, throw in the mushrooms, continue to shake the saucepan over a clear fire that they may not stick to it nor burn, and when they have simmered three or four minutes, strew over them a little salt, some cayenne, and pounded mace, stew them until they are perfectly tender, heap them in a dish, and serve them with their own sauce only, for breakfast, supper, or luncheon. They are very good when drained from the butter and served cold. The butter in which they are stewed is admirable for flavouring gravies, sauces, or potted meats.'

And the bit I like best: 'Persons inhabiting parts of the country where mushrooms are abundant, may send them easily, when thus prepared… to their friends in cities, or in less productive counties. If poured into jars, with sufficient butter to cover them, they will travel any distance, and can be re-warmed for use.'

Baked White Truffle

SERVES 4

anchovies, *cut in half*	2
thick organic double cream	12 dsrtsp
Jerusalem artichokes	4
organic eggs	4
white truffle	

I first ate this outstanding dish at the Ristorante Castello di Mango in northern Italy, where it was cooked by talented chef Silvio Berrino. When I asked how Silvio had made it, I presumed it would be impossible to reproduce, but, thrillingly, it worked perfectly, and I wasn't left with a heap of glass shattered by the heat of the oven. This recipe could, I suspect, be made with any intensely perfumed fungi like ceps, sliced wafer thin, but it will not have the magic of the white truffle. Try and buy one from any good Italian deli, you only need a tiny amount.

→ You need a hot oven, 200°C / 400°F / Gas 6, and one white wine glass per person. In the bottom of each flute put half an ANCHOVY. On top of that put a dessertspoon of thick organic DOUBLE CREAM, Jersey if possible. Above that, spoon a dessert-spoon of JERUSALEM ARTICHOKE PURÉE. (I steamed four artichokes in their skins until soft, popped them out of their skins, and put them through the coarse blade of my mouli.) Then break an organic EGG into the glass. Add another layer of CREAM to cover the egg, you will be within a whisper of the top of the glass by now, and grate some WHITE TRUFFLE over the surface. Miraculously the ingredients stay put in their layers.
→ Put the glasses in a deep roasting tin, and pour boiling water up to the top of the stems. Bake in the middle of the oven. Check after 10 minutes, if the egg is no longer transparent, the dish is done. Mine took just short of 15 minutes. You don't want a really runny egg which will escape into the cream, but one where the yolk is a bit set around the edges. Each layer is a treasure trove of taste as you work your way to the bottom, the artichoke a perfect earthy foil to the truffle's delicacy, the salt, sharp anchovy a brilliant contrast to the creamy richness.

Cold Cucumber and Ricotta Mousse

SERVES 8

organic cucumber	1
sea salt	1 tsp
tarragon vinegar	3 tbsp
powdered gelatine, or the equivalent in leaf gelatine (my preference), see packet for instructions	½oz packet

A delicate summer appetiser or lunch dish, which you can leave in the fridge to set the night before you want it. At the last minute, peel some ribbons of cucumber with a potato peeler, top to bottom, and drop them into the middle of the mousse to serve with it.

→ If you're using fresh RICOTTA, place in a sieve lined with cheesecloth and leave to strain overnight. If you can only get supermarket cheese it doesn't need straining.
→ Peel and seed the CUCUMBER and cut into doll's-size dice. Mix the cucumber, SALT and VINEGAR thoroughly in a bowl. Turn the mixture into a colander, put a plate on top, and leave

organic double cream	300ml/10fl oz
ricotta, fresh if you can get it	500ml/18fl oz
black peppercorns	
chopped chives, parsley and spring onions	a generous handful
a second cucumber for the ribbons if you like the idea	

to drain for at least an hour. Remove the plate, and press down gently with a cloth.

→ Dissolve the GELATINE in 6 tbsp of very hot water, or as per the leaf gelatine instructions in cold water, and cool to tepid. Make sure the gelatine is thoroughly dissolved, then whisk in the CREAM gradually until the mixture is smooth and very thick, but not stiff.

→ Add the RICOTTA by passing it through the small disc of a food mill to aerate it as you go, then stir it in with the cucumber. Taste, and add a touch more TARRAGON VINEGAR and SALT if you think it needs it, but do not make the taste too strong. Grind in some BLACK PEPPER, then stir in the finely chopped HERBS and tiny rings of the white of the spring ONIONS.

→ Turn into a mould which you have oiled with a little OLIVE OIL. Set in the refrigerator overnight. Turn the mousse out onto a large plate just before you serve it, a deep blue or green plate works beautifully, by slipping the mould into a bowl of boiling water for a few seconds, then going round the inside edge of the mould with the point of a long, thin-bladed sharp knife that you have dipped in hot water. It is not difficult. Serve with warm toasted sourdough bread or caraway seed rolls.

Mozzarella in Carrozza

SERVES 4

white bread OR ciabatta	4 slices
buffalo mozzarella, *cut into slices*	1
sea salt and black pepper	
organic milk	120m/4fl oz
large organic egg	1
flour	
vegetable oil OR light olive oil for frying	

Trust the Italians to have a better way than we do with a toasted cheese sandwich, which is really what this divinely oozing mozzarella in a 'carriage' is. Perfect snack food or something to cut into golden squares to pass round with a glass of Prosecco before supper.

→ Cut the slices of BREAD in half and place a piece of MOZZARELLA on four of the halves. Season and cover the cheese with another half of bread. Pour the MILK into a shallow bowl and whisk the EGG in another bowl with some seasoning.

→ Spread some FLOUR on a large plate. Put 1cm/½in of OIL into a frying pan and heat it quickly. Dip the first sandwich into the milk, coat with flour and then dip it into the egg mixture before slipping it straight into the smoking oil. Repeat with the other sandwiches, cooking them in a single layer until they are golden brown on both sides. Drain on kitchen paper and serve.

Gruyère Soufflé

butter, *softened*	a knob
breadcrumbs from a stale loaf OR ground walnuts	1 tbsp
Parmesan cheese, *grated*	2 tbsp
fresh thyme, *chopped*	1 tsp
unsalted butter	55g/2oz
flour	45g/1½ oz
full-cream milk	300ml/10fl oz
large organic egg yolks	4
Gruyère, *Beaufort if possible*	85g/3oz
black pepper, *freshly ground*	
cayenne	tip of a tsp
large organic egg whites, *room temperature*	6

You can make this with a mature unpasteurised Cheddar or a lovely lactic Lancashire like Mrs Kirkham's if you'd rather, but a good Gruyère like Beaufort makes a stunning soufflé. Please don't turn the page in fear of the perils of the sunken, leathery soufflé, or the soufflé that failed to rise to your challenge. If you follow this simple method you will have a light, creamy, tremblingly perfect interior and a crisp, browned crust.

→ You need a soufflé dish that holds 750 ml/1½ pints. Grease it well with the softened BUTTER. Mix together the GROUND WALNUTS or BREADCRUMBS with 1 tablespoon of PARMESAN and the THYME. Sprinkle the mixture on to the dish—it will stick to the buttered edges; discard what doesn't.

→ Preheat the oven to 200°C/400°F/Gas 6. Place a baking sheet in the middle of the oven. Melt the BUTTER in a small pan, add the FLOUR and let it simmer for a minute or two into a blond roux before adding the HOT MILK at scalding point. Take off the heat and whisk fiercely until it becomes smooth, then add the EGG YOLKS one by one, whisking them in. Throw in the CHEESE, PEPPER and CAYENNE and keep warm on a low heat nowhere near boiling point. Whisk the EGG WHITES with a pinch of SALT until they are at stiff peak stage. Stir a tablespoon of the whites into the cheese mixture to slacken it. Lightly fold in the rest, a spoon at a time, with a rubber spatula or metal spoon, keeping the mixture light and airy. Don't overwork it.

→ Scrape the mixture into the prepared soufflé dish. Sprinkle the remaining tablespoon of PARMESAN over the top and put the soufflé onto the baking tray in the middle of the oven. Check after 25 minutes by pushing the dish with your hand and seeing how shuddery it is. It will probably take another 5 minutes, but you need it trembling but not liquid in the middle. The top should be lightly browned. Remove from the oven, rip the collar off if you've used one and set the soufflé on the table immediately.

Vegetable Soufflés

Vegetables that make good, strongly flavoured purées also make good soufflés. Spinach, with a salty hit of a few anchovies, is fantastic; parsnip is good with a teaspoon each of cumin and coriander which has been tempered then ground; mushroom with some dried ceps and chanterelles and plenty of fresh parsley.

→ To start a vegetable soufflé, sweat a very finely chopped

SHALLOT or small ONION with a finely minced clove of GARLIC in 55g/2oz butter. You then add 225g/8oz of cooked, PURÉED VEGETABLE and turn this into the béchamel before proceeding in the normal way.

Smoked Salmon Soufflé
→ Smoked salmon also makes a good soufflé if you have some leftover bits. Omit the garlic from the sweated onion mixture and add 225g/8oz of SMOKED SALMON into the béchamel with some chopped DILL.

Soufflés à la Suissesse

SERVES 4

milk	240ml / 8fl oz
flour	55g /2oz
sea salt, black pepper and nutmeg	
unsalted butter	55g /2oz
Parmesan, *freshly grated*	110g / 4oz
organic egg yolks	3
organic egg whites	2
double cream	340ml /12fl oz
fresh thyme, *chopped* (optional)	a little

These little soufflés are poached, more like quenelles, and gratinéed with cream and cheese. They are cooked twice, so most of the work can be done in advance. Serve them with a small bitter salad of Treviso chicory or radicchio and a dressing of walnut or hazelnut oil.

→ Bring the MILK to scalding point in a pan. Let it cool to blood heat before pouring it into the FLOUR and whisking to stop it going lumpy. Add the SEASONING with a grating of NUTMEG and cook over a gentle heat, stirring all the while until the mixture thickens. Let it cool a little, then add half the BUTTER, a generous half of the PARMESAN and the EGG YOLKS, one at a time, whisking them in well. Whisk the EGG WHITES to stiff peaks. Stir the first spoonful into the cheese mixture, then gently fold in the rest a tablespoonful at a time.

→ Preheat the oven to 180°C/350°F/Gas 4. Scrape the mixture into well-buttered ramekins filling them two-thirds full. Put the ramekins in a small roasting tin and add boiling water to come three-quarters of the way up their sides. Poach for 20 minutes or until set and slightly springy to the touch.

→ Butter a gratin dish and sprinkle in some of the remaining PARMESAN. Remove the ramekins from their water bath. When they have cooled slightly, run a knife blade around each one, turn out onto your hand and plop into the buttered gratin dish. Pour the CREAM over the soufflés and sprinkle each one with PARMESAN and a pinch of THYME. Put them back into the oven for 20 minutes until gratinéed, golden and bubbling, or hold them to finish off later.

Kirkham's Lancashire Cheese and Chive Soufflé

SERVES 6

Kirkham's Lancashire cheese	110g / 4oz
walnuts	about 12
unsalted butter	55g / 2oz
flour	45g / 1½oz
Jersey milk	300ml / 10fl oz
chives, *chopped*	1½ tbsp
salt, pepper and cayenne	
organic egg yolks	4
organic egg whites	5

The beautiful, lactic taste is not lost in the cooking here—the cheese bubbles creamily without melting. Coat the soufflé dish with ground organic walnuts, and sprinkle some more on top. They enhance rather than mask the flavour as Parmesan might.

→ Preheat the oven to 200°C/400°F/Gas 6. Grate the CHEESE and reserve. Grind the WALNUTS moderately finely.

→ Butter a soufflé dish that takes at least 900ml/1½ pints, and throw in most of the walnuts, rolling them round the dish till they cling to the butter. Grease a strip of greaseproof paper and place it like a dog-collar 5cm/2in above the top of the dish. Secure with a paper clip.

→ Melt the BUTTER in a small pan, then make a roux with the flour. Remove from the heat and, with a small whisk, beat in the MILK which you have heated to boiling point. Whisk in the YOLKS one by one, throw in the CHEESE, then return briefly to a low heat, on no account letting it bubble. Remove, SEASON, and add the CHIVES.

→ Whisk the WHITES until stiff. Stir a spoonful of them into the mixture, then lightly and quickly fold in the rest. Spoon into the soufflé dish, sprinkle over the remaining WALNUTS, and put immediately into the oven. Don't look for 30 minutes. Mine was ready then, puffed up, browned, and with the perfect slightly sad centre.

Crab Soufflé

SERVES 4

butter	
breadcrumbs, *made with day-old brown bread*	2–3 tbsp
Parmesan cheese, *grated*	1 tbsp
cayenne pepper	a pinch
curry powder (optional)	1 small tsp
crab meat, brown and white	340g/12oz
French mustard	1 tsp
Tabasco sauce	a few drops
dry sherry	2 tsp

This is the king of the savoury soufflés and one instance when cheese and fish work together, so don't lose the Parmesan.

→ Preheat the oven to 190°C/375°F/Gas 5. First make the béchamel sauce: melt the BUTTER in a saucepan, add the FLOUR and cook, stirring, for 1 minute. Add the BAY LEAF and gradually stir in the MILK. Cook, stirring constantly, until the sauce is thick and smooth. Season to taste.

→ Butter a soufflé dish generously, then roll the BREADCRUMBS and half the PARMESAN around the inside of the dish, tipping out and reserving what doesn't adhere to the butter. Melt a knob of BUTTER in a saucepan, add the CAYENNE and CURRY POWDER if you are using it, and cook for 1 minute. Remove from the heat and add the CRAB MEAT, MUSTARD, TABASCO, SHERRY and SALT and PEPPER to taste. Warm gently, then stir in the

salt and pepper	
béchamel sauce (see below)	150ml/5fl oz
double cream	1–2 tbsp
organic egg yolks	4
organic egg whites	6
Béchamel sauce	
butter	2 tsp
plain flour	2 tsp
1 small bay leaf	
milk	150ml/5fl oz
salt and pepper	

béchamel sauce and the CREAM. Remove from the heat and stir in the EGG YOLKS. (The mixture can be prepared ahead up to this point.)

→ Whisk the EGG WHITES until stiff. Fold them briskly but lightly into the mixture and turn into the soufflé dish. Sprinkle the remaining PARMESAN and BREADCRUMBS over the top. Fix a piece of greaseproof paper around the dish, the top 5cm/2in buttered on the inside, and fasten with a paper clip. When the soufflé has risen and the paper is taken away, this looks spectacular. Bake in the oven for 20–25 minutes: the soufflé should be firm and well risen, with the barest hint of a shudder at the middle if you shake it gently. Bring it directly to the table as soon as you have taken off the greaseproof paper.

Hard-boiled Eggs with Tapenade

SERVES 6 OR MORE IF THERE ARE OTHER DISHES

large organic eggs	6
salted capers	2 tbsp
black olives, *stoned*	24
salted anchovies, *rinsed and de-spined*	6
fillets of anchovy in olive oil	10
best tinned tuna	55g/2oz
Dijon mustard	a scant teaspoon
olive oil	
lemon juice	
eau de vie OR cognac	a few drops
pepper	

A lovely Provençal hors-d'oeuvre, black, oily, salt—perfect to whet the most recalcitrant of appetites. Use good Mediterranean olives, the kind in olive oil not brine.

→ Hard-boil the EGGS. Cut them in half lengthwise and scoop out the yolks to use in the tapenade. Rinse the CAPERS on a slotted spoon under a cold tap to remove the salt.

→ Pound the EGG YOLKS, BLACK OLIVES, ANCHOVIES, CAPERS, TUNA and MUSTARD together in a mortar. Then gradually amalgamate a couple of tablespoons of OLIVE OIL into the mixture, followed by a spritz of LEMON and a breath of SPIRIT. Season with PEPPER to taste; you will not need salt because of the salt ingredients.

→ With a teaspoon, fill the white egg cavities with the black tapenade. Serve cool. The tapenade will keep well for days and is equally good spread like a pâté on fingers of warm toast to be served with drinks.

Tortilla Española

SERVES 4

potatoes	450g/1lb
large organic eggs	6
best olive oil	120ml/4fl oz
sea salt and freshly ground pepper	

There is really no time of day I wouldn't serve a tortilla—late breakfast or brunch, lunch, on a picnic, in the early evening with drinks, or dinner itself. Tortilla can be served hot, warm or cold.

→ Do not use a voluminous frying pan—you are making a cake of eggs, not a flat omelette. Peel the POTATOES and cut them into small dice. Heat the OLIVE OIL, and when it is hot, throw in the POTATOES and coat them all over in the oil. Lower the heat and turn them gently every so often until they are cooked through. Remove the potatoes with a slotted spoon and drain them on kitchen paper in a bowl.

→ Heat the olive oil in the pan again, with a bit extra if you need it. Meanwhile, beat the EGGS with the PEPPER and pour them over the potatoes, then pour the mixture into the hot oil in the pan and cook at a high heat for a minute before turning the temperature down. Add SALT and cook until there is no sign of liquid egg at the top of the mixture. Cover with a plate and flip the tortilla over onto it, add a splosh more olive oil to the pan, then slide the tortilla back into the pan and cook for a further couple of minutes.

→ Serve hot or warm with a tomato sauce, on its own or with some Navarrico piquillo peppers, roasted over beech wood and imported by Brindisa. Or eat it cold and cut into wedges with a tomato salad. Once cooked, a tortilla will keep for a couple of days, and reheats well in a tomato sauce.

Innes Buttons with Toasted Hazelnuts

Innes Button cheeses	1 per person
endives OR treviso	
hazelnuts, *roasted and crushed*	
hazelnut oil	
black pepper	

How difficult is it to produce perfect lemony, fudgy, lactic little buttons of fresh goat's cheese? Well in England they are a rarity. These examples were the overall winners at the British Cheese Awards in 2002 when I was one of the judges. Order them from The Fine Cheese Company on 01225 448748.

→ Innes Button cheeses are best served with some TREVISO or ENDIVES underneath. Add a judicious sprinkling of crushed roasted HAZELNUTS over each button, a slug of HAZELNUT OIL and a scrunch of PEPPER.

Gougère

Serves 4

fine plain flour	110g/4oz
salt	a pinch
black pepper	
cayenne	a knife tip
mustard powder (optional)	1 tsp
unsalted butter	85g/3oz
water	240ml/8fl oz
organic eggs, *beaten*	3
strong farmhouse Cheddar, *diced into small cubes*	55g/2oz

Filling

unsalted butter	30g/1oz
medium onion, *finely chopped*	1
celery stick, *strung and finely chopped*	1
Portobello mushrooms, *sliced*	110g/4oz
OR dried ceps OR morels	30g/1oz
OR crabmeat, half white, half brown	340g/12oz
OR cooked chicken, pigeon, guinea fowl or pheasant	340g/12oz
flour	30g/1oz
chicken stock, OR fish stock if using crab	300ml/10fl oz
sea salt and black pepper	
parsley, *chopped* (for the mushroom or chicken)	1 tbsp
dill/chervil, *chopped* (for the crab)	1 tbsp
double cream	4 tbsp

Topping

Parmesan cheese, *grated*	2 tbsp
dry breadcrumbs	2 tbsp

Think of this as a gorgeous empty vessel that you can fill with crab, chicken, mushrooms or other vegetables. It is made with a cheese choux paste and its golden, crisp crust is best offset by a lovely gloopy-sauced filling of old-fashioned comfort and simplicity.

→ Sift the FLOUR, SALT, PEPPER, CAYENNE and MUSTARD POWDER if you're using it a couple of times from on high; they need to be sifted fine.

→ Put the BUTTER and WATER in a large heavy-bottomed pan and heat them together slowly. When the butter has completely melted into the water let them come to a rolling boil and add the flour mixture. Remove from the heat and beat soundly with a wooden spoon until the mixture starts to leave the sides of the pan. Leave to cool.

→ Preheat the oven to 200°C/400°F/Gas 6. Once the mixture is warm rather than hot, beat in the lightly beaten EGGS a little at a time until the mixture is glossy, shiny, and of a dropping consistency—this may be before you've used up all the egg. Stir in the CHEESE. Grease a baking tray and make a circle of spoonfuls of the gougère mixture around the edge of the tin, so that the ring can be filled with the filling later. Bake until puffed up and golden, about 25 minutes.

→ Meanwhile make the filling. Melt the BUTTER in a pan and gently soften the ONION and CELERY. If you're using DRIED MUSHROOMS soak them in warm water to rehydrate. If you're using cooked CHICKEN or GAME, tear it with the grain into thin strips. Add the mushrooms, crab, chicken or game and cook for 5 minutes. (Dried fungi will take longer so if you are using it, allow 10–15 minutes.) Sprinkle over the flour and stir for 2–3 minutes before adding the HOT STOCK. Bring to the boil, turn down the heat and simmer for 5 minutes, then season and stir. Add the HERBS and the CREAM, check the SEASONING, then turn the filling into the middle of the gougère ring.

→ Sprinkle the topping over the filling and return to the oven for 15 minutes until bubbling and golden on top.

Goujons of Plaice

large fillets of plaice, *skinned*	2
flour	
sea salt and black pepper	
organic egg, *beaten*	1
fine brown or white breadcrumbs made from stale bread	
groundnut oil for deep frying	
lemon	1

→ Cut the PLAICE FILLETS into ribbon strips and dip them in the seasoned FLOUR, then in the beaten egg and finally in the BREADCRUMBS. Pour some GROUNDNUT OIL into a deep-fryer and bring it slowly up to 190°C. I don't have a thermometer, so I watch for the oil to start moving, then drop in a large crumb. If it seizes and starts to fry instantly, the temperature is hot enough for the fish. Put the goujons in the basket and lower them into the hot oil for 3–4 minutes until they are beautifully browned. Drain them on kitchen paper and season with a little salt.
→ Delicious served with the Asian Dipping Sauce on p. 411 or the Crème Fraîche Tartare on p. 407.

Tartare of Tuna with Chicory

heads of chicory	6
fresh tuna steak	285g/10oz
shallots, *finely chopped*	2 tsp
garlic, *finely chopped*	1 tsp
root ginger, *finely chopped*	1 tsp
chives, *finely chopped*	1 tbsp
black peppercorns, *crushed*	½ tsp
Japanese soy sauce	1 tbsp

I first came across these delicious raw mouthfuls a couple of years ago in one of Rowley Leigh's columns, and knew that they must be good.

→ Trim the bases of the CHICORY and carefully pull off the outer leaves, saving the hearts for a salad. Lay 24 of the leaves on a flat plate or tray, like little boats.
→ Slice the TUNA as thinly as you can, then slice it again into strips. Chop the strips into little dice, then chop again until you have a really fine texture. Food processors are out—the result would be a minced mulch.
→ Mix the tuna well with ALL THE OTHER INGREDIENTS. Using two teaspoons, mould small amounts of the mixture into little quenelles and place one on each chicory leaf. Cover with cling-film and chill if you are not going to eat them immediately.

Ceviche of Wild Salmon

wild salmon, *skinned and filleted*	675g/1½ lb
dry white wine	170ml/6fl oz
lime	juice of 1
orange	juice of ½
lemon	juice of ½

This is a dish I have cooked, or should I say assembled, many times over the years, but always obeying one simple rule: use wild salmon. The flavour and texture of the farmed stuff and the method of rearing it, poor, pale, greasy, flabby imitation that it is of the magnificent tail-thrashing wild specimen, is just not something I want anything to do with, or a dish I care to serve or eat.

→ Using a very sharp knife, slice the SALMON, straight from the fridge, into 5mm /¼ in slices. Put into a container with a lid—an old plastic ice cream container is ideal. Add ALL THE OTHER INGREDIENTS, cover and refrigerate. Turn the salmon occasionally, or shake the container gently. The dish is ready to eat after about 8 hours. It will keep well for about 24 hours in a sealed

small onion, *sliced in thin rings*	1
small garlic clove, *sliced*	1
salt and pepper	
olive oil	4 tbsp

container in the fridge, but remember to remove the ONION and GARLIC after the first 8 hours so that they don't overwhelm the fish.

→ To serve, strain off the marinade and put a tablespoon of the cucumber and avocado sambal (see p. 82) alongside the fish, and some brown soda bread if you like.

Home-cured Salmon with Marinated Vegetables and Manchego

SERVES 4

wild salmon, *skinned and boned*	340g / 12oz
sea salt	1 cup
sugar	½ cup
olive oil	
orange	*zest* of 1
lemon	*zest* of 1
Vegetables and marinade	
small carrot	1
small red onion	1
celery stick	1
fennel bulb	1
red pepper	1
butternut squash	1
lime	juice of 1
sherry vinegar	2 tbsp
good olive oil	90ml / 3fl oz
runny honey	1 tbsp
orange	*zest* of 1
coriander seeds, *freshly ground*	1 tsp
sugar	
little gem lettuces	2
Manchego OR Pecorino cheese	

You need to prepare this dish at least 8 hours before you want to eat it. It is simple and spectacular.

→ Pack the SALMON in SALT and SUGAR, cover and leave in the fridge for 4 hours. Wash off the salt and sugar. Pat dry and cover with OLIVE OIL and the ZESTS. Leave covered in the fridge for at least 4 hours, then slice into thin strips.

→ Peel and wash the VEGETABLES. Slice into thin strips with a peeler or mandolin. Season with SALT, PEPPER and the ground CORIANDER SEEDS and a pinch of SUGAR. Mix all the marinade ingredients together and then mix well with the vegetables. Cover and leave to stand for an hour before using.

→ Mix the salmon strips with the marinated vegetables. Pile into a bowl with the LITTLE GEM LETTUCES and some shavings of lovely aged sheep's milk cheese like MANCHEGO or PECORINO on top, making sure they don't get crumbled, or serve on individual plates.

Cucumber and Avocado Sambal

cucumber, *skinned and seeded*	½
red pepper, *skinned and seeded*	1
avocado	1
lemon juice, olive oil and balsamic vinegar	to taste
fresh dill, *finely chopped*	1 tbsp

→ Chop the CUCUMBER as finely as you can — into dice about 3mm / ⅛ in square. Do the same with the RED PEPPER, and chop the AVOCADO into slightly bigger cubes.

→ Sprinkle on some LEMON JUICE, a little OLIVE OIL and BALSAMIC VINEGAR, then add some BLACK PEPPER and finely chopped DILL. Perfect with the ceviche of salmon on p. 80.

Ceviche of Lemon Sole with Tomato and Chilli Salsa

SERVES 2

lemon sole fillet, *boned and skinned*	225g / 8oz
lemon	juice of 1
olive oil	
flat-leaf parsley	a handful
salt and pepper	
Tomato and Chilli Salsa	
small red onion, *very finely chopped*	½
red chilli, *very finely chopped*	1
green chilli, *very finely chopped*	1
ripe tomatoes, *skinned, seeded and diced*	2
yellow and red pepper, *very finely diced*	1 tbsp of each
garlic, *finely chopped*	1 tsp
coriander, *chopped*	1 tbsp
Tabasco and Worcestershire sauce	dash of each
olive oil	
sea salt and black pepper	
avocado (optional)	

When you want light, quick, sharp, fresh, easy, fishy, this is the one. You can make a ceviche with all sorts of different fish, the lemon or lime juice do the job of cooking it.

→ Cut the fillet of SOLE on the diagonal into thin strips. Marinate for at least an hour in the LEMON JUICE, drain well and dress with OLIVE OIL, PARSLEY and SEASONING. Serve with a spoonful of SALSA.

Tomato and Chilli Salsa

→ To make the salsa, mix the finely chopped ONION and CHILLI, then add the tiny diced TOMATOES and PEPPERS. Add the GARLIC and CORIANDER, TABASCO and WORCESTERSHIRE and stir in enough good OLIVE OIL to loosen. Season to taste. You might like to add a few thin slices of cooling avocado to the salsa.

Soft Roes on Toast with Caper Butter

SERVES 2

seasoned flour for coating	
herring roes	225g/8oz
shallots, *finely minced*	1 tsp
capers, *desalinated and chopped*	1–2 tsp
unsalted butter, *softened*	55g/2oz
lemons	2
sea salt and black pepper	
sourdough bread, *toasted and crusts removed*	2 or 4 slices
unsalted butter for cooking	30g/1oz

This recipe and the following one make lovely starters or light lunch or supper dishes. Herring roes are a seasonal thing; the female herring is plump with them in May, but they are available all the year round frozen.

→ Pour a handful of FLOUR and some SEA SALT and BLACK PEPPER into a ziploc bag, add the ROES and shake until they are coated. Put the floured roes onto a plate, shaking off any excess flour, then work quickly so the flour doesn't begin to clog.
→ Mash the SHALLOTS and CAPERS into the softened BUTTER with a fork and add a spritz of LEMON JUICE and some seasoning. Spread it thickly over the pieces of TOAST.
→ Melt the 30g/1oz of BUTTER in a frying pan and when it begins to bubble throw in the ROES. Fry for 2–3 minutes until the roes begin to look firmed up to about half their thickness, then turn them making sure you don't break them up. Fry the other side until it begins to brown. They should take 4–5 minutes altogether. Pile the roes on the spread toasts and put quarters of LEMON alongside to squeeze on top.

Smoked Paprika Roes on Toast

SERVES 2

seasoned flour for coating	
herring roes	225g/8oz
Spanish smoked paprika (piccante pimentón)	a pinch
unsalted butter	30g/1oz
unsalted butter for the toast, *softened*	55g/2oz
sourdough bread, *toasted and crusts removed*	2–4 slices
lemon juice	
sea salt and black pepper	

→ Pour a handful of FLOUR and some SEA SALT and BLACK PEPPER into a ziploc bag, add the ROES and shake until they are coated. Put the floured roes onto a plate and sprinkle a pinch of SMOKED PAPRIKA along the length of each roe.
→ Melt the BUTTER in a frying pan. When it begins to bubble, add the roes, paprika side down, and scrunch over some more BLACK PEPPER. While they are frying, make and butter the TOASTS and put them on the plates. After a couple of minutes or so, add a pinch more PAPRIKA to the tops of the roes just before you turn them, when they have begun to crispen. Cook for another few minutes until they are firm.
→ Turn the roes onto the toasts and squeeze a little LEMON over the tops, adding a little SEA SALT at the same time.

Marinated Mackerel with Potato Salad

SERVES 6

mackerel fillets, *skinned*	6–8

Marinade

good green olive oil	120ml /4fl oz
dry white wine	125ml /4fl oz
white wine vinegar	60ml /2fl oz
water	120ml /4fl oz
Pernod	2 tbsp
lemon, *sliced*	1
bay leaf	1
parsley, dill and thyme	a few sprigs of each
carrot, *finely sliced*	1
celery stick, *finely chopped*	1
shallot, *finely chopped*	1
molasses sugar	a generous pinch
salt and pepper	

Potato Salad

waxy salad potatoes such as Pink Fir Apple or Anya	450g /1lb
shallot, *finely chopped*	1
good olive oil	4 tbsp
white wine vinegar	1 tbsp
flat-leaf parsley, *chopped*	2 tbsp
sea salt and black pepper	

This dish should be marinated for 18–24 hours before you serve it, leaving only the potato salad to do a couple of hours beforehand. It is really a fish 'tartare'—the fish is pickled without cooking it, and the effect of the white wine vinegar is to ameliorate the oiliness of the fish. A wonderful starter if you are cooking for huge numbers, since it cooks itself and you can make it in advance.

→ Cut the MACKEREL into long, thin strips, 7.5 × 1.25cm / 3 × ½in. Put ALL THE MARINADE INGREDIENTS together in a bow, add the strips of FISH and submerge them. Cover the bowl with clingfilm and refrigerate for at least 18 hours. Bring to room temperature before you serve.

→ An hour or two before you want to eat, prepare the potato salad. Boil the POTATOES and skin them while still as hot as you can bear. Pour the various components of the dressing— SHALLOT, OLIVE OIL, WHITE WINE VINEGAR, PARSLEY and SEASONING —over the potatoes while they are still hot and turn them gently to coat them in the dressing. Place a layer of the potato salad on each plate, or on one large plate. Then place some mackerel with its accompanying juices, vegetables and herbs on the potato summit.

Devilled Mackerel with Mint and Tomato Salad

SERVES 4

mackerel	4 × 325g/12oz
butter	45g/1½oz
caster sugar	1 tsp
English mustard powder	1 tsp
cayenne pepper	1 tsp

→ Preheat the grill to high. Slash the MACKEREL skin at 1cm / ½in intervals on both sides, from the head down to the tail, taking care not to cut too deeply into the flesh.

→ Melt the BUTTER in a shallow flameproof dish. Remove from the heat, stir in the SUGAR, MUSTARD, SPICES, VINEGAR, PEPPER and SALT and mix together well. Add the mackerel to the butter and turn them over once or twice until well coated in the mixture, spreading some into the cavity of each fish as well. Transfer them to a lightly oiled baking sheet or the rack of the grill pan and grill for 4 minutes a side, until cooked through.

paprika	1 tsp
ground coriander	1 tsp
red wine vinegar	2 tbsp
black pepper, *freshly ground*	1 tsp
salt	2 tsp

Mint and Tomato Salad

small, vine-ripened tomatoes	225g / 8oz
small onion, *halved*	1
mint, *chopped*	1 tbsp
lemon juice	1 tbsp

→ Arrange the salad on 4 plates, sprinkling the layers with the lemon juice and some seasoning. Put the mackerel alongside and serve, with some fried sliced potatoes if you wish.

Mackerel Rillettes

SERVES 4–6

salt enough to cover the fish fillets	
organic lemon	1
organic lime	1
coriander seeds, *ground in a mortar*	1 dsrtsp
mackerel, *filleted*	750g / 1lb 10oz
sherry vinegar	
garlic clove	1
olive oil	2 tbsp
chilli flakes or OR dried chilli, *finely diced*	¾ tsp
basil leaves	15
cracked black pepper and sea salt	

Here is Heston Blumenthal's way with mackerel and a very good way it is too. This is a dish you can prepare ahead, at least three hours before you want it, but it will sit tight in the fridge for a couple of days if you need it to. Ask your fishmonger to fillet the mackerel for you.

→ Place the SALT in a bowl and finely grate the LEMON AND LIME ZEST over it. Add the GROUND CORIANDER and mix. Spread some of the salt to a depth of 2mm on a flat plate, then press the MACKEREL fillets into it, skin side down. Sprinkle with a little SHERRY VINEGAR and add more SALT so that the fillets are completely covered. You can do this in two layers if your plate isn't big enough to do it in one. Leave for 45 minutes.

→ Meanwhile, peel the GARLIC and press it with the flat of a knife to crush it. Remove the green germ from the middle. Put the garlic, OLIVE OIL and CHILLI in a small pan and warm over a low heat for 10 minutes. Do not let the garlic brown and burn or the oil will become bitter. Remove the pan from the heat and set aside. Once it is cool, strain the oil through a sieve.

→ When the fish is ready, wash it thoroughly to remove all the salt, then remove the skin with a sharp knife. Place the fish in a bowl and add the flavoured oil. Using a fork, mix well, shredding the flesh as you go. Finely chop the BASIL and add it to the fish. Cover and place in the fridge for at least a couple of hours.

→ To serve, place little mounds of fish on small plates and sprinkle over some SEA SALT and freshly ground PEPPER. Have some fingers of granary toast or good warmed bread on the side.

Grilled Herrings with Sweet Smoked Paprika and Coriander

SERVES 2

herrings, *filleted*	1 per person
coarse sea salt	
coriander, *finely chopped*	1 tbsp
garlic clove, *finely chopped*	1
sweet smoked paprika	2 pinches
lemon juice	

I have always found it curious how oily fish—mackerel, smoked salmon, smoked eel—are made less rich by brown bread and butter. Curious but true.

→ Preheat the grill. Place the HERRINGS, butterflied out and skin side up, on the grill rack and scatter over a good sprinkling of SEA SALT. Put the pan as close as you can get it under the preheated grill. The skin will bubble up, and the salt will spit. Leave for about 3 minutes. Turn over the fillets, they should be almost tender when pierced with a skewer, and place back under the grill for only 30 seconds or the flesh will dry out.

→ Remove the herrings and place them on serving plates. Scatter a tiny pinch of the SMOKED PAPRIKA, some CORIANDER and a morsel of GARLIC on each one, spritz with LEMON JUICE and serve with brown bread and butter.

Squid Braised in its Ink

SERVES 4

squid, cleaned, plus ink sacs, OR two sachets of ink	600g/1¼lb
small bulbs fennel	3
small organic onions	3
garlic cloves, *finely chopped*	3
Oloroso sherry	170 ml/6fl oz
large tomatoes	4
tomato paste	1 tbsp
bay leaves	2
orange rind	2 strips
salt and pepper	
fresh peas, podded weight	225g/8oz
olive oil	

→ Preheat the oven to 150°C/300°F/Gas 2. Slice the FENNEL bulbs thinly and finely chop the ONIONS. Skin, seed and chop the TOMATOES.

→ Heat some OLIVE OIL in a heavy-bottomed casserole, then add the fennel, onions and garlic, and cook gently until softened a bit. Add the SQUID and stir to coat. Then add the SHERRY, and bring to a simmer.

→ Add the TOMATOES and TOMATO PASTE, the BAY LEAVES and ORANGE RIND, and SEASON. Squeeze in the SQUID INK, stir, and cover with greaseproof paper and a lid. Put in the oven for an hour, then remove and add the PEAS. Stir, cover and return to the oven for a further hour. Eat hot or warm out of soup bowls.

This dish is is full of strong flavours, beautifully green and black, and perfect as a starter or a main course. It can be made the day before and reheated. Accompany it with a glass of cold Fino or Manzanilla sherry.

Moules Marinière

SERVES 4

medium onions, *finely chopped*	2
OR shallots, *finely chopped*	4
garlic cloves, *finely minced*	3 or 4
flat-leaf parsley, *chopped*	large handful
dry white wine	300ml/10fl oz
mussels, *cleaned and de-bearded*	2kg / 4½lb
extra parsley	
unsalted butter, *cubed*	55g / 2oz
sea salt and black pepper	

→ Put the ONIONS OR SHALLOTS, GARLIC, PARSLEY and WHITE WINE into a large heavy-bottomed pan and bring to the boil. Simmer for 5 minutes. Now slosh in all the MUSSELS, turning up the heat to full blast and stirring the mussels around a bit. Put the lid on and let the steam force the shells open. Check after a couple of minutes and stir the ones that haven't yet opened closer to the heat source, putting the lid back on until they have. Remove and discard any mussels whose shells don't open.

→ Put the opened mussels and the onion, garlic and parsley into a warmed serving bowl with a slotted spoon and keep them warm. Carefully strain the fish liquor into a pan to remove the grit and bring it to the boil. Now reduce the heat and whisk in little cubes of BUTTER until you have a glossy sauce. Sprinkle over the extra PARSLEY, SEASON and return the liquor to the mussels. Serve with crusty bread and more butter and some chilled white wine.

La Mouclade

SERVES 4

saffron	a good pinch
mussels, *cleaned*	1.8kg/4lb
butter	30g/1oz
dry white wine	120ml / 4fl oz
small onion, *finely chopped*	1
garlic cloves, *finely chopped*	2
good curry powder	1 tsp
ground celery seed	1 tsp
cognac	2 tbsp
flour	1 scant dsrtsp
double cream	240ml/8fl oz
flat-leaf parsley OR coriander	
salt and pepper	

A creamily curried dish, good on its own as a starter, or with rice as a main course.

→ Put the SAFFRON in a bowl with a tablespoon of HOT WATER. Put the MUSSELS and WINE into a pan, cover, and cook until they open. Put them in a colander over a bowl, and catch all the juice in it, then keep the mussels warm.

→ Melt the BUTTER in a saucepan, add the ONION, GARLIC, FLOUR and SPICES, and cook gently for 2–3 minutes. Add the CREAM, simmer again for a couple of minutes, season and pour the sauce over the mussels. Scatter with the PARSLEY OR CORIANDER and serve with rice, bread or on their own.

Mussels with a Red Pepper Sambal

SERVES 4

dry white wine	120ml/4fl oz
mussels, *cleaned*	450g/1lb
lemon	a spritz
red pepper, *seeded*	½
cucumber	7.5cm (3in)
paprika	a dusting
salt and pepper	

A delicious cold dish of mussels to eat with drinks, ice-cold Fino or white wine.

→ Heat the WINE in a pan and cook the MUSSELS, covered, until the shells open. Remove the top shells, and put two mussels into each half shell, putting all the liquor back into the pan. Reduce this down to about 4 tablespoons of juice, season, and add LEMON JUICE to taste. Seed the RED PEPPER and chop into minute doll-sized pieces. Skin and seed the CUCUMBER and chop as the pepper. Scatter the pepper and cucumber over the mussels on their serving dish, and brush over the juice. Chill, season, then sprinkle a tiny pinch of PAPRIKA over them.

Potted Crab

MAKES 12 RAMEKINS

best unsalted butter	about 400g/14oz
mace	a blade or good pinch
nutmeg	a good pinch
cayenne	⅓ tsp
salt and pepper	
lemon juice	
crabmeat	85g/3oz

Classic potted crab is only made with the white meat of the crab, but using the brown meat too deepens and intensifies the flavour. If you have a good fishmonger he will pick the crab for you and divide it into light and dark.

→ Preheat the oven to 150°C/300°F/Gas 2. Melt 225g/8oz of the BUTTER gently, then pour it carefully into another pan, leaving behind the milky, curd-like solids. Add the SPICES to the clarified butter, then turn the WHITE MEAT into the spiced butter, amalgamate well and taste. You should have a breath of spiced warmth, but not full-scale heat from the cayenne. Adjust accordingly, then add SALT, PEPPER and a squeeze of LEMON JUICE to taste.

→ Boil a kettle, and in the meantime fill each ramekin with a layer of the buttered white crabmeat, followed by a layer of BROWN MEAT. Finish with a layer of the white meat. Leave just enough room at the top of the ramekin for the final layer of clarified butter, which you will add after cooking. Place the ramekins in a roasting tin, pour boiling water to come halfway up their sides, and place in the oven for 25 minutes.

→ Remove, cool, then clarify the rest of the BUTTER and pour over each ramekin like sealing wax. Place in the fridge. Take them out 20 minutes or so before you make your BROWN TOAST so that they are cold, but not fridge cold. Then slip a slim knife blade all the way around the girth of each ramekin right to the bottom, turn them out on to the palm of your hand, and put each one, butter-side up, on individual plates.

Seafood Plate

Crab

white meat	110g/4oz
brown meat	55g/2oz
dill, lemon juice, olive oil	

Squid

squid, *sliced thinly*	170g/6oz
garlic clove, *finely chopped*	1
red chilli, *finely chopped*	1
flat-leaf parsley	a handful
olive oil	2 tbsp

Salmon

wild salmon	110g/4oz
smoked salmon	4 thin slices
lemon	juice of 1/2
tartare sauce	large spoonful

Scallops

scallops	4
olive oil	
vinaigrette	

Tartare Sauce

home-made mayonnaise	
gherkins and capers	1 tbsp
anchovy fillet, *chopped*	1
shallot, *chopped*	1 tbsp
French mustard	1 tsp
dill, chervil and tarragon	

Stephen Markwick, now chef at Culinaria in Bristol, serves the following five fish dishes together as one incredible starter. You can pick any combination or serve one element.

Crab
→ Simply pick the meat from the CRAB, and dress it with some fresh DILL, LEMON JUICE and OLIVE OIL.

Squid
→ 'Wok' or pan fry all the SQUID INGREDIENTS over a high heat in the hot oil until tender, about 1-2 minutes. SEASON. Serve warm.

Salmon
→ Cut the SALMON into fine dice and marinade briefly with the juice of half a LEMON for about 15 minutes to start the cooking process. Drain well and mix with the TARTARE SAUCE. Tear each smoked salmon slice into two, place a spoon of the salmon and tartare sauce mixture in the middle and roll it up like a miniature pancake.

Scallops
→ Slice each SCALLOP into 2 or 3 discs, and fry briefly in hot OLIVE OIL with the corals; 30 seconds a side should do it. Dress them while still hot with VINAIGRETTE and serve warm.

Tartare Sauce
→ Home-made tartare sauce is easy. To your home-made MAYONNAISE, add chopped GHERKINS and chopped CAPERS, a chopped ANCHOVY FILLET, chopped SHALLOT and a teaspoon of FRENCH MUSTARD. Then throw in some finely chopped DILL, CHERVIL and TARRAGON.

Little Crab Custards

Serves 6

fresh crabmeat, brown and white if possible	225g/8oz
organic eggs, *beaten*	4
whipping cream, Jersey if possible	600ml/1 pint
Oloroso OR Fino sherry	2 dsrtsp
Dijon mustard	2 tsp
cayenne	knife point
Parmesan, *freshly grated*	2 tbsp
sea salt	

I make these almost absurdly easy custards with both the brown and the white meat of the crab, as the richer, creamier brown lends its intense flavour and texture well beyond the milder white. If your fishmonger can't oblige, stick with the white.

→ Preheat the oven to 180°C/350°F/Gas 4. Simply put ALL THE INGREDIENTS together into the liquidiser and blitz briefly until amalgamated and creamy. Taste and adjust everything you need to, remembering that the sherry should be a back-note but not too intrusive; likewise the mustard and cayenne.

→ Place six ramekins in a roasting tin. Pour in the crab mixture. Boil a kettle and surround the ramekins with a moat of boiling water to come up to their middles. Cook for 25–30 minutes in the centre of the oven or until just set to a wobble when you give the tin a little shake to test them. They will go on cooking as they cool.

→ Serve warm with a either a small, peppery salad of wild rocket and watercress, or with some granary toast.

Langoustine Salad

Serves 4

large langoustines (Dublin Bay prawns)	16
organic egg yolks	2
Dijon mustard	1 tsp
garlic clove, *pounded with a little salt in a mortar*	1
vegetable oil	150ml/5fl oz
olive oil	150ml/5fl oz
live yoghurt	to taste
lemon	juice of 1
black pepper	
Pernod (optional)	1 tsp
fennel bulbs with their fronds	2
sharp eating apples	2
celery	1 heart

A perfect Christmas-time starter, or lunch or supper dish.

→ Put 12 of the LANGOUSTINES belly down on your chopping board and run a knife down through the middle of them lengthways. Scoop out the flesh, including the delicious dark meat from the head, which you should keep separate from the white flesh. Keep the other four whole.

→ Now make your mayonnaise. Stir the EGG YOLKS together in a bowl with a wooden spoon before stirring in the DIJON MUSTARD and salty GARLIC. Then begin to add the OILS, mixed together, drip by drip to begin with, then in a steady stream, stirring constantly. (See p. 404 for more on mayonnaise.) When you have used all the oil and have a thick, yellow emulsion, add a tablespoon of YOGHURT followed by a spritz of LEMON. Continue adding the two until you have the desired flavour and texture, which should be pouring consistency, rather like double cream. Add PEPPER and PERNOD if you have some to hand, then the CHOPPED FRONDS from your fennel bulbs and the BROWN MEAT from the langoustines.

→ Remove the tough outer leaves of the FENNEL before slicing the bulbs wafer thin on a mandolin. Now peel, quarter and core the APPLES and slice them thinly, squirting a little LEMON JUICE over them to stop discolouration. Peel the CELERY HEART with a potato peeler before slicing it equally thinly on the mandolin.

→ Combine the vegetables and fruit with the 12 chopped langoustines. Spoon over some mayonnaise, turning the ingredients in it well. You may not need all the mayonnaise, but keep it for later. Place a pile of the salad on each plate, on some green leaves if you like, placing a whole langoustine on each plate.

→ If you prefer, add the fruit and vegetables in thin layers and keep the langoustines for the top, instead of making a mélange.

'Sun's Eye', or Sologa

FOR EACH SERVING:

anchovies, preferably the salted ones, *rinsed and dried*	3–4
capers or cornichons, *chopped*	1 tbsp
white onion, *finely chopped*	1–2 tbsp
pickled beetroot	2–3 tbsp
flat-leaf parsley, *chopped*	2–3 tbsp
raw egg yolk	1
lemon juice (optional)	a few drops

A spectacularly beautiful yet simple dish that I first ate at the house of my Swedish friend Kristina von Wrede. The combination of sweet, sour, astringent and salt, of textures from smooth to crisp and fresh, and the brilliance of the colours, make this dish both startling and original. Use beetroots pickled in white wine vinegar, not malt vinegar.

→ Chop ALL THE INGREDIENTS one by one, keeping them separate. Arrange each plate, starting with a small circle of ANCHOVIES in the middle, so that all you can fit inside it is the egg yolk later. Then do the same with the CAPERS OR CORNICHONS, so that the circle abuts the anchovies, and outside that, the ONIONS then the BEETROOT then the PARSLEY, over which you can sprinkle a bit of LEMON JUICE. Finally put the EGG YOLK in the middle.

→ You eat the dish by breaking into the yolk and mixing it into the other ingredients. Would I be foolish in imagining this to be a good hangover cure if your hands were steady enough to make it? Serve with a home-made wholemeal or caraway roll.

Scallops and Steamed Leeks with Sauce Maltese

SERVES 4

scallops, per person	2 large OR 3 small
fat leek, per person OR slim wands of baby leeks, per person	1 4
Sauce Maltese	
white wine vinegar OR tarragon vinegar	3 tbsp
water	2 tbsp
white peppercorns	10
large organic egg yolks	3
best unsalted butter	170g/6oz
sea salt	
Seville orange OR orange and lemon juice	to taste

When blood oranges are in season, they make a thrillingly beautiful Sauce Maltese, but better still is the sharpness of a Seville orange. The sauce is, after all, just a delectable version of a hollandaise, so perfect with fish. The sweet-with-sweet leeks and scallops is a fine marriage, sharpened by a puddle of the unctuous and glossy sauce.

→ Trim the SCALLOPS, leaving their coral whole and separate. Slice the whites into three discs if the scallops are large, two if they are smaller. SEASON just before you griddle them.

→ I steam my well-washed whites of LEEK whole if they are the baby ones. If it is later in the season and they are thicker, either ruthlessly peel off any tough outer layers and steam them whole, or slice them finely to steam. You want them soft right through to the point of a knife. Keep them hot while you cook the scallops.

→ Cook the SCALLOP WHITES on a hot griddle you have lightly brushed with OIL before heating, or in a frying pan prepared the same way—a minute a side until just stiffened and opaque should do, introducing the whole CORALS for 30 seconds a side. Scatter the scallops over the leeks and hand round the sauce in a jug or pour it over each plate, according to your taste in such matters.

Sauce Maltese

→ Put the VINEGAR, WATER and PEPPERCORNS into a small pan and boil down to about a tablespoon of liquid, then pour it into a bowl and leave it to cool for a few minutes. Beat the EGG YOLKS into the reduced liquor, then place the bowl over a pan of barely simmering water and stir, adding small knobs of BUTTER, bit by bit, as they melt in. If by any ghastly chance the mixture curdles, the remedy is the same as it is for mayonnaise: first hold your nerve, then try to bring it back by stirring in a tablespoon of scalding water. If that doesn't work, start with another egg yolk, whisk it, then add a tiny trickle of the curdled sauce, starting drop by drop, whisking hard as you go, until all is well. Once the sauce looks as thick and glossy as newly washed hair, remove from the heat, season with SALT and add the JUICE to taste. You can leave the sauce for an hour or so before you want it, then heat it through over barely simmering water, making absolutely sure you don't overheat it. Scrambled eggs is not the idea.

Scallops with Parsnip Purée

SERVES 2

medium parsnip, *peeled and cut into chunks*	1
unsalted butter	55g/2oz
cayenne	a knife point
cumin seeds, *tempered and crushed* (optional)	a knife point
sea salt and black pepper	
large scallops	2 per person
flat-leaf parsley, *chopped*	1 tsp

There is no more perfectly pure, sweet, taste-of-the-sea starter than the scallop, with its disc of firm white flesh and its gaudy, soft coral comma. Sweet and sweet work beautifully together; you can serve scallops with a parsnip purée, a minted pea purée or a purée of Jerusalem artichokes.

→ Steam the PARSNIP. Mash it or put it through the smallest disc of your mouli-légumes, adding two-thirds of the BUTTER, the spices if you are using them and the seasoning to taste. Keep warm.

→ Clean and trim the SCALLOPS. Slice the white into 3 discs and leave the corals whole. Melt the rest of the BUTTER in a pan and add the whites of the scallops when it is bubbling. Cook for about 30 seconds a side, or until the white turns opaque, then turn them over, add the corals, and cook for 30 seconds or so longer. Turn over the corals and continue cooking them until just set, about 30–45 seconds. Season, then put a little mound of parsnip on each plate, followed by the buttery scallops and PARSLEY and serve.

→ Cooking the scallops on a griddle is just as good. Brush a griddle with OLIVE OIL, heat it to hot and put the SCALLOPS on it for the same amount of time as above, turning them over at half time. That way, less butter and a satisfying branding of black griddle stripes.

Scallops with Minted Pea Purée

SERVES 2

large scallops	2 per person
fresh OR frozen peas OR petits pois	228g/8oz
chicken stock to cover (see p. 54)	a little
butter	a knob
double cream	2 tbsp
sea salt and black pepper	
fresh mint, *finely chopped*	1 dsrtsp

As far as I know, Rowley Leigh of Kensington Place takes credit for putting the pea with the scallop in such a simple and disarmingly delicious way.

→ Clean and trim the SCALLOPS. Slice the white into 3 discs and leave the corals whole. Cook the scallops in a pan with butter or on a griddle as above. Cook the PEAS in simmering CHICKEN STOCK. Drain, keeping the stock, and place in a food processor with the BUTTER and CREAM and a tablespoon of CHICKEN STOCK. Process roughly; I like texture not baby food. Add the SEASONING and any more stock or butter or cream you think it needs to taste. Scrape out onto a plate and stir in the MINT.

→ Make a mound of brilliant green PEA PURÉE on each plate, arrange the scallops and their corals as you like and serve.

Scallops with Jerusalem Artichoke Purée

SERVES 2

large scallops	2 per person
Jerusalem artichokes, *scrubbed but not peeled*	225g/8oz
sea salt and black pepper	
double cream	2 tbsp
butter	a knob
flat-leaf parsley, *finely chopped*	1 tsp

→ Clean and trim the SCALLOPS. Slice the white into 3 discs and leave the corals whole. Again, cook the scallops in a pan or on a griddle (see p. 93).

→ Steam or boil the JERUSALEM ARTICHOKES until tender. Allow them to cool a little, then remove their skins and mash or mouli, adding plenty of BLACK PEPPER, some SALT, and some CREAM and BUTTER. They are watery; don't let them get sloppy.

→ Reheat the purée in a small pan, then scrape into a little mound on each plate. Add the scallops and inject a burst of colour with a little finely chopped PARSLEY.

Coquilles St Jacques

SERVES 4

large scallops	8
béchamel sauce (of which 60ml / 2fl oz should be double cream)	300ml/10fl oz
breadcrumbs	1 tbsp
Parmesan cheese, *freshly grated*	1 tbsp
mashed potato, *made with about 340g/12oz of potatoes, milk, butter and seasoning*	
Duxelles	
shallots, *finely chopped*	2
unsalted butter	30g/1oz
button mushrooms, *thinly sliced*	110g/4oz
sea salt and black pepper	
dry white wine	100ml/3½fl oz
thyme	a sprig
lemon juice	a little

This wonderful classic Parisian dish, not to be confused with the Provençal version, is really fish pie served in the shell.

→ To prepare the SCALLOPS, separate the corals and halve the white discs around their circumference, gently removing all the sinewy bits.

→ Make the BÉCHAMEL (see p. 402) and keep it warm while you cook the duxelles.

→ First, sauté the SHALLOTS gently in the BUTTER until golden and softened. Throw in the finely sliced MUSHROOMS and cook them down until their juices have started to run. SEASON, add the WINE and THYME and bring to the boil. Simmer until the wine has virtually disappeared. Take the pan off the heat, remove the thyme and squeeze in a little LEMON JUICE.

→ Divide the mixture between four scallop shells. Put the scallop discs over the duxelles with two commas of coral to each portion.

→ Spoon some warm béchamel over each shell and sprinkle over the BREADCRUMBS and most of the PARMESAN. Let the dish cool and set in the fridge for 30 minutes.

→ Preheat the oven to 200°C/400°F/Gas 6. Spoon the MASHED POTATO over the filling or around the edge of the shell and sprinkle over the last of the Parmesan. Bake for 20 minutes. Then put the shells under a hot grill to give them a final burnish before serving.

Smoked Salmon with Saffron-braised Fennel

SERVES 4

fennel bulbs, root left on	2
water	100ml/3½fl oz
olive oil	200ml/7fl oz
star anise	3
green olives in good olive oil, *pitted and halved*	a handful
saffron	a pinch
salt and pepper	
smoked salmon, preferably wild	8 slices
cream cheese	2 tbsp
mascarpone cheese	2 tbsp
shallots, *very finely chopped*	1 tbsp

Richard Corrigan included this unusual, delicately spiced dish on a St Patrick's Day menu we devised. It is beautifully uncheffy, and most of the preparation can be done the day before, so all you need to do on the day of eating is mix the cheeses and minced shallot and arrange the plates with slices of wild smoked salmon.

→ Preheat the oven to 200°C/400°F/Gas 6. Cut each FENNEL bulb in half, then each half into quarters or slices, depending on their size. Put them in a roasting tin or gratin dish with the WATER, OLIVE OIL, STAR ANISE, OLIVES, SAFFRON and SEASONING. Bring slowly to the boil, then cover with tin foil and cook in the oven until tender. Check with a skewer after 20 minutes. Cool and refrigerate—this can be done the day before.

→ Mix the CHEESES with the finely chopped SHALLOT. On each plate, arrange the fennel with a mound made out of a couple of the slices of SMOKED SALMON, then add a spoonful of the cheese mixture. Serve with Irish soda bread.

Smoked Trout and Horseradish Pâté

SERVES 6–8 AS A SMALL STARTER

horseradish, *freshly grated*	1 tsp
crème fraîche	2 tbsp
lemon	a spritz
black pepper	
smoked trout fillets	2
best full-fat soft cream cheese	1 tbsp
lemon	juice of ½, or to taste

Another great idea to pass round with drinks, on little squares or triangles of hot toast, or serve as a light lunch or supper with a salad.

→ Mix together the HORSERADISH, 1 tablespoon of CRÈME FRAÎCHE, LEMON JUICE and a scrunch of BLACK PEPPER. Mash the fillets of TROUT on a plate, then transfer to a bowl. Add the creamed horseradish, CREAM CHEESE, LEMON JUICE and remaining CRÈME FRAÎCHE in that order. Season with BLACK PEPPER. Taste and adjust lemon juice and seasoning. Serve cool on hot toast cut into squares.

Smoked Eel and Horseradish Pâté
→ Use 110g/4oz of skinned SMOKED EEL FILLET instead of the trout and follow the method above.

Smoked Salmon Pâté with Lemon

smoked salmon trimmings	
unsalted butter	equal amount
lemon juice	
cayenne	a knifepoint

This is a delicious bonne bouche or starter and a great way to use up all your trimmings, or, indeed, if you can't afford a side or whole slices of smoked salmon, just buy trimmings in the first place. No one is going to know.

→ Weigh the smoked SALMON, then pound it with an equal amount of unsalted BUTTER. (You can use a food processor if the butter is not fridge cold.) The main seasoning is LEMON JUICE, with a knifepoint of CAYENNE to pep it up.

→ You can use whipped cream instead of half the butter, which lightens the paste. If you use only butter, add a layer of clarified butter to seal the top, cover with foil and keep the pot in the fridge for up to 10 days.

→ The pâté also makes a perfect Sunday supper with hot brown toast and runny scrambled eggs.

Smoked Salmon Pâté with Cream Cheese

→ This is a coarser-textured pâté, with the addition of CREAM CHEESE. The following proportions work best: 50 per cent smoked salmon trimmings, roughly blitzed, to which you add 40 per cent softened unsalted best butter and 10 per cent good full-fat cream cheese. Work everything together with some cracked black pepper and lemon juice. Refrigerate until cold.

Smoked Buckling Pâté

SERVES 4

buckling	2
unsalted butter, *softened*	
lemon juice	
black peppercorns, *cracked with a rolling pin or in a mortar*	1–2 tsp

Buckling are hot-smoked Atlantic herrings eaten cold, rather than cold-smoked like kippers, and they make a wonderful dish for a brunch party. They have a milder, subtler flavour that is really brought out by the smoke. Make this 2–3 hours before you need it or the night before.

→ Skin and fillet the FISH. This is easy and quick, though the tiny bones can be a bit fiddly. The hair's breadth ones you can leave in as you won't notice them.

→ Gently mash the flesh on a plate with a fork, removing any further bones. Add about a tablespoon of BUTTER to start with, mashing it in well to amalgamate but not crushing the fish to a paste. Now add another tablespoon of butter and repeat.

→ Squeeze over the juice of half a LEMON and add a teaspoon of coarsely cracked PEPPERCORNS. Taste and add more lemon juice, peppercorns and even butter if you feel it needs it—this is a dish to make to your own taste. Put in a pot, press down, cover with clingfilm and refrigerate. Simple.

→ Eat the pâté cold with hot toast. It is particularly good with a walnut and rye loaf or with sourdough rye. Or you can spread the pâté on toasted bagels and fill them with peppery fresh watercress.

Blinis with Smoked Fish and Horseradish Cream

SERVES 6

Blinis

fresh yeast	30g/1oz
OR dry yeast	15g/½oz
lukewarm water	6 tbsp
plain flour	200g/7oz
buckwheat flour	110g/4oz
lukewarm milk	240ml/8fl oz
organic eggs, *separated*	3
unrefined sugar	1 tsp
sea salt	
sour cream	3 tbsp
unsalted butter, *melted*	110g/4oz

Serving

smoked salmon
smoked eel fillets
cream, *lightly whipped*
horseradish, *grated*
lemon juice
black pepper

These blinis need a little long-term planning, but no more than that. Think about them in the morning, whisk them into life and leave them. Think about them briefly in the afternoon, stir in the flour and leave them again. Then cook them just before your drinks or supper and let everyone pile their own goodies on top. Any smoked fish works well, though salmon is the classic.

→ Whisk the YEAST into the lukewarm WATER and leave it to froth for 10 minutes. Put the PLAIN FLOUR and half the BUCKWHEAT FLOUR into a large bowl, make a well in the centre and add the yeast mixture and all the milk.

→ Whisk into a batter, cover with a tea towel and leave in a warm place for 3 hours. Stir in the remaining buckwheat flour and leave for a further 2 hours.

→ Beat the EGG YOLKS, SUGAR, SALT, CREAM and 3 tablespoons of melted BUTTER together lightly and mix into the dough. Whisk the EGG WHITES stiffly and fold them in. Leave for an hour. Brush a heavy frying pan with melted BUTTER, warm the pan over a medium heat and cook the mixture, a small ladleful at a time. Cook on each side until small bubbles appear on the surface (about 2 minutes a side). Wrap them in a tea towel or napkin and put them in a warm oven while you make the rest.

→ Serve with a plate of smoked salmon (one slice per person should be enough) and a plate of smoked eel fillets (one fillet per person as it is very rich). Have ready a bowl of lightly whipped cream into which you have stirred grated horseradish to taste, a squeeze of lemon juice and a scrunch of black pepper. Or use sour cream and horseradish with black pepper stirred in.

Crêpes Parmentier with Smoked Eel, Crispy Bacon and Horseradish Cream

SERVES 6

smoked eel fillets	2
organic oak-smoked streaky bacon rashers	8
Crêpes Parmentier	
floury organic potatoes, *peeled and cooked*	450g/1lb
milk	60ml/2fl oz
potato or ordinary flour	2 tbsp
organic eggs	3
egg whites	4
double cream	2 tbsp
salt and pepper	
butter	
Horseradish Cream	
double OR soured cream	1 small carton
fresh horseradish root, *grated*	
lemon	
salt	

I think the affinity between eel and bacon is sublime. Here they are both smoked, so it's a head-on, full-strength flavour, with the creamiest of little starchy potato pancakes and a hit of horseradish. You can prepare the batter a few hours before you want it, and the horseradish, leaving your guests with the assembly job.

→ First make the crêpes. Put the hot POTATOES through the coarse disc of the mouli, or mash by hand. Put them into a bowl with the milk, flour, eggs, whites, cream and seasoning, and whisk together. Heat a tiny bit of clarified, unsalted butter in your pancake pan, and add tablespoons of the mixture, several if your pan is big enough, flipping the pancakes over with a palette knife when they begin to bubble and brown around the edge; a couple of minutes.

→ Keep warm on a plate in a warm oven while you make the rest. Allow a rasher of streaky bacon per person and throw in a couple extra, and fry in their own fat until curled and crispened.

→ Skin and fillet your eel by literally unpeeling it in one swift, satisfying move. Then chop your two fillets into 5cm/2in chunks, and put one on each pancake, followed by the bacon and a dollop of horseradish cream.

Horseradish Cream

→ I use either double cream or soured cream. If you can't get hold of fresh horseradish root, the only commercial brands I know that don't turn it into a noxious paste are the English Provender Company's Hot Horseradish, stocked by good supermarkets, and Source Foods Organic Horseradish Relish. Depending on whether you want a runny or a stiffer result, do or do not whip the cream. Then stir in the horseradish a teaspoon at a time, tasting as you go. There is no going back! A spritz of lemon and a sprinkle of salt, and you have it.

Brandade of Smoked Mackerel

SERVES 6–8

puff pastry	225g/8oz
smoked mackerel fillet, *skinned and boned*	225g/8oz
garlic clove, *peeled*	1
salt, pepper, lemon juice	
good olive oil	50–85ml/2–3fl oz
milk	50–85ml/2–3fl oz
egg yolk for brushing patties	

Dill Cream

cream, *lightly whipped*	generous tbsp per person
lemon juice	
dill seed, *pounded*	
salt and pepper	

Sambal

cucumber, *peeled and cut into doll's-sized dice*	1
onion, *finely chopped*	1
celery, *finely chopped*	
red pepper, *finely chopped*	1
flat-leaf parsley	
olive oil and lemon	
salt and pepper	

This was a delicious starter that George Perry-Smith used to serve at the Riverside in Helston, Cornwall. If you are buying the puff pastry ready-made, do go for an all-butter one.

→ Pound the GARLIC in a mortar with just enough SALT to melt it, add the smoked MACKEREL, and pound energetically until the resultant paste is smoother than you believed possible, checking for escaped bones as you go.

→ Prepare a bain-marie and in it warm the mackerel paste in a decent-sized pudding basin, and the MILK and OIL in two jugs; don't let them get too hot, just warm. Add the oil and the milk to the mackerel alternately, a little at a time, working each addition in thoroughly before adding more. The more you can work it in without making the mixture sloppy, as opposed to soft and light, the more interesting will be the contrast between crisp pastry and moist, light filling. Season to taste with PEPPER and LEMON JUICE, and maybe a little SALT. Chill. Roll out the pastry fairly thinly, and cut into rounds with a 7.5cm/3in cutter. Put a generous teaspoon of mackerel mixture on each, fold over and seal.

→ Keep the patties on a lightly floured tray in the fridge until the meal. Preheat the oven to 230°C/450°F/Gas 8 and bake 3 per person, brushed with EGG YOLK, for about 12 minutes. Serve with a generous tablespoon per person of dill cream and the sambal.

Dill Cream
→ Simply season and sharpen the WHIPPED CREAM with a squeeze of LEMON, and some pounded DILL SEED to taste.

Sambal
→ For the sambal, peel the CUCUMBER, cut into tiny dice and mix with very finely chopped ONION, CELERY, RED PEPPER and PARSLEY, dress with OLIVE OIL, LEMON, SALT and PEPPER, and put a generous tablespoon on each plate.

Duck Liver with Grokes

Duck Liver with Grapes

SERVES 4

duck livers, *any green patches or tubey bits removed*	340g/12oz
sea salt, black pepper, cayenne	
flour	a little
unsalted butter	30g/1oz
brioches, *topknots removed, cut into thick slices*	2
duck or chicken stock (see p. 54)	90ml/3fl oz
Madeira OR Marsala	3 tbsp
muscat grapes, *peeled, halved and pipped*	2 dozen
pomegranate molasses	1–2 tsp

Make this with chicken livers if you like, but it is a treat to find the richer, denser duck livers, the flavour of which is such a foil to the grapes. The discovery of pomegranate molasses, so much a part of Middle Eastern and Moroccan cooking, is a revelation when you want a complex, lemony underscoring without the acidity of the lemon itself. Make sure you buy really good brioche.

→ Remove any green patches or tubey bits from the LIVERS and season them with SALT, PEPPER and a knife tip of CAYENNE. Roll them in a dusting of FLOUR, shaking off the excess—you want just enough to help them crisp delectably. Melt the BUTTER in a small pan, and when it is foaming put in the livers. Turn them after a couple of minutes and cook the other side for another few minutes. They will take about 5 minutes to cook to crisped exteriors and meltingly pink middles. Remove to a warm plate.
→ Toast the BRIOCHE slices on a griddle or in a toaster and keep them warm. Deglaze the pan with the STOCK and BOOZE, scraping as you go. Throw in the GRAPES, just to heat through with the POMEGRANATE MOLASSES. Taste after you have added the first teaspoon of molasses to see if you want to go further. It mustn't overwhelm. SEASON, then remove the grapes with a slotted spoon and let the juices reduce. Meanwhile, put the livers on top of the brioche slices, pile on the grapes and pour the sticky pan juices over the lot. A little more BUTTER added at the juice reduction stage, just a walnut-sized piece, gives extra gloss and butteriness.

Venison Liver Parfait

SERVES 12

venison liver	about 600g/1¼lb
garlic clove, *crushed*	1
juniper berries, *well crushed*	2 heaped tsp
salt and freshly ground pepper	
organic eggs	3
good double cream	800ml/1¼ pints
gin	3 large tbsp

This is a fantastic dish for a celebration, not difficult to make, but when you chill it, turn it out and cut it into rosy pink, lightly creamy slices it will delight even more than the chicken liver version.

→ Preheat the oven to 170°C /325°F /Gas 3. Butter a 30 × 8 × 8cm (12 × 3 × 3in) terrine with a lid, or a 900g /2lb loaf tin. Chop the LIVER into chunks, and throw it into the food processor with the GARLIC, JUNIPER, SALT and PEPPER, and process until liquid and smooth. Add the EGGS, and continue for a further minute, then add the CREAM and GIN, and give it another few seconds. Check for SEASONING: it needs quite a bit of salt and pepper, and you might want more juniper. Then sieve it into your terrine. Do not omit this stage, you want a velvet-smooth texture. Cover with the lid, and stand the terrine in a bain-marie or a roasting tin with hot water up to its middle. Cook for an hour. Check that it is just firming to the touch—it will continue to cook when you remove it from its water bath—and leave it to cool. It could need a further 10 minutes or so, but mine was beautifully pink after an hour.

→ When cool, refrigerate for at least a couple of hours. To serve, dip the terrine into hot water, run a fine-bladed knife carefully around the edges, hold your breath and turn it upside down onto a serving dish. Then make a lot of wholemeal toast, and serve it with the best French unsalted butter you can find. I wrapped the remains of mine in clingfilm and kept it in the fridge for several days.

Chicken Liver Pâté

SERVES 8

organic chicken livers	450g /1lb or thereabouts
unsalted butter, *softened*	110g /4oz
sea salt and black pepper	
small garlic clove, *very finely chopped*	1
thyme OR basil	a sprig a few leaves
cognac	2 tbsp
Madeira, Marsala OR port	2 tbsp

This is an exceptionally rich but simple dish, which you can either spread on crostini to accompany your pre-supper drink or serve fridge cold with hot granary toast as a starter. I only ever use organic chicken livers. Make this 2–3 days before you need it to allow all the flavours to develop.

→ First clean the LIVERS and remove all the gristly bits from them, especially any little green stained bits as they will make everything taste bitter. Melt 30g/1oz of the BUTTER in a frying pan and sling in the livers, cooking them for about 5 minutes and turning them as each surface begins to brown. They should still be rosy pink inside.

→ Plop a further 55g /2oz of softened BUTTER into your food processor or liquidiser with the chicken livers, SEASONING, chopped GARLIC and THYME LEAVES. Reserve the hot butter in the pan, to which you now add the COGNAC. Allow it to bubble furiously before adding the MADEIRA, MARSALA or PORT and heating it through for a minute. Pour the buttery liquor into the processor and process until smooth. Scrape the mixture into a small earthenware tureen or bowl.

→ Melt the remaining butter—or better still, pork, goose or duck fat if you have it. Skim off the white sediment onto kitchen paper with a slotted spoon and pour the butter onto the top of the pâté to form a protective buttery layer. Cover with foil and a lid when it has set and place in the fridge for 2–3 days before you eat it. Eat cold with hot granary, wholemeal or sourdough toast and a few cornichons.

Country Terrine with Prunes, Pistachios and Green Peppercorns

FILLS A 1.2 LITRE/2 PINT TERRINE

Ask the butcher to coarsely mince the following:

belly pork without the rind and small bones	450g/1lb
unsmoked streaky organic bacon	340g/12oz
pig's liver	450g/1lb
pork back fat	170g/6oz
half a pig's kidney	

Other ingredients

unsalted butter	75g/2½oz
onions, *chopped*	450g/1lb
garlic cloves, *peeled and finely chopped*	4
flat-leaf parsley, *finely chopped*	1 bunch
fresh thyme, *chopped*	3–4 sprigs
rosemary, *very finely chopped*	1 sprig
green peppercorns, *drained from their brine*	1 heaped dsrtsp
juniper berries, *crushed in a mortar*	6
whole pistachio nuts	55g/2oz
mi-cuit Agen prunes, *stoned and quartered*	100g/3½oz
organic egg, *beaten*	1
mace and nutmeg	½ tsp each
a fresh bay leaf	
calvados, Somerset cider brandy OR cognac	60ml/2fl oz
Fino sherry	60ml/2fl oz
sea salt and freshly ground black pepper	

This has guts, substance and depth and is remarkably easy to make. Try to make the terrine at least a couple, if not 4 days before you need it so the flavours marry and develop. It freezes well so double up quantities and make a terrine to keep for another time. Ask your butcher to mince all the meat coarsely for you.

→ Melt the BUTTER in a heavy frying pan and gently sauté the ONIONS, coating them in the fat, for about 25 minutes until softened and golden. Put THE MEAT AND ALL THE OTHER INGREDIENTS up to but not including the bay leaf into a huge bowl and mix well to amalgamate. Place the BAY LEAF in the middle of the bottom of the terrine, then turf in the buttery onions when they've cooled down a little. Put the ALCOHOL in the onion pan and warm before setting light to it and letting the alcohol burn off. When the flames have died down, pour the alcohol into the bowlful of mixture and add the seasoning, turning everything together well.

→ Preheat the oven to 150°C/300°F/Gas 2. Put the mixture into the terrine, cover it with foil and its lid and put it in a roasting tin with boiling water poured three-quarters up its sides. Cook on the middle shelf for an hour. Uncover and insert a skewer deep into the terrine, count to ten then see if it is hot on your tongue. The meat juices should be pink. Put back into the oven uncovered for 15–30 minutes, depending on whether the skewer was hot or warm and the juices bloody or pink after the first hour.

→ Take out of the oven and replace the foil while you let the terrine cool. Put in the fridge for a couple of days at least and remove it 30 minutes before you want to eat. Serve with toast or a good sourdough or crusty loaf and a few cornichons or green olives.

Rillettes de Tours

SERVES 4–6

belly pork	1kg/2¼lb
dry white wine	1 glass
garlic cloves, *crushed*	4–6
nutmeg	
salt and pepper	
pork fat	450g/1lb

→ Preheat the oven to 110°C/225°F/Gas ¼. Take the rind off the BELLY PORK and put it to one side. Remove and discard the bones and cut the meat into 2.5cm/1in chunks. Put them into a Pyrex or non-aluminium dish. Pour the WINE over them, then add the crushed GARLIC, a suspicion of NUTMEG and the SEASONING. Cover and bake for at least 5 hours, or until the meat is virtually falling to pieces.

→ Meanwhile, sprinkle the RIND with SALT and roast it in a hot oven, 200°C/400°F/Gas 6 until crisp. Leave to cool on a rack set over a plate to catch any residue. Chop the rind finely. Melt the PORK FAT and strain it. Shred the meat roughly using two forks and mix it with its juices and the garlic; mix in the chopped, roasted rind and its juices. Pour into small pots or jars, or into one larger earthenware dish. When cool, pour the pork fat over it to seal the top.

→ Rillettes can be stored for months in a sealed jar in a cool place, or if you are going to eat them within a couple of weeks, you can keep them in a plastic container in the fridge. Serve with a good crusty bread, some glossy green or black olives, a few cornichons and a good bitter lettuce such as escarole or radicchio.

Grilled Quail Flavoured with Balsamic Vinegar

SERVES 4

quail	4
olive oil	
sea salt	
black pepper	
best aged balsamic vinegar	
chicken stock	

This is almost not a recipe it is so simple; the sort of dish you can cook in front of friends over drinks and eat as an ambulant starter together. Dunk a bit of bread in the sweet-sour juices, balsamic is perfect for small game, and do eat with your fingers—quail and cutlery don't go. I cook mine 'long leg', that is, with the trail still inside them, but if you are squeamish, don't.

→ Preheat the grill. Place the QUAIL on their sides in a large gratin dish, brush with olive oil and rub with sea salt and black pepper. Cook for 5 minutes, then repeat the process with the other side. Finally, splosh a dessertspoon of best aged BALSAMIC VINEGAR over each bird, add a tablespoon of CHICKEN STOCK per bird to the dish and blast the quails under the grill for a final 5 minutes. Gently pull a leg away from the body and pierce here to check the quail are cooked through, then rest them, turning them in their juice for 5 minutes before eating.

Shortcrust Pastry

plain white organic flour	170g/6oz
sea salt	a pinch
unsalted butter, fridge cold	85g/3oz

→ I sift the FLOUR and a pinch of SEA SALT into the food pro-cessor, then cut the fridge-cold BUTTER into cubes on top of it. Pulse several times for 3–4 seconds a time before adding a tablespoon of COLD WATER through the feed tube. If the paste is still in crumby little bits after a minute or two, add a table-spoon more of water, but remember, the more water you use, the more the pastry will shrink if you bake it blind. The moment it has cohered into a single ball, stop, remove it, wrap it in clingfilm and put it in the fridge for at least 30 minutes.
→ If you are making pastry by hand, sift the FLOUR into a large bowl with the SALT, add the chopped BUTTER, and work as briskly as you can to rub the fat into the flour. Use the tips of your fingers only, rather like running grains of hot sand through your fingers. Add the water bit by bit as above; wrap and chill the pastry.
→ Now scatter a bit of FLOUR on your work surface, roll your rolling pin in it, dust the palms of your hands, and start rolling. Always roll away from yourself, turning the pastry as you go, and keep the rolling pin and work surface floured to prevent sticking. Once it is rolled out, slip the rolling pin under the pastry, and pick it up, judging where to lie it in the greased tin. Again, never stretch it because it will shrink back. Try to leave at least 30 minutes for the unbaked tart case to commune with the inside of your fridge. Or put it in the fridge the night before you need it.

Baking blind
→ If you are baking your pastry case blind, preheat the oven to 190–200°C/375–400°F/Gas 5–6.Tear off a piece of greaseproof paper a little larger than the tart tin and place it over the pastry. Cover the paper with a layer of dried beans; the idea is to prevent the pastry from rising up in the oven. When the pastry is nearly cooked (the timing depends on the rest of the recipe), remove the paper and beans and prick the base of the pastry to let out trapped air that would otherwise bubble up. Return the tart to the oven for about 5–10 minutes to dry the pastry base.

Blue Cheese Tarts with Red Onion Marmalade

SERVES 6

shortcrust pastry	
mascarpone	55g/2oz
double cream	60ml/2fl oz
egg yolks	3
blue cheese, *crumbled*	170g/6oz
salt, black pepper and cayenne	a pinch
Red Onion Marmalade	
red onions, *thinly sliced*	2
salt, black pepper and sugar	a pinch
butter	55g/2oz
sherry vinegar	2 tbsp
red wine	4 tbsp

I can't remember when I first went to Judy and Stephen Markwick's wonderful restaurant in Bristol, but I have eaten exceptionally well there over the years. This is one of their recipes, using a mixture of Roquefort, Stilton and Shropshire Blue.

→ Preheat the oven to 190°C/375°F/Gas 5. Line six individual tart tins with PASTRY (see p. 104), and bake blind. Remove from the oven and turn the heat up to 220°C/425°F/Gas 7.

→ Make the red onion marmalade by mixing the ONIONS in a bowl with SALT, PEPPER and SUGAR. Heat the BUTTER in a saucepan until foamy and add the onions, stirring well. When almost cooked down, add the VINEGAR and RED WINE, and simmer gently until well reduced; this will take about 40–50 minutes.

→ Make the tart filling by beating together the MASCARPONE, CREAM and EGG YOLKS until smooth, then stir in the BLUE CHEESE and SEASONING. Place a spoonful of the onion marmalade into each pastry case (you can also add wilted spinach leaves if you like) and then fill each one with the blue cheese mixture. Bake for about 10–15 minutes. Good served with chutney, something like green tomato.

Tomato and Prosciutto Tarts

MAKES 8 SMALL TARTS

puff pastry *made with butter*	300g/10oz
prosciutto, San Daniele if possible	8 slices
best extra virgin olive oil	150ml/5fl oz
garlic cloves	3
black pepper	
plum tomatoes OR organic cherry tomatoes	10 about 40
fresh basil	a handful
fresh thyme OR rosemary	a handful

You can use ready-made puff pastry for this recipe but make sure it is the best, made with all butter. If you want to make your own see p. 517.

→ Preheat the oven to 190°C/375°F/Gas 5. Roll out the PASTRY, and stamp it out into eight 10cm/4in circles. Place them on a greased baking sheet and leave in the fridge until needed

→ Tear the PROSCIUTTO roughly and put it in the food processor with half the OLIVE OIL, the GARLIC CLOVES and the PEPPER. Blitz for a few seconds to make a rough purée. Slice the PLUM TOMATOES or halve the CHERRY TOMATOES. Tear the BASIL leaves and add them to the remaining olive oil, but not more than 20 minutes before you use them, or they will blacken.

→ Spoon a mound of the prosciutto mixture on to each tart base, leaving a good-sized edge free. Place a circle of tomatoes on top, brush with a little of the oil and basil mixture and sprinkle with chopped THYME OR ROSEMARY. Cook for about 15 minutes, until the pastry is puffed up, golden and cooked through. Put the tarts on a rack, brush with more of the oil and basil mixture and serve them warm.

Souffléd Cheese Tart

SERVES 6

shortcrust pastry case, *chilled* (see p.104)	1 × 23cm /9in
egg, *beaten*, for brushing	1
milk	150ml/5fl oz
bay leaves	2
butter	30g/1oz
plain flour	30g/1oz
black pepper, cayenne	
English mustard (optional)	1 tsp
Gruyère, *grated*	55g/2oz
Parmesan cheese, *grated* plus extra for sprinkling	30g/1oz
eggs, *separated*	2
double cream	1 tbsp

→ Preheat the oven to 200°C/400°F/Gas 6. Bake the PASTRY blind for 20 minutes (see p. 104), then remove the beans, prick the base with a fork, brush with BEATEN EGG, and return to the oven for 5 minutes.

→ Heat the MILK gently with the BAY LEAVES. Make a thick béchamel sauce with the BUTTER, FLOUR and warm MILK. Season with PEPPER, a touch of CAYENNE, and the MUSTARD if you're using it. Add the GRUYÈRE and PARMESAN and remove from the heat. Whisk the EGG YOLKS with the CREAM and stir them into the sauce. Leave the mixture to cool, then remove the bay leaves and fold in the stiffly beaten EGG WHITES. Pour into the pastry case, sprinkle on a handful of coarsely grated PARMESAN, and cook for about 15 minutes, until puffed up, browned, and still slightly trembly. Leave to rest for 10 minutes before serving.

Roasted Aubergine, Goat's Cheese and Smoked Paprika Tart

SERVES 6

aubergine	1
extra virgin olive oil	
yellow pepper	1
Vulscombe or similar fresh goat's cheese	1
organic eggs	2
extra yolks	2
double cream	120ml/4fl oz
crème fraîche	120ml/4fl oz
coriander	1 small bunch
mint	1 small bunch
sea salt, black pepper	
smoked paprika	a pinch
shortcrust pastry *made with 170g/6oz flour and 85g/3oz of butter* (see p. 104)	

Brushing discs of aubergine with olive oil and roasting them on a tray in the oven stops their natural tendency to soak up lots of oil. I use a Vulscombe goat's cheese from Devon, but any fresh goat's cheese will do.

→ Preheat the oven to 190°C/375°F/Gas 5. Slice the AUBERGINE into discs, brush with OLIVE OIL on both sides and place on a sheet of silicone paper. Halve, core and seed the YELLOW PEPPER, then cut into thin strips and place them on the same baking tray. Sprinkle over a little OLIVE OIL and turn the peppers in it. Roast for about 20 minutes until the aubergine slices and peppers are tender when pierced with a fork.

→ Make the shortcrust PASTRY, line a 23cm/9in tart tin and bake the pastry shell blind in the usual way for 15 minutes (see p. 104). Remove the dried beans and greaseproof paper, prick the base with a fork and return to the oven for 5–10 minutes until lightly browned and cooked.

→ Crumble the GOAT'S CHEESE. Whisk together the EGGS, YOLKS and CREAMS, then whisk in the chopped HERBS. Season with SALT and PEPPER.

→ As soon as the pastry shell is cooked, cover the base with slightly overlapping slices of aubergine, add spokes of yellow pepper, then scrape in the goat's cheese and distribute it evenly. Add the herby custard, then scatter over a pinch of SMOKED PAPRIKA. Bake until the custard is browned and trembling (about 30 minutes). Leave to cool for at least 10 minutes before eating.

Souffléd Crab Tart

SERVES 6

shortcrust pastry, *made with 170g/6oz flour and 85g/3oz unsalted butter* (see p. 104)	
crab meat, brown and white	450g/1lb
salt, black pepper, cayenne	
organic eggs	3
Parmesan cheese, *grated*	1 tbsp
Gruyère cheese, *grated*	1 tbsp
double cream	240ml/8fl oz
French mustard	2 tsp

→ Make the SHORTCRUST and line a 23cm/9in tart tin. Preheat the oven to 200°C/400°F/Gas 6. Bake the pastry blind for 10 minutes (see p. 104), then remove the beans, prick the base with a fork, and return to the oven for 5 minutes. Remove the pastry case and turn the heat down to 190°C/375°F/Gas 5.
→ Season the CRAB, going carefully with the CAYENNE—you want a bit of heat, but nothing overwhelming. Beat in 1 whole EGG and 2 YOLKS, and then the CHEESES, CREAM and MUSTARD. Whisk the 2 EGG WHITES until stiff, and fold gently and quickly into the mixture. Pour the mixture into the pastry case, and cook for about 30–40 minutes. Check after 30; it should be puffed up but have a slightly wobbly centre, like a soufflé. Remove from the oven and leave to cool for 10 minutes before serving. A spoonful of cucumber and avocado sambal (see p. 82) is a good accompaniment.

Scallop, Artichoke and Smoked Bacon Tart

SERVES 6–8

shortcrust pastry case, (see p. 104)	1 × 23cm/9in
Jerusalem artichokes	170g/6oz
large scallops	6
smoked streaky bacon rashers	4
double cream	300ml/10fl oz
Jersey milk	3 tbsp
organic eggs	2
organic egg yolks	2
salt and black pepper	

→ Chill the pastry case in the fridge while you prepare the filling. Preheat the oven to 190°C/375°F/Gas 5.
→ Peel the ARTICHOKES and slice them into thin coins, 3mm/ ⅛ inch thick. Steam until tender, then leave to cool. Clean the SCALLOPS and separate the whites from the corals. Slice the whites into three discs each, and the corals into two if they are bumper-sized. Snip the BACON into thin pieces and fry in its own fat until really crispy. Drain and dry on kitchen paper.
→ Line the pastry base with the cooled artichokes, then cover with a layer of the raw scallops, distributing them evenly, then dot with the bacon.
→ Whisk the CREAM, MILK, EGGS and YOLKS together, SEASON, and, using a jug, pour gently into the pastry case so as not to displace the filling ingredients. Cook for 35–40 minutes; the corals will stick out of the top in their deliciously gaudy-coloured way, and be just cooked. Leave to cool for 10 minutes, then turn out and serve with a mustardy dressed plain green salad.

Monkfish Tarts with Béarnaise

MAKES 10–12 SMALL TARTS OR ONE LARGE ONE

shortcrust pastry, *chilled* (see p.104)	
egg, *beaten*, for brushing	1
monkfish, *skinned and sliced*	450g/1lb
salt and black pepper	
butter	
chanterelles OR organic mushrooms, *cleaned and chopped*	375g/12–14oz
fresh tarragon	a handful

Béarnaise sauce

tarragon vinegar	2 tbsp
shallot, *finely chopped*	1
tarragon, *finely chopped*	3 tsp
unsalted butter	140g/5oz
organic egg yolks	2

This can be made either as one whole tart, or as little tarts that just need a last-minute assembly job before serving with drinks—an ambulant starter. They only need 5 minutes in the oven, and everything can be prepared in advance. Monkfish is tenderly, juicily fleshy, so there is no chance of the tarts drying out.

→ Preheat the oven to 200°C/400°F/Gas 6. Bake the PASTRY blind (see p. 104) for 20 minutes if it is a large tart, 10 minutes if small, then remove the beans, prick the base with a fork and brush with beaten EGG before returning to the oven, for 10 or 5 minutes respectively. The pastry should be crisp and cooked. Turn the heat up to 220°C/425°F/Gas 7.

→ Season the slices of FISH and fry them in a generous chunk of BUTTER on both sides, until just opaque. Remove the fish from the pan and add the mushrooms, cooking them until they are completely softened.

→ Make the BÉARNAISE by heating together the TARRAGON VINEGAR, SHALLOT and 1 teaspoon of the CHOPPED TARRAGON in a small stainless steel saucepan, until the liquid has almost all evaporated. Melt the BUTTER in a small saucepan and leave to settle for a minute or two. Remove the vinegar mixture from the heat, add the EGG YOLKS and whisk until thick. Then, little by little, very slowly pour in the hot melted butter, leaving behind the white residue, whisking as you go. Sieve the sauce and scatter in another 2 teaspoons of CHOPPED TARRAGON.

→ Put the MUSHROOMS in the pastry cases, followed by the slices of monkfish, then pour over the béarnaise. Sprinkle on a bit more TARRAGON, and put the tart or tarts in the oven for a quick blast of heat: 5 minutes is all they need. Serve at once.

Bitter Leaf and Blood Orange Salad

radicchio	½
red endive	1
white endive	1
blood oranges, *cut into segments*	2
Nyons or good, black olives, *pitted*	12
goat's cheese, such as Ragstone or Golden Cross log, *crumbled*	

Dressing

cider vinegar	1 tbsp
runny honey	1 tbsp
lemon juice	1 tbsp
olive oil	2 tbsp
sea salt and black pepper	

→ Separate out the leaves of the RADICCHIO and CHICORY, wash gently and dry. Place in a bowl with the ORANGE SEGMENTS, pitted OLIVES and crumbled GOAT'S CHEESE.

→ Whisk all the DRESSING INGREDIENTS together, pour over the salad and toss well.

Mustard Leaf, Lettuce, Radish, Grated Parsnip and Carrot Salad

mustard leaves	
lettuce	
radishes	12
small parsnip, *peeled*	1
medium carrot, *peeled*	1
sesame seeds, *toasted*	1 tbsp

Dressing

lemon	juice of 1
yoghurt	1 tbsp
crème fraîche	1 tbsp
cider vinegar	1 dsrtsp
olive oil	to taste
Maldon sea salt	

Hot mustard leaves are lovely in a mid-winter salad if you can get them, tossed with a green lettuce. Use bunched watercress if you can't get mustard leaves, for their earthy, pepperiness.

→ Wash and dry the SALAD LEAVES, and place in a large bowl. Slice in a dozen RADISHES, coarsely grate over a small PARSNIP and a medium CARROT and toss over a large tablespoon of toasted SESAME SEEDS.

→ Mix all the DRESSING INGREDIENTS and SEASON to taste and add to the salad. Toss well with your hands in the bowl to amalgamate.

Chicory Salad

SERVES 4

white chicory OR mixed white and red chicory	6 heads
grain mustard	2 tsp
aged balsamic OR sherry vinegar	2 tbsp
cold-pressed olive oil	8–10 tbsp
sea salt and black pepper	
unsalted butter	30g/1oz
whole shelled walnuts	a handful
maple syrup	1 tbsp
chives, *chopped*	1–2 tbsp

This is a lovely plain winter salad, which you can make with white chicory and red Treviso chicory together if you like. You can dress it up with slices of orange and a little of the juice mixed into the dressing, or add some crunch with salted, buttered walnuts caramelised in a good maple syrup. Or leave well alone and eat it plain.

→ Chop the CHICORY into a combination of stubby circles and leaves. Mix the MUSTARD, VINEGAR, OLIVE OIL and SEASONING to make the dressing to your taste. I like a lot of mustard to coat the leaves.

→ Heat the BUTTER in a small frying pan. When it begins to bubble, throw in the WALNUTS and immediately shake over a little SALT. Turn the walnuts in the butter for a couple of minutes before adding the MAPLE SYRUP. It will splutter and bubble, but keep stirring to amalgamate it with the buttery nuts. Remove from the heat after a couple of minutes when the mixture is still a little liquid. Dress the salad, throw over the hot nuts and toss with the chives before serving.

Tomato Salad

SERVES 4

tomatoes	5
fresh basil	a handful
tarragon, parsley, chives or chervil	a handful
black pepper	
garlic clove	1
salt	
best extra virgin olive oil	to taste

It is all very well thinking this is the easiest of salads to make, but it isn't. We can't even buy tomatoes worthy of it here; ours are acidic and watery and seedy and the skins are tough and unyielding. So, get Italian or Provençal tomatoes if you can and organic ones whenever possible.

→ Always core tomatoes with a small sharp knife. To peel, blanch them in boiling water for 30 seconds and spike them with a knife to help the skin loosen. Drain and refresh them briefly in cold water; you don't want the tomatoes to cook.

→ Slice the TOMATOES and place them slightly overlapping on a large plate. Never dress them until just before serving. Allow a big tomato per person and a little extra for the dish. Strew with torn BASIL, finely chopped TARRAGON, PARSLEY, CHIVES, CHERVIL or whichever herb is to hand, and season liberally with BLACK PEPPER. Add some very finely chopped GARLIC too, if you wish.

→ Just before serving, add a little SALT—no earlier or it will encourage the tomatoes to water—and a liberal libation of the best extra virgin OLIVE OIl you have. You might like to add a good teaspoon of Dijon mustard to the oil before you dress the salad. I like to take this dressing in a screw top jar on bracing Irish picnics!

Provençal Tomato Salad

SᴇRᴠᴇꜱ 4–6

tomatoes	450g/1lb
olive oil and walnut oil	150ml/5fl oz
walnuts	1 tbsp
garlic clove	1
flat-leaf parsley, *chopped*	1 tbsp
basil, *chopped*	1 tbsp
salt and pepper	

The dressing should not be made more than half an hour before you are going to serve it, or it will turn purple.

→ Blanch and skin the TOMATOES, slice them and arrange in rows on a flat dish. Into a food processor or liquidiser put the mixed OLIVE OIL and WALNUT OIL, WALNUTS, GARLIC, chopped PARSLEY and fresh BASIL. Add SALT and PEPPER. Blend briefly to amalgamate, pour over the tomatoes and serve.

Tomato, Olive and Basil Salad with Grilled Ricotta

SᴇRᴠᴇꜱ 6

fresh ricotta	675g/1½lb
summer savory, thyme, parsley and chives, all or any combination	
olive oil	4 tbsp
sea salt and black pepper	
large, meaty tomatoes, *skinned*	6
fresh basil leaves, purple if you can find them	a handful
Niçoise olives	18–24
aged, mellow balsamic vinegar	2 tbsp

A brilliant example of a cooked/raw salad that is made substantial by the addition of the grilled ricotta. If you can find summer savory, it is an underemployed and delightful herb that works incredibly well with fresh goat's cheese too.

→ Spoon the RICOTTA, a tablespoon of finely chopped PARSLEY and CHIVES and a dessertspoon of SAVORY and THYME or to taste, SEASONED, with roughly 2 tablespoon of the OLIVE OIL, into 6 ramekins. Shake a little extra oil over the top of each ramekin and set under the grill until bubbling.

→ Meanwhile, skin the TOMATOES by pouring boiling water over them to cover, piercing each tomato with the sharp point of a knife blade and counting to 30. Pour away the scalding water, adding cold for 10 seconds or so, then pour away that and you should be able to peel the tomatoes without damage to your fingers.

→ Slice and core the tomatoes and overlap them on individual plates. Scatter the BASIL and OLIVES over and around them and dribble over more OLIVE OIL and the BALSAMIC VINEGAR. Season. Let the flavours marry for a few minutes. Turn out each ramekin of bubbling ricotta on the side of the salads and serve with good, crusty warm bread.

Tricolore

large, meaty-fleshed organic tomatoes, *skinned*	1 per person
buffalo mozzarella	1 between 2 people
fresh basil leaves	a handful
good, peppery, grassy extra virgin olive oil	
sea salt and black pepper	

This is probably Italy's most famous export after spaghetti Bolognese and pizza, but as with the two of them, its reputation is only as good as the ingredients used and the cook at the helm. Please buy the best mozzarella di bufala or burrata that you can find. This is not the time to use factory-produced cow's milk mozzarella, which is fine for pizza.

→ Slice the TOMATOES and overlap them on a preferably white plate down one side in a line. Do similarly with the MOZZARELLA on the other side of the plate. Burrata should be left whole. Tear a few BASIL leaves over the salad and pour on some OLIVE OIL. Salt the tomatoes a little with SEA SALT like Maldon. Scrunch some BLACK PEPPER over and serve. If you wish, you could sprinkle some good, aged balsamic over the tomatoes or add slices of avocado to the dish. The Italian flag on a plate.

Caesar Salad

leaves from two heads of romaine or a couple of small cos lettuces	
garlic cloves, *crushed*	2
olive oil	170ml/6fl oz
white sourdough bread, *cubed*	6 tbsp
organic eggs	2
lemons	juice of 2
Worcestershire sauce	8 drops
Parmesan cheese, *freshly grated*	6 tsp

This is the original Caesar salad recipe, as served by Caesar Cardini in Tijuana in Mexico. The salad leaves should not be torn or cut, but plenty of restaurants take no notice of that detail.

→ Wash and chill the LETTUCE leaves. Put the GARLIC in the OLIVE OIL and leave for an hour or more to infuse. Preheat the oven to 200°C/400°F/Gas 6. Brush the bread with some of the oil and bake until golden.

→ Put the lettuce leaves in a big bowl. Place the EGGS in cold water, bring to the boil and boil for 1 minute. Break the eggs over the salad leaves and toss the salad slowly with your hands. Add the LEMON JUICE, OLIVE OIL, WORCESTERSHIRE sauce and SEASONING, then toss the salad very well again. Add the CHEESE, toss one more time and serve.

Courgette, Pine Nut and Sultana Salad

SERVES 4–6

medium courgettes	6
olive oil	
garlic cloves, *peeled and finely chopped*	2
sultanas	a handful
pine nuts	a handful

This can be served as part of a vegetarian lunch or supper and eaten hot, warm or cold. Don't worry about the courgettes being unevenly cooked. That is part of the charm of the dish—some are browned, some firm, some almost cooked to a pale green pulp.

→ Cut the COURGETTES into thick slices and throw them into a heavy-bottomed frying pan in which you have heated a few tablespoons of good OLIVE OIL. Cook, stirring as you go, until the courgettes are no longer completely firm and resistant. I hesitate to offer a time, as size and heat are the deciding factors, but around 7 minutes.

lemon juice

sea salt and black pepper

Then add the SULTANAS, PINE NUTS, GARLIC and plenty of SEASONING. Let the pine nuts brown slightly before adding LEMON JUICE to taste—use at least one whole lemon and possibly more. Cook everything together briefly to marry the flavours, then turn out onto a serving dish, preferably one of a contrasting colour to show them off best.

Beetroot, Broad Bean and Artichoke Salad with Anchovy Dressing

This is a beautifully earthy dish with a wonderful combination of flavours and colours. In winter, use chopped potato instead of the broad beans; don't worry if you can't get artichokes—the salad is just as good without them. Keep all the vegetables separate on the plate. You can use anchovies in olive oil or the salted kind, which need soaking in water.

SERVES 4 AS A STARTER

small raw beetroot	6
lemon, *halved*	1
globe artichokes	4
baby broad beans, *podded*	450g/1lb
duck OR hen eggs	4
oak-smoked bacon rashers, *cut into small strips*	110g/4oz
flat-leaf parsley, *chopped*	2–3 tbsp
Anchovy Dressing	
olive oil	4–5 tbsp
mild onions, *thinly sliced*	450g/1lb
garlic cloves, *thinly sliced*	3
anchovies	55g/2oz
white wine vinegar	1 tbsp
pepper	

→ Preheat the oven to 150°C/300°F/Gas 2. Scrub the BEETROOT but do not peel or trim them or they will bleed their juices. Place on a baking sheet in the oven for about 2 hours or until tender. Peel off the skins, and cut into cubes or thin wedges.

→ Bring a large saucepan of water to the boil, squeeze in the LEMON JUICE and drop in the LEMON HALVES. Add the ARTICHOKES and boil until the leaves come away easily. Leave to cool, strip off the leaves, scrape out the 'choke' and trim off the stem, leaving the heart, which is all you use in this recipe. Cook the BROAD BEANS in boiling salted water until al dente, then skin any that look large and toughish.

→ Boil the EGGS for 6–8 minutes, so that the yolks remain soft; you might like to boil an extra egg first, to test the cooking time. Sauté the BACON until really frizzled; you don't need any fat to do this.

→ Meanwhile, make the dressing. Heat the OIL in a heavy-bottomed frying pan, add the ONIONS and GARLIC, cover the pan and sweat until thoroughly softened, golden and wilted, which will take about 20 minutes. Add the drained ANCHOVIES and put the whole lot into a liquidiser or food processor with the vinegar. Blend until smooth and season with PEPPER. Shell the eggs and cut them in half. Arrange the vegetables in sections on a pretty plate, sprinkle the bacon on top of the broad beans and arrange the halved eggs around the edge of the plate. Pour on the warm dressing and scatter with a generous amount of chopped PARSLEY.

Hot Grated Beetroot and Apple Salad with Horseradish Dressing

SERVES 4

medium beetroots	4
small sharp eating apples like Cox's	2
olive oil	
red wine vinegar	
grated fresh horseradish OR grated hot horseradish	2 tsp, or to taste
sea salt and black pepper	
fresh dill or parsley	

This is a lovely hot salad to give a pickle-sharpness to your cold meat and jacket potato.

→ Preheat the oven to 190°C/375°F/Gas 5. Wash the BEETROOTS but leave the skins on and whiskers intact or they will bleed their juices. Wrap them tightly in foil and bake in the oven for about 40–50 minutes.

→ Five minutes before they are ready, grate the APPLE. Warm the OLIVE OIL and WINE VINEGAR, around 4:1 ratio in tablespoons, and stir in the HORSERADISH to taste and the SEASONING. Pour over the apple to stop discolouration. Remove the beetroot from the foil and peel it with a knife, holding the hot beetroot on the prongs of a fork to make it easier. Grate the beetroot on the large grater holes onto the pile of apple, toss it all together, scatter over your HERBS and serve.

Roasted Beet, Watercress, Orange and Crottin Salad

SERVES 4

baby beets	4
watercress, with its peppery stems if you can get it	1 bunch
green beans, *topped and tailed*	225g/8oz
oranges, *peeled, pithed, pipped and cut into circles*	4
crottin goat's cheese OR goat's curd	110g/4oz
fruity extra virgin olive oil	5 tbsp
sherry vinegar	2 tbsp
sea salt and black pepper	

Not everyone loves the much maligned beet, but I adore its earthy sweetness, particularly when little jewels of young beet have been wrapped in foil and roasted whole, which imbibes them with a seriously intense flavour.

→ Preheat the oven to 200°C/400°F/Gas 6. Wash the BEETS but don't trim them. Wrap them tightly in foil and bake in the oven for 30 minutes. Check with a skewer, and if they are just tender when pierced through to their middles, they are cooked. Unwrap and leave to cool.

→ Wash the WATERCRESS, remove any thick, whiskery stalks at the bases of the stems and pat dry. Throw the topped and tailed GREEN BEANS into boiling water and cook until tender. Drain and refresh under running cold water to arrest the cooking, then pat dry. Peel the ORANGES, remove the pith and pips and cut into circles. Arrange the orange slices, whole baby beets, green beans and watercress in four separate areas of the plate and then crumble over the CROTTIN. Whisk the OIL and VINEGAR together, season it and pour over. Serve immediately, the beans and beet still with a memory of warmth to them, before the beet can paint the cheese purple.

Aubergine, Feta and Mint Salad

SERVES 4

medium aubergines	2
extra-virgin olive oil	
feta cheese	110g/4oz
mint	a few sprigs
lemon juice	
black pepper	

Aubergine slices soak up oil like nobody's business. Cooking them in the oven like this makes sure they are tender but not drenched and sodden with oil.

→ Preheat the oven to 200°C/400°F/Gas 6. Line a baking tray with baking parchment. Cut the AUBERGINES into thick rounds, brush both sides with OLIVE OIL and lay on the baking tray.
→ Cook for 15 minutes until soft and browned—check with a skewer to make sure they are done. Leave to cool slightly. While still warm, layer the slices in a serving dish with crumbled FETA and torn leaves of MINT. Season each layer with BLACK PEPPER. Drizzle over a little OIL but don't overdo it—the slices will be oily already. Spritz with LEMON JUICE.

Aubergine Salad with a Wild Rocket Purée

SERVES 2

large aubergine (the stripy purple and white kind if you can find them)	1
best extra-virgin olive oil to brush over the slices	
rocket, *torn to shreds*	1 bunch
best extra-virgin olive oil	90–120ml/3–4fl oz
lemon juice	
pine nuts	55g/2oz
black pepper	
sheep's milk feta	a small piece
mint	a sprig

The sharply lemony, peppery vibrant green rocket purée is a perfect foil to the aubergine's gentle, smoky flavour.

→ Preheat the oven to 180°C/350°F/Gas 4. Slice the AUBERGINE into discs, brush each side with OLIVE OIL and place them on non-stick paper on a baking tray. Roast for 15 minutes or so: the aubergines should be soft, but not browned and crisp. Place in a single layer on a plate, slightly overlapping.
→ Blend the ROCKET, OLIVE OIL, LEMON JUICE and PINE NUTS with a good scrunch of BLACK PEPPER, making sure you do not over-blend it to a sludge. Spread a little of the purée over each aubergine slice and keep the rest covered in the fridge to use another time.
→ Crumble a small lump of feta into little pieces over the salad, add some finely chopped mint leaves, and sprinkle over a little extra virgin olive oil and a spritz of lemon juice. Serve just warm, or at room temperature.

Roasted Aubergine, Red Onion and Tomato Salad

SERVES 4

chickpeas	a handful
onion, 2 cloves, carrot, celery stick, thyme and 2 bay leaves	
aubergine	1
red onions	2
large tomatoes	4
garlic cloves	4 or 5
fresh thyme	a sprig
baby spinach leaves	a handful
good sheep's milk feta	110g/4oz
olive oil	
a well-aged balsamic vinegar	
sea salt and black pepper	

Another perfect lunchtime salad which you can experiment with, using red peppers, shallots, sweet potatoes, courgettes or any of the good roasting squash such as red onion or butternut.

→ Soak the CHICKPEAS overnight in cold water. Next day, rinse them and just cover with fresh water in a large earthenware casserole. Add an ONION stuck with a couple of CLOVES, a chopped CARROT and stick of CELERY, a sprig of THYME and a couple of fresh BAY LEAVES, bring to the boil, skim, then allow to simmer at a mere burble for 2 hours under cover.

→ Preheat the oven to 220°C/425°F/Gas 7. Cut the AUBERGINE into cubes, peel the ONIONS and cut them into eighths, and halve the TOMATOES. Place them on a roasting tray with the GARLIC and dribble OLIVE OIL over everything. Add the THYME and roast until everything is cooked through, 30–40 minutes. Remove from the oven and add a libation of OLIVE OIL and some BALSAMIC VINEGAR to taste.

→ Place the roasted vegetables on a pretty, flat plate. Toss in the cooked chickpeas and the raw SPINACH, which will wilt gently in the warmth, and crumble over the FETA. Season and serve.

Fennel and Red Onion Salad
→ Follow the recipe above but use 2 bulbs of FENNEL, tough outer layers stripped off and the rest cut into chunks and roasted with the other ingredients

Raw Porcini Salad

porcini
green olive oil
lemon juice
black pepper
salt

→ If the PORCINI are firm fleshed and fresh, slice them as thinly as you can, and merely add a dressing of best green OLIVE OIL and LEMON JUICE and a scrunch of BLACK PEPPER and SALT. A wonderfully hedonistic starter.

Broad Beans with Preserved Lemon, Coriander and Spanish Paprika

SERVES 4

podded broad beans	500g/1lb 2oz
large onion, *thinly sliced*	1
Spanish paprika	1 tbsp
cumin, *roasted in a pan then ground*	1 tsp
extra virgin olive oil	4 tbsp
water	6 tbsp
sea salt and black pepper	
fresh coriander, *coarsely chopped*	1 medium bunch
half a preserved lemon, *thinly sliced*	
lemon	juice of 1

This is one of the many wonderful dishes Sami cooks at Ottolenghi in London's Notting Hill. It is best made with the first little pods of broad beans, but I'm not purist about this one—frozen beans will do, but thaw them first. After all, they're getting revved up with spices and preserved lemons. This dish makes a lovely salad, mezze or starter, or a good accompaniment to lamb or chicken with couscous.

→ Put the BROAD BEANS, ONION, PAPRIKA, CUMIN, OLIVE OIL and WATER in a large saucepan. SEASON, cover and bring to the boil. Turn down the heat and simmer until the beans are just cooked (about 10 minutes). You might need to add a little more water during the cooking.

→ Add the chopped CORIANDER, PRESERVED LEMON and LEMON JUICE, then adjust the SEASONING. Serve hot or warm.

Broad Bean, Feta and Radish Salad

SERVES 4

podded broad beans	225g/8oz or so
peppery radishes	1 bunch
spring onions, *outer skin and tough part of green tops removed*	3–4
best sheep's feta	8 slim slices
mint leaves, *finely chopped*	2 tbsp
flat-leaf parsley, *coarsely chopped*	2 tbsp
seeds from a pomegranate *without any skin* (optional)	
walnut oil	2 tbsp
extra virgin olive oil	1 tbsp
lemon juice OR cider vinegar	1 tbsp
black peppercorns, *coarsely scrunched or crushed*	

Make this in May or June with the youngest, most tender small beans, then they won't need slipping out of their skins to reveal their inner greenness. Scatter over the seeds from a pomegranate to add glamour and sweet juiciness to the equation if you like.

→ Either use the BEANS raw, or throw them into a pan of boiling water for a minute then refresh them in cold water, drain them and pat them dry. Slice the RADISHES on a mandolin or by hand, wafer thin. Thinly slice the SPRING ONIONS and add them to the beans and radishes on a large serving plate. Slice the FETA and drape it over the other ingredients. Scatter over the HERBS and POMEGRANATE SEEDS and then mix the dressing to taste and pour it over. Add a scant teaspoon of crushed BLACK PEPPERCORNS and serve.

Potato Salad

SERVES 4

waxy new potatoes like Jersey Royal, Pink Fir Apples or Anya	675g/1½lb
mint	
Dijon mustard	1 tbsp
red wine vinegar	2 tbsp
vegetable oil	90ml/3fl oz
extra virgin olive oil	2 tbsp
spring onions, *finely chopped with a little of their green shoots* OR a shallot OR mild, small onion, *finely chopped*	a bunch
chives, *snipped*	a bunch
sea salt and freshly ground black pepper	

Like all disarmingly simple things, this can be spoiled by not paying attention to detail and using inferior ingredients. As this is one of the most wonderful and versatile of dishes, as good with chicken or grilled meat as it is with baked fish or a raft of other different salads, it is worth getting right.

→ Scrape the POTATOES if they are Jersey Royals. If they are Pink Fir Apples it is easier to take the skins off when they are boiled and still hot as they are so nubbly and knobbly. Boil them in salted water with a few sprigs of MINT, then drain.
→ While the potatoes are cooking, make the dressing by whisking together the MUSTARD, OILS and VINEGAR, and seasoning to taste. Skin and chop or just chop the potatoes when they are hot and dress them immediately, turning them well with the dressing, SHALLOT or SPRING ONION and the CHIVES. Eat warm.

Moroccan Carrot Salad with Garlic and Coriander

SERVES 4

carrots, *peeled and cut into sticks*	500g/1lb 2oz
garlic cloves, *peeled*	4
olive oil	4 tbsp
cider vinegar	2 tbsp
cumin seeds, *roasted in a pan then ground*	1 tsp
paprika	1 tsp
sea salt and black pepper	
fresh coriander, *chopped*	2 tbsp

Another dish from Ottolenghi in London's Notting Hill.

→ Cover the CARROTS in a saucepan with boiling, salted water, adding the GARLIC, and cook until tender but not soft. Drain, crush the garlic cloves and add them to the carrots with the REMAINING INGREDIENTS, leaving aside half the coriander.
→ Transfer to a serving dish while hot and sprinkle over the rest of the CORIANDER. I like this at room temperature, but it can be served hot or cold.

Cos Lettuce with Cashel Blue and a Cream Dressing

SERVES 6

French mustard	1 tsp
sugar	1 tsp
tarragon vinegar	2 tsp
garlic, *crushed*	a scrap
hard-boiled egg, *white and yolk separated*	1
double cream	200–250ml/ 7–8½fl oz
chives, *chopped*	2 dsrtsp
Cashel Blue cheese	110–170g/4–6oz
cos lettuce, *outer leaves removed*	2 heads

Cashel Blue is a richly creamy blue Irish cheese, fudgy textured with no hint of bitterness. It is delicious crumbled into this salad of cos hearts. Keep the outer leaves of the lettuces for soup.

→ Stir the FIRST FOUR INGREDIENTS together in a bowl with the EGG YOLK, then stir in the CREAM. Thin with a bit of milk or water if it has thickened too much.

→ Pour cold over the washed LETTUCE, then scatter over the chopped EGG WHITE, CHIVES and coarsely crumbled CASHEL BLUE.

Greek Salad with Fried Halloumi

SERVES 4

large ripe organic tomatoes, the meaty sort	4
cucumber	1
red onion	1
radishes	1 bunch
mint leaves, *chopped*	1 bunch
flat-leaf parsley, *chopped*	1 bunch
Kalamata OR other black olives	55g/2oz
extra virgin olive oil	5 tbsp
lemon juice	2 tbsp
sea salt and black pepper	
olive oil	1 tbsp
halloumi, *cut lengthways into ½ inch slices*	255g/9oz

This is a slightly different take on the classic Greek salad which you'll probably know and love already and may not wish to change one iota, in which case stick to your sheep's milk feta.

→ Quarter the TOMATOES and remove the cores. Peel the CUCUMBER in stripes with a potato peeler and cut into chunks. Slice the RED ONION finely on a mandolin or by hand. The RADISHES can be added whole or sliced finely as you prefer.

→ Put the FIRST SIX INGREDIENTS into a large, shallow bowl or onto a large serving dish and dress with the OLIVE OIL and LEMON JUICE and SEASONING. Turn with your hands to amalgamate and taste to check the dressing is to your liking.

→ Place a large frying pan on a medium heat, add the OLIVE OIL and cook the HALLOUMI for a minute on each side or until golden brown. Drain on paper towels before draping warm over the Greek salad and serve with good bread, preferably the twisted plait of Greek white which comes with a lovely sesame seeded top.

Fried Halloumi, Fennel and Orange Salad

SERVES 6

fennel bulbs, *stripped of their outer tough leaves*	2
lemon	juice of 1
Valencia or sweet/sharp organic oranges	4
small red onion	1
fruity extra virgin olive oil	
black olives, Nyons for preference	½ cup
halloumi *sliced 1.5cm/½ in thick*	340g/12oz
brandy (optional)	2 tbsp
sea salt and black pepper	

A salad that brings out the best in halloumi, and in somewhat of a spirited way too.

→ When you have rid the FENNEL of their tough, outer leaves, slice them wafer thin on a mandolin or by hand, keeping the little green fronds to chop and decorate with later. Spread the slices out on a plate, and squeeze LEMON JUICE over them. Leave them to soften and absorb the juice for 30 minutes or so, then pour over some OLIVE OIL and turn with your fingers, tasting to get the right acidity/oiliness for your taste.

→ Meanwhile, remove the peel and pith of the ORANGES and cut them into circles, removing any pips as you go. Slice the RED ONION wafer thin too—the mandolin is a fantastic and indispensable gadget for this. Arrange the red onion and BLACK OLIVES with the fennel and orange, turning them in the dressing.

→ Dunk or brush the slices of HALLOUMI in olive oil on both sides and fry them in a large pan for a couple of minutes or until browned on both sides. Remove to the plate with the other salad ingredients. Deglaze the pan with the BRANDY until it is warmed, then pour it over the halloumi and set light to it. Allow the alcohol to burn off before SEASONING the salad and bringing it to the table.

White Tuscan Salad

SERVES 4

whole fresh buffalo mozzarellas, the best you can find	2
fennel bulbs, *tough outer leaves and stalk removed*	2
celery heart, *the stalks strung with a potato peeler*	1
sea salt and fresh black pepper	
Tuscan olive oil, best fruity, peppery	4–6 tbsp
lemon	juice of 1

This is the haute couture of salads, pure white elegance and depth of flavour, three simple ingredients, the perfect antipasto.

→ Drain the MOZZARELLAS and cut them into thin slices. Arrange them in a single layer on a large, dark blue, green or other coloured plate that will offset the white well.

→ Slice the FENNEL wafer thin without the cores on a mandolin or by hand. Chop the CELERY diagonally into small strips with its leaves. Strew the fennel and celery over the mozzarella together, season, lash on the OLIVE OIL and squeeze over the LEMON JUICE.

→ Leave for an hour for the flavours to marry before serving at room temperature with other antipasti or as a single starter.

Artichoke Heart, Fennel and Red Pepper Salad

SERVES 6

organic red peppers	2
char-grilled artichoke hearts	1 jar
fennel bulbs	2
olive oil, lemon juice, salt and pepper	
chervil if you have it to hand	a sprinkling

You need good char-grilled artichoke hearts for this salad, such as those made by Seggiano.

→ Grill the PEPPERS on all sides and put them in a bowl under clingfilm so the skins begin to steam off. Skin, de-seed and cut them into thin strips. Slice the ARTICHOKE HEARTS thinly.
→ Remove the outer layer of the fennel bulbs down to the firm heart, and slice them as thinly as you can, with a mandolin if you have one. Put all the vegetables into a bowl, then pour in your oil and lemon DRESSING, and mix together gently by hand. Serve with a good crusted bread like Boule de Meule.

Asparagus, Sprouting Broccoli and Goat's Cheese Salad

SERVES 4

asparagus stems	24–30
extra virgin olive oil	
purple sprouting broccoli	225g/8oz
fennel bulbs	2
organic lemons	juice of up to 2
sea salt and black pepper	
goat's cheese such as Ragstone OR Golden Cross	110–170g/4–6 oz
savory, *chopped*	1 dsrtsp

→ Break off the woody bottoms of the ASPARAGUS and then brush a griddle or the base of a heavy-bottomed frying pan with OLIVE OIL. When it is hot put in the asparagus spears and cook for a few minutes before turning with a pair of tongs. Continue to cook until each spear is cooked through to just tender when the base is pierced with a skewer, removing the spears one by one to a plate as they are ready.
→ Meanwhile steam the BROCCOLI until al dente. Strip the FENNEL bulbs of their tough outer leaves and slice them paper thin on a mandolin or by hand. Squeeze a little LEMON JUICE over the slices to prevent them from browning, turning them on the plate to coat. Slice the GOAT'S CHEESE or crumble it, your call.
→ Throw the vegetables, cooked and raw, into a large serving bowl and dress while warm with OLIVE OIL and LEMON JUICE. Season with SALT and a good scrunch of PEPPER. Throw the goat's cheese over the salad and sprinkle the SAVORY over the top. Serve at a bare warmth.

Asparagus and Parmesan Salad

SERVES 4

asparagus spears	at least 36 or so
extra virgin olive oil	
aged balsamic vinegar, the really good, mellow stuff OR lemon juice if you prefer	
sea salt and black pepper	
really good Parmesan cheese to shave	a chunk

The inimitable, indescribable flavour of asparagus is brought further to life with the salty, grainy contrast of thinly sliced shards of aged Parmesan and, in this case, a dressing poured over the spears' warmth. Eat in your fingers please, there is no other way with the sexiest vegetable in the canon. This turning and turning and griddling keeps the colour vibrant and the texture perfect. There is no merit in putting these fragile wands anywhere near water; it does them a grave injustice.

→ First peel the bottom couple of inches of the SPEARS with a potato peeler before chopping off the woody bottoms. This really will make a difference. Brush a generous spoonful or two of OLIVE OIL over a warming griddle or griddle pan. When the oil is hot, line the asparagus up on the pan and allow the spears to cook on one side before turning them over with a pair of tongs. Keep doing this until the spears are just a little more than al dente all the way through the thickest part when pierced with a skewer. Don't let them brown.
→ Remove the spears to a large serving dish as they cook, lining them up like soldiers in a double layer if need be. You might need a little more oil during the cooking process.
→ Pour over a simple OLIVE OIL and BALSAMIC or LEMON dressing while the spears are still hot and season, more PEPPER than SALT as the cheese is salt. Now slice wafers of curling Parmesan to layer over the top randomly. Serve warm with good crusty bread, preferably sourdough, to mop up the juices.

This is also good with Pecorino, and if you like the idea of something more unctuously melting try a good, lactic Taleggio shaved in thin slices and draped over the greenery.

Sprouting Broccoli Salad

broccoli, *broken up into florets*
best olive oil
lemon juice
sea salt
black pepper
red chilli, *finely chopped*
anchovies, *chopped*

→ Steam the little FLORETS, STALKS and LEAVES until al dente. Throw them into your serving dish, and toss when still hot in best OLIVE OIL, LEMON JUICE, SEA SALT and BLACK PEPPER to taste. Very finely chopped RED CHILLI, fried for 30 seconds in the olive oil, is a good addition if you want to turn the heat up, and you can scatter a couple of finely chopped ANCHOVIES into the dish if you feel like it. Serve while still warm.

Spiced Pears with Gorgonzola, Watercress and Salted Walnut Salad

SERVES 6

Spiced pears

red chilli, *halved and seeded*	1
rosemary	1 sprig
bay leaf	1
star anise	2
cinnamon sticks	2
honey	2 tbsp
lemons, *pared rind and juice*	2
Marsala	600ml/1 pint
unrefined caster sugar	450g/1lb
conference pears	6

Filling

Gorgonzola	225g/8oz
best cream cheese	110g/4oz
spring onions, *finely chopped*	1 tbsp
chives, *finely chopped*	2 tsp
thyme leaves, *chopped*	1 tsp
black pepper	

Salad

watercress OR rocket leaves	a handful for each plate

a simple dressing of extra virgin olive oil and good balsamic vinegar

Topping

butter	a knob
walnuts	110g/4oz
maple syrup OR sugar	1 dsrtsp

good sea salt like sel de Guerande

These spiced pears are the most wonderful winter fruit dish and I use them with venison, guinea fowl, partridge and pheasant as well as in this salad. You can cook quinces in the same spice mix, too, to serve with game or pork. A lovely re-working of the classic combination of pears and blue cheese, this is luscious and creamy, salty and fresh-tasting.

→ Put the CHILLI, HERBS, SPICES, HONEY, LEMON RIND and most of the juice, MARSALA and SUGAR into a pan just large enough to hold the pears as well, and bring slowly to the boil. Simmer for 5 minutes.

→ Meanwhile, peel the PEARS, leaving the stalks on. Rub the pears with a little LEMON JUICE so they don't discolour. Put the pears in the pan with the spicy liquid and add a little water to just cover if you need to. Bring back to the boil then simmer for 30–40 minutes or until soft right through when pierced with a skewer.

→ Let the pears cool, then cut them in half and remove the cores. Cream the GORGONZOLA and CREAM CHEESE in a bowl with a fork. Stir in the SPRING ONIONS and HERBS and SEASON. Spoon the mixture into the cavities of the pears and place them on a plate on top of the salad leaves.

→ Melt the BUTTER in a pan and when it is foaming, throw in the WALNUTS. Add the MAPLE SYRUP or SUGAR and turn the nuts to coat. Cook the halved walnuts until they are hot but not browned and add enough SALT FLAKES to give them a deliciously buttery salt/sweet balance. Strew them on the salad when they are still warm. Add the salad dressing and serve.

Watercress, Pear and Roquefort Salad

SERVES 2

organic watercress	1 bunch
ripe pears	2
lemon juice	
best Roquefort	110g/4oz
a fruity olive oil, such as Ravida from Sicily	
a well-aged balsamic vinegar (ideally 20 years or more)	
sesame seeds	a handful
sea salt and black pepper	

Watercress is best eaten raw, and here the peppery leaves are contrasted with creamy, salty cheese, sweet pear, mellow vinegar and fruity olive oil. Simple perfection if you use only the best ingredients.

→ Wash and dry the WATERCRESS and heap it onto each plate. Peel, core and quarter the PEARS and rub with a little LEMON JUICE to keep them from discolouring. Break up the CHEESE and add the pears and creamy lumps of cheese to each plate.
→ Make a dressing with the OLIVE OIL and BALSAMIC VINEGAR (two parts oil to one part balsamic), adding SEA SALT and a scrunch of BLACK PEPPER. Toast a handful of SESAME SEEDS in a hot oven until they turn golden and nutty smelling. Five minutes should do it, but keep checking as they are the easiest of things to burn. Pour a libation of the dressing over each portion of the salad, sprinkle with sesame seeds and eat.

Winter Red Cabbage Slaw

SERVES 8–10

small red cabbage	1
sharp eating apples like Cox's	2
lemon juice	
carrots	2
celery sticks	3
unsalted butter	a knob
walnuts	110g/4oz
maple syrup	up to 1 dsrtsp
sea salt	
blue cheese such as Stilton, Beenleigh Blue or Roquefort	110g/4oz
Slaw Dressing	
seeded mustard	1 tsp
red wine or cider vinegar	1 tbsp
fruity olive oil	3–4 tbsp
walnut oil (optional)	1 tbsp
sugar (optional)	½ tsp

The vibrant flavours and colours of this vitamin-packed salad lift the winter gloom instantly. It is so delicious and full of substance you'll need nothing else for lunch.

→ Start by slicing the CABBAGE razor thin and removing its tough core. Peel the APPLES, slice thinly and sprinkle with LEMON JUICE to prevent discolouring. Peel and grate the CARROTS and string and chop the CELERY.
→ This is not a salad to be assembled in neat layers—you want the flavours to mingle and penetrate. Put the cabbage, apple, carrots and celery together on a large serving platter or in a large bowl. Melt the BUTTER in a pan over medium heat and fry the WALNUTS briefly. Add the MAPLE SYRUP as soon as the walnuts are coated in the butter and sprinkle over some coarse SEA SALT. Taste a walnut to make sure you have the sweet/salt balance you desire.
→ Remove from the heat and throw the warm buttery walnuts over the vegetables. Add the thinly sliced BLUE CHEESE and the dressing. Toss briefly and gently before serving.

Feta, Watermelon and Mint Salad

SERVES 4

sheep's milk feta	225g/8oz
large, ripe watermelon	¼
lemon juice	
extra virgin olive oil, but not too powerful a one for this dish	
fresh mint	a few sprigs
black peppercorns, *coarsely crushed*	1 tsp

→ Peel and chop the MELON into large-ish chunks and remove as many black seeds as you can, or get a suitably fleet-fingered child to do it for you.
→ Break the FETA up by hand as it always seems more more-ish this way than cubed. Toss the feta and melon together gently with a large spoon and fork, then sprinkle with a little LEMON JUICE. Pour over some OLIVE OIL and scatter over the PEPPER. Taste and adjust the lemon or oil if needs be. Roll up a few leaves of MINT and cut into fine cigar strips, scattering them over the top of the salad. What could be easier?

Pasta, Fontina, Walnut and Celery Salad

SERVES 25 IF PART OF A LARGE BUFFET, OTHERWISE USE COMMON SENSE

macaroni OR organic wholewheat penne	450g/1lb
mild extra virgin olive oil	8 tbsp
Fontina cheese	225g/½ lb
Bel Paese	225g/½ lb
Gorgonzola piccante	225g/½ lb
fresh walnuts	4 tbsp
celery	the heart of 1 large head and the leaves
walnut oil	1 tbsp
freshly ground black peppercorns	

I am always looking for great, unusual salads and dishes to serve at a party that are easy to prepare in advance and which marry with the main meat or fish and the other salads. Here is some inspiration from my old favourite, Anna Del Conte, who suggests that the pasta can be cooked and tossed with oil up to 6 hours in advance and the other ingredients added up to 2 hours in advance.

→ Cook the PASTA in plenty of boiling water as per the instructions and drain while very al dente. Refresh in a colander under cold water, drain again, and throw into a large bowl. Toss with the OLIVE OIL and leave to cool completely.
→ Cut the three CHEESES into small cubes and add to the pasta, together with the WALNUTS, breaking them up as you throw them in. String the CELERY with a potato peeler and slice into thin diagonal strips. Add to the pasta.
→ Toss with the WALNUT OIL and plenty of freshly ground BLACK PEPPER. Taste and add SALT if you think it needs it. Leave aside for an hour or so for all the flavours to combine. Sprinkle the chopped CELERY LEAVES over the top just before serving.

Fennel and Parmesan Salad

<small>SERVES 4</small>

fennel bulbs	4 small or 2 large
fruity, pungent olive oil	4–6 tbsp
lemon juice	2 tbsp
sea salt and black pepper	
fresh Parmesan cheese	55g/2oz

→ Strip the tough, outer layers from the FENNEL. Slice the fennel as slim as slim can be on your mandolin or by hand, and dress with the OLIVE OIL, LEMON JUICE and SEASONING. Use very little salt, if any at all, since aged Parmesan is salt enough. Shave paper-thin slivers of PARMESAN and lay beautifully on top of the fennel.

→ Scatter over the green chopped FRONDY BITS from the fennel bulbs and serve. I think this salad looks best on a dark plate as it is pure white and ivory with just a tinge of green.

Hot Bacon and Egg Salad

<small>SERVES 4 AS A STARTER</small>

chicory (white or Treviso)	2 heads
cos lettuce	heart of 1
freshly ground black pepper	
organic smoked streaky bacon rashers, *rinds removed*	4
good white and red wine vinegar	
large organic eggs	4
thick slices of sourdough bread, *crusts cut off*	2
garlic clove	1
a little olive oil	
chives, *snipped*	1 tbsp

If you are making this for lunch or supper rather than as a starter, use two eggs each and an extra rasher. How could something so simple be so delicious? Just try it and see if you don't agree.

→ Put the washed CHICORY and SALAD LEAVES in a large salad bowl and scrunch over some BLACK PEPPER. Start cooking the BACON RASHERS in a small frying pan with no added fat. You want to keep frying beyond the point where the fat has started running and allow the bacon to brown and crisp on both sides.

→ While the bacon is frying, half fill another frying pan with water that you have acidulated with a few tablespoons of WHITE WINE VINEGAR. Bring the water to the boil and then turn it down to a gentle simmer. Break the EGGS into a ramekin, one at a time, and gently drop them into the water. Cook until the whites have set, but the yolks are still soft. I shoosh hot water over them gently as they cook until the yolks have a translucent veil. Remove with a flat, slotted spoon to a plate. You can always return the eggs to the simmering water for 30 seconds if they have cooled down or you have cooked them a little too soon.

→ Rub the BREAD with a cut clove of GARLIC, brush with a little OLIVE OIL and cut into croutons. Bake the croutons in a hot oven briefly until they are crisp on both sides but not too browned. When the rashers are crisp, pour the hot bacon fat on to the salad leaves and break the rashers over the top; they should shatter like glass if they are crisp enough. Heat three tablespoons of RED WINE VINEGAR and let it bubble and reduce a little while you lay the eggs across the leaves and scatter over the croutons. Pour on the reduced vinegar, add the finely snipped CHIVES over the salad and serve.

Spiced Rice Salad

SERVES 4–6 AS A STARTER OR
LUNCH DISH

wild rice	a handful
brown basmati rice	450g/1lb
cinnamon stick	1
turmeric	1 tsp
fresh ginger	about 5 cm/2 in long
ground cloves	1 tsp
nutmeg, *grated*	1 tsp
coriander seeds, *crushed*	6–7
spring onions, *finely chopped*	1 bunch
fresh or frozen peas, *cooked*	110g/4oz
extra virgin olive oil	2–3 tbsp
salt and pepper	
lemon	½
pine nuts	2–3 tbsp
raisins	a handful
coriander (optional), *finely chopped*	

→ Bring a large saucepan of boiling water to the boil and throw in the WILD RICE. After 10 minutes, add the BASMATI RICE, CINNAMON STICK, TURMERIC and GINGER and boil for about 40 minutes. Drain the rice and remove the ginger and cinnamon.

→ Immediately stir in the CLOVES, NUTMEG and CORIANDER SEEDS, then the SPRING ONIONS and cooked PEAS if you're using them. Moisten the rice with OLIVE OIL, but not too liberally, and season with BLACK PEPPER, SALT and a squeeze of LEMON JUICE.

→ Roast the PINE NUTS in the oven for about 10 minutes or until pale brown. Meanwhile, soak the RAISINS in boiling water for 10 minutes until they swell. Drain and scatter over the rice, with the pine nuts. You can add some finely chopped CORIANDER if you like.

Cracked Wheat Salad

SERVES 4–6 AS A LUNCH DISH

cracked wheat (bulgur)	450g/1lb
small onion, *finely chopped*	1
garlic clove, *finely chopped*	
salt and pepper	
flat-leaf parsley, AND/OR fresh mint, *finely chopped*	a handful
fresh coriander, *finely chopped*	a handful
olive oil	6 tbsp
lemon juice	6 tbsp

→ Soak the CRACKED WHEAT in cold water until it has swollen and expanded enormously; this should take about 30 minutes. Drain in a sieve, pressing down firmly, then squeeze out any excess moisture by hand. Mix in the chopped ONION and GARLIC. Season, then add the HERBS, OLIVE OIL and LEMON JUICE. Taste—it should be very lemony and not too oily.

→ If you like, add some or all of the following: skinned, seeded, chopped tomatoes; roasted red peppers, skinned and seeded; skinned chopped cucumber; crumbled feta or goat's cheese; black garlicky olives. Pile onto a serving dish and surround with lettuce leaves.

Bazargan or Cracked Wheat and Nut Salad

SERVES 6–8

cracked wheat (bulgur)	340g/12oz
extra virgin olive oil	6–8 tbsp
pomegranate molasses OR 2 tbsp tamarind paste *dissolved in 4 tbsp boiling water*	3 tbsp
lemon	juice of 1
tomato paste	4 tbsp
ground cumin	1 tsp
ground coriander	1 tsp
ground allspice	½ tsp
ground cayenne OR chilli pepper	½ tsp, or to taste
walnuts, *very coarsely chopped*	140g/5oz
hazelnuts, *very coarsely chopped*	100g/3½oz
pine nuts, *lightly toasted*	55g/2oz
flat-leaf parsley, *finely chopped*	large bunch

This inspirational Syrian dish is from Claudia Roden's seminal The Book of Jewish Food. *The sourness of the pomegranate molasses or tamarind gives the grain a delicious sharp sweet flavour and colours the bulgur, which should be of the coarse kind. Roden advises making it four hours before serving so that the wheat absorbs the dressing properly.*

→ Put the CRACKED WHEAT into a large bowl and cover with plenty of cold, slightly salted water. Leave to soak for an hour or until tender (the coarse bulgur takes much longer). Drain in a sieve and press out the excess water.

→ In a serving bowl, beat the OLIVE OIL with the POMEGRANATE MOLASSES or dissolved TAMARIND PASTE. Add the LEMON JUICE, TOMATO PASTE, CUMIN, CORIANDER, ALLSPICE and CAYENNE and beat well. Pour over the cracked wheat and mix thoroughly. Add the NUTS and flat-leaf PARSLEY, mix again and adjust the SEASONING if necessary.

Puy Lentil, Feta, Roast Tomato and Onion Salad

SERVES 6

Puy lentils	350g/12oz
onions, *peeled*	2
large organic tomatoes	4
olive oil	
baby spinach	3 handfuls
best sheep's milk feta *rinse the feta in cold water when you take it out of its brine.*	175g/6oz
garlic cloves	3

This dish is perfect for a summer lunch, supper or picnic and can be prepared in advance before being left to marinate for a couple of hours. Or you can eat it warm as soon as you have made the dressing.

→ Put the LENTILS in an enamel pot and just cover with water. Bring them to the boil, take any scum off the surface, then simmer them until cooked, about 40 minutes. They do not need to be pre-soaked.

→ Preheat the oven to 200°C/400°F/Gas 6. Cut each ONION into six pieces, halve the TOMATOES and place them all on a baking tray. Pour over a generous libation of OLIVE OIL and put the tray of vegetables in the oven to roast for about 30 minutes. The tomatoes should be weeping juice and soft, and the onions should have caramelly bits and also be soft. Drain the lentils and place them in a bowl with a splosh of good OLIVE OIL and

fresh ginger	4cm/1½in finger
red chilli, *seeded*	1
fresh coriander	large bunch
Dijon mustard	a generous tsp
olive oil	
lemons	juice of 1½
sea salt and black pepper	

the SPINACH, which will begin to wilt in their heat. Stir until it has. Crumble the FETA over the top.

→ Now make the dressing. Chop the GARLIC, GINGER and CHILLI and put them in a food processor with the CORIANDER. Add the juices from the roasted tomatoes and onions, the MUSTARD, then some more OLIVE OIL, about 5 tablespoons, and the LEMON JUICE. SEASON and blitz. Taste and adjust anything that needs it. Place the warm tomatoes and onions in the salad and pour over the dressing, turning the whole salad when you have done so with your fingers. Serve, or leave to marinate for a couple of hours and eat at room temperature.

A Salad of Hot Chickpeas

SERVES 6

organic chickpeas	225g/8oz
onion, *stuck with a couple of cloves*	1
carrot, *chopped*	1
celery stick, *chopped*	1
thyme	a sprig
fresh bay leaves	a couple
olive oil	
wine vinegar	a sprinkle
sea salt	
black pepper	
small onion, *finely sliced into rings*	1
red chilli, *finely chopped* OR spinach (optional)	a little 225g/8oz
flat-leaf parsley, *roughly chopped*	

Tinned simply will not do. I am not saying ever, but texturally you will not accomplish this dish unless you cook them yourself. After all, soaking and cooking chickpeas has nothing to do with skill and time and everything to do with bothering, then leaving well alone. The effect of the libation of grassy, peppery olive oil upon hot, cooked chickpeas, or any other vegetable for that matter, is stimulant enough to the senses, releasing the scent of both and uniting them at the same time.

→ Soak the CHICKPEAS overnight in cold water. Next day, rinse them and just cover with fresh water in a large earthenware casserole. Add an ONION stuck with a couple of CLOVES, a chopped CARROT and stick of CELERY, a sprig of THYME and a couple of fresh BAY LEAVES, bring to the boil, skim for your life, then cover and allow to simmer at a mere burble for 2 hours.

→ Drain the CHICKPEAS, turn them into an earthenware serving dish and douse immediately with your best OLIVE OIL, a sprinkle of WINE VINEGAR and SEA SALT, which you must never add during the cooking, since it will toughen the skins irredeemably. Add a good scrunch of BLACK PEPPER and the ONION, so finely sliced that the rings are papery thin and will wilt on contact with the hot chickpeas.

→ You could also add some finely chopped RED CHILLI if you feel like it, or some spinach, the baby leaves called pousse if possible, which you throw in raw so that they wilt into the warm assembly. Finally the PARSLEY, a good green confetti of roughly chopped leaves. What could be simpler yet more delicious?

Sillsalad

SERVES 6

pickled herring fillets	300g/10oz
medium-sized pickled beetroots	4
waxy-fleshed salad potatoes like Pink Fir Apple or Anya (depending on size)	4–6
tart eating apples, preferably Cox's	2
cornichons	2–3 large or 4–5 small
small onion, *finely chopped*	1
crème fraîche	
fresh dill	

Either pickle your own herring with the very simple recipe given below or buy the Swedish pickled herrings in jars from Swedish Affar in Crawford St, London W1 or from Ikea. If you are salting your own herring and pickling your own beetroot, you need to start this dish three or four days before you want to eat it. If you've already pickled your beetroot and the herring is shop-bought, start 24 hours before you want to serve it. Don't use beetroot pickled in malt vinegar: it is too crude a substitute for white wine vinegar.

→ To pickle herring: Put the fish in a plastic bag with one cup of coarse SEA SALT to 1kg/2¼lb of HERRING and store in a cool dark place for 1–4 days. Remove the backbone, fillet, and soak thoroughly in water to desalinate for 6–8 hours.

→ To pickle beetroot: Put the whole cooked BEETROOTS in a jar and pour over WHITE WINE VINEGAR and SUGAR, 4:1, to cover. Add one clove of GARLIC, a teaspoon of MUSTARD SEED and 6 CLOVES. Screw the lid on and the flavour will be absorbed after 2 days.

→ To make the salad: cook, skin and cool the POTATOES. Cut ALL THE INGREDIENTS into rough 1cm/½in cubes and mix them together in a bowl. Add freshly ground PEPPER. Cover the salad and let it mature in the fridge for 24 hours.

→ When you're ready to serve, mix in the CRÈME FRAÎCHE and chopped DILL. Pile the salad on a serving dish, sprinkle with some more chopped DILL and serve with some thinly sliced rye bread and butter.

Spicy Prawn Noodle Salad

SERVES 4

garlic clove, *finely chopped*	1
red chilli, *seeded and diced*	1
fresh ginger, *grated*	a finger
fresh coriander, *chopped*	1 dsrtsp
organic shoyu sauce	4 tbsp
olive oil	
lime	juice of 1
large raw prawns in their shells	12
organic plain OR spinach egg noodles	255g/9oz

This is a zingy, fragrant, oriental-inspired salad, full of great raw vegetables and vibrant tastes.

→ Mix together the GARLIC, CHILLI, GINGER, CORIANDER, SHOYU SAUCE, OLIVE OIL and LIME in a bowl, add the PRAWNS and leave to marinate. Cook the NOODLES as per instructions for 4 minutes, then coat them lightly with SESAME or OLIVE OIL so they won't stick.

→ Peel the CARROT, then, using the peeler, ribbon it from top to bottom. Throw the ribbons into the bowl with the noodles. Thinly slice the MANGETOUT into strips, throw them into the bowl and add the BEANSPROUTS and MUSHROOMS.

→ Remove the PRAWNS from the marinade. Griddle the prawns until pink and cooked through on both sides, then shell them.

→ Throw half the roughly chopped CORIANDER and MINT into

large carrot	1
mangetout	a handful
beansprouts	a handful
raw chestnut mushrooms	5 or 6
fresh mint and fresh coriander	a bunch of each
Spicy Dressing	
organic lemons	3
organic limes	3
garlic clove	1
fresh ginger, *grated*	a finger
runny honey	1 dsrtsp
olive oil	
stem ginger and the syrup (optional)	a piece 1 tbsp
salt and pepper	

the salad, add the dressing and toss with your fingers to amalgamate well. Add the REST OF THE HERBS and serve.

Spicy Dressing
→ To make the dressing, peel the CITRUS FRUITS thinly with a potato peeler so that you have strips of peel with no pith. Put the slices of peel with the JUICE of the fruit in a pan with the GARLIC, fresh GINGER and HONEY. Bring to the boil and reduce by a half until you have a lovely, syrupy sauce. Strain it into a bowl through a sieve, add the OLIVE OIL until you have a dressing you like the taste of, then add the finely chopped piece of STEM GINGER AND ITS SYRUP. SEASON to taste.

Chilled Crab, Cucumber and Avocado Salad

SERVES 4

crab, *cooked*	1.5kg/3¼lb
ripe Hass avocados	2
cucumber	1
chervil, dill and chives, *finely chopped*	1 tbsp of each
limes	2
a few bunches of watercress and some rocket or the heart of a cos lettuce	
Mustard Dressing	
home-made mayonnaise	1 dsrtsp
seeded mustard	1 tsp
cider vinegar	1 tbsp
olive oil	4–5 tbsp

I think crab is at its best served chilled, but not icy cold. It is rich though, and you do not need a huge amount of it. The crab that I picked for this dish yielded 340g/12oz of brown meat and a little less of white, enough for four.

→ Put the WHITE CRAB MEAT onto a plate with the SALAD LEAVES. Add long slivers of AVOCADO and chunks of peeled, seeded CUCUMBER, the finely chopped HERBS, and a few quarters of LIME to squeeze on. Pour over the dressing, and serve the salad with a loaf of good country bread.

Mustard Dressing
→ Make a dressing with the MAYONNAISE, SEEDED MUSTARD, CIDER VINEGAR and OLIVE OIL. Then sieve a couple of tablespoons of the BROWN CRAB MEAT into it and season to taste. You might like to add a tiny pinch of CAYENNE instead of black pepper.

Cousin Deborah's Salmon

SERVES 4

wild salmon fillets OR salmon steaks	4

Marinade

lime	juice of 1
garlic clove, *chopped very finely*	1
Thai fish sauce	1 tbsp
red chilli, *finely chopped*	1
ginger, *freshly grated*	1 tsp
spring onions, *finely chopped*	2
light soy sauce	4 tbsp
sesame oil	1 tbsp

To finish the dish

Chinese medium egg noodles

crisp lettuce, *finely chopped*

small bunch of coriander, *chopped*

→ Mix ALL THE MARINADE INGREDIENTS in a non-metal dish and add the FISH. Leave for at least an hour, or covered in the fridge overnight. Turn the fish over once while it is marinating to make sure all of it is covered in the marinade.

→ When you are ready to cook the FISH, heat a griddle pan to very hot, remove the fish from the marinade and wipe off all the juice and bits. Reserve the marinade. Sear the fish on both sides until just cooked, remove from the pan and keep warm if you are eating the dish hot. If not, leave the fish on a plate to cool. Cook the NOODLES according to the instructions, drain and return to the pan with the marinade. Toss over a medium heat to warm through.

→ To serve, put the crisp LETTUCE at the bottom of each bowl and place a nest of noodles on top. Add a piece of salmon and garnish with the chopped CORIANDER. This is just as good served in the same way as a cold summer salad dish.

Salade Cauchoise

SERVES 1

cooked ham	55g/2oz
celery stick	1
spring onions, *chopped*	1 tbsp
walnuts, *broken into pieces*	1 tbsp
salt and pepper	
garlic clove, *crushed*	1
new potatoes, *boiled* (optional)	

home-made mayonnaise
(see p. 404)

Adjust the quantities given here to your party; this amount is for one person. You don't need to be too precise about quantities—or even ingredients: if you don't have spring onions, use chives, shallots or onions.

→ Finely shred the HAM into long thin strips, and put in a bowl with the CELERY, SPRING ONIONS and WALNUTS, then season with SALT, PEPPER and GARLIC. Add a few boiled tiny new POTATOES if you want to make the dish more substantial. Mix well, and bind with some home-made MAYONNAISE that you have thinned with cream or milk.

Salade Niçoise

SERVES 4

waxy new potatoes like Jersey Royals	450g/1lb
green beans	450g/1lb
broad beans, podded weight	450g/1lb
organic eggs	6
cos lettuce	1
large, meaty, ripe tomatoes, *skinned and quartered*	4
cucumber, *skinned, split in half, seeded with a teaspoon and chopped into dice*	1
small artichoke hearts, *cut into chunks*	8
best tuna or ventresca (belly of tuna) from Ortiz sold by Brindisa	1–2 tins
OR a couple of seared tuna steaks *cooked rare and broken into chunks*	
anchovies in olive oil	1 tin
black olives, the glossy Niçoise ones if you can get them	16–20
chives, *snipped small*	small bunch
sprigs of tarragon, *chopped small*	1–2

Niçoise Dressing

French mustard	1 heaped tsp
sea salt and black pepper	
tarragon vinegar	2 tbsp
garlic cloves, *finely minced*	2
best extra virgin olive oil	6–8 tbsp

The attraction of Salade Niçoise is the combination of the cooked and the raw, the vibrant and the mild, the known and unexpected with the non-formulaic twist. Here is a little guidance on how I like to play with the theme, and a purely personal one it is too. There are certain ingredients and ways of cooking them that I would always use, while others are a movable feast.

→ Scrape the JERSEY ROYALS, or wash them and cook with their skins on, depending on how rustic you feel. Drain and slice when still hot. While the potatoes are cooking, throw the topped and tailed GREEN BEANS into plenty of boiling, salted water—a handful at a time, so that the temperature doesn't fall below a rolling boil. That way, the beans retain their colour and don't turn khaki. Do not undercook. Al dente green beans are a fad of the food photographers who want their beans emerald green. They should be cooked to tender as the French do! Drain and refresh in cold water.

→ Throw the podded BROAD BEANS into boiling water. If they are new season's and tiny, cook for no more than a minute, then pour cold water over them and drain thoroughly.

→ Boil the EGGS for 6–7 minutes depending on their size, then pour cold water into the pan for a couple of minutes. I like softly hard-boiled eggs whose yolks still have a memory of crocus-coloured goo about them. Peel when you can stand the heat, and slice in half.

→ Mix the FIRST FOUR DRESSING INGREDIENTS together well, then pour in the OIL, whisking as you go, until you have the desired flavour.

→ Find a beautiful, shallow, earthenware dish and strew the washed, torn LETTUCE AND ITS HEART over the bottom of the dish. In the middle of the lettuce, pile a mound of the green and broad beans, potatoes, ARTICHOKES, CUCUMBER and TOMATOES, TUNA and BLACK OLIVES. Artful arranging is fine at this stage. I like things not too regimented, but I always put the halves of egg around the edge with a cross of anchovies over them.

→ Dress the salad with the dressing and HERBS, bring it to the table, and gently toss the central ingredients in front of the assembled company if you feel like it. A bit of a ritual is good with a dish such as this. Good French bread is a necessity.

Jersey Royal, Chicken, Green Bean, Egg and Avocado Salad

SERVES 2

green beans	2 handfuls
small Jersey Royal new potatoes	350–400g/12–14oz
organic Hass avocado	1
organic eggs	2
left-over chicken, *without the skin*	110g/4oz
home-made mayonnaise (see p. 404)	
chives, *snipped*	a handful
flat-leaf parsley, *finely chopped*	a handful
lovage leaves, *finely chopped*	6

A perfectly beautiful pale salad, lightly bound with a herb mayonnaise. Each ingredient adds a different texture and flavour; the whole is a dish of gentle subtlety requiring absolutely nothing else.

→ Soak the GREEN BEANS in cold water for an hour to invigorate them. Top and tail and throw them, a handful at a time, into a large pan of well-salted boiling water. Do not put a lid on the pan or throw all the beans in at once, so lowering the temperature of the water to below boiling. If you do, the beans will turn out khaki rather than sparkling green. Cook until they have just lost their bite. Immediately plunge the beans into cold water, drain and chop into thirds.

→ Meanwhile, scrape and cook the POTATOES and softly hard-boil the EGGS. Halve the eggs and cut each half into three. Slice the larger cooked potatoes in half, leave the pebble-sized ones whole. Cut the AVOCADO into slices. Tear the CHICKEN along the grain into 5mm/¼in strips.

→ Place everything in a roomy, pretty bowl. Add the chopped HERBS to the MAYONNAISE, pour over the salad and turn lightly so that nothing gets broken up. Serve while the beans and potatoes still have a memory of warmth about them.

Warm Chicken and Puy Lentil Salad with Stove-dried Tomatoes

SERVES 4

chicken thighs	675g/1½lb
lemon juice	90ml/3fl oz
garlic cloves	9
extra virgin olive oil	90ml/3fl oz
thyme	10 sprigs
carrot, *peeled and diced*	1
celery stick, *diced*	1
white onion, *peeled and diced*	1
bay leaf	1

This is a stunning salad, served at the healthiest fast-food joint I know—Leon's in Soho's Great Marlborough Street. Remember to start it ahead of time as the chicken needs marinating and the tomatoes need drying. I don't soak the lentils, I just clean them thoroughly. Stove-dried tomatoes are also fantastic in pasta with chunks of goat's cheese, sage leaves frazzled in olive oil, and crème fraîche and a little butter stirred in.

→ Start preparing the stove-dried tomatoes a day or so before you want to eat this salad. Cut the TOMATOES into quarters and lay them on a baking tray, skin-side down. Finely mince the clove of GARLIC and stir it into the OLIVE OIL, then dribble the garlicky oil over the tomatoes. Sprinkle over the THYME LEAVES. Leave the tomatoes on a warmed hotplate, on the Aga hotplate or on a pilot light until they are dried but not shrivelled—this will take 24–32 hours.

→ Dice the CHICKEN into chunky, bite-sized pieces and marinate overnight in 2 tablespoons of the LEMON JUICE, 3 of the GARLIC CLOVES, finely chopped, and 1 tablespoon of OLIVE OIL. Cover with clingfilm and refrigerate overnight.

Puy lentils, *picked and washed thoroughly in a sieve*	100g/3½oz
red wine vinegar	1 tbsp
chicken stock (see p. 54)	850ml/1½ pints
organic egg	1
Greek OR Turkish yoghurt	170g/6oz
sea salt and black pepper	
rocket leaves	140g/5oz

Stove-dried Tomatoes

large vine-ripened tomatoes	4
garlic clove	1
olive oil	40ml/1½fl oz
thyme	2 sprigs

→ The next day, heat the oven to 150°C/300°F/Gas 2. Warm a generous tablespoon of OIL in a heavy-based pan on a medium heat and throw in the CARROT, CELERY and ONION. Add a few sprigs of THYME, 2 chopped cloves of GARLIC and the BAY LEAF, and sweat without colouring for about 10 minutes.

→ Add the drained LENTILS, pour in the RED WINE VINEGAR and reduce until the liquid has evaporated. Pour in the CHICKEN STOCK, cover with a layer of greaseproof paper and foil and bake in the oven for 20 minutes, or until tender but with a slight bite. SEASON to taste and allow to cool.

→ Chop the remaining GARLIC and put it in the blender with the EGG. Whizz for a few minutes until pale and fluffed up, then start pouring in the rest of the OLIVE OIL, a drop or two at a time to begin with. Add 40ml/1½fl oz of lemon juice, then turn out into a bowl and stir in the YOGHURT. (If you prefer to make the sauce by hand with a wooden spoon as I do, use an egg yolk, not the whole egg.)

→ Season the CHICKEN and grill for about 10 minutes, turning halfway through. Meanwhile, put the ROCKET on a large serving dish, followed by the stove-dried TOMATOES and half the LENTILS. Scatter the chicken over the top when it is cooked, then dress with more LEMON JUICE and OLIVE OIL.

→ Spoon over as much of the garlic sauce as you like, but don't drown the salad—you can keep what remains and use it for crudités later. Add the rest of the lentils and thyme, and serve warm with wedges of lemon.

Roast Chicken Salad with Grain Mustard Mayonnaise

SERVES 6

organic chicken, about 1.4–1.8kg/3–4lb	1
onion, *sliced*, olive oil, salt and pepper	
white chicory	4 heads
red Treviso chicory	1
watercress	1 small bunch
butter	a knob
whole walnuts	a handful
maple syrup	1 dsrtsp

Grain Mustard Mayonnaise

egg yolks	2
olive oil (not a strong, extra virgin one)	150ml/5fl oz
grain mustard	1 tbsp
lemon	juice of 1
some Jersey milk OR single cream for thinning	
chives, *snipped small*, plus extra for decorating	2 tbsp
sea salt and black pepper	

→ Place the CHICKEN on its side on a layer of sliced ONION in a roasting tin, pour over some OLIVE OIL and season with SALT and PEPPER. Roast for 20 minutes a side and 20 minutes breast up in a hot oven, 200°C/400°F/Gas 6. When the chicken has cooled down sufficiently for you to be able to tear it apart, remove the skin (and eat it), then pull the pieces of chicken from the legs, breasts and wings along the grain into strips and put them into a large bowl. Reserve the cooking juices.

→ Make the MAYONNAISE: whisk the EGG YOLKS in a bowl at room temperature until they begin to emulsify, then add the OIL—drip by drip to begin with, then in a steady stream— and stir continuously until it has thickened. Stir in the GRAIN MUSTARD, then add the JUICE OF A LEMON, a teaspoon at a time, until the mayonnaise has begun magically to pale and slacken before your eyes. You need something the texture of thin cream, not something a spoon will stand up in, so now begin to slacken it further with the lovely oniony, oily JUICES FROM THE ROAST and some MILK or CREAM. Add a couple of tablespoons of each in turn until you have the desired consist- ency. Check the seasoning, mustard and lemoniness. If it doesn't taste really lemony, add some more now; the acidity will be dulled once you have added the other ingredients. You should also be aware of the mustard and its graininess. Finally stir in the snipped CHIVES.

→ Pour the mayo over the still warm chicken so that all the flavours can mingle and marry and the chicken doesn't dry out now it has been skinned. Chop some of the CHICORY into circles but leave some leaves whole for decorating. Add the chopped chicory and the WATERCRESS to the chicken.

→ In a small frying pan, melt the BUTTER until it begins to foam, then throw in the WALNUTS. Turn them briskly to coat all over and add a little salt. After a couple of minutes, turn up the heat and dribble over the MAPLE SYRUP, tossing the WALNUTS to coat them before the syrup caramelises the pan rather than the nuts. You may need a further spoonful; taste and see, you should be able to taste salt, sweet and butter concomitantly. Remove from the heat before the nuts begin to brown. Break up half the nuts and fold them into the salad.

→ Transfer the chicken salad to a large platter and surround it with the whole LEAVES OF CHICORY; arrange them like the spokes of a wheel, but not as obviously as one white, one red. Snip some more CHIVES over the top and throw the whole warm walnuts in a crusted line along the middle of the salad before serving.

Thai Beef Salad

SERVES 4

rump steaks	4 × 180g/6oz or so
sea salt	
olive oil	
salad leaves	
fresh coriander leaves	2 tbsp
Sauce	
garlic cloves	3
sea salt	
hoisin sauce	4 tbsp
hot chilli sauce OR paste	1 tbsp, or to taste
mirin	4 tbsp
toasted sesame oil	1 tbsp
root ginger, *grated*	2cm/1in
small onion, *finely minced*	1
sesame seeds	2 tbsp
fresh lime juice	1 tbsp
Thai Salad Dressing	
fresh lime juice	3 tbsp
soy sauce	2 tbsp
runny honey	2 tbsp
rice vinegar	1 tbsp
mirin	1½ tsp
ginger root, *grated*	1½ tsp
toasted sesame oil	½ tsp
extra virgin olive oil	4 tbsp

→ Season the STEAKS with sea salt when you take them out of the fridge, an hour before you cook them. Brush the griddle with OLIVE OIL before you heat it. Griddle the steaks so that they are charred but rare, even if you don't like rare meat, as they will then 'cook' in the sauce overnight in the fridge. Slice thickly when still hot.

→ Crush the GARLIC CLOVES to a paste with a little sea salt. Mix this with the rest of the SAUCE INGREDIENTS in a bowl. Drop the warm slices of steak into it, decant the whole lot into a ziploc bag and put it in the fridge overnight.

→ Bring back to room temperature the following day. Mix the SALAD LEAVES with the fresh CORIANDER and add the dressing. Place the strips of beef on top before serving.

PASTA &

gnocchi

Spaghetti with Tomato Sauce

Serves 6

olive oil	3 tbsp
onions, *finely chopped*	2
celery sticks, *finely chopped*	2
garlic cloves, *finely chopped*	6
fresh plum tomatoes, *skinned, seeded and chopped*	1kg/2¼lb
Italian plum tomatoes	1 × 400g/14oz tin
tomato passata, organic if possible	half a 200g/7oz jar
tomato purée	1 tbsp
bay leaves	2
fresh thyme, parsley AND/OR basil, *chopped*	generous bunch
molasses sugar	2 tsp
red wine	about 150ml/5fl oz
salt and pepper	
spaghetti	
butter and olive oil	
extra basil leaves	
Parmesan, *freshly grated*	

This is my tomato sauce recipe for you to add to or subtract from as you wish. If good organic plum tomatoes are not in season, you may wish to use all tinned tomatoes with some good passata from a jar, as our acidic English tomatoes are not really up to the job. Texture is an individual thing too. You may serve it straight from the pan or push it through the coarse blade of the mouli if you like a smoother, but not baby-food style, texture. Quantities of pasta and Parmesan are up to you and your appetite.

→ Heat the OIL in a large, heavy-bottomed frying pan and sauté the ONIONS, CELERY sticks and GARLIC until softened and translucent. Add the FRESH and TINNED TOMATOES, TOMATO PASSATA and PURÉE, and chop the tinned tomatoes down into the liquid. Add the BAY LEAVES and other HERBS, simmer for a minute, then stir in the SUGAR. Simmer, uncovered, until the sauce is beginning to thicken, stirring occasionally, for about 15 minutes. Add a good splash of WINE, season and stir. Keep the sauce simmering happily for up to another 30 minutes, giving it the occasional stir and adding a little more wine or tomato passata if it begins to dry out.

→ Cook the SPAGHETTI in plenty of boiling, salted water according to the instructions on the packet. Drain unthoroughly, without shaking the colander, so that there is still water on the pasta when you return it to the pan. Stir in a knob of BUTTER with a splosh of good OLIVE OIL then stir in the tomato sauce on the heat for a minute. Tear a few BASIL LEAVES over the top of the sauce if you have some. Serve freshly grated Parmesan separately.

Raw Tomato Sauce

Serves 4

small onion	1
large garlic clove	1
ripe, well-flavoured tomatoes, *skinned, seeded and finely chopped*	675g/1½lb
olive oil	6 tbsp
torn basil leaves, chopped chives and flat-leaf parsley	1 tbsp of each
lemon juice	2 tbsp
salt and pepper	

This is a family favourite, not, as you might imagine, only in the summer months when it can be tossed into pasta and eaten warm or cold. In the winter we eat it with hot pasta, and it is fresh, healthy and invigorating. The best pasta to serve it with is of the short, squat variety, say a fusilli or chunky macaroni.

→ Mince the ONION and GARLIC together in a liquidiser or food processor. Put in a bowl with the REMAINING INGREDIENTS, stir, then cover and leave in the fridge for about 30 minutes. Stir again, then stir into a steaming hot bowl of pasta, and serve warm or cold.

Spaghetti Aio e Oio

SERVES 4

spaghetti OR spaghettini	450g/1lb
best extra virgin olive oil	6–8 tbsp
large garlic clove, *very finely minced*	1
red chilli, *chopped and seeded*	to taste
flat-leaf parsley, *chopped*	2 tbsp

Spaghetti or the tinier spaghettini is the right pasta for this cheapest and most deliciously simple of sauces. Just don't stint on the best olive oil and good pasta. Even a dish such as this can only be as good as its raw ingredients, and you need a peppery, grassy, fruity olive oil to come through the hit of chilli and garlic. Always use flat-leaf parsley for this dish.

→ Put the SPAGHETTI in a large pan of salted, boiling water and while it is cooking, make the sauce. Make sure you have SALTED the pan of water as salt does not dissolve well in olive oil, so you don't want to be adding extra salt when you sauce your spaghetti.

→ Put the OLIVE OIL, GARLIC and chopped CHILLI in a small pan over a low heat and cook gently until the garlic turns a pale gold but does not brown. When the pasta is cooked and drained, toss it immediately with the sauce, making sure it is all coated evenly. Add the chopped PARSLEY and serve. What could be easier?

Spaghetti al Cacio e Pepe

SERVES 4

spaghetti	450g/1lb
good extra virgin olive oil	3 tbsp
salt and coarsely ground black pepper	
Pecorino Romano cheese, *grated*	85g/3oz

Another plain Jane but perfect dish—the crucial ingredient is Pecorino Romano, the lovely salt, crystalline, aged sheep's milk cheese that has a lactic graininess and strength of flavour enough to make this dish, with no need for further partnering. Just black pepper and good olive oil.

→ Bring a large pan of salted water to the boil and throw in the SPAGHETTI. Cook it for only 5 minutes before draining, but save the cooking water in another pan. Pour the OLIVE OIL into the hot pan, add the pasta and return to the heat, adding a ladleful of the hot cooking water from time to time and the coarsely ground BLACK PEPPER. Once the pasta is cooked al dente, add the grated PECORINO and stir it in thoroughly. Check the SEASONING and serve.

Spaghetti Carbonara

SERVES 6

garlic cloves	2 or 3
best olive oil	3 tbsp
pancetta, *cut into small strips*, OR prosciutto, *shredded*	225g/8oz
dry white wine	120ml/4fl oz
large eggs	2
Parmesan and Pecorino cheese, *grated*	55g/2oz of each
black pepper	
spaghetti	
flat-leaf parsley, *finely chopped*	

This is one of the great fast suppers that you can make when the fridge is bare of all but the basics. It is really just a glorious Roman version of eggs and bacon served with spaghetti, so if you can, use fat chunks of pancetta, tear up prosciutto or culatello, or opt for oak-smoked back rashers.

→ Smash the GARLIC CLOVES with the flat of a knife blade. Warm the OLIVE OIL and garlic together in a small pan and remove the garlic when it has turned golden brown. Throw in the PANCETTA, and cook until browned and beginning to crisp. Pour in the WINE, let it bubble for a couple of minutes, then turn the heat off.

→ Break the EGGS into the bowl from which you'll serve the pasta, beat them, then throw the CHEESES and the PEPPER in and beat again.

→ Add the cooked, drained SPAGHETTI — I allow 85–110g/3–4oz per person — and toss well to coat the pasta stickily. Reheat the pancetta quickly, pour it over the pasta, toss thoroughly with the PARSLEY and some more BLACK PEPPER and serve.

Spaghetti with Cream, Bacon and Peas

SERVES 6

garlic cloves	2 or 3
best olive oil	3 tbsp
pancetta, *cut into small strips*, OR prosciutto, *shredded*	225g/8oz
butter	
double cream	300ml/10fl oz
cooked peas, fresh or frozen	225/8oz
spaghetti	
black pepper	
Parmesan, *freshly grated*	

→ If you don't want to make the classic Carbonara, cook the GARLIC and BACON as above, then add a nut of BUTTER and the DOUBLE CREAM and PEAS. Bubble the mixture for a couple of minutes before pouring it over the cooked and drained PASTA. Grind over some BLACK PEPPER, throw in a handful of PARMESAN, and serve some extra Parmesan separately.

Spaghetti with Breadcrumbs and Anchovies

SERVES 4

ripe fresh tomatoes	255g/9oz
garlic cloves, *finely sliced*	2
dried chillies, *finely chopped and seeds removed*	1 tsp
flat-leaf parsley, *chopped*	1 tbsp
extra virgin olive oil	6 tbsp
spaghetti OR linguine	450g/1lb
salted anchovies, *de-spined and rinsed*	4
OR bottled anchovy fillets, *drained*	8
unsalted butter	30g/1oz
dried breadcrumbs	6 tbsp
dried oregano	1 tsp
organic lemon	*zest* of 1

In her great work, Gastronomy of Italy, *Anna Del Conte explains that in the poor regions of southern Italy, toasted breadcrumbs were, and often still are, used instead of expensive Parmesan or Pecorino cheese. Anna uses dried breadcrumbs toasted, but I like to cook mine in a little mixed butter and olive oil so that they coat the pasta and have crunch. I also like to add a little lemon zest at the finish.*

→ Peel, halve, seed and chop the TOMATOES. Put the GARLIC, CHILLIES, PARSLEY and half the OLIVE OIL in a large frying pan and sauté for a minute. Add the tomatoes and cook over a medium heat for 5 minutes, stirring frequently. Meanwhile, cook the PASTA according to the instructions on the packet.

→ Chop the ANCHOVY FILLETS. Put all but a tablespoon of the rest of the OLIVE OIL into a small pan and heat, then add the anchovies and mash them down into the pan for a minute until they disintegrate into the oil. In a separate pan, melt the BUTTER with the remaining oil and add the BREADCRUMBS, frying them until they turn golden and crisped. Throw the anchovies and their juice into the tomato mixture. Add the OREGANO and carry on cooking for a minute. Check the SEASONING, then take the pan off the heat.

→ Drain the pasta, but not too thoroughly, and put it back in the pot with a little of its cooking water still dripping from it. Add the tomato and anchovy mixture, give it a good stir and sprinkle the buttered breadcrumbs over the top before serving. A little ZESTED LEMON over the surface adds a lovely zing at this stage.

Spaghetti with Griddled Asparagus

SERVES 4

asparagus	6 spears per person
extra virgin olive oil	
lemon	zest and juice of 1
flat-leaf parsley, *chopped*	1 tbsp
tarragon, *chopped*	1 tbsp
knob of butter	
spaghetti	450g/1lb
Parmesan cheese, *grated*	

→ Snap the woody bottoms of the ASPARAGUS and peel the lower half of each stem with a potato peeler. Roll the asparagus in good OLIVE OIL. Heat the griddle, then add the asparagus spears. When they have scorch marks, roll them over and continue to cook until al dente when pierced with a knife. You may need to pull the tips over the edge of the griddle before the thick ends are cooked through. Cut into 2.5cm/1in lengths.

→ Cook the PASTA as usual, drain, but not too thoroughly. Add the asparagus, LEMON JUICE AND ZEST, HERBS and BUTTER. Serve with grated PARMESAN.

Pasta Puttanesca

SERVES 4

olive oil	3–4 tbsp
medium onion, *chopped fine*	1
garlic cloves, *finely chopped*	2
anchovies in olive oil, or salted anchovies, *finely chopped*	3–4
hot dried chilli, *chopped fine with its seeds* OR cayenne	1 to taste
organic plum tomatoes	2 × 400g/14oz tins
spaghetti	450g/1lb
capers	1 heaped tbsp
good black olives, *pitted and halved*	16–20
fresh basil (optional)	1 bunch
unsalted butter	a knob

This is one of the great store cupboard dishes I can always cook if people turn up unexpectedly. Tinned tomatoes, good olives and anchovies, salted or brined capers, dried chillies or cayenne, onions, garlic and spaghetti are wonderful standbys, and no good kitchen should be without them!

→ Bring a large pan of water to the boil. Meanwhile, heat the OLIVE OIL in a large, heavy-bottomed frying pan and throw in the chopped ONION. Cook over a medium heat until it is beginning to soften, then add the finely chopped GARLIC, the chopped ANCHOVIES (if using salted anchovies rinse them well under the cold tap) and the chopped CHILLI. The anchovies will begin to melt into the oil. Let the garlic begin to soften and turn pale gold, no more, then add the tinned TOMATOES, chopping them down into the sauce with a knife and bringing them up to a bubble. Simmer for 10–15 minutes while you cook the PASTA.

→ Meanwhile, put the brined or salted CAPERS on a slotted spoon and run the cold tap over them to rid them of their saltiness. Throw the OLIVES into the pan when the sauce has reduced, thickened and become quite jammy, then add the capers and heat them through. Remove the pan from the heat.

→ Tear the BASIL, which is optional, and stir it into the sauce. Check the SEASONING —you have chilli, salt anchovy and caper, so may need no more. Drain the pasta and add a knob of unsalted BUTTER. Pour the sauce over the hot pasta in the pan or bowl, toss well and serve immediately in warmed bowls.

Pasta with Pesto

SERVES 6

fresh basil, organic if possible, leaves *stripped from the stems*	110g/4oz
fruity extra virgin olive oil	8 tbsp
pine nuts	3 tbsp
garlic cloves, *chopped roughly*	2
Parmesan cheese, *freshly grated*	55g/2oz
Pecorino Sardo cheese *freshly grated*	2 tbsp
sea salt and black pepper	
pasta of your choice	

Pesto is perfect with trofie, penne, tagliatelle, pappardelle, spaghettini or potato gnocchi. It can also be used with lasagne and béchamel sauce, or with crespelli, Italian pancakes with béchamel and fresh mozzarella. Traditionally the Genoese serve their pesto sauce with waxy new potatoes and green beans mixed in with it and the pasta. I urge you to try it and see for yourself. It is a winner.

→ Wash and dry the basil leaves in a tea towel, then put them in a food processor or mortar with the olive oil, pine nuts, chopped garlic and a little salt, and process until you have a textured purée. If you process for too long, the resulting purée will lose its lovely green colour as the blades will render the basil sludgy and brown. You can also do the whole process with a pestle and mortar for a more authentic version texture-wise. Transfer to a bowl and stir in the two cheeses and grind some black pepper over the pesto. Taste and adjust whatever you need to—you may need a little more oil, more cheese or more pine nuts.

→ When your pasta is cooked, drain it, keeping back a couple of tablespoons of cooking water, which you should stir immediately into the sauce. Then tip the sauce into the warm bowl you have shunted the pasta into and toss everything together thoroughly with a couple of spoons. Add a little extra salt and pepper and pass round an extra bowl of mixed Parmesan and Pecorino.

Sicilian Pesto

SERVES 4

blanched almonds	55g/2oz
garlic clove, *peeled*	1
extra virgin olive oil	4 tbsp
Pecorino cheese, *grated*	2 tbsp
fresh mint leaves, *washed*	1 tightly packed handful
dried red chilli pepper,	½ tsp, or more to taste
ripe, firm, fresh plum tomatoes, *peeled, seeded and chopped*	3 or 4
sea salt	1 tsp

This recipe is by the other doyenne of Italian cookery writing, Marcella Hazan. It is a southern red rather than a northern green sauce—warmer, feistier, riper. This quantity makes enough for 450g/1lb of pasta.

→ Put ALL THE INGREDIENTS in a food processor and process to a creamy consistency. Taste and correct for SALT. Toss with PASTA that has just been drained and is still piping hot. Serve at once. The sauce may be refrigerated in a tightly sealed container for up to a week.

Pasta with Roasted Fennel and Garlic

SERVES 2

fennel bulbs	55g/2oz
extra virgin olive oil	
garlic bulb	1
butter	a knob
black olives, *pitted*	12
fresh rosemary, *chopped*	1 tbsp
breadcrumbs	2 tbsp
anchovies	3
tube pasta such as rigatoni	225g/8oz

→ Peel off the tough outer layers of the FENNEL and cut the bulbs into quarters. Roll in OIL and put on a baking tray. Slice the head off a bulb of GARLIC. Roast the fennel and garlic in a hot oven—200°C/400°F/Gas 6—until the fennel is al dente and starting to brown and the garlic cloves are soft when pressed—20 to 30 minutes. Squeeze the flesh out of the garlic cloves and put in a pan with the OLIVE OIL, BUTTER, OLIVES, ROSEMARY and BREADCRUMBS. Chop in the ANCHOVIES and cook together for a few minutes then tossed into nearly drained tubes of long pasta. No cheese as it's fishy.

Penne with Roasted Squash, Prosciutto, Sage and Parmesan

SERVES 2

red onion squash	1/3
OR butternut squash	1/2
olive oil	
red chilli, *split down the middle and seeded*	1
penne	225g/8oz
butter	
prosciutto	4 slices
fresh sage leaves	a good handful
fresh Parmesan cheese	
sea salt and black pepper	

→ Preheat the oven to 200°C/400°F/Gas 6. For this recipe, I think it is better to remove the skin of the squash before cooking. Peel the SQUASH and cut into small cubes. Roll them in about 4 tablespoons of good OLIVE OIL in a roasting tray, season and add the split CHILLI. Roast until the squash is tender, about 20 minutes. Remove the chilli, which will have exuded enough warmth into the olive oil for this dish.

→ Cook the PENNE in plenty of boiling salted water. I favour the extra-large Carluccio variety, which has apertures large enough to contain, as well as to be coated by, the sauce. Make sure when you drain the penne that you return a little of the cooking water to the pan with it, then slather on a bit of butter.

→ Meanwhile, tear the PROSCIUTTO into bits and cook it separately in a couple of tablespoons of OLIVE OIL for a couple of minutes until crisp. Remove the prosciutto with a slotted spoon and throw in the SAGE, cooking until deliciously frizzled and browned.

→ Throw the squash, prosciutto and sage into the pot with the penne, stir in a tablespoon or two of PARMESAN, adjust the SEASONING and serve. Pass round some more Parmesan at the table. There is great contrast between the salt cheese, sweet, yielding, mealy-fleshed squash, crisp, salt prosciutto and astringent sage.

Penne with Rocket and Fresh Ricotta

SERVES 4

extra virgin olive oil	4 tbsp and extra to pour over
garlic cloves, *peeled and sliced*	2
red chilli, *seeded and chopped*	1
wild rocket, *coarsely chopped but keep a few leaves whole*	450g/1lb
penne	450g/1lb
fresh ricotta cheese	225g/8oz
fresh basil	a handful
butter	a knob
Parmesan cheese, *freshly grated*	140g/5oz

You can make a variation on this theme with spinach or watercress. Use the same amount of spinach as rocket, or three bunches of watercress, preferably with stalks.

→ Heat half the OLIVE OIL in a heavy-bottomed pan and put in the GARLIC and CHILLI. Cook gently just until the garlic begins to turn pale gold, then throw in half the ROCKET and let it wilt for a couple of minutes. Throw the contents of the pan into a food processor and add most of the rest of the ROCKET and OLIVE OIL. SEASON and blitz to a coarse texture.

→ Cook the PASTA and drain, leaving a couple of tablespoons of cooking water in the pan. Add the sauce and then mix in the RICOTTA which you have broken up very gently into the pan. Toss in the whole leaves of ROCKET, the torn BASIL, the knob of BUTTER, SEASON and add a good splash of OLIVE OIL. Pass the PARMESAN round separately in a bowl.

Penne with Aubergine, Tomato and Mozzarella

SERVES 4

large aubergine, *cut into small cubes*	1
extra virgin olive oil	7–8 tbsp
garlic cloves, *peeled and thinly sliced*	2
flat-leaf parsley, *chopped*	a handful
Italian plum tomatoes	1 × 400g/14oz tin
dried chilli, *seeded*	1
penne	450g/1lb
butter	a knob
sea salt and black pepper	
buffalo mozzarella cheese, *cut into small cubes*	1

→ You could sprinkle salt over the aubergine cubes in a colander and leave them for 20 minutes to let the bitter juices drain, but aubergines don't seem to be as bitter as they used to be, so I will leave that bit of the process up to you.

→ Heat 2 or 3 tablespoons of OLIVE OIL in a heavy-bottomed pan and then throw in the GARLIC and PARSLEY, cooking them until they soften, but not until the garlic browns.

→ Add the chopped TOMATOES and all their juice with the CHILLIES and a sprinkle of salt and cook for around 20 minutes on a medium heat. In a separate pan heat 4 tablespoons of OLIVE OIL and throw in the cubed AUBERGINE, frying it until it is browned on all sides and soft right the way through. Unlike many vegetables, aubergine is really not nice if it has bite, so make sure it is cooked through.

→ Drain the aubergine on kitchen towel so it is not too oily. When your PENNE is cooked, drain it and return it to the pan with a couple of tablespoons of cooking water. Lob in a knob of BUTTER then turn the pans of tomatoes and aubergine into the pasta and amalgamate briefly. Throw in the cubed MOZZARELLA, scrunch over some PEPPER and serve.

Penne with Swiss Chard, Blue Cheese and a Walnut Cream Sauce

SERVES 4

chard leaves and their stalks	8
penne or conchiglie	450g/1lb
butter	a knob
organic lemon	*zest* of 1
Roquefort, Gorgonzola or other good, not industrial, blue cheese	170g/6oz
unpasteurised organic double cream	300ml/10fl oz
walnuts, *broken up*	110g/4oz
sea salt and black pepper	
Parmesan cheese, *freshly grated*	110g/4oz

You may use the lovely dark, bubbly-leaved cavolo nero—black cabbage—instead of chard, which gives a bitter rather than sweet note to this dish. Conchiglie pasta also works well with this sauce.

→ Put the CHARD LEAVES and chopped-up STALKS in the top of a double boiler and steam until both are cooked, about 5 minutes. Remove to a plate to cool.

→ Meanwhile, cook the PASTA according to the instructions to al dente, drain it and return it to the pan with a couple of tablespoons of the cooking water and the knob of BUTTER. Zest the LEMON into the pasta and throw in the chard stalks and the leaves, well torn. Crumble in the BLUE CHEESE, pour in the CREAM and throw in the WALNUTS, SEASON and put on a very low heat just until the cream has heated through but not to boiling point. Mix gently, but remember you want the cheese to have texture. Adjust the seasoning and serve with a bowl of Parmesan to pass around.

Taglierini with Baked Fennel, Cherry Tomatoes and Wealden Round

SERVES 2

fennel bulbs, *well peeled and very finely sliced*	2
organic cherry tomatoes	2 dozen
garlic cloves, *sliced*	2
olive oil, butter	
taglierini OR fine spaghetti	225g/8oz
black pepper and garlic Wealden Round, *cut into pieces*	85g/3oz

Wealden Round is a fabulously fresh unpasteurised soft cow's milk cheese. Have some extra to add to each bowl. A creamy goat's cheese such as Ragstone also works well.

→ Preheat the oven to 200°C/400°F/Gas 6. Put the FENNEL, CHERRY TOMATOES and GARLIC into a small roasting tin, splosh on a few tablespoons of OLIVE OIL, and bake in the oven until the fennel is softened through and basking in the tomatoey juices. About 20 minutes.

→ Cook the PASTA according to the instructions, drain, add a good knob of BUTTER to the pan, then the SOFT CHEESE and taglierini, stirring on a gentle heat to coat. Add the vegetables in their juices, season and serve.

→ You can add a good dollop extra of cheese to the top of each bowl to melt in as you eat it.

Pasta with Broccoli, Anchovy and Chilli Sauce

SERVES 4

broccoli OR broccoli rabe	675g/1½ lb
orecchiette, conchiglie or penne pasta	450g/1lb
extra virgin olive oil	8 tbsp
small anchovy fillets in olive oil, *chopped*	12
or salted anchovies, *well rinsed and chopped*	6
medium hot red chilli, *halved, seeded and chopped*	1
a knob of unsalted butter	
Parmesan cheese, *freshly grated*	2 tbsp
Pecorino Romano, *freshly grated*	4 tbsp

Easy, economical and elegantly simple, this sauce is lovely with orecchiette, the little ear-shaped pasta from Puglia in southern Italy. Use more chilli if you like, but note that this dish shouldn't need salt with the salt anchovies and cheese, nor pepper because of the chilli.

→ Remove the BROCCOLI stalks and peel them, cutting off the woody bits at the bottom of them. Chop the peeled stalks into small, juicy chunks. Break the broccoli heads into florets. Get your pasta water boiling in the meantime and cook your PASTA according to the instructions on the packet, making sure it is al dente before you drain it and return it to the pan with a couple of tablespoons of the cooking water. Meanwhile, steam the broccoli until al dente, around 7 minutes, then refresh under cold water in a colander to arrest cooking and keep the colour.

→ Pour the OIL into a large frying pan that will also hold the broccoli, and put over a medium heat. When the oil looks like it is hazy and lively, add the chopped ANCHOVIES and mash them into the oil with a fork. Turn the heat down to gentle. The sauce will be more of a paste at this stage. Add the chopped CHILLI and the broccoli, and turn it all well into the sauce over the heat for 5 minutes.

→ Throw the sauce into the pan with the pasta, to which you have added the knob of BUTTER, and turn everything together with both the cheeses in the pot. Serve immediately.

Pasta with Porcini

SERVES 2

porcini mushrooms	225g/8oz
fresh egg pasta	225g/8oz
olive oil	
garlic clove	1
bay leaf	1
whipping cream	1 small carton
butter	a knob
flat-leaf parsley, *finely chopped*	
salt and pepper	

This dish is best with fresh pasta, such as tagliatelle or pappardelle, but dried will do.

→ Clean the PORCINI and slice them thinly. Heat a film of OLIVE OIL in the bottom of a frying pan, put in the GARLIC and BAY LEAF, and sauté until the garlic begins to brown. Remove it and the bay leaf, throw in the porcini, fry quickly, tossing and turning as you go, until they are just tender and have released their juices, a matter of a few minutes.

→ SEASON, pour in the CREAM, bubble it, and then throw in the pasta that you have cooked and drained and adorned with a knob of BUTTER. Amalgamate briefly, add a dusting of finely chopped flat-leaf PARSLEY, and serve.

Taglierini with Hazelnut Sauce

SERVES 6

butter	a good-sized knob
garlic, *finely chopped*	1 clove
extra virgin olive oil	90ml/3fl oz
hazelnuts	200g/7oz
chilli pepper	1 pinch
taglierini noodles	675g/1½lb

Try to find the best fresh roasted hazelnuts you can for this sauce, preferably from Piedmont.

→ Melt the BUTTER in a large pot. Add the GARLIC, the OLIVE OIL, the HAZELNUTS that you have crushed but not ground (you want them nibbed rather than chunky) and the CHILLI PEPPER, and fry them together briefly.

→ Cook the PASTA, drain and pour into the sauce. Stir well to coat, and serve. I served a sprouting broccoli salad (see p. 122) with mine, which is a delicious accompaniment to any creamy or oily pasta dish.

Spaghetti with Roasted Celeriac, Tomatoes and Goat's Cheese

small celeriac	1
olive oil	3–4 tbsp
cherry tomatoes	8
frozen peas	a handful
chicken stock	ladleful
knob of butter	
goat's cheese, *cubed*	110g/4oz

→ Peel the CELERIAC and cut into cubes, losing the nasty soft bits in the middle. Toss the cubes in OLIVE OIL and roast in a hot oven—200°C/400°F/Gas 6. After about 10 minutes turn the celeriac cubes over, add the CHERRY TOMATOES, and cook for another 10 minutes. Meanwhile cook a handful of FROZEN PEAS in a ladleful of CHICKEN STOCK if you have any. If not, use water.

→ When the vegetables are nearly ready, cook the PASTA, drain, leaving a little water in the bottom of the pan, and add a knob of BUTTER. Add the roasted celeriac, peas and cooking stock. Toss, add the cubed GOAT'S CHEESE at the last minute so it doesn't melt in completely, and serve with some freshly grated Parmesan if you wish.

Bigoli

Serves 4

very large organic onions	2
fruity extra virgin olive oil	
anchovies in olive oil	½ jar
unsalted butter	a knob
black pepper	
spelt OR wholewheat spaghetti	450g/1lb
flat-leaf parsley, *chopped*	

This is my version of the lovely Venetian pasta dish, bigoli. I couldn't find the fatter, wholewheat pasta that they make specially for it, so use skinnier strands of spelt pasta, which work well. I think the idea is to make the dish branny and nutty, so I'm not worried about the switch.

→ Peel the ONIONS and slice them very thinly into rings. Sweat the onions down slowly, slowly, in a large, heavy-bottomed frying pan with a few tablespoons of EXTRA VIRGIN OLIVE OIL for 10 minutes, then continue to cook extra slowly under a lid. I do this in the baking oven of the Aga, stirring every 10 minutes, for about 40 minutes; do the same on top of the stove.

→ Remove the ANCHOVIES from the jar and mash them with a fork down into the onion, cooking them in for 5 minutes. Season with BLACK PEPPER but no salt; the anchovies are salt enough. Throw in a knob of unsalted BUTTER the size of a walnut. Blitz in a food processor until smooth.

→ Co-ordinate the PASTA cooking time so that it's ready just after you've blitzed the sauce — keep it just the dangerous side of al dente as it will be heated through in the pan with the sauce afterwards. Put the not-quite-fully drained pasta into the pan you cooked the onions in and return the sauce to the pan. Turn it over a very gentle heat to coat and cook the pasta through a little more for a couple of minutes. Throw over a fistful of chopped PARSLEY and bring to the table in the pan to serve in warmed bowls.

Gnocchi alla Romana

Serves 4

milk	1 litre/1¾ pints
sea salt	
coarse-ground semolina (semolina flour)	225g/8oz
large organic egg yolks	3
Parmesan cheese, *freshly grated*	75g/2½ oz
grated nutmeg	¼ tsp
unsalted butter	75g/2½ oz

→ Heat the MILK with a little SALT in a heavy pan. When it begins to simmer, add the SEMOLINA in a thin stream, beating quickly to prevent any lumps from forming. Cook for about 15 minutes, beating constantly until the semolina has formed a thick paste and comes away from the sides of the pan. Remove the pan from the heat and allow the semolina to cool a little.

→ Add the EGG YOLKS, one at a time, mixing them in thoroughly. Add all but 4 tablespoons of the PARMESAN, the NUTMEG, 30g/1oz of the BUTTER and a pinch of SALT. Incorporate everything thoroughly, then turn the mixture out onto a slab of marble or work surface previously moistened with cold water. Spread the semolina to a thickness of 1cm/½in and cool it completely for about 2 hours.

→ Preheat the oven to 230°C/450°F/Gas 8. Cut the semolina into 4cm/1½in rounds. Place a layer of rounds in the bottom of a buttered ovenproof dish, put the leftover scraps in between, then cover with another layer of the gnocchi rounds, slightly overlapping.

→ Melt the remaining BUTTER and pour it over the gnocchi. Sprinkle with the remaining PARMESAN and bake in the oven for about 15 minutes, until the gnocchi are heated through. Allow to cool for a few minutes before serving.

Potato Gnocchi

SERVES 4

floury potatoes, *scrubbed*	1kg/2¼lb
sea salt	1 tsp
Italian oo flour	285g/10oz
large organic egg, *beaten*	1
unsalted butter	75g/2½ oz
garlic cloves, *lightly crushed*	2
sage leaves, *torn*	3–4
Parmesan cheese, *freshly grated*	75g/2½oz

→ Boil the POTATOES, drain, and peel them while still hot. Sieve them in a food mill or a potato ricer onto the worktop. Sprinkle a little SALT onto the FLOUR in a bowl and mix well. Add the beaten EGG and half the flour to the potatoes. Knead, gradually adding more flour, until the mixture is soft, smooth and slightly sticky. Shape the mixture into rolls, about 2.5cm/1in in diameter, then cut into 2cm/¾in pieces.

→ To shape the GNOCCHI, take a fork and hold it with the tines resting on the worktop at an angle of 45 degrees. Take each piece of dough, dust it with flour, then press it lightly with the thumb of your other hand against the inner curve of the prongs. With a quick downwards movement, flip it towards the end of the tines. The gnocchi should be concave on the thumb side, and convex with ridges on the fork side.

→ Bring 5 litres/8–9 pints of water to the boil in a large pan. Do not put salt in the pan as this tends to make the gnocchi stick together.

→ Meanwhile, make the sauce. Put the BUTTER, GARLIC and SAGE in a small, heavy pan and cook slowly. The sauce is ready when the foam has disappeared and the butter is light golden. Discard the garlic and keep the sauce warm.

→ Drop the gnocchi into the boiling water – you can cook about 30 at a time in a big pan. Cook for 20 seconds after they come to the surface, then lift out with a slotted spoon, pat dry with kitchen paper and transfer to a heated dish. Pour over a little sauce, sprinkle with some PARMESAN and keep warm. Repeat until all the gnocchi are cooked. Pour the remaining sauce over and sprinkle with Parmesan.

Butternut Squash Gnocchi

Serves 4

olive oil	1 tbsp
butternut squash or red onion squash	500g/1lb 2oz
sweet potatoes	500g/1lb 2oz
Italian '00' flour	200g/7oz
baking powder	2 tsp
salt	
large organic eggs	2
Parmesan, *freshly grated*	4 tbsp
nutmeg	a generous grating
Parmesan and Cinnamon Dressing	
unsalted butter	75g/2½oz
Parmesan cheese, *freshly grated*	30g/1oz
sugar	1 tbsp
cinnamon	1 tsp
Sage Dressing	
unsalted butter	75g/2½oz
fresh sage leaves, *snipped*	6
Parmesan cheese, *freshly grated*	55g/2oz

→ Preheat the oven to 180°C/350°F/Gas 4. Line a baking tray with foil and brush it with oil. Cut the SQUASH in half, scoop out the seeds and fibrous bits and place cut-side down on the foil. Pierce the SWEET POTATOES with a skewer and put them on the foil. Bake for 40 minutes to an hour until both vegetables can be pierced easily with a fork.

→ Peel the sweet potatoes and scoop the flesh out of the squash. Using a mouli-légumes or potato ricer, purée both together into a bowl. Mix in the FLOUR, BAKING POWDER and SALT, then break in the EGGS. Mix everything together well, add the Parmesan and season with nutmeg and more salt to taste.

→ Bring a large pan of salted water to the boil. Flour your hands and shape the GNOCCHI into small balls. Drop into simmering water and cook for 1–2 minutes after they have come to the surface. If you prefer, use a piping bag and a large plain nozzle to shape the gnocchi. Fill the bag with the mixture and hold it over the pan, squeezing it with one hand and cutting the mixture as it comes out of the nozzle. Cut short shapes, about 2cm/¾ in long, letting them drop straight into the simmering water. Cook the gnocchi in 3 batches. Lift them out of the pan with a slotted spoon and place in a large ovenproof dish. DRESS each batch separately and keep the dish in a low oven.

Parmesan and Cinnamon Dressing
→ Melt the BUTTER in a double boiler or a bowl over a pan of simmering water. Pour the butter over the gnocchi and sprinkle with PARMESAN, SUGAR and CINNAMON.

Sage Dressing
→ Put the BUTTER and SAGE LEAVES in a small pan and heat until the butter melts and begin to foam. Spoon the buttery sauce over the gnocchi and sprinkle with the Parmesan.

Spinach and Ricotta Gnocchi

Serves 4

spinach, *cooked*	500g/1lb 2oz
large organic eggs	2
ricotta cheese	200g/7oz

A perfect starter or main course. Try to get fresh ricotta if you can – the flavour and texture is so much better than the industrial version. If you are serving the gnocchi as a starter, remember not to serve anything too heavy afterwards, or anything with cheese for your main course.

→ Press all the water out of the SPINACH with a wooden spoon and a conical strainer if you have one; if not, press through a colander or sieve. Now chop the spinach or push it through the

Italian 00 flour	200g/7oz
nutmeg, *grated*	½ tsp
Parmesan cheese, *freshly grated*	100g/3½oz
sea salt and freshly ground black pepper	
unsalted butter	100g/3½oz

coarse disc of a mouli-légumes. Beat the EGGS together in a bowl and mix in the RICOTTA, beating them both together. Mix in the FLOUR, spinach, NUTMEG and half the PARMESAN. Taste and adjust the seasoning.

→ Dust your hands with flour and form the mixture into balls the size of large marbles. Place them on a baking tray and chill in the fridge for 30 minutes.

→ To cook the GNOCCHI, bring 5 litres/8–9 pints of salted water to the boil in a very large pan. Add the gnocchi, a dozen at a time, and cook them for 3–4 minutes after the water returns to the boil. Lift them out with a slotted spoon and transfer them to a dish. Dot with a little BUTTER, sprinkle over a little PARMESAN and keep them warm while cooking the rest.

→ Meanwhile, melt the remaining BUTTER in a small pan. Just before serving, spoon the butter over the cooked gnocchi and sprinkle with the remaining PARMESAN.

Prawn and Leek Lasagne

SERVES 6

butter	55g/2oz
or olive oil	4 tbsp
white parts of 12 thick leeks, *chopped into 1cm/½ in chunks*	
lasagne sheets	560g/1¼lb
cooked peeled prawns	900g/2lb
Parmesan cheese, *grated*	110–170g/4–6oz
béchamel sauce (see p. 402)	up to 850ml/1½ pints

This is one of those gloriously adaptable dishes that you can dress up or down every which way. Clams, mussels, a tad of smoked haddock, some glistening scallops with great commas of coral or just a plain heap of prawns, whose sweetness has a natural affinity with the leeks. Throw in a handful of fresh or frozen peas if you have them, or some slices of steamed fennel with their feathery fronds to further the pink and green theme.

→ Preheat the oven to 190°C/375°F/Gas 5. Heat the BUTTER OR OIL in a large saucepan, add the LEEKS and cook over a low heat until softened and translucent.

→ Boil the LASAGNE until tender, then spread the pasta sheets on a clean tea towel to drain. (Alternatively, use the sort of lasagne that does not need precooking, but make sure you use a good brand or the texture is like toasted cardboard.)

→ Put a thin layer of BÉCHAMEL SAUCE in a large greased baking dish and sprinkle about one-third of the grated PARMESAN on top. Add a layer of lasagne, and scatter half the leeks and half the PRAWNS on top. Pour over half the remaining béchamel and sprinkle another third of the grated Parmesan on top. Repeat the layers, starting with the lasagne and ending with the Parmesan. Cook in the preheated oven for 30–40 minutes. Test by inserting a knife into the pasta; the top will be golden and bubbling. Serve with a green salad with some finely sliced fennel.

Lasagne al Forno

SERVES 8

olive oil	2–3 tbsp
a knob of butter	
large onions, *finely chopped*	2
celery sticks, *chopped*	3
carrots, *finely diced*	3
garlic cloves, *finely chopped*	3 or 4
minced beef (chuck, or similar, with plenty of fat)	1kg/2¼lb
salt and fresh black pepper	
bay leaves	2
milk	240ml/8fl oz
nutmeg, *grated*	about ¼ tsp
white wine	240ml/8fl oz
plum tomatoes	2 × 400g/14oz tins
1.2 litres/2 pints of béchamel, *made with a bay leaf and nutmeg* (see p. 402)	
lasagne sheets	560g/1¼lb
Parmesan cheese, *freshly grated*	

You may make the ragù sauce a day or two in advance, even freeze it, then all you have to do is perfect your béchamel on the day. Use one-third minced pork with the beef if you wish. Please choose a good-quality lasagne to make the dish with, not the cardboardy kind that will ruin your perfect sauce.

→ Warm the OIL and BUTTER in a heavy cast-iron pot, add the ONIONS, and sauté gently until softened and translucent. Add the CELERY, CARROTS and GARLIC, and cook for another couple of minutes, stirring to coat well. Add the MINCED BEEF and a large pinch of SALT, and grind over some PEPPER. Stir until the beef has lost its raw pink look. Add the BAY LEAVES and MILK, and simmer gently for about 10 minutes, until the meat has absorbed most of the milk. Add the NUTMEG, then the WINE, and let it simmer until it has nearly evaporated. Add the cut-up TOMATOES with their juice and stir thoroughly. Cook at a lazy simmer, uncovered and with just an intermittent bubble breaking through the surface, for 3 hours or more. Stir from time to time. The fat will eventually separate from the sauce, but the sauce will not be dry. Taste and check the seasoning.

→ Boil the LASAGNE until tender, then spread the pasta sheets on a clean tea towel to drain. (Alternatively, use the sort of lasagne that does not need precooking, but make sure you use a good brand or the texture is like toasted cardboard.) Make the BÉCHAMEL (see p. 402).

→ Preheat the oven to 200°C/400°F/Gas 6. Pour just enough béchamel to cover the base of your greased baking dish. Add a layer of lasagne, followed by a layer of the ragù, a layer of béchamel, and a good handful of PARMESAN. Continue with two or three more layers, until your sauces are both used up, add a final sprinkling of Parmesan, and bake in the oven for about 30 minutes, The dish should be bubbling all over, and the knife should slip easily through the layers of lasagne. The ragù is also great with spaghetti.

Lasagne di Magro

SERVES 6

fennel bulbs (optional)	4
best olive oil	120ml/4fl oz
medium onions, *finely sliced*	2
medium courgettes, *chopped*	3
medium carrots, *chopped*	2
shelled or frozen peas	225g/8oz
salt and fresh black pepper	
lasagne sheets	560g/1¼lb
béchamel sauce (see p. 402)	up to 850ml/1½ pints
organic chestnut mushrooms, *sliced*	170g/6oz
Parmesan cheese, *freshly grated*	310g/11oz
tomatoes, *skinned and seeded*	8
buffalo mozzarella	4

A deluxe vegetarian lasagne for which you can alter the combination of vegetables according to season and taste.

→ Preheat the oven to 200°C/400°F/Gas 6. If you are using FENNEL, remove the outer tough layers, quarter the bulbs, then steam until almost tender. Heat the OLIVE OIL in a heavy-bottomed pan, add the ONIONS, and a bit of SALT to release the juices. Fry gently until softened and translucent, then add the COURGETTES, CARROTS and PEAS. Season with SALT and PEPPER. Cook until the carrots are al dente, but unbrowned, about 10 minutes.

→ Boil the LASAGNE until tender, then spread the pasta sheets on a clean tea towel to drain. (Alternatively, use the sort of lasagne that does not need precooking, but make sure you use a good brand or the texture is like toasted cardboard.) Make the BÉCHAMEL (see p. 402).

→ Pour just enough béchamel sauce to cover the bottom of your greased baking dish, then add a layer of lasagne. Cover with a layer of the cooked vegetables, then a mantle of béchamel, followed by a handful of sliced raw MUSHROOMS, one of PARMESAN, and one of TOMATOES. Repeat until you have used up all the ingredients.

→ Cover the top with slices of MOZZARELLA, and bake for 25 minutes. Remove from the oven, and allow it to rest and cool for a few minutes before you serve it. As always, garlic bread (see p. 35) and a plain green salad cannot be bettered as accompaniments.

Lasagne with Aubergines

→ For a different texture and flavour, try making this lasagne with aubergines instead of carrots. Cut the AUBERGINES into 2.5cm/1in cubes, brush them with OIL and roast in a hot oven until tender—about 30 minutes. Add to the other vegetables and continue as above.

Roasted Chicken and Leeks with Lemon and Tagliatelle

SERVES 4

onion, *peeled and quartered*	1
organic lemon, *quartered*	1
organic chicken	1 × 1.2kg/2¼lb
onion, *peeled and sliced*	1
butter	85–125g/3–4oz
sea salt	
black pepper	
leeks, *cleaned and trimmed*	8
olive oil	
Tagliatelle	450g/1lb
lemon	juice and finely zested rind of 1

A small organic chicken will feed four or more people, depending on whether the bird or the vegetables have the starring role.

→ Preheat the oven to 200°C/400°F/Gas 6. Quarter a peeled ONION and a whole organic LEMON and put alternate hunks inside the CHICKEN. Place the bird on top of a peeled sliced ONION in a roasting tin. Rub a generous amount of BUTTER on the breast of the bird, and sprinkle over a good pinch of SEA SALT and a generous scrunch of BLACK PEPPER.

→ Cook for 30 minutes, then baste the bird with the buttery juices and throw in the cleaned, trimmed LEEKS cut into short batons, roll them in the butter, and add a splosh of OLIVE OIL. SEASON. Return to the oven for a further half-hour. I add the chicken LIVER to the roasting tin for the final 5 minutes.

→ Meanwhile, bring a large pan of water to the boil. Test the chicken and leeks with a skewer to check they are cooked through. Transfer the chicken to a carving board to rest and allow for a further rush of fugitive juices to escape.

→ Cook your TAGLIATELLE. When al dente, drain the pasta, leaving a bit of cooking water to lubricate it. Return it to the pot, then add a knob of BUTTER, the meat juices, chicken liver and leeks, the juices from the bird's cavity, everything that has collected in the roasting tray, and the juice of a whole LEMON and its ZEST.

→ Quickly carve hunks of hot flesh with their crispy salt skin from the bird and throw them into the pot, mixing all the ingredients before you serve.

Sicilian Pasta Pie

SERVES 6

aubergines	675g/1½lb
vegetable oil for frying	
penne or rigatoni	400g/14oz
fresh tomato sauce (see p. 140)	900ml/1½ pints
Parmesan cheese, *freshly grated*	55g/2oz
dried oregano	1 tbsp
Italian salami (optional)	140g/5oz
hard-boiled eggs, *sliced*	2

In Sicily this is called Pasta 'Ncasciata, the pie being encased—'ncasciata—in the fried aubergines. The salami is optional since the dish already has a rich flavour and texture. This is a stunning dish worthy of a celebration.

→ Cut the AUBERGINES lengthways into thin slices and fry them a few at a time in plenty of hot vegetable oil. They shouldn't absorb a lot of oil if the oil is hot enough and you don't fry too many at a time. When they are golden on both sides, remove the slices and dry them well on kitchen paper.

→ Cook the PASTA, drain it when al dente, and immediately dress it with the TOMATO SAUCE. Add the PARMESAN and OREGANO, mix well, taste and check the seasoning. Slice the SALAMI thickly if using and cut into strips.

fresh buffalo mozzarella, *sliced*	200g/7oz
caciocavallo cheese, *sliced*	55g/2oz
brown breadcrumbs	2 tbsp
extra virgin olive oil	2 tbsp
salt and freshly ground black pepper	

→ Preheat the oven to 190°C/375°F/Gas 5. Line the bottom and sides of an oiled 20cm/8in springform tin with the aubergine slices. Cover the bottom with a layer of pasta, then add sliced EGG, SALAMI, more aubergine and MOZZARELLA and CACIO-CAVALLO slices. Repeat these layers until all the ingredients are used, finishing with a layer of pasta. Sprinkle with the BREAD-CRUMBS and drizzle over the OLIVE OIL. Put in the oven to bake for 30–40 minutes, or until the dish is heated right through.
→ Remove from the oven and run a spatula between the pie and the inside of the tin. Place a round serving dish upside down over the pan and invert the pan onto it. Leave the pie to stand for a few minutes, then unclip the tin and carefully remove it. Remove the base of the tin and serve immediately. If the pie collapses, it hardly matters; the flavour should overwhelm everyone.

Winter Pasticcio

SERVES 4

medium red onions	4
fat leeks, the whites only	4
courgettes	2
fennel bulb	1
organic cherry tomatoes	2 × 200g/7oz punnets
olive oil	
thyme	2–3 sprigs
salt and pepper	
organic penne pasta	340g/12oz
prosciutto OR culatello	6 slices
anchovies	6
garlic clove	1
basil leaves	a handful
Pannarello OR Fontina cheese, *cut into dice*	170g/6oz
mascarpone	2 tbsp

I used red onions, leeks and cherry tomatoes in this delicious dish of penne baked with roasted vegetables. The cheese melted like butter into the pasta and was sharp and strong in equal measure.

→ Preheat the oven to 190°C/375°F/Gas 5. Peel and quarter the ONIONS, peel the LEEKS and cut into 4cm/1½in barrels, and cut the COURGETTES into 2.5cm/1in chunks. Strip the FENNEL of its outer leaves and cut into quarters.
→ Put the vegetables and TOMATOES on a roasting tray and dribble on OLIVE OIL, rolling everything around to cover. Scatter on the THYME, SALT and PEPPER, and put in the oven until roasted and softened, about 30 minutes. Keep the leeks well bathed in oil so they don't brown.
→ Cook the PENNE until al dente in plenty of fast-boiling salted water. Put the torn PROSCIUTTO, ANCHOVIES, GARLIC and BASIL in the food processor with 2–4 tablespoons of olive oil and blitz briefly. You want a coarse-textured gunge rather than a sludge! Turn the contents of the bowl into the drained pasta, add the vegetables, the PANNARELLO or FONTINA and the MASCARPONE and amalgamate well; grind on some more black pepper. Turn into a greased gratin dish, and bake for 20 minutes. You can sprinkle it with flat-leaf parsley to serve and offer PARMESAN if you wish, but it is delicious as is with a plainly dressed salad.

Macaroni Cheese

SERVES 4

béchamel sauce (see p. 402)	up to 850ml/1½ pints
Cheddar cheese, *grated*	170g/6oz
macaroni or penne	450g/1lb
enough butter to grease the dish and dot little bits over the gratin	
garlic clove, *finely chopped* (optional)	1
breadcrumbs, and Parmesan, *grated*	a handful of each

The most important ingredient in this dish is the Cheddar, so choose a well-matured unpasteurised Cheddar such as Montgomery's, Quicke's, Keen's or Daylesford, or the dish will be bland and unremarkable. You may make the upscale model of this with the classic mornay sauce ingredients of half Parmesan to half Gruyère if you would rather. In this case, rather less cheese will be needed to come to full strength, say 55g/2oz each, but check the flavour and up it if you need to.

→ Preheat the oven to 200°C/400°F/Gas 6. Prepare the BÉCHAMEL while you are bringing a huge pan of water to the boil for the PASTA and add the CHEDDAR off the heat to make mornay sauce. Butter a large gratin dish and scatter over the finely chopped GARLIC if you are including it.

→ Drain the pasta, not too thoroughly, tip it into the gratin dish and immediately begin pouring the sauce over it, stirring as you go and allowing the tubes to start absorbing the sauce. Sprinkle the top with PARMESAN or the PARMESAN AND BREADCRUMB mixture, dot with BUTTER and brown in the oven until the top is bubbling and molten, 15–20 minutes.

Eliza Acton's Macaroni à la Reine

SERVES 4

macaroni	450g/1lb
strong unpasteurised Cheddar, *thinly sliced*	285g/10oz
double cream	450ml/16fl oz
unsalted butter, *cut into small cubes*	55g/2oz
extra butter for greasing the dish	
sea salt and black pepper	
mace OR nutmeg, *freshly ground*	
pinch of cayenne	

When Eliza Acton wrote her influential Modern Cookery for Private Families *in 1845, this unfloured, richly creamed version of macaroni cheese graced the pages. I have made a few small alterations to update it. This is exceptionally rich and needs no more than a plain green salad to follow.*

→ Cook the PASTA as per the instructions. While it is cooking, melt the thinly sliced CHEESE in the CREAM over a low heat, stirring constantly. Stir in the cubes of BUTTER and season with the SALT, PEPPER and SPICES.

→ Drain the macaroni and put it into a buttered gratin dish. Pour the sauce over it and stir well until it has been properly absorbed. Brown in a hot oven, 200°C/400°F/Gas 6 for about 15 minutes. You may, Eliza suggests, substitute Stilton for half of the Cheddar.

Pasta with Chicken Liver Sauce

SERVES 4

fresh organic chicken livers	340g/12oz
milk	
spaghetti, tagliatelle OR pappardelle	450g/1lb
shallot OR small onion, *finely chopped*	1
olive oil	1 tbsp
unsalted butter	30g/1oz
small garlic clove, *finely minced*	1
organic smoked back bacon (optional)	2 rashers
OR prosciutto	2 slices
sage OR basil	6 leaves
frozen petits pois	225g/8oz
sea salt and black pepper	
white wine OR vermouth	4 tbsp
unsalted butter	a knob
Parmesan cheese, *freshly grated*	

Always buy organic chicken livers. Any residue from any chemicals or drugs used in the rearing of animals collects in the organs, and the flavour of organic livers really is better. This is an inexpensive dish even with organic livers.

→ Trim the CHICKEN LIVERS and remove any green patches, fatty bits or tubes. Soak the livers in MILK for about 20 minutes. Put a large pan of water on to come to the boil before adding your PASTA.

→ Meanwhile, put the SHALLOT OR ONION in a heavy-bottomed frying pan with the OLIVE OIL and BUTTER and sauté over a medium heat until it begins to soften. Add the minced GARLIC and cook it for a couple of minutes; you don't want it to go brown. Then add the BACON OR PROSCIUTTO cut or torn into strips and the SAGE OR BASIL LEAVES. In another small pan, boil some water, throw in the PEAS and boil them for a couple of minutes. Drain. Cook the bacon or prosciutto for a minute before adding the chicken livers, which you have patted dry and cut in half. Season with SALT and PEPPER, and turn the livers as each side begins to colour and lose its raw look. When they are coloured all over, add the WINE OR VERMOUTH and allow it to bubble before adding the peas. Check the livers, they MUST stay pink in the middle. The dish is completely cooked once they are rosy-middled without looking raw inside, about 5 minutes after the wine has been introduced to the sauce. Check the seasoning.

→ Turn the pan out over the drained, cooked pasta to which you've added a lump of BUTTER and toss well to coat it all in the sauce. Serve immediately with a bowl of freshly grated PARMESAN on the side.

Spaghetti Bolognese

SERVES 6–8

olive oil	2–3 tbsp
butter	a knob
large onions, *finely chopped*	2
celery sticks, *chopped*	3
carrots, *finely diced*	3
garlic cloves, *finely chopped*	3 or 4
minced beef (chuck, or similar, with plenty of fat)	1kg/2¼ lb
salt, and black pepper, *freshly ground*	
bay leaves	2
milk	240ml/8fl oz
nutmeg	
white wine	240ml/8fl oz
plum tomatoes, *cut up*	2 × 400g/14oz tins
spaghetti	900g/2lb
Parmesan cheese, *freshly grated*	

A ragù is characterised by its mellow, gentle flavour, so don't blanch at the idea of adding milk to the meat first. It protects the meat from the acidic bite of the tomatoes you add later. Whatever you do, don't ask for lean mince. You need a good marbling of fat for a sweeter, tastier ragù than you will ever get without it. You can add ⅓ part pork mince to the beef if you wish.

→ Warm the OIL and BUTTER in a heavy cast-iron pot, add the ONIONS, and sauté gently until softened and translucent. Add the CELERY, CARROTS and GARLIC, and cook for another couple of minutes, stirring to coat well. Add the BEEF and a large pinch of SALT, and grind over some PEPPER. Stir until the beef has lost its raw pink look.

→ Add the BAY LEAVES and MILK, and simmer gently for about 10 minutes, until the meat has absorbed the milk. Add a suspicion of NUTMEG, about ¼ teaspoon. Add the WINE, and let it simmer until it has evaporated, then add the cut-up TOMATOES with their JUICE and stir thoroughly.

→ Cook uncovered at a lazy simmer, with just an intermittent bubble breaking through the surface, for 3 hours or more. Give it a stir whenever you happen to be passing. Eventually the fat will separate from the sauce, but it will not be dry. Taste, and correct the SEASONING.

→ Cook the SPAGHETTI in plenty of boiling, salted water according to the instructions on the packet. Drain unthoroughly, without shaking the colander, so that there is still water on the pasta when you return it to the pan. Stir in a knob of BUTTER with a splosh of good OLIVE OIL, then stir in the sauce. Serve freshly grated PARMESAN separately.

Mozzarella-stuffed Meatballs with Tagliatelle and Fresh Tomato Sauce

SERVES 4–6

onion	1
garlic cloves	2
flat-leaf parsley, *chopped*	handful

→ Mince the ONION, GARLIC and PARSLEY together in a liquidiser or food processor and add them to the MEAT in a large bowl. Sprinkle in the chopped fresh THYME or MARJORAM, some SALT and PEPPER, and then work in the beaten EGG with your fingers or a wooden spoon. Cut the MOZZARELLA into 1cm/½in cubes. Roll into meat mixture into balls the size of an extra-large marble, pushing a cube of mozzarella into the centre of each. Roll very lightly in FLOUR, and cook in a large frying pan in a generous amount of OLIVE OIL, turning to brown all over.

minced beef	450g/1lb
thyme or marjoram, *chopped*	1 tsp
salt and pepper	
egg, *beaten*	1
buffalo mozzarella, *cut into 1cm/½ in cubes*	½
flour	
olive oil	6–7 tbsp
tomato sauce (see p. 140)	
tagliatelle	

→ Remove from the pan to a warmed gratin dish, and pour over a quantity of TOMATO SAUCE (see p. 140). Serve with some tagliatelle.

Pasta con le Sarde

SERVES 4

sultanas and pine nuts	a handful
onion, *peeled and chopped*	1
good olive oil	
fennel bulbs, *finely chopped*	2
anchovies, *chopped*	4
fresh sardines, *chopped*	225g/8oz
fresh sardines, *filleted*	225g/8oz
fennel seeds	1 tsp
pepper	
penne	450g/1lb

This is another of the lovely Italian food writer Anna Del Conte's recipes, which I have cooked for summer lunches and suppers for the last three or four years. It is very hard to get really fresh sardines here, but I find the Portuguese frozen ones that are sold by the box in my fishmongers are probably better tasting than the fresh. They have been frozen so soon after being caught that they haven't lost the oily fresh flavour that turns to rancid so quickly with all the oily fish like sardines, mackerel and herring.

→ Soak the SULTANAS in warm water for 10 minutes and drain, and toast the PINE NUTS. Lightly fry the ONION in OLIVE OIL and add the pine nuts and sultanas. Blanch the FENNEL for 1 minute, before adding to the onion for another 15 minutes. Add a little of the blanching liquor liquid if the mixture is too dry.

→ Add the ANCHOVIES to the pan, with the CHOPPED FRESH SARDINES. Scatter over 1 teaspoon of FENNEL SEEDS, season with PEPPER and cook for a further 10 minutes.

→ Preheat the oven to 200°C/400°F/Gas 6. Meanwhile, cook the PENNE until it is al dente. Drain, turn into the sauce and transfer to an oiled gratin dish. Add the FILLETS OF SARDINES and a further libation of olive oil. Cover with foil and bake in a hot oven for 15 minutes.

Seafood Spaghetti

Everyone has their own favourite version of this, mine varies seasonally and according to what the fish shop has in that day, but it wouldn't be right without a stack of shells and pink carapaces. Carpetshell clams from Devon are as pretty as they are salty-sweet, and with langoustines, mussels and scallops the dish is done.

Serves 2

clams	225g/8oz
mussels	225g/8oz
langoustines OR large, raw prawns	4
scallops with their coral	2 large or 4 small
medium onion	1
garlic cloves	2
fennel bulb	1
celery stick	1
saffron stamens	large pinch
extra virgin olive oil	2–3 tbsp
freshly-podded peas	110g/4oz or so
butter	a knob
Pernod	2 tbsp
dry white wine	½ glass or so
organic tomatoes	4
flat-leaf parsley and basil, *chopped*	1 tbsp each
sea salt and black pepper	
spaghetti	225g/8oz

→ Scrub the CLAMS and MUSSELS and remove any weedy-looking beards. Clean the SCALLOPS and separate the coral from the white, cutting each disc into 2–3 slices. Peel and finely chop the ONION and GARLIC. Remove the tough outer layer of the FENNEL and dice, and string and finely chop the CELERY. Soak the SAFFRON stamens in a few tablespoons of warm water for 20 minutes.

→ Warm the OLIVE OIL in a large, heavy-bottomed pan and stew the onion, garlic, fennel and celery gently until they are softened and translucent. In the meantime, get a large cauldron of water to the boil for the PASTA ready to cook to al dente and co-ordinate with the sauce. Put the PEAS in a small pan with a little water and a knob of butter, and stew gently until tender. Leave in the pan.

→ Heat a little OLIVE OIL in a small frying pan and put in the LANGOUSTINES. Cook until the underside turns pink before turning over and cooking the other side similarly. Remove from the heat. Pour the PERNOD over the softened onion and allow it to bubble and steam for a minute before adding the WHITE WINE and SAFFRON. Bring to the boil, add the clams and mussels and cook under a lid briefly until they have opened.

→ Throw in the scallops with their coral to cook briefly in the pan (they will take no more than a minute), adding the langoustines at the same time. Season and throw in the TOMATOES, which you have skinned, seeded and diced, and the peas. Remove from the heat immediately and sloosh the sauce into the almost drained pasta in the pan, adding a knob of butter. Turn to mix over the heat for a minute. Remove from the heat, throw over the HERBS and serve in hot bowls with an extra bowl on the table to hurl the empty shells into.

Risoni with Seafood and Roasted Vegetables

SERVES 4

risoni (rice-shaped pasta)	350g/12oz
small aubergine, *cut into 2.5cm/1in cubes*	1
onion, *cut into thin wedges*	1
red pepper, *cut into 2.5cm/1in pieces*	1
large plum tomato, *cut into thin wedges*	1
garlic cloves, *finely chopped*	2
olive oil	85ml/3fl oz
coarse sea salt	½ tsp
prepared squid, *cut into thin rings*	110g/4oz
raw tiger prawns	225g/8oz
sundried tomatoes in olive oil, *sliced small*	3
red chilli, *seeded and chopped small*	1
white wine vinegar	1 tbsp
flat-leaf parsley, *chopped*	5 tbsp
salt, and pepper, *freshly ground*	
rocket (optional)	55g/2oz

→ Preheat the oven to 220°C/425°F/Gas 7.

→ Cook the PASTA until al dente, drain and leave to cool. A little slug of OLIVE OIL splashed over after draining prevents it from sticking unpleasantly. Put the AUBERGINE, ONION, RED PEPPER and fresh TOMATO in a bowl with the GARLIC, 2 tablespoons of OLIVE OIL and the SEA SALT, and mix well. Roast, spread out in a small tin, for about 30 minutes until well coloured around the edges. Leave to cool.

→ Heat a tablespoon of OLIVE OIL in a frying pan, add the SQUID, and fry over a high heat for 2½ minutes until lightly browned. Season with SALT and PEPPER and leave to cool. Peel the PRAWNS and fry them in olive oil until pink.

→ When the pasta, vegetables and squid are barely warm, put them in a large bowl with the remaining OIL, PRAWNS, SUNDRIED TOMATO, CHILLI, VINEGAR, 4 tablespoons of PARSLEY, 1 teaspoon of SALT and a few good scrunches of BLACK PEPPER. Toss together lightly, then fold in the ROCKET if you've decided to use it. Spoon everything on to a large plate, and sprinkle with the remaining parsley.

FISH
& Sh

ellfish

Lobster

<small>SERVES 6</small>

lobster	1 per person
olive oil	5 tbsp
Dijon mustard	1 tbsp
parsley, tarragon and chives, *chopped*	a handful
shallot, *finely chopped*	1 heaped tbsp
soya sauce	12 drops
freshly-ground white pepper	
small glass of anisette, pastis or Pernod	

The best-tasting lobsters weigh 675g–900g/1lb 8oz–2lb so don't be cajoled into buying a large brute and assume you'll get more or better for your money. You won't. In fact, the best thing to do is buy a whole lobster per person if they weigh around the 500g/1lb 2oz mark and you want to serve them for a main course.

To my mind, the method of plunging the creatures into fast-boiling water is as acceptably brief a method of killing as possible, but you do have a choice. If you don't like the thought of it, don't do it and don't eat lobster. There's another method for those who know the creature's anatomy to perform it accurately. At the top of the shell where the two side pieces of shell and the head intersect, there is the pattern of a cross. You may spear a thin but firm-bladed sharp knife down through the middle of the cross where the lines meet, which will sever the lobster's central nervous system instantly. Death, therefore, is also instantaneous.

→ A lobster is best cooked in seawater, the water it came from. Failing that, use a heavy hand with the salt. Bring a very large pan of salted water up to a rolling boil, then drop in the LOBSTERS. A 500g/1-and-a-bit pounder should take 10 minutes, add another 10 minutes for each further 500g/1lb or so. The spiny lobster or crawfish, to my mind sweeter, subtler and better-textured than lobster, should be cooked in the same way.

→ To eat your lobster cold with the dressing, take it out of the water it has cooked in and let it cool before serving. You may split the lobster lengthwise if you like, starting at the head with a sharp knife point and cutting straight down through the middle of the shell to the end of the tail. Then pull out the black intestine that runs down the back. Crack the claws if you like. Otherwise, let people tackle their lobster with crackers and picks.

→ For the dressing, simply mix ALL THE INGREDIENTS together. Serve with the lobster or remove the meat from the lobsters, dice and fold into the dressing.

Hot Grilled Lobster with Piquant Cream Sauce

SERVES 6

cooked lobster	
shallots, *finely minced*	2
unsalted butter	45g/1½oz
Madeira OR fino (dry sherry)	1 glass
béchamel sauce (see p. 402)	600ml/1 pint
Dijon mustard	1 dsrtsp
OR chopped anchovies	3
OR mixed Gruyère and Parmesan cheese, *grated*	a handful
sea salt, pepper and cayenne	
breadcrumbs and *grated* Gruyère for the top	a handful each
butter, *melted*	30g/1oz

Rich though it is, the strange thing is that hot lobster is best set off with a rich sauce, even if it is the simplest of them all—melted hot butter with a spritz of lemon and black pepper.

→ First remove the meat from the cooked LOBSTERS and dice. Sweat the SHALLOTS in the melted BUTTER gently until softened, before adding the MADEIRA OR SHERRY and reducing it to 1 tablespoon. Add the hot BÉCHAMEL sauce and either the MUSTARD, ANCHOVIES OR CHEESE to taste. SEASON, going easy on the cayenne (add only a knife tip first) and tasting as you go.

→ Put a little sauce in the base of the shells then add the lobster meat and more sauce. Put the mixed BREADCRUMBS AND CHEESE on top and dribble over the melted butter. Put the lobster shells on a baking tray under a hot grill and let them bubble and brown—keep a close watch on them. Take the lobsters out from under the grill and serve.

A Simple Fritter Batter

plain flour	110g/4oz
salt	a pinch
olive oil	3 tbsp
water	about 150ml/5fl oz
egg white	1

This is great for shellfish such as mussels, clams and scallops.

→ Sieve the FLOUR and SALT into a bowl and whisk in the OLIVE OIL and WATER. Continue whisking for a few minutes. Leave the batter to rest for a couple of hours, then whisk the EGG WHITE stiffly and fold it in. Dip the fish into the batter and fry briefly until delectably bronzed. Drain on kitchen paper and serve with the Asian dressing on p. 411 or the crème fraîche tartare on p. 407.

Tempura Batter

chilled water	200ml/7fl oz
plain flour	55g/2oz
potato flour	55g/2oz
salt	

→ Whisk the chilled WATER with both FLOURS and a pinch of SALT until light and frothy. Despite its lumpy appearance, this makes a light, crisp, coating batter for things like prawns.

Fish Stew with a Rouille

Serves 8

Fish stock

fish bones	1.5–1.8kg/3–4lb
4 litres/7 pints water	
fennel bulbs, *chopped*	2
celery sticks, *chopped with leaves*	2
onions, *chopped*	2
tomatoes, *quartered*	6
tomato purée	1 tbsp
saffron; splash of Pernod (optional)	

Stew

red mullet, *filleted, boned weight*	675g/1½lb
monkfish tail, *boned*	675g/1½lb
squid, *cleaned and cut into rings*	450g/1lb
large prawns in shells	450g/1lb

Rouille

peppers, *roasted and peeled*	150g/5oz
red chilli, *seeded*	1
day-old bread, *crustless*	1 slice
small garlic cloves, *peeled*	5
olive oil	120–170ml/4–6fl oz

→ First make an intensely flavoured fish stock with the FISH BONES. Sole and turbot are good, and I add prawn or crab shells to enhance the flavour and colour. Add the WATER, bring to the boil, remove scum and simmer for 30 minutes. Sieve and discard the bones. Simmer for a further 30 minutes.

→ Add the OTHER INGREDIENTS. Simmer until softened, press through a sieve and SEASON. You can refrigerate this overnight, then the stew will take a mere three minutes to cook after reheating the soup.

Stew

→ I used the fish listed, but improvise if you prefer to use other types. Cut the FISH into generous, 5cm/2in chunks, and throw them into the barely simmering pot of fish stock. They are ready as soon as they lose their translucence, about 3 minutes. Put in the peeled PRAWNS, and serve with toasted slices of baguette and rouille.

Rouille

→ Process together the roasted, peeled PEPPERS – if you are feeling lazy, the supermarkets sell a good brand imported by Brindisa – with the CHILLI, a crustless slice of day-old BREAD soaked in water and wrung out, and the GARLIC. Pour the OLIVE OIL in a steady stream into the processor until you have a sumptuously thickened vermilion ointment. Taste and season.

Zarzuela

Serves 6

mixed fish: tuna, swordfish, squid, monkfish	1kg/2¼lb
limes	pulp and juice of 2
garlic cloves, *chopped*	4
medium onions, *peeled and chopped*	4
fennel bulbs, *thinly sliced*	4
tomatoes, *skinned, seeded and chopped*	6–8

This is the most versatile of recipes, on which you can improvise according to your taste, your budget and what is in season.

→ I always include SQUID. If the squid are large, blanch them in the pulp and juice of two LIMES, then slice into rings. Cut the OTHER FISH into 8cm/3in pieces.

→ Fry the GARLIC, ONIONS and FENNEL in OLIVE OIL until softened and translucent: it takes about 20 minutes. In a large, heavy-bottomed casserole, put a layer of half this mixture, followed by the FIRMER FISH and the skinned, seeded and chopped TOMATOES. Then a layer of CHICKPEAS and squid, followed by another layer of the onion mixture. Top this with

chickpeas, *soaked, cooked*
225g/8oz

yellow peppers,
seeded and finely sliced   2–3

cherry tomatoes   450g/1lb

saffron threads   a generous pinch

dry white wine   300ml/10fl oz

fish stock (see p.168) 300ml/10fl oz

limes   juice of 2

saffron   a generous pinch

olive oil

salt and pepper

fresh coriander   a handful

the YELLOW PEPPERS and the CHERRY TOMATOES. Mix together the WINE, FISH STOCK and LIME JUICE and add the SAFFRON. Pour the saffrony liquid over the fish, it will not cover, then bring the whole dish very slowly up to the boil.

→ I find if you have completed this process slowly enough, it will be cooked when it reaches boiling point, but test the peppers to see if they're soft. A sprinkle of chopped CORIANDER completes the dish.

La Bourride

SERVES 4

white fish, *cut into
bite-sized chunks*   900g/2lb

Court bouillon

white wine vinegar   2 tbsp

white wine   300ml/10fl oz

onion   1

bay leaf   1

orange peel   a strip

fennel

fish heads   2 or 3
—ask the fishmonger

carrot, *chopped*   1

celery stick, *chopped*   1

onion, *quartered in its skin*   1

Aïoli

fresh garlic cloves   6–12

sea salt and black pepper

organic egg yolks   3

best Provençal
olive oil   up to 425ml/15fl oz

lemon   juice of ½

A Provençal bourride of gently poached white fish, with a pungent, heaving-with-garlic aïoli stirred into it, is superb. Use up to three of the following fish: hake, cod, bass, bream, John Dory, monkfish.

→ To make the court bouillon, bring a pan of water to the boil with the white wine VINEGAR, white WINE, ONION, BAY LEAF, ORANGE PEEL, FENNEL and FISH HEADS. Add the CARROT, CELERY and ONION. Simmer for about 30 minutes, then let it cool. Strain.

→ For the fish bourride, bring the COURT BOUILLON to the boil, then add bite-sized chunks of FISH, allowing about 225g/8oz per person, in order of thickness. Monkfish is chunkier and will take a little longer to cook (3–4 minutes), thinner slices will take 2–3 minutes, small hake steaks on the bone 5–6 minutes. The bouillon should be at a gentle simmer. Remove the pan from the heat. Gently place the fish in a warm tureen with a couple of ladles of court bouillon. Put a tablespoon of AÏOLI into a bowl and stir a ladleful of the bouillon into it, before returning the mixture to the tureen with the fish. Sprinkle with PARSLEY. Serve the rest of the aïoli separately.

Aïoli

→ Crush the GARLIC with a little SEA SALT in a mortar until it is a creamy paste. Beat in the EGG YOLKS. Whisk in the OLIVE OIL, first drip by drip, then in a thin, steady stream when you have an emulsion. Add the LEMON JUICE and season.

Fish Pie

SERVES 6

haddock, cod, coley or pollack, *skinned and filleted*	1.4kg/3lb
natural smoked haddock	110g/4oz
milk	300–425ml/10–15fl oz
butter	30g/1oz
leeks, white parts, *chopped small*	2
potatoes	1kg/2¼ lb
plain flour	30g/1oz
bay leaf	1
nutmeg, *grated*	
salt and pepper	
fresh dill, *chopped*	a bunch
flat-leaf parsley, *chopped*	a bunch
prawns, if feeling flush	110g/4oz
eggs, *softly hard-boiled* (optional)	2

The best nursery-cum-comfort food there is, this may be the most basic of fish pies, but none the worse for it. Add some raw scallops, cleaned and sliced, instead of prawns if you like.

→ Preheat the oven to 180°C/350°F/Gas 4. Put the piece of HADDOCK, COD, COLEY OR POLLACK in a gratin dish with the smoked HADDOCK, 300ml/10fl oz of the MILK and a knob of BUTTER, and bake for 15 minutes. Turn the fish into a deeper baking dish, flaking it gently and extracting any bones, but keeping it in largish bits. Reserve the cooking liquid. Gently simmer the LEEKS in the cooking milk until soft. Boil the POTATOES and mash thoroughly.

→ Melt the rest of the BUTTER in a saucepan, add the FLOUR and cook, stirring, for 1 minute. Add the BAY LEAF and a good pinch of NUTMEG, and gradually stir in the liquid from the fish to make a béchamel sauce. Taste and adjust the SEASONING, add the DILL and PARSLEY, then pour the sauce over the fish. Add the PRAWNS if you have them. You could also add a couple of quartered, softly hard-boiled EGGS to the cooked fish before mixing with the béchamel.

→ Top the pie with mashed POTATO and cook in the oven for 15–20 minutes, until browned and bubbling on top.

Fish Pie with Rosti

SERVES 6–8

cod	675g/1½lb
bay leaf	1
peppercorns	1 dsrtsp
dry vermouth OR white wine	150ml/5fl oz
milk	300ml/10fl oz
natural smoked haddock	450g/1lb
quails' eggs	12
spinach	900g/2lb
butter	85g/3oz
plain flour	2 tbsp
crème fraîche	200ml/7fl oz
single cream	300ml/10fl oz

My cousin Deborah, a very fine cook, with whom I always share recipe and restaurant gossip, dreamt up this delicious fish pie with a crisp top of cheesy rosti. The base layer of spinach, such a natural partner to smoked haddock, means the only other thing you'll need is a crisp salad of bitter leaves. The quails' eggs are well worth the trouble.

→ Preheat the oven to 200°C/400°F/Gas 6. Poach the piece of COD with the BAY LEAF and half the PEPPERCORNS in the VERMOUTH and a little water for about 7 minutes, or until just cooked. Bring the MILK to scalding point, pour it over the smoked HADDOCK in a gratin dish with the rest of the PEPPERCORNS, and let it rest for about 10 minutes. You may turn it over; the fish is smoked, so it is already cooked, but it needs to be tender so you can flake it. Drain all the fish, keeping both lots of fish liquor, flake, skin and de-bone it. Boil the QUAILS' EGGS for 3 minutes and shell.

→ Gently steam the SPINACH in no more than the residue from

tiger prawns, shelled weight	225g/8oz
flat-leaf parsley, *chopped*	2 tbsp
salt, pepper	

Topping

good, mature Cheddar cheese	85g/3oz
potatoes, *peeled*	900g/2lb
butter	85g/3oz

the water you have washed it in, until it has wilted, stirring so that it doesn't stick. This will take 3–4 minutes. Drain it thoroughly, and place a layer of it, with a good scrunch of BLACK PEPPER, at the base of an ovenproof dish.

→ Melt the BUTTER, add the FLOUR, and make a nutty golden roux, then whisk in the hot fish liquors. Stir in the CRÈME FRAÎCHE and CREAM, then the TIGER PRAWNS and PARSLEY; season and remove from the heat. Place the COD and HADDOCK on top of the SPINACH, pour over the sauce and prawns. Halve the quails' eggs, and push them into the mixture.

→ Grate the CHEESE, then coarsely grate the POTATOES, a food processor will do it fine, and mix them with the melted BUTTER. Pile on top of the fish and bake for 45–60 minutes, until the top is seductively golden and crunchy.

Cod, Fennel and Smoked Bacon Pie

SERVES 6

cod, *boned, filleted, cut a good 2.5cm/1in thick*	1kg/2¼lb
fennel bulbs	4
organic smoked back bacon	3 slices
béchamel sauce *made with 50g/2oz each butter and flour, and 600ml/1 pint milk* (see p. 402)	
flat-leaf parsley, *finely chopped*	2 tbsp
chives, *finely chopped*	2 tbsp
potatoes, *steamed and mashed with butter and milk*	1kg/2¼lb
salt and pepper	

→ Preheat oven to 180°C/350°F/Gas 4. Cut the COD into the same-sized chunks you would for a meat stew, and put them in the bottom of a deepish ovenproof dish. SEASON.

→ Trim the FENNEL, removing any faintly stringy, woody layers, and cut into quarters vertically. Steam the quarters of fennel until just unresistant at their base, and add them to the fish. Snip the BACON into fine strips, and fry until browned in a small pan, drain and add to the dish. Any more than 3 rashers would, I feel, overwhelm the pie.

→ Pour in the seasoned BÉCHAMEL SAUCE, into which you have stirred the fresh HERBS off the heat. It might not appear to be enough, but remember that cod exudes quite a bit of juice.

→ Cover with mashed POTATO, furrow the surface with a fork, dot with butter, and cook for 35–40 minutes until browned and bubbling.

Leek, Pollack and Smoked Bacon Pie

→ Pollack makes a good alternative for this pie. Watch out for the bones. Use leeks, green parts as well as white, instead of fennel, steaming them before adding to the fish. You can add a small amount of smoked haddock too, if you wish – about 140g/5oz is enough.

Codcakes with Kaffir Lime Leaves and Thai Dipping Sauce

SERVES 2

shallot, *peeled and chopped*	1
garlic cloves, *peeled and crushed*	2
small hot red chillies, *seeded and chopped*	2
fresh coriander leaves, *coarsely chopped*	a handful
kaffir lime leaves, *cut into strips*	8
Thai fish sauce (nam pla)	1 tbsp
sea salt	
cod fillet	450g/1lb
groundnut OR grapeseed oil	

Thai Dipping Sauce

rice vinegar	6 tbsp
light muscovado sugar	4 tbsp
organic shoyu sauce	1 tbsp
small red chilli, *seeded and finely chopped*	1
small green chilli, *seeded and finely chopped*	1
coriander leaves, *very finely chopped*	1 tbsp
kaffir limes	juice of 2
OR lime	juice of 1

You can make the codcake mixture in advance and keep it covered in the fridge until frying time. The dipping sauce keeps equally well and should be served cold. These cod cakes also make a sensational first course, in which case they will feed four.

→ Place the SHALLOT, GARLIC, CHILLIES and CORIANDER in a food processor with the LIME LEAVES and FISH SAUCE and blitz. Scrape into a bowl and season with SEA SALT. Throw chunks of COD into the processor and blitz to a paste, not a sludge. Tip the fish into the other ingredients and mix everything together thoroughly.

→ Flour your hands a little to prevent sticking and form the mixture into 8 flat patties. Cover the patties and put them in the fridge until an hour before you want to use them. Heat about 6 tablespoons of OIL in a frying pan. Fry the codcakes until golden on each side (about 4 minutes). Drain on kitchen paper and serve with the sauce.

Thai Dipping Sauce

Heat the VINEGAR and SUGAR in a small pan until the sugar has dissolved and the mixture is syrupy. Stir in the SHOYU sauce. Leave to cool before adding the CHILLIES, CORIANDER and LIME JUICE. Chill.

Salmon Fishcakes

SERVES 6

wild salmon, *cooked*	about 600g/1lb 4oz
cooked potato, *mashed without milk and butter*	285g/10oz
sea salt and freshly ground black pepper	
flat-leaf parsley, *chopped*	a handful
stale wholemeal bread	85g/3oz

Salmon fishcakes should be made with the leftovers from a perfectly moist wild salmon whose flesh has slightly gelled overnight, been flaked but not crushed to a pulp, and bound with some dry, smooth, unbuttery mashed potato and a healthy seasoning of flat-leaf parsley, coarsely ground pepper and sea salt. If you don't have the amount of salmon listed here, the fishcakes are still delicious with half potato, half salmon.

→ Mash the SALMON into the POTATO roughly so it still has coarse-textured flakes and is not a homogeneous purée. SEASON and throw in the PARSLEY, then shape the mixture into 12 2.5cm/1in thick cakes and place them on a large flat plate. Keep covered in the fridge for an hour or two to firm up, or

organic eggs	2
vegetable or olive oil for frying	

longer if it is convenient. Cut the BREAD into small squares, bake in a slow oven for 15 minutes to dry out, then put in a food processor to whizz into crumbs.

→ Whisk the EGGS and pour onto a large flat plate, and spread the dried BREADCRUMBS on another. Dip the fishcakes first in the EGG on both sides, then turn them in the breadcrumbs, making sure the sides are well crumbed too. Place them on a third large plate. Heat a shallow film of OIL, about 60ml/2fl oz, in a frying pan over a medium heat. Put the fishcakes in and fry for 4 minutes or so a side until golden . Drain on kitchen paper and serve with a dollop of crème fraîche tartare (see p. 407).

Smoked Haddock Fishcakes

SERVES 6

fresh haddock fillet	675g/1½lb
natural smoked haddock	340g/12oz
milk	
butter	
black pepper	
medium potatoes, *peeled, steamed and mashed*	3
celery salt	¼ tsp
cayenne pepper	a scant fork-end
flat-leaf parsley, *chopped*	2 heaped tbsp
egg, *beaten*	1
flour, salt and pepper	
olive oil	

A small piece of smoked haddock with the fresh lifts this dish transcendently. Too much would overwhelm.

→ Preheat the oven to 180°C/350°F/Gas 4. Grease a gratin dish with butter and lay your FISH FILLETS in it. Add a splosh of milk, dot with little pieces of BUTTER, season with BLACK PEPPER and cook in the oven for 15 minutes. With a spoon and fork, flake away the fish from the skin into large chunks, and pile it on the top of the MASHED POTATO. Add the CELERY SALT and smidgen of CAYENNE, then scatter on a confetti of PARSLEY. Season, remembering that the smoked haddock is quite salt. Mash together lightly: you want the fish to be flaky, not pulverised to a paste.

→ Have three large plates in front of you, one empty, one with the beaten EGG, and one with some seasoned FLOUR. Flour your hands, grab a fishcake's worth of the mixture and mould it before dipping it in the egg, then coating in flour. Shake off the excess and place the cake on the clean plate. This quantity should make 12 fishcakes.

→ Heat a good quantity of OLIVE OIL, 6 tablespoons or so, until hot, and cook the fishcakes until well bronzed on both sides. About 5–6 minutes a side should do it. Serve with lemon wedges and a leafy vegetable like purple sprouting broccoli.

Crabcakes

SERVES 4,
ALLOWING 2 CRABCAKES EACH

milk	3–4 tbsp
wholemeal bread, *crusts removed*	2 thin slices
crab meat, brown and white	450g/1lb
mayonnaise	1 large tbsp
cayenne pepper OR harissa	small pinch
dry English mustard	¼ tsp
celery salt	¼ tsp
flat-leaf parsley OR fresh coriander, *chopped*	1 tbsp
Worcestershire sauce	
salt and pepper	
egg, *beaten*	1
olive oil, for shallow frying	

In Britain we make fishcakes with potato to bind them. The Americans often use bread soaked in milk, as one does for taramasalata, and the result is a light-textured but scrumptiously spicy, crisp crabcake.

→ Pour the MILK over the BREAD, let it soak in, then squeeze out the bread until it is moderately dry. Put it in a bowl and mash it with a fork. Add ALL THE REMAINING INGREDIENTS except the egg, mix well and season to taste. Add the beaten EGG, then shape the mixture into eight cakes, working quickly and lightly.
→ Heat the OIL in a large frying pan, drop in the crabcakes and cook until crisp, about 3 minutes on each side. Serve with a herb mayonnaise (see p. 404).

Brandade Tart

SERVES 6 AS A MAIN COURSE

shortcrust pastry case	23cm/9 in
egg, *beaten*, for brushing	
large potato, about 150g/5oz, *peeled*	1
chunk of salt cod	450g/1lb
extra virgin olive oil	150–300ml/5–10fl oz
creamy milk	150–300ml/5–10fl oz
garlic cloves	3
lemon	1
black pepper	
Provençal black olives and flat-leaf parsley	

Make sure you use your best olive oil for this dish. The salt cod has to be soaked in several changes of water for at least 24 hours before using, then drained.

→ Make the SHORTCRUST PASTRY and bake the tart case (see p. 104). Steam the POTATO in chunks until cooked, then mash it or put it through the coarse blade of a mouli-légumes.
→ Run your fingers over the soaked COD and use tweezers to pull out any bones. Either put the fish in a saucepan of cold water, bring to the boil, switch off instantly and leave for a few minutes, or pour boiling water over it to cover and leave for 10–15 minutes, until a fork can flake it without resistance.
→ Preheat the oven to 220°C/425°F/Gas 7. Warm the OLIVE OIL in a saucepan and do likewise with the milk and garlic in another pan. Skin the cod and put it in chunks into a food processor, switch on, and pour in the olive oil and milk alternately, in a slow, steady stream. You can either add or discard the GARLIC. When you have a thick paste, turn it into a bowl and stir in the mashed potato with a wooden spoon. Add the juice

of up to the whole LEMON, to taste, and BLACK PEPPER. You won't need salt. Turn into the pastry case or and place in the preheated oven for 5 minutes. Decorate with the OLIVES and PARSLEY, and serve warm.

Smoked Haddock and Watercress Tart

SERVES 6

shortcrust pastry (see p. 104)	
smoked haddock	325g/12oz
creamy milk	300ml/10fl oz
butter	30g/1oz
small onion, *finely chopped*	1
celery stick, *finely chopped*	1
plain flour	30g/1oz
salt and pepper	
nutmeg, *grated*	
watercress, *finely chopped*	a bunch
eggs, *beaten*	2
Parmesan cheese, *grated*	2 tbsp

This is an unusual way of using smoked haddock, which seems to have as much of an affinity with the peppery, iron-rich leaves of watercress as it does with spinach.

→ Make the SHORTCRUST PASTRY, line a 23cm/9in tart tin with a removable base and bake blind (see p. 104).

→ Preheat the oven to 190°C/375°F/Gas 5. Put the HADDOCK and MILK in a saucepan and bring to the boil, then reduce the heat and simmer very gently for 10 minutes. Skin the fish and flake it into a bowl. Reserve the poaching milk.

→ Heat the BUTTER in a saucepan, add the ONION and CELERY and cook until softened. Stir in the FLOUR and cook for a couple of minutes, then add the reserved POACHING MILK and stir until the sauce has thickened. Season to taste with SALT, PEPPER AND NUTMEG. Remove from the heat and stir into the fish, adding the WATERCRESS and beaten EGGS. Pour into the pastry case and sprinkle the top with PARMESAN. Bake in the oven for 25–30 minutes, when the tart will be risen and crusted with golden brown. Leave to cool slightly and turn out onto a plate.

Smoked Haddock and Spinach Tart

→ You may use spinach instead of watercress if you prefer. Wash 450g/1lb of spinach and cook in the water clinging to the leaves until just wilted. Press through the strainer to extract as much water as possible or you will have a soggy tart.

Hot-roast Salmon, Leek and Potato Tourte

SERVES 6

potatoes, *cooked and skinned*	450g/1lb
leeks, *thinly sliced*	450g/1lb
butter	
filo pastry	a packet
hot-roast salmon	225g/8oz
organic eggs	2
double cream	2 heaped tbsp
mascarpone	1 heaped tbsp
herbs, such as dill, chervil and parsley, as you wish, *chopped*	
sea salt, black pepper	

→ Slice the cooked POTATOES and leave them to cool. Sauté the LEEKS in butter, SEASON and leave to cool.

→ Preheat the oven to 200°C/400°F/Gas 6. Brush a Swiss roll tin with melted BUTTER, line with a layer of FILO and brush that with melted BUTTER. Cover the filo with sliced potatoes, followed by a layer of cold, cooked leeks, then the hot-roast SALMON. Pour over a mixture of the EGGS, CREAM AND MASCARPONE, all whisked together and SEASONED well. Sprinkle over the chopped HERBS.

→ Brush another couple of sheets of filo with melted BUTTER, place them on top and trim the edges. Bake for 20–25 minutes until browned and just set. Leave to rest for a few minutes before serving.

Kulebiaka or Salmon Pie

SERVES 6

filleted wild salmon, *cooked or raw*	675g/1½lb
unsalted butter	225g/8oz
shallots OR onions, *chopped*	225g/8oz
chestnut OR organic mushrooms, *coarsely chopped*	225g/8oz
lemon	juice of 1
brown rice OR kasha	170g/6oz
water OR chicken stock	425ml/15fl oz
fresh dill, *chopped*	2 tbsp
flat-leaf parsley, *chopped*	2 tbsp
hard-boiled eggs, *sliced*	3
sea salt, black pepper, nutmeg	
puff pastry made with 450g/1lb flour (see p. 517)	
egg yolk, *beaten*, for glaze	

→ If the SALMON is raw, cut it carefully into 6mm/¼in slices, then fry them briefly in 85g/3oz of the BUTTER. They should still have a raw colour. Gently sauté half the ONIONS OR SHALLOTS in a little more of the butter until softened and golden, then add the MUSHROOMS and cook for a further 5 minutes. Spritz with the LEMON JUICE and SEASON.

→ Fry the rest of the ONION gently in a little more butter until soft, then add the RICE OR KASHA and stir to coat each grain before adding 425ml/15fl oz of WATER OR CHICKEN STOCK. Simmer gently, adding more liquid if you need to. When the rice or kasha is cooked, add the DILL, PARSLEY, SALT, PEPPER and NUTMEG.

→ Preheat the oven to 200°C/400°F/Gas 6. Roll out half the PASTRY into an oblong and place it on a baking sheet. Put half the rice or kasha on top of it, leaving 2.5cm/1in uncovered all the way round the edge. Add the sliced salmon, followed by the sliced hard-boiled EGGS and lastly the mushroom mixture. Cover with the rest of the rice or kasha.

→ Roll out the rest of the pastry. Brush the rim of the lower piece of pastry with beaten EGG and lay the second layer on top, pressing it down to seal the edges together. Turn over the rim to double it, and mark it all the way around with the tines of a fork. Decorate in any shape or form you like—I make little pastry fish.

→ Cut a cross in the centre of the pie through which the steam can escape, brush the top with the beaten EGG and bake for an hour. If the pastry is colouring too quickly, cover it with buttered greaseproof paper. Just before serving, melt the rest of the BUTTER and pour it through the central hole.

→ I think a bowl of soured cream served alongside the kulebiaka, with or without some more finely chopped dill, is a great addition.

Salmon Baked in Pastry with Ginger and Currants

SERVES 6

wild salmon, *cut from the tail end, skinned and filleted*	1kg/2¼lb
ginger in syrup, *drained and diced very small*	3 pieces
currants	30g/1oz
unsalted butter, *softened*	110g/4oz
sea salt and black pepper	
shortcrust pastry, *made with 450g/1lb flour and 225g/8oz unsalted butter* (see p. 104)	
egg, *beaten*, for glaze	
Sauce Messine	
single cream	600ml/10fl oz
egg yolks	2
French mustard	2 tsp
plain flour	2 tsp
butter, *softened*	110g/4oz
organic lemon	juice of 1
small onion, *very finely chopped*	½
fresh tarragon, parsley, chervil, dill, *chopped*	a small bunch

When I first ate this, cooked by my number one culinary hero George Perry-Smith, it was a revelation. And it has another glory – that of looking as beautiful and difficult to make as you could imagine, but without actually being so. Just make sure you buy wild salmon.

→ Preheat the oven to 230°C/450°F/Gas 8. Check that there are no bones remaining in the pieces of SALMON and season on both sides. Using a fork, incorporate the diced GINGER and CURRANTS into the softened BUTTER. Spread half the mixture over the bottom salmon fillet, place the top fillet over it and spread it with the rest of the butter mixture.

→ Roll out the PASTRY and place the salmon on it. Join the edges of the pastry into a parcel, sealing them with a little MILK and making sure they aren't lumpy. Brush with the EGG YOLK, place on an ungreased baking sheet and bake in the oven for 30 minutes.

→ If you are remotely worried that it might not be quite cooked – and the thickness of salmon does vary – insert a skewer right the way through the fish. If it goes through easily, it's a done deal. Remove from the oven to rest for 5 minutes before cutting it into slices and serving with SAUCE MESSINE.

Sauce Messine

→ To make the sauce, swirl ALL THE INGREDIENTS together in a blender until green. Heat the sauce through gently in the top of a double boiler until thickened, stirring constantly. Serve in a warm bowl.

Stewed Squid with Leeks and Red Wine

SERVES 4

squid, *innards removed and tentacles left whole*	1kg/2¼lb
onion, *peeled and sliced*	1
garlic cloves, *peeled and sliced*	4
leek, *trimmed, sliced and well washed*	1
fennel bulb, *sliced*	1
olive oil	2–3 tbsp
fennel seeds, dill seeds and coriander seeds, *equal quantities ground together*	1 tbsp in all
small hot chillies, *chopped*	2
oranges	zest and juice of 2
red wine	½ bottle
fresh OR frozen peas	110g/4oz
mint leaves, *chopped*	a small handful
a little extra *grated* orange zest and *chopped* garlic mixed together	

The amazingly talented Stephen Markwick, chef/proprietor of what was Bristol's best restaurant Markwick's, and ex-pupil of the great George Perry-Smith, is now at Culinaria in Bristol. Stephen was cooking this dish last time I steamed into his kitchen to watch him at work and write about him. Stephen serves this lovely dish as a first course, with a few croutons of thinly sliced baguette brushed with a little olive oil and crisped in the oven. I think it is as successful as a main course, served with plainly cooked rice.

→ First prepare the SQUID. Cut the body into rings, the wings into strips and leave the tentacles whole.

→ Preheat the oven to 140°C/275°F/Gas 1. In a heavy-bottomed casserole, gently fry the ONION, GARLIC, LEEK and FENNEL together in the OLIVE OIL until softened. Add the GROUND SEED MIXTURE and the CHILLIES, then stir in the squid. Stir around a little until the squid has stiffened and then introduce the ZEST AND JUICE of 2 oranges and the RED WINE. SEASON well— squid absorbs a great deal of salt – and bring everything to a simmer. Cover and braise slowly in the oven for about 2 hours. Add the PEAS for the last 20 minutes of the cooking time.

→ Stir in the chopped MINT, sprinkle over the extra ORANGE ZEST and GARLIC, and serve directly from the pot in one of the ways suggested above.

Thakkali, or Prawn and Tomato Curry

SERVES 4

prawns, shell on	675g/1½lb
vegetable oil OR ghee	1 tbsp 1 dsrtsp
small red onion, *finely sliced*	1
fresh OR dry curry leaves	a handful
fenugreek seeds	2 tsp
garlic cloves, *peeled and chopped*	6
green chillies, *seeded and finely chopped*	2
cumin seeds, *lightly roasted and ground*	1 tsp

I first ate this at an extraordinary Sri Lankan night at a restaurant in Dulverton in Somerset. Nelisha, who cooked the dishes, had learned to cook her native food from her mother and was clearly one of those premier-league home cooks who was offering her customers a unique restaurant experience.

→ Shell the PRAWNS and place the shells in a pan with 1.2 litres/2 pints of cold water. Bring to the boil and simmer for 40 minutes. Strain and reserve the prawn stock.

→ In a heavy pan, heat the OIL OR GHEE, and add the sliced ONION, CURRY LEAVES and FENUGREEK SEEDS. Fry until lightly browned. Add the chopped GARLIC and green CHILLIES and stir them in. Reduce the heat. Add all the SPICES and CHILLI POWDER and stir for a few seconds, then add the prawn stock. Simmer uncovered until the prawn stock has reduced by half.

→ Add the TOMATOES, creamed coconut and ground MALDIVE

coriander seeds, *lightly roasted and ground*	1 tsp
chilli powder	2 tsp
plum tomatoes	1 × 400g/14oz tin
creamed coconut	55g/2oz
Maldive fish, *ground* (optional)	1 tbsp
lime	juice of 1

FISH if using, stir, and then simmer uncovered until the sauce has thickened. Just before serving, add the prawns and heat them through. Add LIME JUICE to taste.

Kedgeree

SERVES 6

naturally smoked haddock	450–675g/1–1½lb
milk	300ml/10fl oz or so
bay leaf	1
butter	a knob
black pepper	
brown or white basmati rice	about 560g/1¼lb
olive oil	3 tbsp
large onions, *thinly sliced*	2
cumin seeds	2 tsp
coriander seeds	2 tsp
garam masala	1 tsp
cayenne	½ tsp
organic eggs	9–12
fresh or frozen peas, podded weight	225g/8oz
double cream	4–6 tbsp
butter	a knob
flat-leaf parsley OR coriander	a bunch
mango chutney	

→ Put the HADDOCK skin-side down in a shallow gratin dish with the MILK, BAY LEAF and a knob of BUTTER and warm over a gentle heat until the milk is at a bare simmer. Season with BLACK PEPPER and continue to simmer for 10–15 minutes, making sure the fish is basted with the cooking liquor. When it is ready, it will pull easily away from the skin with a fork. Meanwhile, cook the RICE according to the instructions on the packet, remembering to start the rice earlier if it is brown as it will take longer. Start the ONIONS off at the same time. Heat the OLIVE OIL in a large heavy-bottomed frying pan, and gently sauté the onions for a couple of minutes.

→ Now add the spices. The CUMIN and CORIANDER can be roasted in a small pan for a minute or until they smell toasty, then crushed in a mortar and added to the onions with the GARAM MASALA. Continue to cook until slightly softened and translucent, then turn down the heat, put a lid on them and cook more slowly until they have completely softened, about 20 minutes. Meanwhile boil a pan of water for the EGGS, and just before it reaches boiling point, drop the eggs in and boil them for 5½ minutes. Plunge into cold water so you can peel them. Cook the PEAS in a little boiling water until tender.

→ Remove the fish and any stray bones from the skin and pull it into large flakes with a fork. Remove the lid from the frying pan and add the drained rice. Then add the peas and fish, season with a little more PEPPER if it needs it and pour in the CREAM over a low heat. Add a generous extra knob of BUTTER and the finely chopped PARSLEY OR CORIANDER, and stir briefly to amalgamate. Remove from the heat and place the halved eggs all around the edge of the pan. Serve straight from the pan with some good mango chutney and a green salad.

Seafood Risotto

Serves 6

dry white wine	150–300ml/5–10fl oz
mussels, *cleaned and de-bearded*	24
scallops, *cleaned*	12
butter	45g/1½oz
strong fish stock (see p. 168)	1.5 litres/3 pints
olive oil	3 tbsp
large onion, *finely chopped*	1
celery sticks, *finely chopped*	
Carnaroli or Arborio rice	450g/1lb
fresh peas, if in season	a couple of handfuls
saffron threads	a pinch
Parmesan cheese, *grated*	50g/2oz
salt and pepper	
cooked prawns, *shelled and de-veined*	up to 450g/1lb
fresh chervil and parsley, *chopped*	1 tbsp of each

This is an elegant and beautifully coloured dish, which needs no more by way of accompaniment than the simplest green salad tossed in the very best olive oil. It is the kind of good-tempered dish that responds well to you throwing in whatever seafood you can lay your hands on. The real prerequisite is some good strong fish stock, which I usually make with an assortment of crab, lobster and prawn and shrimp shells.

→ Heat a little of the WINE in a saucepan, add the MUSSELS, cover and steam just until the shells open. Remove the mussels and put to one side. Cook the SCALLOPS by slicing the white flesh into two or three discs, leaving the corals whole, and sautéing the white parts in a little of the BUTTER for 30 seconds on each side, the coral for 30 seconds altogether. Bring the FISH STOCK to the boil and keep it at simmering point.

→ Heat the OIL in a large, heavy pan, add the ONION and CELERY and cook over a low heat until they have softened and turned golden. Stir in the RICE and keep stirring to coat, until it begins to look translucent. Turn up the heat and add about 150ml/5fl oz of the wine. When it has been absorbed, start adding the hot stock, a ladle or two at a time. Stir the liquid in carefully, and let it simmer until it has been almost absorbed before you add more, and the PEAS if you are using them. Keep adding the STOCK a little at a time, and with the last ladleful add the saffron.

→ After about 20–25 minutes the rice will be slightly resistant to the bite, but almost tender. Stir in a small lump of butter, the grated PARMESAN, SALT and PEPPER. Add the PRAWNS, MUSSELS and SCALLOPS. Scatter the HERBS over the top, and if the dish doesn't appear beautifully liquid, add a final ladleful of fish stock. Season to taste and serve in bowls.

Risotto Nero

Serves 4

Fish stock

fish bones and heads and some prawn or crab shells	1kg/2¼lb
water	2.2 litres/4 pints
onion, *chopped*	1
celery sticks, *chopped*	2

It's blacker than a starless night. Indeed, no food is blacker than a risotto nero, the cuttlefish ink dyeing the rice, the vegetables, the plate, as black as a seam of coal. It feels decadent before you even eat it as you smell its intense fishiness rising like an exhalation from the pan.

→ To make the stock, put the BONES in a large pan with the water, bring to the boil and simmer for 20 minutes. Strain through a muslin-lined sieve into another pan, add ALL THE VEGETABLES and HERBS and bring back to the boil. Simmer for 35 minutes, then strain again. You should now have around 1.2

fennel bulb, *chopped*	1
carrot, *chopped*	1
whole tomatoes	2
bay leaf	1
thyme	a sprig

Risotto

small cuttlefish	450g/1lb
unsalted butter	30g/1oz
extra butter to finish with	a knob
olive oil for the risotto	1 tbsp
olive oil for the cuttlefish	2 tbsp
shallots, *peeled and finely minced*	2–3
garlic cloves, *peeled and finely minced*	3
Carnaroli or Arborio rice	340g/12oz
dry white wine	150ml/5fl oz
flat-leaf parsley, *chopped*	4 tbsp
Parmesan cheese, *freshly grated*	55g/2oz

litres/2 pints of stock. (You can freeze any extra stock once it has cooled.)

→ Clean the CUTTLEFISH. You can use squid or octopus in this dish, but squid ink sacs are not so large, so you will have to buy a few of the little sachets of neat ink fishmongers sell. Cut off the tentacles, removing the beaky mouth, then skin each tentacle separately. Tear away all the tough skin from the body, then pull out the cuttlebone. If you are using squid, remove the plastic-like quill. Open up the body of the cuttlefish and pull out the ink sac and set aside. Discard the entrails and head and wash the body. Slice it into long, thin strips and chop the tentacles similarly.

→ Heat the BUTTER and 1 tablespoon of OIL in a frying or risotto pan and soften the SHALLOTS and GARLIC over a gentle heat until golden. Add the RICE and stir to coat it thoroughly in butter and oil. Squeeze the sachets of ink or the ink sac into the rice, and add a little hot FISH STOCK to the sachets to extract the maximum amount of ink. Add the heated WINE and simmer, stirring all the time until the rice has almost absorbed it. Start adding the hot FISH STOCK, a ladleful at a time and continue to stir to release the starch in the rice. The rice will take about 22 minutes to cook, but keep tasting to make sure you remove it from the heat when it is still al dente. The risotto should be sloppy but not soupy.

→ Heat the remaining 2 tablespoons of OLIVE OIL in a frying pan and when it is really hot, throw in the strips of fish and turn briskly for one and a half minutes. Remove and scatter over the PARSLEY. SEASON and turn the fish into the risotto to paint it black. Throw in 2 tablespoons of the PARMESAN and the BUTTER, add a small, final ladle of FISH STOCK, and cover with a lid. Leave for all the flavours to marry for 5 minutes. Remove the lid and give the pan a final stir before serving. Pass round a bowl of extra grated PARMESAN.

Curried Crab Risotto

SERVES 4

fresh crab meat, white and brown	450g/1lb
small organic onion, *peeled and finely chopped*	1
extra virgin olive oil	3–4 tbsp
fennel seeds, cumin seeds and coriander seeds	1 tsp each
cayenne	¼ to ½ tsp or to taste
garam masala	1 tsp
sea salt and black pepper	
Carnaroli rice	340g/12 oz
dry white wine	150ml/5floz
medium courgettes, *chopped into dice*	2
OR whole baby courgettes with their flowers	8
fish stock (see p. 168)	up to 850ml/1½ pints
unsalted butter	
cream	a little
fresh dill	1 tbsp

It's surprising how the introduction of Indian spices enhances this inimitable Italian dish and accentuates its crabbiness, perhaps more so than even Parmesan would in a more conventional rendering, but it just works beautifully. Make the fish stock with the crab shell, prawn shells and anything else you can get hold of.

→ Pick the CRAB to extract the meat, or get your fishmonger to dress you a freshly boiled crab with no additives like rusk.

→ Sauté the ONION in some warmed OLIVE OIL over a gentle heat for a few minutes. Meanwhile, in a small pan heated over a brisk heat, temper the FENNEL, CUMIN and CORIANDER seeds, erring on the generous heaped side with the cumin, for a minute and then crush them all together in a mortar with the CAYENNE, GARAM MASALA, a little SEA SALT and a few BLACK PEPPERCORNS. Throw most of this mixture over the cooking onion and stir it around for a couple of minutes before adding the RICE and stirring well to coat it on all sides.

→ Add the WINE and let it bubble for a couple of minutes, then start adding the heated FISH STOCK a ladle or two at a time, stirring all the while. After 10 minutes, heat a little more OIL in a separate small pan and throw in the COURGETTE dice, turning to coat in olive oil over a medium heat. You don't want the courgettes to brown or start to exude juice, you want them to cook to al dente and retain crunch and colour. When they have reached this stage, remove from the heat.

→ Keep stirring the risotto and after about 20 minutes, throw in the crab meat and stir it in briefly. Taste and add the rest of the spice mix if you need to, as well as more salt and pepper. Add a good lump of BUTTER, a ladle more hot stock and a few tablespoons of CREAM, remove from the heat immediately and cover with a lid for 5 minutes for the flavours to marry. Remove the lid, add the warm courgettes, give a final stir and bring to the table.

Paella with Monkfish and Saffron

SERVES 4

olive oil	7 tbsp
monkfish tails, *removed from their cartilaginous bone and cut into 2–3cm/1in cubes*	450g/1lb
large onions, *finely chopped*	2
green pepper, *halved, seeded and finely chopped*	2
garlic cloves, *finely chopped*	6
fennel seeds	½ tsp
hot fish stock (see p. 168)	850ml/1½ pints
saffron stamens	a good pinch
Calasparra rice	225g/8oz
white wine OR fino sherry	90ml/3fl oz
flat-leaf parsley, *finely chopped*	small bunch
sweet smoked Spanish paprika	½ tsp
sea salt and black pepper	
piquillo peppers, *torn in strips*	225g/8oz
lemon, *cut into wedges*	1

This is a paella recipe from the Sams of the wonderful Moro restaurant in London. They advise that clams or prawns can be added. I would add, so can mussels, 450g/1lb/1 pint of them. I think this is a great way to use tails of monk, which exude copious amounts of fishy liquor to help flavour the rice. Navarrico and Anko do jars of piquillo peppers, and the ones cooked over beech wood are particularly good.

→ Heat 2 tablespoons of the OIL in a paella or frying pan over a medium heat. Add the MONKFISH and stir-fry until fractionally underdone, a couple of minutes. Pour the monkfish and its juices into a bowl. Wipe the pan clean with kitchen paper and put it back on the heat. Add the rest of the OIL, heat it, then add the ONIONS and PEPPERS. Cook for 15–20 minutes, stirring occasionally. Turn the heat down and add the chopped GARLIC and FENNEL SEEDS. Cook for a further 10 minutes or until the mixture is sweet and has some colour. Meanwhile, bring the STOCK to the boil and infuse the SAFFRON in it off the heat. Add the RICE to the pan and stir for a minute to coat with the vegetables and oil. (The paella can be prepared in advance up to this point; there is a further 20 minutes of cooking time.)

→ Turn the heat up to high and add the WHITE WINE OR SHERRY to the pan, followed by the stock. Now add half the PARSLEY and the PAPRIKA, and season with SALT AND PEPPER. Do not stir from this point. Simmer for 10 minutes or until there is just a little liquid above the rice. Spread the monkfish out evenly over the rice with its juices. Push the monkfish under the stock. Shake the pan to prevent sticking and turn the heat down to low. Cook for 5 more minutes or until there is just a little liquid left at the bottom of the rice. Turn off the heat and cover the pan tightly with foil. Let the rice sit for 5 minutes before serving. Decorate with strips of PIQUILLO peppers, the rest of the chopped PARSLEY and the LEMON. Serve with a green salad.

Salt Cod in Summer Vegetable Sauce

SERVES 4

salt cod, chunk from the middle	450g/1lb
small aubergines, *peeled and cubed*	2
olive oil	
organic green back bacon	2 or 3 rashers
large onion, *peeled and chopped*	1
garlic cloves, *finely chopped*	2
red peppers, *seeded and cut into small squares*	2
tomatoes, *skinned and seeded*	750g/1lb 10oz
molasses sugar	1 tsp
small courgettes, *cubed*	2
dry white wine	170ml/6fl oz
bay leaf	1
salt and pepper	

This is a luscious dish, intensely flavoured by the salt cod, but you could add a teaspoon of harissa or a bit of chilli if you want a bit of additional heat. You can use 'El Navarrico' organic piquillo peppers in a jar, which you add at the end of the vegetable cooking time, instead of ordinary red peppers.

→ Soak the SALT COD, split into 3 or 4 pieces, for at least 24 hours in several changes of water.

→ Remove all the skin and bones from the salt cod, then cut it into fish fingers. Heat some OLIVE OIL in a heavy-bottomed casserole, and fry the BACON in strips with the ONION and GARLIC until the onion is translucent. Add the PEPPERS, TOMATOES, SUGAR, WINE and BAY LEAF and simmer gently for about 25 minutes, until the tomato has collapsed into the sauce.

→ Fry the FISH separately in OLIVE OIL for about 2 minutes a side, until golden. Put it in the tomato sauce. Fry the AUBERGINES gently in the fishy oiled pan with the COURGETTES until softened. Turn into the tomato sauce and simmer gently for about 15 minutes. Check the SEASONING and serve with good crusty bread.

Tonno Balsamico

SERVES 2

thick tuna steaks	2
sea salt and black pepper	
good, extra virgin olive oil	1 tbsp
bruised juniper berries	6
rosemary	2 sprigs
balsamic vinegar, aged, good but not wildly expensive	8 tbsp
Barolo or good, red Italian wine	4 tbsp
best unsalted butter	45g/1½oz or so

→ SALT AND PEPPER the TUNA straight from the fridge on both sides and leave out for an hour at room temperature.

→ Heat the OLIVE OIL in a pan and add the JUNIPER BERRIES and chopped ROSEMARY. Cook very gently together for a few minutes before turning up the heat and adding the BALSAMIC VINEGAR. Reduce it by a third, stirring from time to time before adding the BAROLO OR RED WINE and reducing it further. Taste to make sure the alcohol has lost its raw edge and the balsamic has similarly mellowed.

→ Remove, cover and leave for 30 minutes for the flavours to develop.

→ Griddle the TUNA on both sides until medium rare, then leave to rest while you finish the sauce. Strain the sauce through a sieve and reheat it over a gentle heat, adding a scrunch of PEPPER and the BUTTER, a little at a time, in small knobs, whisking it in as you go. Eventually the sauce will look like dark, shiny velvet. Pour it over the tuna steaks and serve.

Tonno e Fagioli

SERVES 6

cannellini beans	450g/1lb
large tuna steaks	2
large red onion	1
lemons and limes	juice of up to 2 of each
olive oil, salt and pepper	
flat-leaf parsley, *chopped*	a handful

This is a lovely, simple summer dish, to which the addition of fresh lime juice, such a friend of tuna, brings out the true flavour.

→ Soak the CANNELLINI BEANS overnight. Cook until tender, about 40 minutes. Pour some of the OLIVE OIL on to the hot beans once you have drained them.

→ Grill or griddle the TUNA STEAKS until barely cooked through, about 2–3 minutes. Slice the ONION into the finest circles you can muster. When the beans are still warm, add the tuna, more OIL, the CITRUS JUICE to taste, and the onion. Amalgamate gently and season. Sprinkle with chopped flat-leaf PARSLEY.

Halibut in a Green Sauce

SERVES 6

flat-leaf and curly parsley, *finely chopped*	2 tbsp of each
mint, *finely chopped*	2 tbsp
dill and chervil, *finely chopped*	1 tbsp of each
salted anchovies	12
garlic cloves, *almost minced*	6
chopped capers in olive oil; *if in brine rinse carefully*	2 tbsp
black pepper	
hard-boiled egg, *finely chopped*	1
cornichons, *finely chopped at the last minute*	6 or 7
olive oil	
halibut steaks, 2.5cm/1in thick, on the bone	6

A dish of distinction and simplicity. Anchovies in oil will do if you can't get the salted ones.

→ Preheat oven to 200°C/400°F/Gas 6. If you have a mezzaluna it is easy to chop the HERBS finely enough; if not, be patient. Do not do this in a blender or it will look like gunged up grass mowings. Desalinate and de-spine the ANCHOVIES, and chop them so they are almost minced.

→ Add the GARLIC, ANCHOVIES, CAPERS and some BLACK PEPPER to the herbs in a bowl, then dribble in your best extra virgin OLIVE OIL until amalgamated, but not oily or too thick. Stir in the EGG and CORNICHONS and taste: this is a strident sauce and might need more cornichons or garlic.

→ Heat a film of OLIVE OIL in a heavy-bottomed, ovenproof frying pan or gratin dish, and when hot put the pieces of HALIBUT in for about a minute a side just to seal and turn opaque. Turn carefully so they don't flake. Transfer the pan to the top of the hot oven for 6–8 minutes, test with a skewer: the fish should not resist. Put a steak on each plate, and pass round the sauce for everyone to dollop on.

Grilled Hake Steaks with Spring Herbs

SERVES 3

hake steaks, about 2.5cm/1in thick	3
good olive oil	
salt and black pepper	
chives, chervil and dill, *finely chopped*	1 tbsp of each
lemon	a spritz

A deliciously underrated fish, even better line caught, since it dies through lack of oxygen, is put in ice, and consequently has a firmer texture than when it has been netted, and effectively drowned because its gills can't flap in the nets. This is the simplest of recipes to inspire the under-confident fish cook.

→ Get your fishmonger to cut each STEAK thickly, a generous inch. Brush both sides generously with good OLIVE OIL, grind on PEPPER and coarse SALT, and grill for 4–5 minutes a side. You can see if the fish is cooked: the translucent raw flesh will be white all through. Sprinkle the chopped HERBS over the steaks with a spritz of LEMON and the juice that has escaped into the grill pan.

Roast Hake Steaks with Poor Man's Potatoes

SERVES 4

hake steaks on the bone, about 4cm/1½ in thick	4
sea salt and black pepper	

Poor Man's Potatoes

extra virgin olive oil	about 15 tbsp
large onions, *sliced thinly*	3
garlic cloves, *sliced thickly*	5 or 6
red peppers	2
green pepper	1
fresh bay leaves	3 or 4
firm waxy-fleshed potatoes	1kg/2¼lb
cherry tomatoes (optional)	a couple of handfuls
sea salt and black pepper	

→ Start with the potatoes. In a large heavy-bottomed pot, heat 5 tablespoons of the OLIVE OIL, then add the finely sliced ONION and some SALT to help release the juice. Cook gently for about 20 minutes, stirring occasionally, until softened and translucent. Add the sliced GARLIC, roughly chopped PEPPERS and the BAY LEAVES, which you can break a bit to release their flavour, and cook for a further 15 minutes.

→ Cut the POTATOES lengthwise, then cut each slice into two or three chunks and salt them lightly. Add the rest of the OLIVE OIL to the pan, and when it has heated up, throw in the potatoes and the TOMATOES if you are using them. Leave everything to simmer for 40–50 minutes, by which time the potatoes will have cooked through completely when you pierce them with a skewer. Drain the oil through a sieve into a jug, enough will have adhered to coat the vegetables without them swimming, and all the flavours will have married most pleasingly.

→ Preheat oven to 230°C/450°F/Gas 8. About 15–20 minutes before the potatoes are ready, brush the HAKE STEAKS on both sides with OLIVE OIL, put them in a gratin dish and season. Put the fish in the oven, and test it after 15 minutes with the point of a skewer through its thickest part. The flesh should not resist you at all and be flaky, translucent and juicy without having softened to a pulp. The potatoes will keep warm in the warming oven if there is any discrepancy over timing. If you use cherry tomatoes, you will have no need of a further vegetable.

Grilled Hake Steaks with Romesco Sauce

SERVES 4

hake steaks or cutlets, on the bone, 4cm/1½in thick	4
olive oil to brush	
sea salt and black pepper	
fresh thyme, *chopped*	1 tsp

Romesco Sauce

whole blanched almonds	30g/1oz
best olive oil	6 tbsp
garlic cloves, *finely chopped*	2
stale bread, brown or white	a slice
tomatoes, *skinned and seeded* OR the equivalent from a tin, with juice	225g/8oz
red chilli, *seeded and finely chopped* OR cayenne	1 to taste
whole roasted hazelnuts	30g/1oz
red wine vinegar	2 tbsp
fino sherry	4 tbsp

Hake has perfect firmness and bite for a fish stew, a lovely delicate flavour, a flakiness that doesn't collapse on cooking, and it doesn't dry out if you anoint it with oil and show it to the grill or the griddle, either of which works for this recipe.

→ If you are going to grill your fish, line the grill pan with foil and preheat. If you are using a griddle, brush it quickly with a little olive oil when it is hot, trying not to frazzle your pastry brush. Brush the HAKE with OLIVE OIL on both sides, SEASON and add a pinch of THYME to the uppermost side. Place under the grill or on the griddle and watch like a hawk. You will see the heat cook down through the fish under the grill, or work its way up the flesh if it's on the griddle. You will also see the pearly juices begin to collect.

→ When the fish looks cooked halfway through, after about 5 minutes or even less, turn it over gently with a slice, SEASON again and continue to cook. This side might take a little less time. Poke a skewer gently down through the fish — it should not be resistant.

→ Remove the fish from the grill or griddle and pour over the fishy, oily juices. Serve with the ROMESCO SAUCE, as powerful a piece of work as a sauce gets.

Romesco Sauce

→ Roast the ALMONDS briefly in a moderate oven until pale gold. Slowly heat 4 tablespoons of the OLIVE OIL in a pan with the chopped GARLIC. When the oil is hot, remove and reserve the garlic and fry the BREAD briefly on both sides until crisp and golden. Remove the bread from the pan, add 2 more tablespoons of OIL, then the TOMATOES and CHILLI and stir until they are reduced and jammily thickened. This will take about 10–15 minutes.

→ Grind the NUTS in a food processor, or a mortar for a better texture, then add the bread and garlic and continue to pound with the VINEGAR and SHERRY. Stir in the cooled tomato sauce and serve in the mortar.

Plain Grilled Mackerel

SERVES 4

fresh mackerel	4
sea salt and black pepper	
wedges of lemon	
buttered brown bread	

There is really only one way for cooking a straight-from-sea-to-plate mackerel. This method retains all the golden, oily juices and the softness of the fresh flesh while blistering the skin with bubbles of delectable charredness.

→ Gut the MACKEREL if you've caught them yourself rather than bought them from your fishmonger. Now put them upright on a board, belly down, as they would be if swimming. Press down firmly with the flat blade of a knife along the length of their backbones until you can feel and hear something of a crunching separation! The fish should be splayed almost flat now.
→ Turn on the grill and rack up the heat. Place the fish skin side up on the grill pan with the rack in place. That way all the juices will drip through and collect in the pan below. Put the pan as close to the flame as you dare – you might scorch the odd tail, but never fear. An average-sized mackerel, something a little under 450g/1lb, will take about 5 minutes to cook, but keep watching as the flesh chars and splutters. Test with a skewer right through the flesh at the plumpest part, and if it is equally soft right through to the underbelly, the fish is cooked. You do not need to flip the fish and cook it flesh side up, a mistake that many people make and which dries out the fish.
→ Place each mackerel flesh side up on the plate, pour over the oily juices and season. A squirt of LEMON and some slices of good BREAD AND BUTTER and you have one of the simplest and most delicious of foods.

Sea Bass baked with Lemongrass and Dill

SERVES 4

fresh wild sea bass	
	1 × 1.5kg/3¼lb or so
fresh dill	a sprig
lemongrass stalks	a couple
flat-leaf parsley, *chopped*	1 tbsp
butter, *softened*	55g/2oz
lemon	zest of 1
	and a spritz of its juice

I always cook fish on the bone if I possibly can; therein lies the best flavour. In the case of the bass, it is best left for 10–15 minutes after you have removed it from the oven for the flesh to firm up. Serving fish warm, or even at room temperature, is something you don't need to be afraid of.

→ Ask your fishmonger to scale and gut the fish, having made sure it is bright and beady-eyed, as it were, the flesh gluey and shiny, not dull, drab and dry looking. Preheat the oven to 180°C/350°F/Gas 4. Wash the SEA BASS inside and out under a cold tap. Lay a sheet of foil large enough to make a baggy parcel for the fish on a roasting tray.
→ Strip the DILL from its stalks and chop finely – you need about a tablespoon. Unfurl the LEMONGRASS until you have only the inner, bendy, juicy core of it and chop it finely; the

breadcrumbs	4 tbsp
olive oil	
white wine	a splosh
sea salt and black pepper	

exterior is too tough to eat. Mash the dill, lemongrass and PARSLEY into the softened BUTTER with the ZEST OF THE LEMON and a SPRITZ OF JUICE, SALT and PEPPER. Mash in the BREAD-CRUMBS and a little OLIVE OIL if the butter is difficult to work with the breadcrumbs.

→ Score deep, diagonal slashes at intervals along one side of the fish—about four, depending on its length—and stuff the herbed butter in with your fingers as best you can. Turn the fish over and do the same on its other side. If there is any butter left, stuff it into the cavity where the fish has been gutted. Add a good splosh of WHITE WINE and a little libation of OIL to the fish, then SEASON the skin.

→ Close and seal the parcel – it should be baggy but tightly sealed. Bake the fish in the oven for about 35 minutes, or until a knife point or skewer penetrates the whole fish at its widest girth; it should be consistently soft right the way through. Open the parcel and leave for 15 minutes, then serve the fish in fillets with some of the juice poured over them.

Fried Fish in Lager Batter

flour	225g/8oz, plus extra for flouring the fish
lager	240ml/8fl oz
olive oil	1 tbsp
fish of your choice	

This is my favourite batter for fish on the rare occasions I get the deep-fryer out of hibernation. Its light acidity and flavour really complement the fish. Particularly good with a firm white chunk of huss or haddock. Always flour the fish first if you are going to batter it, shaking off the excess before dunking in the batter brew.

→ Sift the FLOUR into a bowl containing the BEER, add the OLIVE OIL and whisk well. Flour the FISH and dunk it in the batter. Put it into the basket of the fryer and lower it into the vegetable oil which should be at 180–190°C. Test with a piece of bread if you don't have a thermometer. It should fizz and splutter and brown within 30 seconds. Do not put too much into a deep-fryer at one time, as it will lower the temperature of the bubbling oil and your food will start to absorb a lot more oil and won't fry properly.

→ Fry until golden, then remove the fish to some kitchen paper and drain thoroughly before serving. If you have to keep the fish warm, don't cover it or the batter will lose its crunch. Put it on some kitchen paper in a medium oven and leave the door open.

Monkfish wrapped in Parma Ham

SERVES 6

olive oil	2 tbsp
rosemary, *very finely chopped*	a sprig
lemon	a spritz
monkfish tails, *cut into 5cm/2in chunks*	1kg/2¼lb
Parma ham, *finely sliced*	200g/7oz
bay leaves	3 or 4
cherry tomatoes	12
salt and pepper	

→ Preheat the oven to 220°C/425°F/Gas 7. Heat the OLIVE OIL gently in a small pan, and when warmed, add the ROSEMARY. Cook for about 30 seconds: you want it to soften slightly but not to brown.

→ Remove the oil from the heat, squeeze on a bit of LEMON JUICE, and brush over the MONKFISH CHUNKS as you go, SEASONING them, and wrapping them up in their PARMA HAM parcels.

→ Tuck them tightly together in a gratin dish, strew the BAY LEAVES and the TOMATOES you've rolled in a bit of extra OLIVE OIL on top, and bake for 15–20 minutes. Insert a skewer, and if they're just unresistant they're cooked. Dish up, pour over the fishy juices.

Roast Stuffed Monkfish with a Lemon and Caper Sauce

SERVES 10

thyme, black peppercorns and sea salt	1 tbsp of each
monkfish, a single tail if possible	2.3kg/5lb
anchovies in olive oil, *drained*	55g/2oz tin
OR salted anchovies, *de-spined and washed*	55g/2oz
red peppers, *roasted, peeled and seeded*	2
OR the wood-roasted piquillo peppers from Brindisa	
saffron threads	a pinch
best olive oil	3–4 tbsp
lemon	1
unsalted butter	55g/2oz
capers, *drained and rinsed*	2 tbsp
flat-leaf parsley, *chopped*	a handful

Ask your fishmonger to remove the bone, leaving the fillets on either side still attached. A summer feast, this is an abstract splash of colour of a dish that you can either prepare or actually cook in advance if you decide to serve it cold. The finished dish will look like a picture, yet presents no challenge to assemble and cook, despite its seeming complexity.

→ Put the THYME, PEPPERCORNS and SALT in a mortar and crush until coarsely ground. Open the FISH out like a book and spread the ANCHOVIES and red PEPPERS evenly over both surfaces. Soak the SAFFRON threads in a tablespoon or two of warm water for 10 minutes. Pour over the saffrony liquor, then half the OLIVE OIL. Close the fish together, and hold it while a friend or child ties string around it at 2.5cm/1in intervals, to make 10 portions.

→ Preheat the oven to 200°C/400°F/Gas 6. Scatter the thyme mixture in a roasting tin, roll the fish in it to coat, then pour on the rest of the OLIVE OIL. Put the fish in the middle of the oven to roast for about 35 minutes. Check with the point of a skewer that it has cooked right through and is not resistant in the middle. Remove it to a warm serving dish if you are going to serve it hot and rest it, shrouded in foil, while you make the sauce.

→ Boil the remaining liquor from the roasting tin down to about half the quantity you started with. Meanwhile, peel the LEMON, removing all the pith with a sharp knife, and divide the fruit into segments. In a small frying pan, melt the BUTTER gently until it begins to turn brown and nutty, add the pieces of lemon, then throw in the drained CAPERS. Add the fish liquor and stir it in, then pour it over the fish. Strew over the PARSLEY and carve the fish into tranches 2.5cm/1in thick. Remember to remove the string before serving.

→ If you are serving the fish cold, do not offer the butter sauce. Make the sauce with olive oil instead or omit it, merely pouring over the reduced liquor while the fish is cooling.

Richard Corrigan's John Dory with Crab Juices

SERVES 4

fresh crab	1 × about 750g/1lb
unsalted butter	
shallot, *finely chopped*	1 tbsp
celery, *finely chopped*	1 tbsp
mushroom, *finely chopped*	1 tbsp
fennel, *finely chopped*	1 tbsp
leek, *finely chopped*	1 tbsp
tomatoes, *chopped*	4
tomato, *peeled, seeded and diced*	1
brandy	1 tbsp
water	about 300ml/10fl oz
sunflower OR olive oil	
John Dory, filleted weight	about 1.3kg/2lb
chives, *chopped*	½ tsp
fresh tarragon and dill, *chopped*	½ tsp
salt and pepper	

→ Remove the CRAB MEAT from the shell and set aside. Bash the SHELL into bits inside a large casserole.

→ Melt a knob of BUTTER in a small saucepan and add the mirepoix of vegetables, the finely chopped SHALLOT, CELERY, MUSHROOM, FENNEL and LEEK, cooking gently for about 10 minutes. Add this to the crushed crab shell with the 4 TOMATOES, stir for 2 minutes, then add the BRANDY and set alight. Pour over water just to cover, bring to the boil, and simmer for 20 minutes. Strain through a sieve into a clean pan, heat to boiling point, and reduce by a half. Whisk in another knob of BUTTER.

→ Fry the FISH FILLETS in a bit of OIL for 3 minutes a side, then add the crab meat and juice and heat through for 2 minutes. Serve, adding the chopped tomato and herbs to each plate.

Baked Skate

SERVES 3–4

filleted skate, per person	225g/8oz
OR skate on the bone, per person	340g/12oz or more
lemon	a spritz
white wine	a splosh
salt and pepper	

Caper Sauce

unsalted butter	85g/3oz
capers	2 tbsp
lemon juice	
salt and pepper	

→ Preheat the oven to 200°C/400°F/Gas 6. BUTTER a roasting tin thoroughly, and lay the SKATE down flat in the bottom of it in one piece. Squeeze on a spritz of LEMON and sprinkle over a splosh of WHITE WINE. Season with SALT AND PEPPER and cook for 5 minutes, before testing the thickest bit with a knife. If it is resistant, return to the oven, another 5 minutes maximum should do.

→ Transfer the fish in serving portions onto a plate and keep warm, while you boil up the roasting tin juices and reduce them a little, beating in a few little extra knobs of BUTTER.

→ If your fishmonger doesn't fillet skate, poach the wings on the bone in water you have brought to the boil and acidulated with a tablespoon or two of WINE VINEGAR. Drop the fish in, keeping the water at no more than a blip, and your fish should be cooked in about 6 minutes; again, test with a knife. Drain carefully, and keep hot.

Caper Sauce

→ Melt the BUTTER in a pan and add the CAPERS, rinsed or desalinated, to the pan. Squeeze on LEMON JUICE to taste, allow it to bubble for a few seconds, then scrunch on some BLACK PEPPER, and add SALT if the capers aren't too salty. Spoon over each piece of skate.

Skate with an Anchovy and Caper Sauce

SERVES 4

white wine vinegar	3–4 tbsp
fresh thyme	a bunch
bay leaves	2
sea salt	a large pinch
skate wings, per person	225g/8oz

Anchovy and Caper Sauce

anchovies in olive oil, *drained*	1 small can (50g/2oz)
butter	55g/2oz

This is one of those magical recipes, not time-consuming, not unduly difficult, which seems to impress well beyond the level of its complexity— a dish to grace either a serious dinner party or an everyday supper. Skate benefits hugely from a piquant, slightly salty accompaniment.

→ Put the VINEGAR, THYME, BAY LEAVES and SEA SALT in a wide, shallow pan, add about 7.5cm/3in of water and bring to the boil. Add the SKATE, bring the liquid back to a faint bubble and simmer for 10 minutes.

→ Take off the skate's skin. Once it is on the plate, liberally anoint the fish with the sauce.

Anchovy and Caper Sauce

→ Swirl the ANCHOVIES and BUTTER to a paste in a food processor. Heat the OIL in a small saucepan and sauté the ONION OR SHALLOTS until softened, then add the WINE and

olive oil	about 2 tsp
shallots, *finely chopped*	2
dry white wine	150ml/5fl oz
double cream	2–3 tbsp
fresh herbs (dill, flat-leaf parsley, chervil), *chopped*	2 tbsp
capers, *thoroughly rinsed*	2 tbsp
pepper	
lemon	½

boil to reduce considerably. Add a couple of tablespoons of the skate's poaching liquid and reduce again. Whisk in little knobs of the anchovy butter until the sauce has emulsified, then add the CREAM, and stir it well in to amalgamate. Add the chopped HERBS, the CAPERS, some PEPPER — but no salt, as the anchovies will provide it — and squeeze on some LEMON JUICE to taste.

Baked Turbot with Sauce Bretonne

SERVES 6

turbot	1 × 2.3–3kg/5–6½lb
chervil and flat-leaf parsley, *chopped*	a small bunch
unsalted butter	55g/2oz
white wine	150ml/5fl oz
sea salt and black pepper	
Sauce Bretonne	
organic egg yolks	4
sea salt and pepper	
Dijon mustard	2 tsp
tarragon vinegar	a few drops
watercress, *chopped*	2 tbsp
chervil, *chopped*	2 tbsp
unsalted butter, *melted the creamy solids removed*	110g/4oz

Sauce Bretonne is great with any firm, white fish, or you may even serve it with wild salmon or sea trout. It has peppery watercress, mustard, the mild aniseed of chervil and the buttery vinegar to give it body, acidity and richness. If you don't have any tarragon vinegar, use white wine vinegar with a teaspoon of fresh tarragon. Turbot is the king of the white fish to my mind, and a real treat that benefits from simple baking in a hot oven.

→ Preheat the oven to 200°C/400°F/Gas 6. Stuff the TURBOT with the HERBS. Grease a large roasting tin with BUTTER, and place the fish in it. Pour over the WHITE WINE, dot the fish with BUTTER and season. Cover the fish with a sheet of greaseproof paper and cook it for about 25 minutes before testing it with a skewer right the way through. How long the fish will take depends on the thickness, so if it is only a tiny bit resistant at its thickest point, check it again in 5 minutes. It is not difficult — fish are not temperamental or more difficult to master than meat, but there is less leeway between being cooked and overcooked. Roughly 10 minutes before you are going to test the fish, start making your sauce.

Sauce Bretonne
→ Stir together the EGG YOLKS, SALT AND PEPPER with the DIJON MUSTARD. Add a few drops of the TARRAGON VINEGAR, then the WATERCRESS and CHERVIL, and slowly stir in the melted BUTTER, a few drops at a time to start with, as you would for mayonnaise. The sauce will hold if you place it over a bowl of hot water, but do not make it in advance — you want the herbs to be green and fresh tasting. Experiment with other herbs like chives, flat-leaf parsley and dill, the best herb if you want to try the sauce with poached wild salmon or sea trout.

Turbot with Sauce Vierge

SERVES 6

turbot	1.4kg/3llb
Sauce Vierge	
ripe tomatoes	4
red wine vinegar	1 tbsp
garlic clove, *peeled and sliced*	1
shallot, *peeled and very finely chopped*	1
salt and black pepper	
best olive oil	150ml/5fl oz
fresh basil	a small bunch

Cook the fish as in the previous recipe and try this simple, raw sauce, which is really just a glorious emulsion of a dressing.

→ Skin, de-seed and chop the TOMATOES. Let them macerate with the VINEGAR, GARLIC and SHALLOT, together with a little SALT and a good scrunch of BLACK PEPPER, for 30 minutes. Stir in the OLIVE OIL and add the torn leaves of BASIL before pouring it over the warm, poached FISH.

Baked Turbot in a Cream Sauce

SERVES 5

turbot	1.4kg/3lb
black pepper	a few screws
coarse sea salt	
butter	several knobs
unsalted butter	55g/2oz
cayenne pepper	a small pinch
whisking crème crue	170ml/6fl oz
flat-leaf parsley, *chopped*	a handful

→ Preheat oven to 200°C/400°F/Gas 6. A glueily grey and tweedy-skinned fresh turbot is the most heavenly of fish, and should be cooked as simply as possible. I placed my TURBOT on a large piece of foil on a baking sheet, scrunching the foil up around the edge of the fish like a protective nest. I then anointed the fish with a few screws of BLACK PEPPER, some coarse SEA SALT and some knobs of BUTTER, and put it on the middle shelf for 25 minutes. It was just unresistant right the way through when spiked with a knife point.

→ I poured the buttery, fishy juices into a small pan with a further 50g/2oz of unsalted BUTTER, and heated it, having closed the fish up in its foil to keep hot. I then added a small pinch of CAYENNE and some SEASONING to the melted butter, and the whisking CRÈME CRUE, and stirred it until it bubbled hard. Throw in a handful of chopped PARSLEY at the last minute, and then slice the fish and pour over the unctuous sauce.

Breaded Plaice

SERVES 2

flour	
sea salt and black pepper	
organic egg, *beaten*	1
brown breadcrumbs	a plateful
parsley, *finely chopped*	2 tbsp
lemon	*zest* of 1 and quartered wedges for serving
large fillets of plaice, *skinned*	2

A simple supper and a lovely one when this milky-fleshed fish is in its prime, particularly when it comes with a fat slick of grainy roe to contrast with the soft, sweet white flesh.

→ Preheat the oven to 180°C/350°F/Gas 4. Put some FLOUR on a large flat plate and SEASON. Whisk the EGG in a separate wide flat dish. Mix the BREADCRUMBS with the PARSLEY and LEMON ZEST and put them on another plate.

→ Dip the PLAICE into the flour, shake the residue off and then dip each fillet into the beaten egg, then into the breadcrumb mixture, coating thoroughly on both sides. Place the fillets on a buttered baking tray and put in the oven for 12–15 minutes or until soft right through when pierced with a skewer.

Baked Cod with Stove-dried Tomatoes

SERVES 4

olive oil	
cod	4 good, thick pieces
sea salt and black pepper	
thyme	a sprig
stove-dried tomatoes (see p. 135)	4 handfuls

This dish shows the pleasure and ease with which you can cook a good piece of fish simply, successfully and succulently. Dry the tomatoes 24 hours before you want to cook the cod. Depending on how many you dry, you can use them with cheese on toast and with pasta over the next couple of days.

→ Preheat the oven to 200°C/400°F/Gas 6. Oil a shallow baking tray with a film of good OLIVE OIL. Place each piece of FISH on the tray, add a few more drops of OIL to the top of the cod, with your fingers over the neck of the bottle to prevent a gush. SEASON well and pull the THYME LEAVES off the sprig onto the pieces of fish. Bake for about 8 minutes, remove from the oven and put a handful of the stove-dried TOMATOES on top of each chunk of cod.

→ Return to the oven for 4–7 minutes, testing after 4 minutes, with a skewer pushed right through the fish at its thickest part. If the skewer slips right down unresistingly, the fish is cooked through. It is as easy as that, but be alert! Overcook a fish by 2 minutes and it's ruined.

→ Serve with oodles of mash and a raw fennel salad grated fine on a mandolin and spruced up with lemon juice and olive oil to taste and some black pepper, 20 minutes or so before you want to eat it to soften the fennel a little. Two slimly shaved bulbs should suffice for four people.

Baked Cod with Greek Potatoes

SERVES 4

thick fillet of really fresh cod	about 1 kg/2¼lb
olive oil	
sea salt and black pepper	
Greek Potatoes	
potatoes	1kg/2¼lb
onion, *peeled and finely chopped*	225g/8oz
garlic cloves	6
fresh thyme OR oregano	a handful
salt and black pepper	
best olive oil	300ml/10fl oz
lemons	juice of 2

The cod—thick, whitely translucent, so tender that it falls away from the skin in giant flakes—is a dish that shuns embellishment, except the best grassy green olive oil. It doesn't even need spritzing with lemon—the Greek potatoes with which you marry the cod bring that, absorbing olive oil, lemon juice and the scent of the herbs and almost braising in their own juice.

→ Preheat the oven to 200°C/400°F/Gas 6. Peel the POTATOES and cut into long, thin pieces rather than chunks—about four pieces if they are medium sized. Put the potatoes into a gratin dish or roasting tin so that they fit snugly in one layer. Throw in the ONION and GARLIC and the HERBS stripped from their stems, SEASON and add the OLIVE OIL and LEMON JUICE. Now add enough water barely to cover. Cook for 45 minutes before turning the potatoes over and cooking for another 45 minutes. An hour and a half should do it. Cook your FISH during the last 15 minutes.

→ Butter a gratin dish thickly and lay your cod to rest in it, skin side down. Dribble some really fine OLIVE OIL over the top, Ravida or Seggiano if possible. SEASON well. Bake for 15 minutes, then test with the point of a sharp knife or skewer. If it goes right through the flesh with no resistance, the fish is done.

Roast Cod with Lentils and Roasted Vegetables

SERVES 2

thick cod fillet	450g/1lb or so
olive oil	2 tbsp
streaky bacon rashers	3 or 4
crème fraîche	2 heaped tbsp
Braised Puy Lentils	
Puy lentils	200g/7oz
fennel bulb	1
onion	1
olive oil	
fresh thyme	small sprig
cherry tomatoes	12

Buy the thickest fillet of cod you can find. The Puy lentils need no soaking, so the whole dish can be made in 50 minutes.

→ Just cover the LENTILS with water in a large, heavy-bottomed pot. Bring them to the boil, then cover and turn down to a simmer. They will take about 40 minutes to cook.

→ Preheat the oven to 220°C/425°F/Gas 7. Chop the FENNEL bulb in half and each half into thirds, cut the peeled ONION into large chunks, and place both in a small roasting tin. Pour a slug of OLIVE OIL over the top, SEASON, add the sprig of THYME and put in the oven to roast. After 20 minutes, add the TOMATOES. All the vegetables should be soft after a further 20 minutes, but pierce with a skewer to test.

→ Put the COD in a gratin dish, pour a good couple of table-spoons of OLIVE OIL over the top, season well and cook in the hot oven for 12 minutes before piercing with a skewer. The flesh should be unresistant right the way through.

While the fish is cooking, snip the BACON into tiny strips and fry them in a little pan until well browned on both sides. Drain the lentils, then add the bacon. Tip in the roasted vegetables with their juice, and the CRÈME FRAÎCHE. Serve the cod alongside or on top of the lentils. You may wish to serve some creamy mashed potato, too.

Roast Loin of Cod with Green Olive Chermoula

SERVES 4

cumin seeds	2 tsp
coriander seeds	1 tsp
onion, *peeled and cut into chunks*	1
garlic cloves, *peeled and chopped*	3
fresh flat-leaf parsley and coriander	a bunch of each
fresh ginger, *peeled and chopped*	a finger
paprika	1 tsp
large Cerignola or similar green olives	6
preserved lemon	1
olive oil	4 tbsp
sea salt, black pepper and cayenne	
thick pieces of cod loin	2 × 600g/1lb 4oz

The chermoula is an exotic species, a musky, chunky, Moroccan spice rub that I use with chicken, lamb or fish. The olives and preserved lemons give it a sharp fragrance and acidity and the cod carries robust flavours with fortitude. A powerful and specially good dish.

→ Heat the oven to 200°C/400°F/Gas 6. Dry-roast the CUMIN and CORIANDER seeds briefly in a small pan for 30–60 seconds, then crush them to powder in a mortar. Put the ONION, GARLIC, HERBS, GINGER, PAPRIKA and dry-roasted spices in the food processor and blitz until they look finely chopped (but don't overdo it).

→ Chop the OLIVES and LEMON together coarsely, discarding the pips. Stir them into the spice mixture, adding OLIVE OIL to make a paste. You may not need all the oil. Season to taste, adding a teaspoon tip of CAYENNE, and slap the paste over the fish. Cover with clingfilm and refrigerate for a couple of hours.

→ Remove an hour before cooking. I cooked my cod in an oiled gratin dish for 15 minutes.

Cod in Grain Mustard Sauce

SERVES 4

coarse sea salt	
cod fillet, about 2.5cm/in thick	4 × 325g/12oz
fresh thyme	
Grain Mustard Sauce	
butter	55g/2oz
flour	55g/2oz
milk	425ml/15fl oz
pepper	
grain mustard	1½ dsrtsp

→ Preheat the oven to 220°C/425°F/Gas 7. Scatter a layer of SEA SALT over the bottom of a roasting tray, then the pulled leaves from a few sprigs of THYME. Sit the pieces of FISH on top, skin side on the salt. Place in the middle of the hot oven. My pieces took 12 minutes, but test with a skewer that they are not resistant, but opaque. Their own liquid will have just started collecting on top.

→ Make a basic BÉCHAMEL SAUCE (see p. 402) in a small saucepan, by melting the BUTTER gently, adding the FLOUR, then pouring on the hot MILK and stirring continuously for 10 minutes until thickened and smooth. Drop in the first spoon of MUSTARD with some freshly ground PEPPER, stir briefly, and taste. Add the other half dessertspoon if you like the robustness; it is a very good foil for the fish.

→ Place the fish on a hot plate—the dissolved salt remains on the tray, and doesn't overwhelm the thyme-scented cod—then pour over some hot mustard sauce.

Poached Salmon

wild salmon	1
white wine	a glass
butter OR olive oil	a lump a splosh
dill, fennel, parsley and chervil	
salt and pepper	

I don't have a fish-poaching kettle, but this en papillote method does the same job just as effectively, and the low cooking temperature retains all the moisture and colour of the fish. Time this carefully—it only takes a few extra minutes to turn juicy succulence to dry desiccation! Use this method for sea trout too, which I favour even above salmon.

→ Preheat the oven to 150°C/300°F/Gas 2. Put the SALMON on a large piece of foil on a baking sheet, raising the edges of the foil a bit so you can anoint the fish with a glass of WHITE WINE. Add a splosh of OLIVE OIL if the fish is to be eaten cold, or a lump of BUTTER for hot. A few branches of any combination of DILL, FENNEL, PARSLEY and CHERVIL stuffed into the cavity will add to the flavour. Scrunch over some salt and pepper, and seal your fish into its baggy parcel. Make two foil straps and put them underneath the parcel at each end so you can lift the fish out more easily when it is cooked.

→ Up to 2 and a bit kilos or 5lb, the fish will take an hour. If it is any larger, allow 12 minutes to the 450g/1lb. Leave the fish to cool to tepid in its parcel, when you can skin it easily. Serve hot with Hollandaise (see p. 403) or cold with Mayonnaise (see p.404).

Grilled Dover Sole

SERVES 2

Dover soles, each about 285–340g/10–12oz weight	2
unsalted butter, *clarified*	55g/2oz
flat-leaf parsley, *chopped*	1 tbsp
unsalted butter, *softened*	55g/2oz
lemon	1

This could be the simplest recipe in the book, but it is undoubtedly one of the finest when the sole is fresh, but not cooked, straight from the sea. The flesh needs a day or two out of the water to firm up to its lovely firm but yielding, juicy texture.

→ The SOLE should be skinned on both sides, the head left on and the roe in if there is any. Your fishmonger will do this.

→ Clarify the BUTTER. Heat it in a small pan and skim the milky residue from the surface before pouring the butter into a bowl, leaving the white solids at the bottom of the pan. Make the parsley butter by mashing the PARSLEY into the softened butter and place in the fridge to firm up.

→ Brush the sole with the clarified butter on both sides. Put them under the grill for about 5 minutes a side or until a skewer slips easily through the flesh and to the backbone. Serve with a couple of knobs of parsley butter placed on the fish and a wedge of LEMON at the side.

Sole Duglère

SERVES 2

sole, *skinned and filleted*	1 × 675g/1½lb
unsalted butter	30g/1oz
flour	25g/scant oz
double cream	90ml/3fl oz
parsley, *finely chopped*	1 dsrtsp
tomatoes, *skinned, seeded and chopped*	2
sea salt and black pepper	

Fish stock

head, bones and skin of sole plus any extra bones from your fishmonger
1 onion, *sliced*
parsley stalks
fennel
chervil
tarragon
half white wine, half water

This was a dish that the late, greatest-of-them-all George Perry-Smith used to serve at Riverside in Helford, Cornwall, although I don't have his own recipe. It is all about refined simplicity, of which George was the master—not one ingredient too many or too few, and all of unimpeachable quality. His cooking, his understanding of how little one had to do to make good food taste superlative, was unequalled.

→ Preheat the oven to 180°C/350°F/Gas 4. BUTTER a gratin dish that will hold the SOLE FILLETS in a single layer, put them in and season. Pour over 200–300ml/7–10fl oz of hot FISH STOCK and poach in the oven for 10 minutes. Pour the fish stock into a jug and keep the fish warm under a piece of butter paper in the warming oven.

→ Melt the BUTTER, add the FLOUR to make a roux and whisk in the strained fish liquor from cooking the fish. Whisk until smooth and keep simmering for a few minutes before adding the CREAM and letting it bubble hard for 2–3 minutes. Take off the heat and add the PARSLEY and TOMATOES. Correct the SEASONING, put the fillets on individual plates and pour some sauce over them.

VEGETA

RIAN
dishes

Flageolet or Haricot Bean Casserole

Serves 4–6

flageolet OR haricot beans	450g/1lb
onion, in its skin	½
celery sticks	3
carrots, *cut into chunks*	3
leek tops	3
bouquet garni	1
olive oil	1 or 2 tbsp
shallots, *finely chopped*	2
garlic cloves, *finely chopped*	3 or 4
salt and pepper	
brown bread	a handful
flat-leaf parsley	a handful
Parmesan cheese, *grated*	2–3 tbsp
butter	30–55g/1–2oz

This makes a wonderful one-pot casserole in its own right. Start the day before by soaking the beans overnight.

→ Soak the BEANS in cold water overnight. Drain, rinse and put them in a large saucepan with WATER OR STOCK to cover the beans. Add the ONION, one of the CELERY sticks cut into three or four pieces, CARROTS, LEEK TOPS and BOUQUET GARNI. Bring to the boil, skim off the scum, cover tightly and simmer until the beans are tender, about 1½ hours.

→ Purée a couple of tablespoons of the beans in a little of the cooking liquid. Remove and discard the other vegetables and drain the remaining flageolets, reserving the cooking liquid.

→ Finely chop the remaining CELERY stick and sauté in the OLIVE OIL with the SHALLOTS and GARLIC until softened. Add the whole flageolets and mix gently. Season with salt and pepper. Stir in the BEAN PURÉE.

→ Preheat the oven to 180°C/350°F/Gas 4. Put the bean mixture in a casserole, and add a little more of the bean cooking liquid so that the mixture almost fills the dish. Whizz together the BROWN BREAD and PARSLEY in a food processor and add the grated PARMESAN. Spread this mixture over the beans, dot with butter, and cook in the oven for 20–25 minutes.

Haveli ke Kofta

Serves 8

small courgettes	4
small carrots	4
cauliflower and broccoli	1 floret of each
fine green beans	55g/2oz
baby sweetcorn	55g/2oz
small green chillies	16
sunflower oil	1 tbsp
black mustard seeds	½ tsp
fresh root ginger	2.5cm/1in piece
salt	
turmeric	½ tsp
chilli powder	½ tsp

These are the most delicious parcels of shredded vegetables and spices formed into miniature aubergine shapes around a green chilli, coated in cornflour, briskly deep fried, and dunked in a spiced tomato sauce. If you think it sounds complicated, don't, it's no more so than making a stuffing.

→ Grate the COURGETTES on the coarse side of the grater, then do the same with the CARROTS. Grate the BROCCOLI and CAULIFLOWER, then shred the BEANS finely. Grate the BABY SWEETCORNS. Slit and chop 3 of the CHILLIES.

→ Heat the OIL in a heavy pan, add the MUSTARD SEEDS and wait until they crackle. Add the chopped GINGER and the chopped green chillies, stir for a moment, add the salt, turmeric and chilli powder. Add the grated vegetables and cook until they begin to soften, then remove from the heat and leave them to cool. Grate the POTATO, mix it into the vegetables, then add the chopped CORIANDER and BREADCRUMBS. Slit the remaining CHILLIES down the middle and briefly fry them.

potato, *cooked, peeled*	55g/2oz
fresh coriander	a bunch
breadcrumbs	30g/1oz
cornflour	2 tbsp
oil for deep frying	

→ Shape the koftas by flattening each one into a 6cm/2½in disc in the palm of your hand, lying a chilli across the middle of it, stalk sticking out, then shaping it into a mini aubergine shape. Dust all over with cornflour, and deep-fry in a flavourless oil until golden brown, about 1–2 minutes.

→ Serve with the kofta sauce and sprinkle with chopped fresh coriander. You can do all the preparation up to the deep frying part in advance.

Kofta Sauce

MAKES ENOUGH FOR 8 TO GO
WITH THE HAVELI KE KOFTA

tomatoes	750g/1lb 10oz
fresh root ginger	2.5cm/1in piece
garlic cloves, *peeled*	4 or 5
unsalted butter	55g/2oz
medium onions, *peeled and chopped*	2
green chillies	2
vegetable oil	1 tbsp
tomato paste	1 tbsp
garam masala	½ tsp
dried fenugreek	½ tsp
chilli powder	½ tsp, or to taste
single cream	60ml/2fl oz
fresh coriander, *chopped*	1 handful
salt and white pepper	

→ Skin, seed, chop and salt the TOMATOES. Purée the peeled GINGER and GARLIC in a blender or pestle and mortar with a tablespoon of WATER to make a smooth paste. Melt the BUTTER in a pan, add the ONIONS, sprinkle over a bit of SALT to get the full impact of the flavour; do the same with the chopped GREEN CHILLIES, and sauté for a minute. Add the tomatoes, reduce the heat, and let everything simmer until the tomatoes are soft. Blitz in a food processor.

→ Heat the OIL, add the ginger and garlic paste, cook for a minute, add the tomato paste and the remaining SPICES, and stir for 30 seconds. As you add the spices, sprinkle over a bit of WATER, which helps release the flavours. Add the tomato sauce, and simmer until it thickens. Carefully place the KOFTAS in the sauce, and simmer for 2–3 minutes. Remove them to a heated serving dish, add the CREAM to the sauce, stir to amalgamate, and pour it over the koftas. Sprinkle over a few chopped CORIANDER leaves and serve.

Stuffed Courgettes, Peppers, Aubergines or Tomatoes

SERVES 4

medium courgettes	4
red pepper	1
yellow pepper	1
aubergine	1 large or 2 smaller
medium tomatoes	8
fresh thyme, *chopped*	1 tsp
medium onions, red or white, *finely chopped*	2
extra virgin olive oil	4 tbsp
large garlic cloves, *peeled and finely chopped*	2
sea salt and black pepper	
flat-leaf parsley, *chopped*	2 tbsp
basil leaves, *torn*	2 tbsp
tarragon, *chopped*	1 tbsp
brown OR white basmati OR long grain rice, *cooked*	110–170g/4–6 oz
feta cheese, *diced*	55g/2oz
Parmesan cheese, *freshly grated*	110–170g/4–6 oz
stale bread, *soaked in warm water and torn to shreds*	2 crustless slices
extra olive oil	
hot vegetable stock (see p. 55)	150–300ml/5–10fl oz

Stuffed vegetables, Provençal-style, are as delicious, if not more so, at room temperature or cold as they are hot. The cooling down seems to bring out the flavours. Just don't get too exercised by the filling ingredients, which you can change and add to or subtract from easily according to the season, the store cupboard, the mood and the purse.

→ Halve the COURGETTES horizontally and remove and dice some of the inner flesh with a teaspoon. Trim off the ends. Cut a circle around the stems of the PEPPERS and remove the stem, seeds and ribs of white core. Halve the AUBERGINE horizontally and remove the stem. Scoop out some of the flesh and dice it. Halve the TOMATOES, scatter over a couple of slivers of GARLIC and a teaspoon of fresh THYME and dribble on OLIVE OIL. Roast the tomatoes in a hot oven, 200°C/400°F/Gas 6, for 15 minutes or until softened.

→ Sweat the ONIONS gently in the OLIVE OIL until softened and pale gold, about 15 minutes, then transfer half the onion to another pan and add the courgettes and half the garlic to one pan and the aubergine and half the GARLIC to the other. Turn the heat up and fry the two sets of vegetables for 10 minutes, stirring and tossing them round the pan. Remove the pans from the heat.

→ In the courgette pan toss in half the roasted, chopped tomatoes with their juices and thyme, add the TARRAGON and half the cooked RICE, and all the FETA cheese. SEASON. In the aubergine pan add the rest of the roasted, chopped tomatoes, the PARSLEY and BASIL and the rest of the RICE.

→ Spoon as much courgette mixture back into the courgettes on a roasting tin as you can pile in, and do the same with the aubergine. Then use the rest of the two mixtures to stuff the PEPPERS, one mixture for the yellow and one for the red. The vegetables should be cheek by jowl so that they support each other in the gratin dish. Cover the tops of the vegetables with the shredded BREADCRUMBS, then with a generous handful of freshly grated PARMESAN.

→ Add a ladle of hot STOCK to the roasting tin so that the vegetables steam and roast at the same time and the dish doesn't dry out. Check at half time and top the stock up if you need to. Dribble over extra OIL and bake for about 45 minutes or until the vegetables are not resistant to a skewer poked right through to their middles. Leave to cool to warm, or cool completely. You may make the vegetables glisten with a little more olive oil just before serving.

→ You may also stuff tomatoes, the large, organic kind, in which case slice off their tops first and scoop out the seeds with a teaspoon. Use their flesh in the stuffing, adding it to the onion when you add the herbs and garlic.

Cauliflower Cheese

SERVES 4

large organic cauliflower, *broken into florets*	1
grain mustard	1 tbsp
OR English mustard powder	1 tsp
mature farmhouse Cheddar, *grated*	85–110g/3–4oz
Parmesan cheese, *grated*	55g/2oz
cream (optional)	tbsp or so

Béchamel sauce (see also p. 402)

milk	850ml/1½ pints
bay leaf	1
onion, *halved*	1
nutmeg, *grated*	
butter	55g/2oz
plain white flour	55g/2oz
salt and pepper	

This simple dish really defines home cooking—if you cook it well. You need a really good, unpasteurised Cheddar like Montgomery's, Quicke's, Keen's or Daylesford so the dish hits the palate with a sharp, tangy, farmyardy note, and you want a touch of grain or English mustard for a little heat.

→ Make the BÉCHAMEL as on p. 402 and while it is cooking, bring a large pan of salted water to the boil. Hurl in the CAULIFLOWER and cook for about 5 minutes or until the stalks are still resistant but not offensively so! A skewer will tell you all you need to know. Drain in a colander. While the cauliflower is cooking, finish the sauce. Stir the MUSTARD into the béchamel and begin to add the CHEDDAR CHEESE on a very low heat. When you have the strength of flavour you like, stop. Adjust the SEASONING or mustard if you need to and add a little CREAM if you feel like it, no more than a tablespoon or two.

→ Put the cauliflower in a gratin dish and pour over the unctuous cloak. Scatter a good handful of PARMESAN over the top and either put under the grill or in a hot oven until you've got a lovely dark mahogany pattern on top and the sauce is bubbling. Don't go past this stage; you don't want it to split and turn oily.

Broccoli and Cauliflower Cheese
→ Make this with half broccoli for a slightly different flavour and a better colour. And you can roast the cauliflower and broccoli instead of boiling. Roll the florets in olive oil, add a little chopped onion and garlic and roast until al dente. Then add the sauce and finish as above.

Hazelnut, Pumpkin and Blue Cheese Fritters

MAKES 8–10 FRITTERS

organic eggs	4
organic self-raising flour	140g/5oz
raw pumpkin or squash, *grated*	1 cup
roasted hazelnuts, *chopped*	55g/2oz
blue cheese, *crumbled*	55g/2oz
parsley, *chopped*	a handful
sea salt and freshly ground black pepper	
vegetable oil	120ml/4fl oz
unsalted butter	55g/2oz
hollandaise sauce (see p. 403) or tomato sauce (see p. 140) to serve	

On a recent trip to give some cooking masterclasses in New Zealand, I breakfasted with Jo Seagar who has a seriously wonderful and homely café, Seagars, in a tiny town called Oxford in Canterbury. These gutsy, unusual fritters are adapted from Jo Seagar Cooks, *a delightful book with 100 recipes from Jo's kitchen. She suggests a hollandaise with them, but if you want to cut the richness, my preference is for a fresh tomato sauce with a little chilli to spice it up.*

→ Beat the EGGS in a bowl then mix in the FLOUR until you have a smooth batter. Add the PUMPKIN, HAZELNUTS, BLUE CHEESE, PARSLEY and SEASONING.

→ Heat the OIL and BUTTER in a large, heavy bottomed frying pan over a medium heat until they begin to bubble. Spoon 3–4 fritters into the pan and cook for approximately 3 minutes, they should look browned, then turn them over carefully and cook the other side. Drain the fritters on paper towel and keep them warm in the oven while you cook the remaining mixture.

→ Grated courgettes work well in place of the pumpkin, and colour the fritters with lovely speckles of green.

Squash, Parmesan and Goat's Cheese Pudding

SERVES 6

red onion OR butternut squash (you need about 450g/1lb pumpkin flesh)	
olive oil	
unsalted butter	85g/3oz
fresh thyme, *chopped*	6 sprigs
lemon juice	
sea salt and black pepper	
double organic cream	150–300ml/5–10fl oz
organic eggs	3
crottins de Chavignol OR small barrels of aged goat's cheese	2
Parmesan cheese, *grated*	

By all means make this dish with carrots if you prefer, in which case slice the carrots and cook them in a pan with water to come half way up them and the butter plopped into the pan. Cook at a fierce heat, tossing and turning the carrots until the water has evaporated and they are coated in butter. Squeeze over some lemon juice and continue as for the pumpkin pud, pureeing the carrots in the food processor so as to make life easier with the thyme and whisked cream and eggs.

→ Preheat the oven to 220°C/425°F/Gas 7. Seed the SQUASH, cut into melon-like wedges, season and dribble with a little OLIVE OIL. Bake in the oven until soft, about 30-40 minutes.

→ When the squash is soft right through when pierced with a skewer, scrape it out of its skin and put the flesh in a large bowl with the BUTTER and mash them together. Add a spritz of LEMON JUICE to take the sweet edge off it, and the THYME and SEASONING.

→ Whisk the CREAM and EGGS together and stir them into the squash mixture. Crumble in the CROTTINS and scrape everything into a well-buttered gratin dish. Sprinkle lightly with grated PARMESAN. Bake for 30-35 minutes or until the top of the pudding is swollen and bursting its browned top.

Pilav

SERVES 2

unsalted butter	55g/2oz
medium onion, *finely chopped*	1
cardamom pods, *lightly crushed*	6
cinnamon stick	1
bay leaves	2
basmati rice	170g/6oz
vegetable stock (see p. 55) or water	about 300ml/10fl oz

A Middle Eastern pilav is a cheap and amazingly versatile dish that lends itself well to the treasures of the store cupboard—use dried apricots, raisins and prunes; pistachios, cashew nuts, almonds and pine nuts; coriander, cardamom, saffron and bay. A pilav is a much drier dish than a risotto and is made with long-grain basmati rice, either brown or white.

→ Melt the BUTTER in a pan and add the chopped ONION. Sauté the onion until it is beginning to soften and turn translucent, about 5 minutes. Throw in the SPICES and stir for a minute or so until they release their heady scent, then pour in the RICE. Stir until the rice is coated all over, then add enough STOCK OR WATER to cover the grain by about 2.5cm/1in. Bring to the boil then reduce to a simmer and cover with a well-fitting lid. Continue to cook for 15 minutes. Keep the lid on, but remove the pan from the heat and leave for 5 minutes.
→ You may eat the pilav on its own with just a knob of butter or with a gently spiced vegetable stew. If you want to add some toasted flaked almonds or pine nuts, stir them in, with or without a handful of raisins you've soaked in a bowl of warm water to plump up for 20 minutes, then drained.

Tomato Pilav

SERVES 6

olive oil	3–4 tbsp
medium onions, *finely chopped*	2
garlic cloves, *peeled*	2
tomatoes, *seeded and skinned* OR the equivalent of tinned tomatoes	about 900g/2lb
sea salt and black pepper	
unrefined brown sugar	1 tsp
bay leaves	2
long-grain rice, *washed and drained*	450g/1lb

→ Heat the OLIVE OIL in a large, heavy-bottomed pan, then fry the ONIONS and GARLIC over a medium heat until the onions have softened and turned translucent. Throw in the chopped TOMATOES with the SEASONING, SUGAR, and BAY LEAVES and sauté for a few minutes. Cover with WATER and simmer gently for about 45 minutes. You may need to add a little water as the sauce reduces to prevent it sticking or turning too jammy.
→ Pour in the RICE and an equal quantity of WATER, bring to the boil, then simmer gently with a tight lid for about 20 minutes, when the rice should be tender. Remove from the heat and leave covered for 5 minutes before serving.

Turkish Aubergine Pilav

Serves 6

aubergines	450g/1lb
sea salt	
olive oil	1 teacup
long-grain rice	450g/1lb
butter	a knob
yoghurt (garlic and cumin optional)	

This is a dish that I found in the wonderful Claudia Roden's classic book Middle Eastern Food, *one of my bibles when I was at university. I have adapted it slightly by roasting the aubergine, as it absorbs less oil that way and is therefore less oily in the finished dish.*

→ Preheat the oven to 200°C/400°F/Gas 6. Cut the AUBERGINE into small cubes and toss them in about half the OIL. Put them in a single layer on a baking tray and roast them in a hot oven until they've softened. Test them with a knife point after 15–20 minutes.

→ Wash and drain the RICE well. Heat the rest of the OIL in a pan, pour in the rice and stir to coat before adding two teacups of WATER. Bring it to the boil, reduce to a simmer, cover and cook for 15 minutes. Now bury the chunks of aubergine in the rice and add a couple of tablespoons of WATER and a large knob of BUTTER. Cover the pan with a clean tea towel and press the lid on firmly so that the dish can steam gently for about 20 minutes. Serve cold with YOGHURT. If you want to spice the yoghurt up a little, add a minced clove of garlic and teaspoon or two of cumin seeds that you've toasted in a hot pan over the heat for a minute, then crushed.

Broad Bean Pilav

Serves 6

coriander seeds	1 tsp
olive oil	3–4 tbsp
OR unsalted butter	75g/2½oz
large onion, *finely chopped*	1
fresh OR frozen broad beans (podded weight)	450g/1lb
sea salt and black pepper	
garlic cloves, *finely minced*	2
fresh dill and flat-leaf parsley, *chopped*	a handful of each
long-grain rice, *washed and drained*	450g/1lb
yoghurt (garlic and cumin optional)	

This is a delicious hot accompaniment to other dishes, or it can be served cold like the aubergine pilav with yoghurt and salad.

→ Toast the CORIANDER seeds in a hot pan for a minute, then crush them in a mortar. Heat the OIL OR BUTTER in a large, heavy-bottomed pan and sauté the ONION over a medium heat until it has softened and turned translucent. Add the BROAD BEANS, SEASONING, GARLIC, coriander seeds and half the fresh HERBS, pour in the rice, and turn to coat everything in oil. Cover the rice with WATER, bring to the boil, then cover with a lid and simmer gently for about 15–20 minutes or until the rice is tender.

→ Add the rest of the fresh HERBS and serve right away if you are using this as a hot accompaniment, or cool and serve with the yoghurt as suggested in the recipe for Turkish Aubergine Pilav above.

Lemon Risotto

(see p. 55)

SERVES 4

unsalted butter	55g/2oz
olive oil	1 tbsp
shallots, *very finely chopped*	2
celery stick, *very finely chopped*	
risotto rice, such as Carnaroli or Arborio	285g/10oz
vegetable stock (see p. 55)	1 litre/1¾ pints
fresh sage leaves, *chopped*	5 or 6
fresh rosemary, *chopped*	a small sprig
organic lemon	zest and juice of 1
organic egg yolk	1
Parmesan cheese, *grated*	4 tbsp
double cream	4 tbsp
salt and black pepper	

Risotto slips easily into the category of food best described as soothing. Comforting as it is in the eating, it is the cooking, with the gradual, gentle application of hot stock and the repetitive, mesmeric stirring of the wooden spoon, that makes it a relaxing ritual which is also simplicity itself—IF you follow the rules. This recipe is from the peerless Italian food writer Anna Del Conte.

→ Heat half the BUTTER, the OIL, and the finely chopped SHALLOTS and CELERY in a heavy saucepan and cook until the soffritto of shallot and celery is softened, about 7 minutes. Mix in the RICE and continue cooking and stirring until the rice is well coated in the fats and partly translucent.

→ While this is happening, heat the STOCK and keep it simmering all through the preparation of the dish. When the rice becomes shiny and partly translucent, after 2 or 3 minutes, pour in about 150ml/5fl oz of the stock. Stir very thoroughly and cook until the rice has absorbed most of the stock. Add another small ladleful of simmering stock and continue in this manner until the rice is ready. You may not need all the stock. Good-quality Italian rice takes about 20–22 minutes to cook.

→ Mix the HERBS with the LEMON ZEST, adding them to the risotto halfway through the cooking. In a small bowl, combine the EGG YOLK, the JUICE OF HALF THE LEMON, the PARMESAN cheese, CREAM and a very generous grinding of BLACK PEPPER. Mix well with a fork.

→ When the risotto is al dente draw the pan off the heat and stir in the egg and cream mixture and the remaining butter. Cover the pan and leave to rest for 2 minutes or so off the heat. Check the SEASONING, and that there is enough lemon juice, then give the risotto an energetic stir, transfer it to a heated dish or bowl and serve at once with more grated PARMESAN in a bowl to pass round.

→ Be warned—risottos do not stand around well, but I have found it absolutely fine to get the risotto to the halfway stage up to an hour before you want to serve it, then leave it with a ladleful of hot stock poured over it and a tight lid on the pan while you have your first course or drinks. Then carry on with another ladleful of stock, cooking the rice for its last 10 minutes.

Leek and Vacherin Mont d'Or Risotto

SERVES 4

slim leeks, *cleaned*	4
unsalted butter	85g/3oz
Carnaroli OR Arborio rice	340g/12oz
vegetable stock (see p. 55)	up to 900ml/1½ pints
small Vacherin Mont d'Or cheese	1
salt and pepper	

You can cook this dish up to the final 10 minutes an hour or two earlier if it suits you, making sure there is a good pool of stock for it to absorb when you leave it. Vacherin Mont d'Or is a rich soft cow's milk cheese.

→ Chop the white parts of the LEEKS only into thin discs. Melt the BUTTER in a heavy-bottomed frying pan, then sauté the leeks gently until wilted and softened. Add the RICE, stirring to coat thoroughly in the butter, then start adding the hot STOCK a couple of ladles at a time, and keep stirring the rice until the stock is almost all absorbed (see p. 209). Add more stock, and continue stirring for about 20 minutes until the rice is just cooked, starchy, with a bite , but neither hard nor porridgey.
→ Season with salt and fresh pepper, remembering that the cheese is quite salty. There should be enough liquid for the risotto to have a slightly soupy quality. Ladle into bowls, then drop a generous spoonful of the golden Vacherin over the summit of each serving.

Risotto Primavera

SERVES 4

leaf artichokes	4
asparagus	1 bundle
extra virgin olive oil	3–4 tbsp
small onion, *finely chopped*	1
Carnaroli OR Arborio rice	340g/12oz
white wine, *heated to simmering point* (optional)	a glass
vegetable stock (see p. 55)	about 850ml/1½ pints
fresh or frozen peas (podded weight)	110g/4oz
small fresh or frozen broad beans (podded weight)	110g/4oz
butter	a knob the size of a couple of walnuts
sea salt and black pepper	
Parmesan cheese, *freshly grated*	170g/6oz
mint, chervil and parsley, *chopped*	1 tbsp of each

In late spring or early summer, this risotto, verdant with green vegetables, is one of the greats. You may use any combination of the vegetables mentioned, and the quantities are very much guidelines, as you may have only a couple of artichoke hearts or be able to afford only a few spears of asparagus at the beginning of the season when it is most expensive. Put the artichokes in cold water with the juice of a lemon to acidulate and stop them from turning black.

→ Bring a pan full of water to a rolling boil and throw in the acidulated ARTICHOKES. Depending on their size they will take 20–30 minutes to cook, but the best test is to try to pull a leaf away from the stem. If it comes away easily the artichoke is cooked. Trim the ASPARAGUS—snap off the bottom of the stems where they are woody, then peel the bottom half of each stem with a potato peeler. Steam the asparagus while the artichokes are cooking—the water beneath them will also contribute to the stock. When the spears are tender, remove from the steamer and chop into chunks, the tips twice the length of the stems.
→ Heat the OIL in a large, heavy-based pan and add the finely chopped ONION, stirring until it begins to soften and turn translucent. Pour in the RICE and turn it in the oil until it is well

coated all over, then add the hot WHITE WINE and let it bubble away until it is nearly all absorbed. Then start adding the vegetable STOCK, a little at a time. Keep adding ladles of hot stock as the rice begins to absorb it, stirring to release the chalky starch that gives the dish its characteristic creamy texture.

→ Meanwhile, cook the PEAS and BROAD BEANS separately in a little water just to cover them until tender. The peas will take about 5 minutes from when you bring them to the boil; the broad beans you can throw into boiling water and they will only take 2 minutes. Drain both, reserving the water for the vegetable stock but leaving a little in the bottom of each pan so the vegetables don't dry out. Remove the leaves from the cooked ARTICHOKES so that all that you have left is the central soft leaves and the choke and the stem. Remove the central leaves in one go and then chop off the stem. Scoop or scrape out the woolly choke and then you have the best bit left, the heart, which you can cut into small pieces. This is a very easy process once you know what to do!

→ When the rice is cooked, gently fold in the artichoke hearts, asparagus, peas and beans and add the BUTTER, SEASONING and a good handful of PARMESAN. Add one more ladle of the vegetable stock, stir gently to amalgamate, and leave covered off the heat for 5 minutes. Remove the lid, scatter over the HERBS and serve, with a bowl of the rest of the grated Parmesan to hand round.

Risotto Automne
→ If you are making your risotto with porcini or chanterelles, each of which have such a distinctive and fugitive flavour, stick to a single type of fungi. I know a lot of other writers suggest a collection of different flavours, but I just prefer to savour one. On the other hand, if you are using dried porcini, it works well texture and flavour-wise to add 225g/8oz of a fresh type like chestnut at the end of the cooking time. If you go this route, leave out the white wine at the beginning of the recipe and add 2 tablespoons of port and madeira to the sautéed mushrooms. Reduce before adding to the rice.

Spinach and Ricotta Pancakes

SERVES 4

Pancakes

plain flour	225/8oz
salt	a pinch
organic eggs	2
whole organic milk	750ml/ 1¼ pints
unsalted butter	a knob

Filling

fresh ricotta	160g/6oz
unsalted butter	85g/3oz
sea salt, pepper and nutmeg	
organic egg	1
spinach	450g/1lb
Parmesan cheese, *freshly grated*	4 tbsp

This is really just a guide, as you may change the main ingredient from spinach to leek, from leek to mushroom, or seafood, whatever takes your fancy. You can make this dish in advance and refrigerate it until an hour before you put it in the oven to bake.

→ Sift the FLOUR and SALT together into a large bowl. Make a well in the centre, break the EGGS into it, and add a splosh of MILK. Whisk the eggs and milk together before gradually working a little of the flour down into the mixture and when it gets too thick to beat, adding more milk.

→ When the mixture is the consistency of thick cream whisk for a few minutes until it is bubbly and frothy. Let the batter rest if you have time for 30 minutes, so that the starch cells can swell and be broken down more easily in the cooking. The batter will thicken while it rests, so you may need to add a little more milk at the end.

→ You need to cook pancakes over a high heat so as to cause a further breaking down of the soaked starch cells and a release of air bubbles within the mixture to produce a lighter texture. Heat a heavy pan, cast iron is perfect for pancakes, and when it is hot, slip in a small knob of BUTTER, swirling it around the pan. The moment it bubbles, add one ladle of pancake mixture and swirl it to cover the base of the pan completely. After about a minute, check the underside of the pancake with a palette knife, and if it has browned, flip the pancake over and cook it similarly on the underside. Stack the pancakes up on a plate as you go. Meanwhile, make the filling.

→ Preheat the oven to 220°C/425°F/Gas 7. Mash the RICOTTA, half the BUTTER, the SEASONING and the EGG with a fork until they are all mixed in well together. Wash the SPINACH and cook with no added water until it wilts. Drain it well and chop in the colander. Stir the spinach into the cheese mixture. Add a table-spoonful of grated fresh PARMESAN at a time to the mixture until you have a firm paste, then put enough mixture into each pancake for it to still roll up tight like a cigar. Place seam edge down in the greased gratin dish as you finish each one. They need to nudge each other in the dish without being squashed like sardines.

→ Sprinkle a generous handful of PARMESAN over the top and either the other half of the BUTTER melted, or knobs of butter.

Bake for about 20 minutes, or until the dish looks plumped and browned and bubbling and irresistible.

Pancakes Layered with Mozzarella and Tomato Sauce

SERVES 4

Pancakes

plain flour	110g/4oz
salt	
eggs	2
milk	300ml/10fl oz
butter	a tiny knob

Filling and topping

tomato sauce (see p. 140)	
béchamel sauce (see p. 402)	
buffalo mozzarella, *diced*	2
Parmesan cheese, *freshly grated*	4 tbsp
fresh basil, *chopped*	a handful

This recipe is the kind of assembly job that lasagne is, a layer-by-layer dish, but it has the advantage that you can make the tomato sauce and the pancakes a day or two in advance, before building, stratum by stratum, this savoury cake. You sprinkle mozzarella and fresh Parmesan cheese between the layers before baking the dish like a pasta gratin.

→ This recipe makes thicker pancakes than you would normally have, but you may add a bit more milk if the batter feels really thick. Make the pancakes as in the previous recipe. Leave the BATTER to rest for 30 minutes and then whisk again. Heat a tiny knob of BUTTER in a heavy pan, pour in a small ladle of batter, wait until it begins to bronze and bubble before flipping and repeating, then place on a plate with a palette knife and repeat. You should end up with 8 good-sized pancakes from this amount of mixture.

→ Make the TOMATO and BÉCHAMEL sauces, and you are ready to assemble the dish. Preheat the oven to 180°C/350°F/Gas 4. Stir the tomato sauce into the béchamel. Butter a gratin dish, place a pancake on the bottom and spread a thin layer of the tomato and béchamel sauce over the top. Sprinkle with MOZZARELLA, PARMESAN, BASIL, SALT AND PEPPER and cover with another pancake. Continue layering the pancakes until you have a sort of leaning tower of Pisa, 8 pancake-storeys high. The top must be sauce, Parmesan, basil, salt and pepper, not mozzarella, which would turn to goo.

→ Cover the dish with a sheet of greased greaseproof paper and bake for about 20 minutes. Remove the greaseproof and continue to cook for a further 10 minutes until bubbling and gorgeous. Leave it to stand outside the oven before before you cut it into triangular wedges like a cake. Serve with a plain green salad. This is substantial with a capital S!

Stirred Polenta

SERVES 4

water	1.5 litres/3 pints
salt	2 tsp
coarse-grain yellow polenta	255g/9oz

Polenta is a wonderful dish, a superb vehicle for strong flavours such as salty blue cheese and Parmesan, but the instant, quick-cook polentas are not very good. Their somewhat acid flavour and their texture are both wanting. There really is no substitute for stirring. Coarse-grained yellow cornmeal is, to my mind, the most satisfying in terms of its robust texture and flavour.

→ Bring the water to the boil in a large, heavy-bottomed pot. Throw in the SALT, then add the POLENTA in a thin stream through the nearly closed fist of one hand, stirring with a whisk and keeping the water boiling. Now start stirring the polenta over a medium heat with a long-handled spoon — the pot needs to be large because the grain will splutter like a Vesuvial eruption to begin with. Carry on cooking and stirring for 10 minutes. For the remaining 30 minutes, stir every minute or so. The polenta is cooked when it forms a single mass that pulls cleanly away from the sides of the pan.

→ When it is ready, plop it into a large bowl moistened with a little water to rest for a few minutes. Now turn the bowl over onto a large serving plate or wooden board and serve it at once. If you are going to cool the polenta and firm it up so that you can slice it and then fry, bake or griddle it, do not pour it into a bowl. Spread it on a board about 7.5cm/3in thick. This stage should be achieved several hours before you want to use it. You may refrigerate it in a block in foil or clingfilm for a few days.

Warm Polenta with Parmesan or Blue Cheese
→ When the polenta is cooked, piping hot and soft, you may stir in some butter and grated Parmesan cheese and serve it just as it is. Little lumps of Gorgonzola stirred and mashed into the polenta are also delicious. Both these ways of serving polenta are good with a branch of roasted vine tomatoes added to the top of the mound of polenta.

Cold Polenta
→ Once it has cooled, polenta can be cut into wedges and fried like fried bread crisply in olive oil, and served with anything from salad to calves' liver and onions. Polenta also makes a great starter with a little ragout of mixed fungi and their winey, garlicky juices poured over it in shallow bowls.

Nigel Slater's Stilton, Onion and Potato 'Frying-Pan' Pie

SERVES 6

floury potatoes	1.5kg/3¼lb
medium onions	4
butter	85g/3oz
Stilton cheese	225g/8oz
milk	150ml/5fl oz
Parmesan cheese, *grated*	30g/1oz

I love Nigel's food, I love Nigel's writing. If anyone can seduce you with words into cooking anything, Nigel is your man.

→ Put a large pan of water on to boil. Peel the POTATOES and cut them into halves or quarters, then add them to the boiling water. When it comes back to the boil, add a little SALT and turn down to a lively simmer. Check the potatoes now and again; they should be tender in 15 minutes or so.

→ While the potatoes cook, peel the ONIONS, cut them in half, then cut each into five or six segments. Put them into a heavy-based frying pan with 45g/1½oz of the BUTTER and let them cook over a moderate to low heat, stirring from time to time. They will need 20–25 minutes to become thoroughly soft and sticky. Bring the MILK to the boil and turn off the heat. Drain the potatoes and tip them into the bowl of a food mixer fitted with a beater attachment. Mix slowly adding the milk and remaining butter. Beat to a smooth mash, stopping well before it becomes gluey.

→ Preheat the oven to 200°C/400°F/Gas 6. BUTTER the base and sides of a heavy 28cm/11in frying pan with a metal handle or a similar diameter baking dish — I use a black cast-iron frying pan — then spoon in half of the mashed potato. Smooth the potato a little, then add the onions and a grinding of BLACK PEPPER. Crumble the STILTON over the onions. Pile the rest of the mashed potato over the top and smooth lightly with the back of the spoon or a rubber spatula.

→ Dust over the grated PARMESAN, then bake in the preheated oven for 25–30 minutes, by which time the top will be pale gold and the filling will be bubbling up around the edges.

Cheddar Cheese and Onion Pie

SERVES 6

good, strong Cheddar, *coarsely grated*	285g/10oz
unsalted butter	30g/1oz
large onion, *peeled and chopped finely*	1
potatoes, *peeled, steamed and diced*	110g/4oz
large organic eggs	2
double cream	4 tbsp
thyme OR flat-leaf parsley, *chopped*	a sprig / a bunch
cayenne pepper	a pinch
sea salt and black pepper	
shortcrust pastry *made with 340g/12oz flour and 170g/6oz unsalted butter* (see p. 104)	
beaten egg for glaze	

A sweet and simple veggie pie that is infinitely more delicious than its ingredients would suggest. Just make sure you use a really mature Cheddar with character, vibrancy and depth of flavour.

→ Preheat the oven to 220°C/425°F/Gas 7. Divide the PASTRY into two balls, keeping one a little larger than the other. Melt the BUTTER in a pan and gently fry the ONION until softened and translucent, then leave to cool. Throw the onions into a bowl with the grated CHEESE, POTATO, EGGS, CREAM, THYME or PARSLEY and the seasoning, and mix thoroughly with your fingers.

→ Roll out the larger ball of pastry and line a shallow greased 23cm/9in tart tin. Tip the cheese and onion mixture into the pastry shell. Moisten the edges of the pastry and cover with the rolled-out top piece, crimping the edges together carefully. Brush beaten EGG over the top and bake in the oven for 30 minutes until crisp and golden brown. You can use leeks instead of onions if you like, or add buttered apple slices instead of the potato.

Vegetable Biriani with a Spiced Pastry Crust

SERVES 6

saffron stamens	a pinch
star anise	3
cardamom pods	8
fennel seeds	1 tsp
blades of mace	2
cumin seeds	1 tsp
turmeric	1 tsp
basmati rice	200g/7oz
mint, basil and coriander, *chopped*	a handful of each
yoghurt	6 tbsp
garlic cloves	2

This is a musky-breathed pie with a spicy, buttery puff pastry top, but you could just as easily heap the filling into little wholewheat picnic pasties instead, to eat warm or cold with Coriander and Mint Chutney (see opposite). You can use ready-made puff pastry for this recipe, but make sure it is the best, made with all butter.

→ Preheat the oven to 190°C/375°F/Gas 5. Soak the SAFFRON in a little hot water for 20 minutes. Half fill a saucepan with water, then add the STAR ANISE, CARDAMOM pods, FENNEL seeds, MACE, CUMIN and TURMERIC and bring to the boil. Throw in the RICE and cook until done, then drain, discarding the pods and mace. Put the HERBS, YOGHURT, GARLIC and CHILLIES in a food processor and blend to a paste. Season with salt and set aside.

→ Heat a large, heavy-bottomed frying pan over a gentle heat, add the PANCH PHORA and roast for a minute. Set aside. In the same pan heat the GHEE, add the VEGETABLES and fry for a couple of minutes. Take the pan off the heat and add the herb paste, panch phora, rice, saffron and its liquid. Stir them all

green chillies, *seeded and thinly sliced*	2
sea salt	
panch phora, an Indian spice mix (optional)	1 tbsp
ghee or clarified butter	1 tbsp
fresh or frozen peas	1 cup
pumpkin OR squash, *peeled, diced, roasted until soft*	1 cup
mushrooms, *chopped*	1 cup
carrot, *diced and steamed*	1
puff pastry	a sheet
egg, *beaten*, for glaze	
extra fennel seeds to sprinkle on top	

together, then scrape them into a pie dish. Wet the outside rim of the pie dish with a brush dipped in water and stick a strip of PASTRY around it. Brush the strip of pastry with beaten EGG and place the pie crust on top, pressing them together gently with the tines of a fork. Brush the top with beaten egg and scatter a handful of FENNEL SEEDS over the surface. Bake for about 30 minutes, or until the pastry is risen and golden.

Coriander and Mint Chutney

→ Put a handful each of fresh CORIANDER and MINT leaves into the blender with a small chopped ONION, a small, seeded, chopped green CHILLI, the JUICE OF A LEMON, SEA SALT and a couple of tablespoons of RED WINE VINEGAR. Process until smooth.

Potato, Garlic and Parsley Tourte

SERVES 6–8

puff pastry	400g/14oz
potatoes, *sliced very finely*	500g/just over 1lb
garlic cloves, *finely chopped*	3
flat-leaf parsley, *finely chopped*	3 tbsp
salt, black pepper, nutmeg	
egg, *beaten*	1
egg yolks	2
organic double cream	240ml/8fl oz

Puffed up and golden, with a flood of garlic-scented cream bubbling under its lid, this is a refined but hearty winter dish. I cook it as I do my tatins, in a Le Creuset frying pan, the kind with a short, enamelled ovenproof handle. Again, you can use ready-made puff pastry for this recipe, but make sure it is an all-butter brand.

→ Preheat the oven to 200°C/400°F/Gas 6. Roll out two circles of PASTRY, one slightly larger than the other. Grease your frying pan or gratin dish and line with the larger pastry circle.
→ In a large bowl, mix the POTATOES—which must be sliced very finely, or they will not cook through before the pastry is perfect—together with the GARLIC, PARSLEY and SEASONING. Layer the potatoes into your frying pan or dish, then cover with the pastry lid, sealing the edges with a fork and brushing the top with beaten EGG. Cut a cross in the middle of the lid for the steam to escape, and bake for 50 minutes.
→ Whisk the EGG YOLKS and CREAM together, remove the pie from the oven and, with a tiny funnel held in the steam-hole, pour in the eggy cream. Please pour slowly, or you'll get a geyser of cream that will then lie on top of your pastry. I know, it happened to me first time round, and with a larger funnel! If you would rather, you can delicately run the tip of a knife around the pastry and gently lever the lid up to pour in the cream.
→ Return to the oven for 10 minutes, then serve the flaky triangular wedges hot from the pan.

A No-Fuss Puff-Pastry Vegetable Pie

SᴇʀᴠᴇS 4

medium onions	5
butter OR oil	enough to cover the bottom of a medium-sized shallow pan
mushrooms, any firm variety	325g/11–12oz
thyme, lemon thyme OR oregano, *chopped*	a handful
crème fraîche	200g/7oz
puff pastry (all butter)	425g/scant 1lb
egg, *beaten,* or milk to glaze the pastry	a little

An irresistible pie from Nigel Slater's book Appetite. *Use an all-butter brand of puff pastry if you don't want to make your own.*

→ Preheat the oven to 200°C/400°F/Gas 6. Peel and roughly chop the ONIONS and let them cook slowly with the BUTTER OR OIL over a low heat for 20 minutes or so, until they are golden, soft and almost transparent. Tear or slice the MUSHROOMS into large, bite-sized pieces and add them to the onions, adding a little more butter or oil if they soak it all up. Leave them to turn golden and tender, but stir them from time to time so they don't stick or burn. Season with the chopped HERBS and stir in the CRÈME FRAÎCHE, grinding in a little SALT AND PEPPER as you go. You want a mixture that is creamy rather than runny, so let it bubble for a minute or two to thicken.

→ The PASTRY needs to be rolled into two rectangles about 35cm × 20cm/14 × 8in (this is conveniently the same measurement as the ready-rolled frozen stuff). Lay one piece on a lightly floured baking sheet and spread the mushrooms and onions over, leaving a good finger thickness of bare rim around the edge. Brush a little beaten EGG, MILK or even WATER around the rim, lay the second rectangle of pastry over the top and squeeze the rims together to seal. It is worth being quite zealous about pinching the pastry, there shouldn't be any possibility of the filling escaping. Brush with more of the beaten egg or milk so that the pastry will take on a rich golden shine in the oven, then cut a couple of little holes in the top to let the steam out.

→ Bake the pie until it has puffed up like a cushion and is the colour of honey. You can expect this to take about 25 minutes. It is worth sneaking a look at the bottom to check if the pastry is crisp underneath (it should be fine because this is not an especially wet filling).

Tourte de Pâques

SERVES 8

Filling

extra virgin olive oil	4 tbsp
onion, *very finely diced*	1
garlic clove, *very finely chopped*	1
spinach, *washed and stalked*	450g/1lb
artichoke bottoms	400g/14oz jar
organic eggs, *boiled for 6 minutes*	6
salt and black pepper	

Pastry

plain flour	450g/1lb
unsalted butter	225g/8oz
organic eggs, *beaten*	2
extra virgin olive oil	3 tbsp
sea salt	½ tsp

More often than not this delectable dish is made with olive oil pastry, but here I've used a buttery pastry with a slug of oil—much easier to work without it collapsing into bits. Don't stint on the artichokes; the briny ones are not right for this dish. Either cook them yourself or use a first-class jar like Seggiano's charcoal-grilled artichokes in olive oil.

→ To make the pastry, rub the FLOUR and BUTTER together until crumbly, then mix in the EGGS, OLIVE OIL and SALT, adding a little cold water if the mixture is too crumbly. Wrap the ball of pastry in clingfilm and put it in the fridge for at least 30 minutes.

→ Heat a tablespoon of OLIVE OIL in a large frying pan and add the chopped ONION, cooking it over a medium heat for about 5 minutes until softened. Add the GARLIC and cook for another couple of minutes. Tip into a large bowl, then add another slug of OLIVE OIL to the pan and cook the SPINACH in batches for 3–4 minutes until wilted. Put it in a colander to drain. Heat a little more OIL in the pan, add the ARTICHOKES and fry them for 3–4 minutes. Mix the spinach and artichokes into the onion and garlic and season well. Leave the mixture to cool.

→ Divide the ball of pastry into two, one piece slightly larger than the other. Roll out the larger disc of pastry and place it in an oiled 25cm/10in tart tin with a removable base. Patch the pastry as you see fit: it rarely makes it in one into the tin. Spoon in the filling, then halve the EGGS and push them, cut side up, into the filling. Brush the rim of pastry with oil, fit the smaller, rolled-out circle on top, crimp the edges and brush with a little more olive oil.

→ Bake for 30–35 minutes at 200°C/400°F/Gas 6. The filling is already cooked, so it's only the pastry you need to watch. Let the pie cool to room temperature and remove it from the tart tin to serve.

La Torta Pasqualina

SERVES 8

Swiss chard	1.8kg/4lb
olive oil	120ml/4fl oz
garlic cloves, *peeled and bruised*	2
fresh marjoram, *chopped*	3 tbsp
fresh ricotta	450g/1lb
Parmesan cheese, *freshly grated*	55g/2oz
unsalted butter	55g/2oz
organic eggs	5
sea salt and black pepper	
filo pastry	340g/12oz

Various forms of this pie are found all over the Mediterranean, where it is traditionally served at Easter. A beautiful centrepiece dish that you can make the day before you want to eat it, then reheat in a low oven to crisp the pastry. The torta is best eaten at room temperature or warm.

→ Tear the washed LEAVES from the CHARD STALKS and cut both into strips. Plunge the stalks into a pan of boiling salted water and add the leaves after 5 minutes. Cook until they are both tender, then drain and press out all the excess water. Pour a couple of tablespoons of the OLIVE OIL into a frying pan and add the GARLIC and MARJORAM. The moment you scent the garlic, remove it, add the chard to the pan and sauté it for 5 minutes, stirring all the time. Season with lots of coarsely ground BLACK PEPPER and leave it to cool. Put the RICOTTA in a bowl and break it up thoroughly with a fork.

→ Preheat the oven to 180°C/350°F/Gas 4. Grease a 25cm/10in springform tin with a little OLIVE OIL and fit 10 sheets of FILO PASTRY, one on top of the other, so that the edges droop over the sides of the tin. Brush each sheet with OLIVE OIL as you go, and keep the filo under a damp cloth—it dries out and tears more quickly than you'd believe possible. Spread the chard over the bottom, then add the crumbled ricotta and half the PARMESAN with a generous scrunch of BLACK PEPPER. Shape 5 hollows around the edge of the filling and place a knob of BUTTER in each, then carefully break an EGG into each hollow.

→ Sprinkle the rest of the PARMESAN over the top, and cover with another 10 sheets of filo, oiling each one as you go. Turn the overhang into the centre and roll it like a cigar to form a ridge at the edge of the pie, then brush the top liberally with OLIVE OIL. Bake for 30 minutes, then turn the heat up to 200°C/400°F/Gas 6 and bake for a further 20 minutes to crisp the top. Let the torta cool in the tin before sliding it onto a serving plate.

La Torta di Porri, or Leek and Rice Pie

SERVES 6

leeks	1.2kg/2½lb
large organic eggs	6
Carnaroli, Arborio or other risotto rice	140g/5oz
extra virgin olive oil	200ml/7fl oz
sea salt and freshly ground black pepper	
Parmesan cheese, *freshly grated*	9 tbsp
organic lemon	1
frozen filo pastry, *thawed*	225–250g/8–9 oz

→ Wash the LEEKS thoroughly, cut away the green parts and slice the white parts into very thin discs. Lightly beat the EGGS and put them in a bowl with the leeks, RICE, half the OIL, two teaspoons of SALT, plenty of PEPPER and the PARMESAN. Add the grated ZEST of an organic LEMON and the JUICE of half of it. Mix very thoroughly with your hands. Set the bowl aside for 4 hours, mixing again when you remember.

→ Preheat the oven to 180°C/350°F/Gas 4. Oil a 25cm/10in springform tin. Pour the rest of the OIL into a small bowl. Carefully unfold the FILO PASTRY leaves, one at a time, taking care to leave the other leaves covered, since filo pastry dries out and cracks very easily. Lift out and lay one leaf over the bottom and up the sides of the prepared tin, allowing the ends to hang down over the outside of the tin. It will tear a little, but don't worry. Using a pastry brush, brush the leaf all over with a little of the oil and then cover with another leaf of the pastry. Lay it across the previous one so that the sides of the tin are covered all round. Brush with oil and lay two more leaves the same way.

→ Now fill the tin with the leek mixture. Fold the overhanging pieces of filo back over the top, one at a time, to make a lid. If the filo is not long enough, lay four more leaves over the top, brushing each sheet with oil. Cut them to fit inside the tin and fold the overlap over to form a ridge around the edge. Brush each one with oil before you place the next.

→ Bake for 45–50 minutes on a preheated baking tray, other-wise the base filo will not cook through and crisp. Let the pie cool for 10 minutes and then remove the side of the tin and turn it over onto an oven tray. Put the pie back in the oven, upside down, for 10 minutes to dry the bottom. Turn onto a pretty round serving dish.

La Torta di Zucchini

→ Use 450g/1lb of COURGETTES, sliced into very fine discs, instead of the leeks. Method and other ingredients as above.

La Torta di Porcini

→ Chop the PORCINI into small pieces and use FLAT-LEAF PARSLEY instead of basil. Take care not to break up the porcini too much when you mix the ingredients with your hands.

Layered Ricotta and Feta Pie

SERVES 6–8

large organic eggs	6
ricotta, fresh if you can get it	500g/a generous 1lb
good sheep's milk feta	500g/a generous 1lb
best olive oil	8 tbsp, plus extra for brushing
fresh dill, *chopped*	2 tbsp
fresh mint, *chopped*	2 tbsp
filo pastry	1kg/2¼lb
unsalted butter, *melted*	55–85g/2–3oz
milk	500ml/18fl oz
organic eggs	2
sea salt and black pepper	

→ Preheat the oven to 200°C/400°F/Gas 6. Whisk the 6 EGGS for the filling together in a large bowl, then add the RICOTTA, sieving it in for lightness, the FETA, which needs crumbling and then whisking in, and 4 tablespoons of OIL. Stir in the fresh HERBS and SEASON cautiously as feta is so salty.

→ Brush a large baking sheet with OLIVE OIL before laying down your first leaf of FILO. Keep the rest of the filo under a damp cloth throughout the process otherwise it dries and tears. Brush with melted BUTTER and add another sheet of filo. Add a layer of the mixture, about 1cm/a scant !in thick, bringing it right to the edge of the filo. Add another two sheets of oiled filo as before, and the same again of the mixture. Repeat this until your last storey of mixture, then add the penthouse roof of a double layer of filo, this time brushing both layers with melted BUTTER.

→ Cut a diamond pattern into the filo roof, then beat together the MILK, any leftover BUTTER AND OIL, and two EGGS. Gently sluice the liquid over the top of the tower. Let it rest and absorb for 15 minutes, then whack the pie into the hot oven for 8 minutes before turning the temperature down to 150°C/300°F/Gas 2 and baking it for another 20 minutes, or until golden and swollen. Best eaten warm.

Feta, Rice and Yoghurt Pie

SERVES 6–8

Jersey milk	600ml/10fl oz
olive oil	1 tbsp
Carnaroli OR Arborio rice	200g/7oz
Greek yoghurt	310g/11oz
feta cheese	340g/12oz
spring onions, *finely chopped*	a bunch
fresh dill, *finely chopped*	30g/1oz
organic eggs	3

Filo is as easy as ordinary pastry. The shop-bought version you're used to seeing in boxes is too fragile for this kind of pie; the homemade version is thicker. But if you prefer, just make a normal shortcrust pastry (see p. 104), but using half butter, half olive oil, and roll it out as thin as you can without it sticking and overstretching.

→ Preheat the oven to 180°C/350°F/Gas 4. Grease a 25cm/10in springform tin with butter. Put the MILK, OLIVE OIL and a little SEA SALT in a heavy-bottomed pan and bring to scalding point, then stir in the RICE. Cover the pan and simmer for 20 minutes.

→ Put the YOGHURT and FETA in a food processor and mix to a smooth paste. Add the SPRING ONIONS and DILL and blitz for a nanosecond. Add the EGGS to the feta mixture, one at a time down the feed tube, then scrape the mixture out of the processor and into the rice. Stir to amalgamate.

→ Roll the FILO out into two long thin sheets in a pasta machine,

sesame seeds	a handful
sea salt and black pepper	
Filo Pastry	
white 00 pasta flour	1kg/2¼lb
sea salt	1 dsrtsp
water	about 250ml/8½fl oz
white wine vinegar	1 tbsp
extra virgin olive oil	4 tbsp
egg, *beaten*, for glaze	

or by hand, as thin as you can. One sheet should be a little larger than the second. Line the tin with the larger piece, don't worry about the overhang at this stage. Then scrape the cooled mixture into the tin, and level the top. Cover the filling with the second piece of pastry. Fold in any short edges towards the centre of the pie and cut the longer ones off. Brush the rim of the bottom layer of pastry with a little milk or water and seal the top to the bottom. Brush the surface of the pie with beaten EGG, prick the surface all over with a fork and scatter over the SESAME SEEDS. Bake for about an hour and eat while warm.

Filo Pastry
→ To make the pastry, sift the FLOUR and SALT into a large bowl, make a well in the centre and add the WATER and VINEGAR. Work the dough until it is smooth, then begin to add the OLIVE OIL, a little at a time, kneading thoroughly until the dough is stretchy and shiny and the oil has been absorbed. Wrap in clingfilm and refrigerate until cold.

Creamy Cheese Bake with Filo Pastry

SERVES 4

feta cheese	140g/5oz
cottage cheese	140g/5oz
large organic eggs	4
flat-leaf parsley, *chopped*	3 tbsp
filo pastry	200g/7oz (5 large sheets)
unsalted butter, *melted*	30g/1oz
milk	425ml/15fl oz

This is one of Claudia Roden's recipes—leaves of filo pastry baked with a light, creamy custard.

→ Preheat the oven to 180°C/350°F/Gas 4. To prepare the filling, mash the FETA with a fork and mix with the COTTAGE CHEESE, one EGG and the PARSLEY.
→ Open out the sheets of FILO, leaving them in a pile. Brush the top one lightly with melted BUTTER and then fit it, buttered side up, into an oiled round baking dish about 30cm/12in in diameter, leaving it overhanging at the sides. Fit the second sheet over it and brush lightly with BUTTER. Spread the filling evenly over the pastry. Cover with the remaining sheets of filo, brushing each with melted butter and finally folding them over the mixture. Fold the top one so that it presents a smooth surface and brush with BUTTER. Bake for 15 minutes until lightly coloured, then remove from the oven.
→ Lightly beat the remaining three EGGS with the MILK and pour over the hot pie; you do not need to add salt as the feta is very salty. Return to the oven and bake for about 30 minutes or until the custard is absorbed and set and the top of the pastry is golden. Serve hot, cut into wedges.

Tomato, Goat's Camembert and Herb Tart

SERVES 6

shortcrust pastry (see p. 104)	
Dijon mustard	1 tbsp
Gruyère cheese, *grated*	100g/generous 3½oz
organic tomatoes, *sliced*	12
Camembert-style goat's cheeses, *sliced*	4 × 125g/4½oz

Herbed brushing oil

extra virgin olive oil	120ml/4fl oz
rosemary, thyme, basil, fennel, *finely chopped*	1 dsrtsp of each
flat-leaf parsley, *finely chopped*	1 tbsp
garlic clove, *crushed*	1
salt and black pepper	
bay leaf	1

→ Combine all the INGREDIENTS FOR THE BRUSHING OIL in a bowl and leave overnight if possible, or at least for a couple of hours.

→ Make SHORTCRUST PASTRY (see p. 104) with 170g/6oz organic white flour and 85g/3oz unsalted butter, but use your best olive oil instead of water—you might need a bit more than 2 tablespoons. Chill, roll out and line a 30cm/12in tart tin.

→ Preheat the oven to 190°C/375°F/Gas 5 and put a baking sheet in the oven. Spread the MUSTARD over the pastry base, then scatter over the GRUYÈRE.

→ Cover with alternate overlapping slices of TOMATO and GOAT'S CHEESE in concentric circles, then brush two-thirds of the herby oil over the surface. Bake the tart on the preheated baking sheet for about 35 minutes until brown and bubbling. Remove from the oven, brush with the remaining oil, and leave to cool for at least 10 minutes before turning out and serving.

Chard, Gruyère and Crème Fraîche Tart

SERVES 6

Swiss chard	2 heads
shortcrust pastry (see p. 104), *chilled*	1 × 23cm/9in tart case
egg, *beaten*, for brushing	
crème fraîche	200ml/7fl oz
Jersey milk	4–6 tbsp
egg	1
egg yolks	4
Gruyère cheese, *grated*	100g/3½oz
cayenne	¼ tsp
salt and black pepper	

Swiss chard has a kind of mild, crunchy earthiness which needs gentle enhancing rather than masking, but it adds good texture and flavour and has the virtue of being somehow unexpected. With some gooey-sharp Gruyère and crème fraîche it makes a delicious tart.

→ Preheat the oven to 200°C/400°F/Gas 6. Strip the leaves off the CHARD, and wash the leaves and ribs carefully. Then slice the ribs rather like you would celery, to about 1cm/½in widthways, and steam them until tender. Drain and leave to cool. Bake the PASTRY blind for 15 minutes (see p. 104), then remove the beans, prick the base with a fork, brush with beaten EGG, and return to the oven for 5 minutes. Turn the oven down to 180°C/350°F/Gas 4.

→ Beat the CRÈME FRAÎCHE, MILK, EGG and YOLKS together until smooth, then stir in the CHEESE and CAYENNE, and, sparingly, some SALT AND PEPPER. Quickly assemble a layer of cooled chard ribs on the pastry base, pour over the custard, and cook until browned, about 30 minutes. I served mine with the steamed chard leaves with a spritz of lemon.

Spinach, Crottin de Chavignol, Tomato and Parmesan Tart

SERVES 6–8

shortcrust pastry (see p. 104)	1 × 23cm/ 9in tart case
spinach	3 big handfuls
double cream	3–4 tbsp
organic eggs	2
organic egg yolks	2
sea salt, black pepper	
nutmeg	a smidgen
crème fraîche	2 heaped tbsp
crottin de Chavignol	1
large tomatoes, *sliced and cored*	2
Parmesan cheese, *freshly grated*	about 3–4 tbsp

The crumbly goat's cheese has so intense a flavour it can stand up to the iron of spinach, the salt strength of Parmesan and the acidity of the soft, fruity tomato. This is an unusual and delicious tart, puffed up until greenly golden and bubbling and crusted with a gratin of Parmesan. Any aged goat's crottin would work well, the Chavignol is one I find particularly splendiferous.

→ Make the PASTRY, refrigerate it and bake it blind (see p. 104), letting it dry out for 5 minutes before you spill the filling ingredients into its midst.

→ Preheat the oven to 200°C/400°F/Gas 6. Meanwhile, wash the SPINACH and put it in a pan with only the residual washing water. Stir briskly over a high heat to stop it sticking and burning—for just long enough for it to wilt and collapse. Blitz in a food processor with the CREAM, but just to the point where the spinach is in large, speckledy blobs, not tiny tweedy ones that are purée rather than texture. It's most important to stop that uniform smoothness that tarts can have if you're not careful!

→ Now beat in the EGGS and EGG YOLKS and SEASON, not too much salt because of the crottin. Add a suspicion of NUTMEG, spinach's best friend. Whisk in the CRÈME FRAÎCHE. Cover the bottom of the tart case which you've just removed from the oven with the shards of CROTTIN, then pour over the green mixture. Turn the oven down to 175°C/350°F/Gas 4 and cook the tart for 15 minutes.

→ Take it out of the oven and carefully plop the slices of TOMATO on the semi-set greenery. Strew over a generous handful of PARMESAN to cover the top, while leaving some of the tomato bare enough to peak through. Continue to cook until the Parmesan has obviously gone from golden to bronzed, crusted gratin and the whole is puffed up and just this side of too much wobble. Leave the tart on a rack for at least 15 minutes to allow the air to circulate beneath it before you venture to cut and eat it.

Butternut Squash and Crottin de Chavignol Tart

SERVES 6–8

shortcrust pastry (see p. 104)	1 × 23cm/9in tart case
small butternut squash, OR red onion squash	1
double cream	3–4 tbsp
organic eggs	2
organic egg yolks	2
crottin de Chavignol goat's cheese	1
sage leaves	a small bunch
best olive oil	2–3 tbsp
crème fraîche	2 heaped tbsp
sea salt and black pepper	

→ Make the PASTRY, chill, then bake it blind for 15 minutes (see p. 104). Remove the foil and beans, dock the base and sides with the tines of a fork to stop them bubbling up, and return the pastry case to the oven to dry out for 5 minutes.
→ Seed the SQUASH and roast it in a hot oven in wedges. When the flesh is soft, scoop it out and purée it in a food processor with the double CREAM. Beat in the EGGS and EGG YOLKS.
→ Preheat the oven to 180°C/375°F/Gas 4. Remove the thin, crusted rind of the CROTTIN, halve it and break it into small, lumpy shards. Sprinkle these over the base of the tart. Heat the OLIVE OIL in a small pan and when it is fiercely hot, throw in the whole SAGE LEAVES, turning them quickly with a spoon so that they frazzle and crisp in a minute or two. Drain off the oil and place most of the leaves in the base of the tart case with the crottin. Set the rest aside. Beat the CRÈME FRAÎCHE into the squash, cream and egg mixture and season well with BLACK PEPPER and only A LITTLE SALT—the crottin is salty.
→ Scrape the mixture into the tart case to just under the top of the pastry and strew the remaining frazzled sage on top. Bake until the tart is puffed up and magnificently burnished in patches. This will take 20–30 minutes—it should be set, but with a faint shudder. Place on a rack and cool for 20 minutes before eating while it is between hot and warm. That way you will really taste it. Serve with a salad of watercress or Treviso chicory—something a little bitter and peppery.

Sorrel Tart

SERVES 6

shortcrust pastry (see p. 104), *chilled*	1 × 23cm/9in tart case
egg, *beaten*, for brushing	
sorrel, *washed, stemmed*	300g/10oz
unsalted butter	55g/2oz
onions, *finely sliced*	285g/10oz
organic eggs	2
organic egg yolks	2
organic double cream	340ml/12fl oz
salt and black pepper	

The lemony-sharp flavour of sorrel in a soup or a hollandaise sauce is always a foil to the richness of eggs, cream and butter. Its tartness here is assuaged by the sweetness of the onions.

→ Preheat the oven to 190°C/375°F/Gas 5. Bake the PASTRY blind for 15 minutes (see p. 104), then remove the beans, prick the pastry all over with a fork, and return to the oven for 5 minutes. Remove from the oven and brush with beaten EGG.
→ Throw the SORREL into a saucepan full of boiling salted water, and take it out and drain it the moment it comes back up to the boil. The leaves will be an unappetising greyish colour, but don't let that put you off. Stew them in 30g/1oz of the BUTTER until all their liquid has evaporated and they have wilted down into a purée; this will take about 20 minutes. Do likewise with

the ONIONS, which will take a bit longer, keeping them covered, and occasionally giving them a stir. They should not brown, but be meltingly translucent, a pale tangle.

→ Mix the onions with the sorrel in a bowl and leave until tepid. Whisk the EGGS and YOLKS with the CREAM and SEASONING and stir into the sorrel mixture. Pour into the pastry case and cook for about 35–40 minutes, until barely set and barely coloured. Leave to cool for at least 10 minutes before turning out and serving.

Cep and Red Onion Tart

SERVES 6

dried ceps	55g/2oz
shortcrust pastry (see p. 104), *chilled*	1 × 23cm/9in tart case
egg, *beaten*, for brushing	
medium-sized red onions	2
unsalted butter	30g/1oz
mascarpone	255g/9oz
large organic egg	1
organic egg yolks	3
sage leaves OR leaves from 2 or 3 sprigs of thyme	8–10
salt and black pepper	

This is a wonderfully intense, musky-flavoured tart. The mascarpone, delicately enhanced by the cep liquor, makes it less rich than if it was full of cream, and it doesn't set in quite the same way as the eggier tarts; it rather slides slowly off its pastry base when sliced, like an earthy, densely flavoured ragout. Use wholemeal flour for the pastry if you like.

→ Soak the CEPS in 300ml/10fl oz of warm water for about an hour, turning them when you remember, to ensure they're all completely rehydrated.

→ Preheat the oven to 200°C/400°F/Gas 6. Bake the PASTRY blind for 10 minutes (see p. 104), then remove the beans, prick the base with a fork, and return to the oven for 5 minutes. Remove from the oven and brush the pastry with a little beaten egg. Turn the oven down to 180°C/350°F/Gas 4.

→ Strain the ceps, pressing gently, and reserve the liquid. Slice the ONIONS finely into rings, and sweat them gently in the BUTTER for a few minutes until they're softened. Chop the ceps coarsely, add them to the onions and cook for a further few minutes. Strain the CEP LIQUID into the pan and let it reduce completely, then tip the mixture into a bowl and leave until it is cold. You can complete the cooking to this stage several hours before if it is more convenient.

→ Whisk the MASCARPONE, EGG and YOLKS together, then add the finely chopped SAGE or THYME and stir in the cep and onion mixture. SEASON, then spread the mixture over the bottom of the pastry case and cook for 10 minutes. Turn the heat down to 170°C/325°F/Gas 3 and cook for a further 25–30 minutes. Check after 25, to see quite how unfirm it is. Remove from the oven, still obviously shuddery, and leave for 10 minutes before turning it out and eating it warm.

Courgette and Basil Tart with a Raw Tomato Dressing

SERVES 6

shortcrust pastry (see p. 104), *chilled*	1 × 23cm/9in tart case
small, firm courgettes	750g/1lb 10oz
salt and black pepper	
olive oil	2–3 tbsp
organic eggs	2
organic egg yolks	2
double cream	150–300ml/5–10fl oz
basil leaves	about 4 tbsp
Tomato dressing	
small onion	1
garlic clove	1
tomatoes, *skinned, seeded and finely chopped*	675g/1½lb
olive oil	6 tbsp
basil leaves, *torn*	1 tbsp
chives, *chopped*	1 tbsp
flat-leaf parsley, *chopped*	1 tbsp
lemon juice	2 tbsp
salt and black pepper	

I don't put Parmesan or Gruyère in this tart as I think they would overwhelm it. If you don't like the idea of a raw tomato dressing, you could make a simple mozzarella and tomato salad to serve at its side.

→ Preheat the oven to 190°C/375°F Gas 5. Bake the PASTRY blind for 15 minutes (see p. 104), then remove the beans, prick the base with a fork, and return to the oven for 5 minutes.
→ Slice the COURGETTES into thinnish coins and layer them in a colander, salting each layer. Leave to drain for 20–30 minutes, then rinse and dry on kitchen paper. Heat the OLIVE OIL in a large, heavy-bottomed frying pan, throw in the courgettes, and cook until they are slightly softened and translucent, but do not allow them to colour. Remove from the pan and drain.
→ Whisk together the EGGS, YOLKS, CREAM and SEASONING: the amount of cream will depend on the depth of your tart tin, so begin with the smaller amount and add more if it doesn't look as if the mixture will fill the pastry case. Put the courgettes into the pastry case with the torn BASIL LEAVES, and pour over the egg and cream mixture. Bake until just set, puffed up and browned, about 30 minutes. Leave to cool for about 10 minutes before turning out, and eat while warm with the gutsy RAW TOMATO DRESSING, made while the tart is in the oven.
→ To make the dressing, mince the ONION and GARLIC together in a food processor. Put in a bowl with the other ingredients, stir, then cover and leave in the fridge for 20 minutes. Stir again, and spoon onto the plates alongside the tart.

L'Aligot Tart

SERVES 6

shortcrust pastry (see p. 104), *chilled*	1 × 23cm/9in tart case
egg, *beaten*, for brushing	1
floury potatoes	1kg/2¼lb
salt and black pepper	
single cream	150ml/5fl oz
unsalted butter	55g/2oz
garlic clove, *crushed*	1
Fontina and Caerphilly cheese, *cut into small dice*	140g/5oz of each

A combination of the most melting of Italian cheeses, Fontina, and crumbled Caerphilly makes a delicious and robustly filling tart. Make a larger-than-you-need quantity of the filling, and you can turn the remainder into potato cakes, flouring them lightly and frying them in butter until crustily bronzed.

→ Preheat the oven to 200°C/400°F/Gas 6. Bake the PASTRY blind for 20 minutes (see p. 104), then remove the beans, prick the pastry with a fork, brush with beaten egg and return to the oven for 5 minutes.
→ Meanwhile, cook the POTATOES in their skins, then peel them and mash them thoroughly with some SALT AND PEPPER. Heat the CREAM and BUTTER together in a saucepan, then mix

with the mashed potatoes, stirring vigorously with a wooden spoon. Add the GARLIC and the diced CHEESES, and stir until well amalgamated.

→ Turn the oven down to 160°C/325°F/Gas 3. Fill the pastry case with the potato mixture, and cook the tart for about 20 minutes. Leave to cool for 10 minutes before turning out and serving.

Tomato and Oatmeal Tart

SERVES 8–10

organic egg	1
double cream	150ml/5fl oz
Parmesan and Gruyère cheese, *grated*	1 tbsp of each
mature Cheddar cheese, *grated*	2 tbsp
salt and black pepper	
fresh thyme	
tomato sauce (see p. 230) *add* fresh thyme, flat-leaf parsley and basil	1 tbsp of each

Oatmeal Pastry

organic white flour	110g/4oz
organic porridge oats	110g/4oz
unsalted butter	110g/4oz

This tart is enough to convert even the most recidivist of meat and two veggers. It is a wonderful picnic tart, the sturdier pastry a better container than thin shortcrust.

→ Make the PASTRY in the normal way (p. 104), but use half organic PORRIDGE OATS with the flour. Chill, then roll out just a little thicker than for normal shortcrust and line a 30cm/ 12 inch greased tart tin. Reserve the remaining pastry in strips for a lattice or, if you can't be bothered, save it for another tart. Preheat the oven to 190°C/375°F/Gas 5. Bake the pastry blind for 10 minutes (see p. 104), then remove the beans, prick the base with a fork, and return to the oven for 5 minutes.

→ Make the TOMATO SAUCE as on p. 230; if you like, you could reverse the proportions of fresh and canned tomatoes. Add the THYME and PARSLEY with the BAY LEAVES and simmer, uncovered, until the sauce is beginning to thicken, stirring occasionally for about 15 minutes. Add a good splash of WINE, season, and simmer for another 30 minutes or so, giving it the odd stir, and adding a bit more wine if it dries out. Sprinkle with the torn BASIL when it has cooled down a bit.

→ Whisk the EGG and CREAM together, then whisk in the PARMESAN, GRUYÈRE and half the CHEDDAR. SEASON and scatter in a few THYME LEAVES. Spread a thick layer of tomato sauce over the pastry to come half-way up the pastry case, then pour over the custard. Arrange your pastry lattice over the top and sprinkle with the remaining Cheddar. Bake for about 25 minutes, until set and palely browned. Leave to cool for about 10 minutes before serving.

Tomato and Saffron Tart

Serves 6

shortcrust pastry (see p. 104), *chilled*	1 × 23cm/9in tart case
egg, *beaten*, for brushing	1
double cream	400ml/13fl oz
saffron threads	1 tsp
organic eggs	2
organic egg yolks	4
basil leaves	12
salt and black pepper	

Fresh Tomato Sauce

olive oil	3 tbsp
onions, *finely chopped*	2
celery sticks, *finely chopped*	2
garlic cloves, *finely chopped*	2
ripe tomatoes, *skinned, seeded and chopped*	1kg/2¼lb
organic Italian plum tomatoes	1 × 400g/14oz tin
organic tomato passata	200g/7oz
tomato purée	1 tbsp
bay leaves	2
molasses sugar	2 tsp
red wine	150ml/5fl oz
salt and black pepper	

When sliced this tart is as brazenly primary-coloured as you could hope for, with its sunset stripes of scarlet and yellow, and with one of the most soothing of saffrony custards imaginable. The texture is ambrosial. The sauce recipe makes double what you need, but it keeps well in the fridge for several days, or you can freeze it.

Preheat the oven to 200°C/400°F/Gas 6. Bake the PASTRY blind for 15 minutes (see p. 104), then remove the beans, brush the pastry all over with BEATEN EGG, and return to the oven for 10 minutes. Remove from the oven and leave to cool. Turn the heat down to 170°C/325°F/Gas 3 and put a large baking sheet into the oven.

→ For the tomato sauce, heat the OIL in a large, heavy-bottomed frying pan and sauté the ONIONS, CELERY and GARLIC until softened and translucent. Add the FRESH AND TINNED TOMATOES; chop the tinned ones once they're in the pan. Add the PASSATA, TOMATO PURÉE, BAY LEAVES and SUGAR, then the RED WINE, and keep at a steady simmer for at least 30 minutes, until the sauce is thick and jammy and the liquid has evaporated. Remove the bay leaves.

→ You can either use it as it is, or, which I prefer, put it through the largest setting of a mouli-légumes to make a coarsely textured purée with enough bite to complement the heavenly, trembly custard that comes to rest on it. Leave to cool while you make the custard.

→ Steep the SAFFRON THREADS in a tablespoon of WATER for at least 5 minutes. Put 4 tablespoons of the CREAM in a small saucepan with the saffron threads and their water. Heat until warm, then leave to infuse for 5 minutes. Beat together the EGGS and YOLKS, and stir in the remaining CREAM and the saffron cream. Do this with a fork: saffron threads wrap themselves around a whisk. Tear the BASIL into small pieces, stir into the custard, and season.

→ Spread a layer of the tomato mixture over the pastry, to come almost half-way up the pastry case. Put the tart with its tomato layer onto the heated baking sheet, on a rack slightly pulled out of the oven, then, using a jug, carefully pour in the saffron custard. Bake until the custard is tremblingly set—about 30–40 minutes—and an intense, goldy colour with brown patches. Allow to cool for at least 10 minutes before turning out.

Leek, Potato and Oatmeal Tart

SERVES 6

oatmeal pastry (see p. 229)	
30g/1oz butter	
large leeks, *white parts sliced 3 mm/⅛ inch thick*	4
garlic clove, *finely chopped*	1
salt and pepper	
large egg, and egg yolk	1 of each
single cream	150ml/5fl oz
nutmeg, *grated*	a pinch
potatoes, *boiled until just tender, then sliced*	3–4
fresh thyme, *chopped*	1 tbsp
strong Cheddar cheese, *grated*	55g/2oz
Parmesan cheese, *grated*	55g/2oz

Leeks and oatmeal are as much a part of Ireland's culinary heritage as potatoes. My idea was to combine all three in one dish, and this is the result.

→ Preheat the oven to 190°C/375°F/Gas 5. Make the PASTRY (see p. 229). Roll out and use to line a 23 or 30cm/9 or 12 inch tart tin. Bake the pastry blind for 10 minutes. Remove the greaseproof paper and beans.

→ Meanwhile, for the filling, heat the BUTTER in a frying pan and sauté the LEEKS and GARLIC until softened, then SEASON them. Whisk together the EGG, YOLK and CREAM and season with SALT, PEPPER and NUTMEG. Spread the leeks over the pastry base, add a layer of POTATOES, the THYME, more SEASONING, and half the CHEESE, then add a second layer of potatoes. Pour over the cream and egg mixture, SEASON, scatter on the rest of the CHEESE, and return to the oven for about 25 minutes until the top is deliciously browned.

Herb Tart

SERVES 6

shortcrust pastry (see p. 104), *chilled*	1 × 23cm/9in tart case
egg, *beaten*, for brushing	
unsalted butter	30g/1oz
flat-leaf parsley, tarragon, basil, thyme, chives and chervil, *chopped*	1 heaped tbsp of each
organic eggs	2
organic egg yolks	2
double cream, OR half cream and half Jersey milk	450ml/15fl oz
salt, black pepper, nutmeg	
Gruyère OR Emmental cheese, *grated*	110g/4oz
Parmesan cheese *coarsely grated* (optional)	2 tbsp

Any combination of the herbs listed makes a good tart, and a thrifty dinner.

→ Preheat the oven to 190°C/375°F/Gas 5. Bake the PASTRY blind for 15 minutes (see p. 104), then remove the beans, prick the base with a fork, and return to the oven for 5 minutes. Brush with BEATEN EGG and leave to cool.

→ Heat the BUTTER in a frying pan, add the HERBS and stir briefly to coat. In a large bowl, whisk together the EGGS, YOLKS and CREAM or CREAM AND MILK, season with SALT, PEPPER and a suspicion of grated NUTMEG, then stir in the GRUYÈRE or EMMENTAL. Stir in the herbs, then pour the mixture into the pastry case and cook for about 25–30 minutes. After about 15 minutes you can sprinkle over a couple of tablespoons of coarsely grated PARMESAN if you like a cheesier flavour. Leave to cool for about 10 minutes before serving.

Fennel, Taleggio and Cardamom Tart

SERVES 6

shortcrust pastry case, *chilled* (see p. 104)	1 × 23cm/9in
fennel bulbs	4
butter	30g/1oz
olive oil, white wine and water	4 tbsp of each
seeds of 8 cardamom pods, *crushed*	
crème fraîche	2 heaped tbsp
organic eggs plus extra egg yolks	2 2
double cream	240ml/8fl oz
Jersey milk	about 250ml/8fl oz
salt and black pepper	
Taleggio cheese	90g/3oz

→ Preheat the oven to 190°C/375°F Gas 5. Bake the PASTRY blind for 15 minutes, then remove the beans, prick the base with a fork, and return to the oven for 5 minutes (see p. 104).

→ Remove all the tough outer layers of the FENNEL, then quarter the bulbs and slice thickly. Put the fennel into a heavy-bottomed frying pan with the BUTTER, OLIVE OIL, WINE, WATER and CARDAMOM SEEDS. Bring to a bubble, reduce to a simmer, cover with a lid and cook gently until the fennel is no longer resistant even at the core. Remove it with a slotted spoon, reserve, and bubble the juices until stickily reduced and syrupy, about 2–3 tablespoons.

→ Whisk together the CRÈME FRAÎCHE, EGGS and YOLKS with enough CREAM and MILK to bring a jugful of the savoury custard to almost 600ml/20 fl oz. Add the fennel liquor to the custard mixture and whisk together thoroughly. SEASON.

→ Cube the TALEGGIO into small squares. Spread the fennel over the pastry base, then scatter the Taleggio over it. Pour on the custard and bake until barely set and browned, about 25 minutes. Eat warm.

Sweetcorn and Spring Onion Tart with a Polenta Crust

SERVES 6

organic quick-cooking polenta	150g/5oz
sea salt	a pinch
spring onions (*outer skins removed*), *finely chopped*	2 bunches
butter	a knob
corn cobs	2
organic eggs plus extra egg yolks	2 2
double cream	300ml/10fl oz
salt, black pepper, cayenne	

You can of course make this tart with ordinary shortcrust but the polenta crust is a stunning yellow colour, with corn's characteristic slight grittiness, and with the fresh corn kernels it is doubly corny!

→ Preheat the oven to 180°C/350°F/Gas 4. For the polenta crust, simply bring 300ml/10fl oz of water to the boil in a saucepan and slowly pour in the POLENTA. Throw a pinch of SEA SALT after it, and stir over a gentle heat for 5 minutes. Remove from the heat and form the polenta into a ball. Using a bit of FLOUR — not polenta, which would make the finished crust too gritty — roll out in the normal way to line a 23cm/9in tart tin, remembering that, unlike flour-based pastry, this is good-tempered enough to be pressed into the tin if it breaks anywhere. Prick the base and bake for 10 minutes. You don't need to bake it blind with beans.

→ Sauté the SPRING ONIONS in the BUTTER until softened and translucent. Cook the CORN COBS and strip off the kernels. Whisk together the EGGS, YOLKS and CREAM, then add the spring onions together with the corn kernels. Season carefully

—there should be enough CAYENNE to give it warmth, but not overpower—and pour the mixture into the pastry case. Bake for 25–30 minutes until golden, puffed up and just set. Leave to cool for 10 minutes before serving, accompanied by peppery watercress or landcress with a garlicky dressing.

Broccoli, Blue Cheese and Crème Fraîche Tart

SERVES 6–8

broccoli, ideally purple sprouting	140g/5oz
olive oil	3 tbsp
medium onion, *finely sliced*	1
thyme	a few sprigs
garlic cloves, *peeled*	4
anchovy fillets, *chopped*	4
blue cheese such as Gorgonzola	85g/3oz
capers, *rinsed*	1 tsp
crème fraîche	200ml/7fl oz
black pepper	
puff pastry (chilled ready-rolled is fine)	400g/14oz
Parmesan cheese for grating	

No one has done as much as Nigel Slater in the way of making people just want to cook, and in inspiring the confidence to do so. His columns are rich, delicious and, like all the best food, wickedly sexy. Try this tart of his; it is perfect as a light lunch or supper.

→ Preheat the oven to 220°C/425°F/Gas 7. Rinse the BROCCOLI thoroughly and drop it into boiling, salted water. Leave it to cook until tender—about 7 minutes depending on the type. Drain, pat dry on kitchen paper and set aside. Return the empty saucepan to the heat and add the OLIVE OIL, ONION, THYME and the GARLIC CLOVES. Leave them to stew to softness over a moderate heat. They should be golden and tender after 10 minutes or so.

→ Chop the drained broccoli roughly and add it to the onions with the chopped ANCHOVIES, crumbled CHEESE, CAPERS and CRÈME FRAÎCHE. Grind in a little pepper and then leave the mixture to cool.

→ Open up the PASTRY, or roll your own into a rectangle measuring 35 × 22cm/14 × 9in, and place it on a lightly floured baking sheet. Score a line, without going right through the pastry, along all four sides, about 3cm/1 inch from the edge. Spread the broccoli mixture over the centre of the pastry, taking it as far as the lines you have scored, and leaving a clear border. This will rise and form a rim during cooking. Scatter with grated PARMESAN CHEESE.

→ Bake for 15–20 minutes. Check after 15; it will cook very quickly. You want the edges to be dark golden brown and crisp. Serve at once, with a salad on the side.

Homity Pies

MAKES 6

shortcrust pastry (see p. 104), *made with 225 g/8 oz organic wholemeal flour*	
potatoes	340g/12oz
butter	30g/1oz
milk OR cream	3–4 tbsp
onions, *finely chopped*	450g/1lb
olive oil	3 tbsp
garlic cloves, *crushed*	2
flat-leaf parsley (or mixed parsley, chives, thyme), *chopped*	2 tbsp
strong Cheddar cheese, *grated*	110g/4oz
salt and pepper	
ripe tomatoes, *sliced*	2

→ Preheat the oven to 220°C/425°F/Gas 7. Roll out the PASTRY thinly and use to line six individual tart tins, 10cm/4in in diameter. If you don't have them, make one larger tart in a 30cm/12 inch diameter tin. Chill for at least 20 minutes. Bake the pastry blind (see p. 104) for 5 minutes (10 minutes if you are making one large tart). Remove the greaseproof paper and beans and return the pastry to the oven for 5 minutes.

→ Meanwhile, boil the POTATOES until soft, drain and mash them with the BUTTER and MILK OR CREAM. Sauté the ONIONS in the oil until golden and softened. Stir into the potato mixture with the GARLIC, HERBS, half the CHEESE, and the SEASONING. Leave to cool.

→ Fill the pastry cases with the mixture, sprinkle with the remaining CHEESE and a slice of TOMATO, and bake in the oven for 20 minutes, until gratinéed and golden on top. Leave to cool slightly and eat warm, or leave to cool completely.

Brown Onion and Basil Pissaladière

SERVES 5–6

Dough

fresh yeast	30g/1oz
salt	
type 'o' pasta flour	300g/10oz
unsalted butter	85g/3oz
organic eggs	2

Topping

olive oil	
organic onions, *thinly sliced*	just under 1kg/2lb
best balsamic vinegar	2 tbsp
molasses sugar	2 heaped tsp
basil	a good handful
salt and black pepper	
anchovies in olive oil, *drained*	2 × 50g/1¾oz tins

This makes a wonderful summer lunch: a tangle of onions browned in balsamic vinegar and spicy green globe basil, with giant Napoletana basil torn over the tomato topping. Of course use ordinary basil if that's all you can find. You can buy small amounts of fresh yeast from most good bakers—or ask for it at the bakery counter of your supermarket.

→ I made my dough in a food processor with the dough hook, but it is easy by hand. Dissolve the YEAST in 4–5 tablespoons of tepid water with a pinch of SALT. Sift the FLOUR, add the BUTTER in small pieces, and process briefly, or rub in using your fingertips. Make a well in the centre and add the EGGS and the yeast mixture. Process until the dough comes away from the bowl in a ball. (If making the dough by hand, mix the eggs and yeast with the flour, gradually drawing the flour in from around the edge of the well, then knead lightly until the dough comes together.) Put it on a floured plate, cover with a floured cloth and leave somewhere warm for 2 hours.

→ For the topping, heat a few tablespoons of OLIVE OIL in a large, heavy-bottomed frying pan, add the ONIONS and cook gently until translucent. Add the BALSAMIC VINEGAR, MOLASSES SUGAR and BASIL LEAVES—ideally green globe basil —keeping a few leaves back to scatter over the pissaladière

garlic cloves, preferably new	4
organic tomatoes, *skinned and sliced*	6

when it comes out of the oven. SEASON, and stir until glossily browned all over, then cover the pan and leave it, but for the occasional stir, for 30 minutes. Pound the ANCHOVIES with the peeled GARLIC.

→ Preheat the oven to 190°C/375°F/Gas 5. After 2 hours the dough will have doubled in size. Knock it back, knead it briefly, then put it in the middle of an olive-oiled baking sheet, about 35 × 22cm/14 × 9in. Press the dough out with your knuckles to cover the sheet, spread the onion mixture evenly over the surface, then the anchovy mixture, and leave the dough to rise for a further 15 minutes.

→ Cook in the centre of the oven for 20 minutes, then turn the heat down to 180°C/350°F/Gas 4 and cook for a further 15–20 minutes. Remove from the oven and lay the slices of TOMATO over the onions. Tear the reserved BASIL LEAVES into pieces and scatter over the top. Dribble over a little OLIVE OIL, slice, and eat hot-and-cold in your fingers.

Polenta Cakes with Rocket Salsa

SERVES 4

quick-cook polenta	140g/5oz
butter	30g/1oz
olive oil	5 tbsp
chives, *finely snipped*	4 tbsp
black olives, *pitted and chopped*	55g/2oz
feta	85g/3oz
sea salt and black pepper	
vegetable oil for frying	
Rocket Salsa	
dry breadcrumbs	55g/2oz
wild rocket	55g/2oz
flat-leaf parsley	55g/2oz
lemon juice	2 tbsp
olive oil	6 tbsp
garlic clove	1

A lovely vegetarian dish from Ottolenghi in London's Notting Hill.

→ In a saucepan bring 600ml/1 pint of water to the boil with some salt. Pour in the polenta while stirring with a wooden spoon, reduce the heat, and keep stirring for four minutes. Remove from the heat, stir in the butter and olive oil, then the chives, olives and feta. Add lots of pepper and taste for salt. While warm, shape into walnut-sized balls, toss in bread crumbs and chill.

→ Heat the vegetable oil in a large, non-stick pan and shallow fry the polenta balls, turning to brown on all sides. Remove to a paper towel. Serve warm or at room temperature on a few rocket leaves with the salsa on the side.

Rocket Salsa
→ To make the salsa, blitz the ingredients with 2 teaspoons of water in a food mixer until thoroughly processed.

PO
and G

ULTRY
AME

Roast Chicken

SERVES 4–6

organic, free-range chicken	1 × 1.5–2kg/3¼–4½lb
onions, *peeled*	2
organic lemon	1
thyme, tarragon OR rosemary	a few sprigs
olive oil OR butter	
sea salt and black pepper	
giblets: neck, heart and liver	

Gravy

chicken liver	
red wine	a glass
cooking water from potatoes and parsnips	

→ Preheat the oven to 200°C/400°F/Gas 6. A chicken of this size will take between an hour and an hour and a quarter to cook and should then rest for 15 minutes to allow the juices to flood back through the meat.

→ Slice a LARGE ONION and lay it on the bottom of your roasting dish. Cut another SMALLER ONION into quarters and the LEMON likewise. Stuff the cavity of the CHICKEN alternately with the lemon and onion, reserving the last lemon quarter to squeeze over the chicken to add zest and freshness to the flavour. Either push the THYME OR TARRAGON into the cavity or finely chop the ROSEMARY leaves ready to sprinkle over the bird later. Season the cavity and place the bird on one side on the onion in the roasting dish. Splosh on about two tablespoons of good OLIVE OIL or rub it with BUTTER, then season the skin.

→ Place on the bottom rack in the oven and cook the chicken for 20 minutes. Turn the bird onto its other side, baste with the pan juices, season and return to the oven for a further 20 minutes. Cooking it on each side helps the heat penetrate to the densest part of the bird, its leg, ensuring it cooks through to the same degree as the breast.

→ Turn the bird upright, baste again, season and sprinkle over the rosemary if you're using it. Add the GIBLETS to the pan and cook for a further 20–35 minutes. If you insert a skewer into the deep part of the leg after an hour and the meat juices run clear rather than bloody, the bird is cooked. Remove the bird from the roasting tin with the carving knife and fork, holding it upside down as you do so that all the delicious lemony meat juices run out from the cavity into the tin. Leave to rest on the carving board with foil tucked around it and a tea towel on top for 15 minutes before carving. Now make the gravy.

Gravy

→ The old school adds FLOUR, the new school doesn't, but it's bound to revert sooner or later. You already have the caramel-ised onions from under the bird and the giblets and meat juices in the tin. Place the tin over a high heat, add a good splosh of RED WINE, about a glassful if you have some open, and stir like crazy so that the sticky onions part company with the tin and break down even further, releasing their flavour and dark colour as they do. Use a fork to crush the CHICKEN LIVER down into the pan, too, so that you have extra intense flavour and texture. Let the wine bubble away merrily for a minute or two so that the alcohol burns off, then add the COOKING WATER from the potatoes and parsnips which will be nice and starchy, and any other cooking water from the vegetables you've cooked. You will not want to add all the potato water if there is lots of it, so pour all but the last half pint down the sink first so that what remains has the starch content which thickens the gravy a little.

→ Bubble this over a high heat to reduce it for 5 minutes or so, longer if you are still finishing other things like the bread sauce (see p. 406) and vegetables. Place a sieve over a large jug and set it in the sink. Pour in the gravy and force through as much of the delicious debris as you can with a wooden spoon, then pour into two dégraisseurs. These lovely little French gravy jugs have two pouring sides, one that releases the fat with the gravy, the other that pours fat free!

Roast Chicken with a Sweetcorn and Ginger Stuffing

SERVES 6

corn cobs	2
large organic corn-fed chicken	1
onion, *sliced*	1
onion, *peeled and chopped*	2
celery sticks, with the leaves, *chopped*	2
fresh ginger, *peeled and very finely chopped*	5cm/2in
the liver of the bird	
seasoning	
breadcrumbs	a handful
egg, *beaten*	1
olive oil and butter	

It did make me slightly uneasy, stuffing a chicken with its daily diet of maize, and its own liver, but I promise you, this is one of the best stuffings ever; the ginger lifts it from ordinary to sublime. Do not add herbs, it would dull the pure flavours.

→ Preheat the oven to 200°C/400°F/Gas 6. Cook the CORN COBS and strip off the kernels. Heat a film of OLIVE OIL and a knob of BUTTER in a frying pan and add the chopped ONION and CELERY. Stir to coat, then add the GINGER, and cook until palely softened. Throw in the LIVER, chopped into 7 or 8 pieces, and cook for a further couple of minutes, until still very pink. Remove from the heat and add the corn, seasoning, BREADCRUMBS and beaten EGG, and amalgamate. Spoon it into the fowl's bottom, pressing it down well. Secure with a cocktail stick.

→ Put your sliced onion on the bottom of the roasting tin, then lay the chicken on its side on top. Season and slather with a bit of olive oil. Cook for 30 minutes a side, then sit the chicken breast up, sprinkle over some coarse sea salt, and cook for a final 30 minutes. Remove and leave to rest for 15–20 minutes under foil. Accompany with the usual roast potatoes, parsnips and other vegetables and gravy.

Aromatic Chicken with Potato, Rocket and Thyme Stuffing

SERVES 4

unsalted butter	55g/2oz
fresh thyme, *chopped*	1 tbsp
lemon juice	a squeeze
salt and pepper	
chicken	1 × 1.5kg/3¼lb
onion, *thinly sliced*	1

Potato, Rocket and Thyme Stuffing

butter and olive oil	
onion, *finely chopped*	1
small new garlic cloves, *peeled*	8–9
medium potatoes, *cut in small dice*	2
fresh thyme	1 tbsp
rosemary	½ tbsp
black olives	4
green olives	8
breadcrumbs	a handful
rocket leaves	8
lemon	*rind* of 1

→ Preheat the oven to 200°C/400°F/Gas 6. Make the aromatic butter by mashing the BUTTER, chopped THYME and a squeeze of LEMON well together, season it and gently spread it with your fingers under the skin of the CHICKEN'S breast and legs.

→ Heat 30g/1oz of BUTTER gently in a frying pan, add the chopped ONION, finely diced POTATO and whole GARLIC cloves, and sauté until softened and translucent. Add the HERBS and OLIVES, stir to coat. Then add a tablespoon of OLIVE OIL, throw in the BREADCRUMBS, and continue cooking until they are crisply golden and coating the potatoes. Test the potatoes with a skewer, they should remain cubed and be almost cooked through. Finally, add the ROCKET, coarsely chopped, for a few seconds. Take off the heat, add the LEMON RIND, season, and stuff the bird!

→ Place it on its side on the sliced onion in a roasting tin, squeeze on a bit of LEMON JUICE, season, and roast for 20 minutes. Repeat on its other side for a further 20 minutes, then turn it breast up for the final 20 minutes, basting it with the juices, and sprinkling it with SEA SALT. Leave to rest for 10–15 minutes, then carve. The pan juices will give you enough unctuously sticky brown gravy.

Spiced Pot-Roasted Chicken

SERVES 4

organic chicken	1 × 2kg/4½lb
coriander seeds	2 tsp
cardamom pods	12
root ginger, *cut into small dice*	1 finger
cloves	6
sea salt	
black peppercorns	6
olive oil	3–4 tbsp

This is a dish I first adapted from a recipe for spiced grilled chicken and cooked two decades ago as an enduring fan of the greatest of food writers, Elizabeth David. The dish is a variation of an Indian kubab chicken which, Mrs David suggests can be fried in butter rather than grilled, or pot roasted, my preferred cooking method. The spices need to penetrate the chicken for 2 hours before cooking, so heat up the oven accordingly.

→ Joint the CHICKEN into 2 breasts and the legs into 2 pieces each. Keep the thighs and carcass for stock. Heat the CORIANDER SEEDS in a small pan on a high heat for 30 seconds or so to temper them. Pound the CARDAMOM PODS in a mortar, removing the husks and leaving the seeds. Add the coriander seeds, diced GINGER, CLOVES, a little SALT and the BLACK PEPPERCORNS. Pound them together with a pestle before

unsalted butter	55g/2oz
organic lemon	1
watercress OR mustard and cress	1 bunch
mango chutney	
Sauce	
olive oil	
butter	
medium onions, *peeled and sliced*	2
turmeric	½ tsp
root ginger, *grated*	1 tsp
salt and pepper	
live yoghurt, goat's or sheep's	1 × small pot
double cream	2 tbsp
currants	1 handful
coriander	1 bunch

adding about 1 tablespoon of the OLIVE OIL and BUTTER and working it into a paste.

→ Gently lift the skins of each bit of chicken by pushing your fingers between the skin and the flesh, without tearing. Score the flesh a little with the sharp point of a knife. Put a teaspoon of paste onto each bit of flesh and spread it across as far as you can go and as evenly as you can. Put the skin back and rub some of the paste onto the cut sides of the chicken too. Leave for 2 hours for the spices to penetrate.

→ Preheat the oven to 180°C/350°F/Gas 4. Heat the OLIVE OIL in a large, heavy-bottomed pot that the chicken will fit into in a single layer. Brown the chicken briefly on both sides, ending up with it cut side down. Cover with a sheet of greaseproof paper and a lid, and pot roast in the oven for 30–40 minutes, checking with a skewer that the juices do not run bloody but are milky pink when it is cooked through.

→ Meanwhile, as the chicken goes into the oven, start on the SAUCE. Melt 30g/1oz of BUTTER and a tablespoon of OLIVE OIL in a frying pan and fry the ONIONS gently for about 20 minutes, until they soften and turn translucent. Shake over the TURMERIC and the grated GINGER and SEASON. Stir and cook for another 5 minutes. Then add the YOGHURT and stir until it thickens. Add the CREAM and CURRANTS. You may make the sauce in advance and heat it through, without bringing it to the boil, when you need it.

→ Put the WATERCRESS or MUSTARD AND CRESS on a serving dish and put the pieces of chicken in their juices on top. Add quartered LEMONS to the dish. Sprinkle chopped CORIANDER lightly over the sauce and serve it in a bowl alongside a bowl of mango chutney.

Chicken Baked with 40 Cloves of Garlic

SERVES 6

chicken, with its liver and giblets	1 × 1.8–2.3kg/4–5lb
lemon, *halved*	1
olive oil	3 tbsp
garlic cloves, *peeled* or unpeeled	40–50
salt and pepper	
thyme	2–3 sprigs

There are two ways of preparing this daunting-sounding dish, and both are equally pleasurable. In the first, the garlic cloves are peeled and stewed in an ivory nest around the bird. In the second, the cloves are put in unpeeled and served with toasted baguette so they can be popped out of their skins and eaten on the toast with hunks of oily, herbed chicken.

→ Preheat the oven to 150°C/300°F/Gas 2. Remove and reserve the LIVER and GIBLETS and tuck the LEMON HALVES inside the CHICKEN. Heat the OIL in a casserole and gently brown the chicken on all sides. Add the GARLIC cloves and turn them to coat with oil. Turn the bird breast down, SEASON, add the giblets (not the liver) and THYME and put on the lid. Cook in the oven for 1½ hours, then turn the bird breast up, put the lid back on and cook for another 30 minutes.

→ Lift the chicken out of the casserole, holding it on end so all the delicious juices run into the pot, then put it on a carving board and wrap in foil. Discard the giblets and add the liver to the casserole to cook briefly, either cut in thin strips, or mashed as you go. Add the juices from the resting bird to the pot, carve, and serve with some of the cloves of garlic on each plate, along with a moat of golden juice.

→ Serve with mash or rice, and a couple of contrastingly coloured vegetables, say carrots and spinach or courgettes.

Mantuan Chicken

SERVES 12

large organic chicken breasts	10
chicken stock (see p. 54)	1 litre/1¾ pints
dry white wine	300ml/10fl oz
Sauce	
light muscovado sugar	5 level tbsp
dry white wine	120ml/4fl oz
sultanas	85g/3oz
lemons	*grated zest* of 2½
best balsamic vinegar	5 tbsp
sea salt	2 tsp
freshly ground black pepper	
best olive oil	120ml/4fl oz

A glorious cold dish for the summer months, this is a 17th-century Mantuan recipe dug out by the great Italian food writer Anna Del Conte. It is the perfect dish to make if you have a huge party of people to feed—it is festive, beautiful and can be prepared in advance. Choose a well-aged, velvety balsamic vinegar; you want rich, mellow velvet not sharp, thin acid.

→ Put the BREASTS in a single layer in as many heavy-bottomed pans as you need (I used three), and cover each with some of the STOCK AND WHITE WINE mixture. Poach at a mere burble, turning every 5 minutes, until cooked through, with only a faint pink in the liquid when pierced with a skewer; 20–25 minutes should do large chicken breasts, and they will continue to cook as the liquid cools. When cool, transfer to one pan with their liquid, cover and keep in the fridge overnight.

→ Just over 3 hours before you want to eat, take the chicken out of the fridge and make the SAUCE. Put the SUGAR and WINE in a small pan and bring it very slowly to the boil, stirring to dissolve the sugar completely. Take off the heat, and add the SULTANAS and LEMON ZEST to infuse. Leave to cool while you cut each breast downwards into 1cm/½in slices, re-assembling them on a large serving dish.

→ Strain the sauce, reserving the zest and sultanas in the sieve. Add the VINEGAR to the sauce, and the SALT AND PEPPER, then start adding the OIL in a trickle, whisking as you go to form an emulsion. Return the zest and sultanas to the sauce, taste, adjust the SEASONING, and pour over the centre of the breasts. Cover with clingfilm and keep at room temperature for 3 hours. Serve with new potatoes or plain rice and some cold white wands of leeks.

Chicken or Pheasant cooked with Red Wine Vinegar and Herbs

SERVES 4

organic chicken OR pheasant	1 × 1.4kg/3lb
organic smoked streaky bacon	55g/2oz
rosemary	1 sprig
sage leaves	4
fresh bay leaves	2
thyme	a little bunch
olive oil and unsalted butter	
dried chilli (optional)	1
large garlic cloves, *peeled and bruised with the back of a knife*	2
Navarrico piquillo peppers, *cut in strips*	4 or 5
good red wine vinegar	100ml/3½fl oz
molasses sugar	1 tsp
butter	55g/2oz
sea salt and pepper	

→ Joint the BIRD so that you have 4 pieces of leg, 4 pieces of breast and 2 wings. Snip the BACON into small strips. With a mezzaluna or sharp knife, chop all the HERBS together really finely and roll them into the bacon.

→ In a large, heavy-bottomed casserole that will fit all the chicken pieces in a single layer, heat a generous splosh of good OLIVE OIL with about 55g/2oz of BUTTER. Gently sauté the bacon and herb mixture with the dried CHILLI if you are using it, and the cloves of GARLIC. Remove the chilli and garlic once you sense the aroma of them has been released into the dish. Add the pieces of chicken, season, and brown on both sides for a total of 15 minutes. Add the strips of PIQUILLO pepper. Raise the heat, add the red wine VINEGAR, then let it bubble furiously for a minute or so before adding 150ml/5fl oz of hot water.

→ Reduce the temperature to a gentle simmer, cover the pot with a lid and cook the chicken for a further 30 minutes. It should be tender when pierced with a skewer. Remove the chicken with all the herbs, peppers and bacon to a heated dish and keep warm.

→ Boil down the juices for a few minutes with a teaspoon of SUGAR until they become more syrupy. Add some small pieces of BUTTER to make the sauce glossy, check the SEASONING and pour the sauce over the chicken. Everyone can have half a breast and a piece of leg, and you still have the wings to suck on. I serve this with brown jasmine rice.

Coq au Vin

SERVES 6

unsalted butter	85g/3oz
olive oil	3 tbsp
organic green back bacon, *diced*	110g/4oz
shallots, *peeled and left whole*	18
garlic cloves	4
organic mushrooms, *halved*	18
large organic chicken, *jointed* OR good-sized legs	1 6
flour	
salt and pepper	
bouquet of fresh thyme, flat-leaf parsley and bay *tied together*	
cognac	4 tbsp
full-bodied red wine	1 bottle
molasses sugar	1 tsp
butter and flour	1 tbsp of each
flat-leaf parsley	1 handful

The classic of classics, this is an old-fashioned '70s bistro dish. But the great joy of that particular ilk and era of restaurant food is that it's the sort you always want to eat and the kind you want to cook at home. Make sure your fowl is the best you can afford, preferably a slow-grown, organically reared, free-range bird. Use a whole chicken or just legs.

→ Preheat the oven to 180°C/350°F/Gas 4. Heat the BUTTER and OLIVE OIL in a heavy-bottomed casserole, and throw in the BACON. Sauté briefly, then add the SHALLOTS, GARLIC and MUSHROOMS and cook gently until the shallots are beginning to turn opaque and pale gold. Remove with a slotted spoon. Shake the CHICKEN PIECES with some seasoned flour in a ziploc bag, then shake off any excess flour. Add them to the pan and brown first on one side then the other for 5 minutes a side. Return the bacon and vegetables to the pot, add the BOUQUET OF HERBS and season. Cover the pot with a lid and cook until tender, about 25 minutes.

→ Set a saucepan on top of the stove on a moderate heat, warm the COGNAC in a ladle, then pour it into the pan and set it alight. Let the alcohol burn off before adding the heated RED WINE and a teaspoon of MOLASSES SUGAR. Reduce by about one-third, then thicken with some old-fashioned beurre manié. (Simply work together a tablespoon each of BUTTER and FLOUR until you have a paste, then break off pea-sized bits and whisk them into a ladle of the hot liquid and add to the sauce.) Strain the sauce into the coq and keep hot until ready to serve. Scatter with the chopped parsley.

Chicken Savoyarde

SERVES 6

organic chicken	1 × 2kg/4½lb
onions, *peeled, one of them stuck with 2 cloves*	2
carrots, *peeled and sliced in half lengthways*	2
celery sticks, *chopped in half*	3
leeks, *trimmed and well washed*	2
bay leaves	2
thyme	2 sprigs
salt	

Poach and cool the chicken the day before you need it if you want to get ahead and make life simple on the night.

→ Put the CHICKEN in a large pot, add the VEGETABLES and HERBS and SALT. Poach very gently for around an hour and a half, skimming off any scum that comes to the surface. Once cooked, lift out the bird and allow to cool. Strain the stock through a fine sieve and discard all solids. Leave to settle and lift off any surface fat with several sheets of absorbent kitchen paper. Set aside until you are ready to make the SAUCE.

→ Remove all the meat from the chicken carcass (discarding skin and also removing all sinews from the drumsticks) and cut into large, bite-sized pieces.

Sauce

butter	55g/2oz
flour	55g/2oz
poaching stock	400ml/14fl oz
dry white wine	300ml/10fl oz
double cream	240ml/8fl oz
Gruyère cheese, *grated*	100g/3½oz
Dijon mustard	1tbsp
tarragon leaves, *chopped*	55g/2oz
salt and pepper	

Topping

breadcrumbs	55g/2oz
Parmesan cheese, *grated*	30g/1oz

→ To make the sauce, melt the BUTTER in a pan, add the flour, and cook for 3 minutes without browning. Gradually add the hot poaching stock, WHITE WINE and CREAM and stir until thickened. Stir in the CHEESE, MUSTARD and TARRAGON, correct the SEASONING and simmer all together for about 20 minutes.

→ Preheat the oven to 230°C/450°F/Gas 8. Put the chicken in a buttered gratin dish, pour over the sauce and sprinkle with the BREADCRUMBS and PARMESAN CHEESE. Bake in the preheated oven for 20–25 minutes until the dish is golden brown and bubbling well around the edges. Eat with buttered new potatoes and a crisp green salad.

Southern-Style Fried Chicken

SERVES 4

flour	
salt and pepper	
celery salt	
paprika	2 tsp
cayenne	2 tsp
organic chicken thighs, *skinned*	8
organic eggs, *beaten*	2
lard	110g/4oz

Classically cooked in bacon fat or lard, and served with sweetcorn fritters (see p. 385), this is a perfect autumn dish. If you don't want to use lard, fry your chicken in 85g/3oz butter and 150ml/5fl oz olive oil.

→ Season the FLOUR and add a knife tip of CELERY SALT and the PAPRIKA and CAYENNE. Put the seasoned flour in a Ziploc bag, throw in the THIGHS, seal and shake. Remove the floured thighs, shaking off any excess flour, and place them on a plate. Turn each thigh in beaten EGG before placing it on a rack for a minute. Repeat with more flour and beaten egg, before a final flouring. Place on the rack while you heat the lard or butter and oil in a heavy-bottomed frying pan.

→ When the fat starts smoking, put the thighs in with a slotted spoon and fry gently for about 10 minutes a side or until bronzed and crisped. You could serve this with a couple of rashers of well-crisped streaky bacon per person.

Chicken in a Cream Sauce

SERVES 4–6

organic free-range chicken	1 × 1.5–2kg / 3¼–4½lb
organic lemon	1
onion, *stuck with 3 cloves*	1
some leek tops	
carrots, *chopped*	2
celery sticks, *chopped with their leaves*	2
bouquet of thyme, parsley, rosemary and bay *tied together*	
peppercorns	12
white wine	½ bottle
chicken stock (see p. 54) or water	1 litre / 1¾ pints or so

Sauce

unsalted butter	55g / 2oz
flour	2 tbsp
chicken stock (see p. 54)	300ml / 10fl oz
double cream	240ml / 8fl oz
organic egg yolks	2
lemon juice	a squeeze
sea salt and black pepper	
tarragon (optional)	1–2 tbsp

Sometimes simple, soothing dishes are the only thing that appeals, and chicken in cream sauce (poulet à la crème) is one of them. Its ivory, creamy tones, rich, smooth softness of flesh and plush velvet sauce somehow defy the word bland that may spring to mind. If you feel like a speckle of green, finish the sauce with some finely chopped tarragon stirred in at the last minute before serving.

→ Rub the CHICKEN inside and out with the cut side of a LEMON, then put the chicken breast up in a large, heavy-bottomed pot. Add ALL THE VEGETABLES, bouquet of HERBS and PEPPERCORNS, followed by the white WINE and enough STOCK OR WATER just to cover the breast. Bring slowly to the boil and remove the scum. Turn down to the gentlest blip of a simmer, then cover with greaseproof paper and a lid and poach. If it's a small bird, turn it breast down after 45 minutes for the last 15 minutes; if it's a large bird do the same after an hour for the last 15 minutes.

→ Start making the SAUCE 30 minutes or so before the chicken is going to be ready. Melt the BUTTER in a heavy-bottomed pan. When it begins to bubble, add the FLOUR and stir it well in until it is a blond roux, pale golden and bubbling. Add the hot CHICKEN STOCK, a ladle at a time, stirring well over a medium heat and making sure there are no lumps. You may wish to do this with a balloon whisk. Now add the CREAM and stir it in. The sauce will be quite thin at this point, but keep cooking it over a gentle heat for about 20 minutes, as it will thicken slowly. You don't have to stir it constantly, but regularly stirring will stop it sticking or forming a skin on top.

→ Just before you are ready to serve, remove the chicken to a carving dish and joint it, putting the pieces on a large warmed serving dish. Beat the EGG YOLKS with a squeeze of LEMON JUICE and add them to the cream sauce, stirring it in but keeping it just under boiling point so that it doesn't curdle. SEASON, taste—you may need more seasoning or lemon juice —and add the herbs if you wish before pouring it over the chicken. You may prefer to add parsley instead.

→ Serve with plain basmati rice and some vegetables or with a plain, green salad. The somewhat sumptuous plainness of the dish should be preserved throughout.

Cold Chicken in a Tarragon Cream Sauce

SERVES 6

organic, free-range chicken	1 × 1.5kg/3¼lb
leek tops, carrots, celery, onions, peppercorns and herbs	
stock you've cooked the bird in	600ml/1 pint
double cream	150ml/5fl oz
organic egg yolks, *well beaten*	6
lemon juice	a little
white wine	a little
sea salt and black pepper	
fresh tarragon	1 handful

This is a lovely summer lunch dish, the cream sauce set and languishing on the poached chicken and a pattern of long, aniseedy tarragon leaves climbing up the snowy slope of sauce like green branches. Make it in advance and eat it cold with an old-fashioned rice salad dressed with a good vinaigrette—sherry vinegar works well with tarragon—and jewelled with fresh young peas.

→ Put the CHICKEN in a tightish-fitting pot with some LEEK TOPS, CARROT, CELERY, ONION, a few PEPPERCORNS and a bouquet of fresh HERBS. Just cover with water, bring to the boil slowly and skim. Cover the pan and poach the chicken for 45–60 minutes, turning it over at half time.

→ Remove the bird from its stock once it is cooked. Set the stock aside. Carve when it is cool enough, the breasts each into two good, thick pieces, the legs into two pieces each and the wings. Remove every last bit of skin.

→ Mix the hot stock with the CREAM and the well-beaten YOLKS. Pour into a wide-bottomed pan and stir or whisk constantly over a gentle heat. Since you are in effect making a custard, there is the danger of its scrambling if you allow it to hit boiling point. You must just have patience and keep whisking until the mixture, all of a sudden, has the consistency of thick cream and coats the whisk or wooden spoon. This usually takes between 10–20 minutes. If you get frightened and feel nothing much is happening, place your pan inside a larger pan containing hot water just under simmering point and leave the sauce, apart from the odd whisk or stir, for 20–30 minutes. It will thicken all by itself and have the added advantage of an even better flavour.

→ Once you have the desirable thick cream texture, season, add a squeeze of LEMON JUICE and a tablespoon of white WINE and a tablespoon of chopped TARRAGON. Keep the rest of the leaves whole for decorating. Stir off the heat until the sauce has cooled a little—it will go on thickening off the heat as all custards do as they are cooling—and pour it over the skinned pieces of chicken on a large serving dish. Dip whole LEAVES OF TARRAGON in the stock and put them, Jack and the beanstalk-like, up either side of the dish on top of the sauce, say a thumbnail in from the edge of the chicken on each side. Serve cold.

Garlicky Stir-Fried Chicken with Ginger and Basil

SERVES 4

chicken breasts	450g/1lb
groundnut oil	2 tbsp
garlic cloves, *chopped*	4–6
fresh ginger, *thinly sliced*	1 finger
chicken stock (see p. 54)	1 ladleful
light soy sauce	1 tbsp
sugar	1–2 tsp
chilli bean sauce	1 dsrtsp
sesame oil	2 tsp
fresh basil leaves, *without their stalks*	a handful

Seared and smoky, this quick chicken stir-fry should only be made with organic or free-range chicken, whatever your budget. It has the pzazz of basil and a hit of chilli bean sauce.

→ Remove the skin from the CHICKEN BREASTS, and the bones if you have bought them on the bone. Cut them into long, thin strips, 4 × 1cm/1½ × ½in. Heat a wok or frying pan over a high heat until it is really hot, then add the OIL. Wait until it begins to smoke before throwing in the GARLIC and GINGER and stir-frying them together for 30 seconds. Throw in the chicken pieces and stir-fry them for 2 minutes, turning them frequently.

→ Add the STOCK, SOY SAUCE, SUGAR and CHILLI BEAN SAUCE, bring to boiling point, then turn down to a simmer for 5 minutes. Stir in the SESAME OIL and tear in the BASIL leaves and stir for a further 30 seconds before removing from the heat and serving with boiled rice and some stir-fried vegetables.

Coronation Chicken

SERVES 6

organic free-range chicken	1 × 1.5kg/3¼lb
leek tops, carrots, celery, onions, peppercorns and herbs	
Cream of curry sauce	
onion, *chopped*	55g/2oz
light olive oil	1 tbsp
fresh Madras curry powder	1 dsrtsp
tomato purée	1 tsp
red wine	150ml/5fl oz
water	120ml/4fl oz
bay leaf	1
salt and pepper	
sugar	1 pinch
lemon slices	2
lemon juice	a squeeze or more
apricot jam, apricot purée OR mango chutney, *sieved*	1–2 tbsp

One of the first cookery books I was ever given as a teenager was The Constance Spry Cookery Book. *She is probably more famous for her coronation chicken with its cream of curry sauce than for anything else. Easy to laugh at what became a stock Sloane party or wedding dish and became mongrelised with a certain proprietary brand of mayonnaise, but when made properly it is a really lovely summer dish.*

→ Put the CHICKEN in a tightish-fitting pot with some LEEK TOPS, CARROT, CELERY, ONION, a few PEPPERCORNS and a bouquet of fresh HERBS. Just cover with water, bring to the boil slowly and skim. Cover the pan and poach the chicken for 45–60 minutes, turning it over at half time. Remove the fowl from its bath of stock when the stock has cooled and joint it. Remove the flesh from the bones and the skin from the flesh.

→ Gently stew the chopped ONION in the OLIVE OIL until translucent. Add the CURRY POWDER and stir to coat the onion. Cook for another couple of minutes. Add the TOMATO PURÉE, the WINE, WATER and BAY LEAF, and bring to the boil. Add the SEASONING, SUGAR and the LEMON SLICES and JUICE. Simmer uncovered for 5–10 minutes. Strain thoroughly through a sieve, pressing down on it hard with a wooden spoon to extract the maximum flavour and cool. Add by degrees to the MAYONNAISE

home-made mayonnaise (see p. 404)	400ml/14fl oz
double cream, *lightly whipped*	about 4 tbsp

with the APRICOT JAM, PURÉE or MANGO CHUTNEY. Adjust SEASONING, adding more LEMON JUICE to taste. Obviously, fresh apricot purée will be sweeter than jam or chutney. Fold in the WHIPPED CREAM. Tear the chicken into pieces along the grain of the meat, the sort you could consider bite-sized, and mix half the sauce in with the chicken. If you are following Constance Spry, arrange at one end of the serving dish with a rice salad of cooked peas, diced cucumber and finely chopped mixed herbs mixed in a well-seasoned French dressing at the other end. Now coat the chicken with the rest of the curry cream sauce. Serve cold.

→ The sauce is also good served with cold lobster or, dare I say it, prawns, if you don't think that a blast from the '70s too far. If you weren't around then in cooking terms it could, of course, all be new to you.

Chicken with Chickpeas

SERVES 4

onion, *finely chopped*	1
sunflower oil	2 tbsp
turmeric	1 tsp
large organic chicken	1
chickpeas, *soaked overnight*	225g/8oz
lemon	juice of 1 or more, to taste
garlic cloves, *crushed*	2–4
black pepper OR cayenne	a pinch
salt	

→ Fry the ONION in the OIL in a large saucepan until golden, then stir in the TURMERIC. Put in the CHICKEN and turn it until it is yellow all over. Add about 600ml/1 pint of water, the drained CHICKPEAS, LEMON JUICE, GARLIC and PEPPER.

→ Bring to the boil and simmer, covered, for 1 hour or longer, turning the chicken occasionally and adding SALT when the chickpeas have softened. Cook until the chicken is very tender, the chickpeas soft, yellow and lemony, and the liquid reduced.

Home-made Chicken Nuggets

SERVES 8

chicken, brown meat, *minced*	750g/1lb 10oz
brown breadcrumbs	175g/6oz
mature Cheddar, *grated*	175g/6oz
mayonnaise to bind	1 tbsp
garlic clove	1
salt and pepper	
egg, *beaten*	
some fine toasted breadcrumbs to coat the nuggets	

→ Preheat the oven to 180°C/350°F/Gas 4. Mix ALL THE INGREDIENTS up to and including the SEASONING together. Form into golf-ball sized nuggets with damp hands to prevent sticking, and roll each one first in beaten EGG and then in the toasted BREADCRUMBS. You can freeze them at this stage if you want to, or if you need only a few of them.
→ Place on a greased baking sheet, and cook for about 25 minutes if fresh, and for 45 if frozen. Serve with some ketchup, or add some finely chopped cornichons, capers and anchovy, with a sprinkling of chives and dill, to your mayonnaise to make a sauce tartare.

Chicken Thighs Stewed with Summer Vegetables

SERVES 6

olive oil	
large onion, *peeled and chopped*	1
plump, organic chicken thighs	6
new potatoes, *cleaned, scraped and left whole*	2–3 per person
chicken stock	to cover
carrots, *cut in thinnish discs*	6
fresh peas, *shelled weight*	450g/1lb
broad beans, *steamed briefly and skinned* (optional)	225g/8oz
fresh mint	1 large handful
salt and pepper	

A simple summer dish that I made with peas picked from the garden seconds before. It can be left to cook for nearly an hour, then brought to the table in the pot.

→ Heat a couple of tablespoons of OLIVE OIL in a heavy-bottomed pan. Sauté the ONION gently with a bit of SALT until softened and translucent, then add the CHICKEN THIGHS skin side down, and brown for a few minutes. Season. Turn them over, and brown the flesh side briefly.
→ Remove the chicken from the pot, and gently turn the POTATOES in the oil and chicken fat for a few minutes. Lay the thighs on top of the potatoes, pour over hot STOCK to cover, then throw in the CARROTS, bring just to the boil, turn down to a bare simmer, and put the lid on. Come back in 50 minutes and pour in the fresh PEAS. Ten minutes later add the cooked BROAD BEANS, SEASON to taste and add the freshly chopped MINT off the heat. With a skewer, test that the potatoes are cooked through, skim some of the chicken fat from the surface if you feel it necessary, and serve.

Chicken Risotto

SERVES 4

chicken stock (see p. 54)	about 850ml/1½ pints
white wine (optional)	1 glass
extra virgin olive oil	a few tbsp
medium onion, *finely chopped*	1
garlic cloves, *finely sliced*	2
carrot, *chopped into very small dice*	1
celery sticks, *strung and chopped small*	1–2 sticks
Carnaroli OR Arborio rice	340g/12oz
remains of a chicken, white and brown meat, *chopped*	
Parmesan cheese, *freshly grated*	170g/6oz
butter	a knob
sea salt and black pepper	
flat-leaf parsley or tarragon, *chopped*	1 tbsp

This is a dish to make when you have the remains of a roasted or poached chicken. You can pick the flesh clean from the carcass before making your stock from the bones, a good stock being the base of the dish before you add your rice, vegetables, chicken, herbs, Parmesan and unsalted butter. If you insist on using stock cubes, there is no point in my trying to convert you, but I always like to have good chicken stock lurking in the fridge or freezer.

→ Heat the STOCK to simmering point, and the WINE if using. Heat 3–4 tablespoons of OLIVE OIL in a large, heavy-bottomed risotto or frying pan. Add ALL THE CHOPPED VEGETABLES together and sauté them over a medium heat until they begin to soften and the onion takes on a translucent glow. Throw in the RICE and stir, turning it to coat it all over in the OIL, before throwing in the white WINE and allowing it to fizz and splutter and begin to become absorbed by the grain. Never let risotto dry out and stick to the pan. You must constantly top it up with liquid, a ladle or two at a time, so that it isn't overwhelmed and submerged and so that you can stir the white stuff continuously while it releases its chalky-thick starch into the stock.

→ When the wine is almost absorbed, add a couple of ladles of STOCK and stir until that too has almost been absorbed, making sure that no grain escapes up the side of the pan. The rice will begin to swell and you must continue to add the stock, a ladle or two at a time, until the rice has swollen, lost its hard-textured edge but kept a degree of firmness that has bite when you test it. Stir frequently—the secret of all good risottos is the stirring, as it releases the chalky starch from the grains of rice. This should take 20–22 minutes.

→ At this point, add the bits of CHICKEN and stir them in. Then add a couple of tablespoons of PARMESAN, the BUTTER (a large knob the size of a couple of walnuts), SALT AND PEPPER, the HERBS and a final ladle of STOCK, and give the dish a last stir.

→ Remove from the heat and cover to allow all the flavours to marry and the butter and cheese to melt as the last of the stock is absorbed. After 5 minutes, serve the risotto straight from the pan, allowing everyone to help themselves to extra grated Parmesan from the bowl. A plain green or simple salad is the only accompaniment this dish needs.

Chicken Liver Pilav

SERVES 4

organic white long-grain rice	450g/1lb
light muscovado sugar	2 tsp
water OR stock	up to 1.2 litres/2 pints
olive oil	2 tbsp
cumin seeds	½ tsp
green cardamom seeds	½ tsp
cloves	½ tsp
ground cinnamon	½ tsp
salt	
organic chicken livers	450g/1lb
saffron threads, *ground and soaked in 1 tbsp warm water*	1 tsp
onions, *peeled and finely sliced in half moons*	2
fresh or frozen peas (*if fresh, cooked and drained*)	225g/8oz
lemon peel, *without the pith*	2 strips
olive oil	
salt and pepper	

→ Preset the oven to 150°C/300°F/Gas 2. Rinse the RICE very well in a sieve under cold water until it runs clear. Add fresh water and soak the rice for at least half an hour and preferably longer.

→ Place the SUGAR in a large flameproof casserole and stir over a medium heat until the sugar melts and turns dark golden brown. Remove from the heat while you add 600ml/1 pint of WATER OR STOCK, the OIL, SPICES and SALT, then bring back to the boil. Drain the rice thoroughly, add it to the boiling liquid, and continue cooking over a low heat, with the lid on, until the liquid has evaporated and the rice is al dente, about 15 minutes. If you are just cooking plain rice, stir it once with a fork, carefully so as not to break the rice, cover with the lid and put in the oven for 20–30 minutes.

→ While the rice is cooking, de-vein the CHICKEN LIVERS but leave them whole, then sauté them briefly on each side. You are not cooking them at this stage, merely browning them, their insides should remain raw-looking. Set aside on a plate, add a little more OIL to the pan if you need to, and start cooking the ONIONS with a bit of SALT to draw out the juices. Continue to cook at a medium heat for the next 30 minutes or so while you finish off the pilav; you want the onions to brown and crisp delectably in the crusty juices, but not be charred and burnt.

→ Meanwhile, add the SAFFRON, PEAS and CHICKEN LIVERS to the pot of rice with the LEMON RIND. Gently bury the livers and peas under the rice with a fork, add up to 600ml/1 pint of extra STOCK, cover and put in the oven for 20–30 minutes. Test the rice, and make sure the chicken livers are jewel pink. Serve in the pot, with the crispy brown onions on top.

Balsamic Tomato Chicken with Basil

SERVES 4

vine tomatoes	500g/1lb 2oz
butter	55g/2oz
olive oil	1 tbsp
garlic clove	1
organic chicken fillet	450g/1lb
good balsamic vinegar, gran reserva if possible	2–3 tbsp
salt, pepper and sugar	
lemon juice	a squeeze
butter	a knob
basil leaves	a handful

I cooked this delicious, summery dish after I had interviewed Lindsey Bareham on publication of her wonderful The Big Red Book of Tomatoes. Lindsey likes this dish because it is full of flavour and quick to make, as easy for one as for six.

→ Core, blanch and seed the vine TOMATOES, and dice them small. Tip all the seed debris into a sieve above a bowl, and press with the back of a wooden spoon to extract all the liquid. Set aside. Crush the GARLIC to a paste with a pinch of SALT.
→ Melt half the BUTTER gently in a pan, add the OIL and GARLIC and cook until aromatic. Cut the CHICKEN into strips 5 × 1cm/ 2 × ½in and put in the pan. Turn up the heat and fry briskly until it is plump and springy. Pour over the BALSAMIC VINEGAR, stir, then add the rest of the BUTTER, the tomatoes and seed debris liquid. Season, and simmer for about 15 minutes until the tomatoes have turned into a sauce and the chicken is completely cooked.
→ Taste, adjust the seasoning with SALT, SUGAR and a squeeze of LEMON, and stir in the knob of BUTTER until it has dissolved. Shred the BASIL leaves over the top and serve with rice, potatoes or pasta.

Chinese Chicken Drumsticks

garlic cloves	4
organic tamari soya sauce	120ml/4fl oz
sesame oil	2 tbsp
fresh ginger, *peeled and grated*	5cm/2in
orange	juice of 1
molasses sugar	2 tsp
chicken drumsticks	2 per person

Marinate the drumsticks overnight if possible, but even 30 minutes is better than nothing.

→ Preheat the oven to 180°C/350°F/Gas 4. Crush the GARLIC to a paste with some SALT in a mortar. Mix together the garlic with the SOYA SAUCE, OIL, GINGER, JUICE and SUGAR in the dish you are going to cook in, in my case a terracotta one, and turn the CHICKEN DRUMSTICKS in it. Cover and leave in the fridge.
→ Bring back to room temperature before cooking. Place in the oven and cook for about 30–40 minutes basting occasionally.
→ A skewer will tell you they're cooked when the blood no longer runs from them. You could reduce the stickily browned juices if you want, but tamari is salty, so be careful.

Elaichi Murg, or Cardamom Chicken

SERVES 4

Greek yoghurt	500ml/16fl oz tub
small chicken	1
fresh ginger, *grated*	2 tsp
fresh garlic, *chopped*	2 tsp
cardamom, *crushed*	2 tsp
ground black pepper	1½ tsp
lime	1
ghee	2 tbsp
coconut milk	400ml/14fl oz tin
large green chillies	6
fresh coriander, *chopped*	1 bunch

→ Empty two-thirds of the tub of GREEK YOGHURT into a J-cloth, and leave overnight in the fridge in a colander over a basin so that it can drain.

→ Joint and skin a small CHICKEN. Liquidise a couple of teaspoons each of fresh GINGER and GARLIC, add 2 teaspoons of crushed CARDAMOM and 1½ teaspoons of ground BLACK PEPPER, grate the zest of the LIME over the paste, and spread it over the chicken pieces. Marinate in the fridge for anything from an hour to overnight.

→ Heat two tablespoonfuls of GHEE in a pan, and brown the CHICKEN PIECES. Tip the drained YOGHURT into the pan, add the tin of COCONUT MILK and bring to the boil. Add 6 large GREEN CHILLIES that you have pricked all over, and half a bunch of chopped fresh CORIANDER. If it makes you go hot just thinking about it, use fewer chillies, and/or fish them out before you serve the dish.

→ Cover with a lid and simmer for 20 minutes, or until the chicken appears cooked through when pierced with a skewer. Adjust the SALT, PEPPER and CARDAMOM just to lift all the flavours, then at the last moment squeeze over some fresh LIME JUICE to taste and the rest of the chopped CORIANDER. Sensational.

Claudia Roden's Chicken with Almonds and Honey

SERVES 8

large onions, *chopped*	2
sunflower oil	4 tbsp
ground ginger	1 tsp
cinnamon	1½ tsp
chickens, *cut into quarters*	2
salt and pepper	
saffron stamens	½ tsp
lemon	juice of ½–1
blanched almonds	225g/8oz
rosewater	1 tbsp
honey	4–5 tbsp

→ In a large saucepan, cook the ONIONS with the OIL until they soften. Stir in the GINGER and CINNAMON and put in the CHICKEN PIECES. Cover with water, add SALT AND PEPPER, SAFFRON and LEMON JUICE and simmer, covered, for about 30 minutes. Taste and adjust the seasonings.

→ Heat the oven to 180°C/350°F/Gas 4. Lift the chicken pieces out of the saucepan and arrange them in a large, shallow baking dish. Pour over enough of the poaching liquid to make sauce for everyone and keep the rest for stock.

→ Grind the ALMONDS coarsely in the food processor and mix with the ROSEWATER and HONEY. Spread this paste over the chicken pieces and place in the oven. They will need about 30 minutes, but check after 20—you want the crust golden and crisp, not brown.

→ Serve with spiced couscous. I add a cinnamon stick and a few cardamom pods while I am steaming it.

Chicken Pie

SERVES 4

organic free-range chicken	1 × 1.5kg/3¼lb
some leek tops, extra carrots, celery, onions and herbs	
medium carrots, *sliced into thick discs*	2
celery, *chopped*	2 sticks
leeks, *white parts sliced into discs*	2
medium onions, *peeled and quartered*	2
unsalted butter	55g/2oz
flour	55g/2oz
full-cream milk	150ml/5fl oz
chicken stock from poaching the bird	150ml/5fl oz
double cream	150ml/5fl oz
sprigs of tarragon and flat-leaf parsley, *chopped*	
sea salt and black pepper	

Shortcrust pastry

plain flour	340g/12oz
salt	1 pinch
unsalted butter OR lard, OR half butter and half lard	170g/6oz
egg, *beaten*, for glaze	

This, to my mind, is the ultimate savoury pie, a dish that deserves serenading for its comfort and homeliness and hidden depths; for its golden crust concealing jewels of vegetables and chicken; and its creamy, satin mantle of a béchamel sauce made slightly aniseedy with tarragon.

→ Put the CHICKEN breast-up in a tightish-fitting pot with some LEEK TOPS, CARROT, CELERY, ONION, a few PEPPERCORNS and a bouquet of HERBS. Just cover with water, bring to the boil slowly and skim. Cover and poach the chicken for 45–60 minutes. Remove the chicken and boil the stock to reduce by half.

→ Make the PASTRY (see p. 104), working it quickly into a ball, then wrap it in clingfilm and chill it in the fridge for half an hour. Steam the VEGETABLES by throwing them into the steamer in the order in which they cook, CARROTS first, CELERY next, then the ONION and LEEK for the last 5 minutes.

→ Preheat the oven to 180°C/350°F/Gas 4 and place a baking sheet on the middle shelf of the oven to heat up. When the bird has cooled down sufficiently to handle, remove all the flesh you can from the bones, peeling off the skin as you go to use with the carcass to make more intensely flavoured stock the second time around. Tear the flesh along the grain, almost pulling it into long bite-sized pieces.

→ Make a roux with the BUTTER and FLOUR, then add the MILK and reduced CHICKEN STOCK, both hot, alternately, until you have a satin-thick sauce. Stirring as you go, cook the sauce long enough to get rid of the flouriness, then stir in the CREAM. Remove from the heat, SEASON and add the chopped fresh HERBS, a couple of tablespoons of each. Stir in the chicken and vegetables and leave to cool.

→ Line your buttered pastry tin or pie dish with two-thirds of the rolled-out PASTRY, then scrape in the filling and spread it out evenly over the pastry base. Cover with the remaining third of the pastry, and crimp the edges together with the tines of a fork dipped in cold water. Brush the top with beaten EGG. Cut a cross in the middle of the pie right through the pastry to allow the steam to escape as the pie cooks. Bake for about an hour, then check. If the pastry is beautifully bronzed, cover the top with greaseproof paper and cook for about another 15 minutes, or until your nose tells you that it is ready. Don't cut into the pie for at least 10 minutes after taking it out of the oven.

Turkey or Turkey and Ham Pie

→ For me, turkey and chicken are right up there as joint ultimate savoury pies, with their nutmeggy, silken béchamel sauce, jewels of meat and earthy sweet vegetables cloaked in crisp buttery pastry. Mostly when making chicken pie I start from scratch by poaching the chicken first. For a turkey pie, you just need the last of your brown and white meat, with, perhaps, a few good chunks of leftover ham and your turkey stock already made, then follow the recipe on p. 254.

Stephen Markwick's Chicken and Mushroom Pie

SERVES 6–8

butter	55g/2oz
flour	55g/2oz
good chicken stock	570ml/1 pint
Dijon mustard	1 tsp
lemon juice	
onion, *finely chopped*	1
mushrooms	225g/8oz
butter	a knob
white wine	a good splash
roasted chicken, cold	1
fresh tarragon, *chopped*	1 handful
flat-leaf parsley, *chopped*	1 handful
sea salt and black pepper	
shortcrust pastry (see p. 104)	
egg, *beaten*, for glaze	

Stephen Markwick is one of the most talented chefs I know, whose reputation, had he cheffed in London instead of Bristol, would have been altogether more legendary.

→ Make a roux-based sauce in the usual way with the BUTTER, FLOUR and CHICKEN STOCK, and season well. Add the MUSTARD and a spritz of LEMON JUICE. Sweat the chopped ONION and sliced MUSHROOMS together in a little BUTTER, add the splash of white WINE and decant the whole lot into the sauce, stirring it over a gentle heat for a few minutes.

→ Strip the CHICKEN FLESH from the carcass, removing all the skin and fat as you go, and tear it into good-sized pieces for the pie. Add the chicken and chopped HERBS to the sauce and check the SEASONING. Set aside to cool. Make the pastry (see p. 104).

→ Preheat the oven to 200°C/400°F/Gas 6. Pile the chicken mixture into a pie dish and top with the pastry lid. Brush with EGG in the usual way and bake for about 30 minutes or until bubbling and golden brown. Serve with mash and a green veg or salad.

Roast Turkey

Bronze organic or free-range turkey	
stuffing (see p. 258)	
large onion, *peeled and sliced*	1
butter, *softened and well-seasoned*	200g/7oz
coarse sea salt	
pepper	

First and all-important is to buy a really good turkey, and by that I mean a Bronze organic or free-range bird that has been properly reared, slaughtered and hung. Intensively reared turkeys are not worth paying less for. By cooking the turkey on its sides before you turn it breast-up you will silence the critics who plead the impossibility of cooking this most delicately delicious of fowl through at the leg/thigh end without cremating and drying out the breast.

→ Preheat the oven to 190°C/375°F/Gas 5. Then weigh your STUFFED BIRD, and calculate the cooking time: 33 minutes per kilo or 15 minutes to the pound applies up to a 6.5kg/14lb bird. So, a 6.5kg/14lb bird will take 3½ hours. Always calculate like this up to this weight, even if the bird is bigger. For each extra pound allow 10 minutes, so, for a 8.7kg/20lb bird, your total cooking time will be 4½ hours. Still not worth getting out of bed early for.

→ Place the bird on its side, on a layer of peeled, sliced ONIONS, and slap the well-seasoned BUTTER on its skin. Shroud the bird in foil, a double layer, clinching it tightly around the roasting tin, so the bird is sealed in. Just before half time, turn the bird on to its other side, baste it with the buttery juices, seal it inside the foil, and continue to cook.

→ About 30–40 minutes before it should be ready, remove the foil, turn the bird breast up and baste it. Season the skin well with coarse SEA SALT and PEPPER, hit the 200°C/400°F/Gas 6 button and allow the bird to crisp up.

→ Rest the turkey, covered with foil and a tea towel, for 20 minutes in a warm place while you make gravy. I simmer the GIBLETS for 30 minutes with the VEGETABLE WATER from parboiling my potatoes and parsnips, adding the LIVER towards the end. I sieve this mixture into the roasting pan with the ONION AND MEAT JUICES, add a splosh of RED WINE and more meat juices from the carving board as frequently as they exude, and stir while they bubble away for a few minutes. I strain the lot into a jug, and then into a dégraisseur.

Chestnut, Apple, Walnut and Celery Stuffing

olive oil	3 tbsp
large onion, *finely chopped*	1
celery, *finely chopped*	½ a head
walnuts, *finely chopped*	110g/4oz
tart dessert apples, *cored, unpeeled and finely chopped*	2
chestnut purée	450g/1lb tin
organic sausagemeat	450g/1lb
wholemeal breadcrumbs	
organic eggs, *beaten*	2
flat-leaf parsley, *finely chopped*	2 tbsp
salt and pepper	
vacuum-packed chestnuts	450g/1lb

This makes enough stuffing to fill the cavity of a large Bronze turkey and a small roasting tin as well. There are lots of very good jars or vacuum packs of organic chestnuts on the market now, and that's what I use for flavour and ease.

→ Heat the OIL gently in a frying pan, and fry together the ONION, CELERY, WALNUTS and APPLE until golden and softened. Turn into a huge bowl and add all the REMAINING INGREDIENTS, mixing well. Add the whole CHESTNUTS last, chopped in quarters so that they don't break up during the mixing. Stuff the bird. Put the rest in a roasting tin and cook separately.

Lemon, Thyme and Parsley Stuffing

stale white bread	225g/8oz
lemons	*grated* zest of 2
lemon	juice of 1
flat-leaf parsley	a large bunch
fresh thyme, *chopped a little to release the oils*	2 tsp
butter, *softened*	110g/4oz
organic eggs	3
sea salt and black pepper	

→ Turn the BREAD to crumbs in a food processor. (If you only have newer bread, toast it in a slow oven until dry on both sides before making into crumbs.) Put the breadcrumbs in a large bowl and add the ZEST and JUICE. Add the roughly chopped PARSLEY and THYME, amalgamate with the softened BUTTER with a wooden spoon, then beat in the EGGS and add the SEASONING.

Pulled and Devilled Turkey

SERVES 6

cooked turkey breast	450g/1lb
turkey leg and thigh	1 of each
Devil sauce	
Dijon mustard	1 tbsp
hot mango chutney	2 tbsp
Worcestershire sauce	1 tbsp
cayenne	½ tsp, or to taste
sea salt	
olive oil	2 tbsp
Pulled sauce	
butter	85g/3oz
double cream	170ml/6fl oz
lemon juice	
sea salt and black pepper	
flat-leaf parsley, *freshly chopped*	a handful

What I love about this dish, almost more than the Christmas roast turkey, is the total contrast between the white meat with its soothing, creamy, bland sauce and the spicy-hot mustardy devil of the sticky brown meat. I have adapted the recipe from Jane Grigson, the late, great scholar-cook.

→ First, pull the BREAST MEAT apart with your fingers into pieces about 4cm/1½in long and the thickness of a large quill. Follow the grain of the meat so that the pieces look somewhat thready. Take the brown meat from the bone and divide it into larger pieces. Slash each two or three times.

→ Mix the DEVIL SAUCE ingredients together, chopping up any large pieces of fruit in the CHUTNEY. Dip the brown meat pieces into it and spoon as much as you can into the slashes. Arrange in a single layer on the rack of a foil-lined grill and grill under a high heat until the pieces are crusted.

→ Meanwhile, melt the BUTTER in a wide frying pan and stir in the CREAM. Let it boil for a couple of minutes and keep stirring until it thickens. Add the pieces of breast and any clinging jelly, and stir until very hot. Spritz with LEMON JUICE and season with SALT AND PEPPER. Put the white meat in the centre of a serving dish and surround it with the brown. Sprinkle with the PARSLEY. Serve with rice, watercress and wedges of lemon.

Honey-blackened Duck Legs

SERVES 6

organic duck legs	6
red wine	1 glass
Marinade	
chestnut honey	2 tbsp
bitter marmalade	2 dsrtsp
star anise, *pounded in a mortar and sieved*	1 tsp
lime	juice of 1
tamari sauce	2 dsrtsp
black peppercorns, *cracked and scrunched in a mortar*	8–10

The mahogany-dark chestnut honey turns to black when you bake these duck legs, and spoonfuls of lumpy bitter marmalade give the dish a sweet-sour taste. Honey used in place of sugar always darkens the food, because the single sugars in it caramelise so readily.

→ Preheat the oven to 200°C/400°F/Gas 6. Mix the MARINADE INGREDIENTS together in a bowl, stirring well, then pour over the DUCK LEGS, and either leave for a couple of hours or cover and put in the fridge overnight.

→ Place the legs in an earthenware dish, spoon the marinade over evenly, and bake. After 20 minutes turn the legs over, the top side will already be a wonderful molassy colour. After another 20 minutes, throw the WINE into the dish. Scrape all the dark, sticky juices into the wine, and turn the legs for a final 20-minute blast.

Roast Duck
SERVES 4

organic or free-range duck	1 × 2–2.5kg/4½–5½lb
onions	2
organic orange	1
sea salt and black pepper	
olive oil	
Gravy	
duck giblets	
thyme	1 sprig
red wine	1 glass
orange	juice of 1
lemon juice	a spritz

Other than a goose, the duck is the fattiest thing you are ever likely to roast, but that does not mean that it is fatty to eat. If you start the bird off in a pan or casserole and then in the hot blast of the oven so you release the fat throughout the cooking, you will end up with lean, pink breast, burnished, salt-crackled skin and shards of confit-like leg that are as sweet and soft as you could wish for. Keep the giblets for the gravy. If you want the full, old-fashioned number, make a sage and onion or onion and thyme stuffing (see opposite).

→ Preheat the oven to 220°C/425°F/Gas 7. Remove the DUCK from the fridge a couple of hours before you are going to cook it and rub the skin all over with SALT and BLACK PEPPER. Leave until it is time to cook. Splosh a little OLIVE OIL in the bottom of a heavy-bottomed pan the duck will fit into, and brown it all over. This should take about 4–5 minutes. You can miss out this part of the cooking if you like and head straight for the oven, but it does get the fat running and the skin crisping.

→ Peel the ONIONS, slice one and quarter the other. Put the sliced onion on the bottom of a roasting tin and put the duck on top. Stuff it with alternating quarters of onion and ORANGE and shove a good sprig of THYME inside the cavity at the same time. Put the bird in the oven.

→ After about 25–30 minutes, remove the duck and spike it all over, not far enough in to hit the meat, with the point of a fork or a skewer to release the fat. Return to the oven and lower the temperature to 200°C/400°F/Gas 6. Repeat the pricking of the fat after another 20 minutes and drain the fat that has collected in the bottom of the pan at the same time into a bowl. This is what you can use for your roast potatoes. If you prefer to cook POTATOES and PARSNIPS around the duck, turn the oven back up to its previous temperature when the duck has cooked and is resting, and put the roasting tin up to the top of the oven to finish off the veg. Put the DUCK LIVER in the tin for the last 10–15 minutes. You can then mash it into the pan juices to flavour the gravy.

→ The duck should take between 1 hour and 1 hour 15 minutes to cook depending on whether you prefer it pink or better-cooked. Duck is not a meat to serve bloody, but the breast should be pink if you like medium-rare meat. When you remove the duck and transfer it to the carving board, cover it lightly so that the crisped skin has no chance of steaming and

losing its texture, and leave for 10 minutes before carving.
→ Duck is notoriously difficult to carve. I favour thinly slicing the breast, then taking the legs off and carving the meat downwards, top to bottom from the meaty tops to the stringy ankles as it were. Then pick your bones!

Gravy
→ While the duck is cooking, put the GIBLETS minus the liver in a small pan and just cover with water. Gently simmer for 30–40 minutes, remove the giblets and keep the liquid for gravy.
→ While the duck is resting, put the roasting tin on a brisk heat on top of the stove and scrape all the CARAMELISED ONION BITS into the juices, mashing down the LIVER into them as you go. You should pour all the JUICES out from the cavity of the bird into the roasting tin before you rest the duck. Now pull the leaves off a sprig of THYME and add it to the pan followed by the red WINE, which should bubble up and cook into the gravy for a few minutes before you add the giblet liquid. Reduce for a few minutes at a brisk simmer before adding the JUICE OF THE ORANGE or orange and lemon. Decant into two dégraisseurs so that the fat doesn't land on your plate.

Sage and Onion Stuffing

a little butter and olive oil	
large onion, *peeled and finely chopped*	1
fresh sage leaves	12–18
fennel bulb, *outer leaves removed, chopped fine*	1
or celery sticks, *strung and chopped small* (optional)	3
the duck liver (optional)	
parsley, *chopped*	1 small bunch
half a small stale white loaf, *the crusts removed, blitzed into breadcrumbs*	
egg, *beaten*	1
sea salt and black pepper	

→ Melt the BUTTER and OIL in a heavy-bottomed frying pan and throw in the ONION, SAGE and FENNEL OR CELERY if you are using them. Sauté gently until soft and translucent but not browned. Add the chopped DUCK LIVER if you're using it and sauté for another couple of minutes before sprinkling over the PARSLEY.
→ Turn the hot stuffing mixture into the BREADCRUMBS in a bowl, season well and stir in the beaten EGG. Plop the mixture in spoonfuls into the duck cavity before roasting the bird.

Crispy Roast Duck with Turnips

SERVES 4

duck	1 × 2.2kg/5lb
onions	2
orange, *quartered*	1
thyme	a bunch
sea salt	

Sauce

butter	
small onion, *chopped*	1
celery, *chopped*	1 stick
duck liver, heart, kidneys and neck	
pomegranate molasses OR *squeezed* juice of pomegranate (If you can't find either, a sweet orange will do)	1 tbsp
red wine	

Glazed Turnips

baby turnips	8
butter	a knob
brown sugar	1 dsrtsp
thyme	

There has always been an affinity between duck and peas, but I think the first miniature-lightbulb-sized turnips of the spring are as much of a match.

→ Preheat the oven high, to 220°C/425°F/Gas 7. This is what I did to really crisp the skin, while keeping the meat pinkly tender. Remove the giblets, prick the skin all over with a fork, and put the DUCK breast-down in the roasting tin on the top of the stove on a moderately hot ring. Leave it as it begins to sizzle. After 2 minutes repeat this on each side, then on the underside. The fat will be beginning to run, and the duck will already have coloured quite deeply. Finally give it another blast breast side down, then remove the tin from the heat, swiftly place a thinly sliced ONION under the bird, a quartered ORANGE, ONION, and a bunch of THYME inside it, and, still breast up, about 8 generous pinches of SEA SALT all over its skin.

→ Roast for 50 minutes, but after 30, remove it from the oven and suck up the fat with your bulb baster, and again prick the skin all over before returning it to the oven. Leave the duck to rest for 10 minutes before carving.

→ Meanwhile, melt a nut of BUTTER in a small pan, add the ONION, CELERY, and the LIVER, HEART, KIDNEYS and NECK of the duck, and brown gently. Then add the POMEGRANATE MOLASSES or JUICE, red WINE to almost cover, and a bit of water, and leave it to simmer for 10–15 minutes, skimming it if you need to. Reheat with the caramelised onions in the roasting tin. Sieve, pushing through as much of the liver as you can, and serve in a dégraisseur alongside the duck.

Glazed Turnips

→ Peel the TURNIPS, cut them into 5mm/¼ inch dice, and cook them in boiling water until just tender, about 7 minutes. Then toss them in BUTTER and DARK BROWN SUGAR with a sprinkling of THYME until soft and caramelised.

Roast Duck with a Wheatberry, Sour Cherry and Sage Salad

SERVES 6

onions	2
orange	1
organic, free-range ducks	2
sea salt and black pepper	

Wheatberry, Sour Cherry and Sage Salad

wheatberries	225g/8oz
dried sour cherries	110g/4oz
spring onions	1 bunch
sage leaves	6–8
parsley	1 small bunch
flaked almonds	55g/2oz
zest of the orange used to stuff the duck	
extra virgin olive oil	
organic lemons	juice of 1–2
sea salt and black pepper	

I always try to find side dishes to accompany roast duck that act like blotting paper and sharpeners to the grease. This makes a dazzling duck dinner.

→ Preheat oven to 230°C/450°F/Gas 8. Peel and slice 1 ONION and put it on the bottom of the roasting tin. Peel and quarter the other ONION.

→ Zest the ORANGE and keep the zest on a plate for the salad. Quarter the orange and stuff it alternately with the onion into the two birds' cavities. Place the DUCKS breast-up on top of the onions and SEASON before putting them into the hot oven.

→ After 30 minutes drain off the fat and gently prick the breast and plump part of the legs with a sharp skewer. Turn the heat down to 200°C/400°F/Gas 6 and continue to cook. Drain off the fat again after a further 30 minutes; if you don't, it will blacken and smoke out your kitchen. Put all the fat into a bowl to cool for the fridge later.

→ The ducks will take 1–1¼ hours to cook—the juices should run pinkish, not red, when the fat part of the leg is pierced with a skewer. Remove from the oven and rest for 20 minutes.

→ Carve the breasts and legs and place them on top of the salad which you have heaped onto a large serving dish. Sprinkle over the ORANGE ZEST and serve.

Wheatberry, Sour Cherry and Sage Salad

→ Boil the WHEATBERRIES until cooked. They have quite a firm texture even when cooked. While they are cooking, roughly chop the SOUR CHERRIES and roll up the SAGE LEAVES and slice them into slim ribbons. Chop the PARSLEY and the SPRING ONIONS. Toast the FLAKED ALMONDS briefly until their edges are tinged mid-brown. This will take 3 or 4 minutes: they turn very quickly.

→ Drain the wheatberries and toss in all the ingredients when still hot. Pour on a few tablespoons of good OLIVE OIL and squeeze over the juice of a LEMON. SEASON. Toss and taste and adjust the seasoning, adding more olive oil and lemon juice if needed. Now add the meat juices from the carving board where the birds have been resting.

Confit of Duck

SERVES 4

sel de Guérande OR coarse sea salt like Maldon	4 tbsp
thyme leaves, *stripped from their stems*	3–4 sprigs
juniper berries	6–8
dried bay leaves	2
sugar	1
black peppercorns	2
nutmeg, *freshly grated*	
free-range duck legs	4
duck or goose fat	600–700ml/ 1–1¼ pints
garlic	half a head

This is resoundingly a midwinter dish, the sort of thing you want to cook after Christmas when you have a giant bowl of goose fat left over, or after you have been roasting a duck and have the duck fat. Traditionally it is made with the legs of the duck or goose; the breast doesn't stand up so well to the salting and cooking ritual, becoming stringy and dry.

→ Grind the FIRST 6 INGREDIENTS together in a mortar with a little freshly grated NUTMEG. Put half the mixture on a plate and put the DUCK LEGS flesh-side down on the mixture. Sprinkle the rest over the top, cover with clingfilm and put in the fridge for 24 hours, turning the legs over once at roughly half time.

→ Preheat the oven to 130°C/250°F/Gas ½. Melt the goose or duck fat very slowly in a heavy-bottomed pan. Wash the brew off the duck legs and pat dry before putting them gently into the warm fat with the GARLIC, slightly bruised with the back of a knife but not peeled. Cook in the oven for 2 hours or until a skewer slides easily right into the flesh.

→ Let the legs cool in the fat before putting them in a bowl or jar. Strain the cold fat over them to cover the legs completely, then keep them in the fridge for at least a month but up to 3 months. Serve with potatoes browned in goose fat.

Slow-stewed Duck's Legs with Celery, Ginger and Star Anise

SERVES 2

duck legs	2
olive oil and butter	a little
head of celery, *using all but the outside stalks*	1
garlic cloves, *thinly sliced*	4
full-bodied red wine	2 glasses
star anise	2
stem ginger, *finely diced, with 2 tbsp of the syrup*	2 knobs
orange peel, *stripped of their pith*	2 pieces
sea salt and black pepper	

A lovely winter's dish of warming spice and fat duck.

→ Warm the oven to 130°C/250°F/Gas ½. Sauté the DUCK LEGS over a high heat in a little heated OLIVE OIL, skin-side down, so that they begin to crisp and release their fat. Lower the heat, turn the legs over and give them a minute on their flesh side before removing them to a plate.

→ String the CELERY with a potato peeler and slice the sticks crossways. Add a knob of BUTTER to the pan and throw in the celery and garlic. Cook for a few minutes, turning them gently to coat, then add the WINE and bubble it for a few minutes. Throw in the STAR ANISE, GINGER, SYRUP, ORANGE PEEL and the duck legs. SEASON, then cover with a layer of greaseproof paper and a lid, and put in the oven.

→ Leave to stew for 3 hours or so, before skimming off the duck fat from the surface. Serve with mash or pommes Anna (see p. 393).

poultry and game / 265

Roast Goose

large onion, *peeled and sliced*	1
goose, (*add the liver and heart to the stuffing*)	4.8–6 kg/10–12lb
stuffing (see p. 258)	
salt and pepper	

Goose is such a marvellous fowl, but many are put off by its apparent richness, fatness, expense and low proportion of meat per pound, or per carcass, so to speak, compared with turkey. I find that you don't need a lot of goose precisely because its succulent richness is a thing to savour sparingly. If you slice it thinly, a goose will easily feed 8–10 people with leftovers for goose and apple sauce sandwiches. And you'll have fantastic stock and fat to cook your roast potatoes in over the winter months.

→ Place the ONIONS in a layer in a roasting tin. Stuff the GOOSE and place it, breast down, in the pan and roast for 1–1½ hours. Turn the bird breast side up, scatter with SALT AND PEPPER, and roast for another hour or so, spiking with a thin skewer every 20 minutes. Drain off the fat at intervals and keep it to make the most delicious roast potatoes.

GAME

Game birds should only be roasted when they are young, so you will have to rely on your butcher, game dealer or the superior wisdom of those you've been shooting with if you are not sure whether the bird in question is a scrawny old boiler or a tender young bird. Soft, pliable feet or ears in the case of rabbits or hares is an indication of youth.

Roasting temperature All roast game birds should be cooked in a high oven, 220–230°C/ 425–450°F/Gas 7–8. Cook larger birds, like pheasant, at the lower temperature and smaller ones, like snipe and woodcock, at the higher temperature.

What to put inside Seasoned butter, onions and fruit are all things that can be put inside the carcass of the birds to increase moisture and flavour and inhibit dryness and toughness.

Hanging times Make sure that the game you are buying has been properly hung. I do not mean hung until it is green and putrid with maggots, as the faint-stomached always imply to those of us who are happy to pluck and gut, but hung until the flesh has begun to break down so that you end up with a tender bird or animal. Pheasants need about 7 days in the winter, though 2–3 days more if the weather is really cold. Partridge should be hung for 3–4 days when it is mild and for up to a week if the weather is cold. The wild duck family need 2–3 days and no more, as their fatty flesh begins to deteriorate. Venison needs up to 10 days; wild rabbit and hare around 3–4 days. Woodcock and snipe need 2–4 days, though some people prefer not to hang them at all.

Plucking	If you've drawn the short straw and been ordered to pluck, usually as the result of road-kill in my case, much to the horror of my children, simply hold the bird over a bin liner so that you pluck inside it. Always pull the feathers with the grain so that you don't tear the skin. Keep a bowl of warm water beside you; feathers stick. Cut off the feet and the wing feathers with a heavy-bladed, sharp knife. To take out the guts, make a small incision by the vent and ease the guts out with your fingers. Keep the liver, heart and gizzard, making sure that you remove the green part from the liver, which will taste bitter as it is stained by the gall sac. Slit the gizzard open to remove the grain before you use it.
	SNIPE need skinning, not plucking; chop off the wings and head and ease off the skin and feathers. Do not draw snipe and woodcock. Their innards are known as the 'trail' and are considered to be a real delicacy, so roast them inside the bird and spread them on toast set underneath it.

Roast Grouse

The 'glorious twelfth' is the day in August when both grouse and snipe come into season. There is always something of a rush to get them down from the moors and into the London restaurants, but they do need to be hung, if only for 24 hours in the August heat, so wait, if but a day, for your first brace. Grouse are in prime condition from the beginning of the season to the middle of October, and only very young birds should be roasted. Pot roasting or turning into a game pie, pudding or pâté should be the fate of those birds who are a little longer in the beak.

Shooting season	12 August–10 December.
Roasting time	30–40 minutes depending on size. Cover with a vine leaf if you have a jar of them and a sheet of pork fat or rashers of unsmoked streaky bacon.
Inside the bird	blueberries, raspberries or seedless grapes and seasoned butter.
Serve with	a bunch of watercress, game chips, some breadcrumbs fried in butter, bread sauce (see p. 406), gravy and rowan or redcurrant jelly; mashed potato is also good and some runner beans, which are in season at the same time.

Roast Partridge

There are two kinds of partridge, the red-legged, or French, partridge and the English grey, or common, partridge, considered to be the king of game birds. You need one partridge per person and that is not negotiable!

Shooting season	1 September–1 February.
Roasting time	30 minutes.
Inside the bird	chopped liver or onion with seasoned butter; a sprig of thyme; mushrooms cooked in butter.
Serve with	braised celery; stir-fried cabbage with bacon and chestnuts; bread sauce (see p. 406), watercress and game chips; mashed potato or roast potatoes; rowan jelly.

Roast Pheasant

A brace of pheasants will feed 4 people. The cock pheasant is always larger and tougher, and you need to make sure the tendons in the legs have been pulled out by the butcher, otherwise the legs are more difficult to eat.

Shooting season | 1 October–1 February.

Roasting time | 40 minutes per kg/20 minutes per lb plus 10 minutes. Either cover the breast of the birds with unsmoked streaky bacon or with softened, seasoned butter. If you use butter, make sure you baste the birds religiously every 10 minutes.

Inside the bird | a knob of thyme or parsley butter and a small quartered onion; some chopped mushrooms or celery cooked in butter with a little ground juniper or black pepper; or a few strips of seasoned fillet steak (extravagant but they add moisture).

Serve with | bread sauce (see p. 406), gravy and game chips; mashed or roasted potatoes and roast parsnips; celeriac and potato purée; spiced red cabbage, breadcrumbs fried in butter.

Wild Duck

There are a large variety of wild duck, some, like the pintail, gadwall, tufted, pochard and goldeneye, are less likely to wind up at the end of the gun barrel and on your plate than others. The ones you are most likely to encounter, depending on where you live and how keen you are to source interesting game, are the mallard, the largest and most frequently eaten duck; widgeon, less strongly flavoured since they graze mainly on grasses, but very good stuffed with apricots or oranges and walnuts or hazelnuts; teal, the smallest duck in the British Isles but the most sought-after by those in the know; and shoveler ducks, which need to be scalded in boiling water to rid them of their muddy flavour from bottom feeding.

Shooting season | Inland: 1 September–31 January.
Foreshore: September–20 February.

WIDGEON AND TEAL

Roasting time | 20–25 minutes, allow 1 bird per person.

Inside the bird | a knob of softened parsleyed butter with a squeeze of lemon juice and the liver mashed into it.

Serve with | orange gravy; orange, endive and watercress salad.

WILD DUCK

Roasting time	30 minutes if you like your wild duck rare, 40 minutes well-cooked.
Inside the bird	a stuffing made with sautéed onion, parsley, walnuts or hazelnuts and dried unsulphured apricots. You may use breadcrumbs as with the classic sage and onion stuffing recipe (see p. 261), or rice. Wild rice is good instead of breadcrumbs too.
Serve with	new potatoes, peas, a bitter leaf salad, braised endives or fennel.

Wild Apricot and Apple Stuffing

Hunza apricots	110g/4oz
apple juice	to cover
breadcrumbs	55g/2oz
butter	
sharp eating apple such as Cox, *peeled, cored and diced*	1
celery stick, *strung and finely diced*	1
parsley, *chopped*	1 tbsp
salt and pepper	

→ Soak the APRICOTS overnight in APPLE JUICE, then stone them. Sauté the CELERY gently in the BUTTER until almost soft, then throw in the APPLE and continue to cook for a few minutes. Add the BREADCRUMBS, PARSLEY and apricots, amalgamate, season and take off the heat. Stuff the birds' cavities before roasting.

Roast Woodcock

It would be a very close call if I had to choose between a grouse or a woodcock. In fact I'd rather not have to make up my mind, but woodcock are a bird you really should try at some stage of your life, difficult though they are both to shoot and thus to lay your hands on. Woodcock are waders with long, straight bills, which can be used as a skewer to truss the bird with.

Shooting season	England and Wales, 1 October–31 January. Scotland: 1 September–31 January.
Roasting time	18 minutes for a rare bird. Allow 1 bird per person.
Inside the bird	leave the trail and add a little knob of butter with marjoram mashed into it. Put a rasher of unsmoked streaky bacon over the breast or smother with butter and baste.
Serve with	fried bread spread with the trail; game chips; mashed potato or roasted potatoes; watercress, green vegetables.

Roast Snipe

They may be in season from the 'glorious twelfth' but these delicious and delicately flavoured little birds are not at their best until October or November.

Shooting season	12 August–31 January.
Roasting time	15 minutes for rare.
Inside the bird	as for woodcock.
Serve with	fried bread spread with the trail and soaked in the cooking juices; redcurrant jelly; game chips; watercress and orange salad.

Braised Partridge with Puy Lentils, Lardons and Shallots

SERVES 4

unsalted butter	55g/2oz
rashers unsmoked streaky bacon, *snipped into small dice*	4
partridges	4
brandy	1 glass
white wine	1 large glass
game or chicken stock (see p. 54), *heated*	150ml/5fl oz pint
a bouquet of thyme, rosemary, parsley and bay *tied together*	
Puy lentils	225g/8oz
onion, *stuck with a couple of cloves*	1
large carrot, *chopped in 3 or 4 pieces*	1
celery sticks, *broken in pieces*	2
leek tops	a few
bay leaf	1
black peppercorns	12
butter and olive oil	
shallots, *peeled and left whole*	12–18
molasses OR dark muscovado sugar	a little

A lovely earthy dish for older birds at the end of the season, this is also delicious made with pigeon, guinea fowl or pheasant.

→ Preheat the oven to 170°C/325°F/Gas 3. Melt the BUTTER in a heavy-bottomed pan with the diced BACON, and fry gently until the fat begins to run from the bacon. Put the PARTRIDGES breast-down in the pot to brown for a couple of minutes, then pour in the BRANDY and set light to it. When the alcohol has burned off, add the white WINE which you have heated first in a small pan. Now add the hot STOCK and the bouquet of HERBS, then cover with greaseproof paper and a lid. Put in the oven for 1½ hours to cook.

→ Meanwhile, rinse the LENTILS under running water (they do not need soaking first), and put them in another large heavy-bottomed pot with the ONION, CARROT, CELERY, LEEK TOPS, BAY LEAF and PEPPERCORNS. Just cover with water, bring to the boil and skim. Cover with a lid and simmer for 35–40 minutes or until the lentils are cooked but maintain their shape.

→ Fifteen minutes before the partridges are due to come out of the oven, put a tablespoon of OLIVE OIL and 30g/1oz unsalted BUTTER in a heavy frying pan. When they are foaming add the whole SHALLOTS. Sprinkle over a teaspoon of SUGAR and cook on all sides until softened, well browned and glazed with sugar.

→ Remove the birds and all the bits from the pot and keep hot on a warmed dish while you reduce the cooking juices by boiling them down to half their original amount. Meanwhile, remove the vegetables you've cooked with the lentils, and spread the lentils with the bits of bacon and the shallots over the bottom of the serving dish. Place the birds on top and pour over the sauce and serve with parsnip or potato and celeriac purée.

Richard Corrigan's Grouse en Croûte

SMALL CAPS Serves 2

mushrooms, *very finely chopped*	110g/4oz
garlic clove, *minced*	1
shallots, *finely minced*	2
unsalted butter OR duck fat	
old grouse, *breasts removed*	1
Savoy cabbage leaves	2
puff pastry (see p. 517)	285g/10oz
egg, *beaten*, for glaze	
Sauce	
grouse carcass, *broken up*	
carrots	2
leek	1
garlic clove	1
butter	walnut-sized piece
red wine OR Madeira	150ml/5fl oz
chicken stock	150ml/5fl oz

Richard Corrigan's food is adjective-defying, and his is one of the handful of restaurants I would rather eat in above all others. You can substitute partridge or pheasant for the grouse. If you don't want to make your own puff pastry, use a good brand made with all butter.

→ To make the SAUCE, roast the GROUSE BONES lightly—don't let them over-colour. Remove the bones and add a mirepoix of the finely diced VEGETABLES to the grouse fat in the roasting tin, then roast them until golden brown. Deglaze on top of the stove with red WINE, scraping all the bits in well, then reduce by half, letting the red wine bubble away merrily. Add the CHICKEN STOCK and reduce that by half too. Strain the sauce through a fine sieve and set aside.

→ Preheat the oven to 200°C/400°F/Gas 6. Make a duxelle with the MUSHROOMS, minced GARLIC and SHALLOTS, cooked in BUTTER—or better still DUCK FAT—until softened. Seal the GROUSE BREASTS lightly and quickly in BUTTER, before laying each one on a Savoy CABBAGE LEAF which you've blanched in boiling water for 30 seconds. Spoon a tablespoon of the duxelle over each breast and spread it evenly over the meat.

→ Wrap into parcels, then roll out two circles of PASTRY, and wrap each parcel in pastry, sealing the edges with beaten EGG. Bake in the oven for 15 minutes until risen and golden. Leave for 4 minutes before serving. Reheat the sauce, adding little bits of butter to enrich it, and serve separately.

Guinea Fowl stewed with Treviso Chicory and Crème Fraîche

SMALL CAPS Serves 6

olive oil	3 tbsp
unsalted butter	55g/2oz
guinea fowl, *jointed*, leg and breast in one large piece	3
chicory	7 or 8 heads
molasses sugar	3 tsp
onion, *finely chopped*	1
lemons	juice of 1½

If you can't find the beautifully autumnal maroon chicory from Treviso, ordinary endives will do fine. Likewise, if you'd rather experiment with pheasant, do. This is an unctuously rich dish, the caramelly juices at once sweet and sharp; all it needs is some mashed potato.

→ Heat the OIL and BUTTER together in a heavy-bottomed casserole, then add the joints of GUINEA FOWL, skin side down, and fry for a few minutes until golden and crispened. Turn over and repeat, then move to a plate with a slotted spoon.

→ Halve the CHICORY vertically and put with the ONION and SUGAR in the casserole, and cook until the chicory begins to caramelise, about 5 minutes. Add the LEMON JUICE, return the guinea fowl to the casserole, and pour in the WINE. Bring to the boil, then simmer gently for a few minutes. Pour in the

white wine	200ml/7fl oz
crème fraîche	240ml/8fl oz
salt, pepper	
flat-leaf parsley, *chopped*	a handful

CRÈME FRAÎCHE, stir it in thoroughly, SEASON, and put the lid on. Cook at a bare simmer for 35–40 minutes. Test that the meat juices run clear with a skewer. Pour the sauce into a saucepan, putting the lid back on the guinea fowl and chicory, and bubble the buttery, creamy juices until they're thickened and amalgamated. Pour over the casserole, add parsley and serve.

Roast Guinea Fowl with a Chestnut, Bacon, Thyme and Wild Rice Stuffing

SERVES 6

guinea fowl	1 × 1–1.2kg/2¼–2½ lb
onion, *peeled and sliced*	1
sea salt and black pepper	
extra unsalted butter	

Chestnut, Bacon, Thyme and Wild Rice Stuffing

mixed basmati and wild rice 85g/3oz	
small onion	1
unsalted butter	55g/2oz
rashers organic smoked back bacon, *cut into small strips*	2
fresh thyme leaves, *chopped*	1 tbsp
juniper berries, *gently crushed*	6
organic peeled, cooked chestnuts	1 × 200g/7oz jar
egg, *beaten*	1

→ Preheat the oven to 200°C/400°F/Gas 6. Stuff the insides of both BIRDS and set them on their sides on top of the sliced ONION in the roasting tin. SEASON THE BUTTER and rub over the leg and breast uppermost of each bird. Cook for 20 minutes like this before putting the birds on their other side and rubbing with more seasoned butter. For the final 20 minutes, turn the birds breast-up, baste them well with the buttery juices and season. The skin should be crisped by then and the birds ready to rest for 10 minutes while you make gravy and finish off your vegetables. Port or Madeira added to the pan juices for your gravy goes very well with guinea fowl, as does Marsala. Roast potatoes and parsnips (see p. 392), Brussels sprouts and bread sauce (see p. 406) are a must.

Chestnut, Bacon, Thyme and Wild Rice Stuffing
→ Cook the RICE according to the instructions on the packet. Meanwhile, chop the ONION finely and sauté in the melted BUTTER over a medium heat for a few minutes until it begins to soften. Add the BACON STRIPS and sauté them until their fat begins to run. Add the THYME LEAVES and JUNIPER BERRIES, then the roughly chopped CHESTNUTS, and continue to cook for a few minutes before adding the rice and stirring everything to amalgamate. You may not need all the rice. Judge the quantity as best you can from the cooked mixture and the size of the birds' cavities. SEASON, remove from the heat and stir in the beaten EGG to bind the mixture together.

Guinea Fowl with Preserved Lemons and Broad Beans

SERVES 4

good olive oil	10 tbsp
large onion, *peeled and finely chopped*	1
guinea fowl, quartered by your butcher	1
broad beans, *after podding*	500g/a generous lb
water	500ml/16fl oz
coriander, *stalks removed and roughly chopped*	1 large bunch
lemon	juice of 1
preserved lemon	1
salt and pepper	

→ In a large, non-reactive saucepan, put half the OLIVE OIL with the chopped ONION, and sauté over a medium heat until soft and transparent.

→ Scrape the onion out of the pan into a small bowl, and add the remaining OIL to the pan. Add the jointed GUINEA FOWL and fry until the skin has browned, turning it as you go.

→ When it has coloured, return the onion to the pan with the BROAD BEANS and water. Simmer for 20 minutes, then add the CORIANDER, LEMON JUICE, strips of peel, thinly sliced, from the PRESERVED LEMON, SALT and PEPPER. Simmer for a further 10 minutes, then remove from the heat and serve with good bread and salad.

Pheasant à la Normande

SERVES 4

pheasants and their giblets	2
unsalted butter	85g/3oz
sharp eating apples like Cox's	6
cinnamon	a little
double cream	300ml/10fl oz
sea salt and black pepper	
Somerset cider brandy OR calvados	1 brandy glass

You can cook the pheasants whole in the pot or joint them first into whole breasts and legs, leaving the wings and the carcass for stock. This is a particularly good way of cooking birds that have got a little long in the beak and would not be tender if roasted.

→ Brown the PHEASANT on all sides in half the BUTTER over a medium heat. Meanwhile, peel, core and slice the APPLES and fry them in the other half of the BUTTER, with a little smidgen of CINNAMON sprinkled over them, for a few minutes. They should still be crisp.

→ Throw a layer of apples into the bottom of a deep, heavy casserole and add the pheasants, breast down. Put the GIBLETS —heart, liver and neck—in the pot, then make a nest of the rest of the apples around the birds. Pour in half the CREAM, cover with greaseproof paper and the lid and cook over a gentle heat for 30 minutes before turning the birds breast-up to finish them. SEASON, cover and cook for a further 20–30 minutes depending on how rare you like your pheasant. I like mine pink, so if the juices flow pink when the birds are spiked through the leg with a skewer and there is no resistance from the flesh, they are cooked. The cock, being bigger, will take a little longer than the hen.

→ *If you prefer*, cook the PHEASANTS in the oven at about 180°C/325°F/Gas 4. Remove the birds from the pot and leave them to rest for 10 minutes, lightly covered with foil, while you add the rest of the CREAM to the apples and heat it through.
→ Remove the GIBLETS, sieving the liver into the sauce. Now pour all the juices from the birds into a frying pan and heat them, adding the glass of CIDER BRANDY OR CALVADOS and setting light to it. Let the flames burn off the alcohol before pouring the liquor into the pot with the cream and apples. Check the SEASONING. Joint the birds and heat them through gently in the sauce before putting the whole of the contents of the pot into a warmed serving dish.

Hot Game Pie

SERVES 6

game birds	2 large or 3 small
enough good game or chicken stock to poach the birds in (p. 54)	
onion, celery, carrots and leek tops	
bouquet of herbs	
unsalted butter	55g/2oz
unsmoked back bacon, *snipped into strips*	4 thick rashers
large onion, *finely chopped*	1
celery, *strung and chopped*	2 sticks
chestnut or Portobello mushrooms, *wiped and sliced*	225g/8oz
garlic cloves, *sliced*	2
flour	1 tbsp
sea salt, black pepper	
fresh thyme	2 tsp
parsley, *chopped*	1 tbsp
Shortcrust pastry	
flour	225g/8oz
salt	1 pinch
butter OR half butter, half lard	110g/4oz

A good way of using up the more geriatric game birds at the end of the season. Serve with redcurrant jelly (see p. 580), cabbage and mash.

→ Make the SHORTCRUST PASTRY and chill (see p. 104).
→ Put the BIRDS in a large heavy-bottomed casserole with some ONION, CELERY, CARROTS, LEEK TOPS and HERBS, and STOCK to cover if you have some; if not use cold water with one-third white wine. Bring to the boil slowly and skim. Cover and simmer at a mere blip until the meat is cooked and comes away from the bone easily. Remove the birds from the pot, and when they are cool enough to handle, strip the meat from the carcasses and put in a pie dish.
→ Preheat the oven to 200°C/400°F/Gas 6. Melt the BUTTER with the BACON and when the fat begins to run, add the VEGETABLES and sauté gently until golden and the mushrooms have begun to exude their watery juices. Stir in the FLOUR at this point, followed by a ladle or two of hot STOCK, and continue to stir so that the sauce becomes silken and lump-free. You want the sauce to remain thick, so don't add more stock than you need. Pour the sauce with the vegetables over the game in the pie dish and season well, adding the HERBS.
→ Cover with the PASTRY, put into the preheated oven and bake for 30 minutes. Turn the heat down to 190°C/375°F/Gas 5 and continue to cook until the pastry is golden and the filling bubbling merrily beneath.

Cold Raised Game Pie

SERVES 6

Hot water crust

water	200ml/7fl oz
lard	170g/6oz
plain flour	450g/1lb
sea salt	½ tsp
organic egg (optional)	1
egg, *beaten* for glaze	1

Jellied stock

bones from the meat used to make the filling	
split pig's trotters OR a knuckle of veal	2
carrots, *chopped*	2
celery, *chopped*	2 sticks
onions, *halved but still in their skins*	2
peppercorns	12
fresh herbs *tied together*	1 bouquet
water to cover	

Filling

game, *well hung*	450g/1lb
pork back fat, *minced*	225g/8oz
lean pork, *minced*	340g/12oz
lean veal, *minced*	225g/8oz
thin rashers of green back bacon, *3 of them* *minced*	225g/8oz
Marsala, Madeira OR dry white wine	a few tbsp
grated nutmeg, cinnamon, cloves	
juniper berries	6
flat-leaf parsley, *chopped*	a handful
sea salt, black pepper	

Use any combination of game for this glorious cold raised pie: pheasant, partridge, grouse, woodcock, wild duck, pigeon. Raised pies are not the big girl's handbags they're cracked up to be. In fact, hot water crust pastry is far more difficult to ruin than ordinary pastry and is curiously satisfying to make as you work it up the pie mould or tin.

→ To make the crust, bring the WATER and LARD to the boil in a small pan. Tip them into the middle of the FLOUR and SALT in a large bowl and swiftly work together with a wooden spoon. You can also do this in a food processor. Add the EGG for colour and richness if you like, but it is not essential. Leave the dough until it has cooled to the stage at which you can handle it, but not so long that it is actually cool.

→ Break off a quarter for the lid and put the rest into the base of a hinged pie mould, or a cake tin if you don't have a mould. Push the pastry up the sides with your hands as quickly as you can, sealing any cracks. If the paste collapses as you are work-ing, never fear, it just means it is a little too hot, so squidge it back into a ball, wait and start again. You can shape small pies around jam jars, but you have to be really careful prising the jars out so the pastry stands proud on its own. It is not impossible— I have done it, and manual dexterity isn't my middle name. If you are going to use this method, I would place a strip of brown paper around the pastry and tie string around the circumference so that the pies keep their shape during the cooking.

→ To make the JELLIED STOCK, put ALL THE INGREDIENTS into a large pan, bring to the boil, skim, then simmer for 3 hours. Strain and boil down the stock until you have about 425ml/ 15fl oz. Set aside to cool. It will set to a solid jelly and is incom-parably better than adding gelatine to your stock, but if needs must, go ahead.

→ Remove the GAME from the bone, cut into small strips, season and set aside. Put the PORK, VEAL and MINCED BACON in a bowl and splash with the ALCOHOL. SEASON, add the SPICES and PARSLEY and mulch it all together with your finger.

→ Line the pastry with the BACON RASHERS, then add layers of game and minced meats, packing them in tightly. Roll out the lid and put it on top with the help of some beaten EGG. Cut a central hole through which the steam can escape, and decorate with pastry trimmings as you will. Brush EGG all over the pie and start the cooking at 200°C/400°F/Gas 6 for the first 30 minutes. Reduce the temperature to 170°C/325°F/Gas 3 and cook for a further hour for small pies, or 2 hours for large ones. Cover the top with greaseproof paper if it is darkening too much.

→ Remove the pie from the oven and take it out of its mould or paper. Brush the sides with beaten EGG once more and return to the oven for 10 minutes for a little colour enhancement. Then pour the jellied stock through the hole with a small funnel; the meat will have shrunk considerably so there will be room. Abandon the pie for at least 24 hours before you tuck in, but longer won't hurt. The beauty of hot water crust pastry is that it absorbs the meat juices and fat on the inside while managing to stay crisp on the outside. Best eaten cold with cranberry sauce (see p. 406) or crab apple jelly (see p. 580).

Rabbit with Mustard Sauce

SERVES 4

unsmoked fat bacon, *cubed*	450g/1lb piece
large onion, *chopped*	1
celery sticks, *strung and chopped*	3
small carrots, *sliced*	6
garlic cloves, *sliced in half*	3
bay leaves	2
thyme, *leaves stripped from their stems*	6 sprigs
salt and pepper	
wild rabbit, back legs and saddle	1
dry cider	150ml/5fl oz
cider brandy OR calvados, OR brandy	2 glasses
organic egg yolks	2
double cream	6 tbsp
Dijon mustard	1 tbsp
moutarde de Meaux mustard	1 tbsp
parsley and chives, *chopped*	a handful

The famous pairing of sweet, mild rabbit meat with sharp mustard is one of those great taste contrasts. Serve with some forcemeat balls (see p. 277) if you like. Joint the rabbit into 2 back legs and the saddle split in 2. Keep the carcass and forelegs for stock.

→ Preheat the oven to 150°C/300°F/Gas 2. Mix the BACON, VEGETABLES, GARLIC, BAY and THYME and put half the mixture in the bottom of a heavy-bottomed casserole. SEASON. Lay the RABBIT JOINTS on top and cover them with the next half of the mixture. Pour over the CIDER and SERIOUS ALCOHOL, cover with greaseproof paper and a lid and put in the oven. Braise for 2½–3 hours or until the rabbit is in danger of falling from the bone with very little provocation.

→ Remove the joints and all the vegetables and bacon to a warm serving dish and keep hot while you make the sauce. Beat the YOLKS and the CREAM together and add a ladle of the JUICES, whisking them together. Return to the casserole and cook at a bare simmer, not letting it come to the boil, until it thickens. Stir in the first tablespoon of MUSTARD and taste. Add the second if it needs it. Adjust the SEASONING. You need to add mustard late to dishes as it tends to make them bitter the longer it is cooked. Pour the sauce over the rabbit, sprinkle over the mixed PARSLEY and CHIVES and serve. Mashed or boiled potatoes and some braised celery are the tops with this earthy dish.

Rabbit Pie

SERVES 6–8

rabbits, *jointed*, with their livers and kidneys	2
prunes d'Agen	12
apple juice OR cider	
large onions, *sliced*	2
sage leaves	6
unsmoked back bacon, *thickly cut*	2 or 3 rashers
hard-boiled eggs	2 or 3
of flat-leaf parsley, *chopped*	a large bunch
good jellied chicken stock	300ml/10fl oz
sea salt and black pepper	
shortcrust pastry (see p. 104), *made with 225g/8oz flour and 110g/4oz butter*	
egg, *beaten*, for glaze	

→ Soak the PRUNES in APPLE JUICE or CIDER and cook gently. Leave to cool, then carefully remove the stones and set aside the liquid.

→ Put the RABBIT PIECES in a large, heavy-bottomed casserole with the sliced ONIONS and SAGE. Add the apple juice or cider used for cooking the prunes, bring to the boil, then simmer very gently for 30 minutes. Strip the meat from the bone as soon as it isn't too hot to handle, then leave it to cool. Meanwhile, cook the BACON and snip into chunky strips.

→ Preheat the oven to 200°C/400°F/Gas 6. Finely chop and season the rabbit LIVERS and KIDNEYS and, using a tiny tea-spoon, stuff this mixture into the prunes. Put the pieces of rabbit and bacon into a pie dish with slices of HARD-BOILED EGG, a good handful of chopped PARSLEY and the stuffed prunes. Season well before pouring in the cold CHICKEN STOCK. Cover with the PASTRY, cut a cross with a sharp knife in the top and glaze with beaten EGG.

→ Cook for about an hour, turning the heat down after the first 20 minutes to 180°C/350°F/Gas 4. I think this is best left until the next day and then served cold, but the choice is yours.

Jugged Hare

SERVES 4

hare, *jointed*	1
flour, salt and pepper	
goose fat OR olive oil and butter	
carrots, *diced*	2
onions, *chopped*	2
garlic cloves	a few
celery sticks, *strung and sliced*	3
Marinade	
robust red wine	1 bottle
cognac	1 tbsp
olive oil	2 tbsp
onion, *thinly sliced*	1
garlic cloves, *bruised*	a few

Hare used to be jugged by those with no ovens, in stone jugs sealed with foil in a pan of simmering water over a flame. Now we still use the delightfully anachronistic term when we really mean stewed hare. The flavour of a hare is one of the great tastes, richly gamey but not fat, its deep ruby flesh falling from the bone if you cook it long enough, adding the liver, heart and blood in an 'aillade' with garlic and red wine vinegar towards the end. Serve with forcemeat balls (see p. 277) as well as or instead of the aillade.

→ Mix the MARINADE ingredients and marinate the JOINTED HARE for as long as it suits you, anything from 1 to 3 days.

→ Preheat the oven to 130°C/250°F/Gas ½. Remove the HARE from the marinade, dry the pieces thoroughly with kitchen paper, then roll them in seasoned FLOUR. I find shaking a few tablespoons of flour with some salt and pepper into a Ziploc bag, and sealing the hare inside it while you briefly toss it around, is the best way to do the job unmessily and without a surfeit of flour adhering to the joints.

orange rind	2 strips
bay leaves	a couple
juniper berries, *bruised rather than crushed*	12
peppercorns	12
Aillade	
liver and kidneys of the hare	
organic green streaky bacon, *finely snipped*	4 rashers
garlic cloves, *chopped into tiny dice*	6 or 7
shallots, *chopped into tiny dice*	4
red wine vinegar	4 tbsp
mace	1 blade
thyme	1 sprig
salt and pepper	

Heat some GOOSE FAT or OLIVE OIL and BUTTER in a heavy-bottomed casserole. Brown the hind legs and the saddle jointed into 2 portions for a few minutes on each side, then remove them to a plate. Scrape up any crusty brown bits from the pan, add more fat if you need to and gently sauté the CARROTS, ONIONS, GARLIC and CELERY together. When they have begun to soften, place the hare joints on the vegetables, season well with salt and pepper, strain the marinade over the meat and bring gently to a simmer. Cover with a layer of greaseproof paper and a lid and cook very gently for about 2 hours, either in the oven or on top of the stove.

→ Meanwhile, make your AILLADE. Chop the HARE LIVER and KIDNEYS and put them, with the BACON, GARLIC and SHALLOTS, in a small pan with 4 tablespoons of red wine VINEGAR, the BLOOD of the hare, MACE and THYME and SEASONING. Simmer at a whisper for a couple of hours, stirring occasionally to prevent anything from sticking. Pour the contents of the pan over the hare before serving. You may feel like offering a tart jelly as an accompaniment—rowan or crab apple (see p. 580) work well.

→ The following day, you can add the ribs and fore legs to the pot of hare bones and remaining sauce, cover with water and add the usual stock vegetables. Simmer for a couple of hours until you have the base for a wonderfully gamey hare soup.

Forcemeat Balls

SERVES 6

stale white bread, *turned into breadcrumbs*	110g/4oz
suet	55g/2oz
parsley, *chopped*	1 tbsp
thyme	2 tsp
organic lemon	*grated zest* of 1
fat bacon, *finely snipped*	2 rashers
sea salt and black pepper	
organic egg, *beaten*	1

If you like the old-fashioned notion of serving forcemeat balls with your hare—or your venison or rabbit—this is a very good recipe.

→ Mix ALL THE INGREDIENTS together in a large bowl then form the mixture into walnut-sized balls. Fry them in BACON FAT or LARD until they are browned all over and serve them round the hare, with more PARSLEY on top.

Medallions of Venison with Red Wine and Juniper

SERVES 2

butter	a generous knob
juniper berries	9 or 10
venison	4 medallions
black pepper, *coarsely ground*	
salt	
wine and port	a slug of each

→ This is the simplest and speediest of venison recipes. Heat a generous knob of BUTTER in a heavy frying pan until golden and bubbling. Grind the JUNIPER BERRIES to as fine a powder as you can. Season the VENISON with coarsely ground PEPPER, then press in half the juniper to the side you are going to cook first, and put the medallions into the pan. After 3 minutes, sprinkle the rest of the juniper over them, grind a bit more PEPPER, and turn them over. They should take 2–3 minutes more if you like them rare. Season with SALT AND PEPPER before the end of the cooking time.

→ Remove, and let them rest in a warm oven while you scrape the pan juices and add a good slug of WINE, and one of PORT if you have it, to the pan. Let this bubble and begin to reduce, then pour it over each portion. A robust root purée, either celeriac and potato or swede and carrot, and some spiced redcurrant jelly, and the dish is complete.

Medallions of Venison with Spiced Beetroot, Cornichons, Tarragon and Sour Cream

SERVES 4

medium beetroot	2 or 3
shallots	2
butter	
juniper berries, *crushed*	6
redcurrant jelly	1 heaped tsp
port	60ml/2fl oz
red wine	120ml/4fl oz
game or chicken stock (see p. 54)	300ml/10fl oz
medallions of venison, at least 1cm/½in thick	675g/1½lb or so
sour cream	60ml/2fl oz
cornichons	4 or 5

You may use loin of venison for this dish if you prefer, in which case take it off the bone and marinate it in red wine, a little olive oil and cognac, a bouquet of thyme, rosemary and bay, and some sliced onions and pepper-corns for a couple of days. There is no fat to speak of on venison, so go gently with the heat and don't let it overcook and dry out.

→ Scrub the BEETROOT, leaving the whiskers attached, wrap in foil and bake in a medium oven until tender. Chop the SHALLOTS finely and sweat them in a little BUTTER with the crushed JUNIPER BERRIES until softened, before adding the REDCURRANT JELLY, PORT and RED WINE. Reduce them by about a half, then add the STOCK and again reduce by a half.

→ While this is happening, cook the MEDALLIONS in a pan with a little melted BUTTER, turning them frequently and making absolutely sure that you don't overcook them. Dried-out venison is not one of the great pleasures of life; tender, pink, stickily oozing venison is. Check with the point of a skewer— you want a little blood, but the meat should feel soft right through, after about 3 minutes a side. Season.

→ When the stock has reduced, finish it with SOUR CREAM, some finely sliced CORNICHONS and a little finely chopped TARRAGON. The beetroot you can cook in advance, peel when it

fresh tarragon, *finely chopped*	
unsalted butter	30g/1oz
salt and pepper	
aged balsamic vinegar	

is not too hot, and grate. Then all you need to do is heat it through in a bit of BUTTER, SALT and PEPPER and a little aged BALSAMIC VINEGAR.

Venison Liver with Gin, Port and Juniper

SERVES 3

venison liver	600g/1¼lb
seasoned flour	
butter	
juniper berries, *ground*	12
gin	2–3 tbsp
port	a slug

→ Slice the LIVER horizontally into the same thickness you would for calves' liver, and toss it in seasoned FLOUR.
→ Add it to a frying pan of bubbling BUTTER, sprinkle over the ground JUNIPER BERRIES and cook it for just over a couple of minutes a side, until a knife blade goes in unresisted. Keep it warm in a serving dish in a warm oven, deglaze the pan with a few tablespoons of GIN, and when that thickens and is beginning to brown, add a good slug of PORT, and simmer it for a few minutes, before pouring it over the liver.

Venison Steak and Kidney Pie

SERVES 4

venison steak and kidney	675g/1½lb
seasoned flour to coat	
small onions, *chopped*	3
large Portobello OR chestnut mushrooms, *sliced*	3
good chicken or game stock (see p. 54)	2–3 ladles
Marsala	1 glass
port OR red wine	1 glass
bay leaves	2
juniper berries, *crushed*	1 heaped tsp
butter	
Shortcrust pastry	
flour	170g/6oz
butter	85g/3oz
egg, *beaten*	1

This makes a wonderful gamey alternative to ordinary steak and kidney.

→ Preheat oven to 150°C/300°F/Gas 2. Sauté the floured MEAT in some BUTTER until just browned on all sides. Remove to a plate, and add the ONIONS and a bit more BUTTER to the pan. Cook until softened and translucent. Cook the MUSHROOMS separately in a bit of BUTTER until they begin to exude their black juice. Return the meat to the pan, add the mushrooms, sprinkle over the JUNIPER, add the BOOZE, allow it to come to a bubble, then add 2–3 ladles of STOCK to just cover, season, and tuck in the BAY LEAVES. Cover with greaseproof paper and a lid, and cook in the oven for an hour, no longer; venison is so unfatty it would start to toughen and dry out. Cool. You can do this a day or two before you want to eat it.
→ Make the SHORTCRUST PASTRY (see p. 104). Spoon the filling into the bottom of your pie dish and place a china bird or egg cup in the dish to funnel out the steam. Add a strip of pastry to the edge of the dish you have brushed with water, then place the rolled-out sheet of pastry over the top. Brush with a beaten EGG wash, and cook in a hottish oven (190°C/375°F/Gas 5) for about 50 minutes. Serve with mashed potato and red cabbage.

BEEF, and PO

LAMB
RK

Roast Beef

joint of sirloin with undercut (fillet) on the bone	2–2.5kg/4½–5½lb
OR a rib of beef weighing the same	
sea salt, black pepper	
English mustard powder	
large onions, *peeled and thinly sliced*	1–2

Roast beef is all about breeding and about choosing a cut and a size of cut that best lends itself to this oldest of British traditions. If you are lucky enough to be able to afford and lay your hands on a good piece of Aberdeen Angus or Shorthorn that has been reared for as long as the breed needs to reach its peak and hung for several weeks, all well and good. Better still, a hunk of Longhorn—the best beef I have ever eaten, with the flavour of rump and the texture of butter. There is no point in cooking your joint off the bone; on the bone there are minimum sizes it is actually worth cooking.

→ Rub your BEEF with some SALT AND PEPPER the night before you are going to cook it if you remember and return it to the fridge.

→ Preheat the oven to 220°C/425°F/Gas 7. Remove the joint from the fridge to bring it to room temperature and rub in a couple of teaspoons of ENGLISH MUSTARD POWDER into the fat. Place the meat on top of the sliced ONION in the roasting pan and place the joint in the oven. It will take a little more than 30 minutes per kg/15 minutes per lb to cook it to rare, and another 20 minutes if you want well-done meat. Baste the meat every 20 minutes or so and insert the tip of a knife blade into the fat all over it when you baste so as to release more of the fat. This you can use to cook the Yorkshire pudding in and save the rest for roast potatoes.

→ Test the meat with a skewer when you think it should be ready. If it feels too raw in the middle and the blood looks very red and comes to the surface immediately, allow another 5–10 minutes' cooking time. Remove to a carving board, shroud tightly in foil with a tea towel loosely placed over it, and leave to rest for 20–30 minutes.

→ Meanwhile make the gravy and finish the Yorkshire puddings and vegetables. Serve with some mustard and horseradish sauce (see p. 409).

Yorkshire Pudding

SERVES 6

plain organic flour	225g/8oz
sea salt	1 pinch
large organic eggs	2
milk	600ml/1 pint

enough hot dripping from the beef to cover the floor of the roasting tin

Make the batter for your Yorkshire pudding a good half hour before you put the roast in. It is always better when it is left to stand and then whisked again before pouring into the hot dripping to be cooked. You can also make the batter the night before if you like and keep it in the fridge, whisking it up just before you use it. The lightness of the batter depends on the quick formation of steam within the mixture and the quick cooking of the flour. That is why you need a hot oven and why the Yorkshire is best when cooked at the top of the oven.

→ Sift the FLOUR and SALT into a large bowl. Make a well in the centre with a wooden spoon and break the EGGS into it. Add a little of the MILK and whisk with a balloon whisk, gradually drawing down the flour from the sides of the bowl and adding more milk when the mixture becomes too thick to work. You should finally have a stiff batter which you should then whisk for as long as your arm will hold out for—up to 5 minutes. Add the remaining milk, whisk it in and leave to stand.

→ Now you need to time things. The fat from the joint needs to be poured onto the base of another roasting tin and returned to the top of the oven, where it will take a couple of minutes to smoke. Then pour in the batter, which will take about 35–40 minutes to cook. You want to deliver the Yorkshire Pudding puffed up to the table once the beef has been rested and carved, so plan accordingly.

Steak and Kidney Pie

SERVES 6

rump steak, *cut into bite-sized pieces*	900g/2lb
ox kidney, *cut similarly*	450g/1lb
flour	2 tbsp
sea salt and black pepper	
butter	85g/3oz
large onion, *chopped*	1
beef stock, OR half stock, half red wine	600ml/1 pint
chestnut OR Portobello mushrooms, *sliced*	225g/8oz
bay leaves	2
fresh thyme, rosemary and parsley *tied together*	a bunch of each
shortcrust pastry (see p. 104)	340g/12oz
egg, *beaten*, for glaze	1

Steak and kidney pies should be made in a proper deep dish, filled with rump, kidney and mushroom, red wine and stock, with a golden crust of lardy or buttery shortcrust pastry cloaking the handsome jewels of meat and offal and rich meaty gravy beneath. You may add 2 dozen oysters once you have cooked and cooled the filling if you want to be seriously retro and true, but whatever you decide, rump steak is the thing to go for here. Chuck steak will work if it's from a lovely well-hung bit of Longhorn, but for flavour it should be rump. You can use puff pastry (see p. 517) if you prefer.

→ You may cook the filling a day or two in advance if you like, so all you need to do on the day is bake the pie.

→ Carefully trim the fat and skin from the MEAT, then toss it and the KIDNEYS in a ziploc bag containing the flour and some SALT AND PEPPER. Add two-thirds of the BUTTER to a frying pan and gently sauté the ONION, then remove it with a slotted spoon. Add the meat in batches in a single layer, letting it colour briefly on all sides. Transfer the meat to a casserole as you go. Pour the STOCK, with or without red WINE, into the frying pan and bring it to the boil, scraping in any crusty bits from the sides of the pan, then pour it over the meat. Fry the MUSHROOMS in the rest of the butter and add them to the casserole, tucking in the herbs. Cover with a lid and cook in the oven at 150°C/300°F/Gas 2 until the steak and kidney is almost cooked. This should take about 1½ hours. Cool and leave until you want to make the pie.

→ Make the PASTRY with 225g/8oz plain white flour, a pinch of sea salt and 170g/6oz unsalted butter (see p. 104). Preheat the oven to 220°C/425°F/Gas 7. Roll out the pastry and cut off strips to fit around the edges of the pie dish. Brush the rim of the dish with water first so that the strips will adhere. Spoon the filling into the pie dish and cover the whole with a sheet of pastry, pressing the edges together firmly. Decorate with pastry leaves or the like if the mood takes you. Cut a cross in the middle of the pastry through which the steam can escape. Brush the pastry with beaten EGG. Bake for 15 minutes, then lower the oven temperature to 170°C/325°F/Gas 3 and cook for a further 45 minutes.

→ Best served with snowy mountains of buttery mashed potato or colcannon (see p. 395), and buttered carrots or cabbage.

Steak and Kidney Pudding

SERVES 6

filling as for the steak and kidney pie, *cooked and cooled* (see p. 284)

Suet crust

self-raising flour	285g/10oz
beef suet	110g/4oz
baking powder	1 tsp
sea salt and black pepper	
fresh thyme	½ tsp

This is the rib-sticking reminder of times past, but with a thin, crisp crust. Cooking and cooling the filling in advance is the secret to perfect suet crust. It reduces the steaming time, thus making the pastry crisper and less damply heavy. I think the sealing in of all the meat and its fine juices in the suet coat makes this one of the great winter dishes. When the spoon sinks through the crust and into the spoon-soft meat and its gluey-dark, thickened juices, you smell heaven on a plate.

→ Mix all the DRY INGREDIENTS for the suet crust together in a big bowl, working the SUET in well. Stir in some cold water — as little as possible — and work it into a firm dough. Roll the dough out into a large circle on a floured surface and cut away one-quarter of it to use for the lid of the pudding. Butter a 1.5 litre/3 pint pudding basin and line it with the larger piece of dough, allowing a little to overhang the rim of the basin. Roll out the quarter piece into a circle big enough for the lid.

→ Spoon the FILLING into the basin, making sure it comes no higher than 2.5cm/1in below the rim. Brush the overhang with water, then put the lid on and press the edges together, sealing them tightly.

→ Cover the pudding with a sheet of pleated foil and tie string around it, making a handle at the same time. Lower the basin onto a trivet or some folded foil at the bottom of a pan of boiling water. The water should come two-thirds of the way up the sides of the bowl. Keep at a gentle boil for 1½ hours, checking the water level after an hour. Don't worry if the pudding is left to steam an extra half hour; it will not spoil.

→ Remove the pudding and cut off the string. Take off the foil and serve the pudding piping hot with good English mustard and some mashed potato.

Fillet of Beef en Croûte

SERVES 8–10

thick piece of fillet	1.8–2kg/4–4½lb
sea salt and black pepper	
beef dripping OR light olive oil	30g/1oz 2 tbsp
puff pastry, bought OR home-made (see p. 517)	
Portobello mushrooms, *chopped very finely*	110g/4oz
unsalted butter	30g/1oz
chicken liver pâté (see p. 101)	110g/4oz
organic egg, *beaten*	1

This is a far swifter and less difficult dish than you might imagine. If you are not prepared to make your own puff pastry, do buy all-butter pastry. If you are making the puff yourself, add 30g/1oz lard to the butter to make it more malleable. You can prepare the fillet right up to cooking point in advance, but make sure the mushrooms, pâté and fillet are all cold when you put them together, and keep loosely covered in clingfilm in the fridge.

→ Preheat the oven to 230°C/450°F/Gas 8. Trim the FILLET of fatty or sinewy bits and season it well. Heat the DRIPPING OR OLIVE OIL in a roasting tin and when it begins to smoke, put in the fillet and brown it all over. Then place in the oven and roast for 20 minutes. Remove to a plate and let it cool.

→ Divide the PUFF PASTRY into a one-third and two-thirds. Roll out the one-third piece to just bigger than the length and breadth of the fillet. Put the oblong of pastry on a baking sheet, prick it all over with the tines of a fork and bake it for 15 minutes until golden. Place it on a rack to cool. Fry the MUSHROOMS briefly in butter in a small pan, stir them into the PÂTÉ and leave to cool. Put the pastry back on the baking sheet and spread it carefully all over with the chicken liver and mushroom mixture. Plop the fillet on top and cut away any pastry that peeps out from the side of the meat.

→ Roll out the big piece of dough so that it is large enough to cover the fillet and tuck underneath it. Pick the sheet up with the rolling pin and place it over the meat. Lift up the underside at one end and brush it with the beaten EGG, then lift the base edge of cooked pastry up with a palette knife and tuck the top side of pastry underneath it. Work your way round the other 3 sides doing the same. If there are any spare bits of pastry, use them to make leaves for the top. Brush the top with beaten EGG and put the baking dish in the fridge. Leave for at least an hour, but if you are going to leave it longer, cover loosely in clingfilm until you want to use it.

→ Bake for 20 minutes if you like your meat rare, by which time the pastry should be browned. If it is not, allow another 5 minutes. If you like your beef cooked medium, bake for 30 minutes in total; if well cooked, 35 minutes in total.

→ This is delicious hot or cold. If you are eating it hot, don't carve it until you bring it to the table so that the meat is still rosy and juicy when people are given their plates.

Pot-Roasted Brisket of Beef with Roast Root Vegetables

SERVES 5–6

brisket of beef	1kg/2¼lb
large parsnip	1
swede	1
carrots	3
onions	3
celery sticks	3
olive oil	
sea salt and pepper	
bay, parsley, thyme and orange peel	1 bouquet
robust red wine	about 750ml/ 1¼ pints

Brisket is a wonderful fat cut of beef to slow roast, with a run of lean stewing meat threaded through its middle. Vary the vegetables as you like.

→ Preheat the oven to 150°C/300°F/Gas 2. Assemble your vegetables. Cube the ROOTS into 2.5cm/1in squares, quarter the ONIONS, or halve them if they are small, and cut the CELERY, carefully strung, into 2.5cm/1in pieces. Brown the BRISKET on all sides in a bit of OLIVE OIL in a heavy-bottomed pot into which it should fit snugly. Throw in the vegetables with a bit more OLIVE OIL, brown, strew on some SEA SALT and PEPPER, tuck in a bouquet of BAY, PARSLEY, THYME and ORANGE PEEL, then splosh on the red WINE.

→ Cover with a sheet of greaseproof paper and roast for 2 hours, but another half hour won't hurt. If the red wine is reducing too much, pour on the same again. The vegetables should be tender when the dish is cooked, but if they are still a bit firm, keep the meat warm for 20 minutes while you finish cooking them separately. Serve this with buttery mashed potatoes.

Creole-style Daube of Beef

SERVES 6–8

pimento-stuffed green olives	20
topside of beef, *boned and rolled*	1.5kg/3¼lb
olive oil	2 tbsp
butter	30g/1oz
large onion, *peeled and sliced*	1
unsmoked streaky bacon	6 rashers
dark rum	about 150ml/5fl oz
large tomatoes, *skinned, seeded and roughly chopped*	8
garlic cloves, *crushed*	4
dark muscovado sugar	1 tsp
thyme, rosemary, parsley, 2 bay leaves and savory	a bouquet
sea salt	
juice of half a lime	

Here is a New Orleans version of the famous daube—topside cooked in a whole, rolled piece, spiked with some piquant pimento-stuffed olives and flamed with dark rum. An unusual and gorgeous winter braise.

→ Preheat the oven to 140°C/275°F/Gas 1. Halve the OLIVES, make incisions all the way around the BEEF and insert the slices of olives. Heat the OLIVE OIL and BUTTER in a large, heavy-bottomed pot and soften the sliced ONION until it begins to turn pale gold. Snip the BACON into strips, add them to the pan and, as soon as the fat starts to run, add the beef and brown it all over. Warm the RUM in a little pan, pour it over the meat and set light to it with a taper. Shake the pan until the flames have totally died down.

→ Throw in the TOMATOES, GARLIC, SUGAR and HERBS, then SEASON with salt and pepper. Cover the meat with a circle of greaseproof and a lid and cook in the oven for 3 hours. It should be really tender when pierced through with a skewer. Remove the bouquet and spritz with LIME JUICE, mixing it into the tomatoey mixture. Serve with some rice.

Boeuf Bourguignonne

SERVES 6

chuck steak OR stewing steak	1.5kg/3¼ lb
unsmoked streaky bacon	225g/8oz piece
rosemary	1 tbsp
thyme	1 tbsp
parsley, *finely chopped*	1 tbsp
olive oil	4 tbsp
red wine	1 bottle
large onions, *chopped*	2
carrots, *diced*	2–3
celery, *strung and chopped*	2 sticks
flour	3–4 tbsp
cognac OR Armagnac	4 tbsp
bay leaves	2
garlic cloves	4
stock	to cover
unsalted butter	45g/1½oz
button mushrooms, *wiped and left whole*	225g/8oz
small shallots	24
parsley, *chopped*	1 bunch

The better the beef, the better the taste. I made this classic recently with Longhorn beef, an ancient breed with wonderful marbling and fat.

→ Cube the STEAK into large chunks, a good mouthful each. Chop the BACON into lardons. Roll the meat in the finely chopped HERBS in a bowl and pour over half the OLIVE OIL and the red WINE. Leave to marinate for 4–6 hours, turning the meat over a couple of times.

→ Pour the marinade into a jug through a sieve, leaving the meat to drain in the sieve. Add the remaining 2 tablespoons of OLIVE OIL to a pan and sauté the bacon lardons over a medium heat, turning them as they brown and begin to crisp. Remove with a slotted spoon and throw in the ONIONS, CARROTS and CELERY. Stir them to coat with oil and bacon fat and cook for about 20 minutes until they begin to soften. Remove the vegetables to the plate with the bacon. Pat the meat dry with kitchen paper. Turn up the heat, adding a little more OLIVE OIL if you need to, and throw in the meat. Turn it to brown on all sides, then spoon over the FLOUR and continue to turn the meat for the next 5 minutes.

→ Return the bacon and vegetables to the pot, pour in the COGNAC and the marinade and stir everything in together well so nothing sticks to the bottom of the pan. Add the BAY LEAVES, the whole cloves of GARLIC and just enough STOCK to cover and return to a simmer. Then cover with a layer of greaseproof paper and a lid, and cook on top of the stove at a bare blip of a simmer for 2½–3 hours or until the meat is tender enough to cut with a spoon. Every so often give the pot a stir and make sure the meat isn't sticking to the bottom.

→ Heat half the BUTTER in a pan and add the MUSHROOMS, turning them over a high heat until their moisture begins to exude. Gently cook the SHALLOTS in the rest of the butter in another pan until they've softened and turned golden. Drain the cooking liquor through a sieve into a pan and return all the ingredients, including the mushrooms and shallots, to the big pot and keep them warm under a lid. Now reduce the cooking liquor by boiling it down, not too hard, for as long as it takes to reduce it by a half. Return the sauce to the pot and reheat gently until piping hot. Scatter fresh parsley over it and serve with plenty of mashed potato.

Shin of Beef with Mustard, Celeriac and Marsala

SERVES 4

shin of beef	1kg/2¼lb
seasoned flour	1 tbsp
olive oil	
medium onions	2
garlic cloves	2–3
carrots, *cut into chunks*	3
small celeriac	1
celery and leaves, *chopped*	2 sticks
Marsala	150ml/5fl oz
bouquet of bay, parsley, thyme and orange peel, *tied together*	
robust red wine	750ml/1¼ pints
seeded mustard	2 dsrtsp
tomato purée	2 dsrtsp
frozen peas (optional)	3 handfuls
salt, pepper	

Preheat the oven to 150°C/300°F/Gas 2. Cut the BEEF into generous 2.5cm/1in cubes and shake them in SEASONED FLOUR. Brown the floured cubes of meat in OLIVE OIL in a heavy-bottomed pot, not too many at a time, on all sides, then set aside.

→ Peel and chop the onions and garlic, and cut the celeriac into 2.5cm/1in dice. Put a bit more OLIVE OIL in the pot and gently sauté the ONIONS and GARLIC for a few minutes until translucent. Add the CARROTS, CELERIAC and CELERY, cook gently on all sides for a few minutes, return the meat to the pot, and add the MARSALA. Set light to it, let it crackle, burn off the alcohol, and let the flames die down before adding the BOUQUET, tucked well in, and the heated red WINE. If it doesn't quite cover, add a bit of hot water.

→ SEASON, cover with greaseproof paper and a lid, and cook for about 2 hours. Take off the lid, stir in the MUSTARD and TOMATO PURÉE to enrich and thicken, and the PEAS if using. Return to the oven for 30 minutes.

Braised Beef with Guinness

SERVES 6–8

chuck steak	1.5 kg/3¼ lb
olive oil	2 tbsp
large onion, *chopped*	1
carrots, *cut into fingers*	450g/1lb
garlic cloves, *peeled but whole*	6
plain flour	2 tbsp
tomato purée	1 tbsp
Guinness	750ml/1¼ pints
bouquet garni with 3 bay leaves, 2 sprigs of rosemary, thyme and parsley and 3 strips of orange peel	
salt and pepper	

→ Preheat the oven to 150°C/300°F/Gas 2. Cut the STEAK into large cubes and trim. Heat the OIL in a heavy-bottomed casserole and seal the meat briefly on all sides. Remove with a slotted spoon and put to one side. Add the ONION, CARROTS and GARLIC and let them begin to colour before sprinkling them with the FLOUR. Add the TOMATO PURÉE, stir and then return the meat to the casserole. Pour in the GUINNESS slowly, stirring and allowing the liquid to thicken. Bury the BOUQUET GARNI in the liquid and bring to boiling point. SEASON, cover with a sheet of greaseproof paper and a lid, and put into the oven for 1½ hours.

→ When the meat is tender, remove and discard the bouquet garni and serve hot, with plenty of mashed potato or colcannon (see pp. 394–395).

Shin of Beef in the Burgundy Style

Real slow food, perfect left to its own devices while you are left to yours. I made this with shin of organic beef on the bone, cut like a sort of grown-up ossobucchi.

SERVES 6

thick pieces of shin of beef, on the bone	6
butter	55g/2oz
green streaky bacon	8 or 9 rashers
large onions, *peeled, chopped*	2
large carrots, *diced*	2
garlic cloves, *peeled, chopped*	4
flour	1 tbsp
beef stock (p. 54)	
rosemary, thyme, parsley and bay leaf	1 bunch
sugar	1 tbsp
salt, pepper	

Marinade

red wine	1 bottle
cognac, OR grappa	1 glass
large onion, *sliced*	1
rosemary, thyme, parsley and bay leaf	1 bunch
peppercorns	12
salt	

To finish

shallots	24
sugar	1 tbsp
butter	55g/2oz
button mushrooms	285g/10oz
salt and pepper	
flat-leaf parsley	

→ Put the BEEF in a large bowl with the MARINADE INGREDIENTS, and leave overnight or for at least 6 hours.

→ Strain off the liquid and reserve, then heat the BUTTER in a heavy-bottomed casserole. Snip the BACON into strips and brown gently. Dry the MEAT, then brown it on both sides briefly. Remove to a plate and brown the VEGETABLES and GARLIC; you may need a bit more BUTTER for this. Sprinkle over a tablespoon of FLOUR, coat the vegetables, then return the meat and add the marinade and stock to cover to the casserole. Bury the bunch of HERBS, add the SUGAR, SEASON and bring to the boil, then cover with a layer of greaseproof paper and a lid and cook at a gentle burble of a simmer for 2–3 hours.

→ About 45 minutes before you are going to serve the beef, put the SHALLOTS in a single layer in a frying pan, add the SUGAR and 25g/1oz of the BUTTER, and cook hard without a lid until the onions are well caramelised and coated in gloopy brown juice. Keep a watch—you don't want the sugar to burn but you want the shallots to have softened right through. Sauté the MUSHROOMS briefly in the rest of the BUTTER, and keep them hot.

→ Remove the meat to a shallow, heatproof dish and keep warm while you bubble the sauce until thickened and reduced. Don't go too far, you don't want an over-concentrated flavour. Pour the sauce over the meat, surround with a heap of shallots and the mushrooms, scatter with PARSLEY, and serve with plenty of buttery mashed potato.

Boiled Salt Beef and Parsley and Horseradish Dumplings

SERVES 6

salted silverside or brisket (*ask the butcher if it needs soaking*)	1.5 kg/3¼lb
large onions, unpeeled, *each stuck with 2–3 cloves*	2
mace	1 blade
nutmeg	a suspicion
black peppercorns, *bruised*	12
Parsley and Horseradish Dumplings	
self-raising flour	110g/4oz
suet	55g/2oz
parsley, *chopped*	2 tbsp
hot horseradish per dumpling	1 tsp tip
sea salt and black pepper	

→ Find a pot that the BEEF will fit into snugly, with the ONIONS tucked in on either side. Put in the SPICES and PEPPERCORNS and cover the beef with half a fingernail to spare of warm water. Bring to simmer point, then cook at a bare blip for 3½ hours, skimming as and when you need to. If the cooking water tastes really salty after the first 10 minutes, drain it and start again. The water should not boil at any stage, so cover the pot only when you are happy the pot is burbling not bubbling.
→ Remove the meat to a warmed serving dish and keep it hot. Boil down half the beef juices in a separate pan while you poach the DUMPLINGS for 10–20 minutes with the rest of the cooking liquor. Remember, they will expand; suet does! And they are filling. Reheat the meat with the dumplings briefly and gently before serving. Serve the reduced sauce separately.
→ Do not cook vegetables with the beef. They will end up like soggy bedclothes and there is enough flavour in the meat and its juices to cook it with nothing but the spices. Serve with carrots Vichy (see p. 372), or stew some leeks in butter to accompany the beef, dumplings and mashed potato, to which you can add some grain mustard if you like.

Parsley and Horseradish Dumplings
→ Sieve the FLOUR into a bowl and mix in the SUET. Throw in the HERBS and SEASON. Stir to mix together. Slowly add cold water and mix with a spoon to a slightly sticky but not too wet dough, finishing it off by hand to make it cohere properly. Flour your hands before pulling bits of the dough away and forming it into walnut-sized balls, into which you push a little HORSERADISH before you start rolling.

Braised Oxtail

SERVES 6

dripping OR butter and olive oil	2 large tbsp
oxtails, ready jointed	4
sea salt and black pepper	
onions, *chopped*	2
carrots, *diced*	2
celery sticks, *strung and chopped*	3
fat leeks, the white parts, *chopped*	2
robust red wine	600ml/1 pint
tomatoes, *peeled and chopped* OR tinned plum tomatoes	450g/1lb
fresh bay, thyme, rosemary and parsley and 2 strips orange peel, *tied together*	
garlic cloves	4
veal, beef OR oxtail stock (see pp. 54–55)	1.5–2.5 litres/3–4 pints
flat-leaf parsley, *chopped*	2 tbsp

If you have an Aga, this is the dish to cook overnight in the slow oven until the meat drops from the gluey bones and the dish is braised to deep, dark perfection. There is no other flavour nor texture so redolent of icy winter, sustenance, ballast and succulence. You need to have made a good potful of veal, oxtail or beef stock before you begin (see pp. 54–55).

→ Preheat the oven to 190°C/375°F/Gas 5. Heat the DRIPPING or OIL AND BUTTER in a large, heavy-bottomed pot. SEASON the OXTAILS, then fry them, a single layer at a time, until browned on both sides. Remove to a plate as you go. Scrape all the crusty bits into the fat and add the ONIONS, CARROTS, CELERY and LEEKS, turning them in the dripping and allowing them to soften but not brown over a medium heat. Lift them out with a slotted spoon, pour the WINE into the pan and turn the heat up so that it boils fiercely and reduces by three-quarters.

→ Now tip the oxtails and vegetables back into the pot, turning the heat down to medium. Add the TOMATOES, bouquet of HERBS tucked down the side of the pot, whole bruised cloves of GARLIC, and STOCK to cover. Bring to boiling point, cover with a layer of greaseproof paper and a lid and braise in the oven until the meat is so tender it is ready to drop from the bone, about 2 hours.

→ Remove the bones from the pot and keep warm. Remove the bouquet and discard it. Now put all the vegetables and sauce through the coarse disc of a mouli so that you have a rough-textured purée—this works extremely well with oxtail. Check the SEASONING and return the meat to the pan with the purée. Simmer gently together for a few minutes.

→ Serve in bowls with plenty of mashed potato, some root vegetable like parsnip or swede roasted in honey, and parsley scattered over the oxtails. There should be 3–4 decent-sized bones per person.

Shepherd's Pie or Cottage Pie

SERVES 6

olive oil	3 tbsp
large onion, *chopped*	1
celery, *strung and chopped small*	2 sticks
medium carrots, *chopped into dice*	2
garlic cloves, *chopped*	3
minced beef OR lamb	675g/1½ lb
tomato concentrate	1 tbsp
Worcestershire sauce	a few shakes
dry white OR red wine OR the equivalent of good gravy from the Sunday roast	1 glass
beef OR chicken stock (see p. 54)	300ml/10fl oz
sea salt and black pepper	
potatoes	1.4kg/3lb
butter and milk for mashing the potatoes	
strong, unpasteurised Cheddar (optional)	2 tbsp

I didn't realise there was any difference between these two until well into my cooking life, despite it being glaringly obvious, lamb being the hungry shepherd's pie and beef the meat used for a cottage pie. Make this with the leftovers from a Sunday joint if you have any, instead of mince.

→ Preheat the oven to 180°C/350°F/Gas 4. Heat the OIL in a large, heavy-bottomed frying pan, then throw in the ONION, CELERY and CARROT, stirring them over a brisk heat but not allowing them to brown. After 5 minutes or so add the GARLIC, reduce the heat and soften everything together. Raise the heat again and add the MINCE, stirring until it has all lost its bloody colour. Add the TOMATO CONCENTRATE, WORCESTERSHIRE SAUCE, WINE and STOCK, SEASON, and simmer for 10 minutes covered. Peel and boil the POTATOES, then mash them with MILK and BUTTER in the usual way until really creamy and well SEASONED.

→ Put the contents of the frying pan into a gratin or baking dish and cover evenly and thickly with the mashed potato. Either dot with BUTTER or sprinkle CHEESE over the top.

→ Bake for 45–55 minutes until golden and bubbling. If it suits you to bake for longer at a lower temperature, begin at 200°C/400°F/Gas 6 for 10 minutes to start browning the top, then turn down to 180°C/350°F/Gas 4.

Italian Shepherd's Pie

→ If you want a more richly Italian version of this classic, call it an Italian shepherd's or cottage pie and just make extra ragù sauce when you are making a Bolognese (see p. 160) and crown it with very un-Italian mashed potato. And gratinée the top, which you have sprinkled with freshly grated Parmesan, to continue the theme.

Robert Carrier's Chili con Carne

SERVES 6

kidney beans, *soaked in plenty of cold water overnight*	340g/12oz
celery	2 sticks
carrots, *chopped*	2
large, unpeeled onion *spiked with a couple of cloves*	1
leeks (to flavour the beans)	2
whole black peppercorns	10
lean beef, *cubed*	1kg/2¼lb
pork, *cubed*	450g/1lb
bacon fat OR butter and olive oil	2 tbsp 1 tbsp of each
large onion, *finely chopped*	1
garlic cloves, *chopped*	4
beef stock (see p. 54) OR if you don't have beef stock, chicken stock (see p. 54)	600ml/1 pint
chili (chile) powder OR chilli powder	4 tbsp ½–1 tsp or to taste
flour	1 tbsp
bay leaves	2
cumin seeds, *toasted in a dry pan for a minute then ground*	1 tsp
oregano	½ tsp
sea salt and black pepper	

I've adapted this dish from Robert Carrier's Great Dishes of the World. *The first time I made it, as a young student, I didn't realise the difference between 'chile' or 'chili' powder and 'chilli' powder. 'Chilli' powder is made entirely from powdered chilli, while 'chili' or 'chile' is a delicate mix of hot peppers, paprika, cumin seed, dried garlic and oregano. One tablespoon of the hot stuff, the chilli, is enough to blow the pan-lid off. Four tablespoons rendered the dish so hot that its even touching your lips was enough to send you into shock. I have made it since and it has been delicious, both with the chili and the chilli. Just don't do what I did first time around. Remember to soak the beans the night before in cold water.*

→ Put the drained BEANS in the bottom of a large, heavy-bottomed pan with the CELERY, CARROTS, ONION, LEEKS and PEPPERCORNS and cover with a thumbnail to spare of cold water. Never salt pulses until they are cooked. It toughens the exterior of them and stops them cooking through satisfactorily. Bring to the boil, scum with a slotted spoon and allow to boil hard for 10 minutes, skimming off the froth as necessary before turning the heat down to a simmer and covering the pot. Check the beans after 1½ hours, though they may take 2 hours to cook.

→ You may cook the beans in advance of making your chilli and just cool them and keep them in their cooking liquor in a covered bowl in the fridge. The other vegetables have given up their goodness and need to be chucked. Keep the bean stock for soup.

→ Trim the fat from the MEAT then brown it, a single layer at a time, in the hot BACON FAT OR OIL AND BUTTER. A minute or two a side is all it needs at this stage. Remove the meat from the fat and throw in the ONION and GARLIC, allowing it to just begin to soften and turn translucent before you put the meat and its juices back in. Add the STOCK, which should be boiling. Bring to the boil, cover the casserole with a sheet of greaseproof paper and a lid and simmer gently for an hour.

→ Blend the CHILI OR CHILLI POWDER with FLOUR in a few tablespoons of the hot pan juices and return to the pot. Go easily if you are using chilli, and taste to get the heat you want. You may always add a little more at the end when you taste the finished dish, but there is no going back if you overdo it. Add the BAY LEAVES, CUMIN, OREGANO and SEASONING, taste and adjust. Continue to simmer the dish under the lid until the meat is completely tender. This could take another hour. Check the SEASONING again, then add a sufficient quantity of beans, without their cooking liquor, to the pot, roughly a ladleful per person. You can always use the leftovers in a soup or add them to the remaining chilli and have a beanier version the next day. Serve with plain boiled rice.

Boiled Rice

SERVES 4 AS AN ACCOMPANIMENT

long-grain white rice	225g/8oz
sea salt	1 tsp

→ Tip the RICE into a measuring jug, noting the plimsoll line that the rice comes up to. Then pour it into the pan you're going to cook it in with the SEA SALT. Measure twice the quantity of water to the rice you've measured in the jug, and pour it over the rice. Bring to the boil, turn the heat down to a simmer and cover with a lid. The rice should take 12 minutes to cook. There should be no water left at this point and when you lift the lid you should just see steam holes in the rice. Remove from the heat and leave for a further couple of minutes under the lid before serving. Never stir around with a spoon, this breaks the grains of rice down into a porridgy pulp. Always use a fork to fluff up and separate the grains of rice.

Steak Tartare

SERVES 6

rump OR fillet steak	450g/1lb
sea salt and black pepper	
olive oil	4 tbsp or so
Worcestershire sauce	
onion, *minced*	2–3 tbsp
cornichons, *finely diced*	1–2 tbsp
parsley, *chopped*	1 tbsp
small organic eggs	4
Little Gem lettuce	1
anchovy fillets (optional)	4

This is one of those dishes that you are more likely to order in a French brasserie than make at home, but if you have some good beef and serious carnivores to feed, it is simple to make.

→ Chop the STEAK very small or mince it coarsely if you have a mincer. Mix it with the SEASONING, OLIVE OIL (start with 3 tablespoons), WORCESTERSHIRE SAUCE to taste, minced ONION, CORNICHONS and PARSLEY. Then make patties or hamburger shapes with your hands and put them on a plate with some leaves of LETTUCE around them.

→ Separate the yolks from the whites of the EGGS, putting a half shell with a yolk in it on top of each steak tartare and an ANCHOVY on top of the meat if you like the salt-fish combination. It does give further depth to this all-meaty treat. Serve with chips or sauté potatoes; the hot and the cold go surprisingly well together.

Steak with Béarnaise Sauce

SERVES 6

steak, 2cm/¾in thick	1 per person
sea salt	
black pepper	
olive oil	
Béarnaise Sauce	
white wine vinegar (or tarragon vinegar)	2 tbsp
French tarragon, *finely snipped*	3 tbsp
shallot, *finely chopped*	30g/1oz
peppercorns, *crushed*	10
organic egg yolks	4
cold water	3 tbsp
unsalted butter, *clarified*	225g/8oz
sea salt and freshly ground black pepper	
chervil, *finely chopped* (optional)	2 tbsp
lemon	juice of ½

If you like your meat blue, don't rest it. It will merely need a minute a side at a very high temperature to char the outside. (The interior will not be cooked, however, so make sure to start with the meat at room temperature.) Otherwise, it is extremely important to rest the meat to allow the heat to warm the blood in the middle of the steak. A good butcher will cut a steak about 2cm/¾in thick.

→ To cook the STEAK, first season the meat with SEA SALT and cracked BLACK PEPPER. If you are using a griddle or pan, rather than a barbecue, brush it with a little OLIVE OIL as it gets hot. Heat until smoking before adding the meat. For a rare steak, cook for 2 minutes a side, then rest it for 6 minutes. For medium rare, cook for 2½ minutes a side, then rest it for 5 minutes. For well done, cook for 5 minutes a side and don't rest it at all.

Béarnaise Sauce
→ Put the VINEGAR, 2 tablespoons of the TARRAGON, the SHALLOT and crushed PEPPERCORNS in a small, heavy-bottomed saucepan and reduce gently by a half.
→ Let it cool, add the EGG YOLKS and COLD WATER, and set the pan over a low heat, whisking continuously. The sauce will gradually emulsify. Be patient; it will take about 10 minutes. Do not allow it to reach boiling point.
→ Remove from the heat and whisk in the BUTTER a little at a time. SEASON, then sieve the sauce and stir in the rest of the TARRAGON, the CHERVIL if using, and the LEMON JUICE to taste. Serve immediately.

Beef Stir-fry

SERVES 4

broccoli, *broken into small florets*	450g/1lb
baby corn	225g/8oz
groundnut oil	2 tbsp
large carrot, *peeled and sliced wafer thin*	1
mangetout	225g/8oz
spring onions, *tough exterior removed, split down the middle* 1 bunch	

Do not worry if you don't have all the vegetables. Just the broccoli and mangetout and carrots work, with onion if you have no spring onions. You do want a range of texture, colour and flavour though. If you don't have a wok, a frying pan will do.

→ Blanch the BROCCOLI and CORN in a large pan of boiling, salted water for 3 minutes and then drain them in a colander, pouring cold water over them to arrest the cooking process. Pat them dry in kitchen paper or they will not fry and maintain a peak of crispness when introduced to the hot oil. They will merely splutter and begin to steam.
→ Heat the wok or a large frying pan over a high heat until it is very hot, then add the GROUNDNUT OIL and heat until it is

sea salt	
black pepper	
garlic clove, *sliced*	1
fresh ginger, *finely sliced or coarsely grated*	1 thumb
sugar	1 tsp
rice wine or dry sherry	1 tbsp
light soy sauce	1 tbsp
dark soy sauce	3 tbsp
beef, cooked or raw, *cubed*	225–340g/8–12oz
sesame oil	2 tsp

smoking. Throw in the broccoli, corn and CARROTS and stir-fry for a couple of minutes. Throw in the MANGETOUT and SPRING ONIONS and stir-fry for another minute. Season, add GARLIC, GINGER, SUGAR, RICE WINE or DRY SHERRY and SOY SAUCES, then the BEEF. Stir-fry for another couple of minutes at a high temperature, turning the beef, lamb and pork well to brown all over and cook through if it's been started from raw. Add the SESAME OIL, stir for another 30 seconds, then transfer the contents of the wok to a warmed serving plate or spoon it over bowls of boiled rice (see p. 295). Serve with a bottle of shoyu sauce to hand round.

Claudia Roden's Filo Triangles with Minced Meat, Onions and Pine Nuts

MAKES ABOUT 20

minced beef	225g/8oz
small onion, *chopped*	1
sunflower oil	2 tbsp
ground cinnamon	¾ tsp
ground allspice	¼ tsp
pine nuts, *lightly toasted*	2 tbsp
filo pastry	5 or 6 sheets
butter, *melted* OR oil	3 tbsp
salt, black pepper	

Filo pastry is the most common of the many doughs used in the Middle East to make pies. Claudia says that meat pies are traditionally made in little triangular shapes and that the classic Arab filling here is called 'tatbila'. You can use lamb instead of beef if you prefer.

→ For the filling, fry the ONION in the oil until golden. Add the MEAT and fry lightly, crushing it with a fork and turning it over until it changes colour. Add SALT, PEPPER, CINNAMON and ALLSPICE. Stir in the PINE NUTS.

→ Preheat the oven to 180°C/350°F/Gas 4. Take out the sheets of FILO only when you are ready to use them, since they quickly dry out. Cut the sheets into four rectangles, measuring about 30 × 12.5cm/12 × 5in), and put them in a pile on top of each other. Brush the top strip lightly with melted BUTTER or OIL.

→ Take a heaped teaspoon of filling. Place it at one end of the strip of filo, about 3cm/1¼in from the edge. Fold the end over the filling. Now pick up a corner and fold diagonally, making a triangle. Continue to fold until the whole strip has been turned into a triangular packet, making sure that you close any holes as you fold so that the filling does not ooze out. If the filo sheets are too thin and look likely to tear, use two strips together and brush with MELTED BUTTER or OIL between.

→ Place the little packets close to each other on a greased baking tray and brush the tops with OIL or MELTED BUTTER. Bake for 30 minutes or until crisp and golden.

Deborah's Luxury Meat Loaf Pie

SERVES 8

best beef mince	450g/1lb
good organic pork sausage meat	225g/8oz
fresh breadcrumbs, white or brown	55g/2oz
large onion, *finely minced*	1
large egg	1
garlic cloves, *finely chopped*	2
fresh parsley, *chopped*	2 tbsp
fresh thyme, *chopped*	1 tbsp
tomato purée	1 dsrtsp
Worcestershire sauce	
sea salt, black pepper	
quails' eggs, *hard boiled and shelled*	12
puff pastry (bought or see p.517)	450g/1lb
egg, *beaten* for glaze	1

If you want to serve this hot, make a spicy tomato sauce to go with it. It's also excellent cold picnic food, needing no more than a good lettuce and some home-made mayonnaise (see p. 404).

→ Preheat the oven to 190°C/375°F/Gas 5. Put the MINCE, SAUSAGE MEAT and BREADCRUMBS into a large bowl. Add ALL THE OTHER INGREDIENTS except the quails' eggs, and gunge them around with your hands to mix thoroughly.
→ Press half the mixture into a loaf tin that you have lightly brushed with OLIVE OIL. Lay the QUAILS' EGGS along the centre of the mixture, pressing them down gently. Cover with the rest of the mixture, put the tin in the oven and cook for 1¼ hours. Remove the meat loaf from the oven and cool completely.
→ Reset the oven to 220°C/425°F/Gas 7. Roll out the PUFF PASTRY. Remove the meat loaf from the tin and wrap it completely in pastry, sealing the edges with beaten EGG. Bake for 35–40 minutes until golden and beautifully risen.

Cornish Pasties

SERVES 4–6

chuck steak	450g/1lb
onion, *chopped*	140g/5oz
mixed carrot and turnip, *chopped*	85g/3oz
potato, *sliced thin on a mandolin*	225g/8oz
fresh thyme	½ tsp
sea salt, black pepper	
pastry *made with 340g/12oz flour, 170g/6oz lard, sea salt and cold water* (see p. 104)	
egg, *beaten* for glaze	

The ultimate crimped parcel, and something well worth making yourself. Here is the classic, but you can experiment with your own combination of textures and flavours. If you can roll out pastry you can make a pasty! And pay attention here. Don't think that this is something to make with butter or any other kind of fat. It ain't. You want the flavour of the lard and the texture it gives to the crust.

→ Make the PASTRY (see p. 104), using LARD instead of butter, and leave to chill in the fridge.
→ Preheat the oven to 200°C/400°F/Gas 6. Trim the MEAT of all its gristle and skin, chop it down fine with a heavy, sharp knife, then mix it with your hands into the VEGETABLES and SEASONING.
→ Roll out the pastry and cut it into two large circles, dinner-plate size, or 4–6 smaller circles for individual pasties.
→ Assemble the steak mixture right down the middle of each circle. Brush the pastry rim with beaten EGG, then bring the two sides of the pastry up to meet over the top of the filling

and pinch them together into a continuous scalloped seam. Pierce two holes on top on either side of the edge through which the steam can escape, and put the pasties on a baking sheet.

→ Brush them all over with beaten EGG and bake for 20 minutes before turning the heat down to 180°C/350°F/Gas 4 for a further 40 minutes. Serve hot, warm or cold.

Italian Meat Loaf

SERVES 8

beef, and veal OR pork, *minced*	450g/1lb of each
organic free-range eggs, *beaten*	4
garlic cloves, *peeled and finely chopped*	2
onion, *peeled and very finely chopped*	1
flat-leaf parsley, *chopped*	2 tbsp
thyme, *chopped*	1 tbsp
sea salt and black pepper	
large, organic tomatoes, *skinned, cored and sliced*	3
organic free-range eggs, *boiled for 6 minutes and sliced*	2
lean smoked ham, *diced*	200g/7oz
Parmesan and Gruyère cheese, *freshly grated*	30g/1oz of each

A firmly set meat loaf, moist with jellied juices and resplendently coloured in strata when you cut into it—what a treat of a dish it is. Serve a meat loaf hot in winter with a cascade of home-made moulied tomato sauce. In the summer it is good clasped warm or cold into a picnic sandwich on a windy or sunny beach.

→ Preheat the oven to 150°C/300°F/Gas 2. In a large mixing bowl, mix the MEATS, beaten EGGS, GARLIC, ONION, PARSLEY, THYME and SEASONING.

→ OIL a loaf tin or terrine and put half the mixture into it, pressing it down firmly with your fingers. Add a layer of TOMATOES, then a layer of HARD-BOILED EGG, followed by the chopped smoked HAM, and sprinkle the grated CHEESES over the top. Cover with the rest of the meat mixture.

→ Put a piece of greaseproof paper under the lid, but if there is no lid use a double layer of foil above the paper, sealed tight against the tin. Cook in the oven in a bain marie for 1½ hours— that means a roasting tin in which you pour boiling water to come halfway up the sides of the terrine. You may remove the lid or foil for the last 30 minutes so that the top browns.

→ When the meat loaf has cooled on a rack in its tin, poke a knife all around the inside of the tin to ease the meat loaf away from the sides, then catch it as it comes out so that you don't turn it upside down, and put it brown side up on a serving dish. Cut into generous slices and press the whole together again before wrapping tightly if this is a travelling meat loaf, then it will retain its juiciness.

Blanquette de Veau

SERVES 4

small whole button mushrooms, *wiped clean*	170g/6oz
lemon	1
unsalted butter	55g/2oz
breast and shoulder of veal, *cut into 4 slices*	1kg/2¼ lb
large carrots, *cut into small chunks*	2
medium onions, *each stuck with a clove*	2
thyme, parsley, rosemary and bay, *tied together*	1 bouquet
small shallots	18–24
flour	1 tbsp
organic egg yolks	3
double cream	6–8 tbsp
sea salt and black pepper	
nutmeg	a little
curly parsley, *chopped*	a handful

Best made with breast and shoulder, and, most importantly, with properly reared veal. This is pinker than the wan, white veal, reared inhumanely in crates, that is now banned in the UK.

→ Put the MUSHROOMS in a small pan with a squeeze of LEMON, a tablespoon of water and half a walnut-sized piece of BUTTER, and cook over a high heat with a lid on for a minute. Put the slices of VEAL in a heavy-bottomed saucepan. Add the mushroom cooking liquor (but set the mushrooms aside) and enough water to cover by about a finger. Bring to the boil, skim, then add the CARROTS, ONIONS and HERBS. Bring back to a bare simmer, cover again and cook at this gentle heat for 1½ hours on top of the stove.

→ Towards the end of the meat's cooking time, cook the SHALLOTS in a little BUTTER, turning them gently for about 15 minutes until softened and golden, not brown. When the meat is cooked, take out the 2 whole onions and discard them, then remove the meat and vegetables to a large dish or bowl and cover.

→ In another saucepan make a roux with the FLOUR and 30g/1oz of the BUTTER. Add the braising liquid and whisk well so there are no lumps and the sauce thickens to a smooth richness. Simmer on a very low heat for about 15 minutes, stirring occasionally. Pour the sauce back into the main pan and add the meat, vegetables and mushrooms. Cover and simmer gently for another 15 minutes.

→ Whisk the EGG YOLKS in a bowl and add the CREAM and a few drops of LEMON JUICE.

→ Add this to the blanquette off the heat and then heat through without letting it reach boiling point. SEASON and add a suspicion of NUTMEG. The sauce should have a wooden-spoon-coating consistency like custard. Remove from the heat and sprinkle with some chopped PARSLEY.

Roast Shin of Veal

SERVES 4

organic, free-range veal	1 shin
garlic cloves, *sliced*	4–6
rosemary	3–4 sprigs
sea salt and black pepper	
flour	
olive oil	4 tbsp
unsalted butter	55g/2oz
onion, *sliced*	1
dry white wine, *heated*	half a bottle or more

Make sure the butcher saws through the bone at the base of the shin as for a leg of lamb. Veal has a natural affinity with rosemary, garlic and lemon but can withstand strong tastes like capers and cornichons in a salsa verde, or being stewed with tomatoes, peas and white wine.

→ Preheat the oven to 190°C/375°F/Gas 5. Make incisions right down into the VEAL with the sharp point of a knife and bury a slice of GARLIC and a bit of ROSEMARY sprig into each slash so that the rosemary sprouts from the top of the flesh. SEASON well and rub a little FLOUR into the meat. Heat the OLIVE OIL and BUTTER together in the roasting tin and add the shin, turning it to brown all over. Put your sliced ONION under the browned shin and put the roasting tin in the oven.

→ After 20 minutes, pull it out of the oven enough to pour over some of the heated white WINE, about 300ml/10fl oz to start with. Reduce the temperature of the oven to 170°C/325°F/Gas 3 and continue to roast for 1½ hours. Baste the joint every so often as veal is a dry meat, and add more white WINE to the pan. Remove the shin to a carving dish and keep warm under foil and a tea towel for 20 minutes.

→ Scrape the browned onion and all the crusty bits from the floor of the pan and stir into the winey juices over a medium heat. You may wish to add a little more white WINE or some of the cooking water from your vegetables. Boil to reduce a little; the colour should be a beautiful mahogany from the caramelised onion. Serve with the usual accompaniments to a roast such as roast potatoes and parsnips (see p. 392).

Scaloppine di Vitello alla Modenese

SERVES 4

lemons	2
veal escalopes, *beaten out by your butcher*	4
sea salt and freshly ground black pepper	
organic free-range egg, *beaten*	1
breadcrumbs *made with about 10cm/4in stale bread*	
unsalted butter	2 tbsp
extra virgin olive oil	1 tbsp
good prosciutto di Parma	4 slices
fresh mozzarella di bufala	225g/8oz
flat-leaf parsley, *chopped* (optional)	1 tbsp

The veal here keeps its taste and tenderness inside the protective elements of ham, cheese and crumb. Simple and easy to prepare, perhaps with some buttered spinach on the side.

→ Preheat the oven to 220°C/425°F/Gas 7

→ Sprinkle the juice of ½ a LEMON over the 4 ESCALOPES and SEASON them before dipping them into the beaten EGG on one plate and the BREADCRUMBS on another. Shake off the excess: you don't want them clogged with crumb, but they should be evenly coated.

→ Melt the BUTTER with the OLIVE OIL in a large, heavy-bottomed frying pan, and when it begins to bubble but before it browns, put in the escalopes and cook over a medium heat for about 6 minutes a side. Transfer to a shallow sided baking tray or gratin dish and place the sliced HAM, then the MOZZARELLA, on top. Bake in the oven for 10 minutes or until the cheese has melted and started to bubble.

→ Serve with quarters of lemon on the side and a little flat-leafed parsley sprinkled over the escalopes if you like.

Breast of Veal Stuffed with Olives

white bread	1 thick slice
milk	a little
garlic cloves	2
flat-leaf parsley	1 bunch
fresh basil	
lean minced pork	110g/4oz
black olives, *stoned*	12
black pepper and nutmeg	
organic egg, *beaten*	1
breast of veal	1 × about 1.8kg/4lb before boning (keep bones)
olive oil	
onion, *sliced*	1
tomatoes, *skinned and chopped*	2
white wine	170ml/6fl oz
meat stock OR water	170ml/6fl oz
salt	

→ Heat the oven to 170°C/325°F/Gas 3. Remove the crusts from the BREAD and soak it in the MILK. Squeeze out and chop it with the GARLIC, PARSLEY and a few BASIL LEAVES. Add the PORK and chopped OLIVES. Season with PEPPER and NUTMEG and add the EGG.

→ Spread the stuffing in a layer over the boned, flattened VEAL, then roll it up like a sausage. Tie securely at 5cm/2in intervals. Heat 2 tablespoons of OLIVE OIL in a heavy-bottomed pan and gently cook the sliced ONION, until wilted and golden, with a little extra garlic if you like.

→ Add the meat and brown lightly on all sides, then add the skinned, chopped TOMATOES and WINE, and reduce a little. Add the STOCK or water, a little SALT, and the MEAT BONES. Cover with greased greaseproof paper and the lid, and cook for 3 hours.

→ This dish is great eaten cold, the meat sliced thinly and served with a salad. The sauce needs to be strained and left to set. Skim off the fat, then spoon the jelly around the meat.

Braised Veal with Fennel and Paprika

SERVES 6

fennel bulbs	4
braising veal, *cut into 2.5cm/1in squares*	1kg/2¼lb
flour	
olive oil	
onions	2
garlic cloves	4
fennel	4 bulbs
celery sticks, *finely chopped with leaves*	2
paprika, Hungarian if possible	1 heaped dsrtsp
white wine	300ml/10 fl oz
organic tomatoes	2 × 400g/ 14oz tins
salt, pepper	
bay leaves	2 or 3

This is what Charlotte Reynolds of Swaddles Green Organic Farm says about their veal: 'Our veal calves are reared in the field with their mothers. It is not white veal, they are not kept in crates, and we keep our calves until they are about five months. They are milk fed and given a bit of hay. We actually need to eat more veal; these calves from the dairy industry do not make good beef because they are from milking herds, so they've got big udders and bony hips, they're short on haunches and well-padded rumps.'

→ Remove the tough outer layers from the fennel and quarter the bulbs carefully to keep them attached at the base. Peel and finely chop the onions and garlic

→ Preheat the oven to 150°C/300°F/Gas 2. Put a few tablespoons of flour in a ziploc bag and shake the veal, a few cubes at a time, to coat it. Brown the veal gently on all sides in 3–4 tablespoons of fruity olive oil in a heavy-bottomed casserole. Remove the meat, add more oil if necessary, and gently sauté the vegetables, keeping the fennel quarters intact. Sprinkle the paprika over the vegetables, return the meat to the pan, add the bay leaves and white wine. Bring to the boil, add the tomatoes, chopping them down as you go, season with salt and pepper, bring up to boiling point again, then cover with a piece of greaseproof paper before putting the casserole in the oven for 1½–2 hours.

Vitello Tonnato with Green Olives

SERVES 8

boned loin of veal	1kg/2¼lb
1 onion, *finely sliced*	
flat-leaf parsley	
Fresh tuna sauce	
tuna steak	225g/8oz
anchovy fillets	6
capers, *drained*	3 tbsp
lemon juice	3 tbsp
olive oil	240ml/8fl oz
salt, pepper	
green olives	12–15
mayonnaise (see p. 404)	

A classic summer dish, this can be made up to five days before you want to eat it. I do not, as is conventional, poach the veal. I roast it.

→ Grill or griddle the TUNA STEAK until just tender, about two to three minutes. Process all the TUNA SAUCE ingredients, bar the mayonnaise and the green olives, until creamy and smooth, but do not overdo it. Stone and roughly chop the GREEN OLIVES, then stir them in. Fold in the MAYONNAISE.

→ Roast the VEAL for an hour on a finely sliced ONION in a hottish oven, 190°C/375°F/Gas 5. Cool, slice and add the warm meat juices to the tuna sauce. Spread a layer of tuna sauce thinly on a serving dish, top with slices of veal, spread another layer of sauce, and repeat until the final layer of sauce.

→ Scatter some chopped, flat-leaf PARSLEY over the top, and decorate sparingly with a few anchovy fillets and black olives. Refrigerate for at least 24 hours.

Calves' Liver with Onions

SERVES 4

unsalted butter	55g/2oz
light olive oil	4 tbsp
onions, *sliced into very fine circles*	675g/1½lb
sea salt	
calves' liver, *very finely sliced*	675g/1½ lb
black pepper	
flat-leaf parsley, *chopped*	1 tbsp
red wine vinegar	2 tbsp

The delicately flavoured calves' liver should be very finely sliced for this dish. You must stew the onions for as long as possible to a soft, sweet tangle, but pay careful attention to the liver. It will be cooked and pink-middled in a matter of seconds.

→ Heat half the BUTTER with the OLIVE OIL in a large, heavy-bottomed frying pan. Cook the ONIONS over a gentle heat for 30 minutes, adding the SALT at the beginning of cooking to draw out the moisture. Stir from time to time. The onions shouldn't go more than a biscuit gold, certainly not brown, as they wilt down and soften. When they are cooked, remove them from the pan with a slotted spoon and set aside.

→ Throw the rest of the BUTTER into the pan and turn up the heat. Add the LIVER in a single layer and fry for about 30 seconds a side, or until pink but not raw in the middle. Transfer the liver to a warm plate and add the VINEGAR to the frying pan with the onions. Toss quickly together, season, add the liver and PARSLEY and serve immediately.

Calves' Sweetbreads in a Cream Sauce

SERVES 2

sweetbreads	
wine vinegar	
dried morels, *soaked in warm water to cover for 30 minutes*	20–24
unsalted butter	55g/2oz
shallots, *finely minced*	3
Marsala	1 glass
double cream	300ml/10fl oz
lemon juice	a little

Sweetbreads are the thymus gland and pancreas of a young animal. They need to be very fresh when you buy them as they deteriorate very quickly, and although they are a bit of a fiddly job to prepare the results are so worth it. Start this dish the day before you want it, or in the morning if you want the sweetbreads for dinner.

→ First prepare the SWEETBREADS. Steep them in a bowl of cold water, changing the water several times, for 2–3 hours. Now put them in a large pan, cover them well with cold water and a couple of teaspoons of WINE VINEGAR, and bring to the boil at a snail's pace. Let them boil for 2 minutes, then plunge the sweetbreads directly into cold water, replenishing it so that they cool really quickly. Now pull off and trim the little fatty, gristly bits, keeping the thin membrane that holds them together intact. Put the sweetbreads in a single layer on a plate, cover with another plate and some weights, and put in the fridge for at least 2 hours, but overnight if it is more convenient. This way they will all be the same thickness when you come to cook them. Lambs' sweetbreads are prepared in exactly the same way.

→ Remove the MORELS from their soaking water and reduce the scented water in a small pan by half to intensify the flavour. Melt the BUTTER in a pan and when it begins to foam, fry the minced SHALLOTS over a medium heat until softened before adding the morels and seasoning. Fry for a further 5 minutes without browning; the shallots should be pale gold. Then splosh in the MARSALA and let it bubble and cook down until only a tablespoon or so is left. Add the reduced liquid from the morels and continue to cook until the mixture is syrupy in appearance.

→ Add the CREAM, bring to a simmer, then add the sweet-breads in a single layer. Cook gently, stirring a little until the sauce has thickened. Adjust the seasoning, add a spritz of LEMON JUICE and serve with mashed or boiled potatoes.

Calves' Kidneys in a Devilled Mustard Cream Sauce

SERVES 4

calves' kidneys	2
unsalted butter	55g/2oz
olive oil	1 tbsp
sea salt and black pepper	
shallots, *finely minced*	3
white wine OR dry sherry, my preference	1 glass
anchovies, *chopped*	2
double cream	150ml/5fl oz
Tabasco a few shakes of the bottle OR cayenne	1 pinch
Worcestershire sauce	1 tbsp
grain mustard	1 dsrtsp

Calves' and lambs' kidneys have equally good flavour and a lovely texture, but I prefer the more delicate flavour of the calves' kidneys whenever I can get them.

→ Remove the suet from the KIDNEYS and trim their core of fat and membrane. Cut the kidneys into small pieces according to their natural divisions. Heat half the BUTTER with the OLIVE OIL. Drop in the kidneys, SEASON, then sear them briefly until the outsides have coloured a little but the middles remain raw-looking. Transfer to a warm plate. Lob in the extra BUTTER and when it is foaming, put in the finely minced SHALLOTS and cook until softened over a moderate heat. Remove from the pan onto the plate with the kidneys.

→ Pour the juice from the kidneys into the buttery pan, add the white WINE and let them bubble away together before adding the chopped ANCHOVIES and turning the heat down. Crush the anchovies into the liquid so they melt into it before pouring over the CREAM, TABASCO and WORCESTERSHIRE SAUCE and plopping in the MUSTARD. Stir and let everything bubble together.

→ Add the kidneys and shallots to the pan over a gentle heat and turn the kidneys in the sauce until coated and cooked — that is, still pink in the middle. Serve on toast if for breakfast or with rice or mashed potato at any other time.

Calf's Kidney with Cabbage and Chorizo

SERVES 4

calf's kidney, preferably organic	1
good chorizo	5cm/2in chunk
savoy cabbage, *shredded tinsel thin*	½
seeded mustard	
good fruity olive oil	
salt and freshly ground pepper	

The sweet, meaty mildness of calves' kidneys is one of life's great treats. I buy organic ones from Swaddles Green Farm; if you cannot get them, use lambs' instead, but it will be a different dish.

→ Remove the fat and gristle from the KIDNEY, then separate the little nuggets and remove the outer membrane. Cut the CHORIZO into matchstick strips, and soak it in a bowl in 2 or 3 tablespoons of the OLIVE OIL. Blanch the CABBAGE in boiling water for a minute, hurl it into a colander, refresh under the cold tap, then drain it thoroughly.

→ Heat a film of OLIVE OIL in a pan and cook the kidney on a high heat for about 3 minutes, turning it to brown on all sides. Remove to a warming oven in a bowl, where it will exude some wonderful bloody juices.

→ Put the chorizo and OLIVE OIL into a heavy-bottomed pan with the cabbage, and heat together thoroughly, adding a good tablespoon, or more to taste, of seeded MUSTARD. Add the kidneys and their juices when all is hot and heavenly, and serve with acres of buttery mashed potatoes.

Ossobucco Milanese

SERVES 8

ossobuchi	8
olive oil	4 tbsp
seasoned organic flour *in a ziploc bag*	
unsalted butter	85g/3oz
large onion	1
shallots	16–20
celery heart with its leaves	1
white wine, *heated*	a generous 300ml/10 fl oz
chicken OR other meat stock, *hot* (see p. 54)	600ml/1 pint

→ Put a few of the OSSOBUCHI in the bag of FLOUR at a time, shake, then remove them, shaking off excess flour. Tie string around each one so they hold their shape, don't skip this bit, or they'll end up misshapen.

→ Heat the OLIVE OIL in a heavy-bottomed casserole, add a single layer of ossobuchi at a time, and brown on both sides. Remove them to a plate, add BUTTER, then the finely chopped ONION and CELERY and the peeled whole SHALLOTS. After about 10 minutes, return the meat to the pan, season with SALT AND PEPPER and pour over the HEATED WINE. Let it all bubble together for a few minutes before adding the HOT STOCK.

→ Turn down to a mere blip, put the lid on, with a sheet of greaseproof paper inside to help seal it, and cook for 1½ hours, turning the veal over every half hour. You can do all this the night before you want it, then reheat it slowly for half an hour on the day.

Italian Meatballs

SERVES 4

veal mince	450g/1lb
pork mince	225g/8oz
capers, *rinsed and chopped*	2 tbsp
anchovy fillets, *chopped*	10
organic lemon	*grated zest* of 1
rosemary needles, *finely chopped*	1 tbsp
flat-leaf parsley, *chopped*	2 tbsp
egg, *beaten*	1
breadcrumbs	75g/2½oz
Parmesan cheese, *freshly grated*	55g/2oz
flour	a little
olive oil	4 tbsp
unsalted butter	55g/2oz
garlic clove, *sliced*	1
dry white wine, *warmed*	240ml/8fl oz
organic whole plum tomatoes	1 × 400g/14oz tin
lemon juice	
pappardelle OR spaghetti	

You may make meatballs with pork, veal, lamb or beef mince, or a combination, as here, of veal and pork. I have stuffed these veal and pork meatballs with capers, anchovies, rosemary and lemon zest. You could also try sage or summer savory, both of which work beautifully with veal and pork.

→ Mix the FIRST TEN INGREDIENTS together well with a wooden spoon, or your hands, in a large bowl. Now pull off chunks of the mixture and roll them into walnut-sized balls. Put some FLOUR on a flat plate so that you can roll each ball in flour, shake off the excess and put each ball ready to fry on another plate.

→ Melt the OLIVE OIL and BUTTER together in a large, heavy-bottomed frying pan. Add the meatballs in a single layer and fry them until browned on all sides. If the fat looks very floury and blackly fatty at this stage, you may pour some of it away, then add the sliced GARLIC and stir for a couple of minutes. Pour in half the warmed WINE, reduce it for a few minutes, then add the TOMATOES. Chop them down into the wine juices and bring to a bubble before you add the rest of the WINE. Simmer for 20 minutes, turning the meatballs from time to time. Remove them with a slotted spoon and keep warm on a large dish while you reduce the sauce for a few minutes longer.

→ Pour the sauce over the meatballs, spritz a little LEMON JUICE over them and serve with some buttered PAPPARDELLE OR SPAGHETTI.

Parsley Pie

SERVES 6–8

breast of veal, *cut into 2.5cm/1in cubes*	900g/2lb
flat-leaf parsley, *chopped*	1 huge handful
stock	290ml/10fl oz
flour	30g/1oz
butter	30g/1oz
double cream	150ml/5fl oz
sea salt and black pepper	
shortcrust pastry *made with 225g/8oz flour and 110g/4oz unsalted butter* (see p. 104)	
egg, *beaten* for glaze	

A beautifully light summer dish of delicate veal, parsley and cream, which you can serve with early summer vegetables—green wands of asparagus, fresh minted peas and tiny violet artichokes.

→ Make the PASTRY (see p. 104) and leave to chill in the fridge.
→ Preheat the oven to 180°C/350°F/Gas 4. Put the VEAL into your pie dish, SEASON it and throw over a green snowstorm of PARSLEY. Add the COLD STOCK and cover with pastry in the usual way (see p. 284). Brush the top with beaten EGG and pierce holes in the centre to allow the steam to escape. Bake for 1½ hours.
→ Work the FLOUR and softened BUTTER into a paste and whisk in the CREAM. Lift the lid of the pie by carefully slitting a corner of the pastry on the join and pour in the cream. Stir it into the stock as much as you can before replacing the lid and returning the pie to the oven for a further 20–30 minutes.

Roast Leg of Lamb

SERVES 6

leg of lamb	2–2.5kg/4½–5½lb
rosemary	6 sprigs
garlic cloves, *peeled and thinly sliced*	6
a few halved fillets of anchovy from a tin (optional)	
olive oil	
sea salt and black pepper	
large onion, *peeled and sliced*	1

A good, grass-fed, well-hung leg of late summer lamb—its fatty jacket studded with garlic, rosemary and perhaps anchovy fillets, which deepen the lambiness in an extraordinarily unfishy way, the fat crisped, the meat pink and cut in thick tranches, served with a blob of home-made spiced redcurrant jelly—is a darn delicious Sunday lunch.

→ Preheat the oven to 200°C/400°F/Gas 6. Cut slits in the fat of the LAMB before sliding in sprigs of ROSEMARY with a slim-bladed knife so that you have a little tussock of rosemary needles poking out of each hole. Do likewise with the ANCHOVIES, if you are using them, having halved the fillets first. Slip the slices of GARLIC into the slits too, avoiding the bone and making sure the leg is scored all over. Pour a little OLIVE OIL over the fat, season and place on a thinly sliced ONION that you have laid on the bottom of the roasting tin.
→ Place the joint on the bottom shelf of the oven and roast for 1¼–1½ hours, basting with a bulb baster every 20–30 minutes. Check with a skewer, and if the flesh is deeply resistant and the blood rises instantly to the surface, leave for another 15 minutes until you check again. You want there to be pink juices, but the feel of the flesh will tell you as much. It needs to yield right the way through. If you like your meat pink, now is the time to remove it from the oven. Place it on the carving

board, covered with well-tucked-in foil and a tea towel placed loosely over it, and let it stand for 20 minutes so the juices can flood back through the meat while you make the gravy and finish off the vegetables.

Roast Shoulder of Lamb
→ Shoulders are usually smaller than legs, so treat in the same way but cook for a little less time. There will be more fatty juices in the roasting pan, but your parsnips will cope with them! If you are 8 people you might wish to buy two slightly smaller shoulders.

Baked Shoulder of Lamb with Pink Fir-Apple Potatoes

SERVES 6

shoulder of lamb, *boned, rolled and tied*	1 × 1.5kg/3¼lb
olive oil and butter	
onion, *peeled and thinly sliced*	1
rosemary, *finely chopped*	1 tbsp
thyme	1 tbsp
redcurrant jelly	3 tbsp
French mustard	1 tbsp
garlic cloves, *crushed*	2
salt and pepper	
breadcrumbs	2–3 tbsp
red wine	1 full teacup
water	1 full teacup
pink fir-apple potatoes	1kg/2¼lb
flat-leaf parsley, *chopped*	a handful

I based this dish loosely on the French lamb boulangère. The lamb's mild sweetness was brought out with a redcurrant and rosemary paste to which I added thyme, French mustard, garlic and breadcrumbs. If you can't find pink fir-apple potatoes, use Anya or similar waxy-fleshed salad potatoes.

→ Preheat the oven to 170°C/325°F/Gas 3. In a deep, heavy-bottomed casserole, brown the LAMB thoroughly on all sides in a bit of OLIVE OIL and BUTTER. Then add the ONION, and sauté until palely golden.

→ Make a paste with the HERBS, REDCURRANT JELLY, MUSTARD, GARLIC and SEASONING, then stir in the BREADCRUMBS until they are amalgamated but the mixture isn't dry. Press them firmly down on top of the lamb along its length. Heat the WINE AND WATER together until boiling, pour around the lamb, not over it, and place the scrubbed whole POTATOES in their skins around the meat. Cover with a layer of greaseproof paper and the lid, and cook in the oven for 1½ hours.

→ Remove, and leave in the covered pot for up to 20 minutes before serving. Scatter some chopped flat-leaf PARSLEY over the top. You can reduce the juices if you like at this stage, although they are deliciously intense without doing so.

→ I serve this dish with carrots and whole fingers of courgettes, flower still attached, sautéed briefly in olive oil and spritzed with lemon.

Gigot d'Agneau with Flageolets

SERVES 8

Flageolets

flageolets, *soaked overnight in plenty of cold water*	450g/1lb
carrots, *chopped into large chunks*	2
celery sticks, *broken into lengths*	2
large onion, skin on, *stuck with 2 cloves*	1
leek tops, if you have them	1 or 2
peppercorns, *bruised*	12
fresh bay leaves	2
rosemary, thyme and parsley *tied together*	

Lamb

leg of lamb	1 × about 2–2.3kg/ 4½–5lb
OR use shoulder of lamb	
garlic cloves	6
rosemary	2 sprigs
olive oil	3–4 tbsp
sea salt and black pepper	
dry white wine	1 glass
a knob of butter	
double cream (optional)	3–4 tbsp

There is something about the marriage of palely green leguminous flageolets and rosily bloody and garlicked leg of lamb that spells harmony and deep satisfaction. This is a king of a dish, scented with rosemary and bay and with some of the flageolets puréed and dosed with cream and butter to give a change of texture. It is just as successful a dish made with shoulder of lamb, which is my preferred cut. I like the more muttony strong flavour of the fuller-fatted meat. Remember to soak the beans the night before you need them.

→ Drain the BEANS and put them in a large heavy-bottomed pot with ALL THE OTHER INGREDIENTS for the flageolets. Cover with water to 2cm/1in above the vegetables. Bring to the boil and scum rigorously with a slotted spoon. Lower to a simmer, put the lid on and cook at a bare bubble for 1½–2½ hours, until the beans are tender right through but not starting to break up.
→ Preheat the oven to 200°C/400°F/Gas 6. While the beans are coming to the boil, spike incisions into the fat of the LAMB and right down into the flesh wherever there is no bone. Push a sliver of GARLIC and a little sprig of ROSEMARY into each fissure. Pour the OLIVE OIL over the meat and SEASON, before putting it at the bottom of the hot oven to roast for about 1½–1¾ hours.
→ When the meat is cooked but still deliciously pink in the middle—the juices run pink rather than bloody when pierced into the deepest part with a skewer, and there is no resistance —remove from the pan to a carving board. Cover with a tight layer of foil and a tea towel. Skim off the fat from the juices in the roasting tin and put the tin on a high heat on top of the stove. Add the white WINE and let it bubble.
→ Remove a large ladle of beans from the pot and liquidise them with about half a ladle of the pot juices. Put the remaining beans in a large warmed dish with a slotted spoon and stir in the puréed flageolets, a large knob of BUTTER and some CREAM if you feel like it. SEASON to taste. Serve with the beans and some mashed potatoes (see p. 394).

Spiced Shoulder or Leg of Lamb in a Gingered, Curried Yoghurt Paste

SERVES 8

shoulder OR leg of lamb	1 × about 2–2.5 kg/ 4½–5½lb
fresh ginger	5cm/2in piece
onions, *chopped*	3
garlic cloves, *roughly chopped*	12
green chillies, *seeded and finely chopped*	2–3
blanched almonds, *roughly chopped*	55g/2oz
live natural yoghurt	500–600ml/ 18fl oz–1 pint
ground cumin	1 tbsp
ground coriander seeds	1 tbsp
cayenne pepper	½ tsp
seeds from cardamom pods	1 tsp
garam masala	1 tsp
salt	1 tsp
olive oil	3 tbsp
cloves	4–5
cinnamon stick	1
peppercorns	4–5
sultanas	1 handful
flaked almonds	1 handful
fresh coriander, *chopped*	

This dish is a stunner, and one you need to get marinating 24 hours before you want to cook it to tenderise the meat and almost suffocate it with the infusion of spice and yoghurt. Marinate the meat in a Pyrex or enamel dish that you can then cook it in. A roasting tin is not the thing; it would taint the flavour.

→ Cut the LAMB into 3 or 4 large pieces on the bone, or get your butcher to do this for you. Peel the GINGER and cut into 5 2.5cm/1in cubes. Put it with the ONIONS, GARLIC, CHILLIES, BLANCHED ALMONDS and one-third of the YOGHURT in a food processor and blend to make a smoothish paste. Pour the rest of the YOGHURT into a bowl, add the onion paste, CUMIN, ground CORIANDER, CAYENNE, CARDAMOM, GARAM MASALA and SALT, and whisk lightly to amalgamate.

→ Make slashes in the lamb flesh and push in as much of the spicy paste as you can, then pour all the remaining paste over the pieces of lamb. Cover the dish with clingfilm and refrigerate, ideally for 24 hours.

→ Take the dish out of the fridge an hour or so before you intend to cook it. Preheat the oven to 190°C/375°F/Gas 5. Heat the OIL in a small frying pan. When it's hot, drop in the CLOVES, CINNAMON and PEPPERCORNS, then pour the whole lot over the lamb.

→ Cover the dish with foil or a lid and bake for about 30 minutes. Remove the lid, sprinkle on the SULTANAS and FLAKED ALMONDS, and put back into the oven, uncovered, for 10 minutes longer. Test that the lamb is cooked—it might need a few more minutes if the legs are huge. Sprinkle with chopped CORIANDER and serve with rice and poppadums and one or two vegetables. A real feast of a dish, not too highly spiced for children.

Spiced Leg of Lamb with Tahini Sauce

SERVES 6

leg of lamb	1
Marinade	
coriander seeds	1 tbsp
cumin seeds	1 tbsp
cardamom seeds	½ tbsp
fresh turmeric root, *grated*	5cm/2in piece
green ginger root, *grated*	5cm/2in piece
cinnamon	1 tsp
allspice	1 tsp
ginger	1 tsp
cayenne	½ tsp
sheep's yoghurt	1 small carton
fresh coriander, *chopped*	1 bunch
olive oil	
sea salt and black pepper	
Tahini Sauce	
garlic cloves, *peeled*	3
dark tahini	4 tbsp
lemons	juice of 1½
sea salt and black pepper	

Serve this spicy lamb with ratatouille (see p. 386). I know it may seem quite a cross-cultural combination but it works superbly.

→ Roast the CORIANDER SEEDS and CUMIN SEEDS in a pan for a minute and then crush in a mortar with the CARDAMOM SEEDS. Put the seeds and the rest of the MARINADE INGREDIENTS into a bowl with the CHOPPED CORIANDER and a tablespoon or two of OLIVE OIL, and stir together.

→ Make some slashes in the LAMB right through the fat so that you can spread the marinade all over the meat and into the slashes. It helps to do this on the clingfilm you're then going to wrap the meat in to keep it sealed tight in the fridge overnight. The paste will spice and tenderise the meat ready to cook.

→ Roast in the normal way in a hot oven. I put my joint on a layer of sliced ONIONS and cook it until pink. For a joint around the 2kg/4lb mark I suggest about 1½ hours at 200°C/400°F/ Gas 6.

Leave the joint to rest for 20 minutes, but I do think lamb needs to be served hot rather than warm, due to the congealing properties of the fat.

→ Carve the meat and pour the spicy juices over the slices. Serve with the TAHINI SAUCE and ratatouille.

Tahini Sauce

→ Put the GARLIC cloves in the mortar with a little SEA SALT and crush them to a wet paste, then whisk in the TAHINI. Thin the paste with LEMON JUICE. Carry on whisking and add water until the sauce has the consistency of double cream. SEASON, taste and adjust the LEMON JUICE if you need to. Serve in a bowl to pass around with the meat. You may add a little sprinkle of crushed, toasted CUMIN to the bowl if you like. The simplest sauce in the world. Also great with lamb kebabs.

Navarin of Lamb

SERVES 6–8

shoulder of lamb, *cubed*	1.4kg/3lb
butter	30g/1oz
olive oil	2 tbsp
large onion, *sliced*	1
flour	2 tbsp
lamb stock, *heated*	600ml/1 pint
sea salt and black pepper	
garlic cloves, *bruised*	2
rosemary	1 sprig
thyme	1 sprig
bay leaf	1
small waxy new potatoes like Jersey Royals	450g/1lb
baby carrots	225g/8oz
baby turnips, *peeled*	12
shelled broad beans	225g/8oz
shelled peas	225g/8oz
asparagus	1 bundle (18–24 spears)
artichoke hearts	6
a little parsley to finish	

This is an early summer dish and one of the great one-pot dinners. You may include any combination of good new potatoes like Jersey Royals, artichoke hearts, asparagus, baby broad beans, tiny lanterns of turnip and baby's fingers of carrots. Later there will be squeaky sweet tiny peas, or you can cheat and add a few frozen ones. With the array of fresh veg no one will notice a single aberrant interloper. The kind of dish that gladdens the heart and makes you feel the sun is beginning to warm itself in readiness for summer.

→ Trim any large bits of fat from the LAMB. Melt the BUTTER with the OLIVE OIL over a medium heat in a large, heavy-bottomed casserole. Throw in the ONION and the meat together and stir to brown the meat and turn the onions golden. Remove both, adding a little extra BUTTER and OIL to the pan if you need. Stir in the FLOUR and let it bubble into a blonde, biscuity-smelling roux before adding the HOT STOCK, a couple of ladles at a time, stirring or whisking it to smoothness as you add more. Return the meat and onions to the pot with the SEASONING, GARLIC and HERBS. Put a sheet of greaseproof under the lid and simmer everything for an hour at a very gentle blip.

→ Add the new POTATOES, whole CARROTS and the whole, peeled TURNIPS and continue to simmer until they are only just resistant, about 40 minutes. Now add whichever of the OTHER VEGETABLES you are using—the BROAD BEANS, PEAS, peeled chopped ASPARAGUS, the spears kept longer than the stalks, and the whole hearts of ARTICHOKE. Cook for about 20 minutes or so, until you can pierce the asparagus and artichokes and they are tender right the way through.

→ If the sauce has become too reduced at any stage of the cooking process, just top it up with a couple more ladles of HOT STOCK. Remove the pot from the heat, skim off any fat from the surface that offends you and scatter fresh chopped PARSLEY over everything.

Braised Lamb Shanks with Rosemary and Balsamic Vinegar

SERVES 4

plain flour	2 tbsp
sea salt and black pepper	
organic lamb shanks	4
olive oil	2–3 tbsp possibly an extra couple of tbsp
rosemary leaves, *finely chopped*	1 tbsp
thyme leaves, *chopped*	1 dsrtsp
large onions, *peeled and sliced thinly*	2
garlic cloves, *roughly chopped*	6
white wine	300ml/10fl oz
balsamic vinegar	150ml/5fl oz
strips of orange peel	2
bay leaves *tied together with string*	2

A hearty dish that will stew happily in its own juice for up to two and a half hours, until the meat is spoon tender and falling off the bone and the sharp rosemary leaves have softened and scented the meat. It is essential to buy a good balsamic vinegar but not one that is life-threateningly expensive. You need the velvet, rich grapey undertones without the sharpness. Seggiano have a good, mellow, musty organic balsamic vinegar.

→ Put the FLOUR and SEASONING in a ziploc bag. Throw in the LAMB SHANKS, seal the bag and give the shanks a good shake to coat them in the seasoned flour. (That way you don't end up wearing it.) Shake off the excess flour and remove the meat.

→ Heat the OIL in a large, heavy-bottomed casserole and brown the shanks on all sides over a medium heat. This should be done quickly, a couple of minutes a side until they begin to brown and crust. Scrape up any burnt bits of flour from the bottom of the pan and remove with a slotted spoon. If the pan looks like it needs more OIL, add it. Then throw in the ROSEMARY LEAVES and let them fizz and hiss for a minute. This begins to tenderise them and draw out their astringent scent. Add the THYME, ONIONS and GARLIC, stir and cook until softened and beginning to turn translucent. Raise the heat and add the WINE AND VINEGAR together, bubbling them furiously for a couple of minutes.

→ Return the shanks and their juice to the pot, lower the heat and add the BUNCH OF ORANGE PEEL AND BAY LEAVES tucked into the side, and cover the pot with a layer of greaseproof paper and the lid. Simmer very gently for 2–2½ hours, turning the shanks in the chocolate-brown liquor every so often. You may add a little more WINE if it looks like the sauce is reducing too much. Serve with champ, a wonderful Irish dish of mashed potato (see p. 395).

Braised Lamb Shanks in Harissa and Tomato Sauce

SERVES 4

flour and seasoning to coat	
organic lamb shanks	4
olive oil	
large onions, *chopped*	2
garlic cloves, *chopped*	4
celery sticks with the leaves, *chopped*	2
harissa (see p. 411)	2 heaped tsp
plus extra to add at the end	
tomato purée	1 tbsp
whole tomatoes	400g/14oz tin
strips of orange peel	a couple

Make the harissa yourself (see p. 411), if possible. It is so much better than the squeezy tube or tinned version, and it will keep for a couple of weeks in the fridge.

→ Heat oven to 150°C/300°F/Gas 2. Put a handful of FLOUR in a ziploc bag with a little SALT and a good scrunch of PEPPER, throw in the LAMB SHANKS, seal the bag and shake until the shanks are coated in seasoned flour.

→ Heat 3–4 tablespoons of OLIVE OIL in a heavy-bottomed casserole and gently brown the shanks on all sides. Remove to a plate.

→ Add a little more OIL if needed, then throw in the chopped ONIONS, GARLIC and CELERY and sauté gently until they begin to soften.

→ Put the shanks back in the pot and add the HARISSA, TOMATO PURÉE and TINNED TOMATOES, and enough water to nearly reach the top of the shanks. Bring to the boil, add the ORANGE PEEL, reduce the heat to a simmer and cover the pot with a layer of greaseproof paper and a lid. Place in the oven for 2–2½ hours—the shanks should be falling off the bone and sweetly tender. Add more HARISSA if you'd like the dish to be even hotter, and serve it with black beans and rice.

Estouffade d'Agneau

SERVES 4

lamb shoulder, *cubed*	1kg/2¼lb
Carluccio's crema di olive nere	200g/7oz

This is so simple, but never use any black olive paste other than Carluccio's. The quality of the olives and olive oil is incomparable, and it has a fragrant hint of capers and oregano. The black oily, olivey juices mingle with the lamb, colouring, scenting and tenderising.

→ Preheat the oven to 150°C/300°F/Gas 2. Simply put the cubed LAMB SHOULDER in the bottom of a heavy casserole, then tip in a whole jar of the CREMA DI OLIVE NERE. Cover with greaseproof paper, then a lid, and abandon in the oven while you work or watch a movie for 2 hours. Then take out and eat.

Lamb and Apricot Tagine

SERVES 4

unsulphured apricots	340g/12oz
fresh orange juice	
olive oil	
shoulder of lamb, *cut into 5cm/2in cubes*	1kg/2¼lb
flour	2–3 tbsp
sea salt and black pepper	
medium onions, *finely sliced*	4
fat garlic cloves, *finely sliced*	3
celery sticks from the heart, *strung and finely sliced*	3
coriander seeds	1 tsp
cumin seeds	1 tsp
cinnamon bark	1 tsp
ground dried ginger root	1 tsp
cayenne	½–1 tsp
fresh bay leaves	2
chicken stock OR water (see p. 54)	
fresh coriander, *chopped*	a handful

The natural affinity betwixt apricot and lamb is a known, surprising sharpness on the palate mollified by the sweet meat. The plush, spiced undertones of this Moroccan dish are mildly subtle and absolutely delicious. Serve with couscous and harissa (see p. 411).

→ Soak the APRICOTS in half fresh ORANGE JUICE, half WATER the night before you want to cook this dish.

→ While you warm 2–3 tablespoons of OLIVE OIL in a heavy-bottomed casserole, dry the MEAT with a piece of kitchen paper and put it into a ziploc bag with the FLOUR, SEA SALT and BLACK PEPPER. Shake the bag until all the meat is lightly covered with flour but not clogged. Put the meat straight into the casserole, in a single layer, while it is still dry. Brown on all sides for a few minutes, then lift out the meat with a slotted spoon and put it on a plate.

→ Add a little more OIL to the pan, throw in the VEGETABLES and sweat them gently. Temper the CORIANDER and CUMIN SEEDS in a small frying pan for a minute or so, until they exude their toasted spice smell, then crush them in a mortar with the CINNAMON BARK. Add them with the OTHER SPICES to the vegetables when they have softened, after about 10 minutes, then add the BAY LEAVES and APRICOTS, without their soaking liquid, a couple of minutes later. Return the lamb to the pan, and just cover with STOCK OR WATER. Bring to the boil, cover, then simmer at a mere blip for about 1½ hours until really tender. Check the SEASONING and, if possible, cool and refrigerate for a day or two before reheating and serving.

→ Sprinkle with chopped fresh CORIANDER before serving.

Breast of Lamb Cooked in the Daube Style

SERVES 8

oak-smoked bacon, *snipped in 1cm/½in pieces*	5 rashers
large carrots *cut in 1cm/½in dice*	5
celery sticks, *chopped*	4
onions, *peeled and chopped*	2

Having abandoned this dish for three hours, I could smell its winey depths three rooms away when I came to take it out of the oven. A sweetly flavoured meat, you could cut it with a spoon after its long, slow cooking.

→ Put the snipped RASHERS in a large, heavy-bottomed casserole, and heat gently until the fat begins to run. Throw in the CARROTS, CELERY, ONIONS and GARLIC, and sprinkle with a tablespoon or two of OLIVE OIL.

→ Tuck the BREASTS in next to each other in the casserole, with the BOUQUET under the flap of one. SEASON. Heat the WINE to boiling point, set light to it, and watch carefully until the flames

garlic cloves	6
olive oil	
whole breasts of lamb on the bone	2 × 1.5kg/3¼lb
rosemary, bay and parsley stalks *tied together with string*	
good red wine	1 bottle
tomatoes	2 × 400g/14oz tins
salt and pepper	

die down. Pour it over the meat. Add the TOMATOES, chopping and sinking them into the wine as you go.

→ Put a layer of greaseproof paper over the top of the pot, cover it with the lid, and cook in a coolish oven, 150°C/300°F/Gas 2, for 3 hours. Remove the casserole dish, unlid it and, with a bulb baster, remove the liquid, tomato-coloured fat as far as you dare. I skimmed off 300ml/10fl oz.

→ Don't carve the meat conventionally: it will be so tender that you can cut right through to the bottom in chunks for each portion. Scoop out the vegetables and bacon with the juices, and anoint the meat with them. Is there anything as good as buttery mashed potato with a dish like this?

Irish Stew

SERVES 4

celery sticks with leaves	2
decent-sized carrots	6
large onions, *peeled and sliced*	2
neck or scrag of lamb, on the bone	8 pieces
lamb stock (optional)	
medium potatoes, *peeled*	2 per person
organic barley	110g/4oz
parsley, *chopped*	large handful
sea salt and black pepper	

A great comforter of an easy, cheap dish to prepare and one that is even better if eaten the day after it has been cooked. Barley and potato provide serious ballast, but should not be introduced at the beginning of cooking time. The starch in them also serves to thicken the juices delectably.

→ String the CELERY STICKS with a potato peeler and chop them into small pieces. Peel the CARROTS and cut into 1cm/½in chunks. Throw the ONIONS, CELERY and CARROTS into a heavy-bottomed pot, then lay the pieces of LAMB on top of them. SEASON, cover with WATER OR LAMB STOCK and bring slowly to the boil. Put a sheet of greaseproof paper over the top, put the lid on and simmer at a gentle blip on top of the stove for the first hour to 1½ hours. If you prefer, you can put the stew in the oven at 150°C/300°F/Gas 2.

→ Remove the lid and tuck the POTATOES into the stew with the BARLEY. You may need a little more HOT STOCK OR WATER as the barley will swell. Bring back to the boil, then turn down the heat and continue to simmer for another hour or until the potatoes are cooked through when you test them with a skewer and the barley is tender. Serve immediately with a large handful of chopped PARSLEY on top, or cool.

→ If you've made the stew the day before you need it, chill overnight. Next day, remove the solid white fat, bring the meat back to room temperature and heat gently through to scalding hot before serving. Best served in wide soup bowls with plenty of juice ladled in with the stew. One of the great one-pot dishes.

Braised Mutton and Caper Sauce

SERVES 8

olive oil	2 tbsp
leg of mutton OR lamb	1.8–2kg/4–4½lb
brandy	1 large measure
garlic cloves	2–3 per person
dry white wine	300ml/10fl oz
thyme	3–4 sprigs
Caper Sauce	
unsalted butter	45g/1½oz
flour	45g/1½oz
cooking juices, wine and brandy and stock	600ml/1 pint
sea salt and black pepper	
organic egg yolk	1
double cream	4 tbsp
capers, *drained and rinsed*	1 heaped tbsp
flat-leaf parsley, *chopped*	1 tbsp

Traditionally, mutton was boiled and often served with boiled onions, as well as the caper sauce, and perhaps a turnip purée. I favour a winey braise, some whole baby steamed turnips and a piquant caper sauce.

→ Heat the OIL in a heavy-bottomed casserole and gently brown the MEAT all over. Add the BRANDY and set light to it with a taper. Wait until it has finished crackling and the flames have died down, then add the GARLIC and WINE. Strew the THYME on top of the joint, cover with greaseproof paper and a tight lid, and simmer very gently for 2–2½ hours. Serve with CAPER SAUCE.

Caper Sauce

→ Melt the BUTTER in with the WINEY JUICES when you have removed the meat to rest. Sprinkle in the FLOUR and allow it to turn biscuit-coloured and begin to cook, before adding ladles of HOT STOCK, whisking as you go, until the sauce has the texture of thin cream. Keep cooking and occasionally stirring for 15 minutes. Then SEASON, beat together the EGG YOLK and CREAM and whisk in off the heat. Put back on a low heat and whisk, but do not allow the sauce to bubble or boil at this stage. Throw in the CAPERS and PARSLEY, stir and serve.

Lamb Boulangère

SERVES 4

butter	
potatoes, *sliced*	675g/1½lb
salt and pepper	
large onions, *thinly sliced*	2
garlic cloves, *sliced*	3–4
meat or chicken stock (see pp. 54–55), *heated*	about 300ml/10fl oz
olive oil	1–2 tbsp
lamb chops	4 large or 8 small

This is really an upside-down Lancashire hotpot, a deliciously warming casserole.

→ Preheat the oven to 180°C/350°F/Gas 4. Butter a gratin or slightly deeper dish. Add a layer of POTATOES, SEASON them, then add a layer of sliced ONIONS and GARLIC, another layer of potatoes, and season again. Pour on the hot STOCK, cover with greaseproof paper and cook in the oven for 1 hour.
→ Heat the OIL in a frying pan and brown the CHOPS on both sides, then lay them on top of the potatoes. Cook for about another 20 minutes.
→ Serve with a root vegetable, preferably puréed to soak up the juice. Either a carrot and swede purée with butter and nutmeg, or a parsnip purée to which you have added a cooked and puréed eating apple (Cox's have the best flavour).

Lancashire Hot-Pot

SERVES 6

scrag OR best end of lamb neck chops	1.4kg/3lb
lamb's kidneys (optional), *membrane and suety fat removed*	6
large onions, *thinly sliced*	3
sea salt and black pepper	
potatoes, *peeled and thinly sliced into discs*	900g/2lb
sea salt and black pepper	
unsalted butter	about 55g/2oz

This is the English version of the French lamb boulangère and the Emerald Islanders' Irish stew. Even the name 'hot-pot' evokes cosiness. A bastion-against-the-cold kind of a dish with its meatily browned potatoes and meat falling from the bone. If you like kidneys, put some into the pot too. They give great depth of flavour and texture to the dish and its cooking liquor.

→ Preheat the oven to 200°C/400°F/Gas 6. Put a layer of CHOPS in the bottom of a large heavy casserole, followed by a layer of ONIONS, SEASONING both as you go. If you are using KIDNEYS, add them with the chops. Build up layers like this, ending with overlapping slices of POTATO on top. Pour in water to come halfway up the contents of the pot, then melt the BUTTER and brush it lavishly over the potatoes.

→ Cover the pot with greaseproof paper and a lid and put in the oven on the middle shelf. After 30 minutes reduce the temperature to 130°C/250°F/Gas ½ and cook for 2 hours. Remove the lid and greaseproof and cook for a final 30 minutes to brown the potatoes. Serve with something green like kale or cabbage.

Saffroned Lamb Stew

SERVES 6

cubed lamb	1kg/2¼lb
lamb's liver, *cut into large chunks*	285g/10oz
lamb's heart, *the fat removed, cut into strips*	1
bread	2 slices
garlic cloves	8
black peppercorns	12–15
saffron, *soaked in a little hot water*	1 generous pinch
thyme	1 bunch
dry sherry	55ml/2fl oz
dry white wine	55ml/2fl oz
sherry OR white wine vinegar	1 tbsp
olive oil, salt	

If you detest lamb's liver or heart, simply replace them with extra cubed lamb.

→ Preheat the oven to 180°C/350°F/Gas 4. Heat a few tablespoons of OLIVE OIL in a heavy casserole, and fry half the GARLIC cloves with the LAMB in batches over a high heat until browned on all sides. Reserve, and do the same with the OFFAL, then reserve it.

→ Tear the BREAD into chunks and fry in the oil with the rest of the GARLIC, finely chopped. Put it in the blender with the PEPPERCORNS, SAFFRON and SHERRY VINEGAR and blitz to a paste. Deglaze the pan with the DRY SHERRY and WINE, add to the blender, and blitz again.

→ Put the cubed meat back in the casserole with the HEART, GARLIC, THYME sprigs and sauce, cover with greaseproof paper and a lid, and cook gently on top of the cooker or in the oven for an hour. Throw in the LIVER, and cook for a further 15 minutes or so; do not let it get grainy.

→ Serve with organic long-grain rice you have cooked with a cinnamon stick, and accompany with a green salad.

Lamb and Apricot Pilav

SERVES 6

unsalted butter	110g/4oz
onion, *finely chopped*	1
cubed lamb shoulder, the fat trimmed a little	450g/1lb
sea salt and black pepper	
ground cinnamon	1 tsp
raisins	a handful
dried unsulphured apricots or Hunza apricots	110g/4oz
long-grain rice	450g/1lb

→ Melt half the BUTTER in a heavy-bottomed pot, then throw in the ONIONS and sauté them until golden and softened. Add the MEAT and brown on all sides before seasoning with SEA SALT, BLACK PEPPER and the CINNAMON. Stir to coat. Add the RAISINS and APRICOTS and coat with butter, then cover with water and bring to the boil. Cover and simmer gently for about an hour.

→ Melt the rest of the BUTTER in another pan, add the RICE, and stir to coat the grains. Pour the rice into the lamb pan and add enough water to the meat juices to cover. Bring to the boil, cover the pan and simmer for 20 minutes. I like to keep this dish more liquid than a conventional pilav.

Lamb Pilav

SERVES 6

olive oil	3–4 tbsp
or unsalted butter	75g/2½oz
large onion, *finely chopped*	1
cubed lamb, *trimmed, but not without fat*	450g/1lb
sea salt and black pepper	
ground cinnamon	1 tsp
tomato purée OR saffron stamens *soaked in hot water for 20 minutes*	3 tbsp / a good pinch
flat-leaf parsley, *chopped*	a handful
large tomatoes, *skinned, seeded and chopped*	2
red pepper, *seeded and sliced into long strips*	1
pine nuts, *toasted in a pan until they colour* (optional)	2 tbsp
raisins (optional)	a handful
long-grain rice, *washed and drained*	450g/1lb

Cubed lamb shoulder is best for this dish as it is slow-cooked so tenderises beautifully and exudes enough fat to flavour the other ingredients. It is also much cheaper than buying a lean cut of lamb. Use either the tomato purée or the saffron—one would cancel out the other, but both are good for colouring and flavouring the rice.

→ Heat the OIL OR BUTTER in a large, heavy-bottomed saucepan and sauté the ONION gently until golden and softened. Add the MEAT and brown it on all sides. SEASON and add the CINNAMON. Cover the pan and continue to cook gently for 10 minutes. Add the TOMATO PURÉE with a little water or the SAFFRON in its water and add more water to cover the meat. Sprinkle over the PARSLEY, throw in the TOMATOES, PEPPER, PINE NUTS and RAISINS and bring to the boil. Then turn down to a simmer and cook slowly for 1½ hours until the meat is tender and the liquid thickened and reduced.

→ Throw in the RICE and just under 600ml/1 pint of water to cover, bring to a rolling boil, cover and simmer gently for 20 minutes, when the rice should be tender. You may scatter over more PARSLEY before you serve.

Tangia

SERVES 6

saffron threads	a pinch
cumin seeds	1 tbsp
large preserved lemon, peel only	1
large onion, *roughly chopped*	1
garlic cloves, *peeled and roughly chopped*	8
olive oil	4 tbsp
fresh coriander, *chopped*	3 tbsp
large onion, *roughly chopped*	1
shoulder of lamb	1 × 2kg/4½lb
2lb or lamb shanks	6
unsalted butter	30g/1oz
sea salt and black pepper	

→ Preheat the oven to 230°C/450°F/Gas 8. Put the SAFFRON THREADS to soak in 6 tablespoons of hot water for 20 minutes. Roast the CUMIN SEEDS for 30 seconds in a small pan, then grind coarsely.

→ Put the cumin seeds in a food processor with the PRESERVED LEMON PEEL, ONION, GARLIC, OLIVE OIL and CORIANDER in the food processor and blitz. Put the LAMB into a heavy-bottomed enamel or earthenware pot and pour the paste over it, adding the SAFFRON and its water, the BUTTER and the SEASONING.

→ Cover the meat with a circle of greaseproof paper, cut to fit inside the pot, then some foil over the top of the pan and the lid pressed tightly down over it. Put the pot into the oven and immediately turn the heat down to 140°C/275°F/Gas 1. In the Aga, I start the pot off for 10 minutes in the roasting oven, then transfer it to the simmer oven. Cook for 5–6 hours—the meat should be beyond stringiness, just butter soft and tender. Serve with couscous.

Baked Kibbeh with Onion and Pine Nut Topping

SERVES 6

fine-ground bulgur	110g/4oz
medium onion, *quartered*	1
lean lamb	500g/1lb 2oz
salt	½ tsp
cinnamon	1 tsp
vegetable oil	2 tbsp
Topping	
onions, *sliced*	500g/1lb 2oz
extra virgin olive oil	3 tbsp
pine nuts	55g/2oz
salt and pepper	
cinnamon, *ground*	½ tsp
ground allspice	a pinch
pomegranate molasses	½–1 tbsp

This is a Lebanese dish which you could eat it as a main course or as part of a mixed mezze. Claudia Roden first came across it when she visited Zahle, the world capital of the Arab mezze.

→ Preheat the oven to 190°C/375°F/Gas 5. Rinse the BULGUR for the kibbeh in a fine sieve under cold running water and drain well. Purée the ONION in a food processor. Add the LAMB, SALT, PEPPER and CINNAMON and blend to a paste. Add the bulgur and blend to a smooth, soft paste. With your hand, press the paste in the bottom of an OILED, round, shallow baking dish, about 10cm/4in in diameter. Flatten the top and rub with the oil. With a pointed knife, cut into 6 wedges through the centre, and run the knife round the edges of the dish. Bake for about 30 minutes until browned.

→ For the topping, fry the ONION in OLIVE OIL until golden brown. Add the PINE NUTS and stir until lightly coloured. Add SALT and PEPPER, CINNAMON AND ALLSPICE and, if you like a slightly sweet and sour flavour, the POMEGRANATE MOLASSES. Cook for a minute or so. Serve the kibbeh hot or cold with the topping.

Curried Lamb Kebabs

MAKES 14 SKEWERFULS

cumin seeds	1 tbsp
fennel seeds	2 heaped tsp
coriander seeds	2 heaped tsp
red chilli, *seeded and finely chopped*	1
garlic cloves	3
salt and pepper	
Geeta's lime and chilli chutney	1 jar
large onions	2
lean leg of organic lamb, *cubed*	1.5kg/3¼lb
cherry tomatoes	4–5 dozen

→ Roast the CUMIN, FENNEL AND CORIANDER SEEDS together in a frying pan until they exude their characteristic toasty smell: a couple of minutes should do it. Throw them into a mortar and grind them into a coarse powder, then add the CHILLI, GARLIC, SALT and PEPPER, and grind them all down together.

→ Pour into a bowl with the LIME CHUTNEY, stir together, then mix thoroughly into the meat. Leave covered with clingfilm in the fridge to marinate for as long as you have.

→ Peel the ONIONS and cut them into chunks. Bring the LAMB to room temperature before you skewer it alternately with the ONIONS and TOMATOES. Barbecue according to your taste. The chunks of lime will crust delectably over the fire.

Galouti Kebabs

SERVES 4

cloves	2
cardamom pods	4
mace	½ a blade
cumin	1 tsp
cinnamon stick	1cm/½in
star anise	1
onion, *peeled and finely chopped*	1
ghee OR clarified butter	75g/2½oz
fresh ginger	1cm/½in piece
garlic cloves	4
mint leaves	6
fresh coriander	½ bunch
fresh pineapple juice	1 tbsp
saffron, *soaked in milk*	a few strands
salt and chilli powder to taste	
lean minced lamb	450g/1lb

→ Dry roast the WHOLE SPICES in a pan for a few seconds, then grind them in a coffee grinder or pestle and mortar. Sauté the onion until softened in a tablespoon of the GHEE. Put ALL THE INGREDIENTS except the lamb mince and the remaining ghee in a food processor, and blitz to a paste. Spread the LAMB out on a flat tray, and pour over the paste of spices. Lightly mix them together with a spoon, then leave covered in the fridge for 4–6 hours to soften.

→ Keeping your hands dampened, shape the meat into patties, each about 6cm/2½in in diameter. Heat some GHEE in a heavy-bottomed pan or on a griddle, then cook the patties for a couple of minutes or so a side, until cooked through, with a slightly blackened crust. Serve with some cucumber you have peeled into ribbons, grated carrot and a spritz of lime juice.

→ To make clarified butter, melt the butter in a small pan, then drain off the yellow part, leaving the white solids at the bottom of the pan.

Moussaka

SERVES 6

aubergines, *sliced* 1cm/½in thick	3
olive oil	
onions, *chopped*	2
garlic cloves, *chopped*	2
lamb mince	675g/1½lb
sea salt and black pepper	
cinnamon	1 tsp
tomato, *skinned, seeded,* and *chopped*	1
tomato concentrate	2–3 tbsp
flat-leaf parsley, *chopped*	1 bunch
dry white wine	a few tbsp
béchamel sauce *made with 600ml/1 pint milk* (see p. 402)	
Parmesan cheese, *freshly grated* (optional)	

This is inexpensive to make, great for a party, served with just a good green salad and a bowl of tzatziki (see p. 20), and if you roast the aubergines in the oven, there will be no lingering frying smells and oozy, oily aubergines. They do tend to absorb tankersful of oil if you fry them in a pan. You may use courgettes or half courgettes and half aubergines if you feel like it.

→ Preheat the oven to 180°C/350°F/Gas 4. Brush the AUBERGINES with OLIVE OIL on both sides, put them on a baking tray in a single layer and roast in the oven. Cook in batches or on two trays if you have them. They are ready when you can prick them with a fork and they are soft right the way through. Don't let them brown too much. They should take 10–20 minutes.

→ Meanwhile, heat 2 tablespoons of OIL in a heavy-bottomed frying pan and sauté the ONIONS until softened and pale gold. Add the GARLIC, sauté for a few minutes, then add the MINCE and fry until it is well-browned and has completely lost its raw look, about 5–10 minutes. Season and flavour with CINNAMON before adding the chopped TOMATO, TOMATO CONCENTRATE and chopped PARSLEY. Stir well, add the white WINE and simmer for 15 minutes. The meat will be cooked and will have absorbed most of the wine.

→ While the meat is simmering, make the BÉCHAMEL SAUCE (see p. 402). Make sure you add a suspicion of NUTMEG. Put alternate layers of aubergine and meat sauce in a deep baking dish or roasting tin, starting and ending with a layer of aubergines. Pour a thick layer of béchamel over the top; you may have some left over. Bake the dish in the oven for about 45 minutes or until it has browned beautifully on top and the meat and aubergine layers have married together. Sprinkle PARMESAN over the top of the béchamel before you bake it if you want a richer dish. Serve piping hot straight from the baking dish.

Moroccan Couscous

SERVES 6–8

stewing lamb like scrag, on the bone	1kg/2¼lb
medium onions, *chopped*	2
chickpeas, *soaked in cold water overnight*	55g/2oz
turnips, *quartered*	2
large carrots, *cut into slices about as thick as a £1 coin*	2
olive oil	2–3 tbsp
sea salt and black pepper	
ground ginger	½ tsp
saffron stamens, *soaked in a little warm water for 20 minutes*	1 pinch
couscous	450g/1lb
light olive oil OR vegetable oil	4 tbsp
raisins, *soaked in warm water for 20 minutes*	1 handful
smallish courgettes, *sliced*	4
frozen or fresh broad beans OR green beans *strung and cut in half*	
fresh or frozen peas instead of OR as well as the broad or green beans	110g/4oz
tomatoes, *skinned seeded and quartered*	4
flat-leaf parsley OR half parsley, half coriander	1 bunch
cayenne and paprika OR a home-made harissa (see p. 411)	a little
unsalted butter	55g/2oz

This is a basic couscous to which you may add or subtract seasonal vegetables, or omit the meat altogether. Cheap, delicious, spiced-up and nourishing.

→ Put the LAMB in a heavy-bottomed casserole with the ONIONS, CHICKPEAS, TURNIPS and CARROTS and cover with cold water. Pour over the OIL and season with the SALT, PEPPER, GINGER and SAFFRON. Bring slowly to the boil, then simmer gently for an hour and a half with the lid on.

→ Ten minutes before the end of cooking time, cover the COUSCOUS with 600ml/1 pint of warm water and a little SALT and allow it to swell and soften for 10 minutes or so. Then add the light OLIVE OIL and work the grain with your fingers to let air into it and rid it of lumps. Add the RAISINS and OTHER VEGETABLES to the stew with the TOMATOES and PARSLEY. Put the couscous into a piece of muslin, tie it loosely and place it in a steamer or a large sieve over the stew. Simmer the stew for 30 minutes.

→ Remove a ladleful of the broth into a bowl and stir in CAYENNE and PAPRIKA to taste, a scant half teaspoon of cayenne for mild heat, a teaspoon for something more intense, and hand it round for people to ladle over their couscous on the plate. Or hand round a bowl of HARISSA instead. In both cases, mound the couscous up high on a large, warmed dish; earthenware is best. Add the BUTTER and fork it into the grain, then arrange the meat and vegetables decoratively on top and pour some broth (without the spices) over it.

Noisettes of Lamb in Vine Leaves and Filo Pastry

SERVES 4

lamb noisettes, 2.5cm/1in thick	8
filo pastry	4 sheets
butter, *melted*	
garlic cloves, *finely chopped*	3
oregano OR marjoram	1 tsp
sea salt	
large vine leaves, *soaked as instructions on the jar*	8
egg white	1
lemon	1
Marinade	
olive oil	6 tbsp
lemon juice	2 tbsp
red wine	120ml/4fl oz
black pepper	

A gorgeous and unusual Greek dish, which you can serve with a chicory and watercress salad, pepped up with some coriander and a good, nutty dressing.

→ Put all the MARINADE ingredients into a bowl and throw in the LAMB NOISETTES, leaving them to absorb everything for an hour. Then drain them and pat them dry with kitchen paper.

→ Preheat the oven to 220°C/425°F/Gas 7. Trim the noisettes of their fat, leaving the 'eye' of lean meat. Cut the sheets of FILO in half lengthwise and brush them with melted BUTTER. Season the lamb noisettes with SEA SALT, sprinkle with a little GARLIC and OREGANO and wrap each one in a VINE LEAF. Place a piece of lamb at the narrow end of a filo strip, flip over the sides and roll up the parcel. Seal each end with a dab of EGG WHITE on your pastry brush. Make the rest of the parcels this way and brush each one with melted BUTTER.

→ Place the parcels on a preheated baking sheet you've whacked in the oven and cook for 10 minutes for pink lamb. Alternatively, deep-fry the parcels in hot OIL for 4–5 minutes until golden. Serve with quarters of lemon and salad.

Lamb Steaks with Green Peppercorns

SERVES 2

lamb steaks	2
green peppercorns	30g/1oz
parsley, *chopped*	1 tbsp
home-made English mustard	2 tsp
egg white	1
breadcrumbs	30g/1oz

Green peppercorn sauce had its short-lived day in the 1980s, so it must be due for a comeback. This combines the muskiness of the crushed spice with heat from the mustard and a souffléed top. It was inspired by a long-forgotten dish by the French chef Roger Vergé.

→ Take the LAMB out of the fridge an hour before you want to use it. Cook on a griddle or barbecue until browned, about 2 minutes a side. Keep any juices from the meat. While the meat is cooking, crush the GREEN PEPPERCORNS finely (leave some texture) and stir in the PARSLEY and MUSTARD. Whisk the EGG WHITE until stiff, then fold it into the peppercorn mixture.

→ Heat the grill. Spread the mixture thickly over the two steaks on the uppermost side, sprinkle with BREADCRUMBS, pour over the fatty cooking juices and grill for 3-4 minutes until golden brown. Serve immediately with new potatoes and green beans.

Lamb Steaks with Sauce Paloise

Serves 6

olive oil	
thyme, rosemary, *chopped*	
garlic, *minced*	
lamb steaks	6
Sauce Paloise	
white wine vinegar	2 tbsp
mint, *finely chopped*	3 tbsp
shallots, *finely minced*	30g/1oz
peppercorns, *crushed in a mortar*	10
organic egg yolks	4
cold water	3 tbsp
unsalted butter, *clarified*	225g/8oz
sea salt and black pepper	
lemon	juice of ½

These need to be cut as thickly as a rump steak. Rub olive oil, thyme, rosemary and minced garlic into the flesh and griddle until cooked as you like—rare, medium rare, medium or well done. Sauce Paloise is the ultimate sauce for lamb, particularly if you've barbecued the meat and want the simple, unctuous tones of butter and mint to accompany lamb and charcoal.

→ Lamb of this quality and cut doesn't need marinating before you barbecue it, neither do you want to mask its intense flavour and sweetness with barbecue sauce. Add the HERBS AND GARLIC to the OIL a few hours in advance so the flavours are released into the olive oil. Take the MEAT out of the fridge an hour before you want to use it. When you're ready to cook, rub in the herbed oil.

→ If you like rare lamb, cook the meat for 2 minutes a side, then rest it for 6 minutes; if you like it medium rare, cook for 2.5 minutes a side and rest for 5 minutes; medium: 3 minutes a side and rest for 4 minutes; well done: 5 minutes a side and no resting time.

Sauce Paloise

→ Put the VINEGAR, 2 tablespoons of the MINT, the SHALLOT and crushed PEPPERCORNS in a small, heavy-bottomed saucepan and reduce gently by a half. Let it cool, add the EGG YOLKS and COLD WATER, and set the pan over a low heat, whisking continuously. Alternatively, make this stage of the sauce in a double boiler over gently simmering water (the pan must not touch the water beneath it). The sauce will gradually begin to emulsify (allow up to 10 minutes). Do not allow it to come to the boil.

→ Remove from the heat and whisk in the BUTTER a little at a time. SEASON, then sieve the sauce and stir in the remaining tablespoon of chopped MINT. Squeeze in the LEMON JUICE to taste. Serve immediately.

Lamb's Liver with Melting Onions

SERVES 2

large onions	3
olive oil	2 tbsp
unsalted butter	55g/2oz
salt	
red wine vinegar	2 tbsp
sugar	1 tsp
marjoram OR oregano (optional)	1 sprig
lamb's liver, *thinly and evenly sliced*	340g/12oz, or 2 decent slices per person

→ Peel and slice the ONIONS into thin moons and then again into half moons and cook them slowly and gently in the OLIVE OIL and half the BUTTER. A little SALT sprinkled over them when you put them into the pan hastens the juices beginning to run. Do not cover the onions, just stir them from time to time to stop them sticking while you let them soften and turn gold for 30 minutes or so. Add the VINEGAR and SUGAR with the stripped sprig of HERBS halfway through cooking and let the vinegar bubble and reduce at a higher heat for a couple of minutes before slowing down the cooking again. Or just add the vinegar to the pan juices once you have removed the liver at the end of its cooking time and scrape all the crusty bits in as you stir over a high heat for a couple of minutes.

→ When the onions are cooked, scoop them to the sides of the pan and melt the rest of the BUTTER. Add the LIVER when the butter is sizzling and cook for 1–2 minutes a side. A knife cut will ensure the middle is really rosy but not raw. Don't wait to poke or you'll be too late. Put a couple of slices of liver on a pile of onions on a warmed plate and consume with much mash!

Chaa Meat

SERVES 5

salt	1 tsp
paste *made with crushed garlic and grated root ginger*	1 tsp
ricotta cheese	85g/3oz
bay leaves	2
shoulder of lamb, *cubed*	1kg/2¼lb
mustard oil	120ml/4fl oz
onions, sliced	85g/3oz
green chilli, *chopped*	1 tsp
coriander seeds, *crushed*	½ tsp
turmeric, cumin and coriander	
gram (chickpea) flour	85g/3oz
whisked yoghurt	500g/1lb 2oz
coriander leaves, *chopped*	

→ Mix the SALT, GARLIC-GINGER PASTE, RICOTTA and BAY LEAVES to make the marinade. Add the cubes of LAMB and leave for at least an hour.

→ When the lamb has marinated, put it in a heavy-bottomed pot, cover it with water and bring it slowly to the boil. Simmer it at a blip until tender, 1– 1½ hours.

→ Heat the MUSTARD OIL, add the sliced ONIONS and chopped CHILLI and sauté. Add the CORIANDER SEEDS and the meat and cook for a few minutes. Then add a pinch each of ground TURMERIC, CUMIN AND CORIANDER, season and simmer. Add the GRAM FLOUR and cook briefly, then blend in the YOGHURT and continue cooking over a slow flame until the gravy is thick. Serve piping hot sprinkled with chopped CORIANDER LEAVES.

Cassoulet de Toulouse

SERVES UP TO 12

Preserved duck

duck legs	6
Maldon salt	1 box
pepper	
cloves of garlic, *peeled*, bay leaves and sprigs of thyme	a few
duck or goose fat	225g/8oz
dry white wine	

Beans

long white haricot beans OR cannellini beans	900g/2lb
salted pig's trotters OR salt pork if you can't cope with trotters	2 / 450g/1lb
pork rind, *cut in squares*	225g/8oz
onions, *peeled, and each stuck with a clove*	3
garlic clove	1
celery with the leaves, *peeled*	3 sticks
carrots	2
the white of a fat leek	
fresh herbs (bay, thyme, rosemary and parsley) *tied together*	1 bouquet

Pork and lamb

shoulder of mutton OR mature lamb	450g/1lb or more
boned loin of pork	450g/1lb
onion	1
Toulouse sausage, or any other coarse-cut pure pork sausage	450g/1lb
garlicky boiling sausage	450g/1lb
tomatoes	6
dry white wine	

This recipe includes preserved duck. You could just roast a duck and then joint it, but this is the classic method for preserved duck or goose. You will need to leave the duck legs in the brine for 36 hours, so plan accordingly. The beans need to be soaked overnight in plenty of water.

→ Begin with the DUCK. Shake a layer of SALT on to a plate, pepper the duck legs, then place them on the salt with the GARLIC and HERBS and cover with the rest of the salt. Cover with clingfilm and refrigerate for 36 hours.

→ Remove the duck from the brine and place in a casserole with the DUCK FAT, a glass of white WINE and one of water. Cover with a layer of greaseproof and a lid and cook gently, at 150°C/300°F/Gas 2 for 2½–3 hours. Leave to cool in the fat.

→ Drain the soaked BEANS. Put them in a large casserole with enough water to just cover, bring to the boil, cover, remove from the heat and leave for 40 minutes or so. This helps make them more digestible. Drain and cover them again with the same amount of cold water. Meanwhile, bring the TROTTERS to the boil in plenty of water and drain immediately. Add them to the beans along with the PORK RIND, ONIONS, GARLIC, CELERY, CARROTS, LEEK and bouquet of HERBS. Bring to the boil, skim, then cover and cook for 2 hours.

→ Meanwhile, roast the LAMB and PORK on a sliced ONION in a roasting tin for 1½ hours in a slow oven, adding the TOULOUSE and GARLIC SAUSAGES, whole TOMATOES and a glass of dry white WINE for the last 20 minutes. Remove from the oven.

→ Cut the meats and sausages into hearty chunks, similarly the trotters if you have used them. Remove the duck legs from their fat and brown them on a roasting tray in the hot oven for 10 minutes. Cool slightly before halving each leg at the joint. Remove the vegetables and the bouquet from the beans and discard.

→ Add the meats, rind, sausage and duck legs to the beans and the sticky tomato juices, without the onions, from the roasting tin. Make sure the meats are in the middle of the dish and the beans on top, before sprinkling some of the BREADCRUMBS and PARSLEY over.

Crust

breadcrumbs	225g/8oz
flat-leaf parsley, *chopped*	1 large handful

→ You can add a little of the duck fat over the crumbs if you like, then return the casserole to the slow oven for a further hour or longer. Serve as is, or break the crust and push it in. Pour in a little water if the cassoulet is drying out, add a second crust and return to the oven until it is golden before serving.

Chickpea and Chorizo Stew

SERVES 6

chickpeas	400g/14oz
chicken OR vegetable stock (see pp. 54–55)	750ml/1¼ pints
organic tomato passata	300ml/10fl oz
good-quality fat spicy chorizo, *cut into hunks*	560g/1¼lb or so
medium onions, *chopped*	2
garlic cloves, *finely chopped*	3–4
olive oil	
Navarrico wood-roasted piquillo peppers from Brindisa OR grill and skin ordinary red peppers	225g/8oz jar
smoked paprika	1 heaped tsp

→ Soak the CHICKPEAS overnight. Next day, drain, rinse and cook in the STOCK and PASSATA until tender.

→ Fry the ONIONS gently in a good glug of OLIVE OIL in a heavy-bottomed casserole until softened and translucent, then throw in the hunks of CHORIZO. Cook for about 10 minutes, turning them as you go. Once they exude some fat, add the GARLIC, then add the chickpeas and their liquor to the pot. Cut the PEPPERS into strips and add them with the PAPRIKA, simmer for another 10 minutes, ladle into bowls and serve. Just as great the second day.

Boiled Bacon and Cabbage

SERVES 8

unsmoked collar of bacon, *without the rind*	1.8–2.2kg/4–5lb
a selection of vegetables, *chopped* (for example, 3 onions, 6 carrots, 2 leeks, 3–4 sticks of celery)	
bunch of fresh herbs, *tied in a bundle*	
chicken stock (see p. 54) OR water	1.5–2.5 litres/3–4 pints
large green cabbage, *chopped and cored*	1

This is THE dish if I want to think of summers in the west of Ireland. It's the one I come home to each summer when I've made the trek across land and inhospitable sea and alighted on the doorstep of my marvellous neighbour Mary Gallagher in Mayo. Somehow, the 13-hour journey is made bearable in the knowledge that we're getting ever closer to this inimitable Irish dinner, the country's best known and best loved.

→ Soak the BACON in cold water for 24 hours, changing the water several times. Put the soaked bacon in a large casserole with the VEGETABLES, HERBS and STOCK OR WATER. Bring just to the boil, skim, turn the heat down and keep it simmering at a mere bubble, with the lid on, for about 30 minutes.

→ Add the CABBAGE and continue to simmer for a further 1 hour. This sounds like a long time, but you are not looking for a crisply al dente result; quite the reverse. The slow cooking will soften the cabbage completely. Turn off the heat and allow the meat to 'settle' for 20 minutes, then remove it from the pot, transfer it to a carving board and keep it hot for a further 10 minutes under a tight layer of foil and a cloth.

→ Using a slotted spoon, lift out the cabbage and discard as much as you can of the other vegetables. Lay a bed of cabbage on each plate, put a couple of thick slices of bacon on top, and serve the cooking liquor in a jug. All you need now is good mustard and some champ (see p. 395) to soak up the juices.

Gammon with Parsley Sauce

SERVES 6

boneless tied piece of gammon	900g/2lb
carrots, *chopped*	3
celery sticks, *chopped*	2
onions, *peeled chopped*	2
bay leaves	2
bouquet of fresh thyme and parsley *with their stalks tied together*	
bruised peppercorns	12

→ Put the GAMMON in a large, heavy-bottomed pot and cover with cold water before bringing it just to the boil and draining it. Put the gammon back in the pan and add the VEGETABLES, 2 BAY LEAVES, the bouquet of HERBS and the PEPPERCORNS. Cover with cold water. Bring up to simmering and cook at this point for 1½ hours with the lid on. Have a look every so often to make sure that the water is murmuring, not bubbling. Check that the gammon is cooked by piercing a skewer right down deep into the gammon—it should be tender right through.

→ Start the sauce about 40 minutes in advance of this by putting the MILK in a small pan with the ONION stuck with cloves and a BAY LEAF. Bring to the boil, then simmer gently for a few minutes. Season with SALT, PEPPER and NUTMEG and put the lid on to let the milk draw the flavours into it. Melt the

Parsley Sauce

milk	600ml/1 pint
small onion *stuck with 2 cloves*	1
bay leaf	1
sea salt, black pepper and nutmeg	
unsalted butter	55g/2oz
flour	55g/2oz
cooking liquor from the gammon	150–300ml/ 5–10fl oz
curly or flat-leaf parsley, *chopped*	1 large bunch

BUTTER and add the FLOUR to make a roux, then make a béchamel in the normal way (see p. 402). Add as much cooking liquor to the milk as you need to get a silky sauce that is about the texture of double cream. Adjust the SEASONING, take off the heat and stir in the PARSLEY, which should not lose its rawness, but look like emerald flecks.

→ Slice the gammon thickly, add a little of the poaching liquid to each plate and pass round the parsley sauce. Mash is a must and butter beans or split peas—anything leguminous really. There's something about gammon and pulses!

Deborah's Baked Gammon

carrots	3
celery sticks	3
leek	1
onion	1
cooking apple	1
parsley	small bunch
thyme	small bunch
bay leaves	2
cloves	about 10
black peppercorns	1 tbsp
star anise	2
unsmoked gammon joint	1 × 1.8kg/4lb
pomegranate molasses (optional)	1 tbsp
Parsley sauce (see previous recipe)	

This recipe from my cousin Deborah can be used for a piece of gammon of any size. Just adjust the cooking times. It is great to eat cold and the remains can be used in risotto, chicken and ham pie, soup and so on.

→ Preheat the oven to 170°C/325°F/Gas 3. Line a roasting tin with two lengths of foil, one lengthwise and the other across the tin. Roughly chop the VEGETABLES and APPLE and lay them on the foil. Add the HERBS and scatter the SPICES and herbs across this mixture.

→ Place the GAMMON JOINT on top and add the POMEGRANATE MOLASSES if used. Loosely seal the foil all round the joint—the air needs to circulate and the juices stay sealed in. Bake in the oven for 65 minutes per kilo/2¼lb plus 30 minutes. Fold back the foil for the last 30 minutes of cooking. When the gammon is cooked, rest for 15 minutes in a warm place. Carefully strain off the cooking juices to use in the parsley sauce (see the recipe for Gammon with Parsley Sauce).

Sausage and Mash

olive oil	
top-quality sausages	2–3 per person
butter	
medium-to-large onion, *thinly sliced into rings*	1 per person
sea salt	
molasses sugar	1 tsp
red wine, Madeira OR Marsala	1 glass
chicken stock (see p. 54) OR leftover gravy	300ml/10fl oz
Worcestershire sauce	1 dash
seeded mustard	1 tsp
black pepper	

Don't be seduced by a cheap, commercial sausage laden with nitrites and preservatives and rusk and salt. For very little more money you can grab yourself a good, porky banger that's never even seen a filler, so will be all the meatier and more filling.

→ Preheat the oven to 180°C/350°F/Gas 4. Heat a little OLIVE OIL in a large gratin dish, then add the SAUSAGES and turn gently (don't break the skins) over a low heat for a few minutes. Remove the sausages to a plate. Add a lump of BUTTER and a slug of OLIVE OIL to the gratin dish and add the sliced ONION, coating well. Sprinkle with SEA SALT so that the onions release their juice and cook down gently for five minutes before adding the MOLASSES SUGAR and stirring in well.

→ Next pour in the WINE, allowing it to bubble away with the onions for a few minutes. If you have some GRAVY left over from a roast, you may add up to 300ml/10fl oz. If not, add the same quantity of CHICKEN STOCK and a slug of WORCESTERSHIRE SAUCE to brown it.

→ Cook gently for a further 20 minutes before dunking the sausages in the gravy, adding the MUSTARD and a good scrunch of BLACK PEPPER. Cook in the oven for about 30 minutes, turning the sausages every 10 minutes, or cook gently in the pan on top of the stove. Some claim that sausages cooked in the oven dry out, but with the onions and their buttery juices in this recipe, it can't happen. Serve with mash (see p. 394).

Toad in the Hole

SERVES 4

lard	2 tbsp
best pure pork sausages	2 per person
grain OR honeycup mustard	

Batter

plain organic flour	225g/8oz
sea salt	1 pinch
large organic eggs	2
milk	600ml/1 pint
enough hot dripping from the beef to cover the floor of the roasting tin	

→ To make the batter, sift the FLOUR and SALT into a large bowl. Make a well in the centre with a wooden spoon and break the EGGS into it. Add a little of the MILK and whisk with a balloon whisk, gradually drawing down the flour from the sides of the bowl and adding more milk when the mixture becomes too thick to work. You should finally have a stiff batter which you should then whisk for as long as your arm will hold out for, up to 5 minutes. Add the remaining milk, whisk it in and leave to stand.

→ Preheat the oven to 220°C/425°F/Gas 7. Heat half the LARD in a frying pan and cook the SAUSAGES briefly all over, 5 minutes will do it. Pour the hot fat into the roasting tin and add the rest of it. Put the tin in the oven for up to 5 minutes or until the fat starts smoking. Meanwhile, roll the sausages in enough GRAIN OR HONEYCUP MUSTARD to coat them. Pour the batter into the smoking fat and place the sausages at intervals across the tin. Bake for 30–35 minutes or until the batter has puffed right up and browned.

→ Serve hot straight from the tin with a couple of green vegetables and some buttery boiled potatoes.

Sausage and Apple Pie

SERVES 4

puff pastry (see p. 517)	450g/1lb
best organic pork sausage meat	450g/1lb
fresh sage leaves, chopped	2 tbsp
large eating apples, peeled and thinly sliced	2
sea salt, black pepper and nutmeg	
beaten egg for glaze	1

→ Preheat the oven to 220°C/425°F/Gas 7. Roll out half the PASTRY and use it to line a 23cm/9in pie dish. Place a layer of half the SAUSAGE MEAT mixed with the chopped SAGE over the pastry base. Cover with the thinly sliced APPLES. Season well, then top with the rest of the sausage meat mixture. Roll out the rest of the pastry and cover the pie, brushing the edges of the base with the BEATEN EGG before sticking and crimping the crust to them. Cut a cross through the centre of the pastry so the steam can escape while cooking. Put the pie in the fridge for half an hour.

→ Brush the pie with beaten egg and put it in the oven on a heated baking tray for 15 minutes. Turn the heat down to 180°C/350°F/Gas 4 and cook for a further 30–40 minutes until puffed up and golden. Use the point of a skewer to make sure the apple is cooked through. Leave to cool for 10 minutes before serving.

How to Cook a Ham

joint of ham	
cider (optional)	
onion, carrot, celery, *chopped*	
bouquet of parsley, bay leaves and thyme, *tied together*	

Ham glaze

French OR grain mustard OR Colman's mustard powder	1 tbsp
dark muscovado OR molasses sugar	1 tbsp
strong runny honey like chestnut	1 tbsp
marmalade OR redcurrant jelly	1 tbsp
organic orange	zest of 1
double cream	1 tbsp
cloves to stud OR ground cloves	1 tsp
black peppercorns, *coarsely cracked in a mortar*	1 tbsp
crushed juniper berries (optional)	1 tsp
orange, *thinly sliced* (optional)	1

Calculate the cooking time in the following way. Up to 2kg/4½lb in weight, 30 minutes to the pound and an extra 15–30 minutes depending on the cut. From 2–4.8kg/4½–10lb: 20 minutes per pound plus an extra 20 minutes. If you are cooking a really large ham, the times are roughly as follows: for a 5.5kg/12lb ham, 3½ hours; for a 7kg/16lb ham, 4 hours; 8.7kg/20lb, 4½ hours; 11kg/24lb, 5 hours.

→ Put the HAM into a huge pan or kettle, cover it with cold water and bring it to the boil. When it has simmered for 5 minutes, taste the water for saltiness; if it is too salty, throw it away. I do this anyway, adding dry local CIDER at this stage, but if you are happy with the water, just add the VEGETABLES and BOUQUET GARNI you would to a stock pot at this stage and calculate your cooking once you've got them all going together. Ham stock with little pink shards of meat, with or without cider, is wonderful for lentil, split pea or pea soup (with frozen peas at this time of year).

→ I tend not to serve my ham hot. If you want to, remove the skin with a long, sharp-bladed knife when the ham is cooked and serve it with an onion or apple and onion sauce or with a mustardy gravy made with some of the stock, some Madeira or Marsala, a little grain mustard and some cream.

→ I prefer a glazed ham for serving cold. Take the ham out of its cooking liquor about 30 minutes before it is fully cooked, remove the skin and carve a diamond pattern with a sharp knife point into, but not right through the fat. Preheat the oven to 190°C/375°F/Gas 5. Mix the GLAZE INGREDIENTS together and spoon and press them onto the fat and into the channels you have cut into it. You may stud the diamonds with WHOLE CLOVES the old-fashioned way if you like or just use GROUND CLOVES in your glaze. Or add some slices of ORANGE, spearing them with cloves so they stick to the ham fat.

→ Glaze the ham in the oven until the glaze has bubbled up and made molten crust on the fat. You may have to keep spooning the brown goo back onto the fat as it does tend to slide off. When the glaze has welded itself to the ham, remove the beast from the tin and leave to cool. Serve with Cumberland sauce (see p. 407).

Roast Leg, Loin or Shoulder of Pork

SERVES 6–8

leg OR shoulder of pork OR a chined loin	2–2.5kg/ 4½–5½lb
sea salt	
black pepper	
olive oil	
onion, *peeled and sliced*	1
Cox's apples	1 per person

A 2–2.5kg/4½–5½lb leg or shoulder will feed 6–8. A chined loin will weigh less and feed 4–6 people. It is also spectacularly easy to carve as the meat cuts down into thick chops. A smaller joint is not really worth cooking—it will shrink and be impossible to carve—so even if there are only two of you, buy a decent-sized joint and enjoy the leftovers whichever way you wish. Make sure the fat has been properly scored. If not, your butcher will do it with a Stanley knife. This is the only way of making sure of tooth-threatening crackling. Serve with apple sauce (see p. 408).

→ If you remember, season the MEAT with SEA SALT and BLACK PEPPER the night before you're going to cook it. When you've brought it up to room temperature on the day, rub the crackling with a little OLIVE OIL with your fingers and sprinkle SEA SALT all over it.

→ Preheat the oven to 220°C/425°F/Gas 7. Place the JOINT on the peeled, sliced ONION in a roasting tin, and after 30 minutes turn the heat down to 170°C/325°F/Gas 3. Calculate the overall cooking time of the joint at 1 hour and 10 minutes per kg/35 minutes per lb. About 40–50 minutes before the end of cooking time, score the skin of the APPLES around their circumference with a knife blade and core them with a corer. Roll them in the fatty meat juices and cook them standing up in the roasting tin until tender when pierced to their middles.

→ If the crackling hasn't achieved the heights of crackle that you would wish for at the end of the cooking time, remove it with a long, thin-bladed knife all in one piece and place it under a hot grill. Keep an eye on it so that it doesn't burn. Alternatively, turn the oven temperature back up to its original, remove the apples if you are baking them, and place the roasting tin with the joint in it at the top of the oven for a further 10–15 minutes. Remove the joint in the normal way and allow it to rest for 15 minutes while you make the gravy and finish off the vegetables. This is not, however, a joint to cover. The crackling will sog with the condensation if you do, so just keep the meat warm somewhere. You may add cider, Calvados or Kingston Black to the cooking juices for your gravy. Just burn off the alcohol by bubbling it hard for 3–4 minutes before you add the vegetable water.

Pork Crumble

SERVES 4

belly pork, *boned*	675g/1½lb
seasoned flour	55g/2oz
lard OR butter	30g/1oz
potatoes, *peeled and sliced*	450g/1lb
onions, *thinly sliced*	225g/8oz
best dry cider	285ml/10fl oz
brown OR white breadcrumbs from a stale loaf	½ cup
strong Cheddar, *grated*	55g/2oz
pinch of cayenne pepper	
thyme leaves, *stripped from the stem*	1 tsp
sea salt and black pepper	

Upper crust, though not in the conventional sense. Crumb rather than crust, but nothing poor man's about this, particularly if you use a good, fruity-strong, aged Cheddar like Montgomery, some oily-scented thyme and a dusky hot hit of cayenne.

→ Preheat the oven to 180°C/350°F/Gas 4. Cut the PORK into cubes and throw into a ziploc bag with the SEASONED FLOUR and toss together. Shake off the excess flour and fry the pork on all sides in LARD OR BUTTER for a few minutes, until golden. Scrape the meat into the dish with the POTATOES and ONIONS. Add the hot CIDER and SEASONING, cover and bake for an hour.
→ Mix the BREADCRUMBS, CHEESE, CAYENNE and THYME together with your fingers, sprinkle over the surface of the meat and put the dish back in the oven, uncovered. Bake for another 30 minutes, or until the top is gratinéed to a gorgeous golden brown.

Shoulder of Pork Braised with Bay, Milk and Potatoes

SERVES 6

shoulder of pork	1.6 kg/3½lb
large onion, *sliced thinly*	1
bay	1 branch, with 10–12 leaves
potatoes, *peeled and sliced into thin discs*	900g/2lb
creamy milk	600–900ml/ 1–1½ pints
salt and pepper	

→ Preheat the oven to 220°C/425°F/Gas 7. Lay the sliced ONION on the bottom of a roasting tin, put the JOINT on top of it, and scatter a good sprinkling of coarse SEA SALT over the scored fat. Roast in the oven for an hour.
→ Heat the MILK, remove the roasting tin from the oven, and strew the BAY LEAVES on the base of it. Arrange the POTATOES in layers around the meat, seasoning as you go, then pour on milk just to cover. Return to the oven; check after 30 minutes that the potatoes aren't drying out. Replenish with milk if you need to. Fifteen minutes later, pierce the potatoes with a skewer, and if they are soft right through to the bottom, all is ready. Let the meat stand for 10 minutes before carving, keeping the potatoes warm while you do.

Pork en Papillote with Prunes and Cream and Armagnac

SERVES 4

thick pieces of organic pork fillet	4 × 170g/6oz
Agen prunes, *soaked in tea or apple juice for a few hours*	16
olive oil	2 tbsp
unsalted butter	45g/1½oz
Armagnac OR cognac	1 glass
sea salt and black pepper	
double cream	150ml/5fl oz or so

Cooking en papillote is a wonderful way of sealing in all the flavours and juices of meat, fish or vegetables. You need good, thick fillets of organic, free-range pork for this dish, and as fillet isn't intrinsically a fatty cut, the tight parcel prevents the meat from drying out. Anyway, prunes and pork are a classic combination, as are prunes and Armagnac. With the slick of cream to lubricate, this is a lovely, easy recipe that's full of depth and flavour.

→ Preheat the oven to 180°C/350°F/Gas 4. Remove any sinewy bits from the MEAT and trim off any thin edges which would over-cook. Remove the PRUNES from their soaking liquor.

→ Heat the OLIVE OIL and BUTTER until it begins to foam, then put the pork fillets in the pan and sear them on all sides until they have browned. Remove the meat from the pan to a plate and slosh in the ARMAGNAC. Light it with a taper and let the alcohol burn off. Add the CREAM and stir until the mixture coheres.

→ Cut 4 oblongs of foil, which will contain the fillets in baggy but tightly sealed parcels. Put the fillets on the four sheets and SEASON, then pull the sides of the foil up so that the liquid won't flow away when you add it. Put 4 prunes on each fillet and pour the sauce over them equally. Scrunch the parcels so that each edge of each one is tightly sealed and put them on a baking tray. Put in the oven for 30 minutes or until the pork is cooked right through and tender. To check, open up a parcel and test the fillet with a skewer—the juices should not run bloody. If the juices look quite thin when the pork is ready, pour them from each parcel into a pan and reduce them by boiling hard, perhaps adding a little more CREAM. Check the SEASONING and return the sauce to each parcel.

→ Seal back up to serve so that everyone opens their own parcel at the table. Serve with mashed potatoes and something a little bitter, perhaps braised endives.

Pork Fillet en Papillote with Dijon Mustard, Fennel and Black Olives

SERVES 6–7

pork fillet	1kg/2¼lb
fennel bulbs, with frondy bits	2
red onions	2
celery sticks, with their leaves	2
good black olives	12
olive oil and butter	
salt and pepper	
Pernod	2 tbsp
Dijon mustard	2 heaped dsrtsp

Inspired by my earthenware pot of Maille mustard after a trip to Dijon, I stuffed some tender, organic pork fillet with a delicious duxelles of vegetables bound with mustard, and breathing aniseedy Pernod fumes, and baked them in foil in the oven.

→ Preheat the oven to 180°C/350°F/Gas 4. Slice the PORK FILLETS almost in half lengthwise, then open them out like butterflies and flatten them slightly with your hands. Trim the bulbs of FENNEL and ONION rigorously to the point of wastefully—you want the tenderest, juiciest parts of both—and chop into a fine duxelles, which means smaller than dice by quite some way. String the sticks of CELERY and chop as for the fennel and onions.

→ Stew all the vegetables together in a little OLIVE OIL AND BUTTER until softened and translucent, season, add the halved, pitted OLIVES, pour on the PERNOD, allow it to bubble briefly, dollop on the MUSTARD, and stir it into the mixture to bind it off the heat. Cool slightly. Spread it in the centre of the pork fillets, then simply press them together, and fix with string, which I tied in a sort of large, raggedy blanket stitch.

→ Place each fillet on its own bit of foil, and seal loosely. Put all the fillets on a flat baking tray, and cook in the oven for 35 minutes. Test with a skewer. In this time, mine were cooked through, with a tinge of pink, and had created a good puddle of juice. Serve with new potatoes and something simple like broad or runner beans, or fresh peas.

Chinese Spiced Belly Pork and Hocks

SERVES 6

extra virgin olive oil	2 tbsp
sesame oil	1 tbsp
star anise	2
onions, *peeled and sliced*	3
belly pork, with the rind and bone	1 piece, weighing about 900g/2lb
pork hocks	2
fresh ginger, *grated*	2 large thumbs

This is one of those earthy, hearty pot-simmered dinners where the meat falls off the bone like a bad cowboy off a horse.

→ Heat the oven to 150°C/300°F/Gas 2. Heat the OILS gently in a heavy-bottomed casserole and throw in the STAR ANISE and the onions. Sauté for 5–10 minutes. Put in the BELLY, rind down, to frizzle with the HOCKS, which you should turn until browned all over. Place the belly rind-side up, add the GINGER and GARLIC and sauté for a minute.

→ Pour in the SHERRY VINEGAR and let it bubble, then add the remaining ingredients. Now add water to almost cover—you don't want the strong flavours to be diluted too much, but the meaty part of the belly should be submerged. Bring to the boil,

garlic cloves, *grated*	3–4
sherry vinegar	4 tbsp
muscovado sugar	3 heaped tbsp
organic shoyu OR tamari sauce	120ml/4fl oz
black pepper	

cover with greaseproof paper and a lid, and braise in the oven for 3 hours or more. The meat should be just on the verge of falling away from the bone.

→ When it is cool enough to handle, slice off most of the thick layer of fat and rind, then cut the belly into large chunks, some of which will be on the bone. Cut the hocks into hunks, too, and put both back into the pot. Cool and refrigerate overnight.

→ Skim the fat from the top with a spoon, then gently heat the casserole through until piping hot. Serve with Thai jasmine rice and pak choi briefly sautéed in sesame and olive oil with a little slivered garlic.

Belly of Pork and Butter Beans

SERVES 6

butter beans *soaked overnight*	450g/1lb
olive oil	2–3 tbsp
large onion	2–3 tbsp
OR shallots, which are good in spring	8 or 9
garlic cloves, *peeled and whole*	6–8
celery	the heart of a head with its leaves
hunk organic belly pork with its rind	600g/1lb 5oz
organic pork sausages	6
organic peeled tomatoes	2 × 240g/8½oz tins
organic tomatoes, *skinned, seeded and roughly chopped*	6
organic passata	½ jar
bay leaves	3
thyme and parsley stalks *tied together*	1 bunch
fresh, flat-leaf parsley	a large handful
black pepper and salt	

→ Bring the BEANS up to the boil in plenty of water, remove the scum, boil furiously for 10 minutes, then simmer with a lid on for 50 minutes. Strain, reserving the water. They will be slightly undercooked. Meanwhile, sauté the chopped ONION or whole SHALLOTS with the GARLIC and chopped CELERY until softened and translucent.

→ Add the BELLY PORK in 2.5cm/1in wide pieces you've cut down to the bone, the bony pieces cut along their length as you would spare ribs. Put them rind-side down and cook until browned, with the SAUSAGES. Turn them over for 2–3 minutes, then add the TINS OF TOMATOES, chopping as you go, the FRESH TOMATOES, and the PASSATA. Tuck the herbs in, and throw in all but a few ounces of the beans, which I then mouli through the medium-sized disc to thicken and enrich the tomato sauce. Season with plenty of coarse ground PEPPER AND SALT.

→ Add a little of the bean liquor if the liquid doesn't come above the stew, bring to the boil, then turn down to a gentle simmer, cover tightly with a lid and forget it for an hour.

→ Sprinkle with flat-leaf PARSLEY and serve with lashings of mashed potato to soak up the juice.

Stir-Fried Pork with Cashew Nuts and Chilli

SERVES 4

organic or free-range pork fillet	450g/1lb
fresh ginger, *grated*	1 tsp
sea salt and black pepper	
cashew nuts, unsalted	55g/2oz
rice wine OR dry sherry	1 tbsp
light soy sauce	1 tbsp
chilli bean sauce	1 tbsp
sugar	2 tsp
spring onions, *chopped*	1 handful
Marinade	
rice wine OR dry sherry	1 tbsp
light soy sauce	1 dsrtsp
sesame oil	2 tsp
cornflour	1 tsp

Pork and cashew nuts are a great duo. All you have to do here is marinade the meat first for 15 minutes while you prepare everything else. You may use chicken if you'd rather.

→ Mix the MARINADE INGREDIENTS in a bowl. Cut the PORK into thin slices about 5cm/2in long and plopthem into the marinade. Heat a wok or frying pan over a very high heat, add the oil and when it is smoking hot, add the GINGER, then the pork 20 seconds or so later. Season it with SALT AND PEPPER and stir-fry for a couple of minutes.

→ Remove the meat, throw in the CASHEW NUTS and stir-fry them for a minute. Add EVERYTHING BUT THE SPRING ONIONS, including the pork, and stir-fry for another couple of minutes. Throw in the chopped SPRING ONIONS and serve.

New York Spicy Spare Ribs

SERVES 2

fresh turmeric root OR dried powdered	2.5cm/1in
turmeric	1 tsp
green ginger root	2.5cm/1in
garlic cloves	6
blackstrap molasses	2 tbsp
chestnut honey	1 tbsp
tomato paste	1 tbsp
tamari sauce	4 tbsp
cinnamon	1 tsp
allspice	1 tsp
ginger	1 tsp
cayenne	1/3 tsp
cider vinegar	1 tbsp

The first time I found little saffron-coloured gnarly fingers of fresh turmeric in a health food shop in New York I was gripped, and used them in every-thing I cooked for weeks. The earthy, deep underscoring they gave each dish was so different to the powdered form and naturally, the healing properties advertised were addictive. If you are unable to buy the real McCoy at a nearby Asian store, back to the jar for the powder, I'm afraid. Note: If you are cooking for four or more people, don't just double up the sauce quantity, a little extra will do nicely with a slug of cider.

→ Preheat the oven to 150°C/300°F/Gas 2. Peel and grate the TURMERIC and GINGER roots and put them in a bowl. Peel and crush the GARLIC cloves with a little SEA SALT under the large blade of a knife. Throw them into the bowl. Add all the other ingredients and stir together.

→ Slice the RIBS so they are single if the butcher hasn't done it for you, and turn them in the spicy brew. Leave for 30 minutes. Put them in a roasting tin and cover tightly with foil. Cook for an hour. Remove the foil and turn the heat up to 180°C/350°F/Gas 4. Continue to cook, turning the ribs every 15 minutes, until

dry cider	90–120 ml/3–4fl oz
organic pork spare ribs	1 rack, to allow 6 to 8 per person

the sauce has gone gloopy brown and thickened a little and begun to cling to the ribs. This could be any time up to an hour, depending on how thin or thick or intense you like the taste.
→ Serve with rice into which you have thrown some cooked peas or broad beans, and any other vegetable you feel like on the side.

Michel Roux's Tourte au Jambon et Tomme de Pyrénées

SERVES 8

best quality ham, *thinly sliced*	675g/1½lb
hard ewe's milk cheese from the Pyrenees, *coarsely grated*	170g/6oz
puff pastry (see p. 517)	600g/1lb 5oz
egg, *beaten*, for glaze	1
Béchamel sauce	
full-fat milk	200ml/7fl oz
butter	30g/1oz
flour	30g/1oz
salt, pepper, nutmeg	
Madeira Truffle Vinaigrette	
Madeira	100ml/3½fl oz reduced to 3 tbsp
black truffles, *chopped*	55g/2oz
truffle juice	2 tbsp
Xeres vinegar	2 tbsp
white truffle oil	1 tbsp
olive oil	1 tbsp
salt, black pepper	

Michel Roux, Michelin-starred chef of Le Gavroche, also happens to be one of the most generous and least egocentric of his profession. If you ask him for a recipe he scurries off mid-service to write it down. Here is his simply delicious, deliciously elegant, classic French tourte.

→ For the béchamel, bring the MILK to the boil and in a separate pan make a roux with the BUTTER and FLOUR. Whisk the milk into this and boil, whisking continuously. Season with salt, pepper and grated nutmeg, loosely cover and leave to cool. (For more on making béchamel, see p. 402).
→ Roll out the PUFF PASTRY into two 23cm/9in circles. Layer the HAM, CHEESE and béchamel on one of the circles, leaving a rim of 4cm/1½in around the outside. The top layer should be ham, pressed well down to form an even dome. Brush the pastry rim with EGG and cover with the other piece of puff pastry. Press well to seal the edges and cut a neat, wave-shaped rim. Refrigerate for 2 hours. Brush with EGG and use the point of a sharp knife to decorate the top with swirling lines like a Pithiviers.
→ Preheat the oven to 190°C/375°F/Gas 5. Cook for 30 minutes or until puffed up and golden. Leave to rest for 20 minutes before cutting. Serve with a little salad and, if feeling extravagant, a Madeira truffle vinaigrette.

Madeira Truffle Vinaigrette
→ For the vinaigrette, simply mix ALL THE INGREDIENTS together and chill.

Bacon and Egg Pie

SERVES 6

shortcrust pastry *made with 340g/12oz flour and 170g/6oz unsalted butter* (see p. 104)	
green organic streaky bacon, *the rind snipped off*	170g/6oz
large organic eggs	6
double cream	4–5 tbsp
sea salt, black pepper and nutmeg	
egg, *beaten* for glaze	

Breakfast in a pie, brunch, lunch or the perfect picnic. You can add all sorts of early morning ingredients if you feel like a bit of serious substance abuse, carbohydrately speaking: slices of black pudding, cooked slices of Cumberland sausage, mushrooms fried in butter. Go with what you've got and who likes what, but here is the basic model.

→ Make the pastry (see p. 104) and chill in the fridge.

→ Preheat the oven to 220°C/425°F/Gas 7. Divide the PASTRY into two balls, the one for the base slightly larger than the one for the top. Line a greased shallow tart tin with the larger piece of pastry. Cook the BACON in a pan until frazzled and burnished brown and drain thoroughly on kitchen paper. When cool, snip the bacon into the pastry base. Break the EGGS into the pie, one at a time, keeping them whole. Pour over the DOUBLE CREAM and season with SALT, PEPPER and NUTMEG.

→ Roll out the remaining pastry, moisten the edges of the pie and cover with the top sheet. Press the edges together and decorate as you will with the trimmings before brushing the pastry with the beaten EGG. Bake in the middle of the oven for 30 minutes until golden brown. Tomato ketchup or brown sauce on the table, please.

Tartiflette

SERVES 4

potatoes, *peeled and boiled to al dente*	675g/1½lb
organic streaky (fat) bacon OR pancetta	140g/5oz
medium onion	1
unsalted butter	55g/2oz
dry white wine	150ml/5fl oz
½ a Reblochon cheese	340g/12oz
sea salt and freshly ground black pepper	

If you don't happen to be in the mountains of the Haute Savoie in France, where tartiflette is something of a national dish, you may just as easily make your own in the marrow-chilling midwinter days. Luxuriate in the glories of Reblochon, an inimitably creamy, fruity, tangy Savoie cheese, which is turned into a tartiflette with onions, ham and potatoes.

→ Preheat the oven to 190°C/375°F/Gas 5. While the POTATOES are boiling, cut the BACON into lardons and slice the ONION into fine rings. Blanch the lardons for a minute in boiling water. Drain the potatoes and let them cool to the point where you can hold them and cut them into 1.5cm/½in thick slices.

→ In a large frying pan melt the unsalted BUTTER and throw in the onions and lardons. Stir to coat and cook gently for about 10 minutes until the onions have softened and are beginning to turn pale gold. Add the sliced potatoes and a little more butter if it's all been absorbed and cook gently, trying not to let the potatoes break up. After 4–5 minutes add the HEATED WINE and continue to cook and turn gently for 5 minutes.

→ Scrape the contents of the pan into a greased gratin dish. Cut the REBLOCHON horizontally through its middle and put each half rind-side down on top of the potato mixture. Bake in the oven for 20-25 minutes or until the Reblochon has formed a lovely sticky crust on top. Cool for 5 minutes before serving with a baguette and a green salad.

Potato and Bacon Pie

SERVES 6

potatoes	450g/1lb
unsalted butter	30g/1oz
medium onions, *sliced*	2
organic streaky bacon, *diced*	85g/3oz
garlic cloves, *crushed with the back of a knife*	2
double cream	270ml/9fl oz
egg yolks	5
green back bacon, *rinds snipped off*	7 or 8 rashers
sea salt and black pepper	

Here the bacon acts as a wrapper, taking the place of pastry in a wonderfully creamy, garlicky pie baked in a terrine. A lovely winter lunch or supper dish.

→ Cook the POTATOES in their skins until they're soft, then drain and peel. Cut into thick slices and set aside. Heat the BUTTER in a frying pan, throw in the ONIONS and stir them over a slow heat for 10 minutes until they have wilted and are beginning to change colour. Add the DICED STREAKY BACON and the GARLIC and continue to cook for a further 3 minutes or so, then pour in the CREAM. Let it boil for a minute, then transfer everything to a bowl and leave to cool.

→ Heat the oven to 180°C/350°F/Gas 4. When the ONION and BACON mixture is nearly cold, stir in the EGG YOLKS and season with PEPPER, then add the sliced potatoes. Line the bottom and sides of a 900g/2lb terrine with the BACON RASHERS and scrape in the mixture. Cover with a layer of greaseproof paper. Put the dish in a roasting tin and pour in hot water to come half way up the sides of the terrine.

→ Bake the pie in the oven for 50–60 minutes, until fairly firm to the touch. Turn out on to a plate and serve piping hot, with nothing more than a well-dressed green salad.

Quiche Lorraine

SERVES 6

shortcrust pastry *made with 110g/4oz flour, 55g/2oz unsalted butter and 1 egg* (see p. 104)	
organic smoked streaky bacon	6 rashers
organic double cream, Jersey if possible	300ml/10fl oz
organic egg	1
organic egg yolks	3
black pepper	

Cream, eggs and smoked bacon are the triumvirate, the final result dependent on the quality of this trilogy as much as on the skills of the cook. This is the real McCoy, a classic.

→ Make shortcrust PASTRY (p. 104) with the FLOUR and unsalted BUTTER, binding the mixture with the EGG and a scant 2–3 tablespoons of WATER. After chilling, line a 20cm/8in tart tin and prick the base with a fork. Preheat the oven to 200°C/400°F/Gas 6.

→ Snip the BACON into strips and cook them gently in a frying pan until the fat begins to run. They should remain pinkly soft, not crispened. Drain, cool slightly, then spread over the bottom of the pastry case. Whisk together the CREAM, EGG, YOLKS and PEPPER, then pour into the pastry case and place in the oven for 20 minutes. Turn the heat down to 180°C/350°F/Gas 4 for a further 10–15 minutes, until the filling is goldenly puffed up like a soufflé.

→ Remove from the oven and leave for 10 minutes before serving. Scalding tarts don't taste of anything.

Leek and Ham Gratin

SERVES 4

leeks	2 per person
Parma ham OR good, thick sliced organic ham, *cut in half*	6 slices
béchamel sauce *made with 30g/1oz each unsalted butter and flour and 600ml/1pint of whole organic milk*	
sea salt, pepper and nutmeg	
breadcrumbs	110g/4oz
unsalted butter	30g/1oz
Beaufort OR cave-aged Gruyère cheese	110g/4oz

→ Preheat the oven to 180°C/350°F/Gas 4. Strip the LEEKS of their tough, outer skins and dark green ends and wash them well. Steam them whole until tender, and if it looks like their outer layer is a little tough, remove it.

→ When the leeks have cooled a little, wrap each one in HAM and place them in a row in a buttered gratin dish. Pour over the BÉCHAMEL SAUCE, which you have seasoned to taste with SALT, PEPPER and a suspicion of NUTMEG.

→ Briefly fry the BREADCRUMBS in BUTTER until golden and crisp, then sprinkle them over the surface of the béchamel. Add the grated BEAUFORT or GRUYÈRE and bake for 25 minutes, or until the sauce begins to bubble through the golden crust.

→ Let the dish stand for 5 minutes, then serve with a simple green salad.

Potato, Leek, Bacon, Sage and Cheese Gratin

SERVES 2

potatoes	675g/1½lb
fat leeks, *well washed*	3 or 4
organic smoked back bacon	6 rashers
fresh sage leaves	a generous handful
unpasteurised mature hard cheese (Cheddar, Lancashire, Cheshire or Caerphilly)	110g/4oz
chicken stock (see p. 54)	600–850ml/ 1–1½ pints
butter	
seeded mustard	1 tbsp
crème fraîche	about 4 tbsp
sea salt and black pepper	

A complete and simple one-pot supper dish that needs no more than a salad to finish with, or perhaps something green like spinach, broccoli or beans if you want an extra vegetable.

→ Preheat the oven to 200°C/400°F/Gas 6. Peel the POTATOES, then slice them finely on the blade of a mandolin or by hand. Place the potato slices in a colander and wash them under a cold tap turning them with your hands to get rid of their milky starch. Pat them dry in a tea towel.

→ In the meanwhile, trim the LEEKS of their dark green leaves and slice thinly. Butter a gratin dish and put in half the potatoes then add all the leeks in a layer. Snip the BACON into strips, removing the rind if necessary and fry in a pan with no added fat until they are crisply frazzled in their own fat and will snap in half. Remove them with a slotted spoon and dot the snippets over the leeks.

→ Now roll up the SAGE LEAVES, cut them into thin strips and frazzle in the bacon fat until they crisp, a few minutes. Dot the sage leaves over the leeks and bacon and pour over the bacon fat. Grate the CHEESE coarsely and sprinkle it over the top, then finish with an overlapping layer of potatoes placed neatly over the top.

→ Heat through the STOCK and pour it hot over the gratin dish until it just reaches the top layer of goodies, but does not submerge them. SEASON and dot with BUTTER then place a layer of buttered wax paper over the dish. Cook for 45 minutes in the top third of the oven. Remove, check under the paper with a skewer pushed right down through the dish that the potatoes are nearly cooked through.

→ Stir the MUSTARD and CRÈME FRAÎCHE together in a bowl and spoon a little ladle of the hot stock from the gratin dish into the crème fraîche mixture, whisking it in well. Pour this mixture over the top of the gratin dish and smooth it right across the top with a rubber spatula. Place the dish back in the oven without the wax paper for 15 minutes longer, by which time it should be bubbling and cooked right through. Leave to stand for 5 minutes before serving.

Quick LUN
& Light

CHES
SUPPERS

Eggy Bread

SERVES 2

eggs	2
bread	2 slices
nut of butter	

A classic breakfast or brunch dish also known as French toast. The Americans sweeten it with maple syrup or icing sugar and cinnamon, with some berries on the side. We tend just to fry the egg-soaked bread in butter and eat it hot, golden, slightly crisp and with a little frill of egg around the side like a pillow edge.

→ Crack the EGGS onto a large plate and beat them carefully with a fork. Soak the BREAD on both sides until nearly all the egg mixture has been absorbed. Melt a little nut of BUTTER in a frying pan and when it begins to bubble, put the bread in, pour any spare egg over the top and cook until the underside is beginning to look slightly crisp and nutty brown in places. Flip over and repeat. Turn onto a warm plate and serve the way you like it.

Gruyère and Ham French Toast

SERVES 4

large, organic free-range eggs	4
whole, organic milk	170ml / 6fl oz
sea salt and black pepper	
good white bread	4 thick slices
Dijon OR seeded mustard (optional)	
organic cooked OR smoked ham OR prosciutto if you prefer	4 slices
Gruyère cheese	4 slices
unsalted butter	

Perfect brunch or lazy weekend food, or a special tea-time treat for the children. This is something of a riff on the French toast theme and gives you the ham and eggs all wrapped together and oozing Gruyère. I say it serves 4, but you may feel more like eating two each because you simply can't help yourself. The slices of bread need to be a good 3cm/1¼in so you can slit them in half and stuff the goodies inside.

→ Beat the EGGS and MILK together with the SEASONING in a bowl and pour the contents of the bowl onto a large plate. Slit open each piece of BREAD very carefully with a sharp knife, to form a complete pocket inside, and cut the HAM and CHEESE to fit inside flat.

→ Spread MUSTARD on one pocket side for those who like it, then slip in the ham and cheese like letters into an envelope. Put as many slices of filled bread as will fit onto the plate into the egg mixture and leave them to soak it up for a couple of minutes. Turn them over and repeat.

→ Preheat the oven to 180°C/350°F/Gas 4. Heat the BUTTER, about a tablespoon, in a frying pan. When it is bubbling gently, slip in a couple of the stuffed slices and fry for a couple of minutes on one side before flipping and repeating for one minute on the other. Repeat with the other two slices. Now put the slices on a baking tray and slip into the oven for 5 minutes before turning over and repeating. They should be bronzed and meltingly gooey.

Oeufs en Cocotte au Parmesan

SERVES 4

organic double cream	150ml/5fl oz
Parmesan cheese, *freshly grated*	55g/2oz
sea salt and black pepper	
large organic free-range eggs	8

There is something both homely and sophisticated about these little ramekins of creamy egg laced with Parmesan, and they are made in a flash.

→ Preheat the oven to 190°C/375°F/Gas 5. Warm 8 ramekins. Heat the CREAM gently in a pan and then add the PARMESAN and SEASONING, not much salt. Put the ramekins in a gratin or baking dish inside a roasting tin, spoon or pour identical amounts of the mixture into each ramekin and plop a carefully broken EGG over the top of each.

→ Pour boiling water into the roasting tin to come halfway up the sides of the ramekins and gently place in the middle of the oven for 7–10 minutes. The eggs should look a little shuddery and have a slight opaque film over the surface when they're done. Serve immediately with hot buttered granary or sourdough toast.

Scrambled Eggs

butter	generous, walnut-sized lump, more if you're cooking more than 6 eggs
organic eggs	2 or 3 per person
milk OR cream	2 tbsp
black pepper	

When they are overcooked, scrambled eggs are very, very nasty—granular and watery with a horrid skin on top – where they should be soft, buttery, creamy, sloppy. Remember that they go on cooking in the pan after you have taken it off the heat, and if you don't continue to stir when you remove the slightly under-set eggs from the pan, the top will be perfect but the bottom dry, crusty and overcooked. Never salt eggs until they are ready: it has the effect of making them watery.

→ Melt the BUTTER in a thick-bottomed pan that will conduct the heat evenly and slowly. Use more if you're cooking, say, 6 eggs for 2 people. Meanwhile, break the EGGS into a small ramekin and throw each one into a bowl large enough to whisk them in. (This way, if you should come across one bad egg, you won't ruin the lot.) Whisk well until the white and the yolk are one, then add a splash, about 2 tablespoons, of MILK OR CREAM and a good scrunch of BLACK PEPPER, and whisk them in.

→ Pour the mixture into the foaming butter and stir on a low heat with a wooden spoon. I find that the slower you cook the eggs the better they taste, so every so often I remove them from the direct heat for a minute and continue to stir them. Just as they are beginning to set, add a few little bits of extra butter. This also has a magical effect on the taste and the texture.

→ When the eggs are sloppy-looking but set, remove from the heat and, still stirring, plop onto hot buttered toast.

Basic Omelette

The pan is as important as the eggs for this sublime, simple dish. You need a heavy-based iron pan, which should never be washed again after its first wash when you buy it. Then cover the base and sides with olive oil and leave it overnight before you wipe it with kitchen paper. Only wipe the pan with a damp cloth or piece of kitchen paper from now on, occasionally adding a little extra olive oil if it doesn't seem oiled, so that it keeps a smooth, slightly greasy surface, and an omelette will never stick to it. However many people you're cooking for, don't make your omelette with more than 4–6 eggs at a time. It's impossible to cook an omelette perfectly, right the way through, if it's too large, so make several instead. An 18cm/ 7in pan is good for 4 eggs, a 23cm/9in pan for 6.

→ Beat the EGGS in a bowl with a fork. I beat until foamy, but some prefer to beat less so that you have just mixed the yolks and the whites. Melt a walnut of BUTTER in the pan and when it begins to bubble and foam but before it browns, tip the omelette mixture in and season with BLACK PEPPER. It will begin to bubble immediately if the pan is hot enough. With a palette knife, worry the edges of the omelette, drawing them to the middle of the pan as they begin to form, so you keep the base of the pan covered with egg. When the egg has begun to set, fold the set part over on each side so that you have an omelette shape. The middle should still appear almost liquid. Flip the omelette onto the plate and serve.

Herb Omelette
→ Add a tablespoon of chopped CHIVES, PARSLEY, CHERVIL, TARRAGON and BASIL in any combination to the egg mixture while it is still in the bowl.

Cheese Omelette
→ Sprinkle a handful of thickly grated CHEESE over the eggs the moment they go into the pan. If you are using Gruyère, you may add it in small cubes to the egg mixture in the bowl.

Bacon or Ham Omelette
→ Dice and cook the MEAT and throw into the egg mixture in the pan. A couple of crisped rashers will do.

Tomato Omelette
→ Either slice a TOMATO and place it into the pan the moment the egg goes in, or skin and seed the tomato, then chop it and add it in the pan. To skin a tomato, put it into a bowl and cover

it completely with boiling water. Make a nick in the side with a knife and after a minute remove it from the water and peel. Cut into quarters, remove the seeds and core, and cut into dice or slices.

Mushroom Omelette
→ Slice 110g/4oz MUSHROOMS per person and cook in a little butter. You need to cook them beyond the point when they stop exuding juice and start to dry out again. Add some chopped chives or tarragon. Add the mushrooms to the pan before folding the omelette.

Tricolour Omelette

SERVES 4–6

olive oil	about 5 tbsp
fresh thyme leaves	1 tsp
plum tomatoes, *skinned, seeded and chopped*	450g/1lb
small, tender spinach leaves	450g/1lb
garlic cloves, *peeled but left whole*	2
organic eggs	9
double cream	100ml/3½fl oz
nutmeg, *grated*	
salt and pepper	
Parmesan cheese, *grated*	30g/1oz
Gruyère cheese, *grated*	30g/1oz

→ Preheat the oven to 150°C/300°F/Gas 2. Heat 2 tablespoons of the OIL in a small frying pan with the THYME LEAVES. Add the TOMATOES and sauté briefly, then put on a plate to cool. Drain away any excess liquid.
→ Heat 3 tablespoons of the OIL in a large saucepan and add the SPINACH leaves and GARLIC. Cook until softened and most of the moisture has evaporated. Remove the garlic, chop the spinach, and leave to cool on a plate. Drain away any excess liquid, otherwise it will make the finished dish watery.
→ Take 3 bowls and break 3 EGGS into each. To one, add the spinach, 3 tablespoons of the CREAM, a suspicion of NUTMEG, SALT AND PEPPER, and whisk together. To the second, add the TOMATOES, 2 tablespoons of the CREAM, SALT AND PEPPER, and whisk. To the third, add the grated CHEESES, the remaining CREAM, SALT AND PEPPER, and whisk.
→ Oil a heavy-bottomed 30 × 10 × 10cm/12 × 4 × 4in loaf tin. Pour in the tomato mixture. Stand the tin in a deep roasting tin with boiling water coming halfway up its sides, and cook in the oven for 20 minutes. It should be just set: not firm, but not runny. If the centre is runny, leave it a bit longer, or the layers will run together. Pour in the cheese layer and cook for a further 20 minutes. Again, it should be just set, so check carefully. Finally pour in the spinach layer and cook for about 20 minutes or until set.
→ Leave to cool down, then slice it in thick wedges straight from the tin when you are ready to eat it.

Omelette Savoyarde

SERVES 2

medium potato	1
unsalted butter	30–45g/1–1½oz
smoked bacon OR good ham, *cut into strips*	55g/2oz
leek, the white only, *cleaned and sliced finely*	1
organic eggs	6
double cream	2 tbsp
sea salt and black pepper	
Beaufort cheese, *freshly grated*	55g/2oz

This is what we eat in the French Alps when we have accomplished a morning's skiing and are in need of hearty delicious food to see us through the coming afternoon's adventures in the snow.

→ Preheat the oven to 220°C/425°F/Gas 7. Peel the POTATO, dice and boil until just al dente, then drain. Melt half the BUTTER over a gentle heat in a non-stick frying pan and add the BACON OR HAM and LEEKS, cooking slowly until they begin to soften. Add the diced potato and the rest of the BUTTER, then pour in the EGGS whisked with the CREAM and half the CHEESE. Cook for a minute without slooshing them around until the omelette is firm enough to fold but still really runny.

→ Fold and transfer the omelette to a well-greased gratin dish. SEASON and sprinkle over the rest of the BEAUFORT. Bake in the oven for 5 minutes. With luck, the omelette will have puffed up and browned but still be runny.

Omelette Arnold Bennett

SERVES 2

milk	300ml/10fl oz
bay leaves	3
onion	2 slices
lemon	2 slices
black peppercorns	6
undyed smoked haddock fillet	285g/10oz
eggs	6
unsalted butter	30g/1oz
double cream	2–3 tbsp
Parmesan, *freshly grated*	2 tbsp
salt and *freshly grated* black pepper	

→ Mix the MILK with 300ml/10fl oz of water, pour into a large shallow pan and bring to the boil. Add the BAY LEAVES, ONION and LEMON SLICES, PEPPERCORNS and smoked HADDOCK and simmer for about 3–4 minutes, until the fish is just cooked. Lift the fish out on to a plate and leave until cool enough to handle, then break it into flakes, discarding any skin and bones. Preheat the grill to high.

→ Whisk the EGGS together with some PEPPER. Heat a non-stick omelette pan over a medium heat, then add the BUTTER and swirl it around to coat the base and sides of the pan. Pour in the eggs, and, as they start to set, drag the back of a fork over the base of the pan lifting up little folds of egg to allow the uncooked egg to run underneath.

→ When the omelette is set underneath but still very moist on top, sprinkle over the flaked haddock. Pour the CREAM on top, sprinkle with the PARMESAN cheese and put the omelette under the hot grill until lightly golden brown. Slide it onto a warmed plate and serve with a crisp green salad.

Piperade, or Piperrada

SERVES 4

organic red peppers	500g/1lb 2oz
ripe, organic tomatoes, *skinned and seeded*	500g/1lb 2oz
large organic eggs	8
olive oil	
onion, *chopped*	1
garlic clove, *chopped*	1
Bayonne ham, pata negra OR prosciutto	4 slices
sea salt and black pepper	

→ Grill the PEPPERS, turning them every few minutes until the skins are charred all over. Allow the peppers to cool before peeling, removing the cores and seeds and chopping them.

→ Heat a couple of tablespoons of OLIVE OIL in a frying pan and gently sauté the chopped ONION over a gentle heat until golden, adding the chopped GARLIC towards the end. Chop the TOMATOES, remove their cores, and add them to the pan with the peppers, cooking them down until you have a meltingly soft texture.

→ Beat the EGGS, season with PEPPER and pour them over the sauce, stirring everything together to make a sunset-coloured mixture. Be patient, worry the eggs a bit and cook very slowly until soft and slightly runny. Fry the HAM separately in a bit of OLIVE OIL until crisp, and serve it atop the eggs. I think warm with a hunk of good bread is preferable to hot.

Tumbled Cracked Black Peppercorn Eggs and Ham

SERVES 4

large baguette, *cut in 4 and sliced in half*	1
olive oil	
garlic clove, *peeled*	1
unsalted butter	55g/2oz
large organic eggs	8–12
black peppercorns, *cracked*	1 tbsp
salt	
basil leaves	a handful
good ham OR prosciutto	4 slices
large tomatoes, *cored and sliced*	2

Half scramble, half omelette, these runny eggs are tumbled on to garlicky toasted baguette with basil and ham. This is also delicious with prosciutto. The cracked black peppercorns make it. I crack mine in a mortar, but a rolling pin works.

→ Scoop out some of the dough from the slices of BAGUETTE to make room for the filling. Pour best OLIVE OIL over each slice and rub over the GARLIC clove to scent the bread and oil. Put the 8 slices on a tray in a hot oven to toast or grill them on both sides.

→ Meanwhile, melt the BUTTER in a frying pan and whisk the EGGS well. Pour in the PEPPERCORNS and then tip the mixture into the pan. You want to tumble and push the eggs with a flat wooden spatula; worry them rather than wait and fold as you would for an omelette, and don't stir to small lumps as you would for scrambled. The end result should be large waves of runny eggs punctuated by tweedy flecks of peppercorn.

→ Remove when still soft as they will keep cooking, and season with a little SALT. Put a few BASIL LEAVES on the bases of the baguette slices, then add the HAM, the TOMATO and finally the egg, finishing with the top pieces of baguette. Then try to get your mouth round one.

Baked Eggs with Spring Vegetables

SERVES 4

large onion, *finely chopped*	1
garlic cloves, *finely chopped*	2
olive oil	4 tbsp
small chorizo, well-spiced sausage OR smoked bacon, *cubed*	110g/4oz
red peppers, *skinned and chopped*	2
tomatoes, *skinned, seeded and chopped*	340g/12oz
fino OR amontillado sherry	1–2 tbsp
small new broad beans	110g/4oz
young peas	110g/4oz
large eggs	8
salt and cayenne pepper	

This is an all-in-one supper, the scarlet and green vegetables flecking the yellow and white eggs like a primary-coloured picture.

→ Preheat the oven to 180°C/350°F/Gas 4. Warm a shallow terracotta baking dish. Heat the OIL in a pan, and add the ONION, cooking gently until it softens. Add the GARLIC, cook for a minute, push aside, add the MEAT, fry until coloured, then remove it.

→ Add the PEPPERS and TOMATOES, and cook until reduced and softened, adding the SHERRY when it starts to look dry. Briefly steam the BROAD BEANS and PEAS until just tender, and add them.

→ Transfer the mixture with the meat to the casserole, whisk the EGGS together briefly—you are looking for an egg white and yolk contrast, not something that looks like an omelette—and season. Pour over the vegetables and bake for about 10–15 minutes, when the eggs are just set.

Oeufs Florentine

SERVES 4

young spinach leaves	675g/1½ lb
béchamel sauce (see p. 402)	425ml/¼ pint
Cheddar cheese, *grated*	110g/4oz
sea salt, pepper and nutmeg	
double cream	3–4 tbsp
organic eggs	8
Parmesan cheese, *freshly grated*	55–85g/2–3 oz

Spinach, eggs and cheese are a lovely triumvirate for this brunch or even light supper dish.

→ Preheat the oven to 220°C/425°F/Gas 7. Wash the SPINACH leaves and remove any tough stalks. Cook the spinach in the water clinging to it from washing just until it wilts, in a large, heavy-bottomed pan. Remove from the heat and drain in a conical strainer or sieve, pressing down hard with the back of a wooden spoon to remove all the excess water. Cut the spinach with a sharp knife until it is well chopped up in the strainer.

→ Warm the BÉCHAMEL through gently and add the grated CHEDDAR to make mornay sauce. Put the spinach in a buttered gratin dish. SEASON it, add a smidgen of NUTMEG and the CREAM, and gently amalgamate with a fork. Shake a little of the PARMESAN over the spinach, which will help prevent the whites from leaking down into it. Carefully break two of the EGGS into a ramekin, gently decant them onto the cheese, and repeat until all the eggs are used.

→ Pour the hot sauce gently over the eggs and cover with the rest of the PARMESAN. Bake in the oven for 5 minutes then put the dish under the grill for a further 5 minutes to brown the top. Serve scorching hot.

Pocket-sized Frittata

MAKES 24

courgette	1
red pepper	1
organic cherry tomatoes, *halved*	24
cooked ham, *cut into thin strips*, (optional)	2 slices
large organic eggs	6
organic double cream	2 tbsp
cornflour	2 tbsp
chives, *chopped*	1 tbsp
basil OR parsley OR tarragon	1 tbsp
feta, *diced*	½ cup
Parmesan, *freshly grated*	½ cup
black pepper	
olive oil, for the tins	

Small muffin tins or deep tart tins are perfect for these irresistible bites of frittata. You can change the doll's-sized dice of veg according to the season, spruce up with crumbled goat or blue cheese or just stick to plain Parmesan and feta. The frittata puff up in the tins to lovely little coolie hats and can be eaten hot, warm or at room temperature.

→ Dice the COURGETTE and fry briskly in a little OLIVE OIL. Remove while still firm. Grill the PEPPER until black, skin and chop into tiny squares.

→ Preheat the oven to 180°C/350°F/Gas 4. Whisk the CREAM, EGGS and CORN·OUR together in a large bowl before adding the courgettes, peppers, HAM, HERBS, CHEESES and BLACK PEPPER, and whisking some more. Put the mixture in a jug and pour into the oiled tins so they are three-quarters full, and add a halved CHERRY TOMATO to each one. Bake for 10–15 minutes, when they will be puffed up and golden. Leave for a couple of minutes before removing with a palette knife.

Fried Eggs

→ Omelette pans are deep enough. Begin by gently heating a walnut-sized piece of BUTTER, or the equivalent splosh of OIL or BACON FAT, until it begins to smoke. Butter will begin to smell nutty, but do not allow it to brown. If that happens, pour it away and start again. Break each egg into a small saucer or bowl and slide it carefully into the hot fat, then spoon the fat gently over the yolk and white to help cook it through.

→ The white will have firmed up to a sort of blueish opaqueness when it has set and the yolk will look cooked but still runny. If you prefer your eggs better cooked, continue or flip the egg over with a slice. Remove carefully from the pan, draining away a little of the butter if you wish to as you go.

Cousin Deborah's Cheese Strata

SERVES 6 BUT CAN BE STRETCHED

streaky bacon, *thinly sliced*	110g/4oz
olive oil	1 tsp
medium onion, *chopped very small*	1
butter, *softened*	about 85g/3oz
good-quality one-day-old bread	5 slices
mature Cheddar cheese, *grated*	170g/6oz
organic eggs, *beaten lightly*	4
single cream	425ml/15fl oz
paprika	¼ tsp
chilli powder	¼ tsp
mustard powder	1 tsp

Deborah and I are first cousins. She is an exceptionally fine cook, wonderful to work with in the kitchen, and I don't believe we've ever quarrelled in or out of it. This is one of her recipes. There is no pastry here, but in every other aspect it meets my demands of a fine savoury tart: cheesy, eggy, creamy, self-contained and great to serve after the theatre or a movie, with a salad. It is refrigerated for 24 hours before cooking, so plan ahead.

→ Fry the BACON in the OLIVE OIL until crisp, drain it on kitchen paper and chop it into small pieces. Fry the ONION in the same pan until soft, but not coloured, then remove with a slotted spoon.

→ Butter the BREAD on one side, and cut into cubes. Line a 23cm/9in flan dish with half the bread cubes. Sprinkle with half the CHEESE and the BACON. Put the rest of the bread into the flan dish and scatter over the rest of the cheese and bacon. Whisk together the EGGS, CREAM and SPICES, and pour them over the top. Refrigerate for 24 hours. Preheat the oven to 180°C/350°F/Gas 4. Bake the strata for an hour and leave to stand for 5–10 minutes before serving.

Haddock and Mushroom Strata
→ This is also delicious made with lightly poached HADDOCK between the layers of bread, and sautéed MUSHROOMS rather than bacon.

Feta and Spinach Parcels

MAKES 15–20

spinach	450g/1lb
sheep's milk feta	1 packet
nutmeg OR cayenne, sea salt and black pepper	a little
olive oil, for brushing	
filo pastry	1 packet

These meltingly salt-sweet, crisp-gooey purses of suspended flavour and texture can be served as a bonne bouche, starter or light lunch.

→ Wash the SPINACH and cook just until it wilts in the residue of water. Drain in a colander and rigorously press out the water with the back of a wooden spoon. Chop the spinach, still in the colander, with a sharp knife until it is quite fine, and leave to cool. Place it on a large plate and season to taste.

→ Preheat the oven to 200°C/400°F/Gas 6. Crumble the FETA into small cubes and shards, and cut the ROQUEFORT into small cubes. Keep the cheeses separate. Place a sheet of FILO on your work surface and brush it with OLIVE OIL before cutting it into 7.5cm/3in squares, circles, or whatever takes your fancy—keep the rest of the filo under a damp cloth as you work. Repeat the process with another two or three sheets of oiled filo.

→ Place a teaspoon of spinach in the middle of a piece of filo, add a few cubes of feta or roquefort, then scrunch the whole into a parcel, leaving a splayed shoot of filo on top. Place on the oiled baking tray, and continue making parcels until you have as many as you want or need. Whack on to the middle shelf of the oven, where they will take between 15–20 minutes to crisp up and goo down. Eat roaring hot off the baking sheet! Or smarten up on plates.

Roquefort and Spinach Parcels
→ Use 110g/4oz of ROQUEFORT or another good blue cheese such as Cashel Blue or Fourme d'Ambert. Cut the cheese into small cubes and follow the method above.

Flamiche

SERVES 6

leeks	1.4kg/3lb
unsalted butter	about 85g/3oz
organic double cream	150–300ml/5–10fl oz
organic egg yolks	3
salt, black pepper, nutmeg	
shortcrust pastry (see p. 104)	1 × 23cm/9in tart case

The scent of leeks sweating gently, sweetly, in butter is one of the great kitchen smells, subsiding as they do into a collective mess that is all buttery white purée. This tart is not baked blind, so allow time for your leeks to cool before spreading the wilted, white heap on the pastry.

→ Trim off the coarse, green outer leaves of the LEEKS and chop the white parts into roughly 1cm/½in rings. Sweat them slowly in the BUTTER, and when thoroughly softened leave them to cool.
→ Preheat the oven to 180°C/350°F/Gas 4. The amount of cream you use will depend on your tart tin: a shallow tin will be fine with the smaller amount, but you will need more to fill a deeper tin. Whisk together the CREAM and EGG YOLKS, and season with SALT, PEPPER and a suspicion of grated NUTMEG. Stir this into the leeks, and spread the mixture quickly and evenly over the PASTRY BASE. Cook for 35–40 minutes, until tremblingly set. Leave for 10 minutes before turning out and serving.

Individual Goat's Cheese Tarts

MAKES 6

all-butter puff pastry, *rolled thinly*	340g/12oz
goat's cheese logs OR soft barrel-shaped goat's cheeses	2
	3
organic egg, *beaten*	1
thyme, rosemary OR savory	3–4 sprigs

Quicker and easier than going shopping in search of a good dinner, this is just a roll-and-bake dish of oozingly delectable goat's cheese, scented with thyme, rosemary or savory, which bursts the banks of the buttery leaves of pastry.

→ Preheat the oven to 220°C/425°F/Gas 7. Cut the PASTRY into six squares. Cut each LOG into three sections or each BARREL in half. Place the cheese in the middle of each square. Brush all round the edge of the pastry with the beaten EGG. Draw the pastry edges together in each corner and press them together from half way up the sides to the top. Throw some chopped HERBS on top of the exposed face of each bit of goat's cheese. Place the tarts straight onto a heated baking tray in the middle of the oven and bake for about 15–20 minutes or until the pastry is puffed up and golden and the cheese looks molten and bubbling. Eat warm rather than scorching.

Little Cheese Croustades

SERVES 4

bread, *crusts removed*	6 slices
unsalted butter	
Gruyère, cave-aged	200g/7 oz
organic eggs	2
crème fraîche OR soured cream	2 tbsp
nutmeg, *grated* and black pepper	
chives, *snipped*	1 tbsp

→ Heat the grill. Butter the BREAD on one side and quarter it in triangles or squares. Grate the GRUYÈRE into a bowl and whisk with the EGGS and CRÈME FRAÎCHE. SEASON to taste and spread the mixture over the bread. Arrange in a gratin dish and grill for a few minutes until golden brown. Serve hot or warm with a pinch of CHIVES over each slice.

Asparagus Tart

SᴇʀᴠᴇS 6

shortcrust pastry (see p. 104)	1 × 23cm/9in tart case
egg, *beaten*, for brushing	1
asparagus	1 good-sized bundle
cream	300ml/10fl oz
Jersey milk	150ml/5fl oz
egg yolks	4
Parmesan, *freshly grated*	2 tbsp
salt and black pepper	

Never, never think you can squeeze more out of each fragile asparagus wand than you really can. Always chop every stem to where it starts feeling woody, and peel the lowest 3–4cm/inch or two just to be safe. I tend to chop the wands into generous 2.5cm/1in lengths, with the spears longer by their spear-head so to speak. Then steam the chopped stems for a few minutes before you throw the tender buds in after them. The point of a sharp knife should pierce the flesh firmly but unresistantly. Then stop cooking immediately. One fat bundle of asparagus will fill your tart case.

→ Preheat the oven to 200°C/400°F/Gas 6 Make the PASTRY, refrigerate it and bake it blind (see p. 104). Remove the pastry case from the oven and brush with beaten EGG. Turn the oven down to 180°C/350°F/Gas 4.

→ Steam the ASPARAGUS as described above and leave to cool. Whisk the CREAM, MILK and EGG YOLKS together, add the grated PARMESAN and SEASON. Spoon the cooled asparagus into the pastry case, then pour over the custard. Cook for 25–30 minutes, until puffed up and just set and browned.

→ Leave to cool for 10 minutes, then serve with a strong-noted salad, say raw fennel, orange and watercress with a walnut or hazelnut and olive oil dressing, which introduces astringency and pepperiness.

Cherry Tomato Tarte Tatin

SᴇʀᴠᴇS 4

puff pastry, an all-butter brand or see p. 517	200g/7oz
extra virgin olive oil	4 tbsp
organic cherry tomatoes, *stalks removed*	about 500g/ 1lb 2oz
balsamic vinegar	8 tbsp
port OR Madeira (optional)	
salt and black pepper	

→ Preheat the oven to 220°C/425°F/Gas 7. Divide the PUFF PASTRY into four and roll into very thin 12cm/5in discs, or one large disc. Pour 1 tablespoon of the OIL into each of four 10cm/4in tart tins, or into one 20cm/8in tart tin, swirl it around, then arrange the TOMATOES in a single layer.

→ Heat the BALSAMIC VINEGAR in a small saucepan and reduce until sticky and caramelised, adding a splash of PORT OR MADEIRA if you have it to hand. SEASON the tomatoes with salt and pepper, then pour over a dribble of the vinegar. Cover with a pastry disc, tucking the pastry in at the sides. Bake for 8–10 minutes, until the pastry is puffed and golden. Check assiduously; a larger tart will take longer.

→ Remove from the oven and run a knife around the edge of the pastry. Place a plate over each tart tin and quickly invert. Be careful—there could be quite a lot of liquid surrounding the tarts, like so many brown moats.

Leek and Parma Ham Gratin

SERVES 4

leeks	2 per person
Parma ham	6 slices, *cut in half*
béchamel sauce, *made with 25g/1oz each of butter and flour, and 600ml/1 pint milk, salt, pepper and nutmeg* (see p. 402)	
breadcrumbs	2 handfuls
butter	25g/1oz
Beaufort cheese, OR the best Gruyère you can find	125g/4oz

Spring leeks are young, long and tender; they can be steamed, wrapped and cooked under a bubblingly rich gratin of buttered breadcrumbs and Beaufort cheese.

→ Preheat the oven to 180°F/350°C/Gas 4. Strip the LEEKS of their tough outer skins and dark green ends and wash well. Steam them until tender, then leave to cool while you make the béchamel.

→ Wrap the leeks in the strips of PARMA HAM and place them in a row on the bottom of a buttered gratin dish. Pour over the BÉCHAMEL. Briefly fry the BREADCRUMBS in butter until golden, then sprinkle a thin layer of them over the surface of the béchamel. Add the grated BEAUFORT OR GRUYÈRE, and put the dish in the oven for about 25 minutes, or until the béchamel begins to bubble through the golden crust. Serve with a salad.

Cheese and Onion Bake with Smoky Bacon

SERVES 4

olive oil	4 tbsp
shallots OR baby onions, *peeled and left whole*	12
fresh thyme leaves	1 tsp
garlic cloves, *peeled and sliced thinly*	2
baguette OR the equivalent of a sourdough loaf *cut or torn into bite-size pieces*	⅓
organic free-range eggs	6
organic whole milk, OR to make it richer, ½ double cream to milk	600ml/1 pint
smoked bacon, *snipped into strips*	4 rashers
chives, *snipped*	2 tbsp
unpasteurised Cheddar, Lancashire OR Caerphilly, *grated*	2 cups

Sometimes you just want simple comfort food, only have scratch ingredients hanging around, and really, really want to turn something delicious out of nothing onto the table and not have to go shopping. Here it is: an easy-peasy supper, lunch or brunch dish that children love too.

→ Heat half the OIL in a large, heavy-bottomed ovenproof pan, and throw in the SHALLOTS and THYME. Cook gently until they're browned on all sides, then add the GARLIC. Cover with a lid and continue to cook so that the shallots begin to release their juices and soften but don't burn. After about 20 minutes they should be soft with just a hint of firmness in the centre when spiked with a skewer. Put them on a plate and reserve.

→ Preheat the oven to 190°C/375°F/Gas 5. While the shallots are cooking, fry the snipped BACON with no additional fat until crisp. Throw the chunks of BREAD into a roasting tin with the other two tablespoons of OLIVE OIL, and shake to coat all over. Put the bread in the oven to bake for 8–10 minutes until crisp and browned. Now scrape the bread into the large ovenproof pan or a gratin dish with the shallots. Pour over the bacon fat and spread out the snippets of bacon. Beat the EGGS and MILK with or without CREAM, SEASON and pour over the contents of the pan. Scatter over the grated CHEESE and CHIVES and bake for 30 minutes in the oven until all puffed up and golden. Bring to the table and serve.

Fasoulia

SERVES 6

dried butter beans	450g/1lb
large onions	2
olive oil	4–6 tbsp
garlic cloves, *chopped*	3
tomatoes, *skinned, seeded and chopped*	3–4
tomato purée	2 tbsp
lemon	½
flat-leaf parsley, *chopped*	3–4 tbsp

The Greeks are particularly good at warm bean dishes, semi-stew, semi-salad in concept. This slightly oily, tomatoey butter bean dish is delicious with a slice of gammon.

→ Soak the BEANS in cold water overnight. Drain, rinse and put them in a large saucepan with fresh water to cover the beans. Bring to the boil and simmer for about 2 hours, or until tender. Drain, reserving some of the cooking liquid.

→ Slice the ONIONS into thin rings and stew gently in about half the OLIVE OIL with the GARLIC. Add the TOMATOES, TOMATO PURÉE and the beans, with just enough of the cooking liquid to thin the sauce without making it liquid. Leave to cool slightly, then pour some OLIVE OIL and a generous squeeze of LEMON JUICE over the beans and turn them gently. Serve warm, scattered with chopped PARSLEY.

Pan Bagnat

SERVES 6–8

large organic tomatoes, *skinned*	6
red pepper OR a jar of roasted peppers	1
shallot OR small onion, *peeled*	1
broad beans, *shelled*	225g/8oz
eggs, *softly hard-boiled*	3
artichoke hearts	4
best bonita tuna OR 'ventresca', belly of tuna	1 small jar
salted anchovies	6
garlic clove	1
red wine vinegar	1 tbsp
olive oil	
pitted olives, Niçoise if possible	a handful
basil leaves, *torn*	a handful
baguette, ciabatta OR rolls	

This is really a Salade Niçoise sealed inside a loaf, the name 'pan bagnat' literally meaning wet bread. If you have time to weight the pan bagnat wrapped in foil on a plate overnight for all the juices and oil to mingle, it is best of all. The types of olives and beans, broad or French, the addition and subtraction of artichokes, eggs, fish, onions, cucumber, and basil or other herbs, is all your own. Use your imagination. Seggiano's artichoke hearts roasted in olive oil are sublime.

→ Cut the TOMATOES into eighths, cut the PEPPER into strips and slice the ONION and ARTICHOKES. Blanch the BROAD BEANS for a minute and slip off the skins if you can be bothered. Mix the vegetables together. Peel the EGGS and slice them. Drain the TUNA. Desalinate and de-spine the ANCHOVIES and split them in half.

→ Slice the BREAD OR ROLLS horizontally and scoop out some of the bread from both halves. Rub both with a cut clove of GARLIC, then sprinkle over the VINEGAR and OIL to dress the loaf. Pile a layer of vegetables on to the bottom half, then add the egg, tuna and OLIVES. Scatter BASIL LEAVES on top and add diagonal strips of anchovy. Put the top deck of bread over the heaped salad and wrap in foil. Place on a plate, weigh down and leave overnight if possible. Cut the pan bagnat into slices to serve.

Risotto Balsamico

SERVES 2

extra virgin olive oil	2 tbsp
unsalted butter	30g/1oz
small shallot, *finely minced*	1
celery, *strung and finely minced*	1 stick
Carnaroli rice	225g/8oz
dry white Italian wine	1 small glass
intense home-made chicken stock (see p. 54)	up to 850ml/1½ pints
more unsalted butter for finishing the risotto	
Parmesan, *freshly grated*	
sea salt and black pepper	
best balsamic vinegar	

No embellishments and no flavours or textures to distract from the rice, the breath of onion, white wine and chicken stock, and the million-dollar moat of aged balsamico. You need the most expensive, velvety, mellow balsamic vinegar for this—mine is a 20-year-old. The thin, sharp stuff good enough for a salad dressing just won't do here. It has to be sweetly sticky, viscous and mellow.

→ Heat the OLIVE OIL and BUTTER together in a shallow pan. I have a special Le Creuset cast-iron risotto pan with an enamelled inside; the large surface area helps the rice to cook evenly. When the oil and butter begin to bubble, add the finely minced SHALLOT and CELERY and a little SALT and stir them gently until they just begin to soften. Meanwhile heat the WINE in a separate pan.

→ Throw in the RISOTTO RICE and keep stirring to coat it with the oil and butter, then add the heated white wine. Stir as it bubbles and begins to be absorbed by the rice. Now add the hot CHICKEN STOCK, a ladle or two at a time. The rice will take around 22 minutes to cook, but the one thing you cannot afford to do is to stop stirring for more than a minute at a time. The stirring is what releases the starch from the rice and gives it the lovely gloopy, starchy texture that a fine risotto should have.

→ When the risotto is still just al dente, or has bite to it, add a final ladle of stock with a knob of BUTTER, a good handful of grated PARMESAN and a scrunch of PEPPER, white if you are being a purist colour-wise. Put the lid on and remove the pan from the heat. Leave for 5 minutes for all the flavours to mingle and settle before giving the risotto a final stir.

→ Put a good tablespoon of best BALSAMIC VINEGAR in the base of each shallow bowl, then carefully heap a mound of white risotto over it. The edges of the puddle should form a black moat around the white mound. Serve with extra cheese in a bowl if you like, though I don't think you need it. Perhaps serve a salad of pure white, shaved raw fennel afterwards, with an olive oil and lemon dressing.

Turkey Tikka on Ciabatta

SERVES 4

small pieces of cooked turkey	450g/1lb
Greek yoghurt	3 tbsp
sea salt	2 tsp
chilli powder	1 tsp
garam masala	1 tsp
lemon	1
olive oil	1 tbsp
dry fenugreek powder (optional)	½ tsp
tomatoes	4
cucumber	½
red onion	1
Romaine lettuce	1
baby ciabattas	4
butter	
coriander chutney (see p. 217)	110g/4oz
mayonnaise	200g/7oz

A good way of using up leftover turkey or chicken.

→ Mix the TURKEY with all the INGREDIENTS FOR THE TIKKA (down to and including the fenugreek) and leave covered in the fridge for at least 2 hours.

→ Heat the oven to 230°C/450°F/Gas 8. Place the turkey in a single layer on a baking tray and roast for about 5 minutes.

→ Slice the TOMATOES and CUCUMBER, chop the ONION and shred the LETTUCE. Spread the CIABATTAS with BUTTER and warm them on a hot pan or under the grill. Spread CORIANDER CHUTNEY on one half of the ciabatta and MAYONNAISE on the other. Layer with shredded lettuce, tomatoes, cucumber, onion and turkey tikka and close the sandwich.

Lox and Bagels

SERVES 4

onion bagels	4
fresh cream cheese, the best you can find	225g/8oz
smoked wild salmon	4 large slices
tomatoes	2
black pepper	

The original, old-style Brooklyn smoked salmon is known as lox, after the Yiddish word for salmon, lachs, Claudia Roden tells us in The Book of Jewish Food. *In the days before refrigeration, Brooklyn salmon was pickled in brine, then desalted and lightly smoked. It would have been much saltier than the smoked salmon we are used to, so it was paired with cream cheese to counteract the salt. This is the favourite American brunch food.*

→ Split the BAGELS in half horizontally around their middles and grill them on both sides. Spread one half thickly with CREAM CHEESE before adding slices of SMOKED SALMON.

→ Top with TOMATO and scrunch over some BLACK PEPPER. Lightly spread CREAM CHEESE over the top half of each bagel and slam them together.

Smoked Salmon and Soured Cream Cheese Rosti

SERVES 4

medium potatoes	6
olive oil	2–3 tbsp
best pure cream cheese	110g/4oz
crème fraîche	1 tbsp
lemon juice	1 tbsp
lemon, *grated zest*	½ tsp
chives, *snipped*	1 tbsp
dill, *chopped*	1 tbsp
black pepper, *coarsely ground*	
wild smoked salmon, *thinly sliced*	170g/6oz
cayenne	

I hardly need to remind you of the celestial combination of smoked salmon and cream cheese, particularly on toasted onion bagels, Irish soda bread or black-as-night rye bread. Here I've used potatoes instead of bread, which is all the more Irish. The wild is the only salmon for me, for flavour, texture, lack of greasiness, and out of kindness and respect to the life of this king of sea fish. Eat it less often, eat better and you will notice the difference immediately if you compare farmed with wild.

→ Peel the POTATOES, grate them on the thick blade of a mandolin or grater onto kitchen paper and pat them dry. Heat the OLIVE OIL in a heavy-bottomed frying pan and add little piles of grated potato. Flatten them down with a spatula, and cook until golden and crisp on one side before turning over and repeating on the other side. You will need 8 piles of rosti. Put the rosti on kitchen paper on a plate as they finish cooking and straight into a warm oven.

→ Stir together the CREAM CHEESE, CRÈME FRAÎCHE, LEMON JUICE, ZEST, HERBS and freshly ground BLACK PEPPER. Put a layer of rosti on each plate, followed by one of the cream cheese mixture, and top it with a slice of SMOKED SALMON. Repeat the layer of rosti, then top with cream cheese mixture on one half of the rosti and a furl of smoked salmon on the other half. A little dusting of CAYENNE on top and it's ready to serve.

Welsh Rarebit

SERVES 4

mature Cheddar, Cheshire, Wensleydale or Caerphilly, *grated*	225g/8oz
unsalted butter, *melted*	30g/1oz
fresh breadcrumbs	2 tbsp
English mustard powder *mixed with 1 tsp water* OR seeded mustard	1 tsp, 1 tsp
organic free-range egg, *beaten*	1
sea salt and black pepper	
Tabasco and Worcestershire sauce (optional)	a few drops
good white OR wholegrain bread	4 thick slices
butter	

Just melting cheese on a piece of toast under a grill can render it stringy and oily, the cheese separating into a pool of buttery liquid. Here is a rather more sophisticated take on this simple classic.

→ Preheat the oven to 220°C/425°F/Gas 7. Mix the finely grated CHEESE with the BUTTER, BREADCRUMBS, MUSTARD and EGG. Beat well and season—you may prefer to omit the salt as the cheese is salty. Add both sauces to taste. Lightly toast the bread, butter it and spread it with the cheese mixture. Bake in the oven for 5–10 minutes until golden brown and bubbling.

American Rabbit

SERVES 4

mature farmhouse Cheddar	255g/9oz
black pepper	
cayenne	1 pinch
mustard	2 tsp
beer or lager	90ml/3fl oz
organic eggs, *separated*	4
good white OR brown crusty bread	

A richer and more refined second cousin of the Welshman opposite.

→ Cube the CHEESE into doll's-size dice and put into a small pan. Scrunch over some BLACK PEPPER and the CAYENNE, and add the MUSTARD and BEER. Cook over a low heat, stirring all the time, until the cheese has melted and is velvety smooth. Beat the EGG YOLKS into the mixture off the heat.

→ Whisk the EGG WHITES in a bowl to firm peaks and stir the first tablespoon into the cheese mixture. Fold in the rest of the whites, a tablespoon at a time, lightly and quickly so as not to let the air out of the mixture. Return to the low heat and stir gently until the mixture thickens a little. Pour the mixture over hot toast and serve immediately. Alternatively, instead of returning the pan to the low heat when you've whisked in the egg whites, pile the mixture on top of the hot toast and put it under the grill until it puffs up and browns like a soufflé. Serve immediately.

Scotch Woodcock

SERVES 4

good white bread, *crusts cut off*	4 slices
unsalted butter OR good olive oil	
capers, *drained and rinsed*	2 tbsp
anchovy paste OR whole anchovies, *crushed*	2 tbsp
black pepper	
Parmesan cheese, *freshly grated*	2 tbsp

This bizarre-sounding dish has traditionally been served as a savoury course in England at formal dinners, but is equally good as a light snack lunch. Often made with the equally weird-sounding Gentleman's Relish (patum peperium), an anchovy paste, you can instead just crush some anchovies with a fork.

→ Toast the BREAD and spread it generously with the BUTTER while still hot. You may prefer olive oil to butter. Chop the CAPERS fine and mash them well into the ANCHOVY PASTE or CRUSHED ANCHOVIES. Season with PEPPER—the anchovies are salt enough. Spread onto the slices of toast. Sprinkle with PARMESAN and put under a hot grill until the cheese has browned. Cut into fingers and devour. Great with a glass of dry fino.

Bombay Vegetable Sandwich

SERVES 4

chilli powder	½ tsp
turmeric	½ tsp
lemon juice	1 tbsp
cumin seed	½ tsp
sea salt	
mashed potato, leftover or *freshly made*	225g/8oz
granary OR wholewheat bread	8 slices
unsalted butter	
coriander chutney (see p. 217) OR mango chutney	
large organic tomatoes, *sliced and cored*	4
small red onion, *sliced in fine rings*	1
sandwich masala, *made with 1 tsp each ground cumin, ground ginger, chilli powder and ground black pepper mixed together*	
Gruyère cheese, *sliced*	225g/8oz

This is a must, a stunning hangover cure but anyway just a stunner of an unusual and simple dish that will impress in a way that simple toasted cheese will never do but is just as easy to make. Once eaten never forgotten and always repeated, this is one of my favourites for brunch, lunch or Sunday supper.

→ Preheat the oven to 220°C/425°F/Gas 7. Add the CHILLI POWDER, TURMERIC, LEMON JUICE, CUMIN and a pinch of salt to the new or old MASH. Butter the BREAD and then turn the slices over so they are butter-side down on your work surface, messy but essential.

→ Spread the CHUTNEY on the unbuttered side of four of the slices of bread. On the other four slices spread the spiced mash, followed by a layer of TOMATO, then the ONION SLICES, a sprinkling of SANDWICH MASALA and the slices of GRUYÈRE.

→ Close the sandwiches and put them on a baking sheet in the oven. After 5 minutes turn them over with a slice if the bottom, buttery slice of bread has toasted and browned. and bake for another 5 minutes. The cheese should be beginning to ooze. Cut each sandwich into two triangles and serve. You can pass around the ketchup and serve with a salad if you like.

Cheesy Crabby Toasts

SERVES 4

fresh crab meat, white and brown	340g/12oz
unsalted butter, *softened*	30g/1oz
Dijon mustard	1 tsp
cayenne	1 pinch
lemon juice	
chervil, *chopped*	½ tbsp
chives, *chopped*	½ tbsp
dry sherry	1 tbsp
sea salt and black pepper	
Gruyère cheese, *grated*	30g/1oz
wholewheat bread	8 slices
Parmesan cheese, *grated*	55g/2oz

Try these little toasts—crab and Gruyère or Parmesan work beautifully together. Make sure the crab is fresh and unadulterated by rusk.

→ Stir the CRAB MEAT, BUTTER, MUSTARD, CAYENNE, a spritz of LEMON JUICE, the fresh HERBS and SHERRY and the grated GRUYÈRE together to amalgamate, and SEASON to taste. Add more lemon juice if you need to.

→ Toast the BREAD and spread the mixture on top of each slice before sprinkling the tops with the PARMESAN. Put the toasts under a hot grill until browned and bubbling.

Smoke-roasted Salmon, Watercress and Horseradish Sandwich

SERVES 1

horseradish, *grated*	
crème fraîche	
lemon juice (optional)	a little
good crusted bread	2 thick slices
organic watercress	a bunch
smoke-roasted salmon	1 portion

→ Stir a teaspoon of HORSERADISH into a heaped dessertspoon of CRÈME FRAÎCHE. Taste and adjust, according to how hot you like it. Add a drop of LEMON JUICE and spread on each slice of BREAD.

→ Put a hefty clump of WATERCRESS, then chunks of smoke-roasted SALMON on one slice, press the other slice on top and eat immediately.

Bruschetta

What we call toast the Italians call bruschetta; what we butter, they slather in olive oil. Here are some savoury toasted snacks, no more than ideas really, that are mere assembly jobs but gustatory delights no less. It goes without saying that the best ingredients will make the best bruschetta, and that means great bread such as sourdough with a nice blackened charcoally crust or a country bread like Pugliese to get the theme in play. Once the bread is toasted or griddled how you like it, rub with a juicy piece of cut garlic on one side, season and daub with the best olive oil in your kitchen. By that I mean extra virgin, fruity, distinctive, peppery, a show-off of an oil. Then add any of the following toppings.

Courgettes, Tarragon and Ricotta
→ Use slim oiled and griddled tongues of courgettes, scattered with tarragon and some lovely crumbled fresh ricotta, sea salt and black pepper.

Aubergine, Basil and Ricotta
→ Cut some long slices of aubergine, paint them with olive oil on both sides and bake in hot oven, 220°C/425°F/Gas 7, until browned. Scattered over some basil leaves, crumbled fresh ricotta, sea salt and black pepper.

Figs and Ricotta with Wild Rocket
→ Cut the figs into eighths, season and turn in a little olive oil and aged balsamic. Pile the three ingredients on top of the bruschetta with a flourish and an extra glug of olive oil.

Asparagus and Pecorino or Parmesan
→ Griddle the asparagus, rolled in a little olive oil, until tender and slightly charred. Spritz over a little lemon juice and cut the asparagus shafts in half. Place on the bruschetta and shave over some Pecorino or Parmesan. Scrunch on the black pepper.

*Buffalo Mozzarella, Green and Black Olives
and Stove-top-dried Tomatoes*
→ I dry my tomatoes or cherry tomatoes cut in half, the cut side brushed with a little olive oil, thyme and a sliver of garlic, overnight on top of the Aga hotplate, turning them at half-time. You may do the same in your warming oven, or just use bought sun-dried tomatoes if it suits you. Stone the olives and add them with the lactic, squishy slices of mozzarella and a scrunch of pepper and salt to the bruschetta. Place a few dried cherry tomato halves on top and glug on a little more oil.

Broad Beans, Mint and Pecorino
→ Use the baby thumb-nail-sized beans at the beginning of the bean season. Blanch them in boiling water for no more than a minute, then slip off their skins to reveal their emerald hearts. Tear a few mint leaves to add to the topping and shave over some Pecorino. Shake over a little more olive oil and devour.

Blue Cheese, Pear, Rocket and Toasted Buttered Walnuts
→ Crumble blue cheese onto the rocket leaves with a juicy ripe pear cored and cut in quarters or eighths and spritzed with lemon juice to prevent discoloration. Warm a nut of butter in a pan, add a few walnut halves sprinkled with a little sea salt and a pinch of sugar and turn them until stickily coated. Put the warm nuts on top of the rocket and cheese and add a dribble of walnut oil if you have it, olive if you don't.

Roast Beetroot, Goat's Cheese, Garlic and Watercress
→ Wrap whole baby beetroot in foil and roast until tender. Slice in half and lay them on watercress and slices of goat's log. If you like, spread roasted garlic cloves onto the oiled toast before adding the topping. Finally, a libation of hazelnut or olive oil and a scrunch of black pepper.

Roasted Red and Yellow Peppers, Taleggio,
Thyme and Watercress
→ Roast the peppers, let them cool under clingfilm, seed, skin and slice into chunky strips. Drape them over watercress on the bruschetta, add some slices of taleggio to cover and a sprinkle of thyme. Seconds under the grill to get the cheese to barely wilt and flop off the toast. Eat me.

Artichoke Hearts and Rocket
→ Use good char-grilled artichokes such as Seggiano's. Warm them through if you like, then slice and pile on top of the rocket. Sprinkle on some toasted pine nuts.

VEGETA and

BLES

PULSES

Carrots Vichy

SERVES 4

organic carrots	450g/1lb
unsalted butter	30g/1oz
molasses OR muscovado sugar	1 tsp
water OR chicken stock (see p. 54)	
sea salt and black pepper	
a little mint, parsley, chervil OR chives, *chopped*	

This classic dish makes sweet carrots sweeter. If you make it with chicken stock it is even better. This is the best thing to serve with a Sunday roast and with so many different meat and fish dishes.

→ If the CARROTS are young and small they won't need cutting or peeling, merely washing; if they are somewhat long in the tooth, peel them and slice them into long, chunky strips.

→ Place them in a heavy-bottomed pan with a wide surface area and throw on the BUTTER and SUGAR. Half cover with cold WATER OR CHICKEN STOCK. Bring to the boil and cook at a brisk boil with no lid on until the water or stock has all but evaporated. Then get in there quick and toss the carrots to coat and caramelise them in the sugary, buttery juices. Do not let them burn. Remove them from the heat the moment they've begun to caramelise and there is no longer any liquid.

→ Season and add chopped HERBS. Do not salt before cooking as the salt will intensify as the liquid reduces.

Cumin-spiced Carrots

large organic carrot	1 per person
cumin seeds	1 heaped tsp for 3 carrots
unsalted butter	15g/½oz
salt and pepper	

→ Cut the CARROTS into thin discs about the thickness of a pound coin—what my children call money carrots. Steam them until on the point of tenderness when spiked with a knife. Toast the CUMIN SEEDS in a dry frying pan until they begin to exude their signature smell, 1–2 minutes should do it. Crush them coarsely, not to a complete powder, in a pestle and mortar.

→ Melt the BUTTER in a pan, throw in the cumin, stir, then throw in the carrots and toss vigorously to coat; you might need a smidgen more BUTTER. SEASON with salt and pepper and serve.

Fresh Pea Masala

SERVES 4

olive oil	2 tbsp
black mustard seed	2 tsp
fennel seeds	1 tsp
fresh ginger, *grated*	2.5cm/1in
onion, *thinly sliced*	1
ground coriander	1 tsp
turmeric	1 tsp
cayenne pepper	to taste
large tomato, *cut into chunks*	1
water	1 ladle
salt and pepper	
fresh peas, *podded*	285g/10oz
coriander, *chopped*	1 bunch

A lovely summer side dish to accompany a spiced lamb, chicken or prawn dish.

→ Heat the OIL in a pan, add the MUSTARD and FENNEL SEEDS, and when they begin to pop, after about 30 seconds, add the GINGER and ONION and sprinkle on some salt. Cook until softened, then add the GROUND CORIANDER, TURMERIC and CAYENNE. Stir together, add the TOMATO and WATER, and cook for a couple of minutes.

→ Stir in the PEAS and SEASON with salt and pepper. Cover the pan and cook until the peas are tender. Adjust the seasoning, throw the CORIANDER over the dish like confetti, and serve.

Stewed Peas

fresh peas	
good chicken stock	
caster sugar	1 tsp
tiny shallot, *finely chopped*	1
butter	a large knob
cos lettuce heart, *finely chopped*	1
small mint leaves	3 or 4

→ Put some fresh PEAS in a saucepan and add CHICKEN STOCK to come one-third of the way up the peas. Add the CASTER SUGAR, finely chopped SHALLOT, BUTTER and finely chopped LETTUCE. Simmer without a lid until the peas are just tender, by which time the liquid will have reduced somewhat and will coat the peas. Finely chop the MINT LEAVES, scatter on top, and serve.

Minted Pea Purée

SERVES 6

onion, *finely chopped*	1
olive oil	
mint	a handful
chicken stock (see p. 54)	600ml/1pint
frozen peas	1kg/2¼lb
sugar, salt and pepper to taste	

Much as I slavishly follow the seasons, and love fresh peas in summer, I love frozen peas, too. Serve this with virtually any fish or meat dish.

→ Sauté the ONION gently in a bit of OLIVE OIL until softened and translucent. Add most of the MINT, and cook briefly. Add the boiling CHICKEN STOCK, bring it back to the boil, and pour on the PEAS, cooking them until they're done.

→ Strain the liquid and reserve. Put the peas in a liquidiser and blend, adding a bit of the stock but keeping the purée thick. Season with SUGAR, SALT and PEPPER, and sprinkle over some really finely chopped MINT LEAVES. Serve immediately so it doesn't lose its green brilliance.

Warm Broad Bean and Pea Purée with Vinaigrette

SERVES 4–6

broad beans, podded weight	1lb/450g
fresh peas, but frozen will do, podded weight	1lb/450g
chicken stock (see p. 54) OR water	
fresh mint	a handful
Vinaigrette	
garlic clove	1
sea salt	
Dijon mustard	1 tsp
white wine vinegar	½ tbsp
lemon	juice of ½
black pepper	
best olive oil	4–5 tbsp

→ First make the VINAIGRETTE by crushing the GARLIC with the SEA SALT in a mortar, then adding THE REST OF THE INGREDIENTS. Add the OLIVE OIL last and whisk into an emulsion as you go. Check the SEASONING.

→ You need baby broad beans, unless you are prepared to take off the leathery jackets from older ones when they're cooked. Throw the BEANS and PEAS into boiling STOCK OR WATER and cook for 5 minutes. Drain, purée in a food processor and stir in the chopped MINT. Dress the purée with vinaigrette when still warm. Good served with pork chops.

Green Beans in an Egg and Lemon Sauce

SERVES 4–6

green beans	450g/1lb
lemon	juice of 1
organic egg yolks	2
black pepper	

Use the long, thin, Kenyan beans which need topping but not tailing.

→ Cook the BEANS until just tender in boiling salted water. Drain them, keeping a ladleful of the cooking water, to which you whisk in the LEMON JUICE and EGG YOLKS. Heat cautiously, whisking all the time, until the sauce thickens miraculously and froths up. Pour warm over the beans, and you have a Greek-style avgolemono dish. Grind some pepper over the dish and leave to cool.

A Dish of Spring Vegetables

SERVES 4

There is nothing as good as a dish of the first squeaky, sweet peas, thumbnails of broad beans, tight-budded asparagus and the tender hearts of violet-tipped artichokes.

→ Allow two ARTICHOKES each, which you should throw into a large cauldron of boiling water acidulated with a splosh of VINEGAR OR LEMON JUICE. Cook until a leaf will peel easily away from the main stem, then cool slightly, remove the leaves so that you can get to the heart, and carefully cut it away from the woody choke.

→ While the artichokes are cooking, trim a large bundle of ASPARAGUS into 5cm/2in lengths, no woody ends included. Steam, adding the tips about 3 minutes after the wands, until unresistant to the knife.

→ Throw 900g/2lb each of BROAD BEANS and PEAS (unpodded weight) into boiling CHICKEN STOCK, if you have it, or water, to not quite cover, in two small pans, and cook briefly, but slightly more than al dente. Remove the broad beans from the stock, and when slightly cooled, pop them out of their grey wrinkly jackets. It really is worth it, and it isn't that much of an effort.

→ Melt a generous lump of BUTTER in a pan, and add the four vegetables. Toss briefly, do not stir or you'll break up the asparagus, sprinkle over some finely chopped MINT, SEASON, and add some COOKING STOCK if you feel like it.

Baby Artichokes Marinated in Olive Oil

SERVES 6

lemons	4
small artichokes	1.5 kg/3¼lb
extra virgin olive oil	150–170ml/5–6fl oz
thyme	2 sprigs
parsley	2 sprigs
bay leaves	
celery	1 stalk
black peppercorns	12

→ Have a large bowl of cold water with the juice of half a LEMON squeezed into it to hand while you trim the ARTICHOKES. Snap off and discard the dark outer leaves, trim the base and the stalk, and rub the other half of the lemon over the cut surfaces as you go. Cut the top 1cm/½in off the remaining leaves, and throw the artichokes into the acidulated water to prevent discoloration.

→ Bring a large pan of water to the boil, add SALT, and boil the artichokes until just tender. Drain well, and place in a bowl.

→ Make the marinade by putting ALL THE OTHER INGREDIENTS into a saucepan with the juice of the three remaining LEMONS and 850ml/1½ pints of WATER. Simmer uncovered for about 20 minutes, then pour the hot liquid over the artichokes and leave to cool. Cover and refrigerate for at least 3 days.

→ When you want to eat them, remove the artichokes with a slotted spoon and serve with an extra splash of olive oil.

Asparagus with Hollandaise

SERVES 2

asparagus	450g/1lb
Hollandaise Sauce	
best unsalted butter	170g/6oz
organic egg yolks	2
sea salt and black pepper	
lemon	juice of ½

I am of the firm opinion that asparagus needs dressing down rather than dressing up, and that its most compatible partners are butter and eggs. Choose the freshest asparagus you can lay your hands on; any sign of dried, withering, scaly stalks and it's not worth buying. Simply dressed, with butter, vinaigrette or hollandaise, asparagus should be eaten warm, and in the fingers. You'll find one method of making hollandaise on p. 403. This is an alternative.

→ Trim the bases of the ASPARAGUS SPEARS if they need it. Stand the bundles upright, tied with string, in a lidded pan with 8cm/3in of boiling, salted water, or lower them diagonally into a steamer, leaving the tips to just poke out from the semi-closed lid so they don't overcook. Check with the point of a knife after 5 minutes, and if it slips in unresisted, the spears are cooked. The fattest stems will take up to 5 minutes longer.
→ Drain well and put on the plate with a deep yellow puddle of HOLLANDAISE. If you're having new potatoes for your next course, cook them around the asparagus; it will scent them deliciously.

Hollandaise (alternative method)
→ Melt the BUTTER in a small pan, take it off the heat and after a minute or so skim the white frothy solids from the top with a spoon and some kitchen paper. Whisk the EGG YOLKS with a dessertspoon of water in a small pan over a very low heat until thick. Add the melted butter bit by bit, whisking as you go. Do not use the milky curd-like solids at the bottom of the pan and remove from the heat before there is any danger of the mixture simmering and curdling. SEASON and add LEMON JUICE.

Creamed Spinach

unsalted butter	30g/1oz
plain flour	30g/1oz
milk	300ml/10fl oz
sea salt, black pepper, nutmeg	
double cream (optional)	3–4 tbsp
spinach leaves	900g/2lb

This is the perfect thing with a piece of rump steak, a veal or pork chop or any meat or fish cooked without a sauce. The secret is not to make too much béchamel sauce and to make the sauce slightly thicker than normal, so any juices from the spinach will not thin it down too much. The cream is not essential, but you might like to enrich the sauce with it.

→ Make the béchamel (see p. 402) with the BUTTER, FLOUR and MILK but rather thicker than usual as mentioned above. A larger grating of NUTMEG than the usual suspicion is good, as the spinach is quite strident and needs standing up to.
→ While the sauce is simmering and losing its flouriness, wash

the SPINACH and remove any tough stalks. Put the spinach in a large pot over a high heat and stir to make sure it doesn't stick to the bottom. There should be some water clinging to the leaves, but they should not be sodden; you just want to cook the spinach until the leaves wilt and begin to exude their juices. This takes a matter of minutes. Now drain the spinach, pressing it in a conical strainer or colander. Keep some juice in case the sauce needs thinning. Put the spinach back in the pan.
→ Add CREAM to the sauce if you like and thin with the spinach juices if necessary. Check the SEASONING and pour the sauce over the spinach.

Cold Spinach with Crème Fraîche

SERVES 4

olive oil	4 tbsp
small garlic cloves, *peeled and finely chopped*	2
spinach, *trimmed and thoroughly washed*	1.8kg/4lb
large lemon	*grated* zest of 1
lemon	juice of ½
crème fraîche	3 tbsp
black pepper, *coarsely ground*	
sea salt	

This is a perfect dish to eat with cold poached salmon or cold rare beef on a summer's day. It comes from one of my great food heroes, Simon Hopkinson.

→ Heat the OLIVE OIL. Add the GARLIC, stir briefly and put in the SPINACH. Stir-fry together, being careful not to allow the garlic to brown. Tip onto a large plate and spread out to cool.
→ When cold, pick up the spinach with your fingers and arrange in loose mounds on individual serving plates. Sprinkle with the LEMON ZEST. Add the LEMON JUICE to the CRÈME FRAÎCHE and stir to thin slightly. Spoon the CREAM over the spinach, grind over plenty of BLACK PEPPER and add a pinch of Maldon SEA SALT.

Gratin of Spinach

SERVES 4

spinach	675g/1½lb
double cream	240ml/8fl oz
organic egg	1
sea salt, pepper and nutmeg	
Parmesan cheese, *freshly grated*	85–110g/3–4oz
unsalted butter	up to 55g/2oz

→ Preheat the oven to 220°C/440°F/Gas 7. Wash the SPINACH and cook it briefly in a large pan, with just the water still clinging to the leaves—no more. Drain the spinach by pushing it with a wooden spoon in a conical strainer or sieve.
→ Grease a gratin dish and put the spinach into it, flattening it down. Beat the CREAM with the EGG, SEASONING and a grating of NUTMEG and pour it over the spinach, stirring it around. Sprinkle the grated PARMESAN cheese over the surface and dot with BUTTER. Bake for 15–20 minutes until golden and bubbling.

Provençal Spinach Gratin

SERVES 4

pousse (young, tender spinach) OR spinach	900g/2lb
sea salt and pepper	
organic plain flour	3 tbsp
fruity extra virgin olive oil	5 tbsp
Parmesan cheese, *freshly grated*	55g/2oz

As you may imagine, this is the olive oil version of the creamy gratin above, suitable for grilled and barbecued meats and summer dishes, and easy to prepare.

→ Wash the SPINACH and remove any tough stalks. Pack it together tightly in fistfuls at a time and cut it into thin ribbons, before cutting it across the other way.

→ Preheat the oven to 230°C/450°F/Gas 8. Oil a gratin dish and press the spinach down into it. SEASON and scatter the FLOUR over the top. Dribble the rest of the OLIVE OIL all over the surface of the spinach and bake in the oven for 10 minutes. Turn the heat down to 180°C/350°F/Gas 4 and bake for another 40 minutes. Strew the PARMESAN over the top with a little more OLIVE OIL and finish cooking for a further 10 minutes. Simple, peasant perfection.

Gratin of Brussels Sprouts

SERVES 4–6

Brussels sprouts	450g/1lb
double cream	150–300ml/ 5–10fl oz
garlic	1 clove
butter, to grease the gratin dish	
salt, pepper, nutmeg	
brown OR white stale breadcrumbs	a handful
Parmesan cheese, *freshly grated* (optional)	2 tbsp

→ Remove the outside leaves from the SPROUTS and cut a cross in the base of each one. Bring a large pan of water to the boil, salt it and throw in the sprouts. They will take 4–5 minutes to be firm but yielding to a knife stuck right through them. Drain and refresh under cold water so they keep their colour and don't continue to cook. Cut them in half roughly.

→ Preheat the oven to 200°C/400°F/Gas 6. Rub the GARLIC CLOVE over the greased gratin dish while you are bringing the CREAM up to scald point, i.e. just short of boiling point. Place the Brussels sprouts in the gratin dish and season. Pour the cream over them then shake over the BREADCRUMBS and the PARMESAN if you're using it. Gratinée for 20–25 minutes in the oven or until crusty, browned and bubbling furiously.

Brussels Sprouts with Chestnuts and Frazzled Bacon

SERVES 8–10

Brussels sprouts	1kg/2¼lb
organic smoked streaky bacon, *rind snipped off*	6 rashers
organic chestnuts OR the vacuum-packed ones	1 × 200g/7oz jar
unsalted butter (optional)	a little
flat-leaf parsley, *chopped*	a handful
nutmeg, *grated*	a suspicion
black pepper	

Allow 10–12 sprouts per person. Any that don't get eaten can have a second chance in a gratin or bubble and squeak the following day.

→ Cook the SPROUTS, drain and refresh under cold water as above. You can do this an hour ahead of needing them and keep them in the colander.

→ Fifteen minutes before serving, snip the BACON into small, slim strips and cook it in a heavy-bottomed frying pan, slowly, until it begins to release all its fat into the pan. Cook it further until it begins to brown and crisp, then throw in the roughly chopped CHESTNUTS and sprouts and coat them in the bacon fat for a few minutes. You may need to add a walnut-sized lump of BUTTER, or you may not want to. Remove from the heat, scatter over the PARSLEY and season with NUTMEG, sparingly, and a little BLACK PEPPER.

Green Cabbage with Chestnuts, Bacon and Juniper

SERVES 6

organic green cabbage	
salt	
organic smoked streaky bacon, *snipped into strips*	3 rashers
olive oil and butter	
juniper berries, *crushed in a pestle and mortar*	6
chestnuts, *cooked and peeled* OR Merchant Gourmet chestnuts	18–20 ½ packet
double cream	150ml/5fl oz
salt and freshly ground pepper	

→ Core the CABBAGE thoroughly, remove the tough stalky bits and shred finely. Blanch for a minute in plenty of boiling salted water, then drain and refresh in cold water to arrest the cooking.

→ In a heavy-bottomed pot, gently fry the BACON RASHERS in their own fat, then add a little OLIVE OIL and BUTTER, the crushed JUNIPER BERRIES, and the cabbage. Stir well to coat the cabbage, season, put on the lid, and cook very gently for 15 minutes or so. This is a very good-tempered dish so a few minutes either way won't hurt. Stir in the halved CHESTNUTS and the DOUBLE CREAM and heat through. Check the SEASONING and serve.

Cabbage with Grain Mustard and Lardons

SERVES 6–8

cabbage	1
organic streaky bacon	4 rashers
olive oil	2–3 tbsp
garlic clove	1
grain mustard	2 dsrtsp or to taste
black pepper	
unsalted butter	30g/1oz

A good winter way with a white cabbage, especially if you are serving something porky or beefy.

→ Halve the CABBAGE, removing any tough, outer leaves and remove the core before slicing as slimly as you can into long shreds. Snip the RASHERS into strips and put them in a large, heavy-bottomed pot over a medium heat, allowing them to begin to release their fat. Add the clove of GARLIC when the rashers are beginning to brown. Stir it around, then turn up the heat, add the OLIVE OIL and heat it through.

→ Hurl in the cabbage and stir to coat it in oil. Cook for a matter of a few minutes until the cabbage is no longer raw but still has crunch. Stir in the MUSTARD — it turns bitter if it goes in any earlier — and add the PEPPER, any SALT you think it needs, and a knob of BUTTER if you like.

Spiced Red Cabbage with Apple, Molasses and Cider Vinegar

SERVES 10–12

large red cabbage, *halved, cored and very thinly sliced*	1
medium cooking apples	3
olive oil	2 tbsp
molasses sugar	
cider vinegar	
apple juice OR the Somerset Cider Brandy Company's Kingston Black Apple Aperitif, OR some dry cider	
cloves (OR juniper berries)	6
salt and black pepper	

It's worth cooking a whole cabbage, however many of you there are, as it's just as delicious, if not better, heated through the next day. The principle is long, slow cooking to leach out all the cabbagey juices. Some sort of agro/dolce or sweet/sour combination shows the cabbage off to best effect, and some spice and fruit enhance it yet further.

→ Cut the CABBAGE in half, remove the core and slice thinly. Peel the APPLES and cut into chunks. Put a layer of cabbage in the bottom of a large, heavy-bottomed pot with the OLIVE OIL. Throw on one-third of the apple chunks, followed by about a dessertspoon of little lumps of dark brown MOLASSES SUGAR, a sprinkle of CIDER VINEGAR with your thumb half covering the neck of the bottle, around 4 tablespoons of APPLE JUICE OR APPLE ALCOHOL, a good splash, and a couple of CLOVES. SEASON. Repeat with another two layers of everything.

→ Bring to a gentle simmer on top of the stove, cover with a layer of greaseproof paper and a tight-fitting lid and simmer on. After an hour, check and stir the cabbage thoroughly so that the top layer cooks through in the liquid beneath and doesn't dry out. Repeat once more. It will be ready 2–2½ hours after the start of cooking time. Taste the cooking juices to make sure you have the right balance between acidic and sweet, and adjust accordingly. If at any time the liquid level looks like it's too low to protect the cabbage and lubricate it, add some more apple juice or apple alcohol.

Red Cabbage with Red Wine, Onion and Chestnuts
→ You may prefer to add RED WINE VINEGAR and RED WINE instead of the apple element, in which case ONION instead of apple works best, and you may like to throw in a few whole CHESTNUTS at the same time.

Red Cabbage with Cranberries and Apple
→ Red cabbage is also delicious if you cook it with 450g/1lb CRANBERRIES and a large, chopped cooking apple in the same way as for this recipe, but with a CINNAMON STICK instead of the cloves. You will need to add extra SUGAR as the cranberries are sharper than sharp.

Fennel Braised with Thyme, Olives and Cardamom

SERVES 4

fennel bulbs	4
olive oil	2 tbsp
garlic cloves	2
black olives, *stoned*	8
cardamom pods, *crushed*	3
thyme	1 bunch
chicken stock (see p. 54) OR half water, half white wine	600ml/1 pint
salt and pepper	

This gently aniseedy braised dish is brought to life with salty olives, thyme, garlic and a breath of fragrant cardamom. It is something I always go back to when I am cooking a special fish or pork dish, as it exudes quiet sophistication and good taste. What's more, you can abandon it while you concentrate on cooking the rest of the dinner.

→ Preheat the oven to 180°C/350°F/Gas 4. Once you have removed the tough outer layer of the FENNEL bulbs, cut vertically down and quarter each one. Sweat them gently in the OLIVE OIL in a heavy-bottomed casserole.
→ Add the GARLIC, OLIVES, CARDAMOM, THYME and LIQUID, SEASON, and bring to the boil. Cover with the pan with greaseproof paper and then with a lid, and bake in the oven for 1¼–1½ hours. Particularly delicious with pork or fish.

Gratin of Fennel

fennel	1 large head per person
unsalted butter and olive oil	
sea salt and black pepper	
Parmesan, *freshly grated*	1 tbsp per fennel bulb

→ Preheat the oven to 190°C/375°F/Gas 5. Remove the tough outer leaves of the FENNEL ruthlessly, then slice the bulbs down through their core so the leaves don't part company with the base. Depending on the size of the bulbs you may wish to quarter them.

→ Steam the fennel pieces until just resistant when pierced through with a skewer and place them cut side down in a gratin dish. Sprinkle with OLIVE OIL and a few little pieces of BUTTER, SEASON and throw over the grated PARMESAN. Bake for 15–20 minutes or until golden and bubbling.

Celery Cooked with Cream

celery	1 head
double cream	150ml/5fl oz
organic egg yolks	2
sea salt and black pepper	

This is a perfect accompaniment to plainly grilled lamb cutlets or French-trimmed rack of lamb.

→ Wash and trim the CELERY and peel each stalk with a potato peeler—this simple process makes all the difference. Chop the pieces into 7.5cm/3in lengths on the diagonal, and steam until tender when pierced.

→ Transfer the celery to a pan. Whisk the CREAM with the EGGS, pour over the celery and heat gently so the sauce thickens without boiling. SEASON and serve immediately.

Caramelised Endives with Melted Taleggio

SERVES 4

endives	4
oil	1 tbsp
unsalted butter	30g/1oz
molasses OR dark muscovado sugar	1 tsp
sea salt and black pepper	
fresh thyme, *chopped*	2 tsp
Taleggio cheese *without its rind, cut into slices*	200g/7oz
breadcrumbs	30g/1oz
Parmesan cheese, *freshly grated*	30g/1oz

Taleggio, like Fontina d'Aosta, is a perfect cheese to melt over pasta or vegetables: it doesn't go stringy, it doesn't separate or go hard, and it has a lovely rich creaminess. Great with pork or beef.

→ Halve the ENDIVES down through their core. Preheat the oven to 190°C/375°F/Gas 5. Take a large, heavy-bottomed frying pan with an ovenproof handle, place onto a medium heat and after a minute add the OIL and BUTTER. Add the SUGAR at the same time, and when the oil is hot, place the endives cut-side down into the oil in a single layer—you may have to do this in two batches. Season and leave for about 5 minutes until the cut side is a lovely golden colour and looks caramelised.

→ Turn the endives over and sprinkle with half the THYME. Cover each endive with TALEGGIO and the rest of the THYME and bake for 10–12 minutes until the cheese starts to bubble. Sprinkle over the mixed BREADCRUMBS and PARMESAN with a scrunch of PEPPER, and return to the oven for 5 minutes or until the top looks browned.

Caramelised Leeks with Melted Taleggio
→ You can make this with fat LEEKS. If using leeks, trim off the dark green leaves and cut the white part in half.

Endives au Beurre

SERVES 4

Belgian endives OR Treviso chicory	4
unsalted butter	45–55g/1½–2oz
black pepper	
lemon juice	

Endives enhance fish and meat equally well. I serve mine alongside a chined loin of pork. The most important thing to remember is not to cut the bottoms off the endives, which will lead to the release of bitter juices. Leave them whole, and complement their mildly bitter flavour with lemon at the end. I added no salt to the dish.

Heat the oven to 150°C/300°F/Gas 2. Pack the ENDIVES into a small earthenware or glass casserole, adding knobs of BUTTER and BLACK PEPPER. Cover and put in the oven for 1–1½ hours until cooked (the base should be tender when pierced with a skewer). Add a good squeeze of LEMON JUICE and serve.

Baked Beetroot

SERVES 4

beetroot	8 small or 4 medium
Optional	
crème fraîche	
lemon juice	
black pepper	
dill OR chives	

The sweet earthiness of the beetroot is inimitable but it is an acquired taste. The bleeding of the ruby juices into their surrounding companions can be off-puttingly institutional, but persevere. Here's how to do it.

→ Wash, but do not peel the BEETROOT. Do not disturb the wispy rooty bits by cutting them as the beetroot will instantly start secreting its dark juices. Wrap each beetroot separately and tightly in foil and bake in a medium oven, 190°C/350°F/Gas 4, until tender when pierced with a skewer.
→ Peel when you can bear to and serve the beetroot as they are, or chopped into cubes with a dollop of CRÈME FRAÎCHE spritzed with a little LEMON JUICE, some BLACK PEPPER and a tablespoon of DILL OR CHIVES.

Baked Beetroot with Sour Cream
→ Bake as above. When the beetroot are tender, peel and slice them, and put them in a shallow serving dish. Pour some heated SOUR CREAM over them, add some chopped CHIVES OR DILL if serving with fish, and SEASON with salt and pepper.

Roast Red Onion Squash with Chilli, Rosemary and Thyme

SERVES 4

red onion squash	1
rosemary and thyme, *exceedingly finely chopped*	a few sprigs
garlic cloves, *finely chopped*	2
red chilli, *seeded and finely chopped*	1
good olive oil	
sea salt and black pepper	
butter OR balsamic vinegar (optional)	

I find the red onion squash as intensely flavoured as the best Italian or French pumpkin. It has yielding, mealy-textured flesh and skin that softens to the point where you can eat it.

→ Preheat the oven to 200°C/400°F/Gas 6. Scoop the seeds out of the SQUASH and cut it in melon-like slices. Put the finely chopped ROSEMARY, THYME, GARLIC and CHILLI into a little bowl of good OLIVE OIL, SEA SALT and PEPPER to macerate, then spoon a little into the boat of each squash. You could use sage instead of rosemary and thyme for a change.

→ Bake the squash for about 30–40 minutes until cooked through, basting the slices a couple of times. You can add a knob of BUTTER at the end if you feel like it, or sprinkle over a little BALSAMIC VINEGAR before serving.

Roasted Butternut Squash with Wild or Chestnut Mushrooms and Cream

SERVES 4

butternut squash, allow half a squash per person	2
butter and olive oil	
garlic cloves, *crushed to a paste with sea salt*	2
black pepper	
rosemary OR sage leaves	2 tsp
organic double cream, unpasteurised if possible	300ml/10fl oz
mushrooms	400g/14oz
flat-leaf parsley, *chopped*	a handful

This is a perfect autumnal dish, timely for the confluence of squash and porcini or chanterelles if, like me, you go out fungi-foraging. If you don't, you can use organic chestnut or Portobello mushrooms.

→ Preheat the oven to 180°C/350°F/Gas 4. Cut the SQUASH in half and take out the seeds and fibrous bits. You will find that the seeds are contained in only one of the halves, but scoop out some space in both cavities. Put a generous lump of BUTTER and a splosh of best OLIVE OIL in each cavity, with a bit of the GARLIC PASTE, the finely chopped ROSEMARY OR SAGE and some ground BLACK PEPPER. Reserve half the garlic for the mushrooms. Roast until the flesh is soft, 30–40 minutes.

→ Brush the earth off the PORCINI, or clean the MUSHROOMS with a damp cloth, before slicing them and frying them in a bit of OLIVE OIL until they begin to weep with juice. Add the GARLIC and CREAM and allow it to bubble, stirring as you go. Scatter over the PARSLEY, season and tip the contents of the pan into the squash cavities, stirring in the cream with the butter. Allow to cool for a few minutes before you bring the squash to the table.

Sweetcorn Fritters

cooked sweetcorn, *kernels cut from cobs*	170g/6oz
flour	55g/2oz
milk	2 tbsp
paprika	1 pinch
cayenne	1 pinch
organic egg	1
egg white	1
sea salt	
unsalted butter	a knob

→ Mix the SWEETCORN, FLOUR, MILK, PAPRIKA, CAYENNE and EGG together in a bowl. Whisk the EGG WHITE until stiff and fold it into the mixture, adding a little SALT. Heat the BUTTER in a pan and drop tablespoons of the thick batter into it, frying them on both sides until golden.

Courgette Gratin

SERVES 4

large onion, *chopped*	1
olive oil	3
garlic cloves, *finely chopped*	3
small courgettes, *cut coin-thin*	450g/1lb
flat-leaf parsley	1 handful
long-grain rice	55g/2oz
sea salt and black pepper	
organic eggs	3
Parmesan OR Gruyère cheese, *freshly grated*	2 handfuls

This is as good served with fresh tomato sauce as it is with grilled meat or fish. A little tarragon can be added as well as the parsley.

→ Heat the oven to 180°C/350°F/Gas 4. Gently sauté the ONION in the OIL until softened and translucent, adding the GARLIC midway through the process. Toss in the COURGETTES and chopped PARSLEY (and some tarragon, if you like) and continue to cook gently until the courgettes have softened but still retain some texture.

→ Throw in the RICE and stir, allowing it to absorb the liquid, and cook for 10 minutes. SEASON. Beat the EGGS with the CHEESE, add to the courgettes and turn into an OILED earthenware dish. Bake in the oven for about 30 minutes until bronzed and bubbling. Serve warm rather than hot.

Sautéed Courgettes

→ Coarsely grate some COURGETTES and cook them in a little OLIVE OIL over a low heat until just tender. Squeeze ½ a LEMON over them, and SEASON with salt and pepper.

Stuffed Courgettes

SERVES 4

medium onion, *finely chopped*	1
olive oil	
garlic cloves, *finely chopped*	2
pork mince	110g/4oz
veal mince	110g/4oz
cooked ham, *diced*	55g/2oz
spinach	110g/4oz
large tomato, *peeled, seeded and chopped*	1
parsley	a handful
breadcrumbs	a handful
organic egg	1
sea salt and black pepper	
Parmesan cheese, *freshly grated*	2 handfuls
courgettes, round ones if possible	4

Think in terms of leftovers, rather than specific quantities, and which flavour you would like to be predominant in this dish. You may use less meat, only one kind of meat, or olives or spinach in the stuffing. If you have some cooked beef, chicken or lamb, simply omit the browning stage. Onion, garlic and herbs are a must, as is the binding force of the cheese. If you can't find round courgettes, use the long ones.

→ Heat oven to 200°C/400°F/Gas 6. Sauté the ONION gently in OLIVE OIL for 15 minutes, adding the GARLIC and the MINCED MEAT when the onion has softened. Cook until the meat has lost its raw colour. Cook the SPINACH briefly, drain well and chop.

→ Put the onion and meat mixture in a bowl with the spinach, add THE REMAINING INGREDIENTS, except the cheese and courgettes, and season. Remove the tops from the COURGETTES and scoop out the inner flesh, leaving a strong wall. Pack the courgettes with the stuffing and top with their 'hats'. Place the courgettes in a gratin dish, sprinkle with PARMESAN and drizzle with OLIVE OIL.

→ Bake for about 40 minutes, then check with a skewer that the courgettes are cooked right through. Remove from the oven to cool and eat while still warm.

Ratatouille

SERVES 4–6

large aubergines	2
red peppers	2
large onion, *finely sliced*	1
garlic cloves, *chopped*	3
olive oil	
courgettes, *sliced*	4
thyme	1 sprig
bay leaves	2–3
sea salt and black pepper	
plum tomatoes	1 × 400g/14oz tin
OR fresh tomatoes, *skinned, seeded and chopped*	450g/1lb
fresh basil	a handful

There are no short cuts for this classic-for-all-seasons. The secret of the best ratatouille is simple: the vegetables have to be cooked separately before they are married. That way they retain their individual flavour, texture and character. You do not, after all, want an amorphous swamp of bland, over-stewed, oily-puddle-on-a-plate apology for this Mediterranean joy. Ratatouille is particularly good with plain roast meat or grilled fish, or as part of a summer lunch with salads and cold meat. Otherwise, just serve it for lunch with some good country sourdough bread to mop up the juices.

→ Slice the AUBERGINES into discs, brush them with OLIVE OIL and place on silicone paper on a baking sheet. Roast them in a hot oven, 200°C/400°F/Gas 6, for 15–20 minutes until tender. This is quite the best way to cook aubergines without them absorbing barrels of oil.

→ Meanwhile, put the red PEPPERS on a baking sheet in the oven and turn them every time a side chars, or hold them with a pair of tongs over a naked flame. Put the charred peppers into a plastic bag or a bowl covered with clingfilm for about 20 minutes until they are cool enough to handle and the steam has eased the skin from the flesh. Peel, core, seed and cut them into strips or larger pieces, depending on your preference.

→ Sauté the ONION and GARLIC gently in a little OLIVE OIL until softened. Add the COURGETTES, THYME, BAY LEAVES and BLACK PEPPER and a little more OIL if necessary. When the courgettes have begun to soften, add the TOMATOES and bring to a bubble before adding the aubergines and red peppers. Stew everything gently for a further 5–10 minutes. Check the seasoning and leave to cool. Ratatouille is best eaten warm or cold rather than hot. Strew the torn BASIL LEAVES over the top before serving.

Palak Aloo

SERVES 1

potato, *boiled*	150g/5oz
vegetable oil	a thin film
cumin seeds	½ tsp
garlic, *finely chopped*	½ tsp
onion	75g/2½ oz
tomato passata	75g/2½ oz
spinach, *briefly cooked and coarsely puréed*	300g/10oz
cumin powder	½ tsp
coriander powder	½ tsp
garam masala	½ tsp
red chilli powder, use at your discretion	¼–½ tsp
fresh coriander, *chopped*	1 heaped tsp
root ginger *in matchstick strips*	½ tsp
salt	

A simple dish of spiced potato and spinach which you can serve as part of a vegetarian thali or with fish or meat. If you have left-over cooked spinach and potato, or can contrive to cook extra and keep some back, you are on your way. Also very good to spruce up cold meat or chicken on a Monday night.

→ Cut the POTATO into large chunks. Heat the OIL in a pan, then add the CUMIN SEEDS until they crackle, 30 seconds or so, before adding the finely chopped GARLIC. Add the chopped ONION and cook until softened, then add the TOMATO PASSATA and continue to cook. Add the SPINACH, then mix the powdered SPICES, MASALA, CHILLI and CORIANDER with a couple of tablespoons of water, a brilliant trick to avoid the subtle spices burning while frying them. Add them with the GINGER to the spinach mix and fry briefly. Add the potatoes and heat through, carefully stirring so they don't break up.

Achari Paneer

Serves 4

mustard oil	30g/1oz
mustard seeds	a pinch
fenugreek seeds	a pinch
cumin seeds	a pinch
onions, *very finely chopped*	55g/ 2oz
tomatoes, *chopped*	110g/4oz
best cottage cheese, *sieved*	225g/8oz
red chilli	½ tsp
coriander powder	1 tsp
salt	
sugar	
lemon juice	
fresh coriander, *chopped*	a bunch

If anything could turn me vegetarian, the cooking of Rajasthan would be the strongest contender. This is a lovely dish: tiny quenelles of cottage cheese cooked briefly in pickling spices and the mustard oil that is the standard oil in this part of India.

→ Heat the MUSTARD OIL in a pan and add the whole dry masala—MUSTARD SEEDS, FENUGREEK and CUMIN SEEDS—to temper. This takes only a minute or so and really brings out the flavour of the spices. Allow the seeds to crackle, then add the ONIONS and sauté until brown. Add the TOMATOES, and cook down for 10–15 minutes. Meanwhile shape the COTTAGE CHEESE into small walnut-sized balls between two spoons.

→ Add the CHILLI and half the CORIANDER POWDER to the mixture in the pan, cook for a few more minutes, then drop in the paneer—the little balls of cottage cheese—coating them well in the spice mixture. Add SALT, a pinch of SUGAR and a spritz of LEMON JUICE to taste. Sprinkle over some FRESH CORIANDER and serve. You can make the paneer mixture in advance and assemble all the spices and chopped onion and tomato an hour or two before you want to cook them.

Mater Tikki

Serves 1

fresh mint	½ tsp
fresh coriander	½ tsp
fresh root ginger	½ tsp
medium green chilli	1
potatoes, *boiled and mashed*	200g/7oz
fresh OR frozen peas, *blanched*	25g/1oz
garam masala	½ tsp
chat masala	½ tsp
salt	
cumin seeds	½ tsp
lemon juice	
vegetable oil	300ml/10fl oz

Another lovely vegetarian side dish which is really little more than spiced potato and pea cakes. Garam masala and chat masala are both mixtures of spices. Garam masala contains cumin, cardamom, coriander and other spices; chat masala is a mix of coriander, cumin, chillies and dry mango powder. Prepare the tikkis an hour or two in advance if you like, spreading them out on a plate ready to fry

→ Mix together the chopped MINT, CORIANDER, GINGER and CHILLI and add to the mashed POTATO with BOTH MASALAS and some SALT. Heat a little OIL in a small pan, then crackle the CUMIN SEEDS for a few seconds till they exude their toasty scent, before adding the PEAS and cooking gently until soft. Mash the cumin and peas together a little with a fork, adding the LEMON JUICE and SALT.

→ To make the tikkis, take lumps of the potato mixture and flatten them with the palm of one hand. Pop a bit of pea mixture into the centre and enclose it in the potato until you have a small potato cake. Use a little FLOUR if the mixture is a bit damp, and coat the palm of your hand with the flour so that you can work the mixture with the heel of your palm.

→ Heat the VEGETABLE OIL until a tiny bit of the mixture thrown in fizzes and begins to brown instantly. Drop in the tikkis and cook them for about 3 minutes a side. Drain and serve with some minted yoghurt and a few thinly sliced mild onion rings.

Tadkeywala Dahi

SERVES 1

turmeric, *grate some root if you can get it*	tip of a tsp
red chilli powder	tip of a tsp
vegetable oil	5ml/1 level tsp
mustard seeds	¼ tsp
coriander seeds	½ tsp
cumin seeds	½ tsp
whole red chilli	1
garlic, *crushed to a paste with a little salt*	½ tsp
onion, *finely chopped*	50g/2oz
tomatoes, *finely chopped*	50g/2oz
fresh coriander, *chopped*	½ tsp
fresh mint, *chopped*	½ tsp
fresh root ginger, *in matchstick strips*	½ tsp
salt	
yoghurt, *hung overnight in muslin to drain*	150g/5oz

Do not be put off by the ingredients list, the process is simplicity itself, the spices are all things you will keep in your store cupboard if you are a keen cook. Just remember to hang the yoghurt the day before. The result, a coolly elegant, subtly spiced, yoghurt-based dish, is perfect alongside any plainly cooked white fish or chicken, alone with rice, or with a peshwari naan or a paratha to dip into the juices. I find a J-cloth or nylon sieve as effective as muslin, which I don't always have when it's not the jam-making season.

→ Put the TURMERIC and CHILLI in a bowl with a couple of spoons of water to prevent their burning. Heat the OIL, add the MUSTARD SEEDS, CORIANDER and CUMIN SEEDS and the whole RED CHILLI. Then add the turmeric and chilli in water and the GARLIC PASTE and stir together. Add the ONIONS, stir them in and cook gently until they have softened. Add the TOMATOES, continue cooking for a few minutes, then add the chopped FRESH CORIANDER, MINT, GINGER and SALT.
→ Take the mixture off the heat, mix in the hung YOGHURT, and serve warm.

Spiced Puy Lentils

SERVES 8–10

puy lentils	225g/8oz
ground cumin	2 tsp
fresh coriander, *chopped*	a large handful
lemon	juice of 1
olive oil	150ml/5fl oz
salt and pepper	

→ Throw the PUY LENTILS into a large pan of boiling water. They don't need soaking, they are the delicious speckledy, earthy blue-black ones. Cook until tender, about half an hour, and drain. Stir in the ground CUMIN, a large handful of fresh, chopped CORIANDER, the LEMON JUICE, OLIVE OIL and SEA SALT AND PEPPER. Taste and make sure it is lemony enough.

Yellow Lentils Tempered with Cumin and Garlic

SERVES 6

split lentils	200g/7oz
turmeric	a pinch
salt	
ghee OR clarified butter	30g/1oz
cumin seeds	½ tsp
garlic	½ tsp
onion, *finely chopped*	55g/2oz
tomato, *chopped*	30g/1oz
chilli powder	½ tsp
cumin powder	½ tsp
fresh coriander, *chopped*	a handful

Serve this lentil dish with some rice or alongside a fish or meat curry.

→ Wash the LENTILS, cover with water and bring them to the boil. Remove the scum from the top with a slotted spoon and some kitchen paper, and simmer. Add the TURMERIC and SALT when the lentils have considerably softened and continue to cook until done.

→ Heat the GHEE in a pan, then add the whole CUMIN and GARLIC, followed by the ONIONS and TOMATO. Sauté them with the CHILLI and CUMIN POWDER. When the mixture has softened, add it to the lentils and heat through to boiling. Add a handful of fresh CORIANDER, check the SEASONING and serve.

Onions Baked with Goat's Cheese and Thyme

SERVES 4

small onions	12
OR shallots	24
olive oil	
soft goat's cheese	200g/7oz
thyme OR marjoram, *chopped*	1 tbsp
garlic cloves, *peeled and finely chopped*	2
cayenne, nutmeg, salt and pepper	

→ Preheat the oven to 180°C/350°F/Gas 4. Blanch the ONIONS in boiling salted water for 5 minutes to soften them. Drain and slice vertically in half. OIL a gratin dish and place the onions in it cut side up. Season with SALT, PEPPER, NUTMEG, a pinch of CAYENNE and add a bit more OIL to moisten. Cut and crumble the GOAT'S CHEESE over the onions, then sprinkle with the THYME and GARLIC, and bake for 40 minutes.

Baby Onions and Tamarind

SERVES 6

shallots OR pickling onions	450g/1lb
olive oil	2 tbsp

You can find tamarind paste in Middle Eastern and Indian stores and many supermarkets these days. It gives the onions an intense sweet-and-sour taste.

→ Poach the SHALLOTS OR ONIONS in boiling water for about 5 minutes (this makes them easier to peel) and peel them when just cool enough to handle. In a pan just large enough to

tamarind paste	1 tbsp
sugar	1 tbsp

contain them in one layer, sauté the onions in the OIL, shaking the pan and turning them to brown them lightly all over. Add the TAMARIND and the SUGAR and half cover with water. Stir well and cook, covered, over a low heat for about 25 minutes or until very soft, adding water if necessary; lift the lid and reduce the sauce over a high heat at the end. Serve cold as a side dish, or as part of a mezze.

Piggy Figgies or Figs in Lardo

black figs	1 or 2 per person
lardo OR prosciutto fat	

Lardo is difficult to come by outside Italy or a good Italian deli, but the fat from some sliced prosciutto works well wound in thin skeins around the figs. The most perfect soft and crisp, salt and sweet bite you ever came across, this is great to serve with drinks or as a starter as well as a side dish.

→ Preheat the oven to 220°C/425°F/Gas 7. Simply open the tops of the FIGS out gently and wind a little LARDO OR FAT through and over the top of them, a strip or two per fig. Place on a baking tray and blast for 3 minutes, by which time the fat will have both crisped and leaked its porky, salt juices into the grainy, red cavity of the black fig.

Saffron-Stewed Jersey New Potatoes with Chicken Stock and Thyme

SERVES 4

Jersey new potatoes, *skins on but scrubbed*	675g/1½ lb
butter	30g/1oz
saffron threads	1 good pinch
bay leaf	1
thyme	1 sprig
hot chicken stock (see p. 54)	120ml/4fl oz
spring onion, *finely chopped*	1
knob of butter (optional)	

These are a marvellous accompaniment to grilled or baked white fish, intensely flavoured with the reduced stock and saffron and the scent of bay and thyme.

→ Sweat the POTATOES in the BUTTER in a heavy-bottomed casserole for a couple of minutes. Add the SAFFRON threads, BAY LEAF and THYME and shake the pan. Add the hot CHICKEN STOCK, cover the pan and simmer gently for about 15 minutes.
→ Remove the lid and boil to reduce the liquid until it is a syrupy glaze. Remove the thyme and the bay leaf, add the finely chopped SPRING ONION and another knob of BUTTER if you like, and cook the potatoes a couple of minutes longer.

Roast Potatoes and Parsnips

potatoes	
parsnips	
dripping, goose OR duck fat OR olive oil	3–4 tbsp

Roast potatoes are a winter thing. You need old season's potatoes, preferably floury ones that you can ruffle up with a fork to make a larger surface area to crisp up. Allow one potato large enough to cut into three big chunks per person and a few extras.

→ Two chunks of parsnip should be enough for each person. Peel and cut them thick enough that they don't burn in the roasting tin, which skinny ones tend to. Peel the POTATOES, cut them and put them with the PARSNIPS in a large pan. Just cover them with cold water, salted if you wish, and bring to the boil with the lid on. Remove the lid and boil rapidly for about 5 minutes, by which time the potatoes will not be totally resistant when you poke a knife tip into them. Place a colander over a large jug. Drain the potatoes into the colander, keeping the water for cooking further vegetables in or just for the gravy if you're braising or steaming the rest of the veg.

→ A couple of minutes before you drain the potatoes and parsnips, place a large roasting tin with either a lump of DRIPPING, GOOSE or DUCK FAT (a well heaped tablespoon and a bit extra) or 3–4 tablespoons of OLIVE OIL in the top of the oven and wait until you hear it splutter, about 3–4 minutes. Olive oil makes good, crisp roast potatoes but the flavour imparted from the dripping or fat is infinitely superior, so try to keep some in the fridge from your last joint of beef or duck.

→ Remove the roasting tin to the top of the stove and slip the drained potatoes into it, standing back as they will begin to splutter madly. Turn each potato in the fat so that they are completely coated, then plough a fork across the surface of each potato until it looks well furrowed.

→ Return the tin to the top of the oven and roast for about an hour, turning every 20 minutes as each side crisps. After the first 20 minutes, throw the parsnips into the middle of the tin —they cook more quickly than the potatoes and will burn more easily in the greater heat at the edge. Turn them when you turn the potatoes. When they are crisp all over and the rest of the lunch is ready to put on the table, drain the fat into a bowl and plop the potatoes and parsnips into a heated serving dish. You may, if you'd rather, cook the parsnips around the joint. This is particularly successful with beef, pork, goose or duck as they then cook in the delicious fat, and more slowly to boot!

Sweet-sour Roasted Parsnips and Sweet Potatoes

SERVES 4

large parsnips	2
large sweet potatoes	2
olive oil	2 tbsp
sesame oil	2 tsp
pomegranate molasses	1 dsrtsp
runny thyme OR other intense, dark honey	1 tbsp
sea salt and black pepper	

→ Preheat the oven to 200°C/400°F/Gas 6. Peel and cut the VEGETABLES into chunky batons—you do not need to par-boil the parsnips for this recipe. Put them on a shallow baking tray and pour over both OILS, turning the batons over to coat all sides completely. Dribble over a thin stream of POMEGRANATE MOLASSES, followed by a thin stream of HONEY and turn to coat evenly. Season and put straight into the oven.

→ After 20 minutes, when the vegetables will have stickily blackened patches (and so will the baking tray), scrape the residue over the vegetables and turn them over. Roast for another 20 minutes or until both sides of the vegetable batons are equally crusted and cooked through to a caramelised, burnished finish.

Pommes Anna

SERVES 3–4

potatoes, *peeled and thinly sliced*	675g/1½lb
unsalted butter, *melted*	85–110g/3–4oz
sea salt and black pepper	

I cook this deliciously simple dish in a cast-iron, heavy-bottomed, stubby-handled frying pan that can go in the oven. Traditionally the pan should be lidded, but mine isn't, so I use greased greaseproof paper.

→ Preheat the oven to 200°C/400°F/Gas 6. Wash the starch out of the potatoes in a colander, pat dry in a cloth, and place the slices in overlapping circles on the well buttered base of the pan. Brush butter over each layer as you go, and season. Cover with greaseproof paper or a lid and cook in the oven. Check with a skewer after 45 minutes, but the potatoes can take up to an hour.

Rosemary Potatoes

SERVES 3–4

large King Edward potatoes	4
olive oil	2 tbsp
garlic cloves, unpeeled	8
rosemary	a few branches
salt and black pepper	

→ Chop the POTATOES into 1cm/1/2in squares, keeping their skins on. Pour the OLIVE OIL onto a baking sheet and warm in the oven, 200°C/400°F/Gas 6, for a few minutes. Add the potatoes and GARLIC and strew over the ROSEMARY. Cook for about 50 minutes, turning every 15 minutes or so. SEASON with salt and pepper. At the end I pop the garlic out of its skin and eat it, but not everyone is that addicted.

Mashed Potato

SERVES 2

potatoes, *peeled and cut into chunks*	450g/1lb
best unsalted butter (more if you like)	55g/2oz
Jersey milk	120ml/4fl oz
salt	
black pepper	

First find the flouriest potatoes, for these make the best mash. Maris Piper or King Edwards are more floury than waxy, and that is what you want. Mash is the number one comfort food, but you have to get the texture silken smooth; there is a world of difference between lumpen, dry mash, mash that is puréed like gloopy baby food, gluey-textured mash and the ideal buttery, satiny, peppery mash that has been moulied and whipped into snowy perfection with a wooden spoon. The butter ratio is yours to decide, but use best unsalted butter.

→ I favour steaming chunks of peeled POTATOES until they are cooked through, then leaving them drained in the top of the steamer for 5 minutes while you gently heat the BUTTER and MILK in a pan. When the butter has melted and the milk is hot, mouli your potatoes into them over a gentle heat on the coarse blade of a mouli-légumes. Some people prefer ricers or mashers, but I find the mouli the perfect tool for the right texture. Now take the pan off the heat, add SALT and a good scrunch of BLACK PEPPER and stir the mixture briskly in the pan with a wooden spoon so that you whip it into a glossy amalgam, ready to serve.

Roasted Garlic Mashed Potatoes
→ I like mashed potatoes the simple way, but the one variation that I think does work is to add a few cloves of roasted GARLIC. Roast the garlic cloves—say 2–3 per person—in their skins, coated in some olive oil, in the oven until soft when spiked with a skewer. Pop them out of their skins and mash them with a fork, adding a little olive oil. As you are mashing the potatoes, add a little of the garlicky oil mixture and a drop of milk at a time—and forego any butter. It gives the potatoes a wonderfully pungent, earthy flavour and is particularly good with fish.

Champ

Serves 6	
floury potatoes, *peeled and cut into chunks*	1kg/2¼lb
creamy milk	300ml/10fl oz
butter	55–85g/2–3oz
spring onions, *finely chopped*	6
salt and pepper	

→ Simmer the POTATOES until tender. Drain off the water, cover the pan and let the potatoes sit for a few minutes. Put the MILK and 55g/2oz of the BUTTER in a saucepan and heat to boiling point. Add the chopped SPRING ONIONS, turn off the heat, and let the onions infuse in the milk.

→ Mash the potatoes, then add the milk, butter and spring onion mixture, stirring until smooth. SEASON to taste. You can make a well in the centre and add an extra lump of BUTTER to melt into the champ if you like.

Colcannon

Serves 6–8	
green cabbage, *finely chopped*	1kg/2¼lb
small leeks, *finely chopped*	2
milk	150–300ml/5–10fl oz
floury potatoes, *peeled and roughly chopped*	1kg/2¼lb
salt and pepper	
nutmeg, *grated*	1 pinch
butter, *melted*	110g/4oz

→ Simmer the CABBAGE and LEEKS in just enough MILK to cover, until soft. Boil the POTATOES until tender, drain and mash them, then season to taste with SALT, PEPPER and NUTMEG.

→ Add the cabbage, leek and milk mixture. Place in a deep, warmed serving dish, make a well in the centre and pour in the melted BUTTER. Serve the vegetables with spoonfuls of the melted butter.

Rumbledethumps

Serves 4–6	
large onion, *peeled and sliced*	1
cabbage, *cut into strips*	450g/1lb
potatoes, *boiled and skinned*	450g/1lb
butter	55–85g/2–3oz
strong Cheddar cheese	125g/4oz
salt and pepper	

A dish said to originate on the Scottish borders, the 'rumbling' is the mashing, the 'thumping' is the beating down. You need a good, strong extra mature Cheddar like Montgomery, Green's or Keen's.

→ Cook the ONION and CABBAGE in boiling salted water until tender, then refresh in a colander with cold water, and drain. Mouli or mash the POTATO with the BUTTER, then mash in the cabbage and onion. Transfer the mixture to a gratin dish, cover with a layer of grated CHEESE, and brown under a hot grill.

Chips

SERVES 2

large, floury winter potatoes	2
groundnut oil for frying	
sea salt	

Remember not to over-fill the fryer or the chips will stick to each other, absorb far too much oil and not crisp up. Make them in batches and keep them warm in a warmed dish on kitchen paper in a medium oven with the door open. There are no shortcuts to making the best, most burnished, bronzed, crisp chips. They simply HAVE to be fried twice or you may as well forget it and go down to the chippy. I like my chips thick, but not so thick that the floury innard overwhelms the crisp outside. Skinny chips seem rather to defeat the object!

→ Peel the POTATOES and cut them however thickly or thinly you like your chips. Wash the chips in a colander under cold running water until you can't see any milky starch, then pat them dry in a tea towel.

→ Half fill your deep-fryer with OIL in the normal way and heat it to 180–190°C. Test with a thermometer or throw in a little bit of bread—if it sizzles and browns the oil is ready. Place as many chips as will fit the basket without crowding. Lower the basket into the bubbling oil and cook the chips for about 7 minutes. They will be cooked through but a pale gold, not darker. Remove and drain that batch on kitchen paper. Do the same with the next batch. You may leave the chips for a couple of hours at this stage if you need to.

→ Return the oil to the same dizzy height of temperature and dunk the basket of chips once again, this time for about 3 minutes until they bronze all over. If they haven't bronzed successfully with this second cooking, a third will do it.

→ Finally put some kitchen paper on top of the chips so the tops will also lose some grease. Shake over a little salt and serve with ketchup, malt or white wine vinegar or garlic mayonnaise.

Gratin of Potatoes with Mustard and Crème Fraîche

SERVES 6

medium, organic, waxy potatoes	12
garlic clove	1
butter	

→ Preheat the oven to 200°C/400°F/Gas 6. Peel the POTATOES and slice into thin discs.

→ Grease a gratin dish with a bit of BUTTER, and put in your potatoes in layers with one finely sliced clove of GARLIC, SEASONING as you go. Pour on the hot STOCK to nearly the level of the top layer, cover with greaseproof paper, and cook for 45 minutes.

→ Mix the CRÈME FRAÎCHE and MUSTARDS in a bowl. Pour and spread over the top of the gratin, and return to the oven until

chicken stock (p. 54) to cover	about 600ml/1pint
salt and pepper	
organic crème fraîche	200ml/7fl oz
seeded mustard	2 dsrtsp
Dijon mustard	1 dsrtsp

the potatoes are tender right the way through, about another 15 minutes. Do not add the cream mixture earlier—mustard turns bitter when cooked for too long.

Pommes Dauphinois

SERVES 4–6

potatoes	900g/2lb
double cream, Jersey if possible	600ml/1 pint
full-cream milk, Jersey if possible	150ml/5fl oz
garlic clove, *finely chopped*	1
nutmeg	
sea salt and black pepper	
unsalted butter for greasing the gratin dish	

The thing that many people get wrong when they cook this dish is the oven temperature. If you nuke the potatoes, the cream will curdle: inexorable fact. There are those who grate Gruyère into their Dauphinois, but the classic way, the best way, to my mind, is the simplest of all: potatoes, a suspicion of garlic, cream, milk and seasoning.

→ Peel the POTATOES and slice them about 5mm/¼in thick on a mandolin or with a Magimix slicing disc. Put them in a bowl of cold water.

→ Preheat the oven to 140°C/275°F/Gas 1. Pour the CREAM and MILK into a pan and add the GARLIC, a good grating of NUTMEG and the SEASONING. Warm through to hot on a low heat.

→ Meanwhile, drain the potatoes, dry them on kitchen paper or a clean tea towel and put them back in the bowl. Pour the cream mixture over them and turn to coat. Scrape the creamy potatoes into a well-buttered gratin dish and push them well down into the dish. Bake in the middle of the oven for an hour before inserting a skewer right down deep. If the potatoes are still resistant, and not golden and bubbling on top, give them a little longer until they are, and flash them briefly under a hot grill to brown. If, on the other hand, you find the potatoes are browning too quickly, cover with a sheet of greaseproof.

Potato and Fennel
→ Try adding sliced FENNEL in between the layers of potato.

Jerusalem Artichoke /Turnip
→ Use JERUSALEM ARTICHOKES with the potatoes, in equal proportion. TURNIPS are good too—half and half.

Parsnip
→ PARSNIPS are lovely too, with CRÈME FRAÎCHE and a table-spoon of GRAIN MUSTARD added in lieu of ordinary cream.

Celeriac, Thyme and Potato Gratin

SERVES 6

potatoes, King Edward or Yukon Gold are good	900g/2lb
celeriac (about ⅓ the weight of the potatoes)	1
double cream, Jersey if possible	600ml/1 pint
Jersey milk	240ml/8fl oz
garlic clove, *finely sliced*	1
nutmeg	
thyme, *leaves stripped from the stems*	1 tbsp
sea salt and black pepper	
unsalted butter for greasing the gratin dish	
Gruyère cheese, *grated* (optional)	

→ Preheat the oven to 140°C/275°F/Gas 1. Peel the POTATOES and thinly slice them on a mandolin or the slicing disc of a food processor, then put them in a bowl of cold water. Peel and slice the CELERIAC in the same way and add it to the bowl.

→ Pour the CREAM and MILK into a pan and add the sliced GARLIC, a grating of NUTMEG (a suspicion only) and warm through to scald point—small bubbles not an eruption. Meanwhile, drain the potatoes and celeriac, dry them on a tea towel and put them back in the empty bowl. Pour the hot cream mixture over the vegetables and turn them to coat.

→ Scrape everything into a well-buttered gratin dish in layers, SEASONING as you go and adding THYME LEAVES, chopped to release their oil. Bake in the middle of the oven for about an hour before testing with a skewer. If the vegetables are still resistant and not gloriously golden and bubbling on top, give them longer. If they are browned but still not cooked through, cover them with a layer of buttered greaseproof and continue to cook until fondant right through. Add a layer of grated cave-aged GRUYÈRE on the top for the last few minutes if you think the richer the better!

Celeriac and Potato Bubble and Squeak

olive oil	2 tbsp
medium onion, *peeled and chopped*	1
leftover celeriac and potato mash	
grain mustard	1 tbsp
leftover cabbage	
sea salt and black pepper	
unsalted butter	55g/2oz

Quantities are not helpful here as this is a leftovers dish, but one that is perfect for brunch, served with smoked bacon and a fried egg on top. If you have only leftover mash, just steam and mash about a third quantity of celeriac to mash and mix the two. If you don't have any leftover cabbage, very thinly slice a quarter cabbage and fry it quickly in oil first.

→ Gently heat 1 tablespoon of OLIVE OIL in a large, heavy-bottomed frying-pan, add the ONION and fry until softened and golden. Tip the cooked onion into the cold CELERIAC AND POTATO, add the grain MUSTARD and shredded cooked CABBAGE and stir to amalgamate. Season and check it is mustardy enough.

→ Add the rest of the OLIVE OIL and the butter to the frying pan and press your large potato cake down to fry. Make individual cakes if you prefer, but I like to bring a whole panful to the table. Fry on one side until browned, then turn it over and fry the other side—you may need extra BUTTER and a little OIL when you turn the cake over. Serve piping hot from the pan with bacon and eggs.

Potato Salad

SERVES 4

waxy new potatoes	675g/ 1½lb or so
mint	
Dijon mustard	1 tbsp
red wine vinegar	2 tbsp
vegetable oil	90ml/3fl oz
extra virgin olive oil	2 tbsp
spring onions OR a shallot or mild, small onion, *finely chopped*	1 bunch
chives, *snipped*	1 bunch
sea salt and freshly ground black pepper	

Like all disarmingly simple things, this can be spoiled by not paying attention to detail and using inferior ingredients. As this is one of the most wonderful and versatile of dishes, as good with chicken or grilled meat as it is with baked fish or a raft of other different salads, it is worth getting right. Use good waxy new potatoes such as Jersey Royal, Pink Fir Apples, Rattes or Anya.

→ Scrape the POTATOES if they are Jersey Royals. If they are Pink Fir Apples it is easier to take the skins off when they are boiled and still hot as they are so nubbly and knobbly. Boil them in salted water with a few sprigs of MINT, then drain.

→ While the potatoes are cooking, make the dressing by whisking the MUSTARD, VINEGAR AND OILS together and SEASONING to taste. Skin and chop or just chop the potatoes when they are hot and dress them immediately. Turn them with the dressing and the SHALLOT OR SPRING ONIONS, finely chopped with a little bit of their green shoots, and the CHIVES. Eat warm.

Lyonnaise Potatoes

SERVES 2–3

potatoes	450g/1lb
bacon fat, beef dripping, goose fat OR unsalted butter	55–85g/2–3oz
medium onion, *sliced very thinly*	1
sea salt and black pepper	

These potatoes absorb all the flavour of the fat you have cooked them in, so whether you use bacon fat, beef dripping, goose fat or butter, know that the fat is the whole purpose of the dish, rich though it is. It is important to cook the onions separately and then introduce them to the potatoes. That way the onions will not burn, nor will either ingredient lose its identity. I favour bacon fat for flavour.

→ Scrub the POTATOES and boil them in their skins until they are cooked but retain firmness. When they have cooled a little, spike them with a fork, and, using a sharp knife, peel, before cutting them into cubes.

→ Melt the FAT in two separate heavy-bottomed frying pans. When the fat is hot, put the potatoes into one pan and the ONION into the other and season both with SALT. Fry both until golden on all sides, turning the potatoes carefully so that they don't break up. Amalgamate the onion with the potatoes and a good scrunch of BLACK PEPPER at the last minute. The finished dish should have crisp potatoes and gooey onion but no trace of greasiness.

SAUC

and acc

ES

ompaniments

Basic Béchamel Sauce

full-cream milk, Jersey if possible	600ml/1 pint
onion, *peeled and stuck with a couple of cloves*	
bay leaf	
unsalted butter	55g/2oz
plain flour	1 heaped tbsp
nutmeg	
sea salt	
black pepper	
double cream (optional)	

Always use hot milk, always whisk, and always cook long enough for the floury taste to gently winnow itself away until the complex, more subtle scent of nutmeg and bay have come to the fore. A little cream at the end if you need a richer sauce passes muster, or strong Cheddar or gooey threads of Gruyère and a spike of mustard if the recipe calls for a cheese sauce. The best milk to use is Jersey because of its creaminess. Just don't attempt a béchamel with skimmed milk: it defeats the object.

→ Bring the MILK slowly to the boil in a small pan to which you have also added the clove-studded ONION and a fresh BAY LEAF. Then remove the pan from the heat and leave the onion and bay leaf in the milk in a covered pan to infuse for 20–30 minutes.

→ Melt the BUTTER over a gentle heat in a small, heavy-bottomed pan. Just as the butter begins to foam and bubble, throw in a heaped tablespoon of PLAIN FLOUR and stir it gently for a few seconds. Too much flour and you'll get a thick floury base layer to the pan instead of a thin bubbling one; too little and the butter won't amalgamate with the flour, so scatter in a little more. Let this bubble together for a minute or so until it begins to turn a pale biscuit colour, but don't let it darken and begin to burn. Add about half a cup of the MILK, which you have heated to hot again, whereupon the mixture will bubble furiously and you will whisk it furiously with a small balloon whisk until it suddenly thickens beyond easy whisking. Add more milk and repeat; the sauce will take a little longer to thicken each time you add more milk.

→ Begin to cook the sauce more slowly while stirring it with a wooden spoon—you should have whisked the lumps out by now—and add more milk as the sauce seems to demand it to keep the texture thick enough but not solid. Cook slowly for 20 minutes, remembering to stir frequently to prevent it sticking to the bottom of the pan and burning, which milk has a tendency to do, and to prevent a skin forming on the surface.

→ I grate a little NUTMEG into the sauce about halfway through the cooking time and season it. When it is cooked, I check the SEASONING and adjust if necessary. Nutmeg is always best when you add a 'suspicion' of it; you don't want the sauce to become a nutmeg sauce.

Mornay Sauce
→ Add 70g/6oz grated CHEDDAR CHEESE off the heat when the béchamel has finished cooking.

Parsley Sauce
→ Add a bunch of chopped PARSLEY off the heat when the béchamel has finished cooking. The parsley should not lose its rawness, but look like emerald flecks.

Hollandaise Sauce

white wine vinegar	3 tbsp
water	2 tbsp
white peppercorns, *bruised*	10
organic egg yolks	3
best unsalted butter, *cut into cubes*	170g/6oz
sea salt	
lemon juice	

An unctuous rich yellow ointment of a sauce, Hollandaise is the perfect accompaniment to hot salmon or sea trout, or fresh asparagus (see p. 376 for an alternative method of making hollandaise).

→ Put the wine VINEGAR, WATER and PEPPERCORNS in a small pan and bring to the boil. Bubble hard to reduce until there is only a tablespoon left. Strain it into a heatproof bowl and let it cool. Beat in the EGG YOLKS and place the bowl over a pan of very hot, but not quite simmering, water. Gradually whisk in the BUTTER with a small balloon whisk, a couple of cubes at a time, making sure the pan of water underneath still doesn't actually simmer.

→ If the sauce gets too hot it will scramble like eggs and you will have to rescue it by beating another egg yolk, then gradually adding the curdled sauce, a drop at a time to begin with, until it thickens and coheres. Season with SALT and a spritz of LEMON to taste.

Mayonnaise

Serves 4

extra virgin olive oil	200ml/7fl oz
large organic egg yolks,	2
Dijon mustard (optional)	1 tsp
lemon, *halved*	1
salt and pepper	a little

People will always eat as much mayonnaise as you make, so the quantity here is more a guide than an instruction. The oil should be good, heavy extra virgin, yet not intrusively bitter, fruity or peppery.

→ Measure the OLIVE OIL into a small jug. Break the EGG YOLKS into a warm glass or china bowl and stir them in one direction with a wooden spoon. They will thicken in a matter of seconds. Either add the teaspoon of Dijon MUSTARD now and continue to stir and thicken, or begin to pour in the olive oil, no more than a drop at a time to begin with. Keep stirring with your wooden spoon as you start to pour the oil a thin trickle now, speeding up the stirring so that the oil is taken up by the yolks instantly without any danger of separating.

→ As the mayonnaise begins to stiffen, rather than thicken, the trickle can become a thin stream, but do not get trigger-happy. Even mayonnaise that looks too thick to do anything aberrant can curdle before your eyes at the last moment. Every so often you may add a tiny squeeze of JUICE from the halved lemon. Once you have used up all the oil, SEASON, add a spritz of LEMON, taste and adjust.

→ If by any chance you've taken your eye off the bowl and have a curdled mass before you, simply do the following: break an egg yolk into another bowl and stir it to thicken. Now add the curdled mayonnaise, a drip at a time to begin with, stirring defiantly as you go until you can begin to add it in a steady stream. The new yolk will absorb the whole mass of curdled mayonnaise and that will be that.

Herb Mayonnaise

→ Simply add a chopped tablespoon each of DILL, PARSLEY, CHERVIL and TARRAGON or whichever combination of them you have to hand once the mayonnaise is made. Watercress is good too, particularly with cold, white fish.

Horseradish Mayonnaise

→ A couple of teaspoons of GRATED HORSERADISH stirred into mayonnaise is very good with smoked eel.

Aïoli

→ Fish or chicken bourride, bacalao, even some raw vegetables all work well with a pungent hit of this classic Provençal sauce.

It should ward off more than the devil if you make it strong enough. Simply pound 2, 3, more if you dare, cloves of GARLIC in a mortar with a little salt until they are crushed to a juicy purée, then continue as for a classic mayonnaise by stirring in the EGG YOLKS.

Mayonnaise Mousseuse
→ This is good for cold chicken, salmon or asparagus. Simply whisk 150ml/5fl oz DOUBLE CREAM until it holds in soft folds, and stir it into your homemade mayonnaise just before amalgamating it with the chicken or serving it alongside the salmon or asparagus. It is also good with a combination of lobster, Jersey Royal new potatoes and avocado—impossibly rich, improbably delicious.

Sauce Rémoulade

organic eggs, *hard-boiled* yolks only	2
tarragon vinegar	a few drops
raw egg yolk	1
grain mustard	1 dsrtsp
olive oil	200ml/7fl oz
lemon	1
chives and tarragon, *finely chopped*	1 dsrtsp of each
capers, *finely chopped*	1 dsrtsp
salt and pepper	

This creamier, more mustardy version of mayonnaise is the perfect piquant sauce for a classic céleri rémoulade, made with celeriac, which is thickly grated, then blanched briefly in boiling water. The sauce is also good with any raw vegetables that need pepping up.

→ Pound the hard-boiled EGG YOLKS to a paste with a few drops of TARRAGON VINEGAR. Stir the RAW YOLK into the pounded hard-boiled ones with a wooden spoon before adding the grain MUSTARD and continuing to stir. Now stir in the OLIVE OIL in the usual way, adding a spritz of LEMON JUICE every so often.
→ Add the chopped HERBS AND CAPERS, SEASON, taste and adjust with more mustard, lemon, herbs, capers or seasoning as you see fit until the sauce has a powerful flavour. It will coat the celeriac and be a foil to its earthy crunchiness.

Bread Sauce

SERVES 4–6

small peeled onion, *stuck with 4 cloves*	1
bay leaf 1	
Jersey or full-cream milk, organic if possible	600ml/1 pint
nutmeg	
sea salt and black pepper	
small white or wholemeal loaf, *crusts removed* 1	
unsalted butter OR double cream (optional)	a knob a couple of tbsp

Until a year or so ago I always made bread sauce with breadcrumbs, but I have now adopted the torn-chunk-of-bread philosophy. It really does give a better texture and stops a tendency to sliminess that the smoother version has. Bread sauce should be made with day-old or stale bread, white or wholemeal according to your taste, though wholemeal can over-whelm with its own nuttier flavour. You will need to cut the crusts off a whole small loaf before tearing it into bits. If you only have a fresh loaf, remove the crusts, slice it into thickish slices and put it in a warm oven until both sides feel dry before proceeding.

→ Place the cloved ONION in a small saucepan with the BAY LEAF and MILK and bring slowly to scald point, just below boiling. The milk surface should have begun to crinkle. Lower the heat and simmer at a bare bubble for 20–30 minutes, grating in a little NUTMEG halfway through. SEASON.

→ Tear the BREAD into smallish shreds and add by the handful until the milk has absorbed most of it. Allow for some milk to still be visible; the sauce will go on absorbing and stiffening when you put it to one side with the lid on, which you may now do for up to 20 minutes, so make it when you have a gap in the cooking.

→ Just before you are ready to serve lunch, take the lid off and if the sauce looks too solid, add a little more MILK. Test the SEASONING—you may want a little more nutmeg and pepper—and reheat very gently until it just comes to the bubble. Stir in the BUTTER OR CREAM if you like a richer finish to what are, after all, poor man's ingredients. I serve my bread sauce in a warmed soufflé dish with the onion still in it, as there is always someone who wants to eat the whole cooked orb.

Cranberry Sauce

SERVES 8–10

cranberries	340g/12oz
caster sugar	170g/6oz or to taste
orange	juice and zest of 1

→ Weed out the squishy or bruised berries first, then put the good BERRIES into a pan with the SUGAR and ORANGE JUICE. Bring to the boil and bubble away until the berries begin to pop, about 7–10 minutes. Remove immediately so that they hold their shape. Taste for sweetness; you may need to add a little more sugar. Gently turn the ZEST into the sauce so that you don't break the berries up. Pour into a bowl and leave to cool, then cover with clingfilm and keep in the fridge.

Crème Fraîche Tartare

Makes enough for 6

organic egg yolk	1
Dijon mustard	1 tsp
sea salt	
Tabasco	
crème fraîche	3–4 heaped dsrtsp
tarragon vinegar	2 tsp
tarragon, *chopped*	1 tsp
flat-leaf parsley, *chopped*	1 heaped tbsp
chives, *chopped*	1 tsp
rinsed capers, *chopped*	1 tbsp
cornichons, *finely chopped*	1 tbsp

This is a stunning accompaniment to most fried or breaded fish, particularly firm-textured white fish.

→ Beat the EGG YOLK with the MUSTARD, SEA SALT and a few dashes of TABASCO until emulsified. Add the CRÈME FRAÎCHE, a dessertspoon at a time, and one teaspoon of the TARRAGON VINEGAR, whisking well with a small balloon whisk. Whisk until thick, but pourable. Stir in the OTHER INGREDIENTS with the second teaspoon of VINEGAR. Adjust the SEASONING.

Cumberland Sauce

orange	1
lemon	1
redcurrant jelly	225g/8oz
French mustard	1 tsp
Port	60ml/2fl oz
salt and pepper	
ground cloves, nutmeg OR ginger (optional)	

This delectably sticky sweet sauce, underscored with spices and mustard and zinging with soft shards of citrus, is the perfect sweet-sour accompaniment to a Christmas ham. Great in ham sandwiches too. If you can get Seville oranges during their short season, do, but pre-Christmas you'll have to make do with oranges and lemons.

→ First comes the time-consuming part. Peel the ORANGE and LEMON with a potato peeler so there is virtually no bitter pith on the strips of peel. Shred the PEEL with a fine-bladed knife into long, impossibly skinny lengths and blanch in boiling water for a couple of minutes. Drain and set aside.
→ Heat the JELLY and MUSTARD together in a pan until well melted, add the PORT, and whisk until hot. Add the ORANGE AND LEMON JUICE, SEASON to taste, and if you feel like a bit of spice add a pinch of GROUND CLOVES, NUTMEG or GINGER. Stir in the peel and simmer for 5 minutes. Pour into a bowl or jar and keep in the fridge until you want to use it; it will keep for several weeks.

Francatelli Sauce

elderberry OR spiced redcurrant jelly	225g/8oz
port	150ml/5fl oz
muscovado sugar	1 tsp
organic lemon	*pared rind* of 1
cinnamon	1 small stick
black pepper	
juniper berries, *crushed*	2–3

This famous sauce, served with roast venison, was invented by Queen Victoria's chef, Charles Elme Francatelli, and is one I have been making ever since I first cooked venison over 20 years ago.

→ Simmer ALL THE INGREDIENTS together for about 5 minutes in a small pan, stirring to melt the jelly, then strain into a gravy jug. Serve with roast venison.

Cox's Apple Sauce

Cox's apples	6
apple juice OR water	3 tbsp
organic orange	*grated zest* of 1
unsalted butter	30g/1oz
scrunch of black pepper	

→ Peel, quarter and slice the APPLES. Simmer them with the APPLE JUICE and ORANGE ZEST gently in a covered pan until the apples have softened. Remove from the heat and either mash or sieve, depending on the texture you prefer. Return to the pan with the BUTTER and PEPPER, and stir to amalgamate.

Cox's Apple Sauce with Thyme
→ For the thyme version, add the leaves you have torn from a couple of sprigs of THYME and bruised in your fingers. Tip into a bowl to cool.

Bramley Apple Sauce

Bramleys, medium-sized	6
apple juice OR water	4 tbsp
unrefined sugar	2 level tbsp
organic orange rind	1 strip
unsalted butter	30g/1oz
black pepper	a good scrunch

→ Put the APPLES, roughly chopped, skins on, cores included, with the APPLE JUICE, SUGAR and ORANGE RIND into a pan and bring to the boil. Simmer gently with a lid on until the apples are soft. Sieve and return to the pan, cooking gently until the sauce isn't too wet and sloppy.
→ Add the BUTTER and the PEPPER off the heat and turn into a bowl to cool. You may refrigerate the sauce from tepid if you are short of time. It will keep, covered, in the fridge for your cold roast pork.

Mint Sauce

boiling water	3 tbsp
mint leaves, *stripped from their stems and chopped*	enough to fill a small bowl
unrefined sugar	3 tsp
white wine vinegar	4 tbsp

This is a late spring and summer sauce to serve with your lamb and tiny waxy pebbles of Jersey Royal new potatoes. The French think mint sauce is barbaric, but I find the way it cuts the fatty richness of the meat—and sheep fat really does congeal quickly on the plate—with the sweet sharp redcurrant jelly is a glorious triumvirate. Make the sauce 2 hours before you need it.

→ Pour the BOILING WATER over the LEAVES and leave to infuse. When it is barely tepid, stir in the SUGAR, then the VINEGAR and stir until the sugar has dissolved. Taste and adjust the seasoning before serving.

Port, Beetroot and Blackcurrant Sauce

SERVES 2

miniature bottle of port	1
duck OR game stock	a ladle
redcurrant jelly	1 heaped tbsp
black- or redcurrants	55g/2oz
beetroot, *cooked, peeled and finely diced*	55g/2oz
salt and pepper	

Omit the beetroot if you want to keep things simpler, but they add a beautiful, garnet-hued earthiness to this sauce.

→ Make this when to go with roast duck or game. When the birds are covered and resting, add the PORT to the juices in the roasting pan, and bring to the boil. Add the STOCK, and bubble merrily for a few minutes to reduce a little. Add the JELLY, BLACKCURRANTS and BEETROOT, bring back to the boil, then simmer for 5 minutes. Season.

Horseradish Sauce

horseradish root, *grated* OR a good brand like English Provender Company	2 tbsp
crème fraîche	150ml/5fl oz
sugar and salt	a little
lemon	juice of ½

→ Plop the HORSERADISH into a small bowl and stir in the CRÈME FRAÎCHE. Add a tiny amount of SALT AND SUGAR and a spritz of LEMON JUICE, then taste for seasoning and sharpness.

Homemade Ketchup

MAKES SEVERAL BOTTLES

cloves	2
bay leaf	1
cinnamon bark	a small piece
cider vinegar	240ml/8fl oz
light muscovado sugar	8 tbsp
celery seeds	1 tsp
ground mace	½ tsp
ground coriander	¼ tsp
ripe tomatoes	1.5kg/3¼1b
sea salt	½ tsp
English mustard powder	1 tsp
garlic clove	1
Tabasco sauce	
tomato purée	1 tbsp

Ketchup equals Heinz, but this is the real McCoy and well worth the effort, if only to do justice to a particularly fine sausage or fish cake. It is different, rather in the way that home-baked beans are an entirely different dish to the tinned version and instant coffee is quite unlike fresh.

→ Tie the CLOVES, BAY LEAF and CINNAMON together in a bit of muslin. Put the VINEGAR and SUGAR in a heavy-bottomed enamel pan and bring to a simmer. Add ALL THE OTHER INGREDIENTS and bring to the boil, stirring to prevent anything from sticking to the bottom of the pan. Reduce to a simmer and let the mixture blip away for about 40 minutes, stirring occasionally.

→ Remove the spice bag, liquidise the sauce and sieve into a bowl. Cool, then pour through a funnel into sterilised bottles. The ketchup will keep for up to a month in the fridge. Something to do at the tomato glut time of year, particularly if you have quantities of your own to pick.

Green Olive Salsa

SERVES 4

celery sticks	2
best extra virgin olive oil	90ml/3fl oz
green olives, *pitted and chopped finely*	225g/8oz
red wine vinegar	1 tbsp
garlic cloves, *finely minced*	2
red chilli, quartered, *seeded and finely diced*	1
organic lemon	*grated zest* of 1
flat-leaf parsley, *coarsely chopped*	2 tbsp
black pepper	

→ String the CELERY STICKS with a potato peeler and dice finely. Put ALL THE INGREDIENTS in a bowl and turn them with your hands before leaving them for at least 30 minutes. Stir everything together once more just before you serve the salsa. Good with something plain, such as grilled chicken.

Asian Dressing or Dipping Sauce

garlic cloves	2
red bird's-eye chillies, *finely sliced* (depending on your love of heat)	1–2
unrefined caster sugar	3 tbsp
fish sauce	4 tbsp
lime juice, *freshly squeezed*	4 tbsp
rice vinegar	4 tbsp

This works as well with a spicy fishcake as it does as a feisty dressing for all manner of noodley prawn, chicken or raw vegetable salads with ribbons of carrot, cucumber and courgette, or grated carrot, radish, mushroom and spinach. If you are using this as a dipping sauce, add a tablespoon of water and you may add either a tablespoon of olive oil or a couple of teaspoons of toasted sesame oil if you feel like it.

→ Crush the GARLIC in a mortar or under the blade of a knife and whisk it together with THE OTHER INGREDIENTS until the sugar has completely dissolved and the dressing no longer feels gritty. Allow the flavours to marry for 30 minutes before serving or mixing into your salad.

Harissa

Navarrico piquillo peppers from Brindisa OR 1 red pepper	85g/3oz
cumin seeds	3 tsp
red chillies, *sliced in half, the seeds removed*	225g/8oz
garlic	4 cloves
tomato purée	1 tbsp
red wine vinegar	1 dsrtsp
sweet smoked Spanish paprika	2 tsp
extra virgin olive oil	6 tbsp
sea salt and black pepper	

This keeps for a couple of weeks in the fridge, and is well worth making as you can add it to so many dishes. It is good with chicken, with plain baked fish or steaming bowls of mussels, even to spice up fried eggs or late-night Welsh rarebit. Please wear rubber gloves when you seed the chillies, and never rub your eyes afterwards.

→ If you're not using PIQUILLO PEPPERS you'll need to start by cooking and peeling the RED PEPPER. Place the pepper in a hot oven on a baking sheet, turning it every 10 minutes until it is softened all over, or place under a hot grill and char each side until it is softened. Put in a bowl covered with clingfilm while it cools, so it will be easy to peel, core and seed. Roast the CUMIN SEEDS for 30 seconds to 1 minute in a small pan, then coarsely crush in a mortar.

→ Chop the CHILLIES and put them in the food processor, blending them with a little salt and HALF THE SPICES with the GARLIC CLOVES until smooth. Then add the peppers and blend until really smooth. Remove to a bowl and add the REMAINING INGREDIENTS. Taste for seasoning: you may need more salt. If you are keeping the harissa in the fridge, cover it with a thin layer of olive oil to seal it from the air.

JELLIES ICE

and other

'CREAM
puddings

Buck's Fizz Jelly

SERVES 6–8

gelatine	8 leaves
champagne	600ml/pint
organic orange juice, *freshly squeezed*	just under 600ml/1 pint

Think of it this way—there are no other ingredients to speak of and you don't even need cream. And if you earmark a bottle of champagne for the jelly, you can always drink the rest.

→ Break the leaves of GELATINE in half and soak them in 2–3 tablespoons of cold water for 10 minutes. Measure the CHAMPAGNE and pour it into a bowl. Put the ORANGE JUICE into a small saucepan with the leaves of soaked gelatine and their water—8 sheets should set 1.2 litres/2 pints of liquid, but check the packet.

→ Gently heat the orange juice, stirring as you go with a wooden spoon to dissolve the gelatine completely. You do not want the liquid to become very hot or it won't taste so fresh, but make sure that there isn't a stringy trace of gelatine to be seen. Pour the orange and gelatine mixture into the champagne and stir it all together. It will fizz as you do. Pour everything through a sieve into a jelly mould. Mine is big enough for 1.5 litres/3 pints, but I never seem to make a jelly quite that big. Leave to cool before putting it in the fridge to set.

→ You can make a jelly from 2 days to 4 hours before you want to eat it. It will keep for longer in the fridge, but the freshness of the flavour starts to diminish. Turn out by dunking the base half of the mould briefly in boiling water and inverting the jelly onto a plate, or serve from the mould.

Fresh Grapefruit Jelly

SERVES 6

lemon	juice of ½
grapefruit	*pared rind* of 1
orange	*pared rind* of 1
caster sugar	85–110g/3–4oz
water	300ml/10fl oz
leaf gelatine	6 or 7 leaves, but check the packet
grapefruit juice, *freshly squeezed*	600ml/1 pint

The astringency of this lovely sharp jelly is just what you need after something such as roast goose or duck. If you can find pink grapefruits the colour will be a dreamy, dusty pink.

→ Put the LEMON JUICE and GRAPEFRUIT AND ORANGE RIND into a pan with the SUGAR and 150ml/5fl oz of the WATER. Place over a low heat and leave to infuse for 10–15 minutes. Soak the GELATINE (read the instructions for how much to use first) for 10 minutes in the other 150ml/5fl oz of water. Add the soaked gelatine with its water to the saucepan, stir to melt, then strain and leave to cool.

→ Add the gelatine liquid to the freshly squeezed GRAPEFRUIT JUICE, stir well, and pour into a mould or into individual long-stemmed glasses. Leave to cool completely, then refrigerate to set further. The jelly will keep well for several days.

Orange, Grenadillo and Muscat Jelly

SERVES 6–8

grenadillos	2
gelatine	8 sheets
organic oranges *(to make up just under 1.2 litres/2 pints of liquid)*	juice of 8–10
Bonterra organic muscat, OR something similar	½ a bottle

These tangerine-coloured shelled fruits with their milky, moonstone interiors and jet-black seeds are exotic and scented and perfect in a sweet boozy jelly.

→ Halve the GRENADILLOS and scoop out the innards and seeds. Heat them gently in a pan and sieve into a jug—it is easier to separate seed from fruit if it is warm.

→ Soak the sheets of GELATINE in 2–3 tablespoons of cold water for 10 minutes.

→ Put the gelatine and its soaking liquid into a small saucepan with the ORANGE JUICE. Heat through gently, stirring as you go. Make sure the gelatine is completely dissolved and then pour the contents of the pan into the jug with the grenadillo fruit, add the WINE and stir everything together.

→ Pour the mixture through a sieve into a jelly mould, leave to cool, then set in the fridge for 4 hours or up to 2 days.

Clementine, Passion Fruit and Muscat Jelly

SERVES 6–8

underripe passion fruit	3 large
Bonterra organic muscat, OR something similar	half a bottle
organic clementines	about 20
gelatine	8 sheets

It doesn't matter if you buy the passion fruit unwrinkly, which means they are under-ripe, as the sharpness is just what the jelly needs, contrasting as it does with the sweet clementines and muscat. This is utterly divine.

→ Scoop the insides of the PASSION FRUIT into a small saucepan and warm over a gentle heat so that the seeds will separate more easily from the fruit. Sieve them into a jug with the WINE. Squeeze the CLEMENTINES until the jug has just under 1.2 litres/2 pints of liquid in it. Soak the sheets of GELATINE in 2–3 tablespoons of cold water for 10 minutes.

→ Stir in the gelatine, and pour the liquid into the saucepan, heating it through very gently to just warm enough to dissolve the gelatine completely. Pour the mixture through a sieve into the jelly mould, cool and then put in the fridge.

→ The jelly will be ready to eat after just 4 hours or up to 2 days later, depending on when you want it. Serve with some thinly sliced oranges.

Fruits of the Forest and Port Jelly

frozen fruits of the forest, organic if possible	1 × 500g/ 1lb 2oz bag
unrefined vanilla caster sugar	110g/4oz
water	300ml/10fl oz
gelatine (check packet for gelatine-to-liquid ratio)	4 sheets
Rock's organic blackcurrant cordial	2 tbsp
port	150ml/5fl oz

Port is very good with a number of fruits: figs, raspberries, blackcurrants, blueberries and blackberries, the sort of fruits I crave in midwinter even though I know I can't have them. I sometimes make this jelly in winter, buying a bag of frozen fruits of the forest and conjuring up the taste of a warm July day in a not-so-warm midwinter cold snap. In the summer, use whatever combination of berries you can lay your hands on. Just don't use strawberries—when cooked they lose both their magical flavour and their texture, and turn to pink squish.

→ Pour the FROZEN FRUITS directly into a large pan with the SUGAR and WATER. Bring to the boil and gently simmer for 10 minutes with the lid on. Place a large nylon sieve over a bowl and tip the contents of the pan straight into it, leaving the juices to drip as you would for a potted jelly. Don't press the fruit down to extract more juice unless you don't mind a cloudy jelly. I prefer mine as clear and dark as the night sky! Throw away the contents of the sieve; they have done their work.

→ Soak the GELATINE leaves in a shallow saucer of water for 10 minutes, turning them over at half time. When the gelatine is softened all over, put it into the drained juice in a pan, add the PORT and BLACKCURRANT CORDIAL, and warm everything through together very gently.

→ Pour the jelly into little plastic pudding basins you can turn out, or into a large jelly mould or glass bowl, or individual ramekins to set. As long as there is a little cold water shaken into whatever option you choose, the jelly will set and turn out. It will need at least 8 hours or overnight, so this is a great pudding to get ahead with. Jelly and ice cream, that standard children's party duo, is still delicious for grown-ups if home-made with the best ingredients.

Raspberry and Redcurrant Jelly with Summer Berries

MAKES 7

leaf gelatine	6 sheets
fresh raspberries	450g/1lb
redcurrants	140g/5oz
unrefined icing OR caster sugar to taste	about 4 tbsp
extra raspberries and redcurrants	1 punnet of each
blueberries	1 punnet

Raspberries and redcurrants make a magical jelly, with little hanging lanterns of redcurrants suspended in the jelly alongside bruised purple blueberries and soft seeded raspberries. A heap of fruits around the plate and you have a summer pudding as toothsome to the very young as it is to the very old. I use individual plastic bowls, the lidded steamed pudding kind, from which the jellies turn out with minimum resistance, so there are no last-minute panics. You can, of course, use a large mould or glass bowl.

→ Soak the GELATINE for 5 minutes in 2–3 tablespoons of cold water. Blitz the 450g/1lb of RASPBERRIES and 140g/5oz of REDCURRANTS in a food processor, then sieve them into a measuring jug. Sweeten to taste, stirring in the SUGAR to dissolve. Err on the tart side. Top up with water to the 900ml/ 1½ pint mark, but remember to fall short of it by the same number of tablespoons of water you have got soaking the gelatine. Heat the fruit liquid gently until hot, stir in the gelatine in its liquid, and stir off the heat until the gelatine has totally dissolved.

→ Pour the mixture into the wet moulds and leave to cool. The liquid will start to thicken as it cools. Then pop in the BERRIES one by one, about 3 raspberries, 6 blueberries and 4 or 5 redcurrants to each bowl. Put in the fridge to set.

→ Eat a few hours or up to two days later. To turn out, dip the base of each bowl in boiling water for 10 seconds, go round the edge of the bowl with a knife point, turn upside down and squeeze. Arrange on a large dish with extra fresh berries or on individual dishes.

Vanilla Ice Cream

vanilla pods	2
large organic egg yolks	6
vanilla caster sugar	140g/5oz
Jersey milk	500ml/18fl oz
double cream, Jersey if possible	600ml/1 pint

There are many recipes for the supposedly best vanilla ice cream, a lot of which use far more egg yolks than the six I always use, or a higher proportion of milk for a more Italian soft-ice texture. I like this one precisely because it is rich without tasting eggy and the vanilla shines through. Only good, sticky-fresh vanilla pods will do, from Madagascar if possible. The dried ones don't cut it any more than does vanilla extract or, God forbid, vanilla essence. Vanilla ice cream is perfect with apple pie, cherry pie, gooseberry pie; it works well with rich chocolate cakes of the pudding kind, and it is great with crumbles. It laps up chocolate or butterscotch sauce, and it's great with a pile of raw summer berries.

→ Split the VANILLA PODS down the middle and scoop out the seeds with a sharp pointed teaspoon. Put the EGG YOLKS in a bowl with the VANILLA SUGAR and the VANILLA SEEDS. Whisk the yolks, sugar and vanilla seeds together until they amalgamate. Heat the MILK with the split pods slowly until it reaches scalding point (that is, the point just before it boils and rises up dangerously). Pour it straight over the yolk and sugar mixture through a sieve, whisking as you go. Return the mixture to the pan over a very gentle heat and continue to whisk, watching carefully so that no bits of the mixture overheat and scramble at the edges of the pan—the mixture should not get to simmer point. This should take 10–15 minutes, whisking continuously. Once the mixture has thickened, remove the pan from the heat and stir in the DOUBLE CREAM.

→ Leave to cool until it is warm rather than hot, stirring every so often so a skin doesn't form on top. Churn in an ice-cream machine and finish freezing in the freezer in its pail.

→ If you are making the ice cream by hand, put the mixture in a sealable plastic container once it has cooled completely and put it in the freezer. Every 30 minutes, remove and whisk the ice cream to stop crystals forming and ruining the smooth, velvety texture. When the ice cream has set enough to be difficult to whisk, even in the middle, just leave it in the freezer until it has set completely.

→ The ice cream can be made a day or two in advance, but the flavour does tend to diminish quite quickly, particularly once you have opened the lid and started eating the ice cream. This is the base for many fruit, spice and other ice creams.

Honey and Lavender Ice Cream

SERVES 6–8

The most unusual and elegant ice cream I have ever made was inspired by some Provençal lavender honey that I brought back from the Luberon in the Vaucluse. How to intensify it, as ice creams lose in the freezing if the flavours aren't strong enough? Lavender is the sublime but obvious answer.

→ Follow the recipe for Vanilla Ice Cream opposite, but steep 2 good-sized branches of LAVENDER, 10–13cm/4–5in long, in the milk you bring to the boil. Continue to simmer, very low, for 20 minutes, then strain the milk on to the yolks and continue to follow the recipe. When the mixture has thickened, pour in about 225g/8oz of lavender honey that you have first heated until liquid in a bowl in some simmering water. Stir well into the custard, and freeze in the usual way.

Chocolate Sauce

SERVES 3 OR 4

best bitter chocolate, such as Valrhona 64%, *chopped*	110g/4oz
black coffee, *freshly made* (optional)	2 tbsp
vanilla caster sugar	1 tsp
single cream	3–4 tbsp
golden syrup	1 tbsp

→ Place ALL THE INGREDIENTS for the sauce in a pan and heat through gently, stirring all the time, until they are melted and hot. You may like a thinner sauce, in which case keep adding cream or a tablespoon or more of milk at the end and stirring it in until you have arrived at the desired consistency.

Rich Chocolate Sauce

single cream	240ml/8fl oz
caster sugar	25g/scant 1oz
bitter chocolate, *chopped*	110g/4oz
unsalted butter	30g/1oz

→ Boil the CREAM with the SUGAR. Remove from the heat and beat in the CHOCOLATE and BUTTER; keep warm but do not boil. This can be refrigerated and gently reheated in a double boiler.

Butterscotch Sauce

light muscovado sugar	200g/7oz
single cream	240ml/8fl oz
unsalted butter	85g/3oz
pure vanilla extract	a few drops

→ Pour EVERYTHING into a small pan and heat gently, stirring constantly until you have a lively, bubbling morass. This sauce is darker and more minerally still if you use dark muscovado or molasses sugar.

Redcurrant Curd Ice Cream

SERVES 6–8

redcurrants	450g/1lb
large organic eggs	2
organic egg yolks	3
unrefined vanilla caster sugar	110g/4oz
unsalted butter	110g/4oz
vanilla ice cream (see p. 418)	

A fruit curd takes a matter of minutes to make and is really not a technical feat of any seriousness or wizardry. As you stir the fruit, sugar, butter and eggs, the cohesion happens as slowly and steadily as a custard. Suddenly you have it, that gel-like buttery-sharp gloopiness that's about as spoon-lickingly good as you can imagine.

→ Strip the REDCURRANTS from their stems with the tines of a fork Throw the redcurrants into a blender and blitz them thoroughly. Pass them through a nylon sieve into a bowl, pressing as rigorously as your wrist and wooden spoon allow. In a separate bowl, beat together the EGGS, extra YOLKS and the SUGAR.

→ I make my curds in an enormous Le Creuset enamel-bottomed pan; the large surface area makes the curd set quicker. Melt the BUTTER in the pan over a very gentle heat, then stir in the egg and sugar mixture and the sieved fruit. Whisk continuously over a low heat until the whole mixture comes together, between 5 and 10 minutes later. Remove from the heat—the idea is to heat rather than cook the fruit, which would then lose some of its raw flavour and its taste. Pour the curd into a bowl and leave to cool. You may cover it with clingfilm and leave it in the fridge for several days or use it as soon as it is cool.

→ Make half the amount of VANILLA ICE CREAM from the recipe on p. 418 or make the full amount and add a different curd to the second half or keep it plain. When you have churned your ice cream to soft-set, scrape it into a container and cut streaks of curd into it with a spoon until you have a lovely rippled ice cream. Clip the lid on and continue to freeze in the freezer.

Raspberry Curd Ice Cream
→ This is equally scrumptious with raspberries. Make raspberry curd following the recipe on p. 504 and continue as above.

Burnt Orange Ice Cream

SERVES 6–8

sugar	2 tbsp
double cream	1 cup
full-cream milk	1 cup
orange, *grated zest*	2 tbsp
orange juice, *freshly squeezed*	2 cups
Cointreau	¼ cup + 1 tbsp
sugar for the caramel	¼ cup + 2 tbsp
large organic egg yolks	10

My great culinary partner-in-greed George Morley originally found this recipe in an American book, Walking on Walnuts, *by Nancy Ring. The caramel matches the reduced, intensified orange juice and Cointreau taste for taste, and is strong enough to withstand the freezing process without losing its strength and subtlety. Quantities are in US cups—we used an ordinary teacup.*

→ Place the 2 tablespoons of SUGAR in a mixing bowl. In a medium saucepan, scald the CREAM and MILK with the ORANGE ZEST. Take off the heat and leave them to steep together with a lid on the pan for about 30 minutes.

→ Simmer the ORANGE JUICE and COINTREAU until reduced to 1 cup. Whisk into the cream mixture and strain, then return it to the pan and keep warm over a very gentle heat. In another pan caramelise the ¼ cup plus 2 tablespoons of SUGAR until very dark (just past the colour of an Irish setter). Do not stir at any time. Swirl gently in the pan if necessary to ensure even colour. Remove from the heat, protecting your stirring hand with an oven glove, and immediately temper the caramel with a small amount of the warm orange cream while stirring vigorously. Keep adding cream slowly until the caramel stops bubbling violently. Whisk all of the tempered caramel back into the remaining cream and place on the stove over medium heat to scald once more.

→ Add the YOLKS to the sugar in a mixing bowl and whisk together when the cream scalds, but not before. Temper the yolks with the scalded cream by pouring a small stream of the hot cream into the yolks while whisking continuously. Pour back into the pan and return to the stove over medium heat. Stir continuously with a spatula until the mixture thickens to a perceptible custard and a line can be drawn through it with your finger. Cook only until it is just thickened or it will curdle.

→ Immediately strain the finished ice cream base and stir to cool, then churn in an ice cream machine or put into a freezer tray. If you use a tray, remember to stir the setting walls of the ice cream into the middle of the tray after the first hour, and then again an hour or two later, to prevent crystals forming.

Peach and Vanilla Custard Ice Cream

MAKES ABOUT 1.2 LITRES/2 PINTS

vanilla pods	2
large organic egg yolks	6
vanilla caster sugar	140g/5oz
Jersey milk	500ml/18fl oz
double cream, Jersey is best	600ml/1 pint
ripe peaches, French or Italian white peaches if possible	5
lemon juice	a spritz

Here is an ice cream where subtlety works. It is particularly good if you have found the best, scented, white peaches with the perfect acid-sweet balance, but we all know how hard this can be.

→ Split the VANILLA PODS down the middle and scoop out the seeds with a sharp-pointed teaspoon. Put the EGG YOLKS in a bowl with the VANILLA SUGAR and the VANILLA SEEDS. Whisk the yolks, sugar and vanilla seeds together until they amalgamate. Slowly heat the MILK with the split pods until it reaches scalding point. Pour it straight over the yolk and sugar mixture through a sieve, whisking as you go. Return the mixture to the pan over a very gentle heat and continue to whisk, watching carefully so that no bits of the mixture overheat and scramble at the edges of the pan; the mixture should not get to simmer point. It should take 10–15 minutes, whisking continuously, for the mixture to thicken. Remove the pan from the heat and stir in the DOUBLE CREAM. Leave to cool until it is warm rather than hot, stirring every so often so a skin doesn't form on top.

→ Cut the PEACHES in half, remove the stones and then cut each half into three. Blitz the peaches to a pulp in the blender and squeeze over a spritz of LEMON JUICE to bring out the flavour. Fold the peach pulp into the custard mixture. Churn in an ice cream machine and finish freezing in the freezer in its pail.

→ If you are making the ice cream by hand, put the mixture in a sealable plastic container once it has cooled completely and put it in the freezer. Every 30 minutes, remove from the freezer and whisk the ice cream to stop crystals forming and ruining the smooth, velvety texture. When the ice cream has set enough to be difficult to whisk, even in the middle, just leave it in the freezer until it has set completely.

Rhubarb and Passion Fruit Ice Cream

SERVES 8

rhubarb	8 thin wands
light muscovado sugar	about 4 tbsp

A clean-fruited pudding that you can make at the end of January when the first fragile wands of forced rhubarb appear and the rigours of Christmas make it all the more desirable.

→ Preheat oven to 150°C/300°F/Gas 3. Chop the RHUBARB into small chunks, turn it in the SUGAR in a baking dish and bake in the oven until softened, about 20–30 minutes. Test for sweetness. Drain and reserve the juice, you can pour it over the ice cream or drink it! Mash the rhubarb with a fork. Halve the

passion fruit	4 large or 6 small
full-cream OR Jersey milk	500ml/18fl oz
vanilla pod	1
organic egg yolks	6
unrefined caster sugar	110g/4oz
double cream, Jersey if possible	300ml/10fl oz

PASSION FRUIT, scoop out the contents into a small pan and heat very gently until warm, which makes the fruit easier to sieve. Keep the juice and the seeds separately.

→ Split the VANILLA POD and scrape out the seeds. Scald the MILK with the split pod and its innards, then strain the hot milk over the well-whisked EGG YOLKS and SUGAR, whisking as you go. Return the mixture to the pan and continue to whisk over a gentle heat until you have a thickened custard. Decant into a bowl to cool. Whisk the CREAM until thickened but by no means rigid. Fold the cream into the cooled custard, then stir in the passion fruit juice and rhubarb. Finally, fold in a dessert-spoon of passion fruit seeds, more would overwhelm with crunch. Churn in the ice cream maker and freeze, or freeze in an ice tray (see p. 418).

Galia Melon Ice Cream

SERVES 6

Galia melon	1
unrefined vanilla caster sugar	125g/4oz
egg yolks	4
kirsch	
lemon juice	
double cream	300ml/10fl oz

→ Cut a lid off the top of a GALIA MELON and remove the seeds through a sieve with a bowl placed under it to catch the juice. Carefully scoop out the flesh and stew it gently in a pan with the juice and the VANILLA CASTER SUGAR for 2–3 minutes. Blitz in the blender briefly, return it to the pan with 4 beaten EGG YOLKS, and cook over a very gentle heat until it thickens.

→ Cool the mixture, then add a splosh of KIRSCH and a good squeeze of LEMON JUICE to taste. Fold in the whipped but slightly slack DOUBLE CREAM, and freeze in your ice cream machine or in an old-fashioned tray. If you use a tray, remember to stir the setting walls of the ice cream into the middle of the tray after the first hour, and then again an hour or two later, to prevent crystals forming (see p. 418.

→ When the ice cream has set, scoop it out in balls and return it to the melon shell, the base of which you may have to shave slightly with a knife so that it will stand upright. Place the filled melon on a white dish lined with fig leaves or any large (non-poisonous) leaves you have in the garden, and serve.

Cinnamon Ice Cream

whole cinnamon sticks	2
full-cream milk, Jersey if possible	700ml/1¼ pints
organic egg yolks	10
unrefined vanilla caster sugar	170g/6oz
double cream	250ml/8½fl oz

→ Snap the CINNAMON STICKS in half and put them in a pan with the MILK. Bring slowly to scald point, remove from the heat, cover and leave to infuse for 20–30 minutes. Beat the EGG YOLKS thoroughly with the VANILLA CASTER SUGAR.
→ Warm the cinnamon milk to scald point again, then pour it into the egg yolk and sugar mixture, whisking as you go, before returning the whole bowlful to the pan. Cook over a gentle heat, stirring constantly with a wooden spoon and making absolutely sure the mixture never reaches boiling point, until you have a custard that coats the back of the spoon and has visibly thickened. Remove from the heat and strain through a sieve into a glass bowl. You can speed up the cooling process at this point if you need to by putting the bowl into a sink full of ice.
→ Whisk the CREAM until it is softly held but not rigid. Fold it into the custard, a large spoonful at a time, until the two are as one. Pour into an ice cream machine or freeze in the usual way (see p. 418).

Stem Ginger and Spice Ice Cream

SERVES 6–8

cloves	6 or 7
cinnamon bark	a few little bits
Jersey milk	450ml/16fl oz
vanilla pods, *split and the insides scraped out*	2
organic egg yolks	6
unrefined caster sugar OR runny honey	170g/6oz 2 tbsp
double cream	300ml/10fl oz
crème fraîche	300ml/10fl oz
stem ginger	8–10 globes
ginger syrup	1 tbsp
stem ginger, *very finely chopped*	2 globes

This feels fresh and Christmassy at the same time and is utterly delicious. You may use two large tablespoons of runny honey—a strong-tasting one such as chestnut—instead of the sugar if you prefer.

→ Crush the CLOVES and CINNAMON together in a mortar. Scald the MILK with the split VANILLA PODS and their innards. Whisk it into the EGG YOLKS and SUGAR OR HONEY that you have put into a bowl. Return the mixture to the pan, and cook it over a low heat, whisking as you go, until it thickens perceptibly. Do not allow the mixture to boil. You do not want it to curdle into scrambled egg.
→ Immediately the mixture has thickened, remove from the heat and whisk in the CREAMS thoroughly. Whizz in the blender with 6 globes of GINGER, GINGER SYRUP and half a teaspoon of the SPICE mixture, and taste until you have the right strength. The ginger should predominate, but you want a musky breath of spice. Add a couple more globes of ginger if you need.
→ Churn in the ice cream maker for 30 minutes. Finely chop 2 more globes of ginger and add to the setting mixture. You can put the mixture in a ice tray and freeze, but remember to stir

the setting walls of the ice cream into the middle of the tray after the first hour, and then again an hour or two later, to prevent crystals forming.

Brown Bread and Brandy Ice Cream

double cream	300ml/10fl oz
single cream	300ml/10fl oz
vanilla caster sugar	170g/6oz
cognac, OR use rum OR whisky tbsp	2
granary breadcrumbs	170g/6oz
unrefined granulated sugar	55g/2oz
water	4 tbsp
organic egg white (optional)	1

This was the first ice cream I ever made. It is cream-, rather than custard-based, so gave confidence to an inexperienced cook. I have seen many recipes for it since but none with granary bread, which gives a better texture than wholemeal and a slightly malty flavour to the ice cream.

→ Whisk the CREAMS together with the VANILLA SUGAR and COGNAC until they have turned to a light, thick cream. Chill in something shallow in the freezer while you toast the breadcrumbs in a hot oven until golden brown. Keep checking and turning them so that they don't burn.

→ Put the GRANULATED SUGAR and WATER in a pan and boil them hard for a few minutes before leaving them to cool. When cool, mix the BREADCRUMBS into the syrup and stir it into the chilled creams, which you have scraped into a bowl. Fold all together then beat well, before putting in an ice cream maker to churn, or freeze as for vanilla ice cream on p. 418.

→ To make a lighter-textured ice cream, beat an EGG WHITE to stiff peaks, then fold it into the ice cream after the breadcrumb and syrup mixture.

Lemon Ice Cream

SERVES 6

organic, unwaxed lemons	4
unrefined icing sugar	170g/6oz
water	240ml/8fl oz
double cream, Jersey if possible	300ml/10fl oz

Pair this with a citrus jelly or just scoop it out and serve it with walnut biscuits (see p. 523).

→ Peel the LEMONS with a potato peeler and put the strips in a pan with the ICING SUGAR and WATER. Simmer for about 20 minutes. Leave to cool, strain and add to the JUICE OF THE LEMONS. Whip the CREAM until it is softly stiff, not beyond, and gently fold in the cooled syrup. Taste for sweetness—you need it to taste slightly sharper than you think you need. Churn in an ice cream maker (see p. 418).

Strawberry Ice Cream

strawberries	225g/8oz
unrefined icing sugar	110g/4oz
lemon	juice of ½
orange	juice of ½
double cream	300ml/10fl oz

Another classic ice cream that doesn't need to have the full custard treatment, just the full cream. It is good for turning raw soft summer fruits into ice cream before they over-ripen. Just make sure you adjust the sugar to the acidity of the fruit, always leaving it a little sharper than you think you need to. That way, when you add the cream, the fruit will retain more of its flavour. I like to serve fresh raspberries with strawberry ice cream and vice versa.

→ Blitz the STRAWBERRIES in a food processor, then put them through a nylon sieve, pushing through as much of the pulp as you can. Stir in the SUGAR and the LEMON AND ORANGE JUICE. Whisk the CREAM until it holds in soft folds and fold the strawberry mixture into it. Churn or freeze in a container (see p. 418 for more details).

Fig Ice Cream

SERVES 6

black figs, *peeled*	450g/1lb
port	2–3 tbsp
unrefined vanilla caster sugar	110g/4oz
Jersey or other rich, full-cream milk	200ml/7fl oz
organic lemon	juice of ½

There is something lethally, sexily appealing about this ice cream. The figs' black-skinned, secret, scarlet interiors are reduced to seedy pulpiness and frozen with a lick of port, a spritz of lemon and a little milk. No custard, no whisking, no critical processes at all—this is a hands-off, make-it-easy ice that is as delicious as it is simple to make.

→ Throw the FIGS into the blender and blend them until creamy. Add the PORT, 2 tablespoons to begin with, SUGAR, MILK and JUICE and blend to smoothness again. Taste and add the third spoonful of port if you feel it is needed. Bear in mind that the port flavour will be more evanescent post-freezing, so if you still think you need a touch more, pour in the final tablespoon.

→ Churn in an ice-cream machine or put in a sealed plastic container and stir every 30 minutes until just set to prevent crystals forming (see p. 418).

Quince and Pralinéed Almond Ice Cream

SERVES 4–6

quince paste (membrillo)	225g/8oz
lemon juice	2 tbsp
water	1 tbsp
Oloroso OR another sherry	1 tbsp
double cream, Jersey if possible	300ml/10fl oz
almonds, whole but blanched	140g/5oz
unrefined caster sugar	55–85g/2–3oz

I dreamt up this pudding with George, my friend and cooking companion. The recipe evolved when I couldn't be bothered to make a torta de Santiago with quince paste and almonds, and George suggested an ice cream instead. We had the membrillo, I suggested the pralinéed almonds, sherry seemed to enhance the flavours—we experimented. Use Valencia almonds (sold in good supermarkets) if possible.

→ Melt the MEMBRILLO gently in a pan with the LEMON JUICE, WATER and SHERRY. Whisk the CREAM until it holds softly, but is not stiff.

→ In a non-stick frying pan over a gentle heat, scatter the ALMONDS in a single layer, and pour the SUGAR over them. Stir as the sugar melts and the brittle turns the colour of butterscotch, but not dark brown. Remove from the heat instantly and pour on to a greased baking tray. Leave to solidify, then bash into small chunks and little shards.

→ Fold the cream into the membrillo mixture, then fold about one-third of the brittle into it, and freeze. Refrigerate for 30 minutes before serving and offer a bowl of the remaining brittle to scatter sparingly over the top.

Zabaglione Ice Cream

SERVES 4

organic eggs	5
unrefined vanilla caster sugar	110g/4oz
ground cinnamon	1 pinch
Marsala	120ml/4fl oz
dark rum	2 tbsp
double cream, preferably Jersey	300ml/10fl oz

I have never cooked anything from one of Anna Del Conte's books and not been ravished by the result, and this is no exception. An exceptionally fine ice cream.

→ Separate the eggs, putting the yolks in one bowl and 3 of the whites in another. Add the sugar and cinnamon to the yolks and beat hard until you can leave a ribbon trail. Add the Marsala and rum while still beating.

→ Put the bowl over a pan of hot, not boiling, water and whisk constantly, using electric beaters if you have them, until the mixture is foamy and has doubled in volume. This will take about 10–15 minutes. Plunge the bowl into cold water and carry on beating every so often until the mixture is cool.

→ Whip the cream until it has slackly stiffened and fold it in, then whisk the whites to stiff peaks and fold them into the mixture a spoonful at a time. Churn in an ice cream machine if you have one, or freeze (see p. 418).

Basic Sorbet

Stock syrup

vanilla caster sugar	225g/8oz
water	300ml/10fl oz

Sorbets are a light alternative to cream ices. They really show off the fruit and are immensely easy to make. It is no more difficult to make two or three sorbets at a time, particularly in midsummer with all the different berries and currants that are available, since all you have to do is make a larger quantity of stock syrup. Just remember to add the same amount of fruit purée as stock syrup, with a spritz of lemon juice to bring out the flavour of the fruit.

→ Bring the SUGAR and WATER to the boil in a pan and boil for a further 3 minutes until you have a thick, sweet syrup. Leave to cool.

→ When it is cold, mix the stock syrup with sieved fruit purée and a matching slug of alcohol if you like — Calvados for an apple sorbet, eau de vie de poire for pear, framboise for raspberry, kirsch with almost any scented fruit. Go easy: a couple of tablespoons should be enough flavour-wise, and too much alcohol inhibits the freezing process. Add a spritz of lemon, or lime if it's a mango or melon ice, and it's ready for the freezer. See the lemon sorbet recipe below for the next stage.

Lemon Sorbet

vanilla caster sugar	285g/10oz
water	600ml/1 pint
lemon juice, *freshly squeezed*	300ml/10fl oz
organic egg whites	2

→ Bring the SUGAR and WATER to the boil in a pan and simmer together for 5 minutes. Cool, then add the fresh LEMON JUICE, tasting to make sure you have the right strength and sharpness.

→ Strain into ice trays, cover and put into the freezer or churn in a sorbetière. Freeze the mixture for 3–4 hours or until you have a firm block of lemon water ice. Whisk the egg whites to stiff peaks. Fold the lemon ice into the egg whites a spoonful at a time until the mixture has bulked up to a foamy mass. Refreeze in a larger container until the sorbet is firm and snowy.

Raspberry Sorbet

raspberries, *blitzed in a food processor and sieved*	450g/1lb
water	450ml/16fl oz
vanilla caster sugar	285g/10oz
organic lemon	juice of 1
organic orange	juice of 1
framboise OR kirsch (optional)	2–3 tbsp
organic egg whites (optional)	2

You don't have to add egg whites when you are making a sorbet. I prefer the foamy light texture they give, but you may wish for the purer, iced fruit-water flavour, or choose to add just a single whisked egg white.

→ Purée and sieve the RASPBERRIES. Simmer the WATER and SUGAR together for 5 minutes. Let it cool and add the LEMON AND ORANGE JUICE. Fold in the raspberry purée and add the ALCOHOL if you're using it. Freeze as for the lemon sorbet. Whisk the EGG WHITES if you are using them an add the raspberry ice into the whites a spoonful at a time. Re-freeze.

Charentais Melon and Mint Sorbet

ripe Charentais melons	2
unrefined vanilla caster sugar	200g/7oz
water	300ml/10fl oz
mint	1 bunch
organic limes	juice of 3
organic lemons	juice of 2
kirsch	1 tbsp

Here is a piece of scented heaven that will fill your kitchen and your mouth with celestial pleasure.

→ Halve the MELONS and scoop out the seeds. Slowly bring the SUGAR and WATER to the boil in a pan, then simmer them together for 3 minutes. Take the pan off the heat, and throw in the MINT LEAVES, stripped from the stems. Put the lid on the pan and let the contents cool and macerate for an hour. Press all the syrup out of the mint leaves either by hand, or by putting the mint in a sieve and pressing down hard with a wooden spoon. Add the JUICE OF THE LIMES AND THE LEMONS to the syrup and taste carefully. Melon is sweet, so if the syrup needs sharpening now, add more lemon juice.

→ Scoop out the melon in spoonfuls and blitz in the blender. When it is a smooth purée, add the citrus syrup and the KIRSCH and blitz again briefly. Taste one final time and make any adjustments. You may need a little more citrus or even a little more kirsch. Freeze in an ice-cream machine or in a container, making sure you whisk the slush from the sides every couple of hours as it is setting to prevent crystals from forming.

Lemon and Basil Sorbet

good organic lemons	8
oranges	2
water	600ml/1 pint
unrefined caster sugar	340g/12oz
large basil leaves, *chopped fine*	2 dozen

Herbs and spices may seem unusual paired with fruit in ice creams and sorbets, but think, for example, how they have been seen as partners to chocolate by the South Americans for centuries. Star anise and chilli, tonka beans and thyme, infusions of tea, geranium, roses and jasmine, ginger and pepper—the list is endless. I think orange and bay, lemon and basil or thyme, strawberries and black pepper or balsamic are all instances of the one enhancing and drawing out the best from the other.

→ Scrub, wash and dry the FRUIT. Remove the rind with a potato peeler so that you don't get any pith and put it in a saucepan. Add the WATER and SUGAR and bring slowly to the boil. Simmer until the sugar has dissolved. Turn the heat up and boil rapidly for 3–4 minutes. Remove from the heat and allow the syrup to cool completely.

→ Squeeze the LEMONS and ORANGES and strain the juice into the cold syrup together with the BASIL LEAVES. Pour the mixture into an ice cream maker and churn, or freeze in a metal bowl for a couple of hours before beating in the sink with a whisk to break down the crystals. Taste to check it is sharp enough. Add more lemon juice than you need as sorbet always tastes sweeter once it is frozen. Continue to freeze and whisk until it is ready. Transfer the sorbet to the fridge about 30 minutes before serving. See p. 428 for more on sorbets.

Lemon and Rosemary Sorbet

SERVES 6

organic lemons	*grated* zest and juice *of 8*
organic oranges	*grated* zest and juice *of 2*
unrefined vanilla caster sugar	340g/12oz
water	570ml/1 pint
rosemary	3 sprigs, about 5cm/2in long

The almost flagrant freshness of this lemon and rosemary sorbet was a revelation—it gave the taste a kind of purity that lemon alone couldn't match. With a restrained approach, tasting every few minutes and taking heed of the quantity, you could experiment with all sorts of summer and winter herbs. I think grapefruit and thyme might be my next.

→ Put the ZESTS into the SUGAR AND WATER mixture in a pan and bring slowly to the boil so that the sugar dissolves, then boil for 4 minutes. Using a mezzaluna if you have one, chop the ROSEMARY so fine that the leaves are no longer needles but flecks, and add them to the pan. Cover with a lid and turn the heat down to a bare simmer for 15 minutes. Remove from the heat and cool.

→ Add the JUICE OF THE ORANGES AND LEMONS and freeze in an ice cream machine or in a sealed container, making sure you whisk the slush from the sides every couple of hours as it is setting to prevent crystals from forming.

Passion Fruit and Lime Sorbet

SERVES 8

water	2 cups
sugar	2 cups
wrinkly passion fruit	8
limes	2

Limes bring out the flavour of melons, mangoes and passion fruit, a point well worth remembering. They have the ability to make the fruit taste more itself than it does without them, so always squeeze on a little lime juice even if you are just eating a plain wedge of cut melon. This sorbet is stunning, a real refresher after a rich main course. It breezes in and blasts the fat away, leaving you feeling almost virtuous.

→ Measure 2 cups of WATER and 2 cups of SUGAR into a pan; each cup should be about 240ml/8fl oz in volume. Dissolve them together, bring to the boil and simmer for 5 minutes.
→ Scoop the pulp from the PASSION FRUITS into another pan, pour over half the hot syrup and set over a gentle heat until the flesh starts to loosen from the seeds. Sieve into a bowl and press through as much of the pulp as you can with a wooden spoon. Reserve half the seeds.
→ Zest the LIMES onto a small plate and squeeze the juice. Add the lime juice and the remaining syrup alternately to the passion fruit until you have the right tang-to-sweet balance for your taste. Mix in the reserved seeds bar one teaspoonful. Freeze in your ice cream machine or as for the Lemon and Basil Sorbet on p. 430. Add a whisked EGG WHITE to the mixture before you freeze it if you like the lighter, airier sorbet it makes. Serve in glasses with a little zest and a few seeds on top.

Charentais Water Ice

SERVES 6

vanilla caster sugar	110g/4oz
water	225ml/8fl oz
Charentais melons	2
lemon AND/OR lime	
egg white	1

A delicate, subtle water ice, this is good served with Galia Melon Ice Cream (see p. 423).

→ Simmer the VANILLA CASTER SUGAR with the WATER for a few minutes. Liquidise enough MELON PULP to give you 300ml/10fl oz of juice, two melons maximum. Add the cooled syrup slowly, tasting as you go, then sharpen with a spritz of LEMON JUICE, and, if you like, one of LIME, which makes melon taste more melony (and, incidentally, mango more mangoey).
→ Freeze until the outside is set, but the middle still slushily liquid. Gently fold in a stiffly whisked EGG WHITE before returning the mixture to the ice tray and to the freezer. You may make this a couple of days before you wish to serve it, but it does tend to lose flavour after that.

Blackcurrant Leaf Sorbet

SERVES 6–8

caster sugar	225 g/8 oz
water	600 ml/1 pint
small blackcurrant leaves	3 good handfuls
lemon	*grated* zest and juice of 1
egg whites	2

The flavour of the blackcurrant leaves is unlike any you will ever have experienced, a real new taste, unguessable and unexpected. Use only the small leaves, not the big, tough ones.

→ Place the SUGAR and WATER in a saucepan, heat gently until dissolved, then boil for 10 minutes. Add the BLACKCURRANT LEAVES and LEMON ZEST and leave to cool and macerate.

→ Pour the cold liquid through a sieve into a bowl, and add LEMON JUICE until you can detect a real tang—freezing will mute the taste if you haven't put in enough lemon. Whisk the EGG WHITES until stiff and incorporate them into the mixture, making sure you have a homogeneous-looking mixture without a layer of liquid under it. Freeze. If you don't have an ice cream maker, beat the mixture after a couple of hours of freezing, paying special attention to the texture. Serve with walnut or almond biscuits (see p. 523).

Lemon Granita

vanilla caster sugar	285g/10oz
water	600ml/1 pint
lemon juice, *freshly squeezed*	300ml/10fl oz

→ Bring the SUGAR and WATER to the boil in a pan then simmer together for 5 minutes. Cool before adding the fresh LEMON JUICE, tasting to make sure you have the right strength and sharpness. Strain into ice trays, cover and put into the freezer or churn in a sorbetière.

→ Every 30 minutes stir the frozen edges of the mixture from the side to the middle of the ice trays. Depending on how deep your freezing tray or box is, the mixture should be ready in 2–3 hours, by which time it will be like slushy granules; a granita to the Italians. Serve it scooped into tall glasses with soft amaretti or any sweet pudding biscuit.

Coffee Granita

ground espresso coffee	12 tbsp
water	1.2 litres/2 pints
sugar	55–85g/2–3oz

→ Put the COFFEE into a tall, warmed jug and pour the boiling WATER over it. Stir with a wooden spoon and leave to brew. After 10 minutes, strain it and stir in the SUGAR. When it is cold, pour through a double sheet of muslin into freezing trays. Taste for sugar. Freeze, stirring the sides away from the edge of the container every 30 minutes until it is the texture of slushy granules. Serve in tall glasses with a cloud of crème chantilly—whipped cream sweetened with a little sugar.

Lemon Mousse

SERVES 4–6

organic eggs	4
unrefined vanilla caster sugar	110g/4oz
organic lemons zest and juice of 2
gelatine OR leaf gelatine	1 packet
double cream	200ml/7fl oz

This is not a difficult thing to make, but you must allow time for it to chill and set in the fridge. What you don't want is one of those rigid creations that has set within an inch of its life. A mousse should be dense compared to an airy soufflé, but light at the same time and have the sharpness of the lemon to cut through the creamy richness. So you must keep tasting to check the sharpness isn't being drowned by the billows of cream.

→ Separate the EGGS, putting the whites into a bowl large enough for them to bulk up into when you whisk them, and the yolks into a bowl with the SUGAR. Whisk the yolks and sugar together in a KitchenAid or with electric beaters until they become very pale and have turned very creamy. Zest the LEMONS into the mixture. Squeeze the JUICE OF BOTH LEMONS into a small pan, add the GELATINE (following the instructions on the packet) and melt thoroughly over a very gentle heat. You don't want to knock out the fresh lemony flavour, so it should not get very hot. Cool slightly.

→ Whip the CREAM until it holds softly, not stiffly. Pour the lemony gelatine mixture into the creamed yolks and sugar and whisk lightly, then fold in the cream with a metal spoon, again gently and lightly. A gentle touch is paramount with a mousse. Taste for sharpness, adding a spritz more LEMON if need be.

→ Whisk the EGG WHITES to stiff peaks, stiff enough to hold over your head without them slipping an inch! Stir the first spoonful of white into the mousse mixture to slacken it, then fold the rest in very lightly, a tablespoon at a time, keeping everything light and lifted and letting the air get into it until you have used up all the mixture. If you are doing it correctly, the mixture will seem to softly sigh and heave and bubble as you fold.

→ Scrape into a soufflé dish with a rubber spatula and put in the fridge to chill for a few hours or overnight. Some people like to decorate with squirls of cream but that is a retro-step too far for me. Some long, skinny grated zesty bits of either lemon or lime for colour are really all the dish needs, but pour over some cold thin cream if you like.

Rich Chocolate and Prune Mousse

SERVES 8–10

organic prunes	about 2 dozen
hot leaf-tea	1 pot
vanilla caster sugar	140g/5oz
whole eggs, *separated*	3
egg yolks	3
Green and Black's cocoa powder	1 tbsp
double cream	200ml/7fl oz
unsalted butter	85g/3oz
best bitter chocolate, 70 per cent cocoa solids	225g/8oz
Armagnac OR cognac	1 tbsp

Do not be alarmed by the unconventional method of making this richest and most delicious of mousses, whose darkly bitter density is cut by the prunes.

→ Pour hot LEAF-TEA, I used Whittard's Afternoon Blend, to cover the PRUNES, and leave them in the bowl overnight. This way you don't need to cook the prunes, just remove them from the liquid and chop each one into thirds when you need them.

→ Put 55g/2oz of the SUGAR, all 6 EGG YOLKS, the COCOA POWDER and the CREAM in the top of a double saucepan of simmering water. Keep whisking it over a gentle heat until it thickens enough to coat a wooden spoon. Take the top saucepan out of the bottom one, and, off the heat, add small pieces of the BUTTER and CHOCOLATE and stir until fully melted. Add the ALCOHOL and stir it in.

→ Whisk the 3 EGG WHITES with the rest of the SUGAR. Do not add the sugar at the end—this method makes a thickly glossy meringue which you want to whisk to soft peak stage. Fold the meringue lightly into the chocolate mixture that you have decanted into a bowl, and add the prunes. They will not sink to the bottom, the mixture is too dense. Pour into a large soufflé dish and refrigerate overnight if possible.

Lemon Cream Pots

SERVES 8

lemon juice (you'll need 3–4 organic lemons)	120ml/4fl oz
pure lemon oil (optional)	a few drops
vanilla caster sugar	85g/3oz
large organic egg yolks	6
organic double cream	375ml/13fl oz

Bring back the ramekin! Individual creams, brûlées and custards are a lovely way to end dinner, as are little chocolate pots and the like. They are symphonies of measured richness—you get one, and it is rich and profound enough for you not to need more. The most you may do is pour a slick of cold, thin cream over it if you want to go too far. Boyajian do a pure lemon oil that is available in supermarkets.

→ Preheat the oven to 170°C/325°F/Gas 3. Combine the LEMON JUICE, LEMON OIL if using, and SUGAR in a bowl and stir well to dissolve thoroughly. Test for sweetness. In a separate bowl whisk the EGG YOLKS, then add the CREAM. Whisk the lemon juice mixture into the eggs and cream, then strain through a sieve into a jug.

→ Boil a kettle. Set 8 ramekins in a roasting tin and pour the cream mixture into them. Pour boiling water into the tin to reach halfway up the sides of the ramekins. Cover the ramekins with a sheet of greaseproof to prevent a skin from forming, and bake in the middle of the oven for about 30 minutes until tremblingly set. They will carry on cooking once removed from the oven. Take the ramekins out of the water and cool on a rack. Refrigerate for at least 2 hours or overnight before serving.

Vanilla Cream Pots with Armagnac and Orange Apricots

MAKES 6 RAMEKINS

double cream	500ml/18fl oz
full-cream milk	100ml/3½fl oz
fresh vanilla pod, *with its scooped-out innards*	1
egg yolks	6
unrefined vanilla caster sugar	75g/2½oz
Armagnac and Orange Apricots	
dried unsulphured organic apricots	18
orange juice *freshly squeezed*	200ml/7fl oz
unrefined caster sugar	100g/3½oz
water	100ml/3½fl oz
Culpeper's sweet orange oil (optional)	a few drops
organic orange	*peel* of 1
Armagnac, cognac, cider brandy OR Calvados	

You can make this unfussy pudding well in advance, and it is as good in the winter with dried fruit as it is with summer berries or fruits.

→ Put the CREAM and MILK in a pan, add the VANILLA POD AND SEEDS, and bring just to scalding point. Cover the pan, remove from the heat and infuse for 30 minutes or so.

→ Preheat the oven to 170°C/325°F/Gas 3. Whisk the EGG YOLKS together with the CASTER SUGAR until thick and pale, then remove the pod from the cream mixture and pour the liquid over the yolks, whisking them together. Strain the cream into ramekins, set them in a roasting tin with hot water to come halfway up their sides, and cover them with a sheet of grease-proof paper to prevent a skin forming as they cook.

→ Bake until quiveringly set. They will continue to cook outside the oven. Test after 40 minutes by nudging them. Remove from the bain-marie and leave to cool completely. Place two or three APRICOTS with some juice and peel on top of each vanilla cream pot.

Armagnac and Orange Apricots

→ Soak the APRICOTS overnight in half the ORANGE JUICE. Next day, remove the pith from the ORANGE PEEL, slice into matchstick shreds and blanch in boiling water for a minute. Put the rest of the juice into a pan with the sugar, water and shreds of blanched peel. Simmer for 10 minutes, then add the apricots and their juice and simmer until tender, about 15 minutes. Cool them in a glass bowl, then add a generous slug of ALCOHOL and stir it in well.

→ These apricots keep well in the fridge for several days and can be served on their own.

Elizabeth Raffald's Orange Custards

SERVES 8–10

Seville orange OR use part orange, part lemon	rind of ½
cognac, Cointreau OR Grand Marnier	1 tbsp
Seville orange OR use juice of half a sweet orange and half a lemon	juice of 1
unrefined granulated sugar	110g/4oz
large egg yolks	4
double cream	300ml/10fl oz
single cream	300ml/10fl oz
orange-flower water (optional)	1 tsp or to taste
Culpeper's sweet orange oil (optional)	a few drops

Mrs Raffald's The Experienced English Housekeeper *of 1769 was one of the greats, and many of the recipes are adaptable to the present time and kitchen. I don't use candied peel as she suggested, but add a little orange-flower water and a few drops of sweet orange oil to the cream to intensify the flavour, and a twist of blanched peel to the top. You may use either, both or neither, but I beg you to try this divinely unctuous recipe. This is a pudding you will go on cooking for ever. It is easy to make in advance, cheap, and will make people believe you are a seriously good cook. Sweet orange oil is available from Culpeper or good delis and supermarkets.*

→ Preheat the oven to 170°C/325°F/Gas 3. Remove the rind from the CITRUS FRUIT with a swivel-bladed potato peeler, making sure there is no pith on the inside. Simmer the PEEL in a little pan in water for 2 minutes. Drain and put it in the blender with the BRANDY, ORANGE (and LEMON) JUICE, SUGAR and EGG YOLKS. Blend hard until the peel has become pulverised to a slight grittiness and there are no large bits of it floating around.

→ Bring the CREAMS to scalding point (that is, the point just before they boil and rise up dangerously), together in a pan. Pour slowly into the blender, whizzing as you go. Check the flavour and add the ORANGE-FLOWER WATER and SWEET ORANGE OIL accordingly, or, if you have neither, extra ORANGE or LEMON JUICE or SUGAR.

→ Place 8–10 small ramekins in a roasting tin. Pour the orange custard into the ramekins and pour boiling water to come halfway up their sides. Place in the oven for about 30 minutes or until the custards are set with a slight shudder in the middle when gently joggled in the tin. Remove from the water to cool, as custard goes on cooking outside the oven. Serve warm or chilled with a slice of orange or a squirl of peel on top if you like.

Trinity Burnt Cream or Crème Brûlée

MAKES 8 RAMEKINS

vanilla pod	1
organic double cream, Jersey if possible	850ml/1½ pints
large organic egg yolks	7
vanilla caster sugar	3 dsrtsp
demerara sugar	

Whatever anyone says, this is easy to make as long as you have the patience to keep stirring. I feel it needs a good 8 hours in the fridge, and that on no account should it be made in the oven in a bain-marie. The consistency will never have that satiny finish of a properly stirred, all-cream custard. The other mistake is to over-sweeten; remember, the top is pure caramel.

→ Chill the ramekins in the freezer while you make the custard. Split the VANILLA POD, extract the seeds, and put them in a pan with the CREAM and the pod. Bring the cream to scalding point, then remove from the heat and leave to infuse for 10 minutes. Whisk together the EGG YOLKS and CASTER SUGAR, then strain in the cream through a sieve, and return to the pan.
→ On a low heat, stir the mixture continuously, until you can feel it thickening. This takes 10–15 minutes. On no account be tempted to turn up the heat or you will end up with scrambled eggs. Eventually you will find that a trail is left behind by your spoon as you stir. I use a little balloon whisk as the custard begins to thicken, which I sort of worry quickly across the custard.
→ Remove from the heat, and pour into the chilled ramekins. Place in the fridge for a good 8 hours. Remove half an hour before you want them, scatter a thin layer of DEMERARA over the surface with your fingers, followed by a tiny sprinkle of water. Blast with a blowtorch or under a very hot grill until the sugar has caramelised. Return to the fridge for 30 minutes before serving.

Geranium Cream

double cream	300ml/10fl oz
caster sugar	75g/2½oz
rose-geranium leaves	2
cream cheese	140g/5oz

I found this cream in Mary Norwak's lovely book, English Puddings Sweet and Savoury. *She also refers to rose-geranium leaves being used to flavour sponge cakes and crab-apple jelly. Make this pudding the day before you want to eat it.*

→ Put the CREAM into a bowl with the SUGAR and ROSE-GERANIUM LEAVES. Put the bowl over a pan of hot water and heat gently until the cream is hot but not boiling. Remove from the heat and leave until just cold. Gradually add the CREAM to the CHEESE, mixing together until smooth and creamy. Put into a bowl, cover and leave in a cool place, not the fridge, for 12 hours. Take out the leaves and put the mixture into a serving bowl. This is delicious with fresh raspberries or blackberries.

Pannacotta

SERVES 6

vanilla pod	a small piece
double cream	425ml/15fl oz
Jersey milk from the top of the bottle	150ml/5fl oz
vanilla caster sugar	85–100g/3–3½oz
gelatine	1 leaf

Here is an Italian pudding that slips down with cool, elegant ease. It could take a lifetime of experimenting with, as you must get that magical, barely set texture that doesn't smack of a heavy hand with the gelatine, and you need to develop your own ideas as to how creamy and rich or milky and mild you like it. If you can get unpasteurised Jersey cream you are more than halfway to pannacotta heaven.

→ Split the piece of VANILLA POD and scrape out the seeds. Heat the CREAM, MILK, vanilla seeds and pod in a pan. Add the SUGAR, bring to the boil and boil for a minute. Take the pan off the heat, cover and leave to infuse for an hour. Remove the piece of pod. Soften the GELATINE in cold water, squeeze and dissolve in 4 tablespoons of hot water.

→ Strain the cream mixture and add a couple of tablespoons to the gelatine, stirring rapidly. Add the gelatine to the cream mixture, stirring thoroughly to dissolve it. Pour into dariole moulds or ramekins and allow to cool. Cover with clingfilm and chill in the fridge for at least 2 hours. Run a palette knife around the side of the ramekins or moulds to turn the pannacotta out onto individual plates.

→ Some people like to eat pannacotta with a fruit purée or compote. I love the simple purity of the dish on its own.

Les Cremets

SERVES 4

fromage frais	285g/10oz
crème fraîche	150ml/5fl oz
egg whites	2

This is a lovely light, lactic, cool accompaniment to soft summer fruits. Fraises de bois, if you can lay your hands on them, are the best. Remember to make this the night before you want it and check you have the muslin before you start. At a pinch you could use a J-cloth.

→ Line your sieve with clean muslin, sparing enough to fold over the top later. Mix the FROMAGE FRAIS and CRÈME FRAÎCHE together well in a cold bowl. In a separate bowl, whisk the EGG WHITES until they form stiff peaks, then fold them lightly but thoroughly into the creams. Do not knock the air out; be brief. Spoon the mixture into the muslin and fold the extra muslin over the top. Put the sieve over a pudding basin in the fridge overnight.

→ The following day, unmould it. The cream will have shrunk and lost a lot of its moisture as it solidified. Serve in a bowl with a separate bowl of soft fruit to hand round. Delicious with cold, thin cream poured over it.

Coeur à la Crème

curd cheese	225g/8oz
organic eggs, *separated*	2
vanilla caster sugar	55g/2oz
gelatine	1 packet
whipping cream	240ml/8fl oz

This is a firmer cream than the cremet on p. 438 because of the gelatine. It is best set in a heart-shaped mould, the kind with holes in the bottom. Wonderful with soft summer fruit and berries or with a fruit compote in the winter.

→ Put the CURD CHEESE through the coarse disc of a mouli-légumes to aerate it. This improves the texture, so if you don't have a mouli, push it through a sieve. Stir in the EGG YOLKS and SUGAR. Dissolve the GELATINE in 6 tablespoons of very hot water in a bowl and set aside. When it is almost cold and smooth, stir in the CREAM and whip until stiff. Fold in the curd cheese mixture thoroughly but lightly. Whisk the EGG WHITES until they form stiff peaks and fold them into the mixture.

→ Line a large mould or several little heart-shaped moulds with muslin and spoon in the cream, folding the muslin over the top. Put the moulds in the fridge until they set. Turn out onto plates or a large serving dish, and pile mounds of soft fruit, sugared until it bleeds a little, around them.

Lemon Posset

SERVES 6–8

double cream, Jersey if possible	600ml/1 pint
vanilla caster sugar	140g/5oz
lemons	juice of 2

Simple, but utterly delicious. Seventeenth-century recipe books were full of possets, the name of a medicinal drink of milk, curdled with wine or ale and spices, which was said to be good for colds. There is nothing curdled about this sharp, delectable cream.

→ Put the CREAM and SUGAR in a pan large enough to allow it room to boil. Bring to the boil and boil for 3 minutes. Remove from the heat and whisk in the LEMON JUICE. Strain the mixture into a jug before pouring into ramekins. Let them cool, then leave them into the fridge for 4–6 hours before serving. Serve with almond and orange florentines.

Almond and Orange Florentines

MAKES ABOUT 16

organic egg whites	3
unrefined icing sugar	140g/5oz
flaked almonds	400g/14oz
oranges	*grated zest* of 2

A gooey delight from the Ottolenghi deli in London.

→ Preheat the oven to 150°C/300°F/Gas 2. Line a baking tray with silicone paper and brush lightly with vegetable oil. Mix THE INGREDIENTS together by hand. Using a wet hand, make little mounds of the almond mix on the tray, spaced well apart. Dip a fork in water and flatten each biscuit until very thin.

→ Place in the oven and bake for about 12 minutes until the florentines are golden brown. Leave them to cool and harden before removing from the tray.

Crème Caramel with Hazelnut Brittle

SERVES 4–6

vanilla caster sugar	85g/3oz
cold water	1 tbsp
whole organic eggs	2
egg yolks	2
vanilla sugar	2 tbsp
vanilla pod	*scraped out seeds* of 1
milk	600ml/1 pint

Hazelnut Brittle

vanilla caster sugar	85g/3oz
hazelnuts, *skinned*	100g/3½oz

The bitter molten sugar contrasting with the creamy, vanilla-ey depths is true inspiration and pure simplicity. The hazelnut brittle turns it into a party piece but is an optional extra.

→ Preheat the oven to 150°C/300°F/Gas 2. Gently melt the 85g/3oz CASTER SUGAR in a saucepan, until it is liquid and has turned a burnished mahogany colour. Just as it starts to bubble, throw on the COLD WATER and quickly pour the mixture into the base of a soufflé dish, rolling it slightly up the sides until it sets.

→ Break the EGGS and YOLKS into a bowl, add the SUGAR and the INNARDS FROM THE VANILLA POD, and whisk. Scald the MILK in the sugar pan, and pour it over the egg mixture. Once the caramel has set, pour the egg and milk mixture over it. Set the soufflé dish in a roasting tin and pour boiling water to come two-thirds of the way up the dish. Cook for 1½–2 hours, making sure that the custard is still trembling slightly in the middle when you remove the dish from the oven. Leave it in the tin of water until the set is complete, then take it out, cool, and finally chill it in the fridge for a few hours. It should be served cold.

→ To turn the crème caramel out, run a palette knife cautiously around the edge of the dish, place a plate with enough of a lip to hold the caramel over the top and invert it carefully onto the plate.

Hazelnut Brittle

→ Scatter the VANILLA SUGAR in the base of a saucepan, and heat it to the same point as the caramel. Throw in the CHOPPED HAZELNUTS, stir briefly, and spread on a buttered baking tray. Leave to cool and set, then bash the brittle up a bit to serve alongside the crème caramel.

Crème au Café

SERVES 4

coffee, *freshly ground*	110g/4oz
Jersey milk	340ml/12fl oz
unrefined granulated sugar	2 tbsp
sea salt	1 tiny pinch
organic egg yolks	3

Richard Olney's Simple French Food *remains one of my all-time favourite cookery books. It is written with elegance; it is sparse yet informative in its guidance and instruction; and it has a keen sense of place and style. Here is a simple pudding of his that I have adapted. It shares the best characteristics of two classic French puddings, the brûlée and the caramel, and is infused with the sultry, deep tones of burnt sugar and coffee.*

→ Stir together the COFFEE and MILK in a saucepan over a medium flame until a full boil is reached. Remove from the heat, cover and leave it to infuse until tepid. Strain through a muslin-lined sieve, extracting as much of the milk as you can.
→ Boil the 2 tablespoons of SUGAR with 1 tablespoon of water in a small pan until it turns a rich, reddish mahogany. Swiftly remove from the heat and pour in another couple of tablespoons of water. Stir to let it dissolve the caramel and briefly return it to the heat if you need to.
→ Combine ALL THE INGREDIENTS, whisk thoroughly and cook in a double saucepan or a bowl above a pan of barely simmering water. Stir constantly until the mixture becomes the texture of a thick sauce and coats the spoon. At no stage let it boil. Pour into ramekins, cool, and chill in the fridge. Serve with double cream and perhaps some tuiles.

Baked Rice Pudding

short-grain pudding rice	75g/2½oz
Jersey milk	850ml–1.2 litres/ 1½–2 pints
butter	30g/1oz
sugar	2 tbsp
vanilla pod, *split* OR cinnamon stick	1 1

→ Put the RICE with 600ml/1 pint of the MILK and the REMAINING INGREDIENTS into a heatproof stoneware or glass dish. Leave in a gentle oven, 140°C/275°F/Gas 1, for 3 hours. After an hour, stir up the pudding and add more milk to slacken the mixture. After 2 hours, do the same thing again, and, if you like, add some single cream. The butter and the cream are what form the delicious skin. Serve with a jug of double cream.
→ If you reduce the heat, say, to 130°C/250°F/Gas ½ or even lower, you can leave the rice pudding in the oven for twice as long. Add more milk occasionally; you may need some extra if you cook it for this long. Beneath the crust, the rice will caramelise slightly to an appetising brown. Rice pudding is the definition of slow food, so don't try to speed it up.

Gooseberry Fool

SERVES 4–6

tart gooseberries, *topped and tailed*	about 450g/1lb
muscovado sugar	4 tbsp or so
unsalted butter	55g/2oz
single cream OR half each single and double cream	240ml/8fl oz
organic egg yolks, *beaten*	3
elderflower syrup (optional)	2–3 tbsp
Elderflower Syrup	
elderflower	6 heads
vanilla caster sugar	3 tbsp

The fool of fools. There is something about the gooseberry—the splurting of the sharp seeds; the pale green, golden or deep pink hairy orbs which hang like miniature lanterns with an armoury of spikes to contend with as you pull them from the branch; the way the berries collapse and yield when cooked. Paired with elderflower they are a classic combination, the scented sweetness matching the acid sharpness to perfection.

→ Stew the GOOSEBERRIES gently in the melted BUTTER and SUGAR in a heavy-bottomed frying pan. Turn frequently as the sugar begins to coat and caramelise, and do not allow them to overcook. The berries are cooked when you can crush them with a fork without resistance. Leave them to cool.

→ Scald the CREAM in a small pan. Pour it over the beaten EGG YOLKS, whisking as you go, then return the mixture to the pan. Continue to cook and stir or whisk over a gentle heat until the custard has thickened. Pay attention at this stage or the mixture will scramble.

→ If you are using ELDERFLOWER SYRUP, stir that into the fruit purée first, then fold the fruit into the custard. Cool and spoon into glasses or a glass bowl. Top with a sprig of redcurrants or a twist of lemon peel to add colour.

Elderflower Syrup

→ Simmer the ELDERFLOWER HEADS with 240ml/8fl oz water and the VANILLA CASTER SUGAR for 15 minutes. Leave to infuse under a lid before straining through a sieve.

Hunza Apricot and Orange Fool

SERVES 4–6

Hunza apricots	200g/7oz
fresh orange juice	to cover
unrefined icing sugar	
lemon juice	a spritz
double OR Jersey cream	300ml/10fl oz

Remember to start this dish the night before by soaking the apricots.

→ Soak the APRICOTS overnight in the fresh ORANGE JUICE, then simmer them gently in the juice until they are soft. This should take 5–10 minutes. Remove the little kernels and blitz the apricots in the food processor or blender.

→ Boil down the remaining juice until it is reduced by a half and is lovely and syrupy. Stir the juice into the fruit purée and add a little ICING SUGAR to taste and a spritz of LEMON. Whisk the CREAM until it holds but is not rigid, and fold the purée into it thoroughly. Plop into glasses or a large glass bowl and serve with biscuits. Hazelnut and almond biscuits or macaroons are the best with this fool.

Raw Blackcurrant Fool

SERVES 4–6

blackcurrants	450g/1lb
unrefined caster sugar	several tbsp, to taste
lemon juice	a spritz
double OR Jersey cream	300ml/10fl oz

It is extraordinary how different the taste is between raw and cooked blackcurrants. Raw is definitely my preference. It seems to be deeper and subtler, and the sharp, almost musky, vitamin-C-rich juice seems almost to taste of the leaves and bush.

→ Pull the currants from their branches with the tines of a fork. Blitz them well in a food processor or blender, then sieve the resulting purée into a bowl. It will be thick and brilliantly purple. Add sugar until you have the desired taste, keeping it on the sharp side—chilling things accentuates the flavour of the sugar rather than the fruit. Add a squeeze of lemon juice.
→ Whisk the cream until softly holding, then fold the purple purée thoroughly into it for a purple cream, or not so thoroughly if you go for a striated look. Plop into glasses or a glass bowl to chill, and serve on its own or with biscuits.

Raspberry Fool

SERVE 4–6

raspberries	450g/1lb
unrefined caster sugar	1–2 heaped tbsp or to taste
lemon juice	a spritz
double OR Jersey cream	300ml/10fl oz

The essence of summer, these creamy fools are simplicity itself, and far less demanding to make than custard-based ones. Just allow chilling time!

→Keep 12–18 of the RASPBERRIES back to decorate with. Blitz the rest in a food processor or blender, then sieve the fruit, adding SUGAR and a squeeze of LEMON to bring out the flavour. Taste to make sure it is to your liking. Whisk the CREAM until it is softly whipped but firm enough to hold. Now fold all or some of the fruit purée into the cream. You may place a few whole raspberries at the bottom of the bowl or individual glasses, or in the middle of the fool, or save one or all of them to decorate the top.
→ If you have kept back some fruit purée without cream, you may like to run a thin seam or two of fruit with the layers of the creamy fool in the bowl. Chill in the fridge for several hours before serving, and serve with little biscuits.

Strawberry Fool
→ Make a strawberry fool in just the same way, making sure the strawberries are ripe but not over-ripe.

Mango Fool

SERVES 4–6

ripe mangoes	2
lime	1
unrefined caster sugar	1–2 tbsp
double OR Jersey cream	300ml/10fl oz

The most luscious and scented fool of them all. Limes bring out the flavour of mangoes as they do melons and pawpaws, so use lime instead of lemon juice to sharpen things up in this recipe. Mangoes, being a tropical fruit, are available all the year round; just make sure you pick ripe ones.

→ First deal with your MANGO. Cut as close to the stone the length of one side and then the length of the other side to remove the two less-than-halves. The bit around the stone is always harder than you would expect so the knife won't be able to get in that close. Then cut away all the rest of the flesh that is biddable and remove it from the skin, cutting it in chunks and putting it straight in the blender with its juice.

→ Blitz, scrape into a bowl, then spritz with LIME JUICE and stir in the SUGAR to taste. No need to sieve as there are no seeds. Whip the CREAM until it is softly held, fold in the fruit purée, and chill. You may want to serve some extra slices of mango at the bottom of the bowl or glass, or sprinkle a few toasted slivered almonds on top.

Pineapple and Yoghurt Fool

SERVES 6

large, ripe pineapple	1 × 1kg/2¼lb
lime	1
unrefined vanilla caster sugar	2 tbsp
kirsch	1 tbsp
thick live yoghurt (cow's, sheep's or Greek)	400ml/14fl oz

The pineapple, one of my favourite exotic fruits, doesn't translate into fool-hood successfully. I don't know why the mix of pineapple and cream should diminish the singularly luscious, full-throated flavour of the pineapple, but diminish it it does. So I wondered what would happen if I tried to keep its sharpness in place with yoghurt rather than cream, and unbelievably it worked. Lime juice brings out the flavour of the pineapple magically, as it does with mangoes and melons. Try it and see. Just be sure to make the fool a good six hours before you need it, or the night before.

→ Cut the ends off the PINEAPPLE and cut down, removing the skin from top to bottom. Make sure you remove all the brown snodgels as you go. Remove the tough central core, too, as you cut the fruit into wedges from top to bottom. Cut the wedges into smaller chunks and blitz in a food processor until turned to pulp but still retaining some texture, rather than being a smooth purée.

→ Scrape the pineapple into a bowl and grate the ZEST OF THE LIME over it. Squeeze over the JUICE OF THE LIME and sprinkle on the SUGAR and KIRSCH. Cover and refrigerate for six hours. Stir the YOGHURT into the pineapple pulp and spoon the fool into glasses or a large glass bowl. Decorate with a little more LIME ZEST over the top.

Syllabub

SERVES 6

Oloroso OR good dry sherry	4 tbsp
cognac	2 tbsp
lemon	*finely grated* zest and juice of 1
vanilla caster sugar	2 tbsp
double cream, Jersey if possible	425ml/15fl oz
nutmeg	a suspicion

blanched lemon peel
OR a sprig of *bruised* rosemary
to decorate each glass

Syllabubs are best left overnight at the stage before you beat them with the cream, so that the lemon juice, zest and liquor—brandy and white wine or sherry being the usual combination—macerate thoroughly. However, I often make an instant syllabub and add soft summer berries, peaches or nectarines and the like in strata between the billowing folds of cream, and can't say that I am unduly worried by the diminution of depth of flavour. Keep the syllabub for a day or two before serving it if you have the time to make it that far in advance.

→ Put the FIRST THREE INGREDIENTS in a bowl, cover and leave overnight if you have time, or for as long as you can.
→ Strain the liquid into a bowl and stir in the SUGAR until it has completely dissolved. Pour in the CREAM, grate over a tiny bit of NUTMEG and begin to beat with a balloon whisk. It seems hard to imagine that the liquid will be taken up and absorbed by the cream, but it does happen and it doesn't take forever. Keep whisking until the syllabub holds in soft folds, then spoon it into glasses. Keep cool but not very cold, or the cream will harden too much. Decorate and serve with little biscuits such as the almond and orange florentines on p. 439.

Cassis Syllabub

SERVES 4–6

cassis OR blackcurrant liqueur	125ml/4fl oz
cognac	2 tbsp
lemon	*pared* rind and juice of 1
caster sugar	50g/2oz
double cream	300ml/10fl oz
blackcurrants	450g/1lb
light muscovado sugar	to taste
lemon	a squeeze

→ Macerate the CASSIS, COGNAC, LEMON RIND and JUICE together for a few hours, or overnight. Strain into a bowl and stir in the sugar until it has dissolved. Stir in the CREAM slowly, then beat everything together with a balloon whisk until it has cohered and thickened. You want it to hold its shape, but softly; if you overbeat, it will begin to curdle and separate.
→ Swirl the raw BLACKCURRANTS in a food processor until puréed, then push them through a nylon sieve. Add SUGAR to taste, and a squeeze of LEMON JUICE to bring out the flavour. You will probably have too much here, but you can use the leftover blackcurrant purée in a wonderful fool or ice cream.
→ Spoon a layer of syllabub into individual glasses or one glass bowl, then add a stratum of the raw blackcurrant purée. You want it to look like thin seam, not a thick stripe. Repeat with a layer of each, then add a final layer of syllabub. Keep cool, but do not refrigerate.

Blackberry Syllabub
→ You can also make this with blackberries and crème de mûres instead of cassis.

Instant Nellie Melba Syllabub

SERVES 6

white peaches, *skinned*	2
raspberries (plus extra to decorate)	4 tbsp
blueberries	2 tbsp
Syllabub	
Oloroso OR good dry sherry	2 tbsp
cognac (a good one if possible)	1 tbsp
lemon	*finely grated* zest and juice of 1
vanilla caster sugar	1–2 tbsp
double cream, unpasteurised Jersey if possible	425ml/15fl oz

There has been much written about syllabub and the importance of steeping the alcohol, lemon and sugar overnight for the flavours to mingle and marry. But sometimes one is in a hurry. I have made two instant versions of this dish. If the cream is chilled when you start and you return the whole to the fridge for 30 minutes, it works delectably. Even if you don't dissolve the sugar in the alcohol properly and end up with a slightly crunchy syllabub, it is still the most poetic of puddings.

→ In a bowl, measure the ALCOHOLS and add the ZEST and JUICE OF THE LEMON and the SUGAR. Stir so the sugar begins to dissolve. Pour in the DOUBLE CREAM and beat with a balloon whisk until the mixture holds, but not rigidly so.
→ Cut two ripe PEACHES, white if possible, into slices. Put a layer of flavoured cream into each glass, add a layer of peach slices, then repeat the cream and add a spoonful of BERRIES. Finish with berries and a final spoon of cream and then put three or four RASPBERRIES OR BLUEBERRIES on top before refrigerating.

Middle Eastern Winter Fruit Salad

SERVES 6–8

organic dried, unsulphured apricots	2 dozen or so
clementines OR enough oranges, to cover the apricots when soaking	juice of 8 or so
organic oranges	4
Medjool dates, *pitted and halved*	12–15
pomegranate	1
orange-flower water	1 tbsp
passion fruits	1–2
organic orange	*peel* of 1
organic lemon	*peel* of 1

This combination of fresh and dried fruit, with exotic passion fruit and pomegranate juice added to the clementine and orange flower water syrup, is a brilliantly festive, scented dish, which involves almost no effort. The organic fresh Medjool dates are the ones to use, not the horribly over-sweetened ones in boxes or the dried version. Allow six hours or more for the apricots to plump up in the juice before you cook them. Keep a steady hand with the orange-flower water, or the dish will remind you of bubble bath.

→ Put the unsulphured APRICOTS in a bowl and pour over the freshly squeezed CLEMENTINE OR ORANGE JUICE to cover. Leave for at least 6 hours.
→ Gently simmer the apricots in the juice in a covered pan until tender right through when pierced with a skewer. Leave to cool.
→ Cut off the ends of the ORANGES with a sharp knife. Stand each one on its end and work the knife down from top to bottom, cutting off the peel all the way around and making sure any extra bits of pith are removed. Now insert the knife blade just inside a peg on one side and cut into the middle. Do the same with the other side of the peg so the segment comes out with no skin. Segment two of the four oranges in this way. The other two should be peeled as before, removing all the pith as well as the skin, then sliced into thin circles.

→ Put the orange pegs and circles in the bowl with the apricots and their juice, and throw in the DATES. Halve the POMEGRANATE and squeeze in a few seeds, then squeeze the juice from both halves in a squeezer and add it to the bowl. Add the ORANGE-FLOWER WATER. Halve one PASSION FRUIT and sieve the juice without the seeds into the fruit salad. Taste for sharpness: you may need two. Remove the peel from an ORANGE and a LEMON with a potato peeler and slice it into fine matchstick strips. There should be no pith on the underside. In a small pan, boil a little water and simmer the strips for a couple of minutes. Drain and add them to the fruit salad before serving.

Spiced Apple Brûlée

SERVES 6–8

medium-sized cooking apples	4
organic double cream	600ml/1 pint
cinnamon bark OR ground cinnamon	a little piece 1 tsp
cloves	5
organic egg yolks	5
unrefined caster sugar	
demerara sugar	

→ Preheat the oven to 190°C/375°F/Gas 5. Core the APPLES and score them around their circumference with a knife tip. Place them on a baking tray, pour on a little cold water and bake them in the oven until soft right through.

→ Meanwhile, scald the CREAM in a saucepan just to boiling point. Scoop out the flesh from the apples and chuck into the food processor. Grind the CINNAMON BARK and CLOVES in a mortar and add them to the apple. Add the EGG YOLKS and process briefly until everything coheres. Add CASTER SUGAR to taste, but leave the purée tart, because you are going to brûlée the top with demerara sugar. Lastly, pour the hot cream into the food processor with the blade still running.

→ Spoon the apple mixture into ramekins and place them in a roasting tin. Pour boiling water around the ramekins to come halfway up their sides, and cook them on the middle shelf of the oven for about 40 minutes. The custards should be set, but with a tremble. They will take longer than conventional custards because of the liquid content of the apples, but hold your nerve.

→ Remove from the tin and cool, then put them in the fridge overnight. In fact, they will keep for several days if you want to get ahead. Sprinkle a thin layer of DEMERARA SUGAR over the surface of each ramekin and spray with a mist of water. Bubble with a blow torch, using a mild flame as close as you can get to the surface. Once you have a beautiful, even mahogany-coloured top, leave to cool before serving.

Pears Baked in Cider

SERVES 6

firm pears, preferably Conference, Anjou or Packham	6
unrefined caster sugar	140g/5oz
dry cider	300ml/10fl oz
lemon	*peel* of 1
hazelnuts OR blanched almonds, *roasted, crushed* (optional)	55g/2oz

If you don't want to use a bottle of red wine for your pears, cider is a sharp and delectable, not a lesser, alternative. Just buy a good bottle of the real stuff, not the violently coloured fizzy commercial brew.

→ Preheat the oven to 150°C/300°F/Gas 2. Peel the PEARS, leaving the stalks on and stand them upright in an earthenware or deep casserole, packed tightly so that they stay standing. Sprinkle them all with SUGAR. Pour the CIDER over, then add the same amount of cold water. Pare the LEMON with a swivel-bladed peeler so you get the peel, but no pith. Put the lemon peel in the pan, cover with greaseproof paper and a lid, and put in the oven for 3–4 hours. The pears should not have broken up but should be tender right through when pierced with a skewer. Carry on cooking them until they really are tender, even if it means another hour. Let them cool to tepid in their liquid.
→ Remove the pears to a bowl and simmer down the liquid to half its volume on top of the stove, by which time it should be a sticky-thick syrup. Put the HAZELNUTS or whole blanched ALMONDS on a baking sheet and roast in a medium-hot oven until they brown. Check after 10 minutes, then check again every few minutes as they can over-brown quite suddenly. Crush in a plastic bag with a rolling pin or with a mezzaluna until nubbly and not too ground. Either let people sprinkle their own nuts over the pears, or add to each pear yourself as you serve them. Serve chilled, with thick cream.

Slow-roasted Pears and Quinces

SERVES 8

firm, ripe pears, Williams OR red Williams	8
quinces	2
lemon	½
red wine	300ml/10fl oz
cinnamon	1 stick
clementines, satsumas OR sweet orange	juice of 2 juice of 1
star anise	1
light muscovado sugar	2–3 tbsp

This is good hot, warm or chilled, perhaps with a home-made vanilla, nutmeg, cinnamon or clove ice cream. By cooking the cubes of quince in the reduced, ruby wine and juice, their flavour will permeate the syrup and, although they take far longer than pears to soften, there will be no danger of them remaining bullet-like.

→ Peel the PEARS, retaining their stalks, and rub them with a cut LEMON to prevent discolouring. Peel the QUINCES, quarter them and remove the cores very carefully; they are rock-like uncooked. Rub with LEMON JUICE. Cut the quince into smallish cubes.
→ While you are doing this, heat the WINE with the CINNAMON and let it boil and reduce by almost half, adding the CLEMENTINE JUICE at the end. Stand the pears snugly in a heavy-bottomed

pot, add the cubes of quince, then pour over the boiling wine. Taste. If the cinnamon has left its mark, remove it. If not, leave it in while the pears begin to cook. Add the STAR ANISE and then throw in 2–3 tablespoons of MUSCOVADO SUGAR. The quinces will need it more than the pears.

→ Cut out a circle of greaseproof to fit inside the pan. Return to boiling point, press the circle of paper down to fit over the fruit, and cover with the lid. Cook slowly, checking after 30 minutes and turning the pears to redden them all over. They may take 1–1½ hours at this temperature, but check every 20 minutes after the first half-hour that the pears are easily poked through with a skewer but not limp and soft. Likewise the quince. Remove the cinnamon at any stage if you think the liquor is spiced enough. Good with clotted or thin cream.

Quinces in Syrup

SERVES 4

lemon	juice of ½
unrefined sugar	225g/8oz
quinces, 4 small OR 2 large	about 900g/2lb
clotted cream	

→ Fill a pan with 1 litre/1¾ pints of boiling water and add the LEMON JUICE and SUGAR. Wash the QUINCES and scrub to remove the light down that covers their skin in patches. Cut them in half through the core but do not peel them. Quinces are extremely hard, so you will need a strong knife and a lot of strength. Do not core them. The pips are important as they produce a wonderful reddish-pink jelly.

→ Cook the quinces as soon as they are cut, as the flesh discolours quickly. Put them, cut side down, into the pan, adding more water if necessary to cover, and simmer until tender. This takes 20–60 minutes. Watch the fruit so that it doesn't fall apart.

→ As soon as the quinces are tender, lift them out. When they are cool enough to handle, cut out the cores with a pointed serrated knife and throw them back into the pan. Reduce the syrup by simmering, then return the fruit to the pan and cook until the syrup becomes reddish and thick. It can take more than an hour to turn into a reddish jelly.

→ Arrange the quince halves, cut-side up, on a serving dish and pour on the syrup through a strainer. It will turn into a jelly when it cools. Serve chilled or at room temperature with dollops of CLOTTED CREAM.

Roasted Quinces

SERVES 4

small quinces	4
unsalted butter	4 tsp
unrefined sugar	8 tbsp
clotted cream (optional)	
pomegranate	*seeds* of 1

Baking the rock-hard fruit whole is a great way to cook a quince. Once they are soft, you can treat them in a number of ways.

→ Heat the oven to 190°C/380°F/Gas 5. Roast the QUINCES whole on a baking tray until they feel soft. Depending on their size and ripeness, this can take 45 minutes to 2 hours, so watch them.

→ Cut the quinces in half down through the cores and cut out the cores with a sharp paring knife. Put them cut-side up on a baking dish with a sliver of BUTTER on top of each and sprinkle with SUGAR—1 tablespoon on the smaller halves and 2 on the larger ones. Put the quinces back in the oven for about 30 minutes until they are very soft and have turned a rich burgundy colour. Alternatively, put them under the grill for a minute until the sugar has caramelised. Serve hot or cold with CLOTTED CREAM. Strew with POMEGRANATE SEEDS just before serving.

Apples Baked with Medjool Dates and Walnuts

FOR EACH PERSON ALLOW

baking apple	1
butter and unrefined caster sugar (optional)	
Medjool dates, *pitted and chopped*	2
walnuts, *broken into pieces*	2
butter, *softened*	a knob the size of a walnut
organic orange, zest	about ½ tsp
light muscovado sugar	1 heaped tsp
unsulphured dried apricot, left unsoaked, but *chopped into small nuggets*	1

→ Preheat the oven to 170°C/325°F/Gas 3. With the sharp point of a knife, score each APPLE around its middle. Core ruthlessly, so that the channel is bigger than just the core, but leave the base intact so that the juices can't escape. If you like, brush each apple with some melted BUTTER and roll it in some unrefined CASTER SUGAR to coat all over before you start.

→ Put the DATES, WALNUTS, knob of BUTTER, ORANGE ZEST, MUSCOVADO SUGAR and APRICOT in a bowl. Mix them all together with a little juice squeezed from the orange until they bind. Sit the apples on a baking tray and push lumps of mixture down into the cavity of each one. Bake in the centre of the oven until the apples are cooked and tender right through to their middles when pierced with a skewer. Beware—if you cook them too fast or too long, they will burst. Eat warm with some good pouring cream.

Baked Berried Apples in Cinnamon Sugar

SERVES 4

large apples	4
cinnamon	½ a stick
unrefined granulated OR demerara sugar	2 tbsp
unsalted butter, *melted*	30g/1oz
blackberries OR blueberries	4 tbsp
sloe gin (see p. 586)	a splash
double cream	

Experiment with this simple but delicious fruit pudding. Why not use prunes and sharp apricots with a few twists of nubbly walnut rather than just vine fruits? Or try an almond paste scented with orange zest, some blackberries with a little kirsch, a few chopped dates and almonds. Always grind the cinnamon in the mortar yourself—very little extra effort for a very much muskier, sweeter, fresher whiff of the lovely bark.

→ Heat the oven to 180°C/350°F/Gas 4. Score the APPLES around their middles with a point of a knife and core thoroughly, nearly to the base. Crush the CINNAMON in a mortar to make about 1 teaspoonful. Mix the cinnamon with the SUGAR, then brush each apple with the warm melted BUTTER before rolling it all over in the cinnamon sugar.

→ Sit the apples on a baking tray, then plop a spoonful of BERRIES into the cavity. Add a little extra melted BUTTER and some SUGAR on top.

→ Bake until soft right through when spiked with a skewer. This should take about 25–30 minutes, unless the apples are enormous. Once they are crustily caramelised, put the apples in bowls and pour a splash of SLOE GIN over them. Serve with a jug of cold, thick CREAM.

Baked Plums with Dark Rum and Demerara

SERVES 6

plums	12
demerara sugar	2 tbsp
dark rum	2 tbsp
water	2 tbsp
clementines	2 or 3
lemon	½

A lovely late summer dish if you have your own plums. If not, use imported ones later in the year. Particularly good with vanilla ice cream.

→ Preheat the oven to 180°C/350°F/Gas 4. Put the PLUMS in an earthenware dish, sprinkle with a couple of tablespoons of DEMERARA SUGAR, the same of DARK RUM, and the same of WATER. Place a sheet of greaseproof paper over the top, and bake for 20–25 minutes or until just tender when pierced with the point of a skewer.

→ Test the juice. It will be too sweet. Squeeze the CLEMENTINES and half a LEMON, and stir the juice into the syrup. Adjust if you need to. The plums will have burst out of their jackets revealing their pretty pomegranate-pink flesh. Cool them in the dish, then refrigerate.

Fruit Salad

A basic, everyday fruit salad.

SERVES 4–6

apples	2
pears	2
lemon	juice of 1
seedless green grapes	1 small bunch
oranges	2
scented melon like Galia, Ogen or Charentais	1
small pineapple	1
stock syrup (see p. 428) OR extra oranges	1 quantity juice of 2–3
passion fruit (optional)	1–2
English strawberries if in season	1 punnet
banana	1
mint	a few sprigs

→ Peel, core and quarter the APPLES and PEARS, cut them into smallish chunks and put them in a glass fruit bowl. Sprinkle over some LEMON JUICE so that they don't discolour. Halve the GRAPES and add them to the bowl.

→ Now, here's how to cut the ORANGES into pithless slices that don't look as though they've been mugged: first cut the ends of the orange off with a small sharp knife so that you just see orange and no pith. Stand the orange up on one end and carve down, following its natural curve and removing the skin to leave just orange, no pith. Once the orange has been de-nuded of its skin, put the blade of the knife just inside the skin of one of the pegs and slice into it, repeat down the other side of the peg and extract it. Work your way round the orange like this, putting the pegs in the fruit salad as you go.

→ Cut the MELON into slices, remove the seeds and cut into wedges, putting them in the bowl with the other fruit and as much juice as you can save. Remove the skin and little brown core-like bits from the PINEAPPLE and cut it into thick circles. Remove the core with the apple corer and cut the rest into chunks, adding them to the bowl. Hull the STRAWBERRIES and split the big ones lengthways down the middle. Put them in the bowl up to 30 minutes before you are going to eat the fruit salad. Add the STOCK SYRUP (see p. 428) or ORANGE JUICE, then scoop out the middles of the PASSION FRUIT and add them as a decoration on top. Cover and chill for 30 minutes in the fridge, and add the chopped BANANA just before serving. A few sprigs of MINT put in at the end freshen up the look and the flavour.

→ You can make a good exotic fruit salad with mangoes, pineapple, passion fruit or grenadillos, scented melon, limes and pink grapefruit. A fresh berry salad is also good, made with whatever you can lay your hands on, such as raspberries, loganberries, strawberries, cherries and blueberries, with a few fresh peaches thrown in.

Figs in Red Wine with Raspberries

SERVES 4

ripe black figs	16
raspberries	16
butter	a tiny piece for each fig
light muscovado sugar	a handful
red wine	

A simple, elegant dish for when you can't be bothered to fuss but need a little something sweet at the end of a meal. The figs can always be served with a good vanilla ice cream.

→ Preheat the oven to 170°C/325°F/Gas 3. Cut a cross down, but not right through, each FIG so that you can splay them open enough to stuff each one with a RASPBERRY. Place a tiny bit of unsalted BUTTER inside each raspberry. The figs should sit packed tight in a gratin dish so they remain upright. Throw over a handful—a small handful—of MUSCOVADO SUGAR, then pour enough decent RED WINE over the bottom of the dish to cover its base entirely.

→ Bake for 20–25 minutes or until the figs are cooked through but holding their shape. Serve hot or warm with cream. A simple yet exotic dish: the red wine reduces and turns dark and syrupy with the sugar, and the marriage of fig and raspberry is a fine one. You could even slip a little burst of raspberry sorbet next to the figs if you are eating them warm rather than hot.

Spice-roasted Figs with Balsamic Vinegar

SERVES 4

figs	12
mild honey, like acacia	3 tbsp
stock syrup (see p. 428)	150ml/5fl oz
cinnamon	1 stick
cloves	3
star anise	3
root ginger	1 thumb
orange peel, *without the pith*	2 strips
vanilla pod, *split*	1
black peppercorns, *bruised*	3–4
aged balsamic vinegar	3 tbsp

A mellow, spicy, delicious way of roasting figs.

→ Heat the oven to 150°C/300°F/Gas 2. Cut off the tips of the FIGS and cut little crosses in the tops of them, as you do on Brussels sprouts. Put them upright, cheek by jowl and tightly packed, in an enamel baking dish.

→ Put ALL THE OTHER INGREDIENTS into a small pan, bring to the boil and boil hard for 3–4 minutes until reduced to a syrupy sauce. Brush the syrup over the figs and cook for about 30 minutes until soft, basting every few minutes. Serve them warm in their syrup or cold with pouring cream or a spice or vanilla ice cream.

Baked Stuffed Nectarines or Peaches

S ERVES 4

nectarines or peaches	4
amarettini de Saronno or amaretti biscuits	75g/2½oz
vanilla sugar	1–2 tbsp
organic egg yolk	1
butter	

White nectarines are the best, or white peaches, with their more delicate, ethereal flavour, but the most important thing is to make sure the fruit is ripe. This dish marries the almondy flavour of the amaretti with the fruit, and you could add a raw raspberry sauce if you like.

→ Preheat the oven to 170°C/325°F/Gas 3. Steep the NECTARINES OR PEACHES in boiling water for a minute, then skin and halve them. Enlarge the stone cavities, keeping the extra pulp and juice in a bowl.

→ Crush the AMARETTINI in a pestle and mortar, or in a plastic bag with a rolling pin. Tip the crumbs into the bowl with the extra fruit pulp, add the SUGAR and EGG YOLK, and pound together until it is a damp, coherent mass of stuffing.

→ Heap the stuffing generously into the nectarine or peach cavities so that it mounds over the fruit, then set the fruit halves in a greased gratin dish and bake for 30–40 minutes. Serve warm or cold. I serve mine warm with some cold raw raspberry sauce dribbled over the summit.

Poached Peaches in an Orange-flower Sabayon

S ERVES 6–8

peaches	8–10
water	500ml/18fl oz
white wine	500ml/18fl oz
caster sugar	200g/7oz
orange, *sliced*	1
lemon, *sliced*	½
vanilla pod	1
Sabayon	
organic egg yolks	6
caster sugar	100g/3½oz
salt	1 pinch
sweet white wine	120ml/4fl oz
fresh lime juice	4 tbsp
fresh orange juice	3 tbsp
orange-flower water	1 tbsp

The sabayon is just the French version of the Italian zabaglione and makes a wonderfully light sauce, less rich than cream or custard, for any poached fruit. It's particularly good with the summer-scented fruits like peaches, nectarines and apricots. You don't have to use sweet white wine, you may use framboise instead if you are making the sabayon for peaches, but 3–4 tablespoons is enough. Use kirsch for poached cherries. White peaches are the ones to go for flavour-wise, and be sure they are ripe.

→ Put the PEACHES in a saucepan with the WATER, WINE, SUGAR, ORANGE, LEMON and VANILLA POD. Bring to the boil, skim, then cover with a circle of greaseproof paper cut to fit inside the pan with a little air hole snipped into the middle of it. Simmer very gently for 15–20 minutes. Let the peaches cool in the syrup, then peel off the skins, halve and remove the stones. Reserve the syrup.

→ For the sabayon, put the EGG YOLKS, CASTER SUGAR and SALT into a bowl and whisk. Add the WINE and 120ml/4fl oz of the poaching syrup and whisk in a double boiler over simmering water for about 10 minutes or until the mixture leaves a ribbon trail when the whisk is lifted. Whisk in the LIME JUICE, ORANGE JUICE and ORANGE-FLOWER WATER. Spoon the sabayon generously over the peach halves.

Stewed Rhubarb with Honey and Orange

SERVES 4

rhubarb (forced if possible)	450g/1lb
organic orange	zest and juice of 1
acacia or other mild-tasting runny honey	2 heaped tbsp
ground ginger	¼ tsp

→ Cut the RHUBARB into 4cm/1½in pieces and put them in a pan. Add the juice and zest of the ORANGE and the HONEY, and sprinkle over the GINGER. Bring to simmering point, then cover and cook for 7–8 minutes. Don't cook it any more or it will turn to threads, unless it is of the older, fatter variety available later in the year. Instead, remove the pan from the heat and let the rhubarb cool with the lid on. It will continue to poach in the juice as it cools.

Baked Rhubarb

young rhubarb	450g/1lb
vanilla caster sugar	110g/4oz

Choose the tender pink wands of early forced rhubarb that you don't even have to peel. The lower the temperature and the slower they are cooked, the more they will exude deliciously syrupy juices, so don't add any water.

→ Heat the oven to 130°C/250°F/Gas ½. Cut the RHUBARB into 4cm/1½ in lengths, or double this if you like the idea of batons, and put it into an earthenware or ovenproof dish that has a lid. Scatter the SUGAR over the top of the rhubarb and cover it tightly with a layer of greaseproof paper and the lid. Bake for 20 minutes before checking, then subsequently every 10 minutes or so, until the rhubarb is tender and has stewed to softness in its own juice but not lost its shape.

Butterscotch Baked Bananas en Papillote

SERVES 4

large bananas (not over-ripe)	4
butterscotch sauce (see p. 419)	
rum (optional)	a little

→ Preheat the oven to 180°C/350°F/Gas 4. Split the BANANAS in two down their middles. Cut 4 sheets of foil or greaseproof paper big enough to make baggy parcels for the bananas. Place the two halves of banana on each one next to each other. Dribble over some sticky SAUCE and a few drops of RUM if you feel like it. Pull the paper or foil up so that you can fold and pinch the edges tightly together yet leave the parcel baggy. Stand on a baking sheet and put in the oven for about 10 minutes or until the bananas have softened and the sauce coated, but they have not started to over-soften and lose their shape. You can do this with the chocolate sauce on p.419 too.

Banana Split with Chocolate Sauce

chocolate sauce (see p. 419)	
some good vanilla ice cream	1 or 2 scoops each
ripe organic banana, *split lengthwise*	1 per person

This is the pudding of all puddings to appeal to jaded children at the end of a bad day. It is one of those things to suggest in a crisis. Their world will automatically feel sunnier and they can help make the chocolate sauce, then scrape and lick whatever clings to the pan.

→ Make the CHOCOLATE SAUCE (see p. 419). You may like a thinner sauce, in which case keep adding CREAM or a tablespoon or more of MILK at the end and stirring it in until you have arrived at the desired consistency.

→ Plop scoops of ICE CREAM between the BANANA HALVES and pour over the hot sauce. You may sprinkle a few coarsely crushed roasted hazelnuts over the top if your children like them. You may even want to eat this yourself!

Passion Fruit Roulade

SERVES 8–10

large organic eggs	6
vanilla caster sugar	100g/3½oz
lemons	2
plain flour	2 heaped tbsp
Filling	
double cream	270–300ml/ 9–10fl oz
lemon or orange curd (see p. 585)	340g/12oz
wrinkled passion fruits	12
unrefined icing sugar	

A recipe from the incomparable Nigel Slater, and it would whet the appetite of even the most doubtful of rouladers.

→ Preheat the oven to 180°C/350°F/Gas 4. You will need a baking tray measuring roughly 36 × 30cm/14 × 12in with shallow sides. Line the tray with a piece of baking parchment, making sure it comes up the sides of the tray.

→ Separate the EGGS. Whisk the YOLKS with the sugar until thick and pale. Grate the zest of both LEMONS, making sure there is no pith, and squeeze the juice of one of them. Beat the EGG WHITES until they are thick and just capable of standing in soft peaks. Fold the juice and zest into the egg yolk and sugar mixture, followed by the sieved FLOUR. Then add the egg whites slowly and gently so the air is not knocked out of them. It is crucial not to over-mix. Scoop the mixture into the lined baking tin, smoothing it gently out to the edges.

→ Bake for about 10 minutes until the top is very lightly coloured and it feels softly set. It should barely colour. Let it cool for a few minutes.

→ Put a large piece of greaseproof paper on the work surface and turn the roulade out onto it. Be fairly forthright: just tip the roulade out in one swift movement. The cake should be crust-side down. Carefully peel away the paper and cover the roulade with a damp tea towel. It will be fine like this for an hour or so, or even overnight.

→ When you are ready to roll, remove the towel and spread the

CURD over the surface. Whip the CREAM to soft peaks and spread it over the curd. Cut 8 of the PASSION FRUITS in half and spread the juice and seeds over the cream. Now take one short end of the greaseproof paper and use it to help you roll up the roulade. If the surface cracks, then all to the good. Dust with ICING SUGAR and serve cut into thick slices, with the remaining passion fruit juice and seeds squeezed over each slice.

Tasmanian Lemon Pie

SERVES 4–6

butter, *softened*	110g/4oz
vanilla caster sugar (sugar that has been stored with a vanilla pod)	285g/10oz
eggs, *separated*	4
plain flour, *sifted*	4 tbsp
milk	400ml/14fl oz
lemons *grated* zest and juice of 2	

I first ate this pudding at Old Head Hotel in County Mayo in the west of Ireland, where our family holidayed for over a decade. It was one of the three puddings, the others being Canadian pie and butterscotch tart, that Mrs Wallace, who owned Old Head, served weekly; none of the guests, old or young, ever tired of them. The Tasmanian Lemon Pie is something I always have the ingredients for and which graces any occasion in the way only the best unpretentious home food can.

→ Preheat the oven to 180°C/350°F/Gas 4. Cream the BUTTER with the SUGAR until light and fluffy. Beat in the EGG YOLKS, then the FLOUR and MILK, a little at a time. Add the grated rind and juice of the LEMONS. Whisk the EGG WHITES until stiff and add to the mixture, stirring in the first spoonful, then folding each subsequent spoonful lightly and quickly into the mixture to incorporate it as you would a soufflé.

→ Pour into a greased baking dish, so the mixture comes about 5cm/2in up the side of the dish. Cook in the oven for about 25–30 minutes, until slightly brown on top and obviously set but faintly shuddery. Serve warm with clotted cream. The pudding should boast two specific textures—the top a light sponge, the bottom a lemony, gloopy custard.

Black Forest Trifle

kirsch OR cognac	
stoned morello cherries	1 × 680g/ 1½lb jar

Syllabub

white wine, muscat if possible	240ml/8fl oz
kirsch	6 tbsp
organic lemon	zest and juice of 1
vanilla caster sugar	2 tbsp
double cream, Jersey if possible	300ml/10fl oz

Sponge

butter, *softened*	140g/5oz
vanilla caster sugar	85g/3oz
organic eggs, *separated*	2
best bitter chocolate, *grated*	85g/3oz
salt	½ tsp
self-raising flour	200g/7oz
strong fresh coffee	1 tbsp
milk	1 tbsp

Custard

Jersey milk	300ml/10fl oz
double cream, Jersey if possible	300ml/10fl oz
organic eggs	2
organic egg yolks	2
cornflour	1 heaped tbsp
cocoa powder	1 tbsp
vanilla caster sugar	to taste

This was an improvised pudding, made with the remains of some chocolate cake. Use whatever is your favourite, or make a plain sponge as here.

→ For the syllabub, put the WINE, KIRSCH, LEMON ZEST AND JUICE in a bowl, cover and leave overnight if possible, or for as long as you have time for. Strain the liquid into a bowl and stir in the SUGAR until it has completely dissolved. Pour in the CREAM and begin to beat with a balloon whisk. It seems hard to imagine that the liquid will be taken up and absorbed by the cream to begin with, but it does happen and it doesn't take forever. Keep whisking until the syllabub holds in soft folds. Keep the mixture cool but not very cold, or the cream will harden too much.

→ Make the cake if you don't have any leftovers to use. Preheat the oven to 180°C/350°F/Gas 4. Grease a 20cm/8in tin and line with baking parchment, the paper rising about 2.5cm/1in above the tin. Beat the BUTTER and SUGAR thoroughly until pale and creamy. Beat the EGG YOLKS and add them to the mixture. Combine the CHOCOLATE, SALT and FLOUR, and stir into the mixture with the COFFEE and MILK. Whisk the WHITES to stiff peaks, stir the first tablespoon into the cake mixture, then fold in the rest. Stir in a teaspoon of boiling water before scraping the mixture into the tin. Bake for about 45 minutes or until a skewer comes out clean. Cool on a rack.

→ Cut the sponge into thin sections to fit into the base of a glass bowl or glasses. Sprinkle over a little KIRSCH OR COGNAC. Drain the CHERRIES and sprinkle a layer of them over the cake.

→ To make the custard, bring the MILK and CREAM to scalding point in a pan. Whisk the EGGS AND YOLKS with the sifted CORNFLOUR and COCOA POWDER in a large bowl, then pour over the hot cream and milk whisking as you go. Return to the pan over a medium heat and whisk the custard until it is lump-free and thickens discernibly. Add SUGAR to taste and whisk it in so that it dissolves. Remove from the heat and leave to cool to warm. Give it an occasional whisk in the meantime so that a skin doesn't form. Pour over the sponge and cherries. Pile on the syllabub so that the top is billowy rather than flat, and decorate as you feel the urge.

Raspberry Christmas Trifle

SERVES 6

macaroons	5
white wine	240ml/8fl oz
raspberry liqueur	4–6 tbsp
milk	300ml/10fl oz
organic double cream	600ml/1 pint
organic eggs	2
organic egg yolks	2
cornflour, *sifted*	1 tbsp
vanilla caster sugar	to taste
raw raspberries	340g/12oz
icing sugar	to taste
lemon	juice and zest of 1
slivered almonds, *toasted*	

This is a rich but softly delicious pudding that slips down surreptitiously, despite your misgivings on the calorific front. If it is impossible to find raspberries out of season, use raspberry jam. Pace yourself. This is no mere trifle and it is full of hidden depths.

→ Put the MACAROONS into a large glass bowl and pour over half the WHITE WINE and 2–3 tablespoons of RASPBERRY LIQUEUR. Beat the 2 EGGS and 2 YOLKS with the sifted CORNFLOUR. Now bring the MILK and 300ml/10fl oz of the DOUBLE CREAM to scalding point, and pour over the egg mixture. Return to the pan and whisk until thickened. Add VANILLA CASTER SUGAR to taste, and pour over the macaroons.
→ Purée the raw RASPBERRIES in a food processor, sieve and add ICING SUGAR to taste. Pour this mixture over the cooled custard.
→ In a bowl, put the juice of a LEMON and the rest of the WHITE WINE and RASPBERRY LIQUEUR, and stir in 30g/1oz SUGAR until dissolved. Taste for sweetness. Pour over the remaining 300ml/10fl oz organic DOUBLE CREAM and whisk with a wire whisk until thickened but not stiff. Pour this over the raspberry mixture and decorate with LEMON ZEST and toasted slivered ALMONDS.

Pavlova

SERVES 6

organic egg whites	6
salt	a pinch
cream of tartar	½ tsp
vanilla caster sugar	400g/14oz
distilled white vinegar	2 tsp
Filling	
double cream	300ml/10fl oz
raspberry eau de vie (optional)	1 tbsp
raspberries	255g/9oz
wrinkly passion fruit, *the flesh and seeds scooped out*	6

→ Preheat the oven to 140°C/275°F/Gas 1. Whisk the EGG WHITES with the SALT and CREAM OF TARTAR until frothy. Incorporate three-quarters of the SUGAR, beating until glossy, very firm and holding stiff peaks. Fold in the remaining sugar and the VINEGAR.
→ Cut out a sheet of parchment paper to fit a heavy, flat baking sheet. Draw a 25cm/10in circle on the paper, dampen it with a little water and place it on the baking sheet. Spoon the egg whites onto the circle and smooth and shape into a nest, making sweeping, scalloped edges with a damp tablespoon. Bake in the bottom of the preheated oven for 1–1½ hours until the meringue is crusty on the outside and just set on the inside. Allow it to cool, then carefully peel off the paper and transfer the meringue to a serving plate.
→ Just before serving, lightly whip the CREAM, with the EAU DE VIE if you are using it, to form soft peaks. Spoon it into the middle of the meringue, spreading it out towards the edges. Decorate the pavlova with RASPBERRIES and PASSION FRUIT.

Blueberry Clafoutis

SERVES 6

blueberries	450g/1lb
butter	25g/1oz
vanilla caster sugar	85g/3oz
kirsch OR vodka	a splosh
whole organic eggs	2
organic egg yolks	3
organic egg white	1
potato flour	1 heaped tsp
whipping cream	250ml/8fl oz
milk	125ml/4fl oz
flaked almonds	a small handful

→ Preheat the oven to 180°C/350°F/Gas 4. Grease a deepish pudding dish. Melt the BUTTER in a pan, and throw in the BLUEBERRIES with a third of the SUGAR. Add the ALCOHOL, and shake until the fruit begins to release its juice. Take off the heat.

→ Beat the WHOLE EGGS AND YOLKS with a further third of SUGAR, then whisk in the POTATO FLOUR and stir in the MILK and WHIPPING CREAM. Whisk the EGG WHITE with the last third of SUGAR until glossy and thick, and fold it into the custard.

→ Put the blueberries in the dish, pour over the custard and place inside a roasting tin half-filled with boiling water. Sprinkle over a scattering of ALMONDS and bake for 25–30 minutes until faintly shuddery-middled. Eat warm with crème fraîche.

Blueberry, Raspberry and Strawberry Cobbler

SERVES 4

berries (strawberries, raspberries, blackberries, blueberries)	900g/2lb
light muscovado sugar	2–3 tbsp
butter, *cut into small pieces*	30g/1oz
unsalted butter, *chilled*	100g/3½oz
plain organic flour	225g/8oz
baking powder	2 tsp
unrefined caster sugar	3 tbsp

To my mind a cobbler is one of the finest puddings there is, with the purple juices bleeding through the crisp golden crust in between its gaps, and the cobbler top is somehow lighter than a fruit pie. Keep the strawberries whole so they don't turn to pink cottonwool—and it was a triumph. I've also made a plum version which was delicious, as would be apple and blackberry.

→ Heat the oven to 200°C/400°F/Gas 6. Put the FRUIT into a baking dish and scatter over the MUSCOVADO SUGAR and little knobs of BUTTER.

→ Rub the 100g/3½oz unsalted BUTTER into the FLOUR and BAKING POWDER in a large bowl. Don't over-mix it because this will make the cobbler too oily. When you have a fine breadcrumb texture, lightly and quickly stir in all but a table-spoon of the CASTER SUGAR and all the CREAM, using a fork.

→ Shape the dough into little biscuits about 5cm/2in in diameter and about 1cm/½in thick, and place them on top of the fruit. Sprinkle the rest of the SUGAR over the top and bake for about 40 minutes. The fruit will peep through a little and bleed delectably into the dough as it bubbles up and bakes. Serve with plenty of cream.

Apple Crumble

SERVES 6

Crumble top

flour	225g/8oz
sugar	85g/3oz
unsalted butter	170g/6oz
OR	
flour	110g/4oz
ground almonds	110g/4oz
sugar	85g/3oz
butter	170g/6oz

Filling

large Bramley apples	5
OR eating apples,	
Cox's are best for flavour	about 10
sugar	to taste
ground cinnamon	
OR cloves (optional)	1 tsp

A crumble has to be the most instant and easy of puddings to make. It is also one you can go on tinkering with, adding spices, using half muscovado sugar for a more toffeed, treacly taste, adding oats, nibbed walnuts, demerara sugar scattered over the top to add crunch, even shunning the sweet for a savoury, herbed crumble top.

→ Mix the FLOUR and SUGAR in a large bowl and add small chunks of BUTTER. Work in the butter, rubbing it in with your fingertips until it has turned to crumble. Or put all three ingredients in a food processor and pulse for a few seconds at a time until you have crumb. Don't overdo this or the butter will start to turn globby!

→ Preheat the oven to 190°C/375°F/Gas 5. Peel, core and slice the APPLES and put them into a shallow baking dish, scattering SUGAR and any SPICING over them and turning them to get the juices running. A tablespoon of sugar is all you'll need for eating apples, and probably treble that amount for cooking apples. You want a nice contrast between sharp interior and sweet top. Spread the crumble over the fruit evenly and bake for about 35–40 minutes or until the crumble top has browned and the bubbling juices risen. Do not let the top burn. Crumbles are pretty good-tempered puds, so you can cook them slower and longer. Leave them in a warming oven once they're cooked, or eat warm or cold rather than hot if you like.

→ Clotted cream, crème fraîche, thin cream or custard are de rigeur with crumble, depending on your taste.

Plum Crumble

→ Cut the PLUMS in half, remove the stones and follow the method above, using some GROUND ALMONDS in the crumble mixture. Add a scattering of FLAKED ALMONDS to the top.

White Nectarine and Walnut Crumble or Crumble Tart

SERVES 6–8

shortcrust pastry
*made with 110g/4oz flour and
55g/2oz butter* (see p. 104)

nectarines	6 or 7
lemon juice	
vanilla sugar	50g/2oz

Topping

walnuts	85g/3oz
flour	85g/3oz
light muscovado sugar	85g/3oz
butter	55g/2oz

Try this with golden plums if you can't get nectarines. Leave out the pastry base if you prefer.

→ Preheat the oven to 190°C/375°F/Gas 5. Make the PASTRY (see p. 104) and line a deepish greased pie dish. Slice 6 or 7 NECTARINES, skin on, and put them in a bowl with some LEMON JUICE and the VANILLA SUGAR.

→ Make the crumble top by crushing the WALNUTS until bitty, but not sandy and greasy, in a pestle and mortar. Whizz the FLOUR with the light MUSCOVADO SUGAR and BUTTER in the food processor until crumby. Add half the walnuts to the mixture.

→ Put the fruit on the pastry, then a layer of crumble on top, and finish with a handful of walnuts. Don't use all the crumble mixture if it looks like making more than a thinnish topcoat—it would make the pudding too solid. Cook for 40 minutes, then serve with clotted cream.

Apple Brown Betty

SERVES 6

Topping

unsalted butter	55g/2oz
bread, *torn to crumbs*	140g/5oz
light muscovado sugar	55g/2oz
cinnamon *ground from cinnamon sticks in a mortar with*	2 tsp
allspice	1 tsp

Apple purée

large Bramley apples, *peeled, cored and chopped*	6
unrefined vanilla caster sugar	110–140g/4–5oz
unsalted butter	30g/1oz

What a lovely autumnal pudding, homely in the best sense of the word without being dowdy or frumpy or plain-Jane-ish. There are versions where the crumb is cooked like a crumble, but I prefer it like this, scattered over all crisp and cinnamony and buttery-crumbed at the last minute when the apple purée has been dolloped onto the plate.

→ Melt the BUTTER in a heavy-bottomed frying pan and when it begins to bubble, throw in the BREADCRUMBS and stir to coat them in the butter. You will need to go on stirring every so often for much longer than you think to get the breadcrumbs really crisp.

→ While that's happening, cook the APPLES with the SUGAR and a couple of tablespoons of water in a covered pan. Stir every so often as the chunks at the bottom soften so that the rest of the apples get near the heat source. After about 10 minutes you should have a coherent purée, but if the apples still look too watery, just cook them down a little longer with the lid off the pan. They should taste sharp, not too sweet. Remove the apples from the heat and stir in the BUTTER.

→ Once the crumbs have crisped, remove them from the heat and stir in the SUGAR, ground CINNAMON AND ALLSPICE. Taste —you want a harmonious hit of spice with the cinnamon's warm tones coming through clearly. Spoon the apple purée into bowls and let everyone sprinkle over their own crumbs. Pouring cream, clotted cream or crème fraîche needed.

Prune Brown Betty
→ Try making a Brown Betty with PRUNES, turning the fruit into a rich purée first.

Whiskied Plum and Muscovado Brown Betty

SERVES 4–6

Fruit

unsalted butter	55g/2oz
plums, *halved and stoned*	14–18
demerara sugar	2 tbsp
dark muscovado sugar	2 tbsp
Irish whiskey	2 tbsp

Topping

unsalted butter	55g/2oz
bread, wholemeal, white or granary, *torn to crumbs and shards by hand*	140g/5oz
light muscovado sugar	55g/2oz
cinnamon *ground from a cinnamon stick in a mortar with*	2 tsp
allspice	1 tsp

I have always loved the scent of cinnamon and apple, the combination of autumnal spiciness with a whiff of the souk. I find this brittle, snappable, rust-coloured stick that unfurls like a fat cigar works as well with savoury as with sweet things if you don't use it recklessly. Cinnamon is also a natural with plums, and so is Irish whiskey.

→ Melt 55g/2oz of BUTTER in a large heavy-bottomed frying pan and when it begins to foam, add the PLUMS in a single layer, cut side down. Sprinkle the SUGARS over them and cook gently for about 10 minutes, turning occasionally. Cook until the plums are not resistant when pierced with a knife tip, but don't let them collapse—you want them to hold their shape. Add the WHISKEY and bubble to amalgamate with the sticky, sugary juices until they form a thick, almost molten-looking goo. Remove from the heat while you make the topping.
→ Melt the BUTTER for the topping in another frying pan. When it begins to bubble, throw in the BREADCRUMBS and turn to coat them in butter. Keep cooking the crumbs, remembering to stir them every so often, until they have turned golden and crisp. This takes longer than you would imagine, so be patient and make sure you don't overdo it and turn them black. Once they have crisped, remove them from the heat and stir in the SUGAR and the SPICES. Taste and adjust.
→ Serve the two separately so people can scatter their hot, butter-crisped crumbs over their sticky, whiskied plums. Serve with clotted or pouring cream.

Eve's Pudding

SERVES 4

Bramley apples	450g/1lb
unrefined granulated OR light muscovado sugar,	85g/3oz, or to taste
cloves OR cinnamon OR allspice	4 1 tsp
unsalted butter, *softened*	140g/5oz
vanilla caster sugar	110g/4oz
organic eggs	2
lemon	*grated zest* of 1
plain flour	110g/4oz
baking powder	1 tsp
a little milk	

An apple sponge that can be made the plain, classic way as below or with half quince, half apple; with orange zest, cinnamon or cloves; with chopped walnuts turned into the apple purée; or ground almonds in place of half the flour.

→ Preheat oven to 180°C/350°F/Gas 4. Peel, core and slice the APPLES thinly, then put them in a heavy-bottomed pan with a couple of tablespoons of water, the granulated or light muscovado SUGAR and the CLOVES. If you are using ground spice, don't put it in at this stage. Put a lid on the pan and cook the apples slowly, stirring from time to time as the slices closest to the heat will soften first. When the apples have begun to lose their shape and are soft, take them off the heat, remove the cloves and stir in 30g/1oz of the BUTTER, with the GROUND SPICE if you are using it. Put the mixture in the bottom of a greased pie dish.

→ Cream together the BUTTER and VANILLA SUGAR until light and pale and fluffy. Beat the EGGS in one at a time. Add the LEMON ZEST and sift in the FLOUR and BAKING POWDER, folding in well with a metal spoon. Mix to a soft dropping consistency with a little MILK. Spread the sponge mix over the apple and bake for 40–45 minutes. Serve with cream or custard.

Apple Charlotte

SERVES 8

Granny Smiths OR firm, tart eating apples such as Cox's	8–10
unsalted butter (you may not need it all)	225g/8oz
unrefined caster sugar	110g/4oz
organic eggs, *separated*	2
good white bread	½ a large loaf
demerara sugar	1 tbsp

This is a classic pudding, as virtuous for its cheapness as for its scrumptiousness. There is something about crisp, warm, buttery bread and a tart apple purée that can only be topped one way: with the best Jersey cream. You may cook the apple, cool it and add the egg in advance. I make this in a 23cm/9in springform tin.

→ Preheat the oven to 200°C/400°F/Gas 6. Peel and quarter the APPLES and slice them thinly. Put a knob of the BUTTER in a saucepan with enough water just to cover the base of the pan, and add the apples and the CASTER SUGAR. Cover and bring to the boil, then remove the lid and bubble furiously until the apple is cooked but retains some of its shape and texture. Remove from the heat, beat the EGG YOLKS and stir them in.

→ Cut the crusts off the LOAF and cut into slices 1cm/½in thick, 3cm/1¼in wide and the height of the tin. Melt the remaining BUTTER gently in a small pan, then skim off the curdy white solids and froth, leaving the yellow, oily mass. Brush a little of the butter on the base and sides of the tin, then add the DEMERARA SUGAR and turn the tin so that the sides and base are sugar-coated. Dip the bread in the butter and press the slices gently against the sides and base of the tin. Brush the joins with lightly beaten EGG WHITE to act as mortar, and fill the tin with the apple mixture.

→ Cover the top with more butter-soaked bread and bake for about an hour, reducing the temperature to 190°C/375°F/Gas 5 after 20 minutes. The charlotte will look gloriously browned. Remove from the oven, snap open the spring and turn out onto a large plate.

Baked Almond Pudding

SERVES 6–8

almonds, preferably Valencia	225g/8oz
unsalted butter	110g/4oz
Culpeper's bitter almond oil	a few drops
large organic eggs	4
Oloroso sherry	2 tbsp
lemon	zest and juice of ½
vanilla caster sugar	110g/4oz
single cream OR half cream/half Channel Islands milk	500ml/18fl oz
good-quality apricot jam	225g/8oz

This almond pudding has intimations of both Yorkshire curd and Bakewell tarts. You can plop the mixture inside a pastry crust if you are looking for something more heavyweight than a gloriously custardy, flourless sponge.

→ Heat the oven to 190°C/375°F/Gas 5. Carefully grind the ALMONDS in a food processor. Melt the BUTTER in a small pan. Pour it into a large bowl in which you have gently whisked ALL THE OTHER INGREDIENTS, EXCEPT THE JAM, and whisk until they are amalgamated and the butter has been absorbed.

→ Grease a shallow pie dish with butter. Melt the JAM very gently with a tablespoon of water until runny, then pour it into the dish. Pour over the pudding mixture, and set aside until you are ready to bake. The pudding takes between 30 and 45 minutes to cook, depending on the depth and circumference of the dish, but should have a distinct wobble in the centre when you remove it from the oven, and will carry on cooking. The top should be golden and slightly crusted.

→ Eat warm with clotted or pouring cream.

Summer Pudding

SERVES 6

raspberries	750g/1lb 10oz
redcurrants	200g/7oz
vanilla caster sugar	110g/4oz
day-old, good white bread	1 loaf
raspberry liqueur	1–2 tbsp

I happen to believe that Elizabeth David and Jane Grigson got it right—the best summer pudding is made with raspberries and redcurrants only, at a ratio of about 4:1 raspberries to redcurrants. This dish is the definition of the perfect pudding for the English summer; our soft fruits are peerless. Don't worry about the raspberry liqueur if you don't keep it. Just make sure there is enough juice left over to pour over the crown of the pudding and render it thoroughly bloodied with trickling pink fruit. Serve with clotted cream.

→ Put the RASPBERRIES AND REDCURRANTS in a heavy pot with the VANILLA CASTER SUGAR. Heat gently and briefly until the fruit begins to bleed and the sugar is dissolved, no more than about 3–4 minutes. The fruit must not cook or lose its shape.

→ Slice the BREAD and cut off the crusts. Line a pudding basin with slices of bread, leaving no gaps. With a slotted spoon, pile in the fruit, leaving some of the juice in the pot. Sprinkle a tablespoon or two of RASPBERRY LIQUEUR over the pudding before finishing with a top layer of bread.

→ Cover with a plate that just fits, add some heavy weights on top, and put the basin in the fridge overnight. Just before you serve the pudding, turn it out onto a not completely flat plate that can hold the juice, and pour over the rest of the juice to which you've added more RASPBERRY LIQUEUR to taste. You should still pass round the bottle too!

White Fruit Summer Pudding

SERVES 10

white nectarines	4
white peaches	2
white cherries, pre-stoned weight	450g/1lb
white currants, *stripped from their stems with a fork*	225g/8oz
vanilla sugar	110g/4oz
day-old, good white bread	1 loaf

A version of summer pudding glowing white and pale gold with waxy Napoleon cherries, white-fleshed nectarines and peaches, and some tart jewels of white currants, milky like moonstones. I made an intense raw raspberry sauce to pour over it. Use all nectarines or peaches, depending on what is available.

→ Start the night before. Plunge the NECTARINES and PEACHES into boiling water for 30 seconds, skin and cut into about 6 slices per half. Stone the CHERRIES, and throw them into a heavy-bottomed pan with the WHITE CURRANTS, nectarines and peaches. Strew over the SUGAR, turn the fruit gently, then let it bleed over a gentle heat until the juices run, about 2–3 minutes. The fruit should not begin to collapse or cook. Remove from the heat. Test the juice for sweetness, you may need a little more SUGAR, but do not over-sweeten.

→ Slice the BREAD and cut off the crusts. Line the bowl with the

Raw Raspberry Sauce

raspberries	640g/1lb 6oz
golden icing sugar	2–3 tbsp
lemon juice to taste	

bread, fitting it tight as slates on a roof to prevent leaks. Spoon in the fruit, leaving the pink juices that collect at the bottom. Pour them into a jug to be kept for later. Cover with a layer of bread cut out to fit exactly, then fit a plate inside the top of the bowl, and put some weights on it to press the fruit down. Refrigerate overnight. Take the pudding out an hour before you want to eat it. Just before serving, turn it out onto a large plate, and pour over the peachy juices. Serve with the RAW RASPBERRY SAUCE and cream.

Raw Raspberry Sauce
→ Liquidise the RASPBERRIES thoroughly in a food processor, then put them through a nylon sieve. Sift over the first couple of spoons of ICING SUGAR and whisk it in well. Add a good spritz of LEMON, taste, and adjust sweet and sour accordingly.

Caramelised Apricots with Mascarpone

SERVES 4

ripe apricots	8
raspberries	16
kirsch	a little
mascarpone	16 heaped dsrtsp
vanilla pod	seeds from 1
demerara sugar	8 dsrtsp

So simple, and you may do the same with peaches, nectarines, greengages, figs or plums.

→ Heat the grill to a fierce heat. Halve and stone the APRICOTS, put them cut-side up in a shallow baking tray and plop a RASPBERRY into each hole.
→ Whisk 2 tablespoons of KIRSCH into the MASCARPONE and taste. It should be evident but not intrusive. Spoon over the fruit. Mix the VANILLA SEEDS into the SUGAR, sprinkle over the fruit and blast under the grill until it caramelises. Some will slip off the fruit, but no matter. A great weekday quick-fire solution of a pudding.

Macerated Apricots and Nuts

SERVES 6

dried apricots	450g/1lb
blanched almonds	55g/2oz
pine nuts	30g/1oz
pistachios, *chopped*	30g/1oz
rosewater	1 tbsp

This delicately fragrant sweet is an old Syrian speciality of Ramadan, the Muslim month of fast. It keeps very well for days, even weeks, covered with clingfilm in the refrigerator. Use unsulphured dried apricots.

→ Soak the APRICOTS in 750ml/1¼ pints of water overnight. Drain, reserving the soaking water. Take 12 of the apricots and blend to a light purée with the water in a food processor. Add to the rest of the apricots in a bowl and stir in the NUTS and ROSEWATER. Add a tablespoon of sugar if you wish. Chill.

Christmas Pudding

MAKES 2 PUDDINGS

wholemeal flour	200g/7oz
mixed spice	1 tsp
grated nutmeg	1 tsp
ground ginger	1 tsp
sultanas	285g/10oz
currants	285g/10oz
raisins	200g/7oz
mixed candied peel, *finely chopped*	200g/7oz
dark muscovado sugar	450g/1lb
blanched almonds, *chopped*	110g/4oz
fresh brown breadcrumbs	200g/7oz
shredded suet	200g/7oz
large carrot, *grated*	1
Cox's apples, *grated with the skin*	3
organic eggs	6
Guinness	300ml/10fl oz
brandy	60ml/2fl oz
orange	juice and *grated* rind of 1
milk to mix	

This Christmas pudding is black, rich and drunk on the black stuff, a good frothy measure of Guinness. I love the bitter note stout adds to the pudding, combined with the darkly treacled molasses backnote of the darkest muscovado sugar. The further in advance you make it, the more time the flavours have to develop, but you mustn't forget to keep pouring brandy, whisky or rum down the little skewer holes you pierce through the pudding. Once a week will do.

→ Grease two 600ml/1 pint pudding basins. Sift the FLOUR into a large bowl with the MIXED SPICE, NUTMEG and GINGER. Add the DRIED FRUIT and PEEL, SUGAR, ALMONDS, BREADCRUMBS and SUET, then the grated CARROT and APPLES.

→ Beat the EGGS well and add the GUINNESS, whisking until frothy. Then add the BRANDY, ORANGE JUICE AND RIND, and stir into the DRY INGREDIENTS. Add enough MILK to get to a soft dropping consistency. Divide the mixture between the two basins, leaving room at the top of the basin for the pudding to rise. Cover with pleated greaseproof paper and foil, tie securely with string, then boil for 7 hours.

→ To store, remove the wrappings and cover with clean grease-proof paper and foil. Store in a cool dark place and feed once a week as mentioned above. The puddings will need a further 2–3 hours' boiling on Christmas Day.

Brandy Butter

best unsalted butter, *softened*	225g/8oz
unrefined icing sugar, *sifted*	110g/4oz
cognac OR Somerset cider brandy	2–3 tbsp
orange	*grated* zest of 1
nutmeg	a small grating
lemon juice	a squeeze

Always best when made, or rather squelched, by hand. I'm sure the warmth of one's hands begins to activate the spice and alcohol and marry them to the butter and sugar. Good with the pud.

→ Start with the soft BUTTER, which you can cream further in a bowl with a wooden spoon, before adding the SIFTED SUGAR, COGNAC, ZEST, NUTMEG—a suspicion only—and LEMON. Now work everything together with your fingers, the aim being to incorporate all the liquid and end up with a slushy alcoholic mixture. It will firm up in the fridge.

Rum Butter
→ Use half unrefined ICING SUGAR, half LIGHT MUSCOVADO SUGAR and some DARK RUM.

Extravagant Christmas Pudding

MAKES 3 PUDDINGS

plain flour	200g/7oz
ground cinnamon bark	1 tsp
ground mace blade	1 tsp
ground cloves	1 tsp
ground dried ginger root	1 tsp
allspice	1 tsp
sultanas	200g/7oz
raisins	200g/7oz
currants	200g/7oz
Agen prunes	225g/8oz
dried apricots	225g/8oz
stoned dates	225g/8oz
molasses sugar	450g/1lb
Brazil nuts	110g/4oz
almonds, *chopped*	110g/4oz
brown breadcrumbs	200g/7oz
sharp eating apples, *grated with their skin*	3
large carrot, *peeled and grated*	1
beef or vegetarian suet, OR tiny bits of cold butter	170g/6oz
organic eggs	6
Guinness	300ml/10fl oz
Somerset cider brandy OR cognac	60ml/2fl oz
orange	juice and *grated* zest of 1
milk to mix	a little

An even fruitier, more exotic pudding than ever, while staying faithful to my balance of ingredients, nuts, fruits, spices, flour, fat, sugar and alcohol. Don't worry if you can't find all the dried fruits, an approximation will be fine. Little bursts of sour cherries or cranberries, the graininess of figs, the sweetness of dates, the deep, sharp, softness of prunes, the firm acidic bite of unsulphured apricots—all can add textures and contrasting flavours that put the pudding way ahead of the ordinary vine-fruits model. A few Brazil nuts are lovely too, with their oily hardness giving the pudding a crunch amid its more yielding softness.

→ Grease three 600ml/1 pint pudding basins. Sift the FLOUR into an exceptionally large bowl. Add the SPICES and DRIED FRUITS, then the SUGAR, NUTS, BREADCRUMBS, APPLE, CARROT, chopped SUET, EGGS, GUINNESS and BRANDY. Add the ORANGE ZEST AND JUICE that you have beaten together with a whisk.

→ Stir the liquid thoroughly into the DRY INGREDIENTS. Add a little MILK, if you need to, to make a soft dropping consistency. Fill the pudding basins to just over three-quarters full. Cover with a layer of greaseproof paper and put a layer of foil on top of it, both pleated in the middle to allow the pudding to rise. Tie securely with string, making a handle, and place the puddings in a large, heavy-bottomed casserole on a trivet or layer of foil. You may need to use more than one casserole.

→ Fill the casserole to halfway up the sides of the puddings with boiling water, cover with a lid and bring to the boil. Cook at a gentle simmer for 6–7 hours, topping up with water every couple of hours if you need to.

→ Take the puddings out of the water, remove the foil and greaseproof, and allow to cool. Re-cover. They can be fed with extra brandy through skewer holes if you have made them well in advance. The puddings will need 2–3 hours further cooking on Christmas Day.

Steamed Treacle Pudding

SERVES 4–6

flour	225g/8oz
suet	110g/4oz
ground ginger	½ tsp
bicarbonate of soda	½ tsp
milk	200ml/7fl oz
light or dark muscovado sugar	170g/6oz
golden syrup	225g/8oz
lemon	*zest* of 1

→ Sift the FLOUR into a large bowl, add ALL THE OTHER INGREDIENTS and mix them together well. Grease an 850ml/ 1½ pint pudding basin and add the mixture—make sure it has at least a thumb's width to spare at the top, as the pudding will expand and rise.

→ Cover the basin with a layer of greaseproof paper with a pleat in the middle of it and then a sheet of foil, also pleated, on top. This, too, leaves room for expansion. Tie string around the rim of the basin to keep the foil on and make a string lid over the top of the pudding so that it is easy to remove from its hot-water bath. Put the pudding in a heavy-bottomed pan and pour boiling water halfway up the sides of the basin. Cover with a lid and keep the pudding at a steady simmer for 2 hours, topping up the pan with boiling water when necessary.

→ Remove the pudding from the water. Cut the string, remove the foil and greaseproof top and leave it for 5 minutes. Then slip a palette knife gently down the sides of the pudding. Put a plate over the top of the pudding basin and invert the pudding onto it. Serve with cream to complete the indulgence.

→ If you prefer, use individual plastic basins with snap-on lids, in which case eschew the greaseproof, foil and string. These little puddings will only take 1½ hours to steam.

Steamed Ginger Pudding

SERVES 4–6

unsalted butter, *softened*	85g/3oz
vanilla caster sugar	85g/3oz
organic eggs, *beaten*	2
self-raising flour, *sifted*	110g/4oz
preserved ginger, *chopped*	110g/4oz
ginger syrup	2 tbsp
ground ginger	½ tsp
organic lemon	*grated zest* of 1
a little milk	

Something of an adult taste compared to the treacle and jam varieties of steamed pudding, this is also somewhat lighter as it eschews the suet.

→ Cream the BUTTER and SUGAR until light and fluffy, then add the beaten EGGS, sifted FLOUR, GINGER, GINGER SYRUP, GROUND GINGER and LEMON ZEST. Mix well and add enough milk to make a soft dropping consistency. Pour into a greased 850ml/1½ pint pudding basin, leaving room for it to rise. Cover and steam in the usual way for 2 hours (see above).

→ Turn the pudding out and serve with custard or cream. If you want yet more ginger, whip the cream with a couple more tablespoons of ginger syrup and about a tablespoon of preserved ginger chopped into tiny dice.

Sticky Toffee Pudding with Apricots

SERVES 8–10

unsulphured dried apricots	170g/6oz
bicarbonate of soda	1 tsp
boiling water	300ml/10fl oz
unsalted butter	55g/2oz
vanilla caster sugar	140g/5oz
organic egg, *beaten*	1
flour	225g/8oz
baking powder	1 tsp

Topping

dark muscovado sugar	200g/7oz
unsalted butter	110g/4oz
double cream	6 tbsp

The famous Sharrow Bay Hotel version of sticky toffee pudding has become a national favourite. It is tooth-achingly sweet, what with its cascade of toffee sauce and addition of the sweetest fruit of all, dates. Joyce Molyneaux, the retired proprietor and chef of The Carved Angel in Dartmouth, made her pudding with apricots instead, and to my mind it is the version I would infinitely rather tuck into. The apricots' acidic sharpness more than stands up to and contrasts with the velvety thick toffee sauce. This pudding is steamed rather than baked, so turns out moister than the baked sponge version.

→ Place the INGREDIENTS FOR THE TOPPING in a small pan and stir over a gentle heat until the butter has melted and the sugar dissolved. Bring to the boil and simmer for 3 minutes. Pour into two buttered 850ml/1½ pint pudding basins.

→ Place the APRICOTS in a bowl with the BICARBONATE OF SODA and pour the BOILING WATER over them. Leave to cool thoroughly. Cream the BUTTER and SUGAR thoroughly until light and fluffy, then beat in the EGG. Sift the FLOUR and BAKING POWDER into the mixture and fold it in. Stir the apricot mixture into the batter and divide between the two pudding basins.

→ Cover each basin in the normal way (see p. 470) and place the basins in heavy-bottomed pans, filling them halfway up the sides of the basins with boiling water. Cover the pans with lids and steam for 1½ hours. Check from time to time to see if the pans need more boiling water. Lift out of the water and turn the puddings out onto warmed serving dishes. Serve immediately. I think you might just find cream to be somewhat supererogatory at this point.

Steamed Apricot and Pecan Pudding with Butterscotch Sauce

SERVES 6–8

Sauce

light muscovado sugar	200g/7oz
unsalted butter	125g/4oz
organic crème fraîche	200ml/7fl oz
organic vanilla extract	1 tsp

Pudding

boiling water	300ml/10fl oz
unsulphured organic dried apricots, *chopped*	200g/7oz
bicarbonate of soda	1 tsp
vanilla caster sugar	175g/6oz
unsalted butter	50g/2oz
organic egg	1
plain flour	200g/7oz
baking powder	1 tsp
pecan nuts, *bashed up but not crushed to death*	85g/3oz

→ Melt ALL THE INGREDIENTS FOR THE SAUCE together in a saucepan. Let them bubble for a further 3 minutes or so before pouring them into the bottom of a large, greased pudding basin.

→ Pour the BOILING WATER over the APRICOTS and BICARB and leave to cool. Cream the SUGAR and BUTTER until light and fluffy, then beat in the EGG. Sift over the FLOUR and BAKING POWDER, and throw in the PECAN NUTS. Stir in the apricot mixture, and scrape into the pudding basin on top of the butterscotch sauce.

→ Cover with foil and secure with string, then steam in a saucepan of water that reaches halfway up the pudding for 1½ hours. Check that the water level remains constant throughout. Turn the pudding out onto a large, warmed serving plate, not too flat for the moat of butterscotch, and serve with more crème fraîche if you dare.

Lemon Bomb or Sussex Pond Pudding

SERVES 6

self-raising flour	225g/8oz
suet	110g/4oz
slightly salted butter	110g/4oz
milk and water	about 150ml/5fl oz
molasses OR demerara sugar	110g/4oz
large organic lemon	1

You need a thin-skinned lemon for this. I guess the detonator doesn't work on a thick-skinned one. The boiling and roiling of the water obviously trigger the explosion, and when you cut into the suet crust, a black sugar puddle pours forth with the remains of the exploded lemon to do battle with the richness.

→ Mix the FLOUR and SUET in a bowl. Add the MILK and WATER to make a soft dough. Roll the dough out into a large circle, then remove one-quarter with a knife to use as a lid.

→ Butter a 1.5 litre/3 pint pudding basin. Drop the larger piece of dough into it and press it together to line the basin. Put half the chopped BUTTER into the basin with half the SUGAR. Prick the LEMON all over with a fine sharp skewer or larding needle to help the juices escape. Place the lemon on top of the butter and sugar and cover with the remaining BUTTER and SUGAR. Roll out the remaining quarter of suet dough and lay it on top to seal the filling inside.

→ Cover with greaseproof paper and foil in the usual way (see steamed treacle pudding, p. 470) and make a string handle. Lower the pudding into boiling water in a large saucepan, making sure the water comes halfway up the basin. Cover with a lid and steam for 3–4 hours. Slip a palette knife gently down the sides of the pudding, then turn the pudding out onto a large plate with plenty of room for the moat. Make sure everyone gets some of the lemon, all of which will be edible. Clotted or thick cream, naturally.

Steamed Lemon Curd Pudding

SERVES 6

caster sugar	170g/6oz
butter	110g/4oz
organic eggs	2
lemon	juice and rind of 2
flour	110g/4oz
baking powder	1 tsp
milk to slacken	a little
lemon curd (or make your own see p. 585)	1 × 310g/11oz jar

I have made this stunning steamed pudding with lime and blood orange curd as well. Curds are simple and satisfying to make and will always taste better than jarred ones, but if you can't be bothered, reach for a top-notch brand like Duchy. My lemon curd recipe is on p. 585. What you want is a molten-thick golden puddle seeping slowly out of the spongy depths, giving tang to the sweetness.

→ Cream the SUGAR and BUTTER together thoroughly, then beat in the EGGS. Add the juice and rind of the LEMONS, then sprinkle over the sifted FLOUR and BAKING POWDER. Add a bit of MILK to slacken to a dropping consistency, but don't let the mixture become sloppy.

→ Scrape the LEMON CURD from the jar into the bottom of your pudding basin, a snap-on lidded plastic one is fine if you don't want to cover and tie an old-fashioned pudding basin (see p. 470 for how to do this). Spoon the pudding mixture over the curd, cover, set on a trivet in a large pan, and pour boiling water to come halfway up the sides of the basin. Simmer for about 1½ hours, then turn out on to a large dish; remember there will be a lake of sauce.

Jam Roly-Poly

SERVES 6

self-raising flour	170g/6oz
salt	1 pinch
suet	75g/2½oz
cold water	150ml/5fl oz
best strawberry jam with whole berries	225g/8oz

A real roly-poly pudding, oozing whole fruit jam, its seeded crimson stickiness penetrating the layers of dense yet light suet, is a wonder to behold and to eat. You may pour more hot red liquid over it—melt another half pot of jam with a tablespoon of water and a squeeze of lemon juice—and serve with a jug of cold cream. Or eat it with a vanilla-scented custard (see p. 514).

→ Heat the oven to 220°C/425°F/Gas 7. Stir the FLOUR, SALT and SUET together and mix them to a firm dough with the WATER. Flour a work surface and your rolling pin and roll out the dough lengthways to about 10 × 25cm/4 × 10in. Don't roll it too thinly, it should be about 1cm/½in thick. Spread a thick layer of JAM over the surface, not going quite to the edges. Roll the dough up like a Swiss roll, tweaking the edges together. Place on a greased baking sheet and bake for 40 minutes until browned.

Queen of Puddings

SERVES 6

day-old brown bread breadcrumbs	110g/4oz
unrefined vanilla caster sugar	1 heaped tbsp
organic lemon	zest of 1
Jersey, Guernsey OR full-cream milk	600ml/1 pint
unsalted butter	55g/2oz
large eggs, *separated*	4
best-quality apricot OR raspberry jam OR bramble jelly	1 jar
vanilla caster sugar	110g/4oz

So is it to be great amber, sticky clots of apricot jam, strawberry, raspberry, peach, plum or damson jam, bramble or blackcurrant jelly? Whichever you choose, there is something about the texture of this pudding, the soothing soft custard spiked with lemon, the sharp, sweet jam, the heavenly light crunch of the meringue on top that is ultimately, terminally, satisfying.

→ Preheat the oven to 180°C/350°F/Gas 4. Put the CRUMBS into the deep, buttered dish you intend to cook the pudding in, with the VANILLA SUGAR and LEMON ZEST. Scald the MILK with the BUTTER, stir them into the crumbs and leave to cool for 10 minutes. Now beat in the EGG YOLKS one at a time. Bake in the oven for about 25 minutes until the custard has set.
→ Heat the JAM gently with a teaspoon of two of water and pour it over the custard. Whisk the EGG WHITES until stiff, stir in a spoon of SUGAR, then whisk in half of the remaining SUGAR until it is satiny. Fold in all but a spoon of the remaining sugar, pile the meringue on top of the pudding, and sprinkle the rest of the SUGAR over the top. Put back in the oven for about 15–20 minutes or until the meringue is golden and crisp. Serve hot with cold, thin cream. You may make the pudding up to the meringue stage a few hours earlier if it suits you.

Bread and Butter Pudding

This classic defines everything that is best about English puddings. You probably always have the ingredients in your store cupboard or the sort of approximations that will make a different version of it. It is simple and comforting while also something you can spruce up for special occasions— try soaking your sultanas in sherry, using panettone instead of bread, adding candied fruit or little jewels of prune and apricot. You can make bread and butter pudding with cream or milk, spread the bread with marmalade or leave it buttered, make it with teacakes or give it a dark mantle of chocolate custard.

SERVES 6–8

white bread, OR chollah if you like sweet bread, *crusts cut off*	10–12 slices
unsalted butter, *softened*	enough to butter all the bread
organic egg yolks	8
unrefined caster sugar	170g/6oz
vanilla pod	1
Jersey full-cream milk	300ml/ 10fl oz
double cream	300ml/10fl oz
sultanas, *soaked in warm water* OR *warmed sherry* OR *rum for 20 minutes or so until they plump up*	a handful
extra caster sugar for the top	

→ Preheat oven to 180°C/350°F/Gas 4. Butter the slices of BREAD. Whisk the EGG YOLKS and CASTER SUGAR together thoroughly in a bowl. Split the VANILLA POD down the middle and extract the black seeds by running a sharp pointed teaspoon down the middle of the pod. Put the seeds and the pod into a pan with the MILK and CREAM and bring them to simmering point. Then pour the contents through a sieve onto the egg yolk and sugar mixture. Whisk a little until frothy.

→ Grease a shallow pudding basin. Cut the buttered bread into triangles and arrange them in overlapping layers in the basin, throwing over the SULTANAS as you go. Pour the egg custard over the bread and allow it to soak in for a few minutes. Put the pudding dish inside a roasting tin with boiling water halfway up its sides.

→ Poach for about 20–30 minutes. The custard will have thickened considerably but not set, as there are only egg yolks in it. Remove the dish from the roasting tin and scatter CASTER SUGAR over the surface in a thin layer and caramelise it briefly under the grill.

→ If you want a firmer set to the pudding, use three whole eggs and three yolks whisked together.

Marmalade Bread and Butter Pudding

→ You may put MARMALADE on the buttered slices of bread before you cook the pudding, in which case leave the top layer of bread just buttered so the marmalade doesn't burn on top. When the pudding is cooked, melt 3 tablespoons of Seville orange marmalade with a dessertspoon of water and brush it over the surface of the pudding.

Simple Chocolate Mousse

SERVES 4

best bitter chocolate, 70% cocoa solids	200g/7oz
espresso coffee	3 tbsp
unsalted butter	30g/1oz
cognac (optional)	1 tbsp
large organic eggs, *separated*	3

The thrill of pushing the spoon into a dark, lightly airy, yet deeply rich ramekin of chocolate mousse is a constant. It is a perfect pudding, a simple pudding and one that wants no more than to be covered in chilled white pouring cream when you serve it—this has the curious effect of making it seem less rich. Or is this an illusion?

→ Break the CHOCOLATE into squares and put it in a bowl with the COFFEE and BUTTER. Place in the top of a double boiler or in a bowl over simmering water; the bottom of the bowl must not touch the water. The water must stay at a bare simmer throughout. Melt everything together, stirring gently, then remove from the heat and stir in the COGNAC if you are using it.
→ While the mixture is still hottish, stir in the YOLKS, one at a time. Whisk the EGG WHITES to stiff peaks. Stir the first tablespoon into the chocolate to slacken the mixture, then fold in the rest in large spoonfuls. Work lightly and gently to keep the air in the mousse.
→ Scrape into ramekins or a single glass serving bowl and cover. Chill in the fridge for at least 6 hours but overnight if it suits you better. Serve with thin pouring cream, which you can pour over the top of the individual ramekins if you like before serving them.

Rich Chocolate Mousse

SERVES 8–10

vanilla caster sugar	140g/5oz
whole organic eggs, *separated*	3
extra egg yolks	3
Green and Black's cocoa powder	1 tbsp
double cream	200ml/7fl oz
unsalted butter	85g/3oz
best bitter chocolate, 70% cocoa solids	225g/8oz
Armagnac OR cognac	1 tbsp
extra double cream and dark chocolate	

This is the Ferrari of chocolate mousses, rich, velvety, louche and luxuriant.

→ Put 55g/2oz of the sugar, all 6 EGG YOLKS, the COCOA POWDER and the CREAM in the top of a double saucepan or a bowl over simmering water. Keep whisking it over a gentle heat until it thickens enough to coat a wooden spoon. Take off the heat, add small pieces of the BUTTER and CHOCOLATE, and stir until fully melted. Add the ALCOHOL and stir it in.
→ Whisk the three EGG WHITES with the rest of the SUGAR, adding the sugar as you whisk, not at the end. This method makes a thickly glossy meringue that you want to whisk to soft-peak stage. Decant the chocolate mixture into a bowl and lightly fold in the meringue. Pour into a large bowl or individual glasses and refrigerate before serving. When you're ready to eat, whisk some more DOUBLE CREAM to hold soft peaks and spoon onto the mousse. Grate over a little dark CHOCOLATE.

Chocolate Roulade

SERVES 6–8

large organic eggs	6
vanilla caster sugar	75g/2½oz
dark cocoa powder, Green and Black's if possible	55g/2oz
double cream	200ml/7fl oz
unrefined icing sugar	

Chocolate and Coffee Sauce

espresso coffee powder	1 tsp
hot brandy OR hot double cream	1 tbsp
best bitter chocolate, 70% or more cocoa solids	140g/5oz
golden syrup	1 tbsp
unsalted butter	45g/1½oz

Here is a positively scrumptious rendering of this well-known pudding, one that might whet your appetite for the joys of dark chocolate and cream.

→ Preheat the oven to 180°C/350°F/Gas 4. Butter and line a 30 × 20cm/12 × 8in shallow-sided baking tray with greaseproof paper. Separate the EGGS and beat the YOLKS with the CASTER SUGAR until pale and thick. Sift in the COCOA POWDER and whisk them together. Whisk the EGG WHITES to stiff peaks, stir a couple of spoonfuls into the chocolate mixture, then cut and fold in the rest lightly and quickly. Pour onto the greaseproof in the baking tray and cook for 15 minutes in the centre of the oven.
→ Take the roulade out of the oven and let it cool for a few minutes before covering it with a damp tea towel to stop it cracking. Meanwhile, make the sauce (see below).
→ Whip the CREAM so that it just holds soft folds. Put a large piece of greaseproof paper down onto the work surface and sift ICING SUGAR over it. Turn the cake upside-down onto it in one fell swoop and remove the top layer of greaseproof. Spread the sauce over it with a palette knife up to 2cm/¾in away from the edges, then cover the sauce with whipped cream. Use the greaseproof to help you roll the roulade into shape. It is bound to crack a little at this point, but that's just how it should look. Put the roulade onto a large serving dish and slice.

Chocolate and Coffee Sauce
→ Mix the teaspoon of COFFEE POWDER with the hot BRANDY or CREAM. Put the broken squares of CHOCOLATE, SYRUP, BUTTER and the coffee in its hot liquid into the top of a double boiler or in a bowl over a pan of barely simmering water, the bowl not touching the water. Stir over a gentle heat while the chocolate melts.

Chocolate and Chestnut Terrine

Serves 10

best bitter chocolate, minimum 70% cocoa solids	200g/7oz
cognac	1 tbsp
water	1 tbsp
unsalted butter, *melted in a pan*	110g/4oz
unrefined vanilla sugar	110g/4oz
organic eggs, *separated*	4
vacuum-packed chestnuts, *chopped*	3 × 200g/7oz packs
almond oil or similar for greasing tin	

You can make this well in advance and really quickly, then leave it in the fridge for a few hours or even days. You may process the chestnuts with the melted butter and all but a tablespoon of the sugar if you want a satin-smooth terrine, or follow the recipe and end up with nuggets of chopped chestnut in the chocolate for a more textured version.

→ Melt the CHOCOLATE in a double boiler with the BRANDY and WATER. Add the melted BUTTER and all but a tablespoon of the SUGAR. Stir in the EGG YOLKS one by one, then whisk the EGG WHITES to soft peak stage. Add the remaining tablespoon of SUGAR and whisk until stiff. Fold in the chopped CHESTNUTS as well as you can; the mixture will be very thick and sludgy at this stage. Plop it into a loaf tin, which you have greased lightly with an unobtrusive oil such as ALMOND OIL, and smooth down the surface. Leave to cool and put it in the fridge when cold.
→ I think this is best eaten after a day or two, so make it in advance. It will turn out beautifully on to a flat dish. Serve with pouring cream, to which you can add a tablespoon of freshly made coffee if you like. A couple of slices each are all you will want. Killer.

Chocolate Bavarois

Serves 4

gelatine	3½ leaves
milk	600ml/1 pint
dark, bitter chocolate, *broken into pieces*	340g/12oz
organic egg yolks	5
double cream	300ml/10fl oz

This recipe comes from one of the all-time great chefs and food writers Simon Hopkinson. You'll need some crushed ice.

→ Put the GELATINE LEAVES in a bowl, cover with cold water and leave to soften. Heat the MILK and melt the CHOCOLATE in it. Gently whisk together until smooth. Whisk the EGG YOLKS and add them to the milk chocolate mixture. Cook over a gentle heat until thickened, like custard. Drain the gelatine and add it to the chocolate mixture while it is still hot. Whisk together well.
→ Pass the mixture through a sieve into a cold bowl. Place over crushed ice and stir with a wooden spoon until starting to set. Lightly whip the CREAM until holding soft peaks, then carefully but quickly fold it into the chocolate. Pour into individual ramekins or a soufflé dish and refrigerate for at least 2 hours before serving with cold crème Anglaise (see p. 514).

Luscious Chocolate Puddings

MAKES 6

organic eggs	5
extra egg yolks	5
vanilla caster sugar	110g/4oz
best bitter chocolate	225g/8oz
unsalted butter	225g/8oz
plain flour, *sifted*	55g/2oz
cocoa powder and icing sugar (optional)	

Everyone has their own version of these dense, dark chocolate puddings, which pour out a river of runny chocolate sauce when spoon sinks into sponge. You can make the pudding mixture the day before if you like, fill the ramekins and put them to bed in the fridge until you want them. Cold pouring cream is needed to add an ivory wave to the hot chocolate lake.

→ Beat the EGGS, YOLKS and SUGAR together until pale. Melt the CHOCOLATE and BUTTER in a bowl over, but not touching, simmering water. Remove from the heat and add to the egg mixture, beating as you go. Fold in the FLOUR. Pour into the buttered moulds immediately. Cool, then refrigerate for a couple of hours.

→ Preheat the oven to 180°C/350°F/Gas 4. Bake the puddings for about 12 minutes; the tops will have risen and feel dry to the touch. Turn out with a bendy palette knife and serve. You can sprinkle a bit of COCOA POWDER and ICING SUGAR over the top if you are feeling decorative.

Chocolate Pots

MAKES 5 LITTLE RAMEKINS

good double cream	170ml/6fl oz
coffee, *freshly ground*	1 heaped tsp
good dark chocolate, Valrhona or similar	140g/5oz
Jersey milk	90ml/3fl oz
organic egg yolks	2
unrefined icing sugar	1 heaped tbsp

Bitter, black and velvety rich, you can plunge a spoon into one of these little pots and it will remain standing. The scent of coffee spiking best Valrhona chocolate is irresistible. You can make the pots the day before you need them and keep them in the fridge. Cold, thin cream can be poured over the top by those who are seriously over the top.

→ Heat the CREAM with the COFFEE until just below boiling. Remove from the heat, cover and leave to infuse for an hour.

→ Preheat the oven to 140°C/275°F/Gas 1. Melt the CHOCOLATE very gently in the MILK. Beat the EGG YOLKS with the SUGAR, then add the chocolate milk. Sieve the coffee and cream, add to the chocolate mixture and and beat together until blended. Pour into the ramekins and put them in a roasting tin with scalding water to reach halfway up the sides of the ramekins. Bake for 45 minutes, remove from their bain-marie and let them cool.

→ Put them in the fridge for a few hours before serving. You can omit the coffee and use half a vanilla pod split, with the black grains extracted and used too, if you prefer.

Hot Chocolate Soufflé

SERVES 8

milk	450ml/16fl oz
vanilla pod, *split*	1
unsalted butter, *softened*	85g/3oz
plain flour	55g/2oz
unsweetened cocoa powder	20g/²⁄₃oz plus extra for sprinkling the dish
organic eggs, *separated*	6
extra egg whites	6
bitter chocolate (70% cocoa solids), *chopped*	85g/3oz
rum or liqueur such as Grand Marnier	1 tbsp
caster sugar	3 tbsp
rich chocolate sauce (see p. 419)	

The best sweet soufflé I've ever eaten was Michel Roux's at Le Gavroche. A pale, fragile cloud of pistachio, it had a hole carved into its top and a scoop of pistachio ice cream sunk into its airy light depths. It doesn't get much better than that, though Michel's chocolate soufflé is divine, and you really can make it at home. For really stiff smooth egg whites, freeze them up to a week ahead and defrost on the day you want to use them.

→ Bring the MILK to the boil with the VANILLA. Beat the BUTTER until smooth, sift in the FLOUR and COCOA POWDER and pour in the hot milk. Bring back to the boil over high heat, whisking continuously. Remove from the heat and whisk in the EGG YOLKS, chopped CHOCOLATE and RUM OR LIQUEUR. Cover with buttered greaseproof paper and set aside.

→ Preheat the oven to 190°C/375°F/Gas 5. Butter 8 ramekins (9cm/3½in diameter × 6cm/2½ in deep) and sprinkle with a little COCOA POWDER, tipping out any excess. Whisk the chocolate mixture until smooth. Whisk all the EGG WHITES in an electric mixer until frothy. Add the CASTER SUGAR, 1 tablespoon at a time, and continue whisking until stiff yet still smooth. Beat one-third of the egg whites into the chocolate mixture until smooth, then gently fold in the rest. Pour the soufflé mixture into the ramekins, smooth the surface with a palette knife and then run the point of a knife around the rim: this helps the soufflé to rise evenly. Place in the oven for 11 minutes; the soufflés should still be creamy in the middle. Serve immediately, dusted with a little ICING SUGAR, along with a jug of hot RICH CHOCOLATE SAUCE (see p. 419).

Chocolate Parfait

SERVES 8

organic egg yolks	7
vanilla caster sugar	110g/4oz
best bitter chocolate, *chopped*	200g/7oz
amaretto, brandy OR strong black coffee, *freshly made*	1 tbsp
double cream	600ml/1 pint

A parfait is like a light, almost moussey ice cream, lifted with a foam of beaten eggs and sugar. It can be made well in advance of when you want it and frozen. Turn it out of its loaf tin or terrine a couple of minutes after you take it out of the freezer and it's ready to eat. Make it with half chest-nuts if you like, and serve it with the coffee crème Anglaise opposite, or just with cold pouring cream.

→ Line a 25cm/10in long terrine or loaf tin with clingfilm. Whisk the EGG YOLKS with the VANILLA CASTER SUGAR over a double boiler in a bowl large enough for the ingredients to expand to well over double their original size; this will take 10–15 minutes. The more you beat, the more the eggs expand in volume, and the lighter the result.

→ In a separate bowl, melt the CHOCOLATE with the AMARETTO, BRANDY or COFFEE, then stir it into the egg and sugar mixture. Pour in the CREAM and whisk until the mixture forms soft peaks. Pour into the lined terrine and freeze until set.

→ When you are ready to serve the parfait, dip the terrine into boiling water for a few seconds, turn out on to a plate and peel away the clingfilm.

Coffee Crème Anglaise

MAKES 850ML/1½ PINTS

organic egg yolks	8
vanilla caster sugar	75g/2½oz
fresh ground coffee	2 tsp
Jersey milk	300ml/10fl oz
double cream	300ml/10fl oz

This can be flavoured with other ingredients depending on what you are serving it with. Try adding some grated ginger and the syrup from a jar of stem ginger, or chocolate.

→ Whisk the EGG YOLKS and SUGAR together thoroughly until pale and creamy and well amalgamated. Put the teaspoons of COFFEE into the MILK and CREAM in a pan and bring slowly to scald point. Put the bowl with the yolks and sugar over a pan of barely simmering water, the base of the bowl not touching the water, or scrape the egg and yolk mixture into the top of a double boiler. Whisk the coffee-flavoured cream and milk into the yolk and sugar mixture over the hot water, and stir or whisk continuously until it thickens. Pour through a fine sieve to remove any coarse coffee granules.

→ When it has cooled, pour a puddle of sauce onto each plate and top with a slice of chocolate parfait (see above).

Cardamom Crème Anglaise

→ Infuse a couple of CARDAMOM PODS in the milk and cream for 30 minutes after it has come to the boil.

Chocolate Profiteroles

MAKES 18–24

Choux paste

unsalted butter	85g/3oz
salt	1 pinch
water	270ml/9fl oz
plain flour, *sifted into a bowl*	140g/5oz
organic eggs	4

Filling

double cream, Jersey if possible	300ml/10fl oz

Dark Chocolate Sauce

good dark chocolate	1 × 200g/7oz bar
butter	55g/2oz
golden syrup	4 tsp
Jersey cream	3 tbsp

A mountain of airy light choux pastry, a thick slick of crème pâtissière or double cream, and a flood of sticky, syrupy bitter chocolate sauce flooding over each ball. Is any pudding such a crowd-pleaser? It may be old-fashioned, but it shouldn't be confined to the chariot des desserts as it is a surprisingly easy and pleasing pudding to make. Choux paste is a knack, but a child could get it right. Splitting the little weightless buns to let the air out and stuff their middles is a pleasurably repetitive task.

→ Heat the oven to 200°C/400°F/Gas 6. Line a baking tray with silicone paper and set aside. To make the CHOUX PASTE, put the BUTTER, SALT and WATER in a pan and bring to the boil. Just as it comes to the boil, remove the pan from the heat and quickly add the FLOUR. Stir with a wooden spoon until it coheres, then return to a low heat and cook for a minute until it comes away from the side of the pan.

→ Remove from the heat again and leave to cool for a couple of minutes—you don't want the eggs to cook when you add them. Break the first EGG into the pan and whisk it vigorously in with a fork. Add the next 2 EGGS one at a time. Then, depending on how resistant the mixture is, whisk the final EGG and add it slowly, a bit at a time, until the mixture is a little easier to work and looks glossy.

→ Choux will solidify if you leave it, so immediately place teaspoons of the mixture on the baking tray and bake in the preheated oven for 15 minutes. Reduce the temperature to 150°C/300°F/Gas 2 and cook for a further 15–20 minutes or until crisp and brown. Remove, and pierce the side of each profiterole to let out the steam. Cool on a rack.

→ Whisk the JERSEY CREAM for the filling until slackly stiffened. Just before you are ready to serve the profiteroles, slit them, add a good spoonful of cream to the middles, re-splice and then pour over the warm CHOCOLATE SAUCE, as thickly as you dare.

→ Alternatively, fill the profiteroles with crème pâtissière. Follow the recipe on p. 502, but stir a teaspoon of espresso coffee or ordinary coffee granules into the milk.

Dark Chocolate Sauce
→ Melt the CHOCOLATE in a double boiler with the BUTTER, GOLDEN SYRUP and 3 tablespoons of JERSEY CREAM. At no stage should the top pan or bowl touch the water, nor should the water boil, or your cocoa solids will separate.

Marquise au Chocolat

SERVES 10–12

vegetable oil that doesn't taste for oiling the tin	a little
bitter chocolate, 64–70% cocoa solids	340g/12oz
unsalted butter, *cubed*	225g/8oz
organic eggs, *separated*	4
egg yolks	4
unrefined icing sugar	170g/6oz
Green and Black's organic cocoa powder	45g/1½oz
double cream	130ml/4½fl oz

A densely rich chocolate terrine, this needs making at least half a day before you want to eat it but can be made up to 3 days in advance.

→ Lightly oil a loaf tin or long terrine, 30 × 10 × 7.5cm/12 × 4 × 3in and line it with clingfilm. Melt the CHOCOLATE with the cubed BUTTER in a double saucepan over, but not touching, barely simmering water, or in a bowl placed in a pan over, not touching, simmering water. Stir until glossy and velvety and completely smooth. Cool to warm, then stir in the YOLKS one at a time. Sift the ICING SUGAR and COCOA POWDER together into the chocolate mixture.

→ Whisk the EGG WHITES to soft peaks. Stir the first tablespoon into the chocolate mixture, then lightly fold in the rest. Whisk the CREAM until it holds, but be careful not to whisk it rigid. Fold the cream into the mixture and pour it into the tin or terrine. Refrigerate covered with clingfilm overnight or for half a day at least before turning it out onto a plate when you are ready to serve it. Dip the knife blade into hot water to slice. Serve with thin cream or cream whisked with a little rum, a tablespoon or so, and a little icing sugar.

Chocolate St Emilion

SERVES 8

dark chocolate	225g/8oz
instant coffee	1 tbsp
water	120ml/4fl oz
eggs	4
large macaroons	3–4
brandy	40ml/1½fl oz

→ Melt the CHOCOLATE in the WATER with the COFFEE. Separate the EGGS, whisk the YOLKS, and add them to the chocolate at room temperature, mixing them in well. Crumble the MACAROONS roughly, sprinkle them with BRANDY, and mash with a fork. Whisk the EGG WHITES stiffly and fold lightly, but thoroughly, into the chocolate mixture which should still be warm. Layer in glasses with the macaroon mixture.

Hot or Cold Chocolate Pudding

SERVES 6–8

bitter chocolate, 70% cocoa solids	150g/5oz
unsalted butter	140g/5oz
pure vanilla extract	1 tsp
warm water	150ml/5fl oz
vanilla caster sugar	125g/4oz
organic eggs, *separated*	4
self-raising flour	30g/1oz
cream for serving	

A simply delicious chocolate pudding that you may serve hot or cold, depending on your mood and what timing suits you. Both are equally good, although the cold tends to be richer, since I add a layer of lightly whipped cream and finely grated chocolate to shroud the chocolate beneath.

→ Preheat the oven to 200°C/400°F/Gas 6. Grease a 2 litre/3–4 pint soufflé dish. Melt the CHOCOLATE, BUTTER and VANILLA in the top of a double boiler over simmering water. Add the WARM WATER and SUGAR and keep stirring until all the sugar has dissolved. Pour the mixture into a bowl and stir in the EGG YOLKS one by one. Stir in the sifted FLOUR, and whisk until the mixture is free of lumps. Whisk the EGG WHITES to stiff peaks, stir the first tablespoon into the mixture, then fold the rest lightly in with a metal spoon.

→ Boil a kettle, put the soufflé dish inside a roasting tin and pour in scalding water to come halfway up its sides. Cook in the hot oven for 10 minutes, then turn the oven temperature down to 170°C/325°F/ Gas 3 and cook for 30 minutes more. Serve hot with thin POURING CREAM, Jersey or Guernsey unpasteurised if you can find it, or leave to cool completely.

→ To serve the cold version, softly whip 300ml/10fl oz of double cream, cover the pudding with it, and finely grate a dusting of bitter chocolate over the surface. Serve at room temperature— the pudding is lighter that way than if you chill it in the fridge.

This recipe doubles up perfectly, so if you have a party, just make double the amount in a larger soufflé dish.

Malted Milk Chocolate Pudding with Bailey's Custard

SERVES 6–8

Green and Black's organic milk chocolate	100g/3½oz
butter	110g/4oz
caster sugar	110g/4oz
organic eggs	2

→ Bash the CHOCOLATE into small chunks. Cream the BUTTER and SUGAR together until really light and fluffy, then add the EGGS, one at a time. Sieve the FLOUR and BAKING POWDER into the mixture and fold in, then add the MALT POWDER and amalgamate. Add a splosh of MILK at a time, until you achieve dropping consistency, i.e. the mixture will slide willingly off the spoon in a smooth heap, then stir in the chocolate, and scrape the mixture into a greased pudding basin.

→ Cover with foil, tie tightly with string, and steam in a large pan of just bubbling water to come halfway up the pudding basin for 2 hours. Turn out, and serve with this gloriously rich BAILEY'S CUSTARD.

flour	110g/4oz
baking powder	1 tsp
Prewett's malted milk drink	45–55g/1½–2oz
milk (see recipe)	
Bailey's Custard	
vanilla pod	1
full-cream milk, Jersey is best	600ml/1 pint
egg yolks	6
vanilla caster sugar	85g/3oz
Bailey's Irish Cream liqueur	1–2 tbsp

Bailey's Custard

→ Split the VANILLA POD, scrape out the seeds and put both into the pan with the MILK. Whisk over the heat until the milk is at scalding point and the seeds dispersed, then take it off the heat, put a lid on it, and leave it to infuse for 20–30 minutes. Whisk the EGG YOLKS and CASTER SUGAR together thoroughly, then strain the milk over them, add the BAILEY'S, taste, return to the pan, and keep whisking. Cook over a gentle heat, whisking constantly. The cream will look light and almost frothy, and begin to thicken imperceptibly after about 10 minutes. On no account try and speed things up by turning up the heat, unless you want sweet scrambled eggs. Pour into a jug, or keep hot for up to 20 minutes over a double saucepan, and release copiously over the pudding.

Budino

MAKES 7

gelatine leaves	4
bitter chocolate, 70% cocoa solids	225g/8oz
short espresso, or the equivalent strong small cup of fresh coffee	1
caster sugar	100g/3½oz
milk	500ml/18fl oz
organic egg yolks	2

→ Soak the GELATINE LEAVES in 2–3 tablespoons of water for about 10 minutes. Melt the CHOCOLATE with the ESPRESSO in a double boiler. Take it off the heat and whisk in the EGG YOLKS. Heat the MILK with the SUGAR until it is dissolved. Add the milk and sugar mixture little by little to the chocolate, whisking all the time, without creating any foam. Once the gelatine has completely dissolved, add it to the mixture and continue whisking. Pour into small moulds, I used my little plastic steamed-pudding moulds. Allow them to cool and leave to set in the fridge.

→ You can serve them several hours or a day later. A palette knife worked around the moulds enables you to plop them out onto plates. Thin pouring cream is a must. It slicks the chocolate tops beautifully before cascading down the sides.

Spiced Apple Pie

SERVES 6

shortcrust pastry *made with 325g/12oz plain flour and 170g/6oz unsalted butter* (see p. 104)	
light muscovado sugar	55g/2oz
dark molasses sugar	55g/2oz
ground cloves	¼ tsp
ground cinnamon	¼ tsp
grated nutmeg	⅛ tsp
plain flour	1 tbsp
lemon	*grated* rind and juice of ½
orange	*grated* rind and juice of ½
Cox's apples, *peeled and sliced*	675g/1½ lb
butter	30–55g/1–2oz
egg, *beaten*	1
granulated sugar for the top (optional)	

This is the first apple pie I ever baked, and although I have made scores of different ones since, the nostalgia factor seems to win each and every time I return to it. It was a stunning recipe in the first place, alerting me to the fact that although apple pie is all about apples cloaked and sealed in a crisp, buttery crust, releasing their sweet sharp juices only when you cut into the pie, it is important to know what helps bring out their flavour and complements it in such a way as to make an everyday dish something ultra-special. Also delicious made with spelt flour, which gives nuttiness and texture to the pastry.

→ Preheat the oven to 200°C/400°F/Gas 6. Make the PASTRY (see p. 104). Roll out half the pastry and use to line a greased large pie dish.

→ Combine the SUGARS, SPICES, FLOUR and GRATED RINDS and strew a little of the mixture on the pastry base. Cover with some of the sliced APPLES and some more of the sugar mixture. Repeat until the dish is densely filled. Add the LEMON AND ORANGE JUICES and knobs of BUTTER. Roll out the remaining pastry to make the top crust. Crimp and flute the pastry edges together with a fork. Decorate with an apple made from the pastry trimmings and make one or two slits in the top crust to let out the steam. Brush lightly with beaten EGG.

→ Bake in the oven for 35–40 minutes. Leave to cool slightly, then strew GRANULATED SUGAR over the top of the warm pie if you wish.

Rhubarb and Apple Pie

SERVES 6

rhubarb	450g/1lb
eating apples (Cox's are best)	4–6
muscovado sugar	140g/5oz or to taste
shortcrust pastry *made with 285g/10oz plain flour and 140g/5oz unsalted butter* (see p. 104)	
egg, *beaten*, for glaze	1

There's rhubarb and ginger, rhubarb and orange—with or without honey—and the perhaps less well-known marriage of rhubarb and apple. I think this last partnership is every bit as successful, and the apple has the merit of somehow reducing and softening the acidity of the rhubarb in a really unexpected and delicious way. Allowing the fruits to begin to bleed into the dusky muscovado sugar before cooking is something you should try and leave time for.

→ Wash the RHUBARB and chop into short lengths. Peel, core and slice the APPLES. In a large bowl, mix the rhubarb, apples and SUGAR together with your fingers. Leave for 20 minutes or so for the juices to begin to run. Meanwhile make the PASTRY (see p. 104) and chill in the fridge.

→ Preheat the oven to 200°C/400°F/Gas 6. Pack the pie dish tightly with fruit, mounding it up in the centre in the usual way. Roll out the pastry. Cut off a strip and attach it to the rim of the dish, brushing the rim with water first. Brush the strip with water and cover the dish with the sheet of pastry. Drape it loosely rather than stretched taut, as there is always some shrinkage. If you feel like it, use a sharp knife point to cut out diamond shapes in the top. Brush the pastry with beaten EGG and place the pie in the oven for 20 minutes. Turn the heat down to 190°C/375°F/Gas 5 and continue to cook for another 20 minutes, when the pie should be golden and the fruit cooked through. Serve warm with cream or custard.

Blackberry and Apple Pie

SERVES 6

sharp eating apples, *peeled, cored and sliced*	4–6
blackberries, *unripe berries and prickles discarded*	450g/1lb
light muscovado or unrefined granulated sugar	110g/4oz, or to taste
cornflour	2 tsp
shortcrust pastry *made with 285g/10oz plain flour and 140g/5oz unsalted butter* (see p. 104)	
egg, *beaten*, for glaze	1

First pick your blackberries. This is THE autumn pie, fruited with the very best of pie-fellows, the blackberry and the apple; a pie that evokes more memories than any other at this time of year. Quantities here are not a fixed thing. They're more to do with what you've picked, so go with what you've got and use the recipe below as a guideline.

→ Preheat the oven to 200°C/400°F/Gas 6. Throw the APPLES and BLACKBERRIES into a huge bowl, scatter over the SUGAR and sifted CORNFLOUR, then turn the fruit gently with your fingers. Leave to stand for 20–30 minutes, then hurl everything into the pie dish.

→ Roll out the PASTRY and cut off a strip. Wet the rim of the dish with water, then stick on the strip of pastry. Wet the pastry strip and cover with the sheet of pastry, crimping the edges together with the tines of a fork. Decorate with a few pastry blackberries and the odd apple if you feel inspired. Brush with beaten EGG, cut a central hole for the steam to escape from, and cook for 20 minutes. Turn the heat down to 190°C/375°F/Gas 5 and cook for a further 20 minutes until the top is burnished. Serve hot or warm with lashings of cream or custard. Great cold too, with rivulets of purple juice staining the cream.

Sour Cream Apple and Walnut Pie

SERVES 6–8

shortcrust pastry *made with 225g/8oz plain flour and 110g/4oz unsalted butter* (see p. 104)	
large eating apples	10
light brown muscovado sugar	a little
soured cream	142ml/5fl oz carton

Topping

sugar, half light muscovado and half molasses	110g/4oz
unsalted butter	110g/4oz
golden syrup	a large tbsp
flour	55g/2oz
walnuts, *bashed into small bits*	85g/3oz
egg, *beaten*	

→ Preheat the oven to 200°C/400°F/Gas 6. Grease a pie dish with butter, then line it with two-thirds of the rolled-out SHORTCRUST PASTRY. Let the overhang hang loose for now.

→ Peel, core and thinly slice the APPLES. Toss them into a bowl with a small scattering of SUGAR and the SOURED CREAM, then mix with your hands until everything is well amalgamated. Pile this mixture into the pastry base, packing it tightly and mounding it up towards the centre.

→ For the topping, process the SUGARS, small bits of cold BUTTER, SYRUP and FLOUR together. Add the WALNUTS when you have stopped the processing and stir them in. Take lumps of the mixture on the palm of one hand and flatten them out with the other palm, so you have a flattened layer rather than a crumble top, and cover the surface of the apples bit by bit. Join the topping to the pastry edge before you cut off the pastry overhang. Brush with beaten egg.

→ Cook for 20 minutes before turning the temperature down to 180°C/350°F/Gas 4 and cooking for another 30–40 minutes. Check that the top layer is not darkening too much, and if it is, cover with a layer of greaseproof or foil and continue cooking. The pie will smell ready when it is ready. I am of the firm belief that apple pie is best when left to cool for at least 3 hours after cooking, so if you want it warm or hot, work out your cooking times accordingly and reheat very gently. Warm pie, with homemade vanilla ice cream, is the business.

Bottom-crust Fruit Pie

SERVES 6

fruit, plums, damsons, greengages, gooseberries, blackberry or apple	750g/1lb 10oz
sugar	75–85g/2½–3oz, depending on the sweetnessof the fruit

Pastry

plain flour	225g/8oz
sea salt	1 pinch

This is a classic, American-style fruit pie with a free-form rough crust that you wrap unsymmetrically and messily around a pile of sugared fruit. It involves no crimping, primping and decorating. You may use any fruit or combination of fruit you choose, though I think plums, damsons and greengages are pretty damn fine.

→ Cut PLUMS or GREENGAGES in half and remove the stones. DAMSONS you have to leave unstoned; GOOSEBERRIES should be topped and tailed; APPLES peeled, quartered, cored and cut into chunks.

→ Preheat the oven to 200°C/400°F/Gas 6. Make the PASTRY (see p. 104) and roll out into a large circle, about 30cm/12in in diameter, and flip it from the rolling pin into a greased baking

unsalted butter	110g/4oz
OR half butter, half lard	

egg white to glaze
and a little extra sugar

tin. Hurl the FRUIT into the middle of it in a reckless pile and sprinkle over the SUGAR. Fold over the edges of the pastry as far as they will go without stretching them—fatal to pastry, which is shrinking by nature. The edges should very definitely not meet in the middle. Brush the pastry with EGG WHITE and scatter over a little more SUGAR, demerara if you prefer.

→ Bake for 20 minutes, then turn the oven temperature down to 180°C/350°F/Gas 4 and bake for a further 25–30 minutes until bubbling with juices and golden brown.

Pear Pies

SERVES 6

ripe but firm pears	6
unrefined caster sugar	285g/10oz
cloves	6
lemons	zest of 2
lemon juice	2 tbsp
cinnamon	1 stick
almonds, *freshly ground*	4 tbsp
bitter almond extract (Culpeper's)	a few drops
brandy	2 tbsp
soft butter	1 tbsp
puff pastry (see p. 517)	225g/8oz
egg, *beaten*, for glaze	

These are really pears stuffed with a boozy frangipane-spiced cream and wrapped in puff pastry. I leave the pear stalks on so they poke out of the bronzed leaves of buttery pastry. Easier than they sound and both beautiful and delicious.

→ Core the PEARS from their bases, leaving the stalks on. Put the CASTER SUGAR, CLOVES, ZEST, JUICE and CINNAMON in a pan with 750ml/1 pint 7fl oz water and stir together. Add the pears, bring to the boil and simmer gently for 6 minutes. Remove the pears and dry them. Reduce the syrup by letting it bubble away for 5 or 6 minutes. In a bowl, mix the ground ALMONDS with the ALMOND EXTRACT, BRANDY and BUTTER. Stuff the cored bases of the pears with this mixture.

→ Preheat the oven to 200°C/400°F/Gas 6. Roll out the PASTRY and divide into 6 pieces. Wrap each pear in a piece of pastry, brush with beaten EGG, and stand them on a baking sheet. Bake for 30 minutes or until the pastry has puffed up and turned golden. Serve with the sugar syrup and splodges of crème fraîche on the side.

Italian Pear Pie

SERVES 6

shortcrust pastry *made with 340g/12oz plain flour and 170g/6oz unsalted butter* (see p. 104)	
pears, *peeled, cored and sliced*	8
lemon juice	
light muscovado sugar	
amaretti	6 large or 12 small
cinnamon	a knife point
Rose-flower Water Icing	
unrefined caster sugar	2 tbsp
unsalted butter	55g/2oz
rose-flower water	3 tbsp
unrefined icing sugar	110g/4oz

The Italian Pear Pie is a simple dish made festive and slightly medieval with crushed amaretti and a rose-flower water icing.

→ Preheat the oven to 200°C/400°F/Gas 6. Grease a deep, 23cm/9in pie tin and line it with a little over half the PASTRY. Toss the PEAR SLICES in a little LEMON JUICE and light MUSCOVADO SUGAR — be sparing with the sugar. Add the crushed AMARETTI and CINNAMON, then put everything into the pastry case. Cover with the rest of the pastry and make a hole for the steam to escape. Bake for 15 minutes, then turn the heat down to 180°C/350°F/Gas 4 and bake until the pie and the fruit are cooked through, about another 30 minutes.

→ Spread the icing (see below) over the warm pie with a palette knife and serve tepid. You can slake whipped cream with a little eau de vie de poire to serve with it if you feel suitably epicurean.

Rose-flower Water Icing
→ Put the CASTER SUGAR, BUTTER and ROSE-FLOWER WATER into a pan and bring to boiling point. Tip the mixture on to the sifted ICING SUGAR in a bowl and beat until satiny smooth.

Blackcurrant Pie

SERVES 6–8

blackcurrants	675g/1½lb
unrefined granulated sugar	110g/4oz, or to taste
cornflour	1 tbsp
demerara sugar for sprinkling	
shortcrust pastry *made with 340g/12oz flour and 170g/6oz unsalted butter* (see p. 104)	
egg, *beaten*	1

Strip the BLACKCURRANTS from their stems with the tines of a fork. Throw the fruit into a bowl, toss it with the SUGAR, and leave to macerate for about 30 minutes. Pour off the accumulated juice into a small bowl, sift in the CORNFLOUR, and stir together until smooth.

→ Preheat the oven to 200°C/400°F/Gas 6. Line a greased deep pie dish with just over half the PASTRY, add the fruits, then tip over the juice. Roll out the topcoat of pastry, and lay it over the fruit, sealing the edges with the tines of a fork. Cut holes for the steam to escape through and brush with beaten EGG.

→ Bake for 20 minutes, then turn the heat down to 180°C/350°F/Gas 4 and continue to cook for a further 30 minutes or until golden brown. Brush with a little more beaten EGG, and sprinkle with a handful of DEMERARA SUGAR at half time if you want a crunchy sugared top. Serve hot with plenty of thin pouring cream.

Gooseberry Pie

SERVES 6

gooseberries, *topped and tailed*	675g/1½lb
demerara sugar	110g/4oz or to taste
cornflour	2 dsrtsp
Rock's elderflower cordial, or your own home-made (optional)	2 tbsp
unsalted butter	30g/1oz
shortcrust pastry *made with 225g/8oz flour and 110g/4oz unsalted butter* (see p. 104)	
egg, *beaten*, for glaze	

Summer berries make the most magical pies, and gooseberries are one of the best. The berries can be very sharp at the beginning of the season, so adjust the amount of sugar accordingly.

→ Put the GOOSEBERRIES in a large bowl and throw over nearly all of the DEMERARA SUGAR. Sift over the CORNFLOUR and add the ELDERFLOWER if you are using it. Leave to macerate for at least 15 minutes, then pour the contents into the bottom of your pie dish. Dot with BUTTER. Make the PASTRY and chill in the fridge.

→ Preheat the oven to 200°C/400°F/Gas 6. Brush the rim of the pie dish with water and stick a strip of pastry around it. Brush the strip with more water and stick the pastry top to it, crimping the edges together and decorating if you feel like it. If you want to cut a shape out of the top of the pastry, do it before you lower it on to the pie dish. Brush the top with beaten EGG, and, if you have cut out shapes, sprinkle the rest of the DEMERARA over the exposed fruit.

→ Cook for 15 minutes, then turn the heat down to 180°C/350°F/Gas 5 and continue to cook for 30 minutes until the fruit is cooked through and bubbling and the sugar has turned a dark treacly brown. Serve hot or warm with home-made custard (see p. 514) or cream if you prefer.

Gooseberry Meringue Pie

SERVES 6

shortcrust pastry *made with 225g/8oz flour and 110g/4oz unsalted butter* (see p. 104)	
unsalted butter	55g/2oz
demerara sugar	2 tbsp
gooseberries, *topped and tailed*	450g/1lb
large egg whites	3
egg yolk	1
flour	1 tbsp
unrefined sugar	85g/3oz

The meringue used here is unusual in that there is an egg yolk folded into the white, but the dry, crunchy texture works beautifully with the sharp, seedy-textured fruit.

→ Bake the PASTRY blind in a 23cm/9in tart tin (see p. 104). Melt the BUTTER in a large, heavy-bottomed frying pan, then add the DEMERARA SUGAR. When it has turned to liquid caramel, throw in the GOOSEBERRIES in a single layer. Cover and cook briefly, until the skin of the berries changes colour, then remove the pan from the heat. Cool the fruit and check the sugar levels for taste before putting it into the pastry case.

→ Preheat the oven to 140°C/275°F/Gas 1. Whisk the EGG WHITES stiffly, then fold in the YOLK, followed by the FLOUR and SUGAR sifted together. Cover the top of the pie with meringue, then bake in the oven for 40 minutes, until the top is cooked and golden. Serve hot, warm or cold with cream.

Chocolate Pie with Mocha Cream

SERVES 8

Cookie-crumb base

chocolate cookies, plain, not covered in chocolate	225g/8oz
Green and Black's organic cocoa powder	1 tbsp
unsalted butter, *melted*	110g/4oz

Filling

eggs	2
egg yolks	3
caster sugar	40g/1½oz
unsalted butter	140g/5oz
best bitter chocolate with 70% cocoa solids, *broken into pieces*	200g/7oz

Topping

instant espresso coffee	2 tsp
double cream, Jersey if possible	300ml/10fl oz
unrefined icing sugar	1–2 tbsp

Yes, this chocolate pie is rich, heavy, cold, dark, wicked, girth—rather than death—defying, and utterly, utterly seductive. What more could you want from a pudding, nay, from life itself!

→ Put the COOKIES and cocoa powder in a food processor and blitz to crumbs. Add the melted BUTTER and process again to combine. Take a 23cm/9in tart tin, deep rather than shallow and with a removable base, line with the mixture, and refrigerate.

→ To make the FILLING, put the EGGS, YOLKS and CASTER SUGAR into a bowl and beat together vigorously, preferably with an electric whisk, until thick and fluffy. Melt the BUTTER and CHOCOLATE together in a bowl over a saucepan of barely simmering water—don't let the bottom of the bowl touch it—and stir until smooth. Pour onto the egg mixture while still warm, and beat together briefly until well amalgamated. Pour into the cold, crumb crust and refrigerate for a few hours.

→ Up to an hour before you want to eat the pudding, dissolve the instant ESPRESSO in 2 tablespoons of the CREAM. Whip the rest of the cream and add the dissolved espresso. Sift over the first tablespoon of ICING SUGAR and continue to beat until it holds softly. Spoon over the pie and refrigerate for an hour before serving. You can grate a little CHOCOLATE finely over the top and add the other spoonful of ICING SUGAR if you feel like it.

Key Lime Pie

SERVES 6–8

egg yolks	4
sweetened condensed milk	1 × 400g/14oz can
lime, *finely grated zest*	1 tsp
lime juice, *freshly squeezed*	150ml/5fl oz
double cream	240ml/8fl oz
unrefined caster sugar	1 tbsp
shortcust tart shell, *fully baked in 23cm/9in tin (see p. 104)*	

This is my rendering of the American classic. It is difficult to find key lime juice, which is bottled in Key West in Florida and has a slightly fizzy, sherberty quality, but good organic limes make a great pie. I normally avoid any contact with condensed milk, but this pie needs it!

→ Preheat the oven to 180°C/350°F/Gas 4. Whisk together the EGG YOLKS, CONDENSED MILK and half the LIME ZEST, then slowly stir in the LIME JUICE. Pour the mixture into the PASTRY SHELL and bake it for 20 minutes. Let the pie cool on a wire rack before refrigerating it for about 2 hours or until chilled.

→ Decorate the top with pinches of LIME ZEST. If you want to go very rich, whip the DOUBLE CREAM, fold in the SUGAR and the rest of the LIME ZEST, then dollop it on top of the pie.

Pecan Pie

SERVES 6–8

dark muscovado sugar	200g/7oz
unsalted butter	85g/3oz
single cream	240ml/8fl oz
cornflour	2 heaped tbsp
pure vanilla extract	1 tsp
egg yolks	2
pecan nuts	110g/4oz
shortcrust pastry *made with 110g/4oz flour and 55g/2oz unsalted butter* (see p. 104)	

Meringue top (optional)

egg whites	3
unrefined caster sugar	55g/2oz

With its gloopy, butterscotch middle, soft nuttiness and crisp pastry, this is the perfect pie for a good Sunday lunch or a special occasion. You can gild the lily and add a topping of marshmallowy meringue, or you can leave well alone, save for the cold stream of pouring cream that matches ivory with fudgy, caramel brown.

→ Preheat the oven to 200°C/400°F/Gas 6. Line a greased 23cm/9in tart tin with the rolled-out PASTRY, then bake blind for 20 minutes (see p. 104). Turn the oven down to 180°C/350°F/Gas 4. Remove the greaseproof paper and beans and return the pastry to the oven for a further 5 minutes.

→ Pour the SUGAR, BUTTER and CREAM into the top of a double boiler, sift over the CORNFLOUR, and whisk over a gentle heat until the mixture thickens and is wondrously free of lumps. Off the heat, add the VANILLA EXTRACT and whisk in the EGG YOLKS, one at a time. Then stir in the PECAN NUTS and scrape the mixture into the pastry shell.

→ If you're adding MERINGUE, whisk the EGG WHITES until stiff, add a third of the SUGAR and whisk again. Fold in the next third of SUGAR, pile the meringue on to the pecan filling and sprinkle over the remaining SUGAR. Bake at 180°C/350°F/Gas 4 for 20 minutes or until the meringue has bronzed and crisped to a crackling top. Remove from the oven and leave for a few minutes before serving.

Sugar-Topped Cherry Pie

SERVES 6

cherries, pre-stoned weight	750g/1lb 10oz
kirsch	1–2 tbsp
unrefined sugar	110g/4oz
cornflour	2 dsrtsp
shortcrust pastry *made with 285g/10oz flour and 140g/5oz unsalted butter* (see p. 104)	
egg, *beaten*, for glaze	1
demerara sugar	1 tbsp

→ Stone the CHERRIES, then macerate them in a large bowl with the KIRSCH and SUGAR for an hour or so. Pour off the juice that has collected into a smaller bowl and stir in the sifted CORNFLOUR to thicken it. Return the thickened juice to the cherries. Make the PASTRY (see p. 104) and chill.

→ Preheat the oven to 200°C/400°F/Gas 6. Divide the pastry into roughly two-thirds and one-third. Roll out the larger piece for the base of the pie and drop it into a greased pie dish. Pour in the cherry mixture. Roll out the second piece of pastry and place it over the cherries, crimping the edges together well with the tines of a fork. Brush the top with beaten EGG, then throw on the DEMERARA. Make a couple of slashes in the crust for the steam to escape through and bake the pie for about 40 minutes, or until the top has browned. Serve warm or at room temperature with cream or ice cream.

Lemon Meringue Pie

SERVES 6

shortcrust pastry *made with 170g/6oz flour and 85g/3oz unsalted butter* (see p. 104)	
egg white, *beaten*	1
organic lemons	juice and *grated* zest of 3
cornflour	45g/1½oz
water	300ml/10fl oz
large egg yolks	3
vanilla caster sugar	85g/3oz
unsalted butter, *cut into small pieces*	55g/2oz
Meringue	
large egg whites	3
vanilla caster sugar	110g/4oz

A classic, great for Sunday lunch or a dinner for friends. You have to have a crisp crackle of meringue, something that rustles magically when you tap it or break into it with a knife, and the interior should be mallowy and soft. This pudding is all about contrasts. The lemon should make your tongue smart and the meringue should shock it back to life with sweetness.

→ Preheat the oven to 190°C/375°F/Gas 5. Make the shortcrust PASTRY (see p. 104). Line a 23cm/9in tart tin and chill. Bake the pastry blind for 15 minutes, then remove the beans, brush the pastry with beaten EGG WHITE, and return to the oven for 5 minutes. Remove the pastry case from the oven and turn the heat down to 180°C/350°F/Gas 4.

→ Put the LEMON ZEST AND JUICE in the top of a double boiler. Add the CORNFLOUR and whisk in with 2 tablespoons of the WATER until you have a smooth paste. Bring the remaining WATER to the boil, add to the lemon mixture and keep whisking over simmering water until the mixture is thick and bubbling. Remove from the heat and whisk in the EGG YOLKS, SUGAR and BUTTER. Leave to cool slightly while you make the meringue.

→ Whisk the EGG WHITES until stiff, scatter in one-third of the SUGAR, and whisk again until stiff. Fold in another third of the SUGAR with a metal spoon. Spread the lemon mixture over the pastry. Pile the meringue on top and sprinkle it with the remaining sugar. Bake for 15–20 minutes. Allow to cool slightly, then turn out. Best served with thin cream.

Bakewell Tart

SERVES 8

shortcrust pastry *made with 170g/6oz flour and 85g/3oz unsalted butter* (see p. 104)	
really good raspberry jam	170g/6oz
unsalted butter	110g/4oz
vanilla sugar	110g/4oz
ground almonds	110g/4oz
organic egg yolks	4
organic egg whites	3
bitter almond extract (Culpeper's)	1 tsp
flaked almonds	1 handful

This is as classic a tart as lemon meringue, and a real old favourite that you will always have the ingredients for in your store cupboard. It really doesn't matter if you use raspberry, strawberry, apricot or blackcurrant jam for the middle or something more esoteric altogether like damson or rhubarb.

→ Make the shortcrust PASTRY in the usual way (see p. 104) and use to line a 23cm/9in tart tin. Chill. Preheat the oven to 200°C/400°F/Gas 6. Spread a layer of the JAM generously over the pastry base.

→ Melt the BUTTER until it smells nutty. Whisk together the SUGAR, GROUND ALMONDS, EGG YOLKS AND WHITES and ALMOND EXTRACT, then pour in the hot butter and whisk to amalgamate. Pour this over the jam and bake for about 30 minutes until lightly browned and just set. After 25 minutes, strew the FLAKED ALMONDS over the top of the tart, so they get a chance to brown slightly. A tart to be eaten 20 minutes after it comes out of the oven, warm, with some cold, thin cream.

Tarte aux Pommes

SERVES 6–8

cooking apples	450g/1lb
vanilla sugar	170–200g/ 6–7oz
vanilla pod, *split lengthways*	1
eating apples such as Cox's	450g/1lb
butter, *melted*	45g/1½oz
Pâte sucrée	
flour	170g/6oz
sea salt	1 pinch
unsalted butter	85g/3oz
icing sugar	1 tbsp
organic egg yolks	2

French apple tarts are legendary and there are many different versions. This one has an underbelly of sharp apple purée beneath the little buttery sugared crescents of apple. Pâte sucrée (sweet pastry) makes a good contrast with the tartness of the purée.

→ Make the PÂTE SUCRÉE (see p. 516). Chill, then roll out and line a 23cm/9in tart tin.

→ Peel, core and roughly chop the COOKING APPLES. Stew them very gently with 110g/4oz of the SUGAR and the VANILLA POD and its scraped-out SEEDS in a covered saucepan until almost puréed. You can then sieve the apples if you wish, or merely leave them to cool, depending on whether you prefer a coarsely textured or smooth result. Taste for sharpness, and stir in a bit more SUGAR if you have a wickedly sweet tooth.

→ Preheat the oven to 200°C/400°F/Gas 6. When the apples are cold, fill the uncooked pastry case with your apple purée. Peel and slice the EATING APPLES and arrange them over the purée as artistically as you like. Brush the slices with the melted BUTTER and sprinkle over the remaining SUGAR. Bake for about 35 minutes.

→ Serve hot, with cold pouring cream. If you want to add a sophisticated note to what is essentially rustic food, make a sabayon (see p. 454) with some Calvados or cider.

Apple Galette

SERVES 8

Dough

strong white organic bread flour	200g/7oz
dried yeast	2 tsp
salt	1½ tsp
eggs	2
unsalted butter, *melted*	5 tbsp
water OR milk *at blood heat*	about 150ml/5fl oz
toasted nuts—hazelnuts, almonds or walnuts, *chopped* (optional)	1 handful

Topping

Cox's apples	8
unsalted butter	150g/5oz
vanilla sugar	100g/3½oz
ground cinnamon	1 tsp
ground allspice (optional)	1 tsp
double cream	150ml/5fl oz
organic egg	1
extra sugar	
extra nuts (optional)	

A galette is a deliciously crisped, doughy crust harbouring a juice-sodden layer of apples, plums, greengages, apricots, or any of the scented fruits. You can scatter chopped nuts into the dough and over the fruit if you desire. This is not a dish that will good-temperedly reheat; it is to be eaten straight from the oven, or warm. However, you can keep the fruit and the rolled-out dough in the fridge, and finish off the pudding when you need it.

→ First, make the DOUGH. Mix together the FLOUR, YEAST and SALT, then add the EGGS, BUTTER and LIQUID to make a soft, coherent and unsticky dough. Knead by hand or in a food processor. Put the dough in a bowl inside a plastic bag and seal; leave to double in size for at least an hour.

→ Turn out and punch down the dough, throwing in a handful of NUTS if you feel like it. Lightly oil the bowl, roll the dough in it gently, and seal in a plastic bag for a second rise—30 minutes should be enough this time. Punch down again and refrigerate; this dough will not roll out properly if it isn't chilled, it will shrink back temperamentally each time you attempt to roll it. It should then be rolled out to about a 30cm/12in circle and placed on a well-greased baking sheet or pizza plate.

→ Peel and core the APPLES and cut into wedges. Fry them in the BUTTER until gently coloured, and then sprinkle them with the SUGAR and SPICE mixture. Let them begin to caramelise, then remove from the heat and cool to tepid.

→ If you are using plums or apricots, make a cut along the obvious division of the fruit and put about 700g/1½lb fruit and 180g/6oz sugar in a baking dish with a tablespoon of water. Bake until soft enough to extract the stones.

→ Preheat the oven to 200°C/400°F/Gas 6. Leaving 2.5cm/1in free at the edge, arrange the fruit and juices over the dough, put in a warm place for 20 minutes, then bake for 25 minutes.

→ Beat the CREAM, EGG and a little SUGAR together and pour over as much of it as you can—the edge will have risen slightly. Scatter over the NUTS if you are using them and cook until set, roughly 10 minutes.

Spelt Apple Tart with Rosemary and Cinnamon Butter

SERVES 6

Spelt pastry

spelt flour	225g/8oz
unsalted butter, *chilled and cut into cubes*	110g/4oz
granulated sugar (optional)	1 heaped tbsp

Filling

medium-sized cooking apples	5
unrefined granulated sugar	3 tbsp, or to taste
Calvados OR water	1 tbsp
butter	30g/1oz

Topping

large eating apples	2
lemon	juice of ½
unsalted butter	55g/2oz
rosemary needles, *very finely chopped*	1 tsp
cinnamon, *ground from a cinnamon stick*	1 tsp
vanilla caster sugar for the top	

Spelt is an ancient kind of wheat which has been used since Egyptian times. It is wonderfully nutty and full of minerals. This sugared spelt pastry is deliciously crisp and buttery, almost shortbread-textured.

→ Heat the oven to 200°C/400°F/Gas 6. Sieve the SPELT FLOUR into a food processor—spelt takes longer to sieve than conventional flour—and at the end, tip the bran into the bowl with the sieved flour. Add the BUTTER and process briefly, then add the SUGAR if you are using it. Process briefly before adding a tablespoon of ICE-COLD WATER, and continue to the point where the pastry starts to form a ball. Wrap in clingfilm and refrigerate for at least an hour.

→ Meanwhile, peel, core and chop the COOKING APPLES into chunks and put them in a pan with the SUGAR and CALVADOS OR WATER. Cook over a medium heat, stirring to help them break down and allowing the juice to run. Then begin to reduce. Keep cooking the apples until you have a purée that is thick and not watery. Remove from the heat and stir in the butter.

→ Grease a 23cm/9in tart ring. Roll out the PASTRY and line the tart case. Prick the base and edges with a fork. Place a sheet of greaseproof paper or foil to cover the pastry, fill it with dried beans and cook for 10 minutes. Remove the greaseproof paper and beans and return the tart case to the oven for 5 minutes.

→ Peel and slice the EATING APPLES into slices the thickness of a pound coin and squeeze over some LEMON JUICE to stop them going brown. Melt the BUTTER in a small pan and add the ROSEMARY NEEDLES when it begins to bubble. Swirl the pan until the butter begins to turn from gold to brown, add the CINNAMON and remove from the heat.

→ Fill the tart case with the cooled apple purée, then top with a layer of apple pieces. Brush them with the rosemary butter, making sure the rosemary is evenly distributed, then shake a little SUGAR over the apple slices from a spoon. Turn the oven down to 180°C/350°F/Gas 4 and cook until the pastry is cooked through and the apples browned. This should take about 30–40 minutes.

→ Remove the tart from the oven and leave for at least 20 minutes. Turn out of the tart ring and serve warm with cream.

Tarte au Citron

SERVES 10

Pastry

plain flour	450g/1lb
unrefined icing sugar	140g/5oz
best unsalted butter, *cubed and cold*	225g/8oz
vanilla pod	*scooped-out seeds from* 1
organic egg yolks	2

Filling

organic eggs	9
unrefined vanilla caster sugar	340g/12oz
organic lemons	juice of 5
organic lemons	zest of 2
double cream	270ml/9fl oz

extra icing sugar to caramelise with a blow torch

These quantities are enough for a 30cm/12in tart ring, which I place directly onto a baking sheet, or the equivalent tart tin with a removable base. If you only have a smaller tart tin, make a few individual tarts with the remainder of the pastry and keep them uncooked in the fridge with the remaining lemon mixture in a jug until you want to use them.

→ Sieve the FLOUR and ICING SUGAR into a bowl and throw in the chilled, cubed BUTTER. Work to a crumb as quickly as you can, or pulse in the food processor. Add the sticky SEEDS from the vanilla pod and the EGG YOLKS, and work into a ball, adding a little ICE-COLD WATER if you need to, a tablespoon at most. Wrap in clingfilm and put in the fridge for 30 minutes.

→ Heat the oven to 180°C/350°F/Gas 4. Flour your marble or work surface and the rolling pin, then roll the PASTRY out to a circle just a little bigger than the ring or tart tin. Grease the tin or the inside of the ring and the baking tray. Gently ease the pastry over the back of the rolling pin and into the tin. It will shrink, so work it loosely into the tin and don't stretch it. Let the overhang remain at this stage. Bake blind for 15 minutes (see p. 104), remove the foil and beans, cut off the shrunken overhang of pastry and prick the bottom and sides of the pastry with the tines of a fork to prevent them bubbling up before returning the tart base to the oven for 5 minutes.

→ Meanwhile make the FILLING. Whisk the EGGS with the SUGAR and LEMON ZEST, then stir in the LEMON JUICE and fold in the CREAM. Put the mixture in a jug so it is easier to pour into the tart case.

→ Reduce the oven temperature to 130°C/250°F/Gas ½. Slide the tart case as far out of the oven as you dare and pour in the filling up to the top of the pastry. Gently push the tart back into the oven and cook for 30 minutes or until the centre is still juddery without being liquid. The custard will go on cooking out of the oven and you don't want it to set solid. Cool completely.

→ Heat the grill. Sieve a thin layer of ICING SUGAR over the top of the tart and flash it under the grill briefly without letting the pastry edges burn. Cover the pastry edges with a strip of foil if necessary to stop them burning. Or get out your blowtorch and blow. Serve warm or cold. This tart has to be made only 3 or 4 hours at the most before you serve it. Pastry is never the same if left for a day or overnight.

Apricot Tart

SERVES 6–8

shortcrust pastry case, *chilled* (p. 104)	1 × 23cm/9in
egg white, *beaten*	1
apricots, *halved and stoned*	about 17 or 18
vanilla caster sugar	285g/10oz
water	600ml/1 pint
sour cream	120ml/4fl oz
double cream	170ml/6fl oz
organic eggs	2
caster sugar	to taste
unsalted butter	55g/2oz

→ Preheat the oven to 200°C/400°F/Gas 6. Bake the PASTRY blind for 15 minutes (see p. 104), then remove the beans, prick the base with a fork, brush with beaten EGG WHITE, and return to the oven for a further 5 minutes. Turn the heat up to 220°C/425°F/Gas 7.

→ Make a syrup with the VANILLA CASTER SUGAR and WATER. Poach the APRICOTS gently in the syrup until barely tender and still holding their shape. Drain and reserve the syrup. Beat the SOUR and DOUBLE CREAM with the EGGS, and SWEETEN to taste. Melt the BUTTER and pour it straight into the cream mixture, stirring it in.

→ Place the apricots cut side up in the pastry case, starting at the edge and working in circles, slightly overlapping. Put the pastry case on the oven shelf, half out of the oven, then pour the custard in from a jug. Bake until tremblingly set and browned, about 20–25 minutes. Remove from the oven and leave to cool slightly.

→ Meanwhile, boil down the apricot poaching syrup to make a glaze, which you can brush on just before you are ready to eat the tart.

Hazelnut and Apricot Tart

SERVES 8

Hunza apricots	225g/8oz
apple juice	
shortcrust pastry case, *chilled* (see p. 104)	1 × 23cm/9in
unsalted butter	110g/4oz
organic egg yolks	4
organic egg whites	3
vanilla sugar	85g/3oz
ground hazelnuts	110g/4oz
single cream (optional)	a few tbsp

→ Soak the APRICOTS in APPLE JUICE until soft, then stew, stone and purée.

→ Preheat the oven to 200°C/400°F/Gas 6. Spread the puréed apricots over the PASTRY base. Melt the BUTTER until it is golden brown. Beat the EGG YOLKS AND WHITES together with the SUGAR. Stir in the melted butter, then the ground HAZELNUTS. The mixture should be dropping consistency—if it doesn't feel quite slack enough you could whisk in a little SINGLE CREAM. Pour into the pastry case and bake for about 30 minutes, until the filling is set. Serve hot or warm.

Apricot Frangipane Tart

SᴇʀᴠᴇS 8

firm blush apricots	16
rich puff pastry (see p. 517)	200g/7oz
soft-set apricot preserve	50g/scant 2oz
Frangipane	
ground almonds	240g/8oz
apricot kernels	3
caster sugar	150g/5oz
unsalted butter, *softened*	200g/7oz
organic eggs	3
plain flour	100g/3½oz

This is a recipe developed by Dan Lepard, bread guru at Baker and Spice in London, after a story told him by a French pâtissier.

> *'The stone of a soft fruit contains not just the heart of the flavour, but also the knowledge of the plant that bore it. It is essential to use a stone when cooking any fruit.'*

The apricots stand proud in this tart, with beautifully singed tips. If you don't want to make your own puff pastry, buy an all-butter brand.

→ Preheat the oven to 180°C/350°F/Gas 4. Halve the ᴀᴘʀɪᴄᴏᴛS with a small, sharp knife, and remove the stones. Crack three of the stones with a hammer to extract the kernels.

→ Roll out the pastry into a thin circle large enough to cover and overlap the sides of a 25cm/10in tart ring. Place the ring on a baking sheet lined with greaseproof paper. Gently press the pastry down into the ring, and prick the base of the pastry lightly with a fork. Put the pastry in the fridge to chill for 10–15 minutes while you make the frangipane (see below).

→ Spread the frangipane over the base of the tart, then sit the apricot halves upright in the frangipane. Place the tart in the centre of the oven and bake for 15 minutes. Reduce the heat to 160°C/325°F/Gas 3 and continue baking for 35–45 minutes, until the pastry is crisp and the frangipane light brown in colour. Warm the ᴀᴘʀɪᴄᴏᴛ ᴘʀᴇSᴇʀᴠᴇ in a saucepan over a low heat, with a little ᴡᴀᴛᴇʀ to make a syrup, and brush this over the tart. Turn out and serve warm with crème fraîche.

Frangipane

→ For the ꜰʀᴀɴɢɪᴘᴀɴᴇ, place the ᴀʟᴍᴏɴᴅS, ᴀᴘʀɪᴄᴏᴛ ᴋᴇʀɴᴇʟS and Sᴜɢᴀʀ in a food processor and process until the kernels have blended with the sugar and almonds. Next add the ʙᴜᴛᴛᴇʀ, and mix until pale and smooth. Beat in the ᴇɢɢS, one by one, then finally lightly beat in the ꜰʟᴏᴜʀ. Transfer the mixture to a small container and leave in a cool place until needed.

Lemon Ice Cream Tart with a Ginger Crust

SERVES 8

Ginger crust

unsalted butter	110g/4oz
ginger biscuits	400g/14oz

Ice cream

white wine	150ml/5fl oz
dry Marsala OR brandy	2 tbsp
organic lemons	juice and *grated* zest of 2
organic orange	juice and *grated* zest of 1
unrefined vanilla caster sugar	4 tbsp
double cream	500ml/18fl oz

→ Line the base of a loose-bottomed tart tin, about 20cm/8in in diameter, with a single piece of greaseproof paper. Melt the BUTTER in a small pan. Crush the BISCUITS in a food processor or bash them in a plastic bag with a rolling pin—you want a fine powder. Stir the biscuits into the butter. Line the base of the tin with the buttered crumbs, pushing some up the sides as far as you can. It doesn't matter if the edges are rough. Put the crumb-lined tin in the freezer.

→ Pour the WINE into the bowl of a food mixer or a large mixing bowl. Add the MARSALA or BRANDY and the finely grated ZEST of the lemons and the orange. Squeeze one of the lemons and add the JUICE. Reserve the orange for later. Add the SUGAR and CREAM to the wine and zest mixture and beat slowly until thick. You want the consistency to be soft and thick, so that it lies in soft folds rather than standing in stiff peaks. Scrape the mixture into the crumb-lined tart tin and freeze for at least four hours.

→ Remove from the freezer 15–20 minutes before you intend to serve it. I find it easier to remove the tart from the tin while it is still frozen, running a palette knife around the edge first. Cut the PEEL from the orange, slice the flesh thinly and serve at the side of each slice. It can be difficult to push the base up and remove the sides for this tart, so if it looks as though it won't work, serve straight from the tart tin.

Strawberry Tart

This is the spirit of summer, the tart that the first June strawberries are all about, set into the thickly creamy, vanilla-scented crème pâtissière right up to their middles and crowned with a sticky gloop of redcurrant. This is not a tart to be served up the following day; the crème pâtissière tends to soften and dampen the pastry within a few hours of making. No hardship there, just eat it all up at one sitting.

SERVES 8 GREEDY PEOPLE

strawberries	about 1kg/2¼lb
redcurrant jelly	about 4 tbsp
Pâte sucrée	
flour	225g/8oz
unsalted butter	110g/4oz
unrefined icing sugar	1 tbsp
vanilla pod	*scooped out insides* of 1
organic egg yolks	2
cold water	a little
Crème Pâtissière	
Jersey milk	340ml/12fl oz
double cream	150ml/5fl oz
vanilla pod, *split lengthways, the seeds scooped out with the sharp tip of a teaspoon*	1
large organic egg	1
large egg yolks	3
vanilla caster sugar	75g/2½oz
cornflour	45g/1½oz

→ Make the PÂTE SUCRÉE (p. 516) and chill for at least an hour. Preheat the oven to 200°C/400°F/Gas 6. Line a 30cm/12in tart tin with the pastry and bake blind (see p. 516), then remove the beans and return to the oven for 10–15 minutes, until golden and cooked. Watch closely: the edges burn swiftly, and you don't want scorch marks on the bottom. Leave to cool.

→ Turn the cold pastry case out onto a plate or bread board and scrape in the CRÈME PÂTISSIÈRE (see below) with a rubber spatula. Hull the STRAWBERRIES. Starting at the edge of the tart and with the largest strawberries, place them upright into the crème pâtissière in a circle. Work your way in, using smaller strawberries for each circle. Melt the REDCURRANT JELLY with a tablespoon of WATER and brush it liberally over the strawberries and the custardy gaps. Stand back and admire before you cut into slices.

Crème Pâtissière

This is a very amenable custard to make. The cornflour stops it splitting, and you just need to beat the hell out of it to get rid of the tiny, floury lumps. To avoid a skin forming on the top of the custard when it has been cooked and is cooling, rub a little butter over the surface with a knife.

→ Pour the MILK and CREAM into a heavy-bottomed pan. Split the VANILLA POD lengthways and scoop out the seeds with a tip of a teaspoon. Add the pod and scraped-out seeds to the pan and bring to scald point over a gentle heat. Meanwhile, whisk the EGG, EGG YOLKS and SUGAR together with a balloon whisk until light, creamy and pale. Sift one-third of the CORNFLOUR into the bowl and whisk thoroughly until the mixture is smooth. Then do the same with the next third and the last third, making absolutely sure you have beaten out the lurking lumps.

→ Remove the vanilla pod from the hot milk and pour one-third of the milk into the egg and sugar mixture, whisking well. Pour this back into the rest of the milk in the pan, and continue to whisk as vigorously as you can over a gentle heat as the custard begins to thicken. Keep whisking as it simmers for another 5 minutes to cook out the floury taste, just as you do for a béchamel. Pour it into a bowl, cover and cool before using. Crème pâtissière can also be used for sweet soufflés and choux pastry, either as is or flavoured with chocolate.

Brûléed Blackcurrant or Blueberry Tart

SERVES 6

shortcrust pastry *made with 170g/6oz flour, 1 tbsp caster sugar and 85g/3oz butter* (see p. 104)	
blackcurrants OR blueberries	300g/10oz
ground cinnamon	1 pinch
light muscovado sugar	a little
large eggs	2
egg yolks	2
double cream	250ml/8fl oz
kirsch	4 tbsp
granulated sugar	about 3 tbsp

This is a real show-off of a tart, which I started making when my children gave me a blowtorch for Christmas one year. It is still a fantastic thrill aiming a jet of blue flame at the sugary surface and watching the beaded brown bubbles form, crystallise, and turn into a caramelised mahogany sheet. It is just as much of a thrill to crack it, like an egg, with the back of a spoon, and eat the splintery shards of sugar with the strong, tart blackcurrants. If you use blueberries, the cinnamon works equally as well; the result is just milder to the palate, as you would expect.

→ Make SHORTCRUST PASTRY (p. 104), using 1 tablespoon caster sugar to sweeten it. Chill, then roll out and line a 23cm/9in tart tin. Preheat the oven to 190°C/375°F/Gas 5. Bake the pastry blind for 10 minutes (see p. 104), then remove the beans and bake for a further 10 minutes. Remove the pastry from the oven and turn the heat down to 180°C/350°F/Gas 4.

→ Put the FRUIT in a saucepan with 2 tablespoons of WATER and a pinch of CINNAMON, and simmer very briefly. Sweeten to taste with light MUSCOVADO SUGAR. In a bowl, beat together the EGGS, YOLKS, CREAM and KIRSCH, and add a little more SUGAR to taste. Place a single layer of fruit in the pastry case, then pour in the cream mixture and return to the oven for about 30 minutes, until just firm but with a slightly 'sad' centre. Leave to cool.

→ Just before you want to serve it, strew a thin layer of GRANU-LATED SUGAR over the tart. If you don't have a blowtorch and are going to perform this feat under the grill, cover the pastry edges with a strip of foil, then blast the tart until the sugar bubbles and caramelises. The thin, burnt brown skating rink top marries beautifully with the creamy, fruity middle.

Raspberry Curd Tart

SERVES 8

Raspberry curd

raspberries	450g/1lb
organic eggs	2
organic egg yolks	3
unrefined caster sugar	110g/4oz
unsalted butter	110g/4oz

Sweetcrust pastry

flour	225g/8oz
unsalted butter, fridge-cold	110g/4oz
unrefined organic icing sugar	2 tbsp
vanilla pod	scraped-out seeds from 1
organic egg yolk	1
ice-cold water	a little

This should be served fridge-cold so that set curd and crisp pastry vie for attention and contrast. The curd is not stiff enough to stay entirely with the pastry base when you cut into the tart, but don't let that worry you. Once you taste it you will know why. It is quite simply so delicious, the fondant texture so perfect, it doesn't matter.

→ Sift the FLOUR into a large bowl and add the cubed BUTTER straight from the fridge. Sift in the ICING SUGAR and add the VANILLA SEEDS. Work quickly to a crumb with your fingers. Add the beaten EGG and work it in with a tablespoon of COLD WATER. It should cohere without any more water fairly quickly, but if it doesn't, add another tablespoon. Form the pastry into a ball and wrap it in clingfilm. Put it in the fridge to rest for an hour while you make and cool the RASPBERRY CURD.

→ Throw the RASPBERRIES into a blender and blitz them thoroughly. Pass them through a nylon sieve into a bowl, pressing as rigorously as your wrist and wooden spoon allow. In a separate bowl, beat together the EGGS, extra YOLKS and the SUGAR.

→ I make my curds in an enormous Le Creuset enamel-bottomed pan; the large surface area makes the curd set quicker. Melt the BUTTER in the pan over a very gentle heat, then stir in the egg and sugar mixture and the sieved fruit. Whisk continuously over a low heat until the whole mixture comes together, between 5 and 10 minutes later. Remove from the heat—the idea is to heat rather than cook the fruit, which would then lose some of its raw flavour and its taste. Pour the curd into a bowl and leave to cool. You can cover it with clingfilm and leave it in the fridge for several days, or use it as soon as it is cool.

→ Grease and line a tart case with the pastry and bake blind for 20 minutes at 200°C/400°F/Gas 6. Remove the beans and foil, dock the tart with the tines of a fork and return it to the oven for about 8 minutes to dry and crisp the pastry. It should have begun to colour but not brown. Set aside to cool.

→ When cold, scrape the curd into the tart shell and place the tart in the fridge overnight or for at least 6 hours. Remove the sides of the tart case and slide the tart off its base onto a large white plate to serve. No cream required here; the intense raspberry and butter richness is all.

Vanilla and Raspberry Tart

SERVES 6–8

pâte sucrée (see p. 516)
*made with 170g/6oz flour
and 85g/3oz unsalted butter*

organic double cream	300ml/10fl oz
crème fraîche	100ml/3½fl oz
Jersey milk	about 200ml/7fl oz
vanilla pod, *split*	1
egg yolks	6
vanilla sugar	about 3 dsrtsp
vanilla extract	1–2 tsp
raspberries	300g/10oz

→ Preheat the oven to 180°C/350°F/Gas 4. Make a PÂTE SUCRÉE (p. 516) and chill, then roll out and line a 23cm/9in tart tin. Bake the pastry case blind for 10 minutes, then remove the beans, prick the base with a fork, brush lightly with beaten EGG white, and return to the oven for 5 minutes.

→ Scald the CREAMS and MILK with the VANILLA POD and its SCRAPED-OUT INSIDES. Put the YOLKS into a 900ml/1½ pint measuring jug and whisk in 2 dessertspoons of the VANILLA SUGAR. Add the VANILLA EXTRACT, 1 teaspoon to start with. Whisk in the scalded creams, taste, and add more vanilla extract if necessary. I like mine strongly, but not overpoweringly, vanilla-ey. Add the last spoon of sugar if you think you need it.

→ Pull the tart case half out of the oven and shoot the RASPBERRIES on to it in a single, generous layer. Pour in the custard from the jug: this is the easiest, quickest way to decant liquid into a tart and ensure it carries on cooking, doesn't go soggy, and doesn't do the dreaded trick of seeping out of the pastry case and anointing the oven. Turn the oven down to 170°C/325°F/Gas 3 and bake for 40–50 minutes. Check after 40, and if set with a slight wobble, remove and leave to cool for 15–20 minutes. Turn out and eat warm.

St Clement's and Marmalade Tart

SERVES 6–8

shortcrust pastry
*made with 170g/6oz
plain white flour and 85g/3oz
butter, chilled (see p. 104)*

tart orange marmalade	2–3 tbsp
oranges	*grated* rind and juice of 3
lemon	*grated* rind and juice of 1
butter, *softened*	110g/4oz
vanilla caster sugar	225g/8oz
large organic eggs, *beaten*	4

→ Preheat the oven to 180°C/350°F/Gas 4. Make the PASTRY (see p. 104) and chill. Roll out and use to line a 23cm/9in tart tin. Bake blind for 15 minutes (see p. 104), then remove the greaseproof paper and beans and bake for a further 5 minutes. Spread the MARMALADE over the bottom of the tart.

→ Put the grated ORANGE AND LEMON RIND in a bowl. Beat in the BUTTER and SUGAR, then add the beaten EGGS and whisk everything together. Place the bowl over a saucepan of simmering water and stir until the mixture has melted and dissolved. Remove from the heat and stir in the ORANGE AND LEMON JUICE. Test the sharpness and adjust if necessary. Pour over the marmalade-lined tart and return to the oven for 15–20 minutes, or until barely set. Serve warm, with thick cream if you like.

Peach, Vanilla and Amaretti Tarte Tatin

SERVES 8

Amaretti pastry

amaretti biscuits	8
plain flour, *sifted*	170g/6oz
unsalted butter, *cut into pieces*	85g/3oz
iced water	2–3 tbsp

Topping

ripe peaches	8
lemon	juice of 1
vanilla pod	1
caster sugar	85g/3oz
unsalted butter	55g/2oz

This is another of those rare occasions on which I do feel somewhat proud of making a dish I feel I can call my own. It's not the first time amaretti and peaches or peaches and vanilla have become bedfellows, but I did dream up this tart, with its amber peaches speckled in vanilla caramel and the sandy, almondy amaretti pastry that shrouds the fruit until it is upturned to serve. White peaches are the absolute best, but yellow-fleshed are fine. Use nectarines if you prefer.

→ To make the PASTRY, crush the AMARETTI in a food processor, add the FLOUR and BUTTER and process briefly to combine. Add 2–3 tablespoons ICED WATER and process until the mixture comes together. Wrap in greaseproof paper and chill for at least 20 minutes.

→ Preheat the oven to 190°C/375°F/Gas 5. Roll out the pastry to 1cm/½in more than the circumference of the pan—I use a heavy, 25cm/10in diameter Cousances enamelled cast-iron frying pan with a metal handle that I can put in the oven. Set the pastry to one side.

→ Scald the PEACHES in boiling water for 30 seconds. Peel, and sprinkle them with LEMON JUICE to prevent discolouration.

→ Split the VANILLA POD and scrape the seeds out into the SUGAR. Warm the sugar in the frying pan until it is a deep, dark brown and totally liquid. Do not stir, but move the pan around to prevent burning. Remove from the heat and dot with half of the BUTTER. Put half a peach in the middle of the sugar mixture, cut-side up. Quarter the rest, and, starting at the outside of the pan, lay them next to each other in a tightly packed wheel. Arrange the remaining quarters in an inside wheel. Dot with the rest of the BUTTER and put the pan back over the heat for 2–3 minutes to gently start the cooking.

→ Remove from the heat, cover with a mantle of pastry that you tuck down round the edges, and bake for 25–30 minutes. Remove from the oven and leave for 10 minutes before inverting onto a plate. Delicious with crème fraîche.

Pear and Ginger Tarte Tatin

SERVES 8

shortcrust pastry *made with 170g/6oz flour and 85g/3oz unsalted butter* (see p. 104)	
pears	7
lemon	juice of 1
vanilla caster sugar	85g/3oz
unsalted butter	55g/2oz
ginger syrup	2–3 tbsp
ginger, *cut into small dice*	3 knobs

→ Make the shortcrust PASTRY (p. 104) and chill. Preheat the oven to 180°C/350°F/Gas 4 and put a baking sheet in to heat. Roll out the pastry to 1cm/½in more than the circumference of the pan; I use a 25cm/10in cast-iron frying pan that I can put in the oven. Peel, core and halve the PEARS; turn them in LEMON JUICE to prevent discolouration.

→ Warm the SUGAR in the frying pan until it liquifies. The moment the sugar is treacly brown all over but not burnt, remove it from the heat and dot with half the BUTTER; it will bubble up and become absorbed. Then pour over some GINGER SYRUP, a couple of tablespoons or three; any more will be intrusive. Fit the pears head to tail in spokes, sardine style, around the pan. Or, halve the halves vertically into quarters and tuck them on their sides, then cut circular shapes to fill the gaps in the middle, core side up. Sprinkle the GINGER PIECES over the pears, and then cover the whole in a blanket of pastry, tucking it in under the pears around the edges.

→ Bake on the middle shelf of the oven on the preheated baking sheet for about 30 minutes. The juices should be bubbling stickily away around the edge. Remove from the oven and leave to cool for about 10 minutes before inverting onto a plate. The mahogany-tinted pears that gaze up at you should be perfectly cooked and glossily glazed with caramel.

→ Pass round thick cream, and a bottle of eau de vie de poire if you are lucky enough to have any, and feel the ginger's warming presence as it hits your insides.

Sally Clarke's Prune Tart

SERVES 8

Pastry

butter	110g/4oz
icing sugar	55g/scant 2oz
small egg yolks	2
plain flour	170g/6oz

Filling

pitted prunes	12
tea, cognac, orange juice	
organic egg	1
extra egg yolks	2
caster sugar	85g/3oz
vanilla pod	scraped-out contents of 1
double cream	300ml/10fl oz
milk	75ml/2½fl oz

→ Soak the PRUNES overnight in a splash each of TEA, COGNAC and ORANGE JUICE.

→ To make the PASTRY, put the BUTTER, ICING SUGAR and EGG YOLKS in a bowl or food processor and work together quickly. Blend in the FLOUR, and work to a homogeneous paste. Chill for at least 1 hour.

→ Preheat the oven to 180°C/350°F/Gas 4. Roll out the pastry thinly and line a 23cm/9in tart tin. Bake blind for about 25 minutes, or until crisp and golden. Remove from the oven and turn the heat down to 150°C/300°F/Gas 2.

→ For the FILLING, beat the EGG and YOLKS with the SUGAR and VANILLA until smooth. Heat the CREAM and MILK together until hot, and pour over the egg mixture. Strain and leave on one side to cool slightly. Place the prunes in the tart shell and pour over the custard. Bake for 20–25 minutes or until lightly set. Serve cool, with whipped cream.

Ricotta Tart with Amaretto-soaked Raisins

SERVES 6–8

shortcrust pastry *made with 170g/6oz flour and 85g/3oz butter* (see p. 104)	
amaretto	2 tbsp
organic golden raisins	110g/4oz
fresh ricotta, *drained through a muslin-lined sieve for an hour*	450g/1lb
organic eggs	5
potato flour	3 tbsp
unrefined vanilla sugar	6 tbsp
organic orange OR lemon	1
best bitter chocolate (optional)	55g/2oz
unsalted butter (optional)	55g/2oz

If you are worried about the taste of the alcohol for children, don't be. There is a back-note of almonds but no lethal taste nor effect. You may use sherry or rum instead if you can't lay your hands on a miniature bottle of this Italian treat. The soufflé-like lightness of the topping can be taken a step further with a little chocolate swirled into it. I'll leave that decision to you.

→ Preheat the oven to 190°C/375°F/Gas 5. Make the PASTRY (see p. 104) and line a 23cm/9in tart tin. Bake the tart shell blind for 15 minutes, then remove the beans and prick with the tines of a fork before returning to the oven for 5 minutes. Remove to a rack to cool and turn the oven down to 180°C/350°F/Gas 4.

→ Heat the AMARETTO gently in a pan with the GOLDEN RAISINS and remove from the heat before it comes to the boil, allowing them to absorb the liquor for 10 minutes.

→ Push the RICOTTA through the coarse disc of a mouli-légumes or sieve into a large bowl, add one EGG and four YOLKS, keeping the whites in another bowl. Mix thoroughly before adding the POTATO FLOUR and VANILLA SUGAR. Pour the raisins in their liquor into the ricotta mixture and incorporate. Grate in the ZEST OF THE ORANGE OR LEMON.

→ Whisk the EGG WHITES until they form stiff peaks, then stir one tablespoon into the ricotta mixture before lightly folding in the rest. Spoon the mixture into the tart shell. Bake for 40–50 minutes until set, but not rigidly so.

→ If you want to take things a step further, melt the CHOCOLATE and BUTTER gently in a double boiler or in a bowl over, but not touching, a pan of simmering water. Pour the barely warm mixture over the ricotta mixture and then pour it into the tart shell, minimally disturbing the chocolate with a skewer into marbled swirls. Bake as above.

Best eaten warm or cold.

Chocolate and Pralinéed Nut No-Pastry Tart

SERVES 10–12

almonds, *skinned and chopped*	55g/2oz
walnuts, *chopped*	55g/2oz
unrefined icing sugar	1 tbsp
best bitter chocolate	140g/5oz
unsalted butter, *cut into small pieces*	55g/2oz
double cream	60ml/2fl oz
organic egg yolks	5
egg whites	7
caster sugar	55g/2oz
ground almonds	55g/2oz
ground coffee	1 heaped tsp
organic cocoa powder	30g/1oz

Topping

best bitter chocolate	140g/5oz
milk	about 90ml/3fl oz

→ Put the chopped NUTS in a gratin dish, throw the ICING SUGAR over them and place under a hot grill, turning the dish every so often. You want the sugar to dissolve and adhere to the browning nuts. Watch carefully: the nuts should be brown, not black.

→ Preheat the oven to 180°C/350°F/Gas 4. BUTTER and FLOUR a 30cm/12in tart tin. Melt the CHOCOLATE in the top of a double boiler. Stir the BUTTER into it, then the CREAM and remove from the heat.

→ In a large bowl, whisk the EGG WHITES with the CASTER SUGAR until stiff, then gently fold in the YOLKS, followed by the GROUND ALMONDS, COFFEE and COCOA. Then fold in the chocolate, butter and cream mixture and mix gently to incorporate. Pour half the mixture into the tart tin, add the pralinéed nuts to cover the surface, then pour on the rest of the mixture. Cook for 15 minutes. Remove from the oven and leave to cool slightly before turning out on to a wire rack. Leave until completely cold.

→ For the top, melt the CHOCOLATE and MILK together in a double boiler and spread over the tart.

Coffee and Raspberry Bavarois Tart

SERVES 8

Cocoa crust

flour	170g/6oz
Green and Black's organic cocoa powder	2 heaped tsp
unrefined icing sugar	2 tbsp
unsalted butter, fridge-cold	85g/3oz
organic egg yolk	1
cold water	

Bavarois

good coffee, *freshly ground*	2 heaped tbsp
Jersey milk	300ml/10fl oz
vanilla pod	1
gelatine	2 leaves
organic egg yolks	4
unrefined vanilla caster sugar	85g/3oz
double Jersey cream	300ml/10fl oz
unrefined icing sugar	1 tbsp
raspberries	1 punnet, 170g/6oz or so

→ Make the PASTRY in the usual way (see p. 104): sift the DRY INGREDIENTS (including the cocoa powder) together, then work in the cubes of cold BUTTER or do the whole thing in a food processor. Add the YOLK and a tablespoon of WATER, and pulse or work until it coheres. When you roll it out, add a little COCOA to the flour on the board too. Chill, then bake blind (see p. 104) for 20–25 minutes before drying out without the beans and foil for a further 5–8 minutes. The pastry needs to be completely cooked for this recipe.

→ In the meantime, make the BAVAROIS. Put the COFFEE and milk together in a pan with the split VANILLA POD AND ITS SEEDS scraped out with a teaspoon, and bring slowly to boiling point. Remove from the heat, cover with a lid and leave to infuse for 30 minutes.

→ Soak the GELATINE LEAVES in a little cold water according to the instructions on the packet, while you make the custard. Whisk the EGG YOLKS and SUGAR together vigorously, then strain the coffee-scented milk into them through a muslin-lined sieve and whisk them together. Heat the custard slowly in the pan and whisk constantly over a low heat until it thickens and coats the proverbial spoon! This should take about 10–15 minutes.

→ Remove from the heat and stir in the squishy gelatine leaves until they have completely dissolved. Let the custard cool to tepid. Whip the CREAM with a tablespoon of unrefined ICING SUGAR until it holds softly. Fold the cream into the tepid custard, followed by the RASPBERRIES, as gently as you can so that they don't break up. Scrape the mixture into the cooled cocoa crust and set it in the fridge to chill until you can keep your hands off it no longer!

Simon Hopkinson's Chocolate Tart

SERVES 8

Pastry

butter	180g/6oz
icing sugar	75g/2½oz
egg yolks	2
plain flour	225g/8oz

Filling

organic eggs	2
organic egg yolks	3
caster sugar	45g/1½oz
unsalted butter	150g/5oz
best bitter chocolate, *broken into pieces*	200g/7oz

If there is a heaven, this is it. I speak as a hopeless chocoholic, not that I am remotely interested in weaning myself off the stuff. We had briefly corresponded, and Simon had kindly agreed to my using any of his recipes I wanted to; this one is from his book Roast Chicken and Other Stories, *which I go back to time and time again. The only tinkering I have ever done is to make a cocoa pastry with Green and Black's organic cocoa, but the original way is unparalleled.*

→ To make the PASTRY, put the BUTTER, ICING SUGAR and EGG YOLKS in a bowl or food processor and work together quickly. Blend in the FLOUR, and work to a homogeneous paste. Chill for at least 1 hour.

→ Preheat the oven to 180°C/350°F/Gas 4. Roll out the pastry as thinly as you can, and line a 25cm/10in tart tin. Bake blind for about 25 minutes, or until pale biscuit coloured, but thoroughly cooked through. Remove from the oven and increase the temperature to 190°C/375°F/Gas 5.

→ To make the FILLING, put the EGGS, YOLKS and caster sugar in a bowl and beat vigorously together, preferably with an electric whisk, until really thick and fluffy. Melt the BUTTER and CHOCOLATE together in a bowl over a saucepan of barely simmering water, stirring until smooth. Pour on to the egg mixture while just warm. Briefly beat together until well amalgamated, then pour into the pastry case. Return to the hot oven for 5 minutes, then remove and leave to cool. Serve with thick cream.

Treacle Tart

SERVES 6–8

shortcrust pastry *made with 170g/6oz flour and 85g/3oz unsalted butter* (see p. 104)	
golden syrup	up to 8 heaped tbsp
unsalted butter, *cut into small cubes*	30g/1oz
large egg, *beaten*	1
double cream	2–3 tbsp
organic lemons	*grated zest* of 2
brown breadcrumbs, preferably granary	4 heaped tbsp

The sweetest of them all, this is the divinely gloopy, gooey toothache of a tart that is impossible not to love and impossibly easy and quick to make. Sharpen it up with lemon zest and lash on the cream.

→ Preheat the oven to 190°C/375°F/Gas 5. Make the SHORTCRUST PASTRY (see p. 104). Line a 23cm/9in tart tin and chill. Save the trimmings to make a lattice top if you like. Bake blind for 15 minutes (see p. 104), then remove the beans, prick the base with a fork, and bake for 5 more minutes. Turn the heat down to 180°C/350°F/Gas 4.

→ Warm the SYRUP gently, then, off the heat, add the BUTTER and stir until melted in. Beat together the EGG and CREAM and add to the syrup, with the LEMON ZEST and BREADCRUMBS. Stir to mix evenly. The syrup should be thick with breadcrumbs and not too liquid, then pour into the pastry case. Add a lattice top if you like and bake for 25–30 minutes. The filling will have set to a gel.

→ Leave for about 20–30 minutes before serving warm — there is nothing like hot treacle tart for taking the roof off your mouth. Dollop on some clotted cream, then go for a brisk artery-clearing walk afterwards.

Walnut, Fig and Hazelnut Treacle Tart

SERVES 8

shortcrust pastry *made with 170g/6oz flour and 85g/3oz unsalted butter* (see p. 104)	
organic dried figs	8
roast hazelnuts	55g/2oz
organic walnuts	55g/2oz
unsalted butter, *softened*	110g/4oz
light muscovado sugar	110g/4oz
organic eggs	3
golden syrup	170g/6oz
blackstrap molasses	1 heaped tbsp
organic lemon	*juice and zest* of 1

However much you are addicted to treacle tart, you will certainly feel that here is something that doesn't just gnaw at your jaw with its saturation sweetness. Here you have different textures, the dense-textured graininess of the figs and the lemony sharpness cutting the blackstrap molasses and muscovado.

→ Make the PASTRY (see p. 104). Preheat the oven to 200°C/400°F/Gas 6. Bake the tart case blind for 15 minutes, then remove the beans and foil and put the pastry back in the oven for 5 minutes to dry it out. Dock the base and sides with a fork to prevent them bubbling up.

→ Trim the stalks from the FIGS, cut them into small nubbly pieces and put them in a bowl. Chop the roast HAZELNUTS and WALNUTS coarsely and add them to the bowl. Cream the softened BUTTER and MUSCOVADO SUGAR thoroughly in a KitchenAid or by hand, making sure the mixture has turned really pale and light. Beat in the EGGS one at a time.

→ Warm the GOLDEN SYRUP and BLACKSTRAP MOLASSES gently

in a pan until just beginning to turn slightly liquid. Pour them into the creamed mixture, then scrape it all into the bowl of fruit and nuts. Add the JUICE AND ZEST OF A LEMON and tip the contents into the baked-blind pastry shell. Return it to the oven, turn the temperature down to 180°C/350°F/Gas 4 and cook until the tart has set, browned and puffed up a little, but still has a faint quake at its middle. This should take 25–35 minutes. Remove from the oven and cool to warm. Serve with clotted cream or homemade vanilla ice cream (see p. 418).

Butterscotch Tart

SERVES 6–7

shortcrust pastry case
made with wholemeal flour
(see p. 104)

egg white, *beaten*, for brushing	1
Butterscotch filling	
dark muscovado sugar	200g/7oz
single cream	250ml/8fl oz
butter	85g/3oz
cornflour, *sifted*	55g/2oz
egg yolks	3
vanilla extract	1 tsp
Meringue	
egg whites	3
caster sugar	55g/2oz

→ Preheat the oven to 190°C/375°F/Gas 5. Make the PASTRY (see p. 104), using wholemeal instead of white flour. Line a 23cm/9in tin and bake the pastry blind for 15 minutes. Remove the beans, prick the base with a fork, brush with beaten EGG WHITE and return to the oven for 10 minutes. Turn the heat down to 180°C/350°F/Gas 4.

→ Put ALL THE INGREDIENTS FOR THE FILLING in the top of a double boiler and whisk together over a low heat until thick, creamy and lump-free. Then scrape the filling into the baked pastry case.

→ For the MERINGUE, whisk the EGG WHITES until stiff, add one-third of the CASTER SUGAR and whisk again. Add another third of the SUGAR and fold it in gently with a metal spoon. Either spread the meringue over the filling, or mould it into six or seven quenelle-shaped portions with two large spoons. Sprinkle the remaining SUGAR over the top and return to the oven for about 20 minutes, or until beautifully browned and crunchy on top.

Tiramisu

SERVES 6

organic egg	1
organic egg yolks	3
white wine	50ml/2fl oz
Marsala	50ml/2fl oz
amaretto OR cognac and a drop or two of Culpeper's bitter almond essence	2 tbsp
unrefined vanilla caster sugar	100g/3½oz
mascarpone cheese	225g/8oz
espresso coffee powder	1 tsp

Biscuit layer

Italian savoiardi biscuits, OR good boudoir biscuits	175g/6oz
espresso coffee	3 small cups
caster sugar	1½ tbsp
Marsala	2 tbsp
best cocoa powder for sifting over the top, I use Green and Black's	2 level tbsp

Francesco Zanchetta's peerless rendering of this classic Italian pudding. Make this the night before you want it so the cream has time to bind with the layer of biscuit and the flavours develop.

→ Whisk together the EGG YOLKS and WHOLE EGG, WHITE WINE, MARSALA and AMARETTO in a double boiler; I have my grandmother's old enamel one. The top pan should not touch the water simmering in the bottom pan. Whisk until the mixture becomes very thick, you are making zabaglione. Once it is firm and fluffy, remove the bowl from the pan and carry on whisking for a few more minutes. Now add the SUGAR, which will dissolve very quickly. Gently fold in the MASCARPONE with the ESPRESSO POWDER, and then beat everything together for another minute or so to lighten the cream.

→ Mix together the cups of ESPRESSO, SUGAR and MARSALA in a dish deep enough to soak the biscuits. Dip in the BISCUITS so that they absorb the liquid but do not start to break up. Hot coffee helps.

→ Cover the base of a large, shallow rectangular dish with a layer of soaked biscuits, laid tightly together in the same direction, then pour over half of the CREAM before adding a second layer of biscuits, placed at right angles to the layer beneath. This helps to hold the tiramisu together when you serve it. Cover with the rest of the CREAM, and sift the COCOA POWDER thickly over the surface. Cover and chill in the fridge overnight.

Custard or Crème Anglaise

vanilla pod	1
Jersey full-cream milk	600ml/1 pint
large organic egg yolks	6
vanilla caster sugar	110g/4oz

This is a recipe you will use for ever, for ice creams and fools, as a sauce for crumbles, puddings and pies.

→ Split the VANILLA POD down the middle and extract the seeds with the point of a teaspoon. Put the MILK with the pod and the seeds in a pan with a good heavy base and bring slowly to scalding point, whisking the seeds to break them up. Remove from the heat, cover and leave to infuse for 30 minutes if you have time. This is not essential but does intensify the vanilla flavour.

→ Whisk the EGG YOLKS with the VANILLA CASTER SUGAR until pale and thick. Strain the milk mixture over them, whisking as you go and forcing the little beads of vanilla through the sieve with a wooden spoon. Return the mixture to the pan over a low heat and stir or whisk continuously—don't let it get to simmer point. The mixture will begin to look frothy, but make sure the underneath isn't beginning to stick to the base of the pan. Whisk all over the pan right down to the bottom.

→ Eventually—it may take 15 minutes—the custard will have thickened perceptibly. Take off the heat and test with your finger—you will be able to feel and see whether it has the texture of a proper custard. When it is ready, whisk a little longer off the heat as the base of the pan will still be hot and you don't want any scrambly bits. When cooled, this is your base for all the best ice creams and fools. It can also be served hot, warm or cold as a pouring custard for puddings.

Ricotta Fritters

SERVES 4

fresh ricotta	285g/10 oz
organic egg, *beaten*	1
vanilla pod	1
lemon	*grated zest* of 1
cinnamon	a pinch
unrefined caster sugar	1 tbsp
flour, *sifted*	2 tbsp
butter, *clarified*	55g/2oz

A tender, light and unusual pudding which works well with stewed rhubarb, apricots or plums or a barely-bled-in-the-pan combination of berries. Lighten up on the sugar and keep the fruit sharp.

→ Strain the RICOTTA through a cloth in a sieve for an hour. Crumble the sieved ricotta into a bowl and mix it with the beaten EGG. Scrape out the SEEDS FROM THE VANILLA POD and add them with the ZEST, CINNAMON, SUGAR and FLOUR. Whisk lightly.

→ To clarify butter, melt it gently in a pan, then tip the scummy froth away. Lay a piece of kitchen paper on the surface to remove any remaining froth.

→ Heat the CLARIFIED BUTTER in a heavy frying pan and drop tablespoons of the batter not too closely together into the pan. Fry until golden and then flip over and repeat. Drain on kitchen paper and keep warm on a plate in a warm oven while you make the rest. Serve alongside poached fruit.

Pâte Sucrée

flour	170g/6oz
unsalted butter	85g/3oz
icing sugar, *sifted*	1 tbsp
organic egg yolks	2

This pastry, enriched with egg yolks, is perfect for summer fruit and chocolate tarts. This makes enough to line a 23cm/9in tart tin. It is even more important than usual to chill this pastry thoroughly.

→ Sift the FLOUR and a pinch of SEA SALT into the food processor, then cut the fridge-cold BUTTER into cubes on top of it. Add the ICING SUGAR and pulse several times for 3–4 seconds a time before adding the EGG YOLKS. Pulse again and the moment it has cohered into a single ball, stop, remove it, wrap it in clingfilm and put it in the fridge for at least 30 minutes. Chill thoroughly.

→ If you are making pastry by hand, sift the FLOUR into a large bowl with the SALT, add the chopped BUTTER, and work as briskly as you can to rub the fat into the flour. Use the tips of your fingers only, rather like running grains of hot sand through your fingers. Add the ICING SUGAR and EGG YOLKS as above; wrap and chill the pastry.

→ Now scatter a bit of FLOUR on your work surface, roll your rolling pin in it, dust the palms of your hands, and start rolling. Always roll away from yourself, turning the pastry as you go, and keep the rolling pin and work surface floured to prevent sticking. Once it is rolled out, slip the rolling pin under the pastry, and pick it up, judging where to lie it in the greased tin. Never stretch it because it will shrink back. Try to chill the unbaked tart case for at least 30 minutes.

Baking blind

→ If you are baking your pastry case blind, preheat the oven to 190–200°C/375–400°F/Gas 5–6. Some recipes also tell you to put a baking sheet in the oven to heat up. This can be invaluable if you are using a porcelain or other non-metal tart dish, as the hot baking sheet gives it an initial burst of heat to crisp up the bottom of the pastry. If you are using a tart tin with a removable base (my preference, as they are by far the easiest to turn out), placing the tart tin on a baking sheet makes it easier to slide in and out of the oven.

→ Tear off a piece of greaseproof paper a little larger than the tart tin and place it over the pastry. Cover the paper with a layer of dried beans; the idea is to prevent the pastry from rising up in the oven. When the pastry is nearly cooked (the timing depends on the rest of the recipe), remove the paper and beans and prick the base of the pastry to let out trapped air that would otherwise bubble up. Return the tart to the oven for about 5–10 minutes to dry the pastry base.

Glazing
→ Brush the partly baked pastry case with a light coating of beaten EGG or EGG WHITE to ensure a crisp, finished tart.

Pâte Sablée (*sandy pastry*)
→ This is even sweeter, and crumbly, like a buttery biscuit. I use 170g/6oz FLOUR to 110g/4oz BUTTER, 55g/2oz ICING SUGAR and 2 EGG YOLKS. I put the butter, sugar and egg yolks into the food processor and work them together quickly, then blend in the sifted flour and work it into a paste. This needs longer chilling, a minimum of an hour, before rolling out.

Puff Pastry

plain flour	340g/12oz
salt	a pinch
unsalted butter	225g/8oz
cold water	1–2 tbsp

→ Sift the FLOUR and SALT into a mixing bowl, then rub in 25g/1oz of the BUTTER, as for shortcrust pastry, or use a food processor. Mix in the WATER, using as little as possible, and gently knead the dough on a floured surface, preferably marble. Wrap it in clingfilm and refrigerate for 30 minutes.
→ Keep the rest of the BUTTER out so that it softens, then flatten it into a rectangle 2.5cm/1in thick. On a lightly floured surface, roll out the dough into a rectangle 3 times the length and 2.5cm/1in wider than the rectangle of butter. Place the butter in the centre of the pastry, then fold over the top and bottom of the pastry to cover the butter.
→ With the rolling pin, press down on the edges to seal in the butter, then give the dough a quarter turn clockwise. Now roll the dough out so that it returns to its original length. Fold over the ends again, press them together with the rolling pin, and give a further quarter turn clockwise. Repeat the process once more, then rest the dough in the fridge for at least 30 minutes, remembering which way it is facing.
→ Repeat the rolling and turning process twice more, then refrigerate for a final 30 minutes before using or freezing. If the pastry gets warm and buttery at any stage during the process, put it in the fridge to chill.

CAKES,
and COO

BISCUITS
KIES

Muesli Cookies

MAKES ABOUT 24

muesli	225g/8oz
light OR dark muscovado sugar	55g/2oz
wholemeal OR plain flour	110g/4oz
Valencia almonds, *grind them yourself*	85g/3oz
unsalted butter	170g/6oz
flavoured honey, like lavender or chestnut	3 tbsp
bicarbonate of soda	½ tsp

A moreish, solid, substantial cookie that you should not shun on the grounds that it might smack of the health food shop. Just make sure you find a good organic muesli, full of fruit and nuts. Use light or dark muscovado, depending on how treacly a taste you like.

→ Preheat the oven to 190°C/375°F/Gas 5. Put the MUESLI, SUGAR, FLOUR and ALMONDS, which you should grind but not over-grind so that they start looking oily, in a bowl and stir together well. Melt the BUTTER and HONEY together, remove from the heat and stir in the BICARB. Stir this into the dry mixture and mix it all in together well.

→ Plop dessertspoons of the mixture onto greased baking trays or non-stick baking paper, leaving about 5cm/2in between them. Flatten the cookies down with a fork. Bake in the oven for 10–15 minutes or until golden. Cool on a wire tray, then store in an airtight container.

Vesuvial Chocolate Cookies

MAKES DOZENS

butter, unsalted	340g/12oz
good-quality chocolate, 70% cocoa solids	340g/12oz
organic eggs	340g/12oz
light muscovado sugar	450g/1lb
double espresso	1
self-raising flour	500g/1lb 2oz
baking powder	1½ tsp
unrefined icing sugar to roll the cookies in	

These are the best ever, the recipe imparted by the brilliant cooks at Ottolenghi in Notting Hill. You may keep some of the dough in the deep freeze if you make enough. The end result is a pile of oozing, dark chocolate cookies, risen until they crack like parched earth and sweetly crisped by their crackly coat of icing sugar. Serve with tea, coffee or ice cream, or just pile into them as you work, play or watch the television.

→ Gently melt the BUTTER and CHOCOLATE together in a double boiler or in a bowl over, but not touching, hot water. Whisk the EGGS and SUGAR in a KitchenAid or with electric beaters for 3 minutes, then add the warm chocolate mix and the ESPRESSO. Sift the FLOUR and BAKING POWDER and fold them into the mixture by hand. Wrap the dough in clingfilm and leave it to cool for a couple of hours before baking, or put it in the fridge overnight.

→ When you are ready to bake the cookies, preheat the oven to 180°C/350°F/Gas 4. Take the dough and roll walnut-sized balls in your hand. Roll them in ICING SUGAR and put on silicone paper with some space between each one. Bake for 10–12 minutes and allow to cool on a rack.

Snickerdoodles

MAKES ABOUT 4 DOZEN

plain flour	340g/12oz
bicarbonate of soda	1 tsp
unsalted butter, *softened*	225g/8oz
unrefined vanilla caster sugar	255g/9oz
organic eggs	2
walnuts, *very finely chopped*	55g/2oz
unrefined vanilla caster sugar	5 tbsp
ground cinnamon, *ground in a mortar is best*	1 tbsp

A thoroughly American cookie which has a light, cakey texture and a crunchy, cinnamon-sugared exterior. Children will want to cook them for the name alone.

→ Preheat the oven to 190°C/375°F/Gas 5. Sift the FLOUR and BICARB into a bowl. Cream the BUTTER and 225g/9oz of SUGAR until light, then gradually beat in the EGGS, one at a time. Stir in the flour and bicarb and the NUTS. Form the dough into rolls about 2.5cm/1in in diameter, wrap them in clingfilm and refrigerate for about 30 minutes until firm.

→ Stir the 5 tablespoons of SUGAR and the CINNAMON together on a plate or pastry marble. Quickly roll walnut-sized lumps of dough into balls in your hands, rolling them in the cinnamon sugar afterwards. Place them on non-stick parchment paper or greased baking sheets, placing them about 5cm/2in apart. Bake for 10–12 minutes until they are golden brown around the edges. Leave them on the baking tray for a minute before transferring to a rack to cool. Great with poached fruit or some vanilla ice cream.

Black and White Chocolate Cookies

MAKES ABOUT 24

unsalted butter, *softened*	225g/8oz
light muscovado sugar	200g/7oz
unrefined sugar	255g/9oz
eggs	3
plain flour	285g/10oz
baking powder	1 tsp
dark cocoa powder like Green and Black's organic	55g/2oz
dark chocolate, *broken into small chunks*	130g/4½oz
white chocolate, *broken into small chunks*	130g/4½oz

→ Preheat the oven to 150°C/300°F/Gas 2. Beat the BUTTER and SUGARS together in a KitchenAid or with electric beaters until light and fluffy. Add the EGGS, one by one, beating them in well. Sift in the FLOUR, BAKING POWDER and COCOA, throw in the CHOCOLATE CHUNKS and mix well, folding with a large metal spoon.

→ Use about 2 tablespoonfuls of mixture per cookie, putting them on baking trays lined with non-stick baking paper. Place them about 5cm/2in apart as they will spread! Flatten them down a little and bake in the middle of the oven for 20–25 minutes or until their bottoms have darkened to chocolate brown. Cool on wire racks.

Hazelnut and Orange Biscuits

unsalted butter	200g/7oz
unrefined caster sugar	140g/5oz
large egg	1
self-raising flour	225g/8oz
organic orange	*finely grated zest* of 1 (use a nutmeg grater)
Culpeper's sweet orange oil	a few drops
whole roasted hazelnuts, *bashed into bits with a mezzaluna or sharp knife*	85–125g/3–4 oz

Once you have made the mixture for these delicious biscuits, you can keep it wrapped up like a fat sausage in greaseproof paper in the fridge. Slice it like a salami and cook the biscuits whenever you want them—warm for tea, as petit fours with coffee, or to go with puddings like the burnt orange ice cream on p. 421 or a fruit fool. Use the freshest hazelnuts you can find.

→ Cream the BUTTER and SUGAR thoroughly in a KitchenAid or by hand. Then add the EGG, sifted FLOUR, ZEST, OIL and NUTS, and amalgamate. Form the mixture into two balls and roll each one out on a lightly floured surface with both hands, until you have a sausage about 5cm/2in in diameter. Wrap these in waxed paper and foil, and refrigerate. Overnight is best.
→ Preheat oven to 190°C/375°F/Gas 5. Slice the sausage into as many biscuits as you want, place them on a greased baking tray or two, not touching, and cook in the middle of the oven for about 8 minutes. They should not have coloured significantly. Remember, a minute too far and they will burn.
→ Using a palette knife, remove the biscuits immediately to a rack. Be careful: they are soft and bendy and can break at this stage, but they firm up very quickly. They should be beautifully crisp and nutty and scented with orange. Serve them warm with the burnt orange ice cream, which you should remove from freezer to fridge 30 minutes before you want to eat it.

Ginger Biscuits

caster sugar	225g/8oz
butter	125g/4oz
small egg	
golden syrup	1 tbsp
plain flour	225g/8oz
cinnamon	2 tsp
ground ginger	1 level tsp
bicarbonate of soda	1 tsp

→ Cream the SUGAR with the BUTTER until light and fluffy. Add the EGG, then the SYRUP, and beat together well.
→ Mix the DRY INGREDIENTS with the sieved FLOUR and amalgamate well with the egg mixture. Knead into a lump, then break off walnut-sized pieces, roll into a ball, and place on a greased baking tin. This quantity makes about 30 biscuits. Bake for about 45 minutes in a slow oven, or until golden brown. Remove and leave to cool a minute before transferring to a rack to cool further.

Walnut Biscuits

MAKES ABOUT 40

walnut oil	85ml/3fl oz
butter, *softened*	110g/4oz
caster sugar	140g/5oz
salt	a pinch
self-raising flour	225g/8oz
walnuts, *coarsely chopped*	55–85g/2–3oz
egg, *beaten*	1

→ Mix all the ingredients together with enough of the egg to bind. Shape the dough into a roll and refrigerate for at least 30 minutes.
→ Preheat the oven to 190°C/375°F/Gas 5. Slice off very thin circles of dough and bake on a greased baking sheet for 10–15 minutes, until crisp and lightly browned.

Almond Biscuits
→ Use chopped ALMONDS instead of walnuts for equally delicious biscuits that go well with vanilla ice cream.

Melting Moments

MAKES ABOUT 18

unsalted butter, *softened*	170g/6oz
unrefined icing sugar	30g/1oz
pure vanilla extract	a few drops
plain flour	135g/4½oz
cornflour	25g/scant oz
pecans OR almonds	a handful

→ Preheat the oven to 180°C/350°F/Gas 4. Tip the BUTTER, ICING SUGAR and VANILLA into the bowl of the KitchenAid or use your electric beaters to beat the mixture thoroughly until light and fluffy. Sieve the FLOUR and CORNFLOUR into the bowl and stir in until combined.
→ Either plop spoonfuls of the mixture onto a baking tray lined with non-stick baking parchment, or scrape the mixture into a piping bag with a fluted nozzle and pipe 2.5cm/1in circles onto the paper. Push a NUT onto each summit. Leave room to spread between each Moment. Cook for 12–14 minutes or until golden, then cool on a rack.

Flapjacks

MAKES 12

unsalted butter	75g/2½ oz
golden syrup	2–3 tbsp
light muscovado sugar	75g/2½ oz
rolled oats	140g/5oz

→ Preheat the oven to 170°C/325°F/Gas 3. Melt together the BUTTER, GOLDEN SYRUP and MUSCOVADO SUGAR, very gently. Pour them over the OATS in a bowl and mix together until everything is stickily combined. Press the mixture into a greased 18 × 28cm/7 × 11in shallow baking tin and bake for 15–20 minutes until golden and set. Cool and then cut into squares. They will only harden as they cool, so be patient.

Parkin

plain flour	170g/6oz
medium oatmeal	340g/12oz
light muscovado sugar	1 tbsp
ground ginger	½ tsp
sea salt	a pinch
treacle	450g/1lb
unsalted butter	110g/4oz
milk	70ml/2½ fl oz
bicarbonate of soda	1 tsp
flaked almonds (optional)	a handful

This is a deliciously old-fashioned sticky, treacly version, as good served at lunch, with a hunk of strong, unpasteurised Cheddar like Montgomery's or Keen's, as for pudding or tea. Dollop on crème fraîche if it's for pudding. Make the parkin at least a day before you want to eat it, preferably a week, and store it wrapped in foil in a tin.

→ Preheat the oven to 180°C/350°F/Gas 4. Sift the FLOUR into the bowl and add the OATMEAL, SUGAR, GINGER and SALT. Warm the TREACLE gently with the BUTTER, then remove from the stove. Heat the MILK to blood temperature, add the BICARB and pour it into the dry ingredients with the treacle and butter. Fold together. Grease and flour a roasting tin and line it with non-stick baking parchment. Pour in the mixture and bake for about 40 minutes or until firm to the touch. You may sprinkle a handful of FLAKED ALMONDS over the parkin about 15 minutes into baking if you feel like it. Keep the parkin for a day or two before cutting it into squares and serving as suggested above.

Shortbread

unsalted butter, *softened*	110g/4oz
unrefined caster sugar	55g/2oz
fine plain flour	110g/4oz
rice flour	55g/2oz
more caster sugar for dredging	

Shortbread made without butter, best unsalted butter that is, is not worth eating. The butter is the whole point, so no false economising.

→ Preheat the oven to 180°C/350°F/Gas 4. This is a hands-on, hands-in thing. You don't want the BUTTER to become broken up, so plonk it in a large bowl or on a board with the SUGAR and FLOURS and knead everything together into a dough. Then roll it out into a circle or oblong, about 2.5cm/1in thick, on a floured board.

→ Slide it onto a baking tray on a piece of non-stick baking parchment. Decorate the edges by marking them with the tines of a fork and the middle by pricking with the fork, and bake for 15–20 minutes or until pale biscuit colour. Dredge with CASTER SUGAR when cooked. Cool in the baking tray. Great with ice creams and fools too.

Apple and Carrot Shortbread

MAKES ABOUT 20 WEDGES

semolina	55g/2oz
unbleached white flour	170g/6oz
baking powder	¼ tsp
salt	a pinch
soft, unsalted butter	140g/5oz
unrefined caster sugar	100g/3½oz
carrot, *grated*	55g/2oz
apple, *grated*	30g/1oz
milk	

→ Preheat the oven to 180°C/350°F/Gas 4. Sift together the SEMOLINA, FLOUR, BAKING POWDER and SALT. Cream together the BUTTER and SUGAR until light and fluffy. Throw the GRATED CARROT and APPLE into the flour mixture, then fold into the creamed butter. Knead into a soft dough. Rest for half an hour in the fridge.

→ When you're ready to cook the shortbread, roll into 23cm/9in discs, 1cm/½in thick, and mark into wedges. Fork the edges, brush over a MILK WASH, and bake on a non-stick surface for about 10 minutes. Leave to cool before cutting.

Sticky Black Gingerbread

SERVES 8–10

butter	110g/4oz
molasses sugar	55g/2oz
demerara sugar	55g/2oz
organic eggs	2
blackstrap molasses	⅔ of a 450g/1lb jar
dried ginger root, *grated* (or powder if you can't get it)	1 tsp
plain flour, *sifted*	225g/8oz
stem ginger	5 knobs
stem ginger syrup	2 tbsp
milk	2 tbsp
bicarbonate of soda	scant ½ tsp

This is my absolute favourite recipe for that most palate-clinging of sticky cakes, the molasses-rich treacly gingerbread.

→ Preheat the oven to 170°C/325°F/Gas 3. Grease and flour an 18cm/7in loaf tin.

→ Cream the BUTTER and SUGARS thoroughly, then mix in the EGGS one at a time, followed by the BLACKSTRAP MOLASSES. Add the DRY GINGER ROOT with the sifted FLOUR, finely chopped STEM GINGER and SYRUP to the cake mixture. Warm the MILK slightly and stir it into the BICARB until dissolved, then add to the mixture and fold in. Pour the mixture into the loaf tin, and bake for about 1½ hours. Check with a skewer. I favour a sticky, gooey cake, slightly sunken in the middle, so when you turn it out to cool on a rack, it looks like a depressed, blackened brick. When cool, wrap it up in greaseproof paper and foil. It keeps very well for a few days.

Macaroons

ground almonds, Spanish organic ones are the best	170g/6oz
unrefined caster sugar	300g/10oz
egg whites	3
flour OR arrowroot	30g/1oz
vanilla extract	
rice paper OR baking parchment	
split almonds	a handful

→ Preheat oven to 190°C/375°F/Gas 5. Mix the GROUND ALMONDS and SUGAR in a bowl, add the EGG WHITES, and cream together thoroughly. Add the FLOUR OR ARROWROOT and flavour to taste with VANILLA extract, a few drops.

→ Place the rice paper or baking parchment on baking sheets, and spread the mixture out in little rounds with a teaspoon. Press a SPLIT ALMOND into the centre of each one and bake for about 20 minutes. Cool thoroughly on a rack before storing.

Blueberry Shortcakes

blueberries, sharp well-flavoured ones like 'Herbert'	225g/8oz
sugar	
double jersey cream	240ml/8fl oz
Shortcake	
flour	225g/8oz
unrefined granulated sugar	1½ tbsp
salt	a pinch
baking powder	2½ level tsp
unsalted butter	140g/5oz
double Jersey cream	150ml/5fl oz

As long as they have a good, strong, fruity flavour, any sort of berries will work well squished between these little circles of shortcake with cream. Use strawberries, raspberries, blueberries or blackcurrants, or a mixture of any or all of them. This is a perfect impromptu summer recipe that can be put together swiftly. The doughy scones are cooked in 15 minutes and served warm, making the fruit go further and turning it into a substantial pudding.

→ Keep the BERRIES whole if they are small, or halve them. Put them in a bowl and sprinkle them with a little SUGAR to get the juices going. Whip the CREAM so that it holds softly and put it in a bowl in the fridge to chill.

→ Preheat the oven to 230°C/450°F/Gas 8. Sift together the DRY INGREDIENTS for the shortcakes and rub in half the BUTTER, just as you would for shortbread. Mix to a soft dough with the cream, then knead like bread for a minute. Roll out on a floured board, keeping the dough thick enough to cut out six 7.5cm/3in rounds with a scone cutter.

→ Grease a baking sheet and put three of the rounds on it. Melt a little of the remaining BUTTER and brush it over the circles, then put the last three rounds on top. Bake for 10–15 minutes, but check at 10; you want golden scones, not burnt and brown. Separate the double rounds and put the sugared berries on half of them, with or without some whipped cream. Cover with the top decks and more berries and cream.

Gingerbread Men

unsalted butter, *softened*	110g/4oz
light muscovado sugar	100g/3½ oz
golden syrup	170g/6oz
plain flour, *sifted*	400g/14oz
ground ginger (use dried ginger root and *grind it yourself if possible)*	2 tsp
bicarbonate of soda, *sifted*	1 tsp
Icing	
egg white	1
unrefined icing sugar, *sifted*	55g/2oz
lemon juice	a squeeze

→ Preheat the oven to 190°C/375°F/Gas 5. Put the BUTTER and BROWN SUGAR in the bowl of the KitchenAid or whisk with electric beaters until light and creamy. Add the GOLDEN SYRUP, sifted FLOUR, GINGER and sifted BICARB, and mix until you have a smooth dough.

→ Roll out the dough between sheets of non-stick baking parchment to about 5mm/¼in thick. Cut out the gingerbread men with the cutter and place them on baking trays lined with non-stick baking parchment. Bake for 8–10 minutes or until golden. Cool on racks.

→ To make the icing, mix the EGG WHITE and sifted ICING SUGAR together thoroughly with a little squeeze of LEMON. Pipe buttons onto the gingerbread men. Plunge edible silver balls into their middles if you have some. Leave them to set.

Fairy Cakes

unsalted butter, *softened*	110g/4oz
unrefined caster sugar	110g/4oz
eggs	2
self-raising flour, *sifted*	110g/4oz
pure vanilla extract	½ tsp
milk	2–3 tbsp
Icing	
unrefined icing sugar	170g/6oz
water OR lemon/orange/lime juice	2 tbsp
lemon zest, *grated*	1 tsp

The only food colouring allowed in my house is strictly of the turmeric, saffron or blackberry variety, so if you want lividly iced day-glo toppings, invent your own or just make a simple icing and stick on silver balls, Smarties, fresh fruit or what you will. Fairy cakes, like musical bumps, are mandatory children's party fare and every bit as necessary for the comfort and well-being of the parents. They are also a one-step, easy-peasy thing for children to do all by themselves.

→ Preheat the oven to 200°C/400°F/Gas 6. Put the BUTTER, SUGAR, EGGS, FLOUR and VANILLA in a KitchenAid or food processor and whisk until really smooth. Add a little MILK at the end until you have what's known as a soft, dropping consistency, which means the mixture slips off the spoon with ease. Spoon the mixture into a dozen little cake papers which you've put in a tray of muffin or tart tins, and bake for 15–20 minutes or until cooked and golden on top. Cool for 10 minutes before putting the cakes on a rack to cool down.

→ To make the icing, sift the ICING SUGAR into a bowl. Mix in the LIQUID AND ZEST until smooth. Utterly simple.

Muffins

self-raising flour	170g/6oz
baking powder	1 tsp
caster sugar	110g/4oz
ground cinnamon, *best ground in a mortar*	1 tsp
unsalted butter, *melted*	75g/2½oz
egg	1
milk	100ml/3½fl oz
live plain yoghurt, cow's, goat's OR sheep's	100ml/3½ fl oz
pure vanilla extract	1 tsp
blueberries OR raspberries, redcurrants, etc	140g/5oz
Crumble topping (optional)	
butter	30g/1oz
light muscovado sugar	30g/1oz
flour	45–55g/1½–2oz

Warm, light and buttery with a splurt of fruit bled into them so the sponge is stained like blotting paper, the muffin is a cake for all seasons. You can scent them with spice or spike them with berries blue or black; lace them with cherries, colour them red, white or black with currants, add dried fruit, apples, pears or chocolate. Here is the basic mix. The yoghurt is my friend Sally Edwards's touch and she bakes better than almost anyone I know.

→ Preheat the oven to 180°C/325°F/Gas 4. Sieve the FLOUR and BAKING POWDER into a bowl and tip in the SUGAR and CINNAMON. Then add the MELTED BUTTER, EGG, MILK, YOGHURT and VANILLA to the bowl and stir everything together well. Tip in the FRUIT and fold in very gently so it doesn't break up.

→ Butter 10 muffin tins, put in muffin papers if you have them, and plop in the mixture. Place in the middle of the oven on a preheated baking sheet for 35–40 minutes. Leave in the tins for 10 minutes, then turn out onto a rack and eat warm.

Crumble topping

→ If you like the crumble topping idea, rub the BUTTER, SUGAR and FLOUR together briefly and sprinkle on top of the muffins before putting them in the oven.

Chocolate Brownies

MAKES 12–16 SQUARES

best bitter chocolate, at least 64% cocoa solids	200g/7oz
unsalted butter, *softened*	110g/4oz
unrefined vanilla caster sugar	225g/8oz
eggs	2
egg yolk	1
strong coffee, *freshly made*	4 tbsp
plain flour	140g/5oz
baking powder	1 tsp
whole hazelnuts	a handful

Please don't overcook these. You need to push a skewer right through them to check they are done and, unlike a cake where the skewer comes out clean if it's ready, you need a bit of chocolate goo on the skewer. If they tremble in the middle when you wobble the tin, they are still undercooked. Brownies should emerge with what's known as a 'sad' centre and a thin, dry, slightly crunchy crust.

→ Preheat the oven to 180°C/350°F/Gas 4. Line the bottom and sides of a small roasting tin or gratin dish, about 30 × 22cm/ 12 × 9in, with foil, then grease it with BUTTER. Gently melt the CHOCOLATE in a double boiler, or a bowl placed over a pan of simmering water. The bowl should not touch the water.

→ Cream the softened BUTTER and SUGAR until really light and fluffy, by hand or with electric beaters or a KitchenAid. Add the EGGS, one at a time, then the extra YOLK, with the mixer running. Pour in the melted chocolate and the COFFEE, amalgamate, then switch off the machine and sift in the FLOUR and BAKING POWDER. Fold them in with a metal spoon.

→ Pour the mixture into the tin, push in hazelnuts at intervals so they just stand proud, and bake for about 25 minutes. Check with a skewer as above. Leave to cool in the tin on a rack, then cut the brownies into squares and remove them from the tin. Serve with crème fraîche and a scattering of Green and Black's organic cocoa powder if you feel particularly indulgent.

Chocolate Chip and Hazelnut Brownies

MAKES 12–16 SQUARES

unrefined vanilla caster sugar	285g/10oz
eggs	4
unsalted butter	225g/8oz
Green and Black's organic cocoa	85g/3oz
plain flour	85g/3oz
best bitter chocolate, at least 64% cocoa solids	200g/7oz
roasted hazelnuts	110g/4oz
cooking chocolate chunks (The Chocolate Society do them in bags, 70% cocoa solids)	110g/4oz

→ Preheat the oven to 180°C/350°F/Gas 4. Prepare the roasting tin as in the recipe for Chocolate Brownies. Beat the SUGAR and EGGS together really well until they have thickened and the sugar has completely dissolved. Melt the BUTTER in a small pan and pour it into the sugar and egg. Sieve the COCOA and FLOUR together into the mixture, then melt the 200g/7oz of CHOCOLATE in a double boiler as in the previous recipe and add it into the mixture. Stir it in.

→ Put the HAZELNUTS and CHUNKS OF CHOCOLATE into a plastic bag and whack as hard as you dare with a rolling pin, keeping things chunky and in shards. The nuts will inevitably be more pulverised than the chocolate. Fold into the mixture and scrape it into the tin.

→ Bake for about 25 minutes. Test with a skewer, which should not come out completely clean. Leave to cool in the tin on a rack before cutting into squares. Serve warm or cold with crème fraîche and a scant scattering of extra cocoa powder.

Chocolate Cornflake Cakes

MAKES ABOUT 20

cornflakes	55g/2oz
bitter chocolate, 70% cocoa solids	170g/6oz
unsalted butter	30g/1oz

No children's party is complete without these moreish, crunchy chocolate cornflake cakes. Child's play to make, too.

→ Preheat the oven to 150°C/300°F/Gas 2. Spread the CORNFLAKES on a shallow baking tray and put into the oven, on a low shelf, for 10 minutes. Let them cool for a while before bashing them up a little. Warm the CHOCOLATE and BUTTER together in a pan over a low heat until just melted, then stir in the cornflakes. Spoon the mixture into paper cases or use teaspoons to shape into little conical hills on a greased baking tray. Leave to set.

Chocolate Cheesecake Brownies

MAKES 16 SQUARES

Cheesecake mixture

full fat fresh cream cheese, *softened*, so not straight from the fridge	340g/12oz
vanilla caster sugar	85g/3oz
egg yolk	1
plain flour	30g/1oz
organic orange	grated zest of 1
orange juice, *freshly squeezed*	1 tbsp

Brownie mixture

unrefined vanilla caster sugar	285g/10oz
eggs	4
unsalted butter	225g/8oz
Green and Black's organic cocoa	85g/3oz
plain flour	85g/3oz
best bitter chocolate, at least 64% cocoa solids	200g/7oz
hazelnuts, *roasted*	110g/4oz
cooking chocolate chunks, 70% cocoa solids	110g/4oz

Here is a wondrously rich, claggy, hedonistic recipe gleaned from the lovely book Baking With Passion *by Dan Lepard and Richard Whittington. I have somewhat simplified the original, which was made in piped and swirled layers of chocolate brownie mixture and cheesecake mixture. I think it is every bit as successful if you make it in the same way as the chocolate marble cake, just dolloping the mixture into the tin in alternate spoonfuls or doing a chocolate bottom and a cheesecake top, according to your creative bent. If you have done the latter, then you may swirl the top with a skewer before you put the brownies in the oven to give the top a rippled effect.*

→ Preheat the oven to 180°C/375°F/Gas 4. Line the bottom of a 23cm/9in × 5cm/2in deep square tin with foil and grease with BUTTER. First make the cheesecake mixture. Cream together the CREAM CHEESE and SUGAR, then add the EGG YOLK followed by the FLOUR. Finish by mixing in the ORANGE ZEST and JUICE. Set aside.

→ Then make the brownie mix. Beat the SUGAR and EGGS together really well until they have thickened and the sugar has completely dissolved. Melt the BUTTER in a small pan and pour it into the sugar and egg. Sieve the COCOA and FLOUR together into the mixture, then melt the CHOCOLATE in a double boiler, or a bowl over a pan of simmering water, and pour it into the mixture. Stir it in. Put the HAZELNUTS and CHUNKS OF CHOCOLATE into a ziploc bag and whack it as hard as you dare with a rolling pin, keeping things chunky and in shards. The nuts will inevitably be more pulverised than the chocolate.

→ Spoon alternate dollops of brownie mixture and cheesecake mixture into the tin, or do a black bottom and a white top, swirling the mixture with a skewer when you have finished. Bake for 20–25 minutes or until a skewer comes out warm at the tip with slightly sticky crumbs clinging to it. You do not want a dry sponge, which is always a danger with brownies, so err on the side of underdone for this recipe.

Chocolate Biscuit Cake

unsalted butter	110g/4oz
dark chocolate, Valrhona 64% cocoa solids is good for this	110g/4oz
golden syrup	2 tbsp
digestive biscuits	225g/8oz
Icing (optional)	
dark chocolate as before	55g/2oz
full cream milk	1 tbsp or a little more

This is better known as chocolate fridge cake. It is uncooked and reliant on two joyously untechnical techniques—melting and bashing. You can make it a day or two in advance.

→ Melt the BUTTER, CHOCOLATE and SYRUP together very gently over a low heat until liquid, making sure they come nowhere near boiling point. Remove from the heat. Put the DIGESTIVES into a plastic bag, seal it, then smash them around with a rolling pin until they're bashed to crumbs. A few small chunks are fine, as they will add texture. Pour the crumbs into the chocolate mixture and stir together. Press into a shallow tin that you have greased well with butter and leave to set in the fridge. Add icing if you like.

Icing
→ Melt the CHOCOLATE and MILK together very gently over a low heat, adding a little more milk if the mixture seems very thick. Spread over the top of the cake and chill. Turn out, slice and serve with cream or crème fraîche.

Honey-spiced Madeleines

Serves 6

sultanas	30g/1oz
flour	15g/½oz
caster sugar	75g/2½oz
ground almonds	15g/½oz
ground ginger	½ tsp
cinnamon	½ tsp
liquorice	½ tsp
ground mace	a pinch
5-star spice	a pinch
nutmeg	a suspicion
unsalted butter	55g/2oz
acacia OR other runny honey	1 tbsp
organic egg whites	2

Serve with ice creams, fools, a fruit compote, or warm for tea.

→ Preheat oven to 180°C/350°F/Gas 4. Soak the SULTANAS in hot water for 20 minutes to plump them up. Mix ALL THE DRY INGREDIENTS, BAR THE SULTANAS, together in a bowl. Melt the BUTTER in a pan until it turns nut brown, then remove from the heat and stir in the HONEY.

→ Cool slightly, then add to the dry ingredients. Beat together in an electric mixer. Gradually add the EGG WHITES until well mixed: the consistency should be like runny paste. Cover and chill for 30 minutes.

→ Chill a 12-mould madeleine sheet—a Yorkshire pudding tin will do. Brush the moulds with melted butter, dust with flour, shaking out any excess, and scatter the drained SULTANAS over the bases. Spoon in the mixture, and bake for 10–15 minutes until golden and just firm to the touch.

Blondies, Date and Walnut Brownies

unsalted butter	55g/2oz
light muscovado sugar	200g/7oz
organic egg, *beaten*	1
flour	100g/3½oz
baking powder	1 level tsp
sea salt	½ tsp
vanilla pod	*scraped-out seeds* of 1
pitted dates	55g/2oz
walnuts	55g/2oz

An alternative to chocolate brownies. They have the squidgiest, gooeyest middles and the thinnest of crisp, fragile-to-the-touch sugared tops hiding the sweet nuggets of date and squirls of chopped walnuts. It is impossible to eat only one. The fragrant note of the muscovado and the way the slice pulls apart in your hand with sticky resistance are compulsive. Beware.

→ Preheat the oven to 180°C/350°F/Gas 4. Melt the BUTTER in a pan over a low heat, and the moment it is liquid, add the light muscovado SUGAR. Stir it in, still over a gentle heat, only to the point at which the sugar, too, is melted. If you take it too far to bubbling toffee, it will harden instead of staying liquid.

→ Remove the pan from the heat and whisk in the EGG while the mixture is still warm. Sift the FLOUR, BAKING POWDER and SALT into the pan and scrape in the VANILLA SEEDS. Cut the DATES into good-sized nuggets and break the WALNUTS likewise, adding them both to the mixture.

→ Line a shallow baking tin, 18cm/7in, or a small loaf tin, with greased Bakewell paper so that it covers two of the sides, and make sure you grease the other two sides thoroughly. Pour the mixture into the tin. Bake for around 25 minutes, but insert a skewer at 20 minutes and see if it comes out clean. Place the tin on a rack for 10 minutes before cutting the brownies into rectangles and cooling them on the rack.

Blueberry and Cinnamon Friands

MAKES 10–12

unsalted butter	170g/6oz
ground almonds	140g/5oz
organic lemon, *grated zest*	1 tbsp
ground cinnamon	1 tsp
unrefined icing sugar	285g/10oz
organic plain flour	5 tbsp
organic egg whites	2
blueberries	200g/7oz punnet

These charming little friands are good with coffee or at tea time and for pudding, with ice cream or a bowl of chilled fresh berries. Make them in the same tins you would use for jam tarts or individual Yorkshire puds. Great made with blackcurrants or cranberries too.

→ Heat the oven to 200°C/400°F/Gas 6. Melt the BUTTER gently in a pan and cook it until it is golden, not brown. Put the ground ALMONDS, LEMON ZEST, CINNAMON, sifted ICING SUGAR and FLOUR into a bowl and mix together, then stir in the EGG WHITES and combine. Stir in the melted butter, then pour the mixture into the greased tins and scatter over the BLUEBERRIES.

→ Bake for about 15 minutes or until light and springy to the touch, then leave to cool on a rack. Serve with a little extra ICING SUGAR sifted onto them.

Victoria Sponge

unsalted butter, *softened*	110g/4oz
unrefined caster sugar	110g/4oz
eggs	2
self-raising flour, *sifted*	110g/4oz
water	
jam, the best, whatever flavour you like, damson, raspberry, loganberry, strawberry, apricot	about 2 tbsp
unrefined icing sugar for dusting	

Baking your first Victoria sponge is one of those classic culinary landmarks that should prove a triumph and lead to greater things. There is nothing quite like the satisfaction of assembling the double-decker sponge, golden, light, buttery, smoothing on the best seeded strawberry or raspberry jam, adding fresh fruit and thick, whipped cream if you will, then closing the top lid of sponge upon it until the scarlet stickiness just squishes out. A dusting of unrefined icing sugar and the world is definitely a better place.

→ Preheat the oven to 180°C/350°F/Gas 4. Grease two 15cm/6in sandwich tins, non-stick if possible, with a butter paper. Line the bottom of each with a circle of non-stick baking parchment to fit the base and grease that with the butter paper.

→ Cream the BUTTER and SUGAR together until light and fluffy. Beat the EGGS together in a bowl and gradually beat them into the creamed mixture a little at a time, adding a tablespoon of sifted FLOUR if the mixture begins to curdle. Fold in the flour with a metal spoon, lightly and swiftly, adding a little WATER to bring the mixture to a soft, dropping consistency. Scrape the mixture into the tins immediately and smooth the tops with a rubber spatula.

→ Bake in the middle of the oven for about 20 minutes, or until the cakes are well risen, golden and feel spongy when touched with a fingertip. Let the cakes cool for about 5 minutes before turning them out onto a wire rack and peeling away the greased paper. Invert them so that they cool right side up. Cool completely.

→ Spread the JAM with a palette knife over the top of the sponge that is going to be your base or add some freshly sliced strawberries or whole raspberries if you feel like it and they are in season. You can, on the other hand, whisk some Jersey or double cream until slackly stiffened, a small carton will do, and spread that over the jam and then proceed with or without the fresh fruit. Place the top sponge on the jammy sponge and sieve over a restrained amount of unrefined ICING SUGAR.

Nigel Slater's Big Fruit Cake

unsalted butter at room temperature	340g/12oz
soft dark brown sugar	340g/12oz
ready-to-eat figs, prunes, apricots, candied peel, glacé cherries	1kg/2¼lb
large organic eggs	5
ground almonds	100g/3½oz
shelled hazelnuts	140g/5oz
vine fruits (raisins, sultanas, and currants)	500g/1lb 2oz
brandy	5 tbsp
orange	zest and juice of 1
lemon	zest and juice of 1
baking powder	½ tsp
plain flour	340g/12oz

There is no cook or food writer more in touch with what we want to cook, what we REALLY feel like eating, than Nigel Slater. And I've always thought that baking is where he is truly at home; it is one of his real strengths. This is a wonderfully old-fashioned, moist and boozily fruity cake.

→ You will also need a 23cm/9in cake tin with a removable base. Line it with buttered greaseproof paper, which should come 5cm/2in above the top of the tin. Preheat the oven to 170°C/325°F/Gas 3.

→ Beat the BUTTER and SUGAR until pale and fluffy. I needn't tell you that this is much easier in an electric mixer, but I have occasionally done it by hand. Don't forget to push the mixture down the sides of the bowl from time to time with a spatula. While the butter and sugar are beating to a cappuccino-coloured fluff, cut the FIGS, PRUNES, APRICOTS, CANDIED PEEL and CHERRIES into small pieces, removing the hard stalks from the figs. Add the EGGS to the mixture one at a time—it will curdle but don't worry—then slowly mix in the ground ALMONDS, HAZELNUTS, all the DRIED FRUIT, the BRANDY and the CITRUS ZEST and JUICE.

→ Now mix the BAKING POWDER and FLOUR together and fold them lightly into the mix. Scrape the mixture into the prepared tin, smoothing the top gently, and put it in the oven. Leave it for an hour, then, without opening the oven door, turn down the heat to 150°C/300°F/Gas 2 and continue baking for 2 hours. Check whether the cake is done by inserting a skewer into the centre. It should come out with just a few crumbs attached but no trace of raw cake mixture. Take the cake out of the oven and leave to cool before removing from the tin.

→ To make the cake boozier, pierce holes in it and pour a little BRANDY into the holes every 3—4 days for a fortnight. Wrap the cake tightly in greaseproof paper, then in foil or clingfilm and lower it into a tin. Covered, it will be fine for several weeks.

Christmas Cake, or Rich Plum Cake

MAKES A 18CM/7IN CAKE

unsalted butter, *softened*	225g/8oz
light muscovado sugar	225g/8oz
organic eggs	6
lemon *grated* zest and juice of 1	
ground cinnamon	½ tsp
cloves	½ tsp
mixed spice	½ tsp
nutmeg	½ tsp
black treacle	½ teacup
plain flour	340g/12oz
currants	340g/12oz
sultanas	225g/8oz
undyed glacé cherries	55g/2oz
candied orange peel	55g/2oz
strong, dry cider	1 teacup
bicarbonate of soda	1 level tsp
dark rum	¼ teacup

Marzipan

unrefined icing sugar	225g/8oz
ground almonds	450g/1lb
large organic egg	1
lemon juice	3–4 tsp
apricot jam	1 tbsp
water	1 tbsp

Royal Icing

small egg whites	2
lemon juice	2 tsp
icing sugar, *sieved* (I prefer unrefined)	450g/1lb

Do try to make your Christmas cake a couple of weeks ahead of Christmas, so that it may mature and flower at the right time.

→ Preheat the oven 150–170°C/300–325°F/Gas 2–3. Line an 18cm/7in cake tin with three layers of greaseproof paper and a final layer of Bakewell paper.

→ Cream the softened BUTTER and SUGAR together well until pale and fluffy. Separate the EGGS and beat the EGG YOLKS into the creamed butter and sugar one by one. Add the LEMON ZEST and JUICE, the SPICES and the TREACLE. Work in half the FLOUR and FRUIT and pour over enough CIDER to moisten the mixture. Mix the BICARBONATE OF SODA with the rest of the FLOUR and add it with the remaining FRUIT. Whisk the EGG WHITES to stiff peaks, stir the first spoonful into the mixture, then quickly and lightly fold in the rest, a large tablespoon at a time. Add the ALCOHOL and gently fold it in.

→ Pour into the lined tin and bake in the centre of the oven for 2–3 hours, until a skewer comes out clean when sunk into the cake. Leave the cake to cool in its tin. Keep in a tin with a lid on it for a couple of weeks.

Marzipan
→ Sift the ICING SUGAR and mix it with the GROUND ALMONDS. Beat the EGG thoroughly, add the LEMON JUICE and mix with the dry ingredients. Use a wooden spoon to beat everything to a firm paste, then knead it on a board or marble which has been sprinkled with icing. Boil the JAM and WATER in a small pan, sieve it into a bowl and while still hot brush it over the cake. Roll out the marzipan and cover the cake. Leave for 2 days before icing.

Royal Icing
→ Whisk the EGG WHITES until they are white and foamy but not stiff. Stir in the LEMON JUICE, then the sieved ICING SUGAR. Do this bit by bit, using a wooden spoon. When everything is mixed together, continue to beat the mixture until it is a dazzling white — although it will not be dazzling white with unrefined icing sugar! Cover the basin and leave it for an hour or so before using it. Cover the cake all over, then put on the remaining icing, either roughly to make a snowy effect, or in an elegant design with the aid of a forcing bag and nozzles.

Country Christmas Cake

MAKES A 20–23CM/8–9IN CAKE

First list

mixed dried fruit	1.2kg/2lb 8oz
candied peel, *chopped*	55g/2oz
glacé cherries, *halved*	55g/2oz
preserved ginger, *drained and chopped*	85g/3oz
large orange	*grated* zest and juice of 1
large lemon	*grated* zest and juice of 1
bitter orange marmalade	1 tbsp
apricot jam	1 tbsp
stewed apple	225g/8oz

Second list

lightly salted butter, *softened*	225g/8oz
soft dark brown sugar	225g/8oz
organic eggs	4
pure vanilla extract	1 tsp
almond essence	a few drops

Third list

plain flour, *sifted*	340g/12oz
ground cinnamon	1 tsp
ginger	1 tsp
nutmeg	1 tsp
cloves	1 tsp
mixed spice	1 tsp
baking powder	1 tsp
enough blanched almonds to decorate the top of the cake	

After baking

whisky or brandy	1 tbsp

The fruit and spices for this cake need to sit and commune with the juice overnight before you actually make and bake, so plan accordingly. The recipe comes from one of my cooking heroines, Jane Grigson, from whose books I largely taught myself to cook. Start the night before you want to bake the cake.

→ MIX ALL THE INGREDIENTS ON THE FIRST LIST in a large basin. Turn them over thoroughly. Cover and leave overnight.

→ The following day, preheat the oven to 170°C/325°F/Gas 3. Gather the ingredients from the second list. Cream the BUTTER and SUGAR until light and fluffy. Beat in the EGGS one by one and add the VANILLA EXTRACT and ALMOND ESSENCE.

→ Put the FLOUR, SPICES and BAKING POWDER from the third list in a bowl and stir them together. Mix the fruit and flour mixture alternately into the creamed butter and sugar, a little at a time. Line a 20–23cm/8–9in cake tin with three layers of greaseproof paper and a final layer of Bakewell paper. Pour in the mixture and decorate with BLANCHED ALMONDS, unless you intend to cover the cake eventually with marzipan and icing.

→ Bake for 2 hours before turning down the heat to 150°C/ 300°F/Gas 2 for a further 2 hours. Remove the cake from the oven, puncture it with a few holes with a skewer and pour in the BOOZE; an extra tablespoon or two won't hurt. Leave the cake to cool in its tin.

→ Next day, remove the cake and peel off the greaseproof and Bakewell paper. Wrap it in fresh greaseproof paper and keep it in an airtight tin or in firmly sealed foil for at least a month before using it. If you want to finish the cake with marzipan and icing, make your own (see p. 535). The ready-made stuff is never very good. Home-made is easy and tastes much better.

Chocolate Marble Cake

good bitter chocolate, *chopped*	100g/3½oz
milk	120ml/4fl oz
unsalted butter, *softened*	110g/4oz
vanilla caster sugar	140g/5oz
eggs	2
self-raising flour	225g/8oz
baking powder	1 tsp
soured cream	55g/2oz

The quality of the chocolate is paramount here. Use Valrhona, Callebaut or The Chocolate Society's chocolate drops, which are all around 70 per cent cocoa solids for that lingering, velvety, bittersweet taste. The mixture makes enough for one loaf tin so double up if you've got hordes of people or simply want to freeze one. This is another adaptation from Baking With Passion *by Dan Lepard and Richard Whittington.*

→ Preheat the oven to 170°C/325°F/Gas 3. Grease and line a loaf tin, then grease the greaseproof paper and shake a little flour inside it all around, getting rid of the excess.

→ Melt the CHOCOLATE with 60ml/2fl oz of MILK in a double boiler or in a bowl over a pan of simmering water that the bowl doesn't touch. In the KitchenAid or using electric beaters, cream the BUTTER and SUGAR until pale and fluffy. Beat in the EGGS, one at a time, stopping the mixer and scraping the mixture down the sides if you need to.

→ In another bowl, sift the FLOUR with the BAKING POWDER. Stir the SOURED CREAM into the remaining MILK. Fold one-third of the flour into the creamed butter, sugar and egg mixture, followed by one-third of the soured cream mixture. Fold in another third of the flour, then another third of the soured cream, then repeat with the final third of each. Spoon half of this mixture into another bowl and add the chocolate mixture to one half, folding it in thoroughly.

→ With two separate spoons, spoon the mixtures into the tin alternately so that the result will be marbled. Put the tin on to a heated baking tray in the middle of the oven and bake for 50–55 minutes or until a skewer comes out clean.

→ Cool in the tin for 10 minutes. Run a knife between the cake and the sides of the tin, and gently upturn the cake onto your cloth-covered hand, then place upright to cool on a wire rack to finish cooling.

Miranda's Birthday Cake

good dark chocolate, *chopped*	170g/6oz
unsalted butter, *softened*	170g/6oz
caster sugar	170g/6oz
organic eggs, *separated*	4
ground almonds	85g/3oz
plain flour, *sifted*	85g/3oz
Rich Chocolate Icing	
good dark chocolate, *chopped*	110g/4oz
butter	45g/1½ oz
caster sugar	55g/2oz
double cream	90ml/3fl oz

There is nothing like the first cake your daughter—or son—bakes for you, particularly if it has been made almost secretly for your birthday, and the kitchen, which will have been reduced to rubble, with seemingly every implement used, has also, magically, then been cleaned up. It is even better if the recipe isn't one of those moronic apologies for children's cooking that are just as time-consuming and difficult to cook, and disgustingly inedible. This is the wondrously sticky chocolate cake my eldest daughter Miranda cooked for me one birthday.

→ Preheat the oven to 180°C/350°F/Gas 4. Grease two 18cm/7in sandwich tins or one deeper, 20cm/8in round tin. Melt the CHOCOLATE in a bowl over a saucepan of hot water. Cream the BUTTER with the SUGAR (this is easily done in a food processor), then add the EGG YOLKS one by one, then the ALMONDS, FLOUR and the melted chocolate. Whisk the EGG WHITES until they form soft peaks, then gently fold them into the mixture, little by little.

→ Divide the mixture between the sandwich tins and cook in the oven for about 20 minutes. If using one deeper tin, cook for slightly longer. Miranda undercooks hers slightly for a damp, sticky centre. Leave to cool slightly in the tin, then turn out onto a wire rack.

Rich Chocolate Icing

→ For the icing, put ALL THE INGREDIENTS into a bowl over a saucepan of hot water and stir gently over the heat. When smooth, leave to cool and then put into the fridge—it thickens as it cools, and becomes much easier to spread. If you have two sponges, sandwich them together with half the icing and spread half on top. If you have one sponge, cover the top and sides copiously with icing.

Devil's Food Cake

MAKES A 23CM/9IN CAKE

Valrhona OR similar top-quality dark chocolate	140g/5oz
vanilla caster sugar	110g/4oz
milk	120ml/4fl oz
Green and Black's organic cocoa powder	40g/1½oz
organic eggs, *separated*	3
extra yolk	1
soft unsalted butter	150g/5oz
light muscovado sugar	85g/3oz
plain flour	225g/8oz
bicarbonate of soda	1 heaped tsp
salt	1 tsp
soured cream	1 small pot

Bitter Chocolate Icing

best bitter chocolate	200g/7oz
cocoa powder as above	55g/2oz
water	100ml/3½fl oz
golden syrup	1 heaped tbsp
butter, *softened*	55g/2oz
unrefined icing sugar, *sifted*	225g/8oz
egg yolks	2

→ Preheat oven to 180°C/ 350°F/Gas 4. Butter two 23cm/9in springform cake tins, and line the bases with baking parchment. Put the CHOCOLATE, CASTER SUGAR, MILK, COCOA POWDER and 2 EGG YOLKS in a bowl set over simmering water. Stir until melted and custardy.

→ In your KitchenAid or mixer, beat the BUTTER and MUSCOVADO SUGAR until light and fluffy. Beat in the remaining YOLKS, then the FLOUR, SALT and BICARB. Fold in the SOURED CREAM then the chocolate custard. Whisk the EGG WHITES until stiff and fold them into the mixture.

→ Put half the mixture in each of the tins, and bake in the oven for 35–40 minutes. You want the skewer to come out almost clean. Cool briefly in the tins then turn out onto a rack.

→ Cut each sponge into two, then lash the ICING on to each layer and sandwich together, keeping enough to spread all over the top and sides of the cake. Leave in a cool, but not cold, place overnight.

Bitter Chocolate Icing

→ Melt the CHOCOLATE as above. Warm the COCOA POWDER, WATER and GOLDEN SYRUP until runny. Add the chocolate and stir to amalgamate. Remove from the heat and beat in the BUTTER, ICING SUGAR and EGG YOLKS until smooth and creamy. Taste for sweetness. Cool until thick but spreadable.

Wholewheat Chocolate Hazelnut Cake

MAKES AN 18CM/7IN ROUND CAKE

unsalted butter	170g/6oz
light muscovado sugar	170g/6oz
eggs, *beaten*	3
milk	2 tbsp
wholemeal flour, *sifted*	170g/6oz
baking powder	2½ tsp
best bitter chocolate, *chopped quite small*	200g/7oz
ground hazelnuts	110g/4oz
chopped hazelnuts	30g/1oz

This is a surprisingly subtle and delicious cake, with a melting chocolate and toasted hazelnut top, which my cousin Deborah first cooked for me some years ago. It might appear plain—it absolutely isn't.

→ Preheat the oven to 180°C/350°F/Gas 4. Grease and line an 18cm/7in round cake tin; it should be springform so you can cool the cake without having to turn it upside down.
→ Cream the BUTTER with the SUGAR until light and fluffy. Add the EGGS, a little at a time, beating between each addition. Then fold in the MILK, sifted FLOUR and BAKING POWDER, mixing them thoroughly. Add about two-thirds of the chopped CHOCOLATE, together with the GROUND HAZELNUTS, and spoon the mixture into the prepared tin.
→ Finally, sprinkle the CHOPPED HAZELNUTS and the remaining CHOCOLATE over the mixture and bake in the centre of the oven for about 1½ hours, or until the centre is springy when lightly touched. After the first hour, cover the cake with a sheet of greaseproof paper to prevent the nuts from burning.
→ Leave to cool slightly in the tin, then carefully release the springform clip and transfer the cake to a wire rack. Best eaten while still just warm, with or without cream.

Chocolate, Mocha and Roasted Hazelnut Cake

SERVES 8

organic OR good bitter chocolate	185g/6½oz
unsalted butter, *cut into cubes*	185g/6½oz
extra butter for greasing the tin	
very strong, *freshly brewed* good coffee	60ml/2fl oz
organic eggs, *separated*	6
unrefined caster sugar	185g/6½oz
roasted blanched hazelnuts, *coarsely ground in a food processor*	185g/6½oz
crème fraîche for serving	

Here is a bitter-dark, flourless pudding cake, which will grace your grandest dinner or sex up the simplest lunch, tea or supper. There is no time of day this cake isn't good for, especially with a soft, shiny squirl of sharp crème fraîche at its side and a little dark cocoa sprinkled over it if you are in the mood. Use really good chocolate, minimum 70 per cent cocoa solids, and Piedmont hazelnuts if you can find them.

→ Preheat the oven to 190°C/375°F/Gas 5. Break the CHOCOLATE into pieces. Melt the BUTTER and chocolate together with the COFFEE in a double boiler or in a bowl above, but not touching, a pan of simmering water. While they are melting, cream the EGG YOLKS and SUGAR in a KitchenAid or electric mixer until really pale and light. This will take 8–10 minutes. Continue to whisk, adding the melted chocolate, butter and coffee.
→ Fold the roasted HAZELNUTS into the mixture with a clean metal spoon. In a large, clean bowl whisk the EGG WHITES to stiff peaks. Stir a spoonful of egg white into the chocolate mixture to lighten it before folding in the rest.

→ Grease the sides of a 25cm/10in springform tin and line the base with a circle of buttered greaseproof paper. Pour in the mixture and bake for 20 minutes. Turn the heat down to 170°C/325°F/Gas 3 and continue to cook for a further 40 minutes or until a skewer comes out clean. Remove the tin from the oven and set on a rack until completely cool before turning the cake out of the tin and removing the paper. Dust the cake with cocoa powder if you feel like it. Serve with a bowl of CRÈME FRAÎCHE or some home-made vanilla ice cream.

Chocolate Mocha Cake with Irish Whiskey

MAKES A 20CM/8IN CAKE

dark chocolate, minimum 70% cocoa solids	170g/6oz
strong mocha coffee, *freshly made*	4 tbsp
Irish whiskey	2 tbsp
unrefined vanilla sugar	85g/3oz
unsalted butter, soft enough to cream	110g/4oz
organic eggs, *separated*	3
almonds, *freshly ground*	55g/2oz
Culpeper's natural bitter almond essence	a few drops
plain flour, *sifted*	55g/2oz
Icing	
best bitter chocolate	55g/2oz
Irish whiskey	2 tbsp
unsalted butter	55g/2oz

A delicious birthday cake, which needs little more than a perfectly made vanilla ice cream with fresh Madagascan vanilla pods.

→ Preheat oven to 180°C/350°F/Gas 4. Butter and flour a 20cm/8in cake tin. Melt the CHOCOLATE in a double boiler with the COFFEE and WHISKEY. Remove the top pan and allow them to cool. Cream together all but a tablespoon of the SUGAR with the BUTTER until it is pale and fluffy, then beat in the EGG YOLKS, one at a time. Whisk the EGG WHITES with a pinch of SALT to soft peak stage, then add the last tablespoon of SUGAR and beat to firm peaks. Blend the chocolate mixture into the creamed butter and sugar with a rubber spatula, then stir in the ground ALMONDS and bitter almond essence. Fold in a spoonful of the egg white, followed by a spoonful of FLOUR, and continue until it's all blended in.

→ Scrape the mixture into the cake tin and bake it in the centre of the oven for 25–30 minutes. A skewer should come out clean. Cool in the tin for 10 minutes, then run a knife round the edge of the tin and turn the cake out on to a rack.

→ Ice it when it is completely cool. Melt the CHOCOLATE and WHISKEY in the top of the double boiler until satiny smooth. Remove from the heat and beat in the BUTTER, a tablespoon at a time. Stand the bowl over iced water and continue to beat, otherwise the butter and the chocolate will separate. You can always add a little cream if this happens—whisk and the mixture will cohere. Spread the icing over the cake, leaving a rough finish.

Caramel and Chocolate Fudge Cake

Serves 8

unrefined caster sugar	340g/12oz
unsalted butter, *cut into cubes and chilled*	285g/10oz
good chocolate, *melted*	450g/1lb
large organic eggs, *separated*	6
sprinkling of cocoa powder, *sifted*	

The first time I made this sensationally rich, dark, flourless cake it was a little too bitter. Second time around I used a mix of chocolates containing 70 per cent and 50 per cent cocoa solids.

→ Preheat the oven to 180°C/350°F/Gas 4. Grease and line a 25cm/10in springform cake tin.

→ Use a clean saucepan to caramelise the CASTER SUGAR with 2 tbsp water (to help avoid crystallisation). Try to reach a dark caramel colour without burning the sugar, so watch carefully, and don't stir—although you may move the pan.

→ Remove from the heat and add the cubes of chilled BUTTER, carefully but quickly, to arrest the caramelisation. Stir with a whisk. Add the melted CHOCOLATE, whisking constantly, then the six EGG YOLKS, which you must whisk in really well, one at a time, to stop the mixture from splitting. Let the mixture cool to room temperature.

→ Whisk the EGG WHITES until stiff. Stir in the first tablespoon of whisked egg white, then fold the remaining whites gently and lightly into the mixture. Pour the mixture into the tin and bake for about an hour, until a skewer comes out almost clean. The cake should still be slightly wet inside.

→ Let the cake cool totally before removing it from the tin and dusting the top with COCOA POWDER.

Chocolate Pudding Cake with Chocolate Ganache

Serves 8–10

organic eggs, *separated*	4
whole egg	1
vanilla caster sugar	170g/6oz
best bitter chocolate, 70% cocoa solids	225g/8oz
blanched almonds, *freshly ground*	140g/5oz
ground coffee	1 heaped tsp
Chocolate Ganache	
dark chocolate	225g/8oz
double cream	120ml/4fl oz

The marvellous thing about this most sumptuous of cakes is that it can be made well in advance and kept in a tin or sealed container before you adorn it with a rich chocolate ganache. A truly special chocolate cake. Serve with vanilla ice cream.

Preheat the oven to 170°C/325°F/Gas 3. Whisk the EGG YOLKS and EGG together with half the SUGAR until pale and doubled in volume. Melt the CHOCOLATE in a double saucepan or in a bowl over simmering water. Whisk the EGG WHITES, adding the rest of the sugar a bit at a time, until they are at the satiny, soft peak stage. Add half of them to the egg and sugar mixture, folding them in gently. Add the chocolate and the rest of the whites, folding as you go. Then do likewise with the ALMONDS and COFFEE.

→ Grease and flour a 20cm/8in springform tin and line the base with a circle of greased greaseproof paper. Scrape the mixture into the tin and bake for 30 minutes. Then turn the oven off and leave the cake in for another 15 minutes or until a skewer comes out clean from the centre. Remove from the oven and leave to cool in the tin.

Chocolate Ganache
→ Scald the CREAM in a small pan, remove from the heat and stir in the broken up CHOCOLATE until it has melted into the cream. Cover the cake with the ganache and leave to cool.

Chocolate Espresso Cake

SERVES 8–10

unsalted butter, *diced*, plus extra for greasing the tin	185g/6½oz
best dark chocolate, *broken into pieces*	185g/6½oz
very strong coffee, *freshly brewed*	60ml/2fl oz
organic eggs, *separated*	6
unrefined caster sugar	185g/6½oz
almonds, *blanched, roasted and coarsely ground*	185g/6½oz

Simply one of the best pudding cakes I have ever come across with its deep, rich, undertones of coffee under the black velvet chocolate. Sally Edwards used to serve this cake every day at her café in Taunton. There would have been a riot if she hadn't, and now she's gone we have to make our own.

Preheat the oven to 190°C/375°F/Gas 5. Melt the BUTTER and CHOCOLATE together with the COFFEE in a bowl over a pan of barely simmering water.
→ While they are melting, cream the EGG YOLKS and SUGAR in an electric mixer for 8–10 minutes until pale and light. Continue to whisk, adding the melted chocolate and butter. Stop the machine, remove the whisk and fold in the ALMONDS with a metal spoon. In a clean glass or metal bowl, whisk the EGG WHITES to stiff peaks. Stir a spoonful of egg white into the chocolate mixture to lighten it before folding in the rest.
→ Grease the sides of a 25cm/10in springform tin and line the base with a circle of buttered greaseproof paper. Pour in the mixture and bake for 20 minutes. Turn the oven down to 170°C/325°F/Gas 3 and continue cooking the cake for a further 40 minutes.
→ Remove the cake and leave in the tin set on a rack until completely cool. Turn out of the tin and remove the greaseproof paper. Delicious served with crème fraîche or ice cream as a cake or pudding.

Marmalade Layer Cake

bitter, fine-cut marmalade	1 × 450g/1lb jar
double cream, Jersey if possible	250ml/8fl oz
plain flour	140g/5oz
baking powder	1 tsp
large, organic eggs	2
unrefined vanilla caster sugar plus extra for whipping	110g/4oz 1 tbsp
milk	1 tbsp
vanilla extract	1 tsp

I have long been a fan of bread guru Dan Lepard and his books and articles. A few months ago, I found a newspaper cutting with this cake recipe and knew its bitter orange marmalade filling would be worth trying. Dan advises that the only tricky part of this cake is folding the flour into the beaten eggs, which has to be done quickly and with a very light hand to keep the cake airy. Other than that, the only real challenge, if you don't make your own marmalade, is to find one bitter and gloopy enough. I make my version of this cake in a single layer and cook the sponge a little longer. I also change the topping, making it in two different ways as you will see.

→ Preheat the oven to 180°C/350°F/Gas 4. Butter and lightly flour two 20cm/8in round cake tins and put a disc of greaseproof or Bakewell paper in the base of each. Warm 140g/5oz of the MARMALADE over a low heat in half the CREAM, and keep it warm while you mix the cake.

→ In a clean bowl, beat the EGGS with the SUGAR until thick and creamy, using an electric whisk or a KitchenAid. Lightly beat in the cream and marmalade mixture, then sift over the FLOUR and BAKING POWDER. Fold the flour and batter together quickly and evenly using the spatula, so that the mix does not deflate. Divide it evenly between the tins and bake for 20–25 minutes or until risen and barely firm. Remove from the oven and leave to cool in the tins on a rack. If you prefer, make one larger sponge and adjust the cooking time accordingly; start testing by piercing with a skewer after 25 minutes and cook longer if you need to. Test again every 5 minutes.

→ Remove the cakes from the tins and peel off the paper. Whip the remaining half of the CREAM with the MILK, VANILLA and the tablespoon of SUGAR until fluffy, then spread half on top of each layer. Stack one on the other as evenly as you can and serve. I like to fold a large tablespoon of MARMALADE into the cream. It gives it bitterness and texture, assuaging the richness of the cream a little. I also like to add a heaped tablespoon of MARMALADE to the top of the sponge once it has cooled—you may need to gently warm it first. Let this cool before adding the whipped marmalade cream topping. Great served with a blood orange salad.

Almond Macaroon Cake

SERVES 6–8

unsalted butter, *softened*	170g/6oz
unrefined vanilla caster sugar	140g/5oz
salt	a pinch
organic lemon	*zest* of 1
organic eggs	2
crème fraîche	4–5 tbsp
unbleached self-raising flour	140g/5oz
almonds, *freshly ground*	85g/3oz

Topping

organic egg whites	2
unrefined vanilla caster sugar	110g/4oz
ground almonds	85g/3oz

This is really a pudding cake, and should be eaten with a memory of warmth to it, alongside some spiced plums, apricots or pears. The top should be both crunchy and gooey at the same time.

→ Grease a 15cm/6in cake tin, then place a circle of greased greaseproof paper in the bottom of it. Cream the softened BUTTER and SUGAR together thoroughly. Add a pinch of SALT, the LEMON ZEST and the EGGS, one by one, beating as you go. Fold in four tablespoons of CRÈME FRAÎCHE, the sifted FLOUR and the ALMONDS. If the mixture is a little heavy, slacken it with another tablespoon of crème fraîche. Bake in the centre of the oven for 30 minutes.

→ Five minutes before you are due to take the cake out, whisk the WHITES stiffly, incorporate half the SUGAR and whisk again until stiff. Fold in the ALMONDS and the rest of the SUGAR lightly and quickly. Take the cake out of the oven and gently but swiftly pile the macaroon mixture on top and spread it across. Return the cake to the oven for about 20 minutes. The top should be biscuit-coloured and crisp to the touch. Cool for 10 minutes, turn out and serve warm with crème fraîche. You can also leave the cake to cool completely, and warm it gently a few hours later when you want to eat it.

Chestnut Cake

best bitter chocolate	110g/4oz
blanched almonds OR walnuts	100g/3½oz
chestnuts	450g/1lb
organic eggs, *separated*	5
caster sugar	225g/8oz
butter, *softened*	110g/4oz
lemon	grated rind of 1
Strega OR cognac	2–3 tbsp

Claudia Roden calls this her favourite chestnut cake in her lovely book The Food of Italy. *You do not have to be purist and use fresh chestnuts; I use excellent whole vacuum-packed ones which good supermarkets sell.*

→ Preheat oven to 180°C/350°F/ Gas 4. Butter and flour a 25cm/10in cake tin. Grate the CHOCOLATE and finely chop the ALMONDS OR WALNUTS.

→ Blitz the CHESTNUTS to a pulp in a food processor. Beat the EGG YOLKS with the SUGAR. Add the BUTTER, chestnut purée, nuts, GRATED LEMON RIND, chocolate and ALCOHOL, and stir thoroughly. Beat the EGG WHITES until stiff, then fold them in and pour into the cake tin. Bake for 50–60 minutes. Cool and remove from the tin. Serve cold.

Malt and Apple Loaf

MAKES A 450G/1LB LOAF

sultanas	55g/2oz
raisins	55g/2oz
apple juice concentrate	2 tbsp
hot water	300ml/10fl oz
unsalted butter	55g/2oz
malt extract	55g/2oz
sharp eating apple like a Cox	1
lemon juice	
plain OR wholemeal flour	285g/10oz
bicarbonate of soda	½ tsp
ground mixed spice	1 tsp
ground cloves	½ tsp

This is a delicious, densely fruited moist loaf, which needs no more than spreading with a thick slice of unsalted butter.

→ Soak the SULTANAS and RAISINS in the APPLE JUICE concentrate mixed with the HOT WATER for 30 minutes. Then place them in a saucepan with the BUTTER and MALT EXTRACT, and heat through until the butter and malt has melted and dissolved.

→ Preheat the oven to 170°C/325°F/Gas 3. Peel and dice the APPLE and spritz with LEMON JUICE. Combine the DRY INGREDIENTS and the diced apple in a bowl, then pour on the hot ones and stir together thoroughly. Plop the mixture into a greased 450g/1lb loaf tin and bake for 1–1½ hours, when a skewer will come out clean. Leave to cool in the tin for about 15 minutes, then turn out and cool on a wire rack.

Banana Bread

self-raising flour	225g/8oz
ground mixed spice	¾ level tsp
sea salt	½ tsp
vanilla caster sugar	100g/3½oz
unsalted butter, *cut into small pieces*	100g/3½oz
good runny honey	1 tbsp
sultanas	100g/3½oz
chopped walnuts (optional)	55g/2oz
ripe organic bananas, *peeled and mashed with a fork*	450g/1lb
organic eggs	2
lemon	juice of 1

→ Preheat the oven to 180°C/350°F/Gas 4. Sift the FLOUR into a bowl and add the MIXED SPICE, SALT and SUGAR. Add the BUTTER, beat in ALL THE REMAINING INGREDIENTS and pour the batter into a greased loaf tin.

→ Bake for an hour, then turn the oven temperature down to 170°C/325°F/Gas 3 for a further 15–30 minutes. Check with a skewer, which should come out clean. Cool in the tin on a rack before turning out. Eat warm with crème fraîche or on its own.

Date and Walnut Loaf

MAKES A 900G/2LB LOAF

pitted dates, *chopped*	225g/8oz
light muscovado sugar	110g/4oz
unsalted butter, *chopped into small pieces*	140g/5oz
bicarbonate of soda	2 level tsp
boiling water	120ml/4fl oz
organic egg	1
plain OR wholemeal flour	400g/14oz
salt	a pinch
walnuts, *chopped*	55g/2oz
vanilla extract	1 tsp

A plain but good sweet and nutty cake that you may also eat with butter and which you can stir up in a trice. Child's play.

→ Put the chopped DATES, SUGAR, chopped BUTTER and BICARB in a mixing bowl. Pour over the BOILING WATER and stir thoroughly. Add the beaten EGG, sifted FLOUR and SALT, WALNUTS and VANILLA EXTRACT and beat together well. Grease and line a loaf tin and scrape the mixture into it. Bake for 1–1½ hours. Check with a skewer after an hour—it should come out clean when the cake is ready.

Madeira Cake

MAKES AN 18CM/7IN ROUND CAKE

butter, *softened*	170g/6oz
caster sugar	170–200g/6–7oz
large organic eggs, *beaten*	3
plain flour, *sifted*	225g/8oz
baking powder	1 tsp
milk	2 tbsp
lemon	*grated rind* of 1
caster OR icing sugar	
strips of lemon rind	

This is the classic recipe. For cherry or fruit cakes, add 225g/8oz glacé cherries or mixed dried fruit.

→ Preheat the oven to 160–180°C/325–350°F/Gas 3–4. Grease and flour an 18cm/7in round cake tin. Cream the BUTTER with the SUGAR until soft and light—the larger amount of sugar gives the cake a very fine texture. Gradually beat in the EGGS. Fold in the FLOUR and BAKING POWDER, then the MILK and the LEMON RIND.

→ Spoon the mixture into the prepared cake tin and bake for 35–40 minutes, then, if the cake is getting too brown, cover the top with greaseproof paper. If you like a moist cake, test (by inserting a skewer into the centre) after a further 40 minutes; if you prefer a slightly drier cake, give it 50–55 minutes. Leave to cool in the tin for a couple of minutes, then turn out onto a wire rack and leave to cool completely. Decorate with CASTER OR ICING SUGAR and a couple of strips of LEMON RIND.

Carrot Cake

self-raising flour	285g/10oz
baking powder	1 tsp
cinnamon, *grind your own for the best flavour*	1 tsp
ground nutmeg	½ tsp
cloves	½ tsp
vegetable oil	250ml/8½fl oz
light muscovado sugar	225g/8oz
organic eggs	4
organic carrots, *grated*	110g/4oz
sultanas, *soaked in warm water for 20 minutes and drained*	55g/2oz
walnuts, *chopped*	110g/4oz
Cream Cheese Icing	
unsalted butter, *softened*	140g/5oz
fresh cream cheese	285g/10oz
unrefined caster sugar	140g/5oz

An American classic, though I prefer to make mine without the customary desiccated coconut that reminds me of old toe nails. You may add pecans instead of walnuts, make it with sultanas or sultana-free, or even add a cup of homemade apple sauce to the mixture if you feel like it. If you feel the icing is a shade too rich, leave the cake plain.

Preheat the oven to 180°C/350°F/Gas 4. Grease two 23cm/9in cake tins, line them with a circle of non-stick baking parchment and grease the parchment. Shake a little flour inside the tin, then pour away the excess.

→ Sift the FLOUR and BAKING POWDER into a large bowl, then add the SPICES. Beat the OIL and SUGAR together thoroughly in a KitchenAid or by hand, then add 2 OF THE EGGS, one at a time, beating in each thoroughly. Separate the remaining 2 eggs and add the final 2 YOLKS. Remove the bowl and stir in the grated CARROTS, SULTANAS and WALNUTS, or throw the walnuts onto the top of the mixture before cooking each sponge. Sift in the FLOUR and BAKING POWDER and add the GROUND SPICES, then fold everything in together. Whisk the EGG WHITES stiffly in a clean bowl, then fold them quickly into the mixture.

→ Divide the mixture equally between the tins. Set the tins on baking trays in the middle of the oven for about 45 minutes, or until a skewer comes out clean. Cool on a rack until the cake has shrunk away from the sides of the tin and can be turned out onto the rack to cool further.

Cream Cheese Icing
→ Beat ALL THE INGREDIENTS together thoroughly until they become a thick, smooth cream. Spread a bit of the mixture over the top of one of the cakes, put the other cake on top, and spread the rest of the topping all over the top and sides of the cake. Refrigerate for at least 2 hours before serving and in between use so the topping doesn't soften.

Lemon and Poppyseed Yoghurt Cake

This is a gloriously lemony cake with the slight acidity of the yoghurt and the unexpected crunch of zillions of tiny poppyseeds, an under-used seed with a lovely nutty flavour. This is so easy to make and works well with a fruit ice cream. It is one of the cakes I bake most frequently, adored by children and grown-ups.

MAKES A 900G/2LB LOAF

poppyseeds	45g/1½ oz
sheep's milk OR good organic yoghurt	150ml/5fl oz
unsalted butter, *softened*	200g/7oz
organic lemons	*zest* of 2
vanilla caster sugar	140g/5oz
eggs	3
plain flour	255g/9oz
baking powder	1½ tsp
organic lemons	juice of 2

→ Preheat the oven to 170°C/325°F/Gas 3. Put the POPPYSEEDS into the YOGHURT and stir to amalgamate. Cream the softened BUTTER, LEMON ZEST and SUGAR in a KitchenAid or with electric beaters until light and fluffy. Scrape the mixture down the sides of the bowl to incorporate it all as you go and, keeping the beaters switched on, add the EGGS one at a time beating in between each addition. Sift the FLOUR and BAKING POWDER onto the creamed mixture. Stir with a metal spoon, adding the LEMON JUICE and yoghurt and poppyseed mixture, which you must fold in thoroughly.

→ Grease and line a loaf tin. Scrape in the cake mixture and bake on a heated baking sheet in the middle of the oven for 55–60 minutes or until a skewer comes out clean. Cool in the tin for 10 minutes or a little longer, then turn out onto a wire rack to cool.

Sally Clarke's Buttermilk, Cinnamon and Pecan Cake

Sally Clarke has been a landmark of a cook with a landmark of a restaurant, her eponymous hostelry at the upper end of Kensington Church Street in London, for over two decades. Here, next door to her food shop, a treasure trove of good things, she has espoused clean, simple, magnificently sourced ingredients with a pure vision of how the food should speak for itself and really taste.

flour	225g/8oz
salt	
ground cinnamon	1 tsp
sugar	140g/5oz
light muscovado sugar	140g/5oz
pecans, *chopped*	55g/2oz
vegetable oil	150ml/5fl oz
baking powder	½ tsp
bicarbonate of soda	½ tsp
small organic egg	1
buttermilk	240ml/8fl oz

→ Heat the oven to 170°C/325°F/Gas 3. Mix the FLOUR with the SALT, CINNAMON, SUGARS, PECANS and OIL. Mix the RAISING AGENTS with the EGG and the BUTTERMILK and mix into the flour until smooth.

→ Pour into a greased and lined cake tin and bake for about 40 minutes. Test with a skewer before cooling on a rack.

Honey and Walnut Cake

walnuts	1 teacup
caster sugar	1 tbsp
lightly flavoured honey, such as a flower honey	225/8oz
organic eggs, *separated*	6
sifted flour	1 teacup
cream	½ teacup

This is more a heavy, sticky sort of soufflé than a cake. Elizabeth David made this cake with honey and hazelnuts, but it is every bit as good with walnuts. Serve it with raspberries and cream, or blackberries bled with caster sugar and Crème de Mûre in the autumn.

→ Preheat the oven to 180°C/350°F/Gas 4. Pound the WALNUTS in a mortar with the CASTER SUGAR. Put the jar of HONEY in a pan of boiling water so that it is workable. Beat the EGG YOLKS in a large bowl, then pour the honey over them. Gradually add the sifted FLOUR and the walnuts and sugar, then bind the mixture with the CREAM, stirring it all together thoroughly. Whisk the EGG WHITES stiffly. Stir the first tablespoon into the mixture, then lightly fold in the rest with a metal spoon.
→ Butter and line a soufflé dish or cake tin and coat the buttered sides with a few extra ground WALNUTS. Pour in the mixture and cook for about 40 minutes. Cool before turning out onto a rack.

Somerset Apple Cake

SERVES 6

sultanas	170g/6oz
good, dry cider	150ml/5fl oz
unrefined caster sugar	225g/8oz
unsalted butter	170g/6oz
organic eggs	2
plain flour	285g/10oz
baking powder	1½ tsp
cinnamon	1 tsp
organic lemon	zest of 1
large Bramley apples, *peeled and thinly sliced*	2

The best cakes to my mind are always the ones that double up as teatime treats or are good enough for pud, which this one, laced with a lovely dollop of sweetened, cider-brandied crème fraîche, certainly is.

→ Soak the SULTANAS in the CIDER for 30 minutes. Preheat the oven to 170°C/325°F/Gas 3. Cream the SUGAR and BUTTER thoroughly, then add the EGGS, one at a time, beating as you go. Fold in the DRY INGREDIENTS, the LEMON ZEST and the thinly sliced APPLES.
→ Add the sultanas soaked in cider, along with any remaining CIDER. Bake in a greased, lined 20cm/8in springform tin for 45–50 minutes, or until a skewer comes out clean.
→ Cool in the tin, then remove the cake to a rack. Reheat it if you are going to eat it as a pudding, and serve with crème fraîche. Lace the crème fraîche with a little Calvados or Somerset cider brandy if you like.

Plum and Hazelnut Pudding Cake

MAKES A 23CM/9IN CAKE

butter, *softened*	85g/3oz
sugar	85g/3oz
organic white flour	140g/5oz
baking powder	1 tsp
salt	a pinch
organic eggs, *beaten*	2
milk	2 tbsp
ground hazelnuts	55g/2oz
good, not overripe red plums	12
Topping	
butter	55g/2oz
demerara sugar	65g/2½oz
allspice	1½ tsp
organic eggs, *beaten*	2

This is a sort of triple-decker cake, with the plums poached inside it, and a deliciously crunchy, sugary spiced glaze.

→ Preheat oven to 180°C/350°F/Gas 4. Butter a 23cm/9in springform cake tin, and line the bottom with greased baking parchment.

→ Beat the SOFTENED BUTTER and SUGAR together well until light and creamy. Sift the FLOUR, BAKING POWDER and a pinch of SALT into a bowl. Whisk the EGGS and MILK together in a bowl, and beat them alternately with the flour into the creamed butter. Spoon into the cake tin, and sprinkle with the ground HAZELNUTS. Halve and stone the PLUMS, and arrange them cut side up in concentric circles.

→ For the topping, melt the BUTTER, stir in the SUGAR and SPICE, and amalgamate. Cool slightly, then whisk in the beaten EGGS. Pour this over the plums and bake in the oven for about an hour and ten minutes, but test with a skewer after an hour, it should come clean even in the middle. Serve warm with thick cream.

Caramelised Apple Cake with Calvados Crème Fraîche

SERVES 8–10

sharp eating apples such as Cox's	1kg/2¼lb
unsalted butter	225g/8oz
extra butter to cook the apples in	55g/2oz
good runny honey	55g/2oz
unrefined icing sugar	225g/8oz
organic eggs	4
plain flour	225g/8oz
dry yeast	½ a sachet
sea salt	a pinch
demerara sugar	

Another of those lovely pudding cakes, you can also make this with pears. More pudding than cake, it can be served with some crème fraîche laced with Somerset cider brandy, Calvados or rum.

→ Preheat the oven to 180°C/350°F/Gas 4.

→ Peel the APPLES and cut them into small dice. Brown them in 555g/2oz of butter, adding the HONEY after a few minutes. Remove from the heat and drain the juice from the apples, keeping it to pour over the cake later.

→ Cream the 225g/8oz of BUTTER and the ICING SUGAR until white and fluffy, then whisk in the EGGS, one by one. Add the YEAST, sifted FLOUR and SALT, and fold in the apples. Grease a large springform tin and line the base with a disc of greased greaseproof. Sprinkle a thin veil of DEMERARA around the sides. Pour in the mixture and scatter a bit more demerara over the surface of the cake.

→ Bake for about 1½ hours, or until a skewer comes out clean. Cool for 15 minutes before removing from the tin. Serve warm with the crème fraîche and a small jug of the apple juice.

Upside-down Cape Gooseberry and Almond Cake

Cape gooseberries, weighed after removing their leaves	350g/12oz
unrefined caster sugar	200g/7oz
unsalted butter	200g/7oz
organic ground almonds	200g/7oz
vanilla extract	a few drops
organic eggs	3
organic orange	*finely grated zest of 1*
organic orange	juice of 1
crème fraîche	1 tbsp
Shipton Mill's soft pastry and cake organic white flour	110g/4oz
baking powder	1 tsp
salt	a pinch
demerara sugar to sprinkle	

This is a lovely pudding-cake, the sharp, orange orbs of Cape gooseberry bursting on to the tongue, the sponge moist with almonds. Use Shipton Mill's soft pastry and cake organic white flour. It's made from English organic wheat which is soft to grind, with lower protein levels, so is good for cakes and pastry.

→ Preheat the oven to 170°C/325°F/Gas 3. Butter a 20cm/8in springform cake tin. Cover the base with a layer of Cape GOOSEBERRIES, leaving just under a third of them to add to the cake mixture.

→ Cream the SUGAR and BUTTER until light and fluffy, then stir in the ground ALMONDS and VANILLA extract. Beat in the EGGS, one at a time, fold in the ORANGE ZEST AND JUICE, then the CRÈME FRAÎCHE, sifted FLOUR, BAKING POWDER and SALT. Fold the remaining GOOSEBERRIES into the mixture. Sprinkle a bit of DEMERARA SUGAR over the layer of gooseberries in the tin, then plop the mixture over them and smooth it down with a rubber spatula.

→ Bake in the middle of the oven for 1 hour and 10 minutes, but check with a skewer every 5 minutes after 1 hour. Leave to cool in the tin on a rack until just warm, then turn out upside down on to a large plate and serve warm with crème fraîche.

Pineapple and Walnut Upside-down Cake

large pineapple	1
unsalted butter	55g/2oz
light muscovado sugar	55g/2oz
unsalted butter, *softened*	225g/8oz
large eggs	4
unrefined granulated sugar	225g/8oz
self-raising flour	200g/7oz
baking powder	2 tsp
walnuts, *coarsely ground*	55g/2oz

This pineapple cake looks beautiful and tastes refreshingly good. It is as delicious for tea as it is for pudding, and can be eaten warm or cold. Use a normal gratin dish, or pudding dish, to bake it in—I used a rectangular terracotta dish measuring about 35 × 25cm/14 x 10in. If you prefer, use half walnuts and half almonds.

→ Peel the PINEAPPLE to remove all the little brown sharp bits. Slice in circles and remove the cores with an apple corer.

→ Melt the 55g/2oz of BUTTER and MUSCOVADO SUGAR together, then bubble them up, stirring as you go, until they are well amalgamated. Pour this mixture over the bottom of the dish and brush it up the sides. It will drop back into the base, but don't worry.

→ Put a layer of whole fresh pineapple slices over the mixture in the middle of the dish (mine took three). Cut the rest of the pineapple into semicircles and arrange them down the sides.

I fill in the joins with pineapple triangles as I like the cake to be as fruity as possible.

→ Process the 225g/8oz of BUTTER, EGGS, SUGAR, FLOUR, BAKING POWDER and WALNUTS together and pour them over the pineapple. Bake for 50–60 minutes, checking with a skewer after 50. The top will be golden brown.

→ Cool to warm, then run a knife around the edge of the cake and turn it upside down onto a plate, where the pineapple will be glazed with a gorgeous butterscotch goo.

→ Serve with or without cream and a pineapple syrup made with extra pineapple juice and sugar.

Orange and Pine Nut Cake

SERVES 8

caster sugar	190g/6 and a bit oz
organic eggs, *separated*	6
flaked almonds, *toasted and roughly ground*	175g/6oz
pine nuts	275g/10oz
oranges	zest and juice of 2 (keep separate)
runny honey	2 tbsp

This recipe comes from James Webb, head pastry chef at Baker and Spice.

→ Preheat the oven to 180°C/350°F/Gas 4. In a bowl, whisk 85g/3oz of the SUGAR with the EGG YOLKS until thick and pale. Fold in the ground ALMONDS, whole PINE NUTS and ORANGE ZEST.

→ In another bowl, whisk the remaining SUGAR with the EGG WHITES to a thick, glossy meringue. Fold, a third at a time, into the orange and pine nut mixture, then pour into a buttered cake tin, with a buttered greaseproof paper lining. My loaf tin was just too small, I will try a springform tin next time.

→ Bake in the centre of the oven for about an hour, or until a skewer comes out clean. Leave to cool for 15 minutes. Warm the HONEY until it thins, mix with the ORANGE JUICE, and pour this mixture over the cake in the tin.

→ Leave to cool, then remove from the tin and serve with thick cream and fresh fruit.

Auntie Fei's Sour Cream Coffee Cake

Cake batter

butter	55g/2oz
unrefined caster sugar	340g/12oz
organic eggs	4
flour	225/8oz
bicarbonate of soda	½ tsp
baking powder	1½ tsp
soured cream	200ml/7fl oz
vanilla extract	1 tsp

Filling

cream cheese	110g/4oz
egg	1
sugar	1 tbsp
dried cranberries	30g/1oz
OR cooking apple, *peeled and diced*	1
walnuts, *toasted and roughly chopped*	30g/1oz

Topping

flour	110g/4oz
sugar	110g/4oz
salt	1 tsp
ground cinnamon	1½ tsp
walnuts, *toasted and roughly chopped*	85g/3oz
melted butter	30g/1oz
vanilla extract	½ tsp
almond extract	½ tsp

It has taken me until now to realise that in America a coffee cake isn't a coffee cake. It is a cake to eat while you drink coffee, but it has absolutely no coffee in its make-up. This recipe comes from my friend Su's Aunt Fei and relies on the best ingredients, such as really good cream cheese. Please don't think that a proprietary brand like Philadelphia will do: it won't. Get the real stuff and make sure it is without hideous gelling agents and additives. You can vary the fruited middle. I often use dried cherries or cranberries instead of apples, but some sharpness is a must. You will need a bundt tin if possible, though don't worry unduly if you haven't got one.

→ Cream the BUTTER and SUGAR until light and fluffy. Add the EGGS one at a time, mixing well between each one. Sift the DRY INGREDIENTS together and combine the SOURED CREAM and VANILLA in a separate bowl. Alternately add the soured cream mixture and dry ingredients to the butter and sugar in three phases, combining well each time.

→ For the filling, beat together the CREAM CHEESE, EGG and SUGAR until smooth. To make the topping, mix together the FLOUR, SUGAR, SALT, CINNAMON and WALNUTS. Add the BUTTER and EXTRACTS and stir.

→ To assemble the cake, pour half the cake batter into a greased bundt pan and sprinkle with the CRANBERRIES OR DICED APPLE and the toasted WALNUTS. Pour the cream cheese mixture evenly over the nuts and berries and cover with the remaining batter. Sprinkle the topping over the whole cake. Bake at 180°C/350°F/Gas 4 for 50–55 minutes.

Cranberry Streusel Cake

Cake

large organic egg	1
unsalted butter, *softened*	55g/2oz
demerara sugar	85g/3oz
self-raising flour	85g/3oz
baking powder	½ level tsp
cranberry juice OR orange juice *freshly squeezed*	2 tbsp 2 tbsp

Topping

cranberries, left whole	85g/3oz
demerara sugar	85g/3oz
plain flour	85g/3oz
unsalted butter	55g/2oz
cinnamon, *ground in a mortar*	1 tsp

A streusel is just a crumble-topped cake, Austrian in origin, with the crumble providing a good crunch to an otherwise plain, spongy-textured cake. I think this is delicious eaten warm with clotted cream, but you could also eat it American coffee-cake style, with your coffee. I have adapted this from the wonderful Fruit Book *that Jane Grigson published in 1982.*

→ Preheat the oven to 180°C/350°F/Gas 4. Tip ALL THE INGREDIENTS FOR THE CAKE into a KitchenAid or electric mixer and beat well until smooth, or mix by hand. Line the sides and the base of an 18cm/7in square tin or a round springform tin with greaseproof or Bakewell paper and grease everything well. Pour in the mixture and flatten it down level with a palate knife. Throw the CRANBERRIES over the mixture in an even layer.

→ Mix the REMAINING TOPPING INGREDIENTS together by hand or in a food processor as you would for a crumble. Pour the mixture over the cranberries, making sure it is in an even layer with the side of a sharp knife.

→ Bake in the centre of the oven for about 50 minutes or until cooked. Test with a long skewer poked right down through the crumble into the cake—it should come out clean. Cool in the cake tin on top of a rack for 10 minutes to allow the air to circulate, then lift the cake out of the tin with the ends of the Bakewell paper. Cool to warm on the rack before serving if it is for a pudding, or leave to cool completely.

Blackcurrant Streusel Cake
→ This cake works as well with BLACKCURRANTS, which also have a zingy, sharp acidity like the cranberry.

Rhubarb and Ginger Crumble Cake

SERVES 8

Crumble

plain flour	110g/4oz
light muscovado sugar	4 tbsp
unsalted butter	85g/3oz

Fruit

rhubarb, *cut into 1cm/½in chunks*	750g/1lb 10oz
unrefined vanilla caster sugar	1 tbsp, or to taste
dried ginger root, *ground*	1 tsp

Cake

unsalted butter, *softened*	170g/6oz
unrefined vanilla caster sugar	170g/6oz
organic eggs, *beaten*	3
plain flour	170g/6oz
baking powder	2 tsp
milk	1 tbsp

I often go to the shop Books For Cooks in Notting Hill, London, and their small café at the back. Every so often they bring out a small volume of recipes from their staff of cooks who cook in the café and from some of their favourite food writers. I have always made fruit muffins with crumble tops and they have expanded the form to this cake, which could be made with any seasonal fruit, such as cranberry, blackcurrant, black-berry and apple, peach, pear or plum. I use dried ginger root in my version as the intensity of its flavour works so well with rhubarb, but if you can't get it, the ground stuff will do.

→ Preheat the oven to 190°C/375°F/Gas 5. Butter a 25cm/10in springform cake tin and line the base with baking parchment. Pulse ALL THE CRUMBLE INGREDIENTS together briefly until they cohere in a crumbly way. Toss the chopped RHUBARB with the SUGAR and SPICE in a bowl. You may like to add a little more sugar.

→ Beat the BUTTER and SUGAR for the cake together with an electric beater or in a KitchenAid until they are pale and fluffy. Beat in the EGGS, a little at a time, sprinkling in a tablespoon of sifted FLOUR when you have added about half the beaten EGG to stop it curdling. Sift in the rest of the flour and BAKING POWDER and fold in gently but thoroughly. Fold in the MILK.

→ Scrape the cake mixture into the cake tin, followed by the rhubarb, and sprinkle the crumble on top. Bake for about an hour. The crumble should be golden and crunchy and the rhubarb cooked through by then. Place on a rack and cool for 15 minutes, then either release the spring and unmould the cake to serve warm with cream, preferably clotted, or leave until cold to turn out and eat for tea.

Buttery Lemon and Lime Cake

SERVES 6–8

butter	200g/7oz
vanilla caster sugar	340g/12oz
organic eggs	2
self-raising flour	110g/4oz
baking powder	1 tsp

This cake was a happy accident. I found myself following the instructions for one recipe while using the ingredients for another, but it wasn't too late to change tack and invent something totally different that would be as good for a pudding as warm from the oven for tea. You can get the lime and lemon oil from good supermarkets, but they are optional.

→ Preheat oven to 180°C/350°F/Gas 4. Grease and flour a 23cm/9in springform tin.

→ Cream the BUTTER and SUGAR thoroughly, then add the EGGS one by one. Sift in the FLOUR and BAKING POWDER together, add the JUICES and FRUIT OILS, then the CRÈME

lemons	juice of 2 (5 tbsp)
lemon	rind of 1
limes	juice of 1½
lime	rind of 1
Boyajian pure lime oil	a few drops
Boyajian pure lemon oil	a few drops
crème fraîche	1 tbsp
Icing	
unrefined icing sugar	30g/1oz
lemon juice	2–3 tsp

FRAÎCHE, and fold in lightly. Pour into the tin and bake for 45–50 minutes: a skewer should come out clean. Stir the 2–3 teaspoons of LEMON JUICE into the ICING SUGAR for the icing, then spread it over the top. It should just cover it in a thin, sticky veil.

Polenta, Almond and Lemon Cake

SERVES 12

unsalted butter, *softened*	325g/12oz
golden caster OR icing sugar	325g/12oz
organic ground almonds	325g/12oz
vanilla extract	2 tsp
large organic eggs	4
lemons	zest of 3
lemon	juice of 1
organic polenta	225g/8oz
baking powder	1½tsp
sea salt	½ tsp

I have adapted this from the original River Café Cook Book. *This golden-crusted cake should ooze a slightly sad, grainy, almondy centre.*

→ Preheat oven to 160°C/325°F/Gas 3. Butter and flour a 23cm/9in springform cake tin.

→ Beat the BUTTER and SUGAR together in an electric mixer, or by hand, until light and fluffy. Stir in the ground ALMONDS and VANILLA. Beat in the EGGS, one at a time. Fold in the LEMON ZEST AND JUICE, the POLENTA, BAKING POWDER and salt. Spoon into the tin and bake. I kept checking mine from 45 minutes, but it wasn't ready until it had cooked for an hour.

Lemon and Cardamom Cake

MAKES A 23CM/9IN CAKE

cardamom pods	2 heaped tsp
unsalted butter	170g/6oz
light muscovado sugar	110g/4oz
eggs	3
plain flour	200g/7oz
baking powder	1½ tsp
bicarbonate of soda	½ tsp
fine maize meal	55g/2oz
Greek yoghurt	10 tsp
large organic lemons	*grated* zest and juice of 2
demerara sugar to sprinkle	

Citrus works wonderfully with cardamom. This is a light, sticky pudding of a cake, perfect with crème fraîche or orange ice cream.

→ Preheat the oven to 180°C/350°F/Gas 4. Grease and line a 23cm/9in springform cake tin. Crush the CARDAMOM PODS with a pestle and mortar to split them, remove the husks and crush the seeds.

→ Cream the BUTTER and SUGAR until light and fluffy, then beat in the EGGS one by one, adding a little sifted flour if the mixture begins to curdle. Sift the FLOUR, BAKING POWDER and BICARB into the mixture, then add the cardamom seeds. Fold in the MAIZE MEAL and Greek YOGHURT, add the LEMON ZEST AND JUICE, and plop the mixture into the tin, smoothing the top. Bake for 35 minutes, then gingerly open the oven door, pull the cake towards you, and throw a handful of DEMERARA over the top of it. Carry on baking for a further 15 minutes, then test with a skewer. Almost clean means that it is cooked—you want a slightly damp centre with a crust of crunchy sugar on top.

→ Cool for 10–15 minutes, then finish cooling on a rack. Eat it, if your timing is impeccable, with a memory of warmth to it.

Drenched Ginger and Lemon Cake

SERVES 6–8

unsalted butter	170g/6oz
light muscovado sugar	170g/6oz
large organic eggs	2
lemons	*grated* zest of 2
lemons	juice of 2
baking powder	1 tsp
salt	a pinch
self-raising flour	175g/6oz
milk	3–5 tbsp
ginger from a jar of stem ginger in syrup	4 pieces
demerara sugar	35g/1½oz
ginger syrup	2 tbsp

This is my take on the classic lemon cake, whose top you attack with deep skewer holes and trickle down a sticky, tangy lemon syrup. This is the same with ginger and lemon, but the ginger's heat and strength does not overwhelm the citrus. The top ends up looking rather like a glossy, caramel-coloured brandy snap. I used half Shipton Mill's wholemeal, and half Dove's Farm organic plain white.

→ Preheat the oven to 180°C/350°F/Gas 4. Butter a 15–18cm/6–7in cake tin and line the base with a circle of buttered greaseproof paper.

→ Cream the BUTTER and MUSCOVADO SUGAR until light and fluffy, then beat in the EGGS one at a time. Grate the LEMON ZEST into the mixture, then sift over the BAKING POWDER, SALT and FLOUR, and fold them in lightly with a metal spoon. Stir in enough MILK to give a dropping consistency, then add the finely chopped GINGER and fold in lightly. Plop into the tin, smooth the top, and bake in the centre of the oven for about 40–50 minutes until springy to the touch in the centre.

→ Remove from the oven, and leave for 15 minutes before turning out onto a rack. When still warm, place on a plate, and with a long skewer, pierce holes all over the cake from the top through to the bottom. Put the DEMERARA SUGAR, LEMON JUICE and GINGER SYRUP in a pan, stir as it heats to dissolve the sugar, then bubble it up fiercely for a minute or so. Pour it as slowly as you can over the top of the cake, allowing it to seep down the holes. Serve warm or cold with crème fraîche.

Lemon Drizzle Cake

SERVES 6–8

unsalted butter	170g / 6oz
light muscovado sugar	170g / 6oz
large eggs	2
organic lemons	*grated* zest of 2
organic lemons	juice of 2
baking powder	1 tsp
salt	a pinch
organic self-raising flour, (I used half wholemeal, half white)	170g / 6oz
milk	3–5 tbsp
demerara sugar	45g / 1½oz

Do use some wholewheat flour, which gives this cake its great texture, and taste the lemon drizzle to make sure it is lipsmackingly tart—you may need to use three lemons if they are small and not very juicy. It's worth doubling the ingredients and making two cakes so you can eat one and freeze one.

→ Preheat the oven to 180°C/350°F/gas 4. Butter a 15–18cm/ 6–7in cake tin and line the base with a circle of buttered greaseproof paper. Cream the BUTTER and MUSCOVADO SUGAR until light and fluffy, then beat in the EGGS one at a time. Grate the LEMON ZEST into the mixture, then sift over the BAKING POWDER, SALT and FLOUR and fold them in lightly with a metal spoon. Stir in enough MILK to give a dropping consistency. Plop into the tin, smooth the top, and bake in the centre of the oven for 40–50 minutes until springy to the touch in the centre.

→ Remove from the oven, and leave for 15 minutes before turning out onto a rack. When still warm, place on a plate, and with a long skewer, pierce holes all over the cake from the top through to the bottom. Put the DEMERARA SUGAR and LEMON JUICE in a pan, stir as it heats to dissolve the sugar, then bubble it up fiercely for a minute or so. Pour it as slowly as you can over the top of the cake, allowing it to seep down the holes. Serve warm or cold with crème fraîche.

Summer Lemon and Raspberry Cake

ENOUGH FOR 10–12 SLICES

organic eggs, *separated*	6
unrefined granulated sugar	170g/6oz
lemon juice	2 tbsp
organic lemon	zest of 1
salt	a pinch
flour	85g/3oz
cornflour	30g/1oz
Topping	
organic egg	1
unrefined granulated sugar	140g/5oz
lemon	zest and juice of 1 made up to 150ml/5fl oz with water
flour	30g/1oz
double cream, Jersey if possible	300ml/10fl oz
passion fruit	juice of 2
passion fruit seeds OR passion-fruit curd (optional)	1 tsp 2 tbsp
raspberries	340g/12oz

A lusciously rich, primrose-yellow cake, sharp with lemons and raspberries, to which you can add a seam of passion fruit or passion-fruit curd for a more intense sharpness to contrast with the cream-laden topping. Serve an extra bowl of summer berries on the side. If you want to make this when raspberries are out of season, add a handful of toasted flaked almonds to the ingredients, pressing them on to the creamy sides of the cake when you have added the topping. Or just stick with the passion fruit.

→ Preheat the oven to 180°C/350°F/Gas 4. Beat the 6 YOLKS with the SUGAR, LEMON JUICE AND ZEST, and SALT in a KitchenAid or electric mixer. Mix thoroughly for at least 5 minutes until the mixture is pale, light and fluffy. Sift in the FLOUR and CORNFLOUR bit by bit, folding them in as you go.

→ Whisk the EGG WHITES to stiff peaks. Stir the first table-spoonful into the cake mixture, then fold in the rest a tablespoon at a time. Grease three 18cm/7in cake tins well and dust them with flour. Divide the mixture between them and bake for 45 minutes or until the cakes are golden and dry when spiked with a skewer. Cool on wire racks in inverted tins then turn out onto the racks.

→ To make the topping, beat the EGG, SUGAR and LEMON ZEST until foamy, then add the sifted FLOUR and LEMON JUICE. Cook in a double boiler, stirring continuously until velvety smooth and thickened. Cool. Whip the CREAM until it holds softly, then fold it into the lemon mixture. Fold in the PASSION FRUIT JUICE OR CURD at this stage if you are using it.

→ Put half the RASPBERRIES on top of the first layer of sponge, add some of the lemony cream, then repeat with the second layer of cake and the rest of the raspberries and another layer of cream. Plop on your third deck, making sure you leave enough mixture to coat the whole top and sides of the cake.

→ If you do want to use passion-fruit curd, follow the recipe for redcurrant curd on p. 420, substituting 10 passion fruit for the redcurrants. Scoop the flesh out of the passion fruit into a sieve over a bowl and using as much muscle power as you can, stir and push the juice and some of the pulp through the sieve, then transfer the flesh and seeds still in the sieve to a small pan. Warm gently and stir so flesh parts company more easily from seed. Follow the recipe, adding the sieved juice of the passion fruit with the eggs and sugar, and stirring in the pulp at the end of the cooking time.

Orange-Scented Ricotta Cake

SERVES 8

unsalted butter	85g/3oz
vanilla caster sugar	140g/5oz
large organic eggs	2
organic orange and lemon	*grated zest* of ½
potato flour	3 tbsp
baking powder	1½ tsp
pinch of salt	
fresh ricotta, *drained through cloth or kitchen paper for a few hours*	450g/1lb
organic raisins, *soaked in a little hot freshly squeezed orange juice to plump up*	55g/2oz
orange-flower water	1 tbsp
Grand Marnier OR Cointreau	2 tbsp
unrefined icing sugar to sprinkle	

This is the lightest of cakes, made with potato flour and with the ricotta sieved to aerate it. Grand Marnier and orange-flower water intensify and perfume the cake giving it a more Middle Eastern than Mediterranean feel. Serve some summer fruits like strawberries alongside it, turned in a little sugar and freshly squeezed orange juice.

→ Preheat the oven to 180°C/350°F/Gas 4. Beat the BUTTER and all but a tablespoon of the SUGAR together until pale and creamy. Add the EGGS and continue to whisk. Add the ZESTS, POTATO FLOUR, BAKING POWDER and SALT.

→ Push the RICOTTA through the small disc of a mouli or through a sieve, and blend it into the other ingredients. Fold in the RAISINS in their orange brew and sprinkle over the ORANGE-FLOWER WATER and GRAND MARNIER.

→ Butter a 23cm/9in springform tin, scatter the rest of the SUGAR into it and roll it around the base and sides, discarding any excess. Scrape in the cake mixture and bake in the middle of the oven for about 55 minutes, or until a skewer comes out clean. Leave to cool on a wire rack.

→ Turn out onto a plate and sprinkle over a light dusting of UNREFINED ICING SUGAR if you like.

Torta di Santiago

SERVES 8

vanilla caster sugar	110g/4oz
organic lemon, *grated zest*	1 tsp
organic eggs, *separated*	7
almonds with skins, *finely ground in a food processor*	225g/8oz
cinnamon, *ground in a mortar*	1/2 tsp
unrefined icing sugar to sprinkle	

This recipe is for almonds with their skins still on, but if you don't like the idea, blanch and skin them or use almonds that have already been skinned.

→ Preheat the oven to 180°C/350°F/Gas 4. Cream the SUGAR, LEMON ZEST and EGG YOLKS until light and fluffy, then stir in the GROUND ALMONDS and CINNAMON. Beat the EGG WHITES to stiff peaks, stir the first tablespoon into the almond mixture, then fold in the rest gently to incorporate as much air as you can.

→ Pour into a greased 20cm/8in springform cake tin and bake for 45 minutes or until a skewer comes out dry. Cool on a rack before turning out and serving with a little icing sugar sprinkled over it.

Lemon Devil's Food Cake

Green and Black's organic cocoa powder	3 tbsp
unrefined granulated sugar	3 level tbsp
water	3 tbsp
milk	150ml/5fl oz
vanilla pod	*scraped-out seeds* of 1
unsalted butter	110g/4oz
light muscovado sugar	225g/8oz
organic eggs, *separated*	3
plain flour	85g/3oz
cornflour	30g/1oz
baking soda	1 tsp
salt	a pinch

Icing

unrefined icing sugar	285g/10oz
unsalted butter, *softened*	225g/8oz
organic lemons	zest and juice of 2
Grand Marnier OR Cointreau	2 tbsp

A deviation, if such a term can be considered applicable to something as diabolically, devilishly rich as the devil's food cake. Lemon and chocolate are great bedfellows, and the black and white combination of exterior and interior here is more heaven than hell, though still rich enough to be pronounced as wicked as the original sin.

→ Preheat the oven to 170°C/325°F/Gas 3. Put the COCOA, SUGAR and WATER in the top of a double boiler and cook over a gently simmering heat until thickened and velvety smooth. Whisk in the MILK and VANILLA SEEDS, and set aside to cool.

→ Cream the BUTTER and SUGAR until light and fluffy, then beat in the EGG YOLKS one at a time. Beat in the chocolate mixture. Sift the FLOURS and BAKING SODA a couple of times and beat them into the mixture. Whisk the EGG WHITES stiffly and fold them into the cake mixture. Scrape the mixture into two 18cm/7in cake tins, and bake for 30–35 minutes or until a skewer comes out clean. Cool the cakes in their tins on a rack.

→ To make the icing, cream the ICING SUGAR and softened BUTTER until pale and fluffy, then fold in the LEMON ZEST AND JUICE and the GRAND MARNIER. Beat until really smooth and creamy, then spread the icing on top of the first layer and over the whole cake.

Vanilla Cheesecake

SERVES 6–8

Base

Dove's organic digestive biscuits	1 × 340g/12oz packet
unsalted butter	55g/2oz

Middle

fresh full-fat cream cheese, best you can find	450g/1lb
organic eggs	2
organic egg yolk	1
organic double cream	170ml/6fl oz
vanilla caster sugar	55g/2oz
split vanilla pod, *the seeds scraped out with a teaspoon*	1
organic lemons	zest of 2

How sixties the cheesecake feels, yet though it may have gone from glossy and fashionable to a tad tarnished and passé, I can't help but admire its tenacity. Sometimes it is exactly what one wants, the cool, creamy, clagginess, dense and deep above a gently sodden crumb base, with the faint echo of vanilla bean. Use the best cream cheese you can find, additive and thickener-free. Make your own vanilla sugar: wash and dry vanilla pods when you have scraped out the seeds, put them in a jar with unrefined caster sugar, and they will keep for ages.

→ Preheat the oven to 190°C/375°F/Gas 5. Put the BISCUITS OR CRACKERS in a ziploc bag, seal it tight and do maximum damage with a rolling pin, bashing and crushing and rolling to crumbs. Tip the crumbs into an 20cm/8in loose-bottomed cake tin and pour over the melted butter. Stir to amalgamate, then press the mixture down into the bottom of the tin with a wooden spoon. You may keep a little of the mixture back to decorate the edge of the soured cream topping at the end if you like.

Top

soured cream	150ml/5fl oz
vanilla sugar	1 dsrtsp

→ Bake for 10 minutes. Meanwhile, put the CREAM CHEESE, EGGS and YOLK, DOUBLE CREAM, SUGAR, VANILLA SEEDS and ZEST together in a huge bowl and whisk by hand until utterly smooth. Pour into the tin and cook for 25 minutes or until still5trembling in the middle when nudged, as the filling will continue to cook out of the oven on a rack and needs to be light and creamy not solid and claggy.

→ When the cheesecake has cooled on the rack, remove the sides of the tin. Beat the SOURED CREAM and SUGAR together and spread gently over the top of the cheesecake with a palette knife. Add a little LEMON ZEST, grated sparingly on top, or some bright berries in summer. You may refrigerate it and serve it cold, or with a memory of warmth to it.

John Farley's Fine Cheesecake

SERVES 8

shortcrust pastry *made with 170g/6oz flour and 85g/3oz butter* (see p. 104)	
best fresh cream cheese	225g/8oz
organic double cream	2½ tbsp
large organic egg yolks	4
butter, *melted*	55g/2oz
amaretti, *crushed*	85g/3oz
Marcona almonds, *roasted, blanched and ground*	85g/3oz
unrefined vanilla caster sugar	85g/3oz
orange-flower OR rose water	1 tbsp
nutmeg, *grated*	

At the risk of creating an international incident, I feel here is the time and the place to say that cheesecake was not invented by the Americans. Heresy. The very idea! In fact, John Farley of the London Tavern, one of the most illustrious cooks of his time in the 18th century, offered eight different cheesecake recipes in his London Art of Cookery. *I have adapted to the modern taste, using shortcrust instead of puff pastry, and amaretti instead of macaroons. The orange-flower or rose water scents the cheese-cake delicately and distinctively, but err on the side of caution so as not to overwhelm; too much is akin to bubble bath.*

→ Preheat the oven to 180°C/350°F/Gas 4. Line a greased 23cm/9in tin with a removable base with the PASTRY.

→ Mix the CREAM CHEESE, CREAM, EGG YOLKS, BUTTER, AMARETTI, ALMONDS and SUGAR in a large bowl and beat together. Add the FLOWER WATER and NUTMEG carefully, tasting the mixture for the right degree of flavour. Scrape the mixture into the pastry case and bake for 30–40 minutes until the top is browned all over. Eat warm with pouring cream.

BREA
and

D

scones

White Loaf

MAKES 2 LOAVES

organic strong white flour	1kg/2¼lb
fresh yeast	45g/1½oz
fine sea salt	3 tsp
warm water	600ml/1 pint

I make this bread on a terracotta pizza stone, which does two loaves beautifully. It radiates the heat evenly and there are no tin sides to give you a less crusty crust. Heat transfer is critical during baking, and stones radiate heat in a totally different way to a metal tin. I also throw in a splash of water or squirt it into the oven with my iron spray—the steam helps to caramelise the surface of the loaf. I think it works best after the loaf has been in the oven for 10 minutes, but see what you think. You can buy fresh yeast at the bread counter of your supermarket IF they have a bakery in the store. The water should be 30°C in summer, 40°C in winter. To guess it, it needs to be hand-hot, not boiling.

→ Allow approximately 14½ hours from the time you start the dough to cooking your bread. Dissolve a piece of YEAST the size of a pea in 120ml/4fl oz of WARM WATER. I stir the yeast in with a tiny whisk in a jug. Leave it for 10 minutes, then add it to 200g/7oz of the FLOUR to which you have added half a teaspoonful of fine SEA SALT. Mix the dough a little with your fingers until it just coheres, then cover it with a tea towel soaked in cold water and wrung out—this prevents a skin forming on the dough. Leave it for 12 hours at room temperature in the kitchen. I have left it a couple of hours longer when convenient and it has not come to any harm.

→ Twelve hours later, dissolve the remaining FRESH YEAST in 120ml/4fl oz of WARM WATER, whisking it as before. Leave it for 10–15 minutes in the warmth of the kitchen. It won't froth up as it does with a quick-rise bread when you add sugar to the yeast and water at this stage.

→ Mix the rest of the bag of FLOUR with the remaining SALT and throw in a handful of WHEATGERM. Add the starter dough, which will be spongy, to the mixture, then the yeasty liquid followed by the remaining 340ml/12fl oz of WARM WATER. Work it in the bowl with your fingers until it coheres, then remove it to the work surface and knead energetically for 8–10 minutes.

→ Put it back in the large bowl, cover with the damp cloth again, and leave it for an hour to rise; it will double in volume. Put the dough back on the work surface. Seize it, and bash the air out of it, then leave it uncovered for 15 minutes.

→ Preheat the oven to 220°C/425°F/Gas 7 and put the baking stone on the middle shelf to heat up. Divide the dough into two pieces with a knife and bash out the air again. Form each piece into a ball and cover with a damp cloth for 50 minutes.

It will double in size again. Snip a little decorative hole or two in the middle of the top, scatter a tiny bit of FLOUR over and, with a flat spatula, plop the loaves on to the hot stone. After 10 minutes, spray or throw a little water into the oven until the steam hisses. The loaves will need 35–40 minutes. Check that the bottoms sound hollow before leaving them to cool for an hour on a rack.

Wholemeal Caraway Rolls

MAKES ABOUT 20

butter	55g/2oz
milk	340ml/12fl oz
fresh yeast	55g/2oz
organic stoneground wholemeal flour	200g/7oz
boiling water	340ml/12fl oz
sea salt	1½ tsp
molasses sugar	2 tbsp
organic stoneground wholemeal flour	285g/10oz
organic strong unbleached white flour	255g/9oz
caraway seeds (optional)	a handful

→ Melt the BUTTER in a pan. Pour in the MILK and heat to luke-warm. Crumble the YEAST into a bowl, pour in the liquid and stir until the yeast has dissolved. Mix the 200g/7oz of WHOLE-MEAL FLOUR with the BOILING WATER, and add the SALT and SUGAR, the 300g/10oz of STONEGROUND FLOUR and most of the WHITE FLOUR. Mix everything together into a pliable dough, then cover the bowl with a tea towel you have rinsed in hot water and squeezed out, and leave the dough in a warm place to rise for about an hour.

→ Using the rest of the WHITE FLOUR, knead the dough with determination for about 7 minutes on a floured surface, then separate into two pieces. Cut each piece into 10 and shape them into rolls. Place them on two greased baking sheets, cover with tea towels and leave for a further 30 minutes. Preheat the oven to 220°C/425°F/Gas 7.

→ Bake in the middle of the oven for 10 minutes, then let the rolls cool on a wire rack under a tea towel. Serve warm.

Malted Grain Loaf

MAKES 3 LOAVES

organic malted grain flour	1kg/2¼lb
strong organic wholemeal flour	500g/1lb 2oz
sea salt	3 heaped tsp
fresh yeast	45g/1½oz
molasses sugar	3 heaped tsp
hand-hot water (feels neither boiling, nor tepid)	850ml/1½ pints
extra virgin olive oil	3 tbsp
sesame, sunflower or poppyseeds and a little milk for the top of the loaves	

I leave it to you to vary the flavour with the different flours and seeds.

→ Tip the FLOURS out into a very large mixing bowl and add the SALT. Boil a kettle, and put about 200ml/7fl oz of BOILING WATER in a measuring jug, topping up to the 425ml/15fl oz mark with water from the cold tap. The water should now feel hand hot. Drop in the MOLASSES SUGAR and fresh YEAST and stir vigorously for a few seconds until the liquid looks creamy. Leave it for 15 minutes to rise. I still find this as absorbing as I did when I baked my first loaf, the living organism fizzing, popping, bubbling, and the sudden rush and rise in volume like a geyser with a will of its own inhabiting the jug.

→ Pour the contents of the jug into the flour, and then another 425ml/15fl oz of HAND-HOT WATER immediately afterwards, then pour in the three tablespoons of OLIVE OIL. With one hand, start working the wet dough together until it coheres completely into a ball. Remove it from the bowl onto the work surface and start kneading it. Sometimes the dough will appear too dry to work, sometimes too wet and claggy. Simply add a little more water for the former, and sprinkle with a little more flour for the latter; the dough should not feel sticky. After you have started working the dough vigorously with both hands on the work surface, you will, from time to time, probably need to shake a little more FLOUR on to the work surface. The dough will elongate into a sausage each time you work it, which you need to furl back into a ball shape each time before repeating the process.

→ After 10 minutes, place the ball back in the bowl and cover the top with a clean linen tea towel, which you have wetted in hot water and wrung out. Leave at the side of the stove for about an hour, or until it has swollen to about twice its original volume and appears light and spongy.

→ Turn the oven to 230°C/450°F/Gas 8 to warm up. Brush the insides of your bread tins with OLIVE OIL. Turn the dough out onto the work surface, and divide it into 3 pieces with a sharp knife. Knock the air out of each loaf for 3 or 4 minutes, without kneading it, and place each loaf in its tin.

→ Re-cover with a hot, damp cloth, and leave in the warmth close by or on top of the oven for 20–25 minutes. Brush the top of each loaf with a little MILK, and sprinkle over a handful of

SEEDS. Put 2 loaves together on a higher shelf and one on a lower. Set the timer for 35 minutes, but they could take 40. You want a distinctive hollow sound when you tap the base of the bread while turning it out on to a rack with a palette knife.
→ Allow the loaves to cool for at least 40 minutes: bread is steamy, doughy and indigestible if you eat it too soon after coming out of the oven.

Walnut and Onion Spelt Loaf

MAKES 2 LOAVES

spelt flour	675g/1½lb
sea salt	1 tsp
dark molasses sugar	1 heaped tsp
easybake yeast	1 × 7g/¼ oz sachet
milk, *tepid*	425ml/15fl oz
walnut oil	150ml/5fl oz
good, fresh, oily walnuts, *chopped, but not too small*	110g/4oz
medium onion, *finely chopped*	1
egg white	a little
sesame seeds (optional)	a handful

The spelt flour gives this loaf a lovely coarse, branny nuttiness. You can use ⅓ white flour to ⅔ spelt if you prefer.

→ Sift the FLOUR and SALT into a bowl and add the SUGAR. Empty the YEAST into the MILK and pour it straight into the flour, then pour in the WALNUT OIL. Knead well for 10 minutes, adding extra milk if you need to, to obtain a springy dough.
→ Put back in the mixing bowl, cover with a damp cloth and leave to rise for 2 hours. When the dough is about 3 times its original size, take it out of the bowl and knock it back, throwing in the NUTS and ONION and working them in briefly. Divide into 2 with a sharp knife and form into balls.
→ Leave to prove on a greased baking tray in the warm for 45 minutes. Preheat the oven to 190°C/375°F/Gas 5. Brush with a little EGG WHITE and throw a handful of SESAME SEEDS over the top of the loaves. Bake in the centre of the oven for 40–45 minutes or until the crust is brown and the loaves sound hollow when you tap their undersides. Leave to cool on a rack.

Pane Pugliese

easy-blend yeast	½ tsp
strong white flour	140g/5oz
sparkling bottled water, *warmed*	200g/7oz
honey	1 tsp
chickpea flour (optional)	1 tbsp
Italian 'oo' flour OR strong white flour and semolina	340g/12oz 85g/3oz 255g/9oz
sparkling water	110g/4oz
fine salt	2 tsp
extra virgin olive oil	1 tbsp + 1 tsp

The increased bi-soda content of the sparkling water gives a lighter, crisper loaf.

→ Whisk together the YEAST, STRONG WHITE FLOUR, 200g/7oz warm SPARKLING BOTTLED WATER, HONEY and teaspoon of CHICKPEA FLOUR until smooth. Cover the bowl with clingfilm and leave in a warm place for an hour. This is called the 'sponge' and it will be the ferment that aerates the final dough.

→ To this sponge, add the ITALIAN FLOUR or FLOUR AND SEMOLINA, 110g/4oz of SPARKLING WATER, SALT, the tablespoon of CHICKPEA FLOUR if using. Mix until you have a soft, slightly sticky dough. Tip an extra teaspoon of OLIVE OIL on to the palms of your hands and knead the dough 12 times (20 seconds). Cover with clingfilm for 10 minutes. Knead another 12 times and cover again for 10 minutes. Repeat and leave to prove for 30 minutes.

→ Take a small bowl and line it with a tea towel. Dust lightly with flour, then knead the dough into a ball and place it seam-side up in the cloth-lined bowl.

→ Lightly fold the corners of the cloth over the top of the dough, and leave in a warm place for 45 minutes. Heat the oven to 230°C/450°F/Gas 8.

→ Dust a metal tray with SEMOLINA or POLENTA. Peel back the cloth and upturn the dough on to your hand, placing the dough seam-side up in the centre of the tray. Place the tray on the centre rack of the oven and bake for 45–55 minutes, or until the loaf is dark golden brown and sounds hollow when tapped underneath. Leave to cool on a wire rack before serving.

A Simple Flatbread

MAKES 6

strong, white plain flour	500g/1lb 2oz
sea salt	½ tsp
dried yeast	1 × 7g/¼ oz sachet
warm water	300ml/10fl oz
olive oil	a glug or tbsp

From the divine Nigel Slater, a must for the mezze.

→ Put the FLOUR into the bowl of a food mixer with a beater attachment and add the SALT. Empty the YEAST into a small glass, pour on enough of the WARM WATER to make a thin paste, then stir in the rest of the water. Pour the water onto the flour and turn the mixer on slow. Introduce the OLIVE OIL, mixing until you have a stiffish dough. Tip it out onto a floured board and knead with your hands, pushing and folding the dough until it feels springy and elastic to the touch. Set aside in a warm place in a bowl covered with a clean tea towel and leave to rise for an hour or so.

→ Heat the oven to 230°C/450°F/Gas 8. When your dough is about 4 times the size it was, break it into 6 pieces and push each one into a slipper shape. Dust with FLOUR and put them flat on a baking sheet. Bake for 5 minutes then turn the temperature down to 220°C/425°F/Gas 7 and continue baking for a further 5 minutes or so until the underside of the bread sounds hollow when you tap it.

Brown Soda Bread

MAKES A 450G/1LB LOAF

coarse (stoneground) wholewheat flour	170g/6oz
organic wholewheat flour	285g/10oz
bicarbonate of soda	1 heaped tsp
salt	1 tsp
molasses sugar	1 tsp
butter	30g/1oz
buttermilk	500–600ml/16–20fl oz

→ Preheat the oven to 230°C/450°F/Gas 8. Mix ALL THE DRY INGREDIENTS together with your hands, lightly rubbing in the BUTTER. Make a well in the centre and add about 500ml/16fl oz of the BUTTERMILK. Working with a knife, from the centre, gather the mixture to make a soft, wet dough. You may have to add more buttermilk to make the mixture 'sticky wet'.

→ Grease a 450g/1lb round or oblong loaf tin, spoon in the dough and bake for 30 minutes. Cover the top with greaseproof paper and bake for a further 10–15 minutes. Turn out on to a wire rack and cover with a tea towel. Leave to cool slightly before attempting to slice the bread.

John's Bread

MAKES A 450G/1LB LOAF

strong unbleached organic white flour	340g/12oz
organic wholewheat flour	55g/2oz
bran	55g/2oz
butter	30g/1oz
bicarbonate of soda	1 heaped tsp
sea salt	1 tsp
molasses sugar	1 tsp
buttermilk	500–600ml/16–20fl oz

→ Preheat the oven to 230°C/450°F/Gas 8. Mix ALL THE DRY INGREDIENTS together with your hands, lightly rubbing in the BUTTER. Make a well in the centre and add about 500ml/16fl oz of the BUTTERMILK. Working with a knife, from the centre, gather the mixture to make a soft, wet dough. You may have to add more buttermilk to make the mixture 'sticky wet'.

→ Grease a 450g/1lb round or oblong loaf tin, spoon in the dough and bake for 30 minutes. Cover the top with greaseproof paper and bake for a further 10–15 minutes. Turn out on to a wire rack and cover with a tea towel. Leave to cool slightly before attempting to slice the bread.

Cheese and Onion Bread

MAKES 2 SMALL OR 1 HUBCAP-
SIZE ROUND LOAF

strong white organic flour	500g/1lb 2 oz
salt (too much salt will kill the yeast)	a pinch
fresh yeast	15g/1/2oz
organic sunflower oil	1 tbsp
medium onion, *coarsely chopped*	1
water	up to 300ml/10fl oz
mature organic Cheddar cheese	55g/2oz

Use a good, strongly flavoured cheddar like Montgomery or Keen's for this bread. The red onions give it a wonderful colour. The water in the onions slackens the dough considerably, so mix carefully.

→ Sieve the FLOUR and SALT into a bowl, and crumble the YEAST in. Pour in the OIL, mix it in a bit with your hand, throw in the ONION, then start pouring in the WATER. Work the mixture into a stiff dough, then sit it in a warm place for an hour until it has doubled in size.

→ Knock it back vigorously, and either leave it whole or divide it into two. Form it into a flat round, and place it on an OILED baking sheet. Leave it for another hour to double in size, then sprinkle grated CHEESE over the top.

→ Preheat the oven to 220°C/425°F/Gas 7. Bake for about 25 minutes until the loaf is starting to change colour and sounds hollow when tapped. Cool on a wire rack. Delicious eaten warm with unsalted butter, or try it with Marmite and watercress or goat's cheese.

Blue Cheese and Onion Bread
→ Use half BLUE CHEESE, such as Stilton, with the cheddar for a a different flavour.

Eric Treuille's Focaccia

MAKES 1 LARGE LOAF

Dough

strong white flour	500g/1lb 2oz
sea salt	2 tsp
tepid water	325ml/11fl oz
dried yeast	2 tsp

Topping

baby potatoes	500g/1lb 2oz
Gruyère cheese, *grated*	110g/4oz
fresh thyme leaves	2 tsp
sea salt and black pepper	
crème fraîche	4 tbsp
coarse salt to sprinkle	

Eric Treuille and his wife Rosie Kindersley are the owner-managers of my favourite playing-truant shop, Books for Cooks in Notting Hill, London. Eric has a lovely version of focaccia with thyme, Gruyère and crème fraîche that makes the centrepiece of a light lunch, needing no more than a Provençal tomato salad or roasted tomato soup alongside. Eric suggests making and kneading the dough and leaving it to rise in the fridge all day or all night, for 8–12 hours, before letting it stand at room temperature, knocking it back and shaping it.

→ Put the FLOUR in a bowl, make a well in the middle and put the SALT on the raised ridge of flour around the sides. Pour the WATER into the well and sprinkle over the YEAST. Leave for 5 minutes to soften, then stir to dissolve. Draw in enough of the flour to make a soft paste. Cover with a cloth and leave to sponge for 20 minutes until bubbly and slightly puffed up. Draw in the rest of the flour to make a rough, sticky dough. Turn out on to a lightly floured surface and knead for 10 minutes until smooth, light and elastic. Put back into the bowl, cover with a cloth and leave until doubled in size, about 1½ hours.
→ Preheat oven to 220°C/425°F/Gas 6. Scrub the POTATOES and cut into 5mm/¼ in slices. Bring a pan of salted water to the boil, add the potatoes and bring back to the boil. Cook for about 5 minutes until the centres are just tender when pricked with the tip of a knife. Drain well and cool.
→ Deflate the dough by pressing down with the palm of your hand. Roll out into a flat round, about 23cm/9in across, and place on an OILED baking sheet. Spread about half the CHEESE evenly on top of the bread dough, arrange the potatoes on top, scatter with THYME and sprinkle with a little SALT AND PEPPER. Cover with a cloth and leave until risen, about 30 minutes. Dot teaspoons of CRÈME FRAÎCHE over the potatoes and scatter on the remaining CHEESE.
→ Bake for about 30 minutes or until the potato topping is crisp and golden and the bread sounds hollow when tapped underneath. Cool on a wire rack. Serve warm or at room temperature, sprinkled with coarse salt and cut into wedges.

Potato and Porcini Focaccia

sparkling bottled water, *warmed*	340g/12oz
easy-blend yeast	1 tsp
runny honey	1 tsp
strong white flour	480g/1lb 1oz
malt extract	1 tsp
fine sea salt	2 tsp
extra virgin olive oil	10 tbsp

Topping

large potato, *washed, unpeeled and finely sliced on a mandolin if you have one*	1
small onion, *finely sliced*	1
fresh porcini mushrooms OR sliced dried porcini	2 a handful
extra virgin olive oil	2 tbsp
Maldon salt	2 tsp

A little honey helps speed the dried yeast, but if you're using fresh yeast, there is no need for it. You can buy malt extract at health-food shops.

→ In a small bowl, mix together 200g/7oz of the WATER with the YEAST and the HONEY. Whisk together until the yeast has dissolved, then whisk in 140g/5oz of the FLOUR. Cover the bowl with clingfilm and leave in a warm place for 2 hours, giving the mixture a stir after the first hour. By this time it should be bubbling and have risen to double its original height.

→ Scrape the sponge into another larger bowl, then add the remaining WATER and the MALT EXTRACT and whisk together until the sponge has combined roughly with the water. Add the remaining FLOUR and the SALT and squidge the mixture together with your hand (try to do this with one hand to keep the other clean and dry). The mixture will be very soft, slightly lumpy and very sticky. This is good.

→ Scrape the dough down from around the sides of the bowl, then give your hands a good wash to remove any excess dough. Tip 1 tablespoon of the OLIVE OIL on to your hands, remove the dough from the bowl and rub the oil all over the surface of the dough.

→ Place the oiled dough on the worktop and knead 5 times (about 10 seconds). Cover with clingfilm and leave for 10 minutes. Rub another tablespoon of OIL over the surface and knead 12 times (about 20 seconds). Cover and leave to prove for 30 minutes.

→ Knead a further 12 times, then cover and leave for 30 minutes. Heat the oven to 230°C/450°F/Gas 8. Take two 30 × 40cm/ 12 × 16in trays and rub the insides liberally with OLIVE OIL. In a bowl mix together the thinly sliced POTATOES, ONIONS and MUSHROOMS with 2 tablespoons of OLIVE OIL and a pinch of SALT. Stir until the potato slices are well coated with the oil.

→ Divide the dough in two and knead each piece into a ball. Place each ball on a tray and lightly flatten with a rolling pin. Don't worry if the dough springs back. Cover with clingfilm and leave in a warm place for 20–30 minutes.

→ Pick up the corners of the dough and stretch them out until they reach the corners of the tray. Tip the potato mixture evenly on top of each sheet of dough. Cover with clingfilm and leave a further 15 minutes. Remove the clingfilm, dimple the surface of the dough with your fingers, add a little extra SALT if you wish and bake for 30–45 minutes, until the surface is golden brown and the potatoes tender. Remove from the oven and slide the focaccia on to a cooling rack.

Parmesan Grissini

full-cream milk	110g/4oz
dry active yeast	1 tsp
unsalted butter	55g/2oz
Parmesan cheese, *freshly grated*	55g/2oz
strong white flour	200g/7oz
fine sea salt	½ tsp

This is bread guru Dan Lepard's version of the chef Giorgio Locatelli's Parmesan grissini.

→ Heat oven to 180°C/350°F/Gas 4. Warm the MILK until tepid, then whisk in the dried YEAST. Melt the BUTTER in a small saucepan over a low heat and pour the butter into the warm milk. Add the grated PARMESAN and stir together, then add the FLOUR and SALT and work the mixture until a dough is formed.

→ Knead lightly for 10–15 seconds, then wrap the dough in a damp tea towel and leave for 10 minutes. Knead the dough once more for a further 10–15 seconds, cover again, and leave for 30 minutes. Knead a final time for 10–15 seconds, cover and leave for 45 minutes. Lightly flour the work surface and roll the dough until it's about 1cm/½in thick. With a sharp knife or pizza cutter and a ruler, cut strips of dough about 1cm/½in wide. Roll each strip into grissini and place them on a non-stick baking sheet.

→ Bake for 15–20 minutes until crisp and lightly golden. Remove from the oven and cool on a wire rack, and continue with the remaining dough until it is finished.

Basic Scones

MAKES 24–30

plain flour	450g/1lb
salt	½ tsp
unsalted butter	55–85g/2–3oz
bicarbonate of soda	2 level tsp
cream of tartar	2 level tsp
soured cream OR buttermilk	300ml/10fl oz

The lightest scones are made with soured cream or buttermilk, but if you don't have any you can use milk. Use either 2 level teaspoons of bicarbonate of soda and 4½ level teaspoons of cream of tartar with 300ml/10fl oz fresh full-cream milk, or 4–6 level teaspoons of baking powder. Measure the raising agents carefully as too much will ruin the mix. Keep everything cool: cold air expands with the heat and helps make the scones lighter.

→ Preheat the oven to 220°C/425°F/Gas 7. Sift the FLOUR and SALT into a bowl. Cut the BUTTER into little pieces and rub into the flour with the tips of your fingers as quickly as you can. Sift in the RAISING AGENTS and mix well. Add ALL THE LIQUID at once and mix lightly into a spongy dough. Knead very lightly to make the dough smooth and roll out to 1–2cm/½–¾in thick. Handle the scones as little and as lightly as possible.
→ Cut out with a 5cm/2in cutter and leave the scones to stand for 10 minutes — they just seem to turn out better. Brush with EGG OR MILK if you wish before placing on a greased baking sheet in the middle of the oven. Cook for 10–15 minutes, then cool on a rack to keep the outside crisp.

Cheese Scones
→ Add 140g/5oz good strong unpasteurised grated CHEDDAR such as Montgomery's or Keen's to the mixture and add a sprinkle of grated cheese to each top before the scones go into the oven.

Cheese and Thyme Scones
→ Add a couple of teaspoons of finely chopped THYME or ROSEMARY to the top with the cheese. Delicious with soup.

Fruit Scones
→ Add 55g/2oz VANILLA CASTER SUGAR and 55–110g/2–4oz CURRANTS or SULTANAS or RAISINS to the basic recipe.

Treacle Scones
→ Add 30g/1oz SUGAR, 1 teaspoon of GROUND CINNAMON, 1 teaspoon of MIXED SPICE and 2 tablespoons of BLACK TREACLE to the basic recipe. Put the treacle in with two-thirds of the milk, then add the rest as required.

Wholemeal Scones
→ Use half WHOLEMEAL FLOUR and half PLAIN FLOUR for any of the above recipes.

Drop Scones

SERVES 5

self-raising flour, *sifted*	225g/8oz
bicarbonate of soda	½ tsp
baking powder	½ tsp
cream of tartar	½ tsp
sugar	1 tbsp
golden syrup	1 tbsp
full-cream milk	300ml/10fl oz
organic egg	1
butter	a little

→ Mix ALL THE DRY INGREDIENTS together and add the SYRUP. Add half the MILK, whisking it in well, then add the EGG and beat that in thoroughly. Add the rest of the MILK. The mixture should just plop off the spoon. Let it stand for 15 minutes.

→ Brush a heavy, cast-iron pan with butter. I have a wonderful Swedish pan that feels leaden enough to have been forged by the god Thor. When the butter begins to smoke, drop table-spoons of the mixture into the pan, 2 at a time, with a ladle. Leave until you begin to see bubbles forming on the surface and a skin, about 3 minutes. Turn gently with a palette knife and cook until golden brown on the underside. Keep warm in a napkin or cloth before serving with butter, jam, syrup or what you will.

Potato Scones

potatoes	450g/1lb
flour	110–140g/4–5oz
salt	1 tsp
unsalted butter	45g/1½oz

These are deliciously soft, crumbly crumbed and buttery—divine with oak-smoked organic rashers fried until crisped, then draped with their fat running into the scones for breakfast or brunch. You must make the scones with hot potato, so réchauffez if it's last night's potato.

→ Peel the POTATOES, steam and put through a mouli-légumes or potato ricer. Sieve the FLOUR with the SEA SALT. Work all the ingredients together with your fingers, then roll out the dough lightly into thin circles, more biscuit than scone depth, with a very well floured rolling pin. Cut with a scone cutter into circles and either cook on an ungreased griddle top or fry until brown in a little BUTTER. Serve hot and buttered.

PRESER

&

VES
sweet treats

Crab Apple Jelly

fruit	as much as you can pick
water	
unrefined sugar	450g/1lb for each 600ml/1 pint of juice

My affection for crab apple jelly is a deep and enduring one. This was my father's favourite breakfast treat, so it has to be mine.

→ Wash the FRUIT, put it in a huge preserving pan and just cover with water. Bring to the boil and simmer slowly, covered, until the apples are softened to a pulp. Put this into a jelly bag or piece of muslin and suspend it above a bowl so the juice can strain through. Leave it to drip overnight. You do not want to squeeze or hurry any of the juice through: this will make your jelly cloudy instead of sparkling.

→ Measure the beautiful pink juice in a jug, and add 450g/1lb of unrefined SUGAR to each 600ml/1 pint of juice. Bring to the boil, scum and keep boiling until you reach setting point. I start testing after 10 minutes. Put a small saucer in the fridge to cool, then place a teaspoon of boiling juice on the saucer, and put it in the freezer for a couple of minutes. If the liquid on the saucer wrinkles when you push it with a finger, the jelly has reached the setting point.

→ I scald the jars with boiling water in the sink as I wait for the setting point. Ladle the jelly through a funnel into the jars as soon as you have reached setting point. Cover immediately with cellophane and an elastic band.

Spiced Redcurrant Jelly

MAKES 3 OR 4 JARS

redcurrants	1.5kg/3¼lb
water	850ml/1½ pints
cloves	3
cinnamon bark	a short length
cider vinegar	240ml/8fl oz
unrefined granulated sugar	1.5kg/3¼lb

I have a particular affection for this lovely glowing ruby jelly as it was the first jelly I ever attempted a couple of decades ago. Not only did it work, I found its cider-vinegar sharpness and musky spiciness far preferable to the commercial over-sweet confections or even the home-made sugary jellies I had been used to. I have stuck with it and it's great for lamb, venison, hare and grouse.

→ Throw the REDCURRANTS into a large preserving or enamel pan as they are, with their stalks. Add the WATER and SPICES, bring to the boil and simmer until the redcurrants are soft. Strain the juice by putting the fruit into a muslin or jelly bag and leaving it suspended above a bowl to drip through overnight. Do not squeeze or hurry any of the juice through: this will make your jelly cloudy instead of sparkling.

→ Add the VINEGAR and SUGAR to the liquid in the pan, and boil until it reaches setting point. See Crab Apple Jelly above for how to test for the setting point. Pour into warm jam jars and cover while the jelly is still very hot.

Blackcurrant or Whitecurrant Jelly

granulated sugar	340g/12oz to each 450g/1lb of blackcurrants or whitecurrants

The most intense and scented fruit of them all, the blackcurrant makes a jelly so highly flavoured and strong that it is the perfect one to use in a queen of puddings or with a branny slab of home-made soda bread.

→ Put the CURRANTS, along with their STALKS and LEAVES, into a large pan. Add the sugar. Bring to the boil, skimming off the scum as it comes to the surface, then boil fast for 10 minutes. Pour into a bowl through a hair or nylon sieve. Press the fruit down lightly—not firmly, or the jelly will cloud. Test for setting as p. 580. Pour it warm into warm jam jars and seal. The blackcurrant jelly is wonderful in puddings.

Blackcurrant Jam

blackcurrants	1kg/2¼lb
water	850ml/1½pints
unrefined granulated sugar	1.4kg/3lb

→ Simmer the FRUIT with the WATER until it is soft right through, about 45–50 minutes, then add the warmed SUGAR, bring to the boil, and boil until setting point has been reached. Test after 10 minutes—see p. 580.

Strawberry Jam

unrefined granulated sugar	340g/12oz to every 450g/1lb strawberries
lemon	juice of 1 for every 1.4kg/3lb fruit

→ Crush a large spoonful of BERRIES with a fork and put them in a preserving pan with an equal amount of SUGAR. Warm gently until the sugar has dissolved, then add the rest of the HULLED FRUIT and bring slowly to the boil, giving it an occasional stir.

→ Warm the SUGAR in a low oven (this stops the temperature in the pan from lowering), and add it to the fruit with the LEMON JUICE—the lemon provides extra pectin. Boil rapidly for 10–12 minutes, or until setting point has been reached. (See p. 580 for how to do the wrinkle test.)

→ Sometimes the fruit rises to the top (this happens with strawberries and cherries particularly), but if you leave the fruit in the pan after it has finished cooking for about 30 minutes, then stir and pot the jam, all should be well.

Strawberry Jam with Redcurrants

strawberries	1kg/2¼lb
unrefined granulated sugar	1kg/2¼lb
redcurrant juice	300ml/10fl oz

The fruits stay whole exceptionally well in this jam and the syrup is really good. There is a lot of pectin in the currants to help the set.

→ Pour the SUGAR over the HULLED BERRIES in a large bowl and leave them overnight so that the juice starts to bleed from the fruit. Tip the contents of the bowl into a large preserving pan with the REDCURRANT JUICE. Bring to the boil slowly, then boil until setting point is reached. (See p. 580 for how to do the wrinkle test.)

Loganberry Jam

The minimal cooking in this method naturally results in a wonderfully intense flavour. It works just as well for raspberries.

→ Preheat the oven to 180°C/350°F/Gas 4. Put equal weights of LOGANBERRIES and granulated SUGAR in a large dish in the oven. Let them get very hot, but do not allow to boil. Check after 20 minutes, although it could take 30 minutes.
→ Turn the fruit and sugar into a bowl and mix together thoroughly with a wooden spoon. Pour warm into warm jam jars and cover with discs of paper that you have first dipped in brandy, then seal.
→ If mould forms on top of the jam, don't worry; the jam underneath will be fine, and it keeps extremely well.

Plum Jam

plums	2kg/4½lb
water	300–600ml/10fl oz–1 pint, depending on the juiciness of the plums
unrefined granulated sugar	2kg/4½lb

→ Halve the PLUMS to remove the STONES, then bash about half the stones with a hammer or rolling pin to extract the kernels. The French believe the secret heart of the fruit is contained in the kernels, and their best apricot jams always contain little halves of kernel, adding the most intensely almondy, scented taste to the jam. Blanch the kernels in boiling water then set aside on a plate.
→ Tie the plum stones in muslin to cook with the jam. Simmer the fruit with the WATER and stones until soft. Meanwhile, warm the SUGAR in an ovenproof bowl in a moderate oven, then add to the softened fruit and continue to simmer. Test after 15 minutes (see p. 580), although the jam will probably take 15–20 minutes to set. Add the plum kernels before you pot the jam.

Gooseberry Jam

under-ripe gooseberries	1.4kg/3lb
water	600ml/1 pint
sugar	1.8kg/4lb
elderflowers, *tied in a muslin* (optional)	2–3 heads

→ Simmer the FRUIT with the WATER until it is soft, about 20 minutes. Warm the SUGAR as above and add it to the pan. Let the sugar dissolve, add the ELDER·OWERS, then bring the jam to the boil. Test after 10 minutes for setting point (see p. 580), though it may take as long as 20 minutes. Remove the elderflowers if using, and pot the jam. You can use elderflower cordial instead of elderflowers.

Raspberry Jam

→ Allow equal weight of RASPBERRIES to SUGAR. Tip the sugar in an ovenproof dish and warm it through in a moderate oven for 15 minutes. Heat the fruit slowly in the preserving pan until the juices begin to bleed, then add the warm sugar and bring to the boil. This jam shouldn't take longer than 3 minutes to cook if the fruit is fresh and ripe. You don't want it to collapse too much. Test and pot in the usual way.

Uncooked Raspberry Jam

→ Again, allow equal quantities of FRUIT to sugar, UNREFINED CASTER SUGAR in this case. Put the sugar in one ovenproof dish and the raspberries in another and place in a moderate oven for 15 minutes. Remove from the oven and scrape the warmed sugar into the raspberries, stirring the two together for 10 minutes. Leave them to stand for 20 minutes. Repeat the stirring and standing a further couple of times each and then pot the jam. Put the pots uncovered into a cool oven for 1 hour, then cover them.

Quince Paste, or Membrillo

quinces	2kg/4½lb
water	300ml/10fl oz
granulated sugar	

This scented, deep amber paste is one of the great treats of life, perfect eaten with Manchego or an English sheep's milk cheese like Wigmore.

→ Remove the bloom from the QUINCE skins with a cloth. Wash them, cut into quarters and stew them in the WATER until they're soft. Sieve them and weigh the purée, then return it to the pan with an equal amount of unrefined granulated SUGAR. Boil slowly until the mixture comes away from the sides of the pan, stirring with a wooden spoon constantly and carefully.
→ Pour into metal trays lined with Bakewell paper and dry out for a few days in the airing cupboard or on top of the Aga if you have one. Store in a sealed container somewhere cool.

Organic Seville Orange Marmalade

ENOUGH FOR 17 POTS OF VARYING SIZES

organic Seville oranges	2kg/4½lb
organic lemons	3
organic unrefined granulated sugar	3.2kg/7lb
water	5 litres/9 pints

This has become an enshrined ritual in my kitchen every January, which my great friend and superlative marmalade-maker Gale partners me in. It was she, after all, who got me going, disabusing me of my prejudice against the glowing amber pots of bitter orange that I had previously managed to burn or cook to rigidity, setting them in stone rather than soft, golden gel.

→ Wash the ORANGES and LEMONS, halve and squeeze them, reserving the juice and the pips from the squeezing separately. Extract the remains of the pulp, pith and pips from the orange halves with your fingers and put them into a muslin bag with the other pips. Halve the halves, and pile the quarters into a tight stack that you can feed down the feeder tube of a food processor through the slicer disc. Trim any bits of peel that have not been properly shredded.

→ Put the sliced PEEL into a large preserving pan with the squeezed juice, the water and the muslin bag of pips tied to the side and bring gently to the boil. Cover with a lid and put into the simmering oven of an Aga, or continue to simmer very gently on top of the stove. It will take about 2½ hours inside the Aga or rather less, about 2 hours, on top of the stove, for the peel to have absolutely no bite to it right the way through.

→ Remove the muslin bag and suspend it over a bowl for the juice to drain through for about 30 minutes, then add the juice to the liquid in the pan. Now divide the mixture accurately into three batches for the next stage, because it sets better in small quantities. Put one-third of the mixture back into the preserving pan, with one-third of the SUGAR, and heat gently, stirring to dissolve the sugar completely. The mixture mustn't boil until the sugar has completely dissolved. Now boil hard until you reach setting point; ours took about 15 minutes, but start testing after 10. Put a small saucer in the fridge to cool, then place a teaspoon of boiling juice on the saucer, and put it in the freezer for a couple of minutes. While you do this, remove the marmalade from the heat so that it doesn't cook any further. If the liquid on the saucer wrinkles when you push it gently with a finger, it has reached setting point.

→ Now leave the pan off the heat for 30 minutes before you ladle the marmalade into warm clean jars, otherwise the shreds will rise up the jar to the top, and you'll have half-overshredded, half-gel marmalade. Don't fall at the last fence. Be patient, the waiting is all. Repeat with the remaining two-thirds of ingredients.

Lemon Curd

large, organic lemons	2
unsalted butter, *cut into cubes*	85g/3oz
unrefined granulated sugar	225g/8oz
large organic eggs	3

→ I make my curd in a heavy-bottomed, wide-based pan. The wide surface area speeds up the gelling of the curd. Grate the zest from both LEMONS into the pan with a zester and add the juice of the lemons, the BUTTER and the SUGAR. Stir over a gentle heat until the sugar is dissolved, making sure the mixture doesn't come to the boil. Beat the EGGS and add them to the mixture, then keep stirring and watching like a hawk until the curd thickens. Remove from the heat instantly and pot.

Lime Curd/Orange Curd
→ You can make lime and orange curds in the same way, altering the sugar balance to taste. Seville oranges make a lovely curd for a tart.

Rumtopf

strawberries, *hulled*	1kg/2¼lb
sugar	500g/1lb 2oz
rum (the French use brandy)	1 litre/1¾ pints
other fruits such as cherries, raspberries, loganberries, blackberries, peaches, pears, plums, apricots as and when they come into season	

Rumtopf is a lovely thing to make in the strawberry season and dispense in cold times. This has to be started in June or July when strawberries are in season.

→ Once the STRAWBERRIES are hulled, put them in a bowl, sprinkle them with the SUGAR and leave them overnight. The next day, tip the entire contents of the bowl into a rumtopf and pour over the BOOZE. Put a saucer down onto the fruit so that it can't float above the surface of the liquor, cover the jar with clingfilm and the corked lid and keep it in a cool dark place like a larder or outhouse. Keep on adding more fruit and sugar prepared in the same way in whatever quantities you have as the summer fruits season progresses, and keep on topping up the booze in proportion to it.

→ Once the rumtopf is full, add a final slug of booze and hide it until around Christmas. You may serve it straight from the jar, ladling it into glasses and topping them with cream, or pour it lusciously over ice cream, pannacotta, creams or possets.

Damson Gin

MAKES A LARGE JAR

damsons	850ml/1½ pints
unrefined sugar	340g/12oz
good gin	1.2 litres/2 pints

half a dozen kernels from inside the damson stones, *cracked open with a hammer*

After the autumnal hedgerow foraging, the dark staining of fingers, the pricking of the fruit with a fork or silver pin to get the juices flowing, the cracking of the kernels and jarring and sealing of the wine-coloured brew, there is the waiting, turning and shaking as alcohol, sugar and fruit turn to a perfect purple linctus.

→ Prick the DAMSONS with a needle and put them into a large Kilner jar. Add ALL THE OTHER INGREDIENTS, seal the jar and give it a good shake. Shake every week until Christmas, when you may strain and bottle the gin. The fruit will be delicious with a bit of the sticky purple linctus eaten with some home-made vanilla ice cream.

Sloe Gin/Mulberry Gin
→ Prepare sloe gin exactly as above, but use a few drops of CULPEPER'S BITTER ALMOND ESSENCE instead of the damson stones. If you make mulberry gin, use equal measures of MULBERRIES and gin.

Apricot Chutney

apricots, *halved and stoned*	1kg/2¼lb
sharp apple, *chopped*	225g/8oz
onion, *sliced*	225g/8oz
carrot, *coarsely grated*	110g/4oz
raisins	110g/4oz
light muscovado sugar	225g/8oz
sea salt	1 dsrtsp
star anise	1
ground cloves	1 tsp
ground dried ginger root	1 tsp
ground allspice	1 tsp
small dried red chilli	1
white wine vinegar	600ml/1 pint

This is a lovely spicy chutney, all the better for using proper white wine vinegar instead of the throat-wrenching malt vinegar.

Put the APRICOTS in a large bowl with the ONION, CARROT, RAISINS and SUGAR and mix it all together. Put the SALT, SPICES and VINEGAR into a pan and bring slowly to the boil. Add the fruity mixture, stirring it all in together and bringing it back up to the boil. Let it simmer away steadily until the mixture is thick and gloopy and has turned to chutney.
→ Pot into warmed jars, cover and keep somewhere cool and dark for at least 6 weeks before using.

Plum Chutney
→ You can also make this with plums instead of apricots for a glorious autumn chutney.

Courgette Chutney

MAKES 900G/2LB

small lemons	2
medium courgettes	3
onions, *peeled and thinly sliced*	2
Riesling OR other dry white wine	100ml/3½fl oz
brown sugar	2 tsp
black peppercorns, *coarsely crushed*	24
fresh ginger, *peeled and finely chopped*	2.5cm/1in piece
sea salt	

→ Peel the LEMONS, cutting away all the pith, then slice them thinly and discard the pips. Cut the COURGETTES in half lengthwise, then across into 2.5cm/1in pieces. Combine ALL THE INGREDIENTS in a saucepan, adding a little SEA SALT. Cover and cook over a moderate heat for 1 hour, stirring from time to time. There will be quite a bit of liquid at the end of the cooking time, but once the chutney has cooled, the consistency will be perfect.

→ Either bottle, or put in a bowl to serve. It will keep in the fridge for 4–5 days.

Cape Gooseberry Chutney

MAKES A GOOD BOWLFUL

vegetable oil	30ml/1fl oz
mustard seeds	¼ tsp
cumin seeds	¼ tsp
onion, *chopped*	55g/2oz
fresh ginger, *chopped*	1 tsp
green chilli, *chopped*	1 tsp
salt	
red chilli powder	¼ tsp
cumin powder	¼ tsp
coriander powder	¼ tsp
Cape gooseberries, *hulled*	400g/14oz
unrefined sugar	½ tsp

Simple to prepare, this chutney is unusual and highly versatile. Its sweet sharpness is a foil for any rich or fatty meats, and I think it takes the place of our own green gooseberry sauce with a humble herring or mackerel.

→ Heat the OIL, then add the MUSTARD and CUMIN SEEDS. After the mustard seeds have started to splutter, add the chopped ONION. Cook until translucent, then add THE OTHER CHOPPED INGREDIENTS. Cook for 2–3 minutes, add the powdered SPICES and SALT, cook over a low flame, then add the GOOSEBERRIES and SUGAR. Gently sauté over a low flame for a few minutes, making sure the gooseberries retain their shape and do not collapse. Allow the chutney to cool to room temperature before storing in the fridge.

Tomato Chilli Jam

MAKES TWO LARGE JARS

very ripe organic tomatoes	750g/1lb 10oz
red chillies, with their seeds	4
fat cloves of garlic, *peeled*	6
fresh ginger, *peeled and roughly chopped*	3 thumbs
Thai fish sauce (nam pla)	40ml/1½fl oz
unrefined golden caster sugar	450g/1lb
red wine vinegar	150ml/5fl oz

Quite simply, your kitchen should never be without this jam, and it keeps in the fridge for weeks if it is allowed the chance to do so. Great with a Montgomery Cheddar sandwich, in a toasted sandwich or slicked onto bruschetta under a row of slices of Ragstone or Golden Cross goat's cheese; serve it with cold pork, on griddled scallops, or come up with your own idea. Versatile it is.

→ Blend half the TOMATOES, the CHILLIES, GARLIC, GINGER and FISH SAUCE to a fine purée in a blender. You need the chilli seeds for the heat, which is not intense, and the tomato seeds for the pectin, which will make the jam set.

→ Put the purée, SUGAR and VINEGAR into a deep pan and bring to the boil slowly, stirring all the time. When it reaches the boil, turn down to a gentle simmer and add the remaining TOMATOES cut into tiny dice, about 5mm/¼in, skin and all. Skim off the foam and cook gently for 1¼–1½ hours, stirring every so often to release the solids that settle on the bottom and prevent them from burning. Be sure to scrape the sides of the pot too, so the entire mass cooks evenly.

→ When the jam is done, pour it into warmed glass jars. Allow it to cool to room temperature before storing in the fridge or a cold larder for later use.

Pickled Cucumber

SERVES 4

caster sugar	½ tbsp
tarragon white wine vinegar	3 tbsp
cucumber, *peeled and finely sliced on a mandolin or by hand*	1
dill, *finely chopped*	1 tbsp
black pepper	

This is perfect served as a vegetable with a cold poached salmon or sea trout. Its sharpness, with a hint of a sweet note, perfectly complements the rich oily flesh of the fish.

→ In a bowl, stir the SUGAR into the wine VINEGAR until it has dissolved. Throw in the CUCUMBER slices and DILL, and scrunch over a goodly amount of BLACK PEPPER. Leave to macerate for at least an hour before serving, turning the slices 2 or 3 times in the liquor; the cucumber will continue to exude juice as it macerates. Serve straight from the bowl, with as little of the liquid as possible.

Fudge

vanilla caster sugar	500g/1lb 2oz
unsalted butter	50g/scant 2oz
evaporated milk	90ml/3fl oz
pure vanilla extract	a few drops

Fudge and toffee are easy to make and make good presents.

→ Put the SUGAR, BUTTER and MILK into the pan and bring to the boil. Continue to boil it gently, stirring from time to time, until the mixture reaches 115°C. Check the temperature with a sugar thermometer, warming it in a pan of hot water before putting it upright into the pan.

→ If you don't have a sugar thermometer, test to see if little bits of the mixture plopped into cold water harden up immediately. This should take somewhere between 5–10 minutes of boiling.

→ As soon as the fudge is ready, take the pan off the heat, stir in the VANILLA EXTRACT and continue beating until the mixture thickens and becomes distinctly grainy. Pour into a greased baking tray and leave it to cool. Cut into squares and remove when cold.

Chocolate Fudge

loaf OR granulated sugar	450g/1lb
milk	170ml/6fl oz
unsweetened cocoa like Green and Black's organic cocoa	3 tbsp
unsalted butter, *cut into small chunks*	55g/2oz
pure vanilla extract	a few drops

→ Stir together the SUGAR, MILK and COCOA until the sugar has dissolved. Cook gently, allowing the temperature to rise gradually until it reaches 115°C on a sugar thermometer. Warm the thermometer in a pan of hot water before putting it upright into the pan and then allow the syrup to boil rapidly without shaking or stirring it.

→ Once the fudge has reached the desired temperature, remove the thermometer and place it back in the pan of hot water. Take the pan off the heat and dip the base in cold water for a minute to stop the mixture boiling. Then drop in the little chunks of the butter off the heat, still without stirring. Cool. When nearly cold add the VANILLA EXTRACT and beat well. Pour into an oiled tray, mark into squares with a knife blade and cut up when cold.

Toffee

demerara sugar	340g/12oz
unsalted butter	225g/8oz
golden syrup	200g/7oz
lemon	zest and juice of ½

→ Boil everything together in a pan until a tiny quantity of toffee dropped into a bowl of cold water hardens at once, then pour it into an oiled tin. Allow the toffee to cool, then mark off into squares with a knife. Cut into pieces when cold.

Index

First published in Great Britain in 2008
by Weidenfeld & Nicolson
10 9 8 7 6 5 4 3 2 1

Text © Tamasin Day-Lewis 1997–2008
Design and layout © Weidenfeld & Nicolson 2008

A CIP catalogue record for this book
is available from the British Library.

ISBN: 978 0 297 84483 9

Design director David Rowley
Editorial director Susan Haynes
Designed by Ken Wilson | point918
Edited by Jinny Johnson
Assistant Joanna Cannon
Proofread by Jill Williams
Index by Elizabeth Wiggans

Printed and bound in Italy

Weidenfeld & Nicolson
The Orion Publishing Group Ltd
Orion House
5 Upper St Martin's Lane
London WC2H 9EA

www.orionbooks.co.uk

An Hachette Livre UK Company

The Orion Publishing Group's policy is to
use papers that are natural, renewable
and recyclable products and made from wood
grown in sustainable forests. The logging
and manufacturing processes are expected to
conform to the environmental regulations
of the country of origin.